W9-BAN-919

Fodor's 06

CARIBBEAN PORTS OF CALL

Where to Stay and Eat
for All Budgets

Must-See Sights
and Local Secrets

Ratings You Can Trust

Portions of this book appear in *Fodor's Caribbean 2006*
Fodor's Travel Publications   New York, Toronto, London, Sydney, Auckland
www.fodors.com

FODOR'S CARIBBEAN PORTS OF CALL 2006
Editor: Douglas Stallings

Editorial Production: Bethany Cassin Beckerlegge
Editorial Contributors: Isabel Abisláiman, Carol M. Bareuther, John Bigley, Melissa Bigner, Naomi Black, Cathy Church, Harriet Edelson, Kandace Power Graves, Paul A. Greenberg, Molly Jahncke, Melissa Klurman, Adam Kowit, Baty Landis, Lynda Lohr, Diane P. Marshall, Elise Meyer, Kristen Milavec, Paris Permenter, Vernon O'Reilly Ramesar, Christine Ricard, Sara Roahen, Elise Rosen, Eileen Robinson Smith, Jordan Simon, Lan Sluder, Roberta Sotonoff, Kerry Speckman, Tom Steele, Troy Thibodeaux, Jim and Cynthia Tunstall, Chelle Koster Walton, Jane E. Zarem
Maps: David Lindroth, *cartographer;* Bob Blake and Rebecca Baer, *map editors*
Design: Fabrizio La Rocca, *creative director;* Guido Caroti, *art director;* Moon Sun Kim, *cover designer;* Melanie Marin, *senior photo editor*
Production/Manufacturing: Colleen Ziemba
Cover Photo: Norwegian Cruise Line

SPECIAL SALES
This book is available for special discounts for bulk purchases for sales promotions or premiums. Special editions, including personalized covers, excerpts of existing books, and corporate imprints, can be created in large quantities for special needs. For more information, write to Special Markets/Premium Sales, 1745 Broadway, MD 6-2, New York, New York 10019, or e-mail specialmarkets@randomhouse.com.

AN IMPORTANT TIP & AN INVITATION
Although all prices, opening times, and other details in this book are based on information supplied to us at press time, changes occur all the time in the travel world, and Fodor's cannot accept responsibility for facts that become outdated or for inadvertent errors or omissions. So **always confirm information when it matters,** especially if you're making a detour to visit a specific place. Your experiences—positive and negative—matter to us. If we have missed or misstated something, **please write to us.** We follow up on all suggestions. Contact the Caribbean Ports of Call editor at editors@fodors.com or c/o Fodor's at 1745 Broadway, New York, New York 10019.

Be a Fodor's Correspondent

Your opinion matters. It matters to us. It matters to your fellow Fodor's travelers, too. And we'd like to hear it. In fact, we *need* to hear it.

When you share your experiences and opinions, you become an active member of the Fodor's community. That means we'll not only use your feedback to make our books better, but we'll publish your names and comments whenever possible. Throughout our guides, look for "Word of Mouth," excerpts of your unvarnished feedback.

Here's how you can help improve Fodor's for all of us.

Tell us when we're right. We rely on local writers to give you an insider's perspective. But our writers and staff editors—who are the best in the business—depend on you. Your positive feedback is a vote to renew our recommendations for the next edition.

Tell us when we're wrong. We're proud that we update most of our guides every year. But we're not perfect. Things change. Hotels cut services. Museums change hours. Charming cafés lose charm. If our writer didn't quite capture the essence of a place, tell us how you'd do it differently. If any of our descriptions are inaccurate or inadequate, we'll incorporate your changes in the next edition and will correct factual errors at fodors.com *immediately*.

Tell us what to include. You probably have had fantastic travel experiences that aren't yet in Fodor's. Why not share them with a community of like-minded travelers? Maybe you chanced upon a beach or bistro or took a great shore excursion that you don't want to keep to yourself. Tell us why we should include it. And share your discoveries and experiences with everyone directly at fodors.com. Your input may lead us to add a new listing or highlight a place we cover with a "Highly Recommended" star or with our highest rating, "Fodor's Choice."

Give us your opinion instantly at our feedback center at www.fodors.com/feedback. You may also e-mail editors@fodors.com with the subject line "Caribbean Ports of Call Editor." Or send your nominations, comments, and complaints by mail to Caribbean Ports of Call Editor, Fodor's, 1745 Broadway, New York, NY 10019.

You and travelers like you are the heart of the Fodor's community. Make our community richer by sharing your experiences. Be a Fodor's correspondent.

Bon Voyage!

Tim Jarrell, Publisher

CONTENTS

Maps and Charts

ABOUT THIS BOOK

What's In This Book

Up front you'll find a **Cruise Primer**, with some basic information about cruising and cruise ships.

Cruising the Caribbean gives you the low-down on the cruise lines and cruise ships that regularly ply the waters of the Caribbean. This section will help you understand what to expect on your cruise.

Ports of Embarkation gives you background on the most important U.S. ports for joining a cruise, including suggestions for where to stay and eat, and what you might want to do if you spend an extra day or two there before or after.

Ports of Call gives you our best advice on what to do in each major Caribbean cruise port if you want to go your own way, as well as a run-down of our favorite shore excursions offered by most ships if you don't.

Disagree with any of our choices? Care to nominate a place or suggest that we rate one more highly? Visit our feedback center at www.fodors.com/feedback.

Budget Well

Hotel and restaurant price categories from ¢ to $$$$ are defined in the opening pages of each chapter. For attractions, we always give standard adult admission fees; reductions are usually available for children, students, and senior citizens. Want to pay with plastic? **AE, D, DC, MC, V** following restaurant and hotel listings indicate if American Express, Discover, Diner's Club, MasterCard, and Visa are accepted.

Restaurants

Unless we state otherwise, restaurants are open for lunch and dinner daily. We mention dress only when there's a specific requirement and reservations only when they're essential or not accepted—it's always best to book ahead.

Hotels

Hotels have private bath, phone, TV, and air-conditioning and operate on the European Plan (a.k.a. EP, meaning without meals), unless we specify that they use the Continental Plan (CP, with a Continental breakfast), Breakfast Plan (BP, with a full breakfast), or Modified American Plan (MAP, with breakfast and dinner) or are all-inclusive (including all meals and most activities). We always list facilities but not whether you'll be charged an extra fee to use them, so when pricing accommodations, find out what's included.

Many Listings
- ⭐ Fodor's Choice
- ★ Highly recommended
- ✉ Physical address
- ✛ Directions
- 🏠 Mailing address
- ☎ Telephone
- 📠 Fax
- 🌐 On the Web
- ✉ E-mail
- 🎫 Admission fee
- ☉ Open/closed times
- ▶ Start of walk/itinerary
- Ⓜ Metro stations
- 💳 Credit cards

Hotels & Restaurants
- 🏨 Hotel
- 🛏 Number of rooms
- ♨ Facilities
- 🍴 Meal plans
- ✕ Restaurant
- 🐚 Reservations
- 👗 Dress code
- ↘ Smoking
- 🍸 BYOB
- ✕🏨 Hotel with restaurant that warrants a visit

Outdoors
- ⛳ Golf
- ⛺ Camping

Other
- ☺ Family-friendly
- 🔢 Contact information
- ⇨ See also
- ✉ Branch address
- ☞ Take note

Cruise Primer

WORD OF MOUTH

"My wife and I (late 60s) went on three different cruises 15 or so years ago. . . . We are planning on going on a Caribbean cruise for about 9 days in the next month or two. How has cruising changed over those 15 years? What differences can we expect? Thanks in advance."

—Gerhardt

"We were going crazy trying to decide on which island to vacation. Then, a waitress at a local restaurant suggested a cruise. . . . So, here we are, never having considered cruising before and seeing all the choices—wow! Do we ever need help!"

—tabcourt

By Linda
Coffman

IF YOU'VE NEVER BEEN ON A CRUISE BEFORE, it's tempting to ask, "What's so special about a cruise vacation?" It's a good question. Until the age of the airplane, ocean travel was simply a means to get to your far-flung destination—often the only way. But even in the early decades of the 20th century, venerable ocean liners such as the *Normandie* offered the occasional round-trip cruise to an exotic locale.

The passengers on the earliest cruises didn't have a fun-in-the-sun mindset as they sailed to faraway ports. They sailed to broaden horizons and learn about ports of call that couldn't be reached by overland travel. Perhaps they booked a cruise to Panama to observe the construction of the canal or, like the *Normandie*'s passengers, were bound for Brazil and the daring excitement of Carnival.

Regardless of *why* they were cruising, early cruisers steamed toward the unfamiliar with many fewer comforts than contemporary passengers. On the *Normandie,* air-conditioned comfort was available only in the ship's first-class dining room, though at least passengers could find relief from Rio's heat in one of the era's few outdoor swimming pools at sea. If an ocean liner had a permanent swimming pool, it was often indoors and deep in the hull.

Carnival Cruise Line executives like to reminisce about the tiny "gyms" on their early ships, which were converted ocean liners, and then point to how far ship designs have evolved. I remember them well. It was even difficult to find the casino on Carnival's first "Fun Ship" *Mardi Gras,* let alone the indoor swimming pool. That's hardly the case today. Designed for contemporary travelers and tastes, modern cruise ships carry passengers amid conveniences unheard of in the heyday of the North Atlantic ocean liner or even in the earliest vessels permanently dedicated to cruises. There's a lot to like on ships these days.

The allure of a modern sea cruise is its ability to appeal to a wide range of vacationers as a safe and convenient way to travel. Today's cruise ships are lively and luxurious floating resorts that offer something to satisfy the expectations of almost everyone. The first thing you'll find is that although cruise ships differ dramatically in the details and how they craft and deliver the cruise experience, most ships have the same basic features. And although the decisions and considerations in booking one cruise over another can be complex, the more you know about cruise travel in general, the better prepared you will be when it comes to making your choices.

BEFORE YOU GO

To expedite your pre-boarding paperwork, some cruise lines have convenient forms on their Internet Web sites. As long as you have your reservation number, you can provide the required immigration information, pre-reserve shore excursions, and even indicate any special requests from the comfort of your home. Be sure to print copies of any forms you fill out and bring them with you to the pier.

Documents

It is every passenger's responsibility to have proper identification. If you arrive at the port without it, you may not be allowed to board, and the line will issue no fare refund. Most travel agents know the requirements and can guide you to the proper agency to obtain what you need if you don't have it.

Everyone must have proof of citizenship and identity to travel abroad. For American citizens on most cruises to the Bahamas and the Caribbean, that means a valid passport, which was expected at this writing to become a requirement for Americans traveling to the Caribbean and the Bahamas on January 1, 2006. Canadian citizens can often use a valid passport or an original or certified birth certificate (with an official seal) *as well as* a government-issued photo ID, but that will also be changing at the end of 2006, when a passport will be required to travel to the U.S., where virtually all Caribbean cruises depart, from Canada. These requirements are made by the U.S. government and are a change from previous policies. Some countries that normally require a passport for all incoming Americans and Canadians—including Barbados, Belize, and Martinique—have historically waived that requirement for cruise passengers. It is unclear whether that policy will change with regard to Canadians when the new U.S. passport regulations take effect. However, should you miss the ship due to flight delays or other complications, you would need a passport to fly into those countries to join your ship. If your Western Caribbean cruise continues to South America, you will need a passport. Additionally, some countries, including Brazil, require visas.

Children under the age of 18, who are not traveling with both parents, almost always require a letter of permission from the absent parent(s). Airlines, cruise lines, and immigration agents can deny minor children initial boarding or entry to foreign countries without proper proof of identification and citizenship *and* a permission letter from absent or non-custodial parents. Your travel agent or cruise line can help with the wording of such a letter.

Getting or Renewing a Passport

In the past, cruise lines sailing to the Caribbean rarely asked to see the passports of American passengers. Since that policy is now changing, you should apply for a passport as far in advance of your cruise as possible. The process usually takes at least six weeks and can take longer during very busy periods. You can expedite your passport application if you are traveling within two weeks by paying an additional fee of $60 (in addition to the regular passport fee) and appearing in person at a regional passport office. Also, several passport expediting services will handle your application for you (for a hefty fee, of course) and can get you a passport even sooner. You can read all about the passport application process at the web site of the **U.S. Department of State** (⊕ travel. state.gov/passport). A passport costs $97 if you are 16 or older, $82 if you are under 16. It is valid for 10 years.

What to Pack

As far as clothing goes, cruise wear falls into three categories: casual, informal, and formal. Cruise documents should include information indicating how many evenings fall into each category. You will know when to wear what by reading your ship's daily newsletter—each evening's dress code will be prominently announced.

For the day, you'll need casual wear. For warm-weather cruises, you'll typically need swimwear, a cover-up, and sandals for pool and beach. Time spent ashore touring and shopping calls for shorts topped with T-shirts or polo shirts and comfy walking shoes. Conservative is a rule to live by, and mix-and-match will save room in your suitcase. Forget denim, which is too hot, and concentrate on lighter fabrics that will breathe in the Caribbean heat. At night, casual means khaki-type slacks and nice polo or sport shirts for men. Ladies' outfits are sundresses, skirts and tops, or pants outfits. By sticking to two colors and a few accessories, you can mix up tops and bottoms for a different look every night.

Informal dress is a little trickier. It applies only to evening wear and can mean different things depending on the cruise line. Informal for women is a dressier dress or pants outfit; for men it almost always includes a sport coat and sometimes a tie. Check your documents carefully.

Formal night means dressing up, but these days even that is a relative notion. You will see women in everything from simple cocktail dresses to elaborate glittering gowns. A tuxedo (either all black or with white dinner jacket) or dark suit is required for gentlemen. If you have been a "Mother-of-the-Bride" lately, chances are your outfit for the wedding is just perfect for formal night. For children, Sunday-best is entirely appropriate.

Men can usually rent their formal attire from the cruise line, and if they do so, it will be waiting when they board. Be sure to make these arrangements in advance; your travel agent can get the details from the cruise line. But if you are renting a tux, buy your own studs: a surefire way to spot a rented tuxedo is by the inexpensive studs that come with it. Also, many men with a little "girth" consider a vest more comfortable than a cummerbund.

An absolute essential for women is a shawl or light sweater. Aggressive air-conditioning can make public rooms uncomfortable, particularly if you are sunburned from a day at the beach.

Put things you can't do without—such as spare eyeglasses, toiletries, a swimsuit, and change of clothes for the first day—in your carry-on. Most cruise ships provide soap, shampoo, and conditioner, so you probably won't need those.

And plan carefully. In fact, we'd strongly advise you to make a list so you don't forget anything.

Accessibility Issues

As recently as the early 1990s, "accessibility" on a cruise ship meant little more than a few inside staterooms set aside for passengers with mobility issues. Most public restrooms and nearly all en suite bathrooms had a "step-over" threshold. Newer ships are more sensitive to the needs of passengers with disabilities, but many older ships still have physical barriers in both cabins and public rooms. And once you get off the ship—particularly in some Caribbean ports—your problems will be compounded.

All cruise lines offer a limited number of staterooms designed to be wheelchair- and scooter-accessible. Booking a newer vessel will generally assure more choices. On newer ships, public rooms are generally more accessible, and more facilities have been planned with wheelchair users in mind. Auxiliary aids, such as flashers for the hearing impaired and buzzers for visually impaired passengers, as well as lifts for swimming pools and hot tubs, are available upon request. However, more than the usual amount of preplanning is necessary for smooth sailing if you have special needs.

For example, when a ship is unable to dock—as is the case in Grand Cayman, for instance—passengers are taken ashore on tenders that are sometimes hard for the able-bodied to negotiate under adverse conditions. Some people with limited mobility may even find it difficult to embark or disembark the ship when docked due to the steep angle of gangways during high or low tide at certain times of day. In some situations, crew members may offer assistance that involves carrying guests, but if the sea is choppy, that might not be an option.

Passengers who require continuous oxygen or have service animals have further hurdles to overcome. You can bring both aboard a cruise ship, but your service animal may not be allowed to go ashore with you if the port has strict laws regarding animal quarantines.

Insurance

It's a good idea to purchase travel insurance, which covers a variety of possible hazards and mishaps, when you book a cruise. One concern for cruise passengers is being delayed en route to the port of embarkation and missing the ship. Another major consideration is lost luggage—or even the delay of luggage. Both of these possibilities should be covered. You may miss the first day or two of your cruise, but all will not be lost financially. A travel policy will insure you can replace delayed necessities secure in the knowledge you will be reimbursed for those unexpected expenditures. Save your receipts for all out-of-pocket expenses to file your claim and be sure to get an incident report from the airline at fault.

No one wants their cruise vacation spoiled by a broken arm, heart attack, or worse, but if one of life's tragedies occurs, you want to be covered. The medical insurance program you depend on at home might not extend coverage beyond the borders of the United States. Medicare assuredly will not cover you if you are hurt or sick. It is worth noting that all ships of foreign registry are considered to be "outside the United States" by Medicare. Without basic coverage, travelers should be prepared to pay for any care they require, either by credit card or wire transfer of funds to the provider.

Some independent insurers such as Travel Guard, Access America, or CSA offer very comprehensive policies at attractive rates. Nearly all cruise lines offer their own line of insurance. Compare the coverage and rates to determine which is best for you. Keep in mind that insurance purchased from an independent carrier is more likely to include coverage if the cruise line goes out of business before or during your cruise. Although it is a rare and unlikely occurrence, you do want to be insured in the event that it happens.

🗐 U.S. Travel Insurers **Access America** ✉ 2805 N. Parham Rd., Richmond, VA 23294 ☎ 800/284-8300 🖷 800/346-9265 or 804/673-1469 ⊕ www.accessamerica.com. **CSA Travel Protection** ✉ Box 939057, San Diego, CA 92193-9057 ☎ 800/873-9855 🖷 800/336-6409 or 858/810-2428 ⊕ www.csatravelprotection.com. **Travel Guard International** ✉ 1145 Clark St., Stevens Point, WI 54481 ☎ 800/826-1300 or 715/345-1041 🖷 800/955-8785 or 715/345-1990 ⊕ www.travelguard.com.

ARRIVING & EMBARKING

Most cruise ship passengers fly to the port of embarkation. If you book your cruise far enough in advance, you'll be given the opportunity to purchase an air-and-sea package, which can save you money on your flight.

If you buy an air-and-sea package from your cruise line, a uniformed cruise line agent will meet you to smooth your way from airport to pier. You will need to claim your own bags and give them to the transfer driver so they can be loaded on the bus. Upon arrival at the pier, luggage is automatically transferred to the ship for delivery to your cabin. The cruise line ground transfer system can also be available to independent fliers. However, be sure to ask your travel agent how much it costs; you may find that a taxi or shuttle service is less expensive and more convenient.

In addition to the busiest embarkation ports such as Miami, Fort Lauderdale, and New York City, cruises now leave from less-familiar port cities all around the East and Gulf coasts. Since 2001, Galveston and New Orleans have become major home ports and are considered now to be among the nation's top 10 cruise ports. Many people prefer to drive to these ports if they are close enough to home; happily, secure parking is always available, either within the port itself or nearby.

Boarding

Once the planning, packing, and anticipation are behind them, veteran cruise passengers sometimes view embarkation day as anticlimactic. However, for first-time cruise travelers, embarking on their first ship can be more than exhilarating—it can be downright intimidating. What exactly can you expect?

Check-In

Once inside the cruise terminal, you'll see a check-in line. Actual boarding time is often scheduled for noon, but some cruise lines will begin processing early arrivals and then direct them to a "holding" area. During check-in, you will be asked to produce your documents and any forms you were sent to complete ahead of time, plus proof of citizenship and a credit card (to cover onboard charges). You are issued a boarding card that often also doubles as your stateroom "key" and shipboard charge card. At some point—either before you enter the check-in area or before proceeding to the ship—you and your hand luggage will pass through a security procedure similar to those at airports.

The lines for check-in can be long, particularly at peak times. If check-in starts at noon but continues to 4 PM, you can expect lines to trail off as the boarding deadline approaches. Everyone is anxious to get on board and begin their vacation, so if you arrive at one of the busy times, keep in mind that this is not the time to get cranky if you have to wait.

Boarding the Ship

Once boarding begins, you will inevitably have your first experience with the ship's photographer and be asked to pose for an embarkation picture. It only takes a second, so smile. You are under no obligation to purchase any photos taken of you during the cruise, but they are nice souvenirs.

Procedures vary somewhat once you are greeted by staff members lined up just inside the ship's hull; however, once again you'll have to produce your boarding card for the security officer and, possibly, a picture ID. Depending on the cruise line, you will be directed to your cabin, or a steward will relieve you of your carry-on luggage and accompany you. Stewards on high-end cruise lines not only show you the way, but hand you a glass of champagne as a welcome-aboard gesture.

ON BOARD

Check out your cabin to make sure that everything is in order. Try the plumbing and set the air-conditioning to the temperature you prefer. Your cabin may feel warm while docked but will cool off when the ship is underway. You should find a copy of the ship's daily schedule in the cabin. Take a few moments to look it over—you will want to know what time the muster drill takes place (a placard on the back of your cabin door will indicate directions to your emergency station), as well as meal hours and the schedule for various activities and entertainments.

Rented tuxedoes are either hanging in the closet or will be delivered sometime during the afternoon; Bon Voyage gifts sent by your friends or travel agent usually appear as well. Be patient if you are expecting deliveries, particularly on mega-ships. Cabin stewards participate in the ship's turnaround and are extremely busy, although yours will no doubt introduce himself at the first available opportunity. It will also be a while before your checked luggage arrives, so your initial order of business is usually the buffet. Bring along the daily schedule to check over while you eat.

While making your way to the Lido buffet, no doubt you'll notice bar waiters offering trays of colorful and exotic drinks, often in souvenir glasses that you can keep. Beware—they are not complimentary! If you choose one, you will be asked to sign for it. Again, like the photos, you are under no obligation to purchase; however, the glasses are fun souvenirs.

Do your plans for the cruise include booking shore excursions and indulging in spa treatments? The most popular tours sometimes sell out, and spas can be very busy during sea days, so your next stops should be the Shore Excursion Desk to book tours and the spa to make appointments.

Dining room seating arrangements are another matter for consideration. Some people like to check the main dining room to determine where their table is located. If it is not to your liking, or if you requested a large table and find yourself assigned to a small one, you will want to see the head waiter. He will be stationed in a lounge with his charts handy to make changes. The daily schedule will indicate where and when to meet with him.

Paying for Things on Board

Let's step back a moment and take a look at what happened when you checked in at the pier. Because a cashless society prevails on cruise ships, an imprint was made of your credit card or you had to place a cash deposit for use against your onboard charges. Then you were issued a charge card that usually doubles as your stateroom "key." Most onboard expenditures are charged to your shipboard account with your signature as verification, with the exception of casino gaming—even so, you can often get "cash advances" against your account from the casino cashier.

An itemized bill is provided at the end of the voyage listing your purchases. In order to avoid surprises, it is a good idea to set aside your charge slips and request an interim printout of your bill from the Purser to insure accuracy. Should you change your mind about charging onboard purchases, you can always inform the Purser and pay in cash or traveler's checks instead. If your cash deposit was more than you spent, you will receive a refund.

Tipping

One of the most delicate—yet frequently debated—topics of conversation among cruise passengers involves the matter of tipping. Who do you tip? How much? What's "customary" and "recommended?" Should parents tip the full amount for children or is just half adequate? Why do you have to tip at all?

When transfers to and from your ship are a part of your air-and-sea program, gratuities are generally included for luggage handling. In that case, do not worry about the interim tipping. However, if you take a taxi to the pier and hand over your bags to a stevedore, be sure to tip him. Treat him with respect and pass along at least $5.

During your cruise, room service waiters generally receive a cash tip of $1 to $3 per delivery. A 15% to 18% gratuity will automatically be added to each bar bill during the cruise. If you use salon and spa services, a similar percentage is generally added to the bills there. If you dine in a specialty restaurant, you will usually be asked to provide a one-time gratuity for the service staff.

There will be a "Disembarkation Talk" on the last day of the cruise that explains tipping procedures. If you are expected to tip in cash, small white "tip" envelopes will appear in your stateroom that day. If you tip in cash, you usually give the tip envelope directly to each person on the last night of the cruise. Tips generally add up to about $10 to $12 per person per day. You tip the same amount for each person who shares the cabin, including children, unless otherwise indicated.

Most lines now either automatically add gratuities to passengers' on-board charge accounts or offer the option. If that suits you, then do nothing further. However, you are certainly free to adjust the amounts up or down to more appropriate levels or ask that the charge be removed altogether if you prefer distributing cash gratuities.

Dining

All food, all the time? Not quite, but it is possible to literally eat away the day and most of the night on a cruise. A popular cruise directors' joke is, "You came on as passengers, and you will be leaving as cargo." Although it is meant in fun, it does contain a ring of truth. Food—tasty and plentiful—is available 24 hours a day on most cruise ships, and the dining experience at sea has reached almost mythical proportions. Perhaps it has something to do with legendary midnight buffets, the absence of menu prices, or maybe it's the vast selection and availability.

Restaurants

Every ship has at least one main restaurant and a Lido, or casual, buffet alternative. Increasingly important are specialty restaurants. Meals in the primary and buffet restaurants are included in the cruise fare, as are round-the-clock room service, midday tea and snacks, and late-night buffets. Most mainstream cruise lines levy a surcharge for dining in alternative restaurants that may, or may not, also include a gratuity, although there generally is no additional charge on luxury cruise lines.

You may also find a pizzeria or a specialty coffee bar on your ship—increasingly popular favorites cropping up on ships old and new. Although pizza is complimentary, expect an additional charge for specialty coffees at the coffee bar and, quite likely, in the dining room as well. You will also likely be charged for sodas and other drinks during meals other than iced tea, regular coffee, tap water, and fruit juice.

There is often a direct relationship between the cost of a cruise and the quality of its cuisine. The food is very sophisticated on some (mostly expensive) lines, among them Crystal, Cunard, Seabourn, and Silversea. In the more moderate price range, Celebrity Cruises has gained renown for the culinary stylings of French chef Michel Roux, who acts as a consultant to the line. But on most mainstream cruise lines, the food is the quality that you would find in any good hotel banquet—perfectly acceptable but certainly not great.

Seatings

If your cruise ship has traditional seatings for dinner, the one decision that may set the tone for your entire cruise is your dinner seating. Which is best? Early dinner seating is generally scheduled between 6 and 6:30 PM, while late seating can begin from 8:15 to 8:45 PM. So the "best" seating depends on you, your lifestyle, and your personal preference.

Families with young children and older passengers often choose an early seating. Early seating diners are encouraged not to linger too long over dessert and coffee because the dining room has to be readied for late seating. Late seating is viewed by some passengers as more romantic and less rushed.

Cruise lines understand that strict schedules no longer satisfy the desires of all modern cruise passengers. Many cruise lines now include alternatives to the set schedules in the dining room, including casual dinner menus in their buffet facilities where more flexibility is allowed in dress and mealtimes. À la carte restaurants are showing up on more ships and offer yet another choice, though usually for an additional charge.

Open seating is primarily associated with more upscale lines; it allows passengers the flexibility to dine any time during restaurant hours and be seated with whomever they please.

Led by Norwegian Cruise Line and Princess Cruises, more contemporary and premium cruise lines are exploring this adaptation of open seating to offer variety and a more personalized experience for their passengers. More mainstream Carnival Cruise Line and Holland America Line have added a twist with four seating times instead of the usual two, plus casual evening dining in the Lido buffet.

CHANGING TABLES Some cruise lines advise that, although dining preferences may be requested by your travel agent, no requests are guaranteed. Table assignments are generally not confirmed until embarkation; however, every effort is made to satisfy all guests. Should there be a problem, see the maître d' for assistance. Changes after the first evening are generally discouraged; however, there will be a designated place to meet with dining room staff and iron out seating problems on embarkation day. Check the daily program for time and location.

Special Diets

Cruise lines make every possible attempt to insure dining satisfaction. If you have special dietary considerations—such as low-salt, kosher, or food allergies—be sure to indicate them well ahead of time and check to be certain your needs are known by your waiter once on board. In addition to the usual menu items, "spa," low-calorie, low-carbohydrate, or low-fat selections, as well as children's menus are usually available. Requests for dishes not featured on the menu can often be granted if you ask in advance.

Wine

Wine typically costs about what you would expect to pay at a nice lounge or restaurant in a resort or at home (depending on where you live). Wine by the bottle is a more economical choice at dinner than ordering it by the glass. Any wine you don't finish will be kept for you and served the next night. Gifts of wine or champagne ordered from the cruise line (either by you, a friend, or your travel agent) can be taken to the dining room. Wine from any other source will incur a "corkage" fee of approximately $8 to $10 per bottle.

The Captain's Table

Legend has it that a nouveau riche passenger's response to an invitation to dine with the captain during a round-the-world cruise was, "I didn't shell out all those bucks to eat with the help!" Although there are some cruise passengers who decline invitations to dine at the captain's table, there are far more who covet such an experience. You will know you have been included in that exclusive coterie when an embossed invitation arrives in your stateroom on the day of a formal dinner. RSVP as soon as possible—if you are unable to attend, someone else will be invited in your place.

Who is invited? If you are a frequent repeat cruiser, the occupants of an owner's suite, or if you hail from the captain's hometown or speak his native language, you may be considered. Honeymoon couples are sometimes selected at random, as are couples celebrating a golden wedding anniversary. Attractive, unattached female passengers often round out an uneven number of guests. Requests made by travel agents on behalf of their clients sometimes do the trick.

Entertainment

It's hard to imagine, but in the early years of cruise travel, shipboard entertainment consisted of little more than poetry readings and recitals that exhibited the talents of fellow passengers. Those bygone days of sedate amusements in an intimate setting have been replaced by lavish showrooms where sequined and feathered showgirls strut their stuff on stage amid special effects not imagined in the past.

Seven-night Caribbean cruises usually include two original production shows. One of these might be a Las Vegas–style extravaganza and the other a best-of-Broadway show featuring old and new favorites from the Great White Way. Other shows highlight the talents of individual singers, dancers, magicians, comedians, and even acrobats. Don't be surprised if you are plucked from the audience to take the brunt of a comedian's jokes or act as the magician's temporary assistant. Sit in the front row if appearing onstage appeals to you.

Whether it is relegated to a late-afternoon interlude between bingo and dinner, or a featured evening highlight, the Passenger Talent Show is often a "don't miss" production. From pure camp to stylishly slick, what passes for talent is sometimes surprising but seldom boring. Stand-up comedy is generally discouraged; however, passengers who want their performance skills to be considered should answer the call for auditions and plan to rehearse the show at least once.

Enrichment programs have become a popular pastime at sea. It may come as a surprise that port lecturers on many large contemporary cruise ships offer more information on shore tours and shopping than insight into the ports of call. If more cerebral presentations are important to you, consider a cruise on a line that features stimulating enrichment programs

DRINKING ON BOARD

T'S HARD TO AVOID THE SHIP'S BARS since they are social centers, but alcoholic drinks are not usually included in your cruise fare, and bar bills can add up quickly. Drinks at the captain's welcome-aboard cocktail party and at cocktail parties held specifically for past-cruisers are usually free. But if you pick up that boldly colored welcome-aboard cocktail as your ship pulls away from the dock, you may very well be asked to sign for it, and the cost will then be added to your shipboard account. You should expect to pay about the same for a drink on board a cruise ship that you would pay in a bar at home: $3 to $4 for a domestic beer, $4 to $9 for a cocktail, $5 to $7 for a glass of wine, $1 to $1.50 for a soft drink. On virtually all ships, an automatic 15% gratuity will be added to your tab. What most people don't consider is that specialty coffees are also added to your bar tab, so if you order a cappucino—and on some ships that applies even if it's in the dining room after dinner—you'll see a charge of $2 to $3 on your bar bill. To save money on your bar bill, you can follow a few simple strategies. In lounges, request the less-expensive bar brands or the reduced-price drink-of-the-day. On some ships, discounted "beverage cards" for unlimited fountain soft drinks and/or a set number of mixed drinks are available.

In international waters there are, technically, no laws against teenage drinking, but almost all ships require passengers to be over 18 or 21 to purchase alcoholic beverages.

and seminars at sea. Speakers can include destination-oriented historians, popular authors, business leaders, radio or television personalities, and even movie stars.

Lounges & Nightclubs

If you find the show lounge stage a bit intimidating and want to perform in a more intimate venue, look for karaoke. Singing along in a likely piano bar is another shipboard favorite for would-be crooners. Some passengers even take the place of the ship's pianist during breaks to demonstrate their skill.

Other lounges might feature easy-listening music, jazz, or combos for pre- and post-dinner social dancing. Later in the evening, lounges pick up the pace with music from the 1950s and '60s; clubs aimed at a younger crowd usually have more contemporary dance music during the late-night hours.

Casinos

A sure sign that your ship is in international waters is the opening of the casino. On most ships, lavish casinos pulsate with activity. The most notable exceptions are the family-oriented ships of Disney Cruise Line, which shun gaming in favor of more wholesome pastimes.

On ships that feature them, the rationale for locating casinos where most passengers must pass either through or alongside them is obvious—the unspoken allure of winning. In addition to slot machines in a variety of denominations, cruise ship casinos might feature roulette, craps, and a variety of poker games—Caribbean Stud Poker, Let It Ride, and blackjack, to name a few. Cruise lines strive to provide fair and professional gambling entertainment and supply gaming guides that set out the rules of play and betting limits for each game.

Casino hours vary based on the itinerary or location of the ship; most are required to close while in port, while others may be able to offer 24-hour slot machines and simply close table games. Every casino has a cashier for convenience, and you may be able to charge a cash advance to your onboard account.

Other Entertainment

Most vessels have a room for screening movies. On older ships and some newer ones, this is often a genuine cinema-style movie theater, while on other ships it may be just a multipurpose room. Over the course of a weeklong voyage a dozen films may be screened, each repeated several times. Theaters are also used for lectures, religious services, and private meetings.

With a few exceptions, ocean liners equip their cabins with closed-circuit TVs showing movies (continuously on some newer ships), shipboard lectures, and regular programs (thanks to satellite reception). Ships with in-cabin VCRs or DVDs usually provide a selection of movies at no charge (a deposit is sometimes required).

Most medium and large ships have video arcades, and nearly all ships now have computer centers.

Sports & Fitness

Onboard sports facilities might include a court for basketball, volleyball, tennis—or all three—a jogging track, or even an in-line skating track. Some ships are even offering innovative and unexpected features, such as rock-climbing walls and bungee trampolines on some Royal Caribbean ships. For the less adventurous, there's always table tennis and shuffleboard.

Naturally, you will find at least one swimming pool and, possibly, several. Cruise ship pools are generally on the small side—more appropriate for cooling off than doing laps—and the majority contain filtered salt water. But some are elaborate affairs, with waterslides. Princess Grand-class ships have challenging, freshwater "swim against the current" pools for swimming enthusiasts who want to get their low-impact exercise while on board.

Golf is a perennial seagoing favorite of players who want to take their games to the next level and include the Caribbean's most beautiful and challenging courses on their scorecards. Shipboard programs can include clinics, use of full-motion golf cages, and even individual instruction from resident pros using state-of-the-art computer analysis. Once ashore, escorted excursions include everything needed for a satisfying round of play, including equipment and tips from the pro, and the ability to schedule tee times at exclusive courses.

Fitness Centers

Cruise vacations can be hazardous to your waistline if you are not careful. Eating "out" for all meals and sampling different cuisines tend to pile on unaccustomed calories. But shipboard fitness centers have become ever more elaborate, offering state-of-the-art exercise machines, treadmills, and stair steppers, not to mention weights and weight machines. As a bonus, many fitness centers with floor-to-ceiling windows have the world's most inspiring sea views.

For guests who prefer a more social atmosphere as they burn off sinful chocolate desserts, there are specialized fitness classes for all levels of ability. High-impact, energetic aerobics are not for everyone, but any class that raises the heart rate can be toned down and tailored to individual capabilities. Stretching classes help you warm up for a light jog or brisk walk on deck, and there are even sit-for-fitness classes for mature passengers or those with delicate joints. Fees are sometimes charged for specialty classes, such as Pilates, spinning, and yoga. Personal trainers are usually on board to get you off on the right foot, also for a fee.

Spas

With all the usual pampering and service in luxurious surroundings, simply being on a cruise can be a stress-reducing experience. Add to that the menu of spa and salon services at your fingertips and you have a recipe for total sensory pleasure. Spas have also become among the most popular of shipboard areas.

Some spa offerings sound good enough to eat. A Milk-and-Honey Hydrotherapy Bath, Coconut Rub and Milk Ritual Wrap or Float, and a Javanese Steam Wrap incorporating cinnamon, ginger, coffee, sea salt, and honey are just a few of the tempting items found on spa menus. Not quite as exotic sounding, other treatments and services are nonetheless therapeutic for the body and soul. Steiner Leisure is the largest spa and salon operator at sea (the company even operates the Mandara and the Greenhouse spas), with facilities on more than 100 cruise ships worldwide.

In addition to facials, manicures, pedicures, massages, and sensual body treatments, other hallmarks of Steiner Leisure are salon services and products for hair and skin. Founded in 1901 by Henry Steiner of London, a single salon prospered when Steiner's son joined the business in 1926 and was granted a Royal Warrant as hairdresser to Her Majesty Queen Mary in 1937. In 1956, Steiner won its first cruise ship contract to operate the salon on board the ships of the Cunard Line. By the mid-1990s, Steiner Leisure began taking an active role in creating shipboard spas offering a wide variety of wellness therapies and beauty programs for both women and men.

HEALTH & SAFETY AT SEA

Fire Safety

The greatest danger facing cruise ship passengers is fire. All cruise lines must meet international standards for fire safety, which require sprinkler systems, smoke detectors, and other safety features. Fires on cruise ships are not common but they do happen, and these rules have made ships much safer.

Once settled into your cabin, locate life vests and review posted emergency instructions. Make sure vests are in good condition and learn to secure them properly. Make certain the ship's purser knows if you have a physical infirmity that may hamper a speedy exit from your cabin so that in an emergency he or she can quickly dispatch a crew member to assist you. If you are traveling with children, be sure that child-size life jackets are placed in your cabin.

Within 24 hours of embarkation, you will be asked to attend a mandatory lifeboat drill. Do so and listen carefully. If you are unsure of how to use your vest, now is the time to ask. Only in the most extreme circumstances will you need to abandon ship—but it has happened.

Health Care

All large ships have an infirmary to deal with minor medical emergencies, but these infirmaries are not suitable for dealing with major procedures. The ship's doctor should be able to treat you as well as any general practitioner or clinic ashore for minor problems. For really complicated medical conditions, such as a heart attack or appendicitis, the ship's medical team evacuates passengers to the nearest hospital ashore. While at sea, evacuation expenses can rise as fast as the helicopter that whisks the patient away. You'll need supplementary insurance to cover these costs.

Many first-time passengers worry about seasickness. Modern vessels are equipped with stabilizers that eliminate much of the motion responsible for seasickness. Unless your cruise includes the open sea and wind-whipped water, you may not even feel the ship's movement—particularly if your ship is a mega-liner. If you do become seasick, you can use common drugs such as Dramamine and Bonine. Worn behind the ear, the Transderm Scop "patch" is a remedy that dispenses a continuous metered dose of medication which is absorbed into the skin and enters the bloodstream. It requires a prescription. If you have a history of motion sickness, do not book an inside cabin.

Two of the most prevalent diseases that spread through cruise ship populations are influenza and Noroviruses. Annual influenza vaccination is the primary method for preventing influenza and its complications.

Noroviruses are a group of related viruses that cause acute gastroenteritis in humans. Infection usually causes vomiting, diarrhea with abdominal cramps, and nausea. Low-grade fever also occasionally occurs and vomiting is more common in children. Dehydration is the most common complication, especially among the young and elderly, and may require medical attention. Symptoms generally last 24 to 60 hours. To avoid illness, first and foremost: wash your hands thoroughly and often. The Centers for Disease Control (CDC) also advise the use of an alcohol-based hand sanitizer (they come in travel-size bottles) along with hand washing. If you become ill, the ship's doctor will probably quarantine you in your cabin.

Shipboard Services

Communications

Just because you are out to sea does not mean you have to be out of touch. Ship-to-shore telephone calls can cost $5 to $15 a minute, so it makes economic sense to use e-mail to remain in contact with your home or office. Most ships have basic computer systems, while some newer vessels offer more high-tech connectivity—even in-cabin hookups or wireless connections for either your own laptop computer or one you can rent on board. Expect charges in the 35¢- to $1-per-minute range for usage. Ships usually offer some kind of package so that you get a reduced per-minute price if you pay a fee up front.

The ability to use your own mobile phone from the high seas is a relatively new alternative that is gaining popularity. It's also cheaper than using a cabin phone if your ship offers the service. A rather ingenious concept, the ship acts as a cell "tower" in international waters—you use your own cell phone and your own number when roaming at sea. When in port, depending on the agreements your mobile service-provider has established, you may be able to connect to local networks. Rates for using the maritime service, as well as any roaming charges from Caribbean islands, are established by your mobile service carrier and are worth checking into before you leave home.

Laundry & Dry Cleaning

Most cruise ships offer valet laundry and pressing (and some also offer dry-cleaning) service. Expenses can add up fast, especially for laundry, as charges are per item and the rates are similar to those charged in hotels. If doing laundry is important to you and you do not want to send it out to be done, most cruise ships have a low-cost or free self-service laundry room (they usually feature an iron and ironing board in addition to washer and dryer). If you book one of the top-dollar suites, laundry service may be included for no additional cost. Upscale ships, such as those in the Radisson Seven Seas Cruises, Silversea Cruises, and Seabourn fleets, have complimentary self-service launderettes. On other cruise lines, such as Princess Cruises, Oceania Cruises, Carnival Cruise Lines, Disney Cruise Line, and Holland America Line (except Vista-class ships), you can do your own laundry for about $3 or less per load. None of the vessels in the Royal Caribbean or Celebrity Cruises fleets has self-service laundry facilities.

Shore Excursion Desk

Manned by a knowledgeable staff, the Shore Excursion Desk can offer not only the sale of ship-sponsored tours, but may also be the place to learn more about ports of call and garner information to tour independently. Although staff members and the focus of their positions vary widely, the least you can expect are basic information and port maps. Happily, some shore excursion staff members possess a wealth of information and share it without reservation. On some ships the port lecturer may emphasize shopping and "recommended" merchants, with little to impart regarding sightseeing or the history and culture of ports.

CRIME ON SHIPS

Crime aboard cruise ships has occasionally become headline news, thanks in large part to a few well-publicized cases. Most people never have any type of problem, but you should exercise the same precautions aboard ship that you would at home. Keep your valuables out of sight—on big ships virtually every cabin has a small safe. Don't carry too much cash ashore, use your credit card whenever possible, and keep your money in a secure place, such as a front pocket that's harder to pick. Single women traveling with friends should stick together, especially when returning to their cabins late at night. Be careful about whom you befriend, as you would anywhere, whether it's a fellow passenger or a member of the crew. Don't be paranoid, but do be prudent.

DISEMBARKATION

All cruises come to an end eventually, and it hardly seems fair that you have to leave when it feels like your vacation has just begun, but leave you must. The disembarkation process actually begins the day before you arrive at your ship's home port. During that day your cabin steward delivers special luggage tags to your stateroom, along with customs forms and instructions.

The night before you disembark, you'll need to set aside clothing to wear the next morning when you leave the ship. Many people dress in whatever casual outfits they wear for the final dinner on board, or change into travel clothes after dinner. Also, do not forget to put your passport or other proof of citizenship, airline tickets, and medications in your hand luggage.

After you finish packing, attach your new luggage tags (they are color- or number-coded according to post-cruise transportation plans and flight schedules). Follow the instructions provided and place the locked luggage outside your stateroom door for pickup during the hours indicated.

A statement itemizing your onboard charges is delivered before you arise on disembarkation morning. Plan to get up early enough to check it over for accuracy, finish packing your personal belongings, and vacate your stateroom by the appointed hour. Any discrepancies in your onboard account should be taken care of before leaving the ship, usually at the Purser's Desk.

Room service is not available on most ships on the last day; however, breakfast is served in the main restaurant as well as the buffet. After breakfast, there is not much to do but wait comfortably in a lounge or on deck for your tag color or number to be called. Disembarkation procedures can sometimes be drawn out by passengers who are unprepared. This is no time to abandon your patience or sense of humor.

Remember that all passengers must meet with customs and immigration officials before disembarkation, either on the ship or in the terminal. Procedures vary and are outlined in your instructions. In some ports, passengers must meet with the officials at a specified hour (usually very early) in an onboard lounge; in other ports, customs forms are collected in the terminal and passports/identification papers are examined there as well.

Once in the terminal, locate your luggage and proceed to your motor coach, taxi, or retrieve your vehicle from the parking lot.

Customs & Duties

U.S. Customs

Before a ship lands, each individual or family must fill out a customs declaration. If your purchases total less than the limit for your destination, you will not need to itemize them. Be prepared to pay whatever duties are owed directly to the customs inspector, with cash or check. Be sure to keep receipts for all purchases, and be ready to show curious officials what you've bought.

U.S. Customs preclears some ships sailing into and out of New York and other ports—it's done on the ship before you disembark. In other ports you must collect your luggage from the dock, then stand in line to pass through the inspection point. This can take up to an hour.

ALLOWANCES U.S. residents who have been out of the country for at least 48 hours may bring home good valued at up to $600, $800, or $1,600 depending on which countries they have visited. The lowest exemption applies to most Caribbean countries, including Antigua & Barbuda, Aruba, Barbados, Bonaire, the British Virgin Islands, Curaçao, Dominica, the Dominican Republic, Grenada, Jamaica, Montserrat, Saba, St. Eustatius, St. Kitts & Nevis, St. Lucia, St. Maarten (the Dutch side only), St. Vincent & the Grenadines, and Trinidad and Tobago. The $800 exemption applies to Anguilla, the Cayman Islands, Guadeloupe, Martinique, St. Barths, St. Martin (the French side only), and the Turks and Caicos Islands. The $1,600 exemption applies to the U.S. Virgin Islands only (there is no exemption for Puerto Rico, which is considered a part of the U.S.). You can usually bring back goods valued at the highest possible exemption if you visit countries in a higher group provided that the goods valued above the lowest limit come from the country with the highest limit (i. e., buy the most expensive stuff in St. Thomas if your cruise visits that island).Whichever allowance applies, travelers 21 and older may bring home 1 liter of alcohol (2 liters if one of the liters was produced in a CBI country or 5 liters if returning from the USVI and at least 1 liter was produced there). Travelers of any age may also bring back 200 cigarettes (1,000 if returning from the USVI and at least 800 were acquired there), and 100 non-Cuban cigars. Family members from the same household who are traveling together may pool their personal exemptions.

SENDING
PACKAGES HOME Although you probably won't want to spend your time looking for a post office, you can send packages home duty-free, with a limit of one parcel per addressee per day (except alcohol or tobacco products or perfume worth more than $5). You can mail up to $200 worth of goods for personal use; label the package "personal use" and attach a list of the contents and their retail value. If the package contains your used personal belongings, mark it "personal goods returned" to avoid paying duty on your laundry. You may also send up to $100 worth of goods as a gift ($200 from the U.S. Virgin Islands); mark the package "unsolicited gift." Items you mailed do not affect your duty-free allowance on your return.

NONCITIZENS Non-U.S. citizens who are returning home within hours of docking may be exempt from all U.S. Customs duties. Everything you bring into the United States must leave with you when you return home, though. When you reach your own country, you will have to pay duties there.

Canadian Customs

Canadian residents who have been out of Canada for at least seven days may bring in C$750 worth of goods duty-free. You may not pool allowances with family members. If you meet the age requirements of the province or territory through which you reenter Canada, you may bring in, duty-free, 1.5 liters of wine *or* 1.14 liters (40 imperial ounces) of liquor *or* 24 12-ounce cans or bottles of beer or ale. Also, if you meet the local age requirement for tobacco products, you may bring in, duty-free, 200 cigarettes, 50 cigars or cigarillos, and 200 grams of tobacco. You may have to pay a minimum duty on tobacco products, regardless of whether or not you exceed your personal exemption. Check ahead of time with the Canada Border Services Agency or the Department of Agriculture for policies regarding meat products, seeds, plants, and fruits.

You may send an unlimited number of gifts (only one gift per recipient, however) worth up to C$60 each duty-free to Canada. Label the package UNSOLICITED GIFT—VALUE UNDER $60. Alcohol and tobacco are excluded.

U.K. Customs

Caribbean nations—even those that are *départements* of France and use the euro as their official currency—are not part of the European Union (EU) with regard to customs. From countries outside the European Union, including those in the Caribbean, you may bring home, duty-free, 200 cigarettes or 50 cigars; 1 liter of spirits or 2 liters of fortified or sparkling wine or liqueurs; 2 liters of still table wine; 60 milliliters of perfume; 250 milliliters of toilet water; plus £145 worth of other goods, including gifts and souvenirs. Prohibited items include meat products, seeds, plants, and fruits.

Cruising the Caribbean

WORD OF MOUTH

"Have never been on a cruise before. Looking for some advice on a Caribbean Cruise. . . . What is a good cruise line for a beginner cruiser age 28 for activities and night life? Is it best to book flight separate or package together? Any tips I need to be aware of? Thanks."

—Newmarket Cruiser

"For first time cruisers, the variety of cruise lines can be confusing. . . . Which cruise line is more appropriate for the 35–55 age group? Which one has the most relaxed atmosphere (no formal nights)? Looking for fun, relaxation, casual elegance, not stuffy and country clubby, some activities and a casino but nothing over the top. Also what's your favorite itinerary on these cruise lines? "

—bosco

www.fodors.com/forums

By Linda
Coffman

MORE SHIPS PLY THE WATERS of the Caribbean than any other spot on Earth. Some are huge ships carrying more than 2,000 passengers; some are midsize ships welcoming about 1,000 cruisers; and others are comparatively small ships on which you'll find yourself with 300 or fewer other passengers. There are fancy ships and party ships, ships with sails, ships that pride themselves on the numbers of ports they visit, and ships that provide so much activity right on board that you hardly have time or inclination to go ashore. In peak season, it's not uncommon for thousands of passengers to disembark from several ships into a small town on the same day—a phenomenon not always enjoyed by locals. With such an abundance of cruise ships in this area, however, you can choose the ship and the itinerary that suit you best.

CHOOSING YOUR CRUISE

Some of the best "islands" in the Caribbean are the ones that float and move—they are called cruise ships. Just as Caribbean islands have distinct histories and cultures, cruise ships also have individual personalities. Determined by their size, the year they were built, and their style, on one hand, they can be bold, brassy, and exciting—totally unlike home, but a great place to visit. Big ships offer stability and a huge variety of activities and facilities. On the other hand, small ships feel intimate, like private clubs. For every big-ship fan there is someone who would never set foot aboard a "floating resort." Examine your lifestyle—there's sure to be a cruise ship to match your expectations.

After giving some thought to your itinerary and where in the Caribbean you might wish to go, the ship you select is the most vital factor in your Caribbean cruise vacation, since it will not only determine which islands you will visit, but also how you will see them. Big ships visit major ports of call such as St. Thomas, St. Maarten/St. Martin, Nassau, and San Juan; when they call at smaller islands with shallower ports, passengers must disembark aboard shore tenders (small boats that ferry dozens of passengers to shore at a time). Or they may skip these smaller ports entirely. Small and midsize ships can visit smaller islands, such as St. Barths, St. Kitts, or Tortola, more easily; passengers are often able to disembark directly onto the pier without having to wait for tenders to bring them ashore.

Itineraries

You'll want to give some consideration to your ship's Caribbean itinerary when you are choosing your cruise. The length of the cruise will determine the variety and number of ports you visit, but so will the type of itinerary and the point of departure. **Loop cruises** start and end at the same point and usually explore ports close to one another; **one-way cruises** start at one point and end at another and range farther afield.

Most cruises to the Bahamas, Mexico's Mayan Riviera, and other points in the Caribbean are loop cruises. On Caribbean itineraries, you often have a choice of U.S. mainland departure points. Ships sailing out of San Juan, Puerto Rico, can visit up to five ports in seven days, while loop cruises out of Florida can reach up to four ports in the same length of time. The Panama Canal can also be combined with a Caribbean cruise: the 50-mi (83-km) canal is a series of locks, which make up for the height difference between the Caribbean and the Pacific. Increasingly popular are partial transit cruises that enter the Panama Canal, anchor in Gatun Lake for a short time, and depart through the same set of locks.

Eastern Caribbean Itineraries

Eastern Caribbean itineraries consist of two or three days at sea as well as stops at some of the Caribbean's busiest cruise ports. A typical cruise will usually take in three or four ports of call, such as St. Thomas in the U.S. Virgin Islands, San Juan, or St. Maarten/St. Martin, along with a visit to the cruise line's "private" island for beach time. Every major cruise line has at least two of those popular islands on its itineraries. Some itineraries might also include others, such as Tortola, Dominica, Barbados, St. Kitts, or Martinique.

Western Caribbean Itineraries

Western Caribbean itineraries embarking from Galveston, Ft. Lauderdale, Miami, New Orleans, Mobile, or Tampa might include Belize, Cozumel or the Riviera Maya Cruise Port in Mexico, Key West, the Cayman Islands, or Jamaica—all perfect choices for passengers who enjoy scuba diving and snorkeling and look forward to exploring Mayan ruins. Ships often alternate itineraries in the Western Caribbean with itineraries in the Eastern Caribbean on a weekly basis.

Southern Caribbean Itineraries

Southern Caribbean cruises tend to be longer in duration with more distant ports of call. They often originate in a port that is not on the U.S. mainland. Embarking in San Juan, for example, allows you to reach the lower Caribbean on a seven-day cruise with as many as four or five ports of call. Southern Caribbean itineraries might leave Puerto Rico for the Virgin Islands, Guadeloupe, Grenada, Curaçao, Barbados, Antigua, St. Lucia, Martinique, or Aruba. Smaller ships leave from ports as far south as St. George's, Grenada, and cruise through the Grenadines. Every major cruise line offers some Southern Caribbean itinerary, but these cruises aren't as popular as Western and Eastern Caribbean cruises.

Other Itineraries

In recent years, shorter itineraries have grown in appeal to time-crunched and budget-constrained travelers. If you are planning your first cruise in the tropics, a short sailing to the Bahamas allows you to test your appetite for cruising before you take a chance on a longer and more expensive cruise. Embarking at Fort Lauderdale, Miami, Port Canaveral, or Jacksonville, you will cruise for three to five days, taking in at least one port of call (usually Nassau or Freeport in the Bahamas) and possibly a visit to a "private" island or Key West. Four- and five-night cruises may also include a day at sea.

When to Go

Average year-round temperatures throughout the Caribbean are 78°F–85°F, with a low of 65°F and a high of 95°F; downtown shopping areas always seem to be unbearably hot. Low season runs from approximately mid-September through mid-April. Many travelers, especially families with school-age children, make reservations months in advance for the most expensive and most crowded summer months and holiday periods; however, with the many new cruise ships that have entered the market, you can often book fairly close to your departure date and still find room, although you may not get exactly the kind of cabin you would prefer. A summer cruise offers certain advantages: temperatures are virtually the same as in winter (cooler on average than in parts of the U.S. mainland), island flora is at its most dramatic, the water is smoother and clearer, and although there is always a breeze, winds are rarely strong enough to rock a ship. Some Caribbean tourist facilities close down in summer, however, and many ships move to Europe, Alaska, or the northeastern United States.

Hurricane season runs a full six months of the year—from June 1 through November 30. Although cruise ships stay well out of the way of these storms, hurricanes and tropical storms—their less-powerful relatives—can affect the weather throughout the Caribbean for days, and damage to ports can force last-minute itinerary changes.

Cruise Costs

The average daily price for Caribbean itineraries varies dramatically depending on several circumstances. The cost of a cruise on a luxury line such as Radisson Seven Seas or Seabourn may be five or more times the cost of a cruise on a mainstream line such as Carnival or Holland America. When you sail will also affect your costs: published brochure rates are usually highest during the peak summer season and holidays. When snow blankets the ground and temperatures are in single digits, a Caribbean cruise can be a welcome respite and less expensive than land resorts, which often command top dollar in winter months.

Solo travelers should be aware that single cabins have virtually disappeared from cruise ships. Taking a double cabin can cost twice the advertised per-person rates (which are based on double occupancy). Some cruise lines will find same-sex roommates for singles; each then pays the per-person, double-occupancy rate.

Extras

In addition to the cost of your cruise there are further expenses to consider, such as airfare to the port city. These days, only the most expensive cruises include airfare, but virtually all cruise lines offer air add-ons, which are sometimes less expensive than the lowest available airline fare. Shore excursions can also be a substantial expense; the best shore excursions are not cheap. But if you skimp too much on your excursion budget you'll deprive yourself of an important part of the Caribbean cruising experience. Finally, there will be many extras added onto your shipboard account during the cruise, including drinks (both alcoholic and nonalcoholic), activity fees (you pay to use that golf simulator), dining in specialty restaurants, spa services, and even cappuccino and espresso.

CloseUp
SAVING MONEY ON YOUR CRUISE FARE

Y OU CAN SAVE ON YOUR CRUISE FARE in several ways. Obviously, you should shop around. Some travel agents will discount cruise prices, though this is becoming a thing of the past. One thing never changes—do not ever, under any circumstances, pay brochure rate. You can do better, often as much as half off published fares. These are a few simple strategies you can follow:

• Book early: Cruise lines discount their cruises if you book early, particularly during the annual "Wave" season between January and March.

• Cruise during the off-season: If you take a cruise during the latter months of hurricane season (especially October and November) or the period between Thanksgiving and Christmas, you'll often find specials.

• Book late: Sometimes you can book a last-minute cruise at substantial savings if the ship hasn't filled all its cabins.

• Choose accommodations with care: Cabins are usually standardized and location determines the fare. Selecting a lower category can result in savings while giving up nothing in terms of cabin size and features.

• Book a "guarantee": You won't be able to select your own cabin because the cruise line will assign you one in the category you book, but a "guarantee" fare can be substantially lower than a regular fare.

• Cruise with friends and family: Book a minimum number of cabins, and your group can generally receive a special discounted fare.

• Reveal your age and affiliations: Fare savings may be available for seniors and members of certain organizations, as well as cruise line stockholders.

• Cruise often: Frequent cruisers usually get discounts from their preferred cruise lines.

Tipping

Tipping is another add-on. At the end of the cruise, it's customary to tip your room steward, dining room waiter, and the person who buses your table. You should expect to pay an average of $10 to $12 per person per day in tips. Most major cruise lines are moving away from the traditional method of tipping the service staff in cash at the end of the cruise, instead adding the recommended amount per day to your onboard account to cover tips, which you may adjust upward or downward according to the level of service you receive. Bar bills generally include an automatic 15%–18% gratuity, so the one person you don't need to tip is your bartender. Some cruise lines have tipping-optional policies, though most passengers tip anyway. Each cruise line offers guidelines.

CRUISE LINES & CRUISE SHIPS

For each cruise line, we list the ships (grouped by similar configurations) that regularly cruise in the Caribbean. However, not all ships spend the entire year in the Caribbean; for example, some go to Alaska or the Mediterranean during summer months, while others spend part of the year in Hawaii. We've excluded entirely those that have no regular itineraries in the Caribbean. Thus, not all ships owned by the cruise lines we cover are described below.

When two or more ships are substantially similar, their names are given at the beginning of a review and separated by commas. Passenger-capacity figures are given on the basis of two people sharing a cabin (basis-2); however, many of the larger ships have three- and four-berth cabins, which can increase the total number of passengers tremendously when all berths are occupied. When total occupancy figures differ from basis-2 occupancy, we give them in parentheses.

Luxury Cruise Lines

With less than 5% of the market, the ultraluxury cruise lines, which include Crystal, Radisson Seven Seas, Seabourn, Silversea, SeaDream, and Windstar, offer high staff-to-guest ratios for personal service, superior cuisine in a single seating (except Crystal, with two assigned seatings), and a highly inclusive product with few onboard charges. These small and midsize ships offer much more space per passenger than you will find on the mainstream lines' vessels. Lines differ in what they emphasize, with some touting luxurious accommodations and entertainment and others focusing on exotic destinations and onboard enrichment.

If you consider travel a necessity rather than a luxury and frequent exclusive resorts, then you will appreciate the extra attention and the higher level of comfort that luxury cruise lines offer.

Itineraries on these ships often include the big casino and beach resorts, but luxury ships also visit some of the more uncommon Caribbean destinations. With a shallow draft and intimate size, the smaller luxury ships can visit such ports as Anguilla, St. Barths, Tobago, and Jost Van Dyke and Virgin Gorda in the British Virgin Islands.

Crystal Cruise Line

Crystal's three midsize ships stand out for their modern design, amenities, and spaciousness. Built to deliver the first-rate service and amenities expected from a luxury line, these vessels have many of the onboard facilities of a big ship. Crystal ships have long set standards for pampering—one reason these vessels spend several days at sea rather than in port. White-glove service, stellar cuisine, and tasteful understated surroundings create a comfortable cocoon for passengers. Large spas offer innovative therapies, body wraps, and exotic, Asian-inspired treatments by Steiner Leisure. Feng shui principles were scrupulously adhered to in their creation, so the spa areas are havens of serenity. To the typical litany of cruise liner diversions, Crystal adds destination-oriented lectures and talks by scholars, political figures, and diplomats; deluxe theme cruises emphasize such topics as food and wine or the fine arts.

Crystal's target clientele is affluent and older but still active. On select cruises highly trained and experienced youth counselors are brought in to oversee activities for kids and teens. Baby food, high chairs, and booster seats are available upon request.

Staff are well trained, friendly, highly motivated, and thoroughly professional. However, alone among the luxury lines, Crystal's fares do not include tips, so the crew can be noticeably solicitous of gratuities. Suggested tipping guidelines are as follows: steward, $4 per day (single travelers, $5 per day); waiter, $4 per day ($6 per day in alternative restaurants); assistant waiter, $2.50 per day; butler penthouse and suites, $4 per day; 15% is added to bar bills. Tips for other personnel are at your discretion. Gratuities may be charged to your shipboard account.

🖉 *Crystal Cruise Line, 2049 Century Park E, Suite 1400, Los Angeles, CA 90067* ☎ *310/785–9300 or 800/446–6620* 🖷 *310/785–9201* ⊕ *www.crystalcruises.com.*

THE SHIPS
OF CRYSTAL
CRUISE LINE
☁

Crystal Symphony. *Crystal Symphony*'s sleek and sophisticated hull harbors classy, uncluttered interiors and understated decor. Best of all, she is roomy, with one of the highest ratios of passenger to space of any ships afloat. Suites deliver space in abundance; however, the standard outside staterooms are somewhat smaller than would be expected on a luxury ship—the smallest measuring 198 square feet. An advantage is that all have an ocean view and more than half have private verandas. Even the lowest-category staterooms have a separate sitting area (love seat with coffee table), a desk/vanity, and queen or twin beds—with space left over to comfortably move about. Large closets, ample drawer space, and bathtubs are standard. Cabins are equipped with voice mail, fine linens, thick towels, and selections from a "menu" of four different pillow types. Onboard amenities include grand lounges, enrichment programs, and Broadway-style entertainment. All soft drinks, specialty coffees, and bottled water are complimentary. ⋑ *480 cabins, 940 passengers, 8 passenger decks* ⌧ *2 specialty restaurants, dining room, café, buffet, ice-cream parlor, in-cabin safes, refrigerators, in-cabin DVDs, 2 pools (1 indoors), fitness classes, gym, hair salon, 2 hot tubs, sauna, spa, steam room, 5 bars, casino, cinema, dance club, library, showroom, video game room, children's programs (ages 3–17), dry cleaning, laundry facilities, laundry service, computer room; no children under 6 months* ⊟ *AE, D, MC, V.*

☁ **Crystal Serenity.** *Crystal Serenity* is Crystal Cruise Line's long-awaited third ship—the first introduced to the fleet since 1995. Although over a third larger than Crystal's earlier ships, it is similar in layout and follows their successful formula of creating intimate spaces in understated yet sophisticated surroundings. In the Crystal tradition, *Crystal Serenity* has one of the highest passenger-to-space ratios of any ship. As expected on a luxury vessel, there are no inside cabins and all have sitting areas and refrigerators stocked with complimentary bottled water and soft drinks. However, although suites have extra features such as entertainment centers and are generous in size, the least-expensive categories are somewhat smaller than industry standard at this level. All accommodations have ample closet and drawer/shelf storage, as well as bathroom shelves and twin sinks. An impressive 85% boast private balconies furnished with chairs and tables that add additional living space. Spacious public lounges, enrichment programs, and lavish, Broadway-style entertainment are signature amenities. Soft drinks, specialty coffees, and bottled water are complimentary throughout the ship. *548 cabins, 1,080 passengers, 9 passenger decks & 3 specialty restaurants, dining room, café, buffet, ice-cream parlor, in-cabin safes, refrigerators, in-cabin DVDs, in-cabin data ports, 2 pools (1 indoors), fitness classes, gym, hair salon, 2 hot tubs, sauna, spa, steam room, 6 bars, casino, cinema, 2 dance clubs, library, showroom, video game room, children's programs (ages 3–17), dry cleaning, laundry facilities, laundry service, computer room, no children under 6 months ▤ AE, D, MC, V.*

Cunard Line

One of the world's most distinguished names in ocean travel since 1840, Cunard Line's history of deluxe transatlantic crossings and worldwide cruising is legendary for comfortable accommodations, excellent cuisine, and personal service. Though the line is now owned by Carnival, its high-end ships still carry on with a decidedly British sensibility. The line's newest ship, the Queen Mary 2, has a short season of Caribbean cruises, which are highly prized by fans of the line.

In the tradition of multiple-class ocean liners, dining room assignments are made according to the accommodation category booked. The line's ships also have highly regarded specialty restaurants with menus by acclaimed chefs Daniel Boulud and Todd English. Discerning, well-traveled American and British couples from their late-30's to retirees are drawn to Cunard's traditional style and the notion of a cruise aboard an ocean liner. Although resort casual clothing prevails throughout the day, Cunard vessels are ocean liners at heart and, as expected, are dressier than most cruise ships at night. Although most crewmembers are international rather than British, service is formal and sophisticated.

Suggested gratuities of $13 per person per day (for Grill Restaurant accommodations) or $11 per person per day (all other accommodations) are automatically charged to shipboard accounts for distribution to stewards and waiter staff. A 15% gratuity is added to beverage tabs for bar service. At passengers' discretion, gratuities for special services may be presented directly to individual crewmembers.

Cunard Line, 24303 Town Center Dr., Valencia, CA 91355 ☎ 661/ 753–1000 or 800/728–6273 ⊕ www.cunard.com.

THE SHIPS OF CUNARD LINE

Queen Mary 2. With the clever use of design elements, the largest passenger liner ever built bears a striking external resemblance to the smaller, older Queen Elizabeth 2. The world's grandest and most expensive liner is something of a transitional ship, incorporating classic ocean liner features—sweeping staircases, soaring public rooms, a promenade deck, and a grand ballroom—all comfortably within a hull that also sports a trendy Canyon Ranch Spa and a full-scale planetarium. Interior spaces blend the traditional style of early twentieth century liners with all the conveniences twenty-first century passengers expect. Forward and aft on nearly every deck you'll find public spaces tucked here and there—the library, children's center, beauty salon, and even swimming pools and hot tubs. Bring your deck plan instead of dropping bread crumbs to find your way. Most accommodations (78%) are outside cabins and over 86% of these feature spacious private balconies. All are designed with ample closet, drawer/shelf storage, and bathroom shelves. Warm wood cabinetry, quality fabrics, interactive television, and a sitting area with sofa or chairs and dual-height table are typical standard amenities. ➽ *1310 cabins, 2,620 (3,090 at full occupancy), 14 passenger decks ♧ 2 specialty restaurants, 3 dining rooms, buffet, ice cream parlor, pizzeria, in-cabin safes, refrigerators, some in-cabin DVDs, in-cabin data ports, 3 pools (2 indoor), 2 children's pools, hair salon, health club, 7 hot tubs, sauna, spa, steam room, 11 bars, casino, cinema, 2 dance clubs, library, showroom, video game room, children's programs (ages 1–17), dry-cleaning, laundry facilities, laundry service, computer room; no kids under 1.*

Radisson Seven Seas Cruises

Radisson Seven Seas Cruises (RSSC) is part of Carlson Hospitality Worldwide, one of the world's major hotel-and-travel companies. The cruise line was formed in December 1994 with the merger of the one-ship Diamond Cruises and Seven Seas Cruises lines. From these modest beginnings, RSSC has grown into a major luxury player in the cruise industry. With the launch of the *Seven Seas Mariner* in March 2001, RSSC introduced the world's first all-suite, all-balcony cruise ship. *Seven Seas Voyager*, a second 700-passenger all-suite, all-balcony ship entered service in April 2003.

The line's spacious ocean-view cabins have the industry's highest percentage of private balconies; you'll always find open seating at dinner (which includes complimentary wine); tips are included in the fare and no additional tipping is expected. Activities are oriented toward onboard enrichment programs, socializing, and exploring the destinations on the itinerary. Spa and salon services are provided by the high-end Carita of Paris. Although passengers tend to be older and affluent, they are still active. Radisson Seven Seas Cruises manages to provide a high level of personal service and sense of intimacy on small-to-midsize ships, which have the stability of larger vessels.

Radisson Seven Seas Cruises, 600 Corporate Dr., Suite 410, Fort Lauderdale, FL 33334 ☎ *954/776–6123, 800/477–7500, or 800/285–1835* 🖷 *954/772–3763* ⊕ *www.rssc.com.*

THE SHIPS OF RADISSON SEVEN SEAS CRUISES **Seven Seas Navigator.** The spacious *Navigator* is a midsize ship with a big-ship feel. Every stateroom is a superbly appointed, ocean-view suite ranging in size from 301 square feet to 1,067 square feet—90% with private teak balconies. All standard suites have walk-in closets and marble bathrooms with separate tub and shower, cotton bathrobes, hair dryers, TV, CD/DVD players, refrigerators stocked with soft drinks, and a bar set up upon embarkation. At 301 square feet, even the smallest stateroom is sufficiently roomy for comfortable en suite dining—course by course, ordered from the Compass Rose dining room. One crew member for every 1.5 passengers insures personal service. ➽ *245 cabins, 490 passengers, 8 passenger decks ♧ Specialty restaurant, dining room, buffet, in-cabin safes, refrigerators, in-cabin DVDs, pool, fitness classes, gym, hair salon, hot tub, sauna, spa, steam room, 4 bars, casino, dance club, showroom, some children's programs (ages 6–17), dry cleaning, laundry facilities, laundry service, computer room* ▤ *AE, D, MC, V.*

🕭 *Seven Seas Mariner, Seven Seas Voyager.* The world's only all-suite, all-balcony ships are also Radisson Seven Seas' largest, with the highest space-per-passenger ratio in the fleet. All cabins are outside suites ranging from 301 square feet to 2,002 square feet, including the verandas, and feature entertainment centers with DVD/CD player. Butler service is available to all but the least-expensive Deluxe Suite categories. The ships' dining rooms include Signatures, the only restaurants at sea staffed by chefs wearing the Blue Riband of Le Cordon Bleu of Paris, the famed culinary institute. On certain voyages the chefs offer Le Cordon Bleu "Classe Culinaire des Croisiers," workshops that offer a hands-on introduction to the art of French cooking. ⤵ *328 cabins, 700 passengers, 8 passenger decks ⚓ 2 specialty restaurants, dining room, buffet, in-cabin safes, refrigerators, in-cabin DVDs, Wi-Fi (Seven Seas Voyager), pool, fitness classes, gym, hair salon, 2 hot tubs, sauna, spa, steam room, 5 bars, casino, dance club, library, showroom, some children's programs (ages 6–17), dry cleaning, laundry facilities, laundry service, computer room* ▤ *AE, D, MC, V.*

Seabourn Cruise Line

Ultraluxury cruise pioneer Seabourn Cruise Line has earned accolades from repeat guests, traveler polls, and consumer publications since its founding in 1987. Its fleet of three nearly identical, all-suite ships, *Seabourn Legend, Seabourn Pride,* and *Seabourn Spirit,* the latter two deployed to far-flung ports, is known as the "Yachts of Seabourn." The crowd tends to be older and affluent, and people are inclined to dress up. Complimentary "Massage Moments" on deck are minipreviews of the relaxing treatments available in the spa, which offers a variety of massages, body wraps, and facials designed by Steiner Leisure.

These sleek-lined 10,000-ton ships are celebrated for extraordinary levels of personalized service, suites of 277 square feet or more—40% with balconies—and exceptional cuisine designed by famed chef-restaurateur Charlie Palmer. All drinks, including wine and alcohol, are complimentary throughout the voyage, and tipping is neither required nor expected. Shore excursions often include privileged access to historic and cultural sites when they are not open to the public.

🖅 *Seabourn Cruise Line, 6100 Blue Lagoon Dr., Suite 400, Miami, FL 33126* ☏ *305/463–3000 or 800/929–9391* 🖷 *305/463–3010* ⊕ *www. seabourn.com.*

THE SHIPS OF
SEABOURN
CRUISE LINE

Seabourn Legend. Striking and sleek, *Seabourn Legend* feels like a swank private club—elegant, but not stifling. All cabins have a fresh daily fruit basket, stocked bar, thick terry robes and slippers, designer soaps and toiletries, an aromatherapy bath menu, twin sinks, and large tub and shower. In rooms without balconies, the sitting area is adjacent to a 5-foot-wide picture window; about 40% of the cabins have balconies, the majority of which are minibalconies designed for fresh air only—there is no room to stand or sit outside on them. Cuisine is exceptional and prepared to order; service is unfailingly superb. Waterskiing, sailing, and windsurfing may be enjoyed directly from the ship's stern: when at anchor, and weather permitting, the water-sports marina is lowered. An integral 30- by 30-foot submersible steel mesh tank is also available for a protected saltwater swimming experience. ⌖ *106 cabins, 208 passengers, 6 passenger decks* ♿ *Specialty restaurant, dining room, buffet, in-cabin safes, refrigerators, in-cabin DVDs, pool, fitness classes, gym, hair salon, 3 hot tubs, sauna, spa, steam room, 3 bars, casino, dance club, library, showroom, dry cleaning, laundry facilities, laundry service, computer room* ▭ *AE, D, MC, V.*

SeaDream Yacht Club

Launched in 1984 as Sea Goddess mega-yachts, these boutique ships have changed hands through the years, evolving into their present incarnations after total renovations in 2002 as the pride of SeaDream Yacht Club. Voyages are all about personal choice. Passengers enjoy an unstructured holiday at sea doing whatever pleases them, giving the diminutive vessels the feel of true private yachts with a select guest list. SeaDream's unique Asian Spa facilities are on the small side, yet offer a full menu of gentle Asian treatments that includes massages, facials, and body wraps utilizing Eastern techniques.

Ports of call almost seem an intrusion on socializing amid the chic surroundings, although a picnic on a secluded beach adds the element of a private island paradise to each Caribbean cruise. Although the ambience is sophisticated, all cruises are "yacht" casual, and you can leave your formal clothing at home. Every meal is prepared to order, and all drinks, including wine and alcohol, are complimentary. Tipping is neither required nor expected.

🖅 *SeaDream Yacht Club, 2601 S. Bayshore Dr., Penthouse 1B, Coconut Grove, FL 33133* ☎ *305/856–5622 or 800/707–4911* 📠 *305/856–7599* ⊕ *www.seadreamyachtclub.com.*

THE SHIPS OF
SEADREAM
YACHT CLUB

SeaDream I, SeaDream II. With their dark blue hulls and sleek profiles, SeaDream's mega-yachts appear elegant and exclusive. Public areas are quite spacious for such small vessels—the main salons and dining rooms are large enough to comfortably accommodate all passengers at once, although much of the appeal is outside. Topside are unique Balinese Sun Beds with such thick comfortable pads that passengers occasionally choose to spend the night on them. Cabins range from 195 square feet to 450 square feet and have flat-screen plasma televisions, entertainment systems, refrigerators stocked with complimentary beer, soft drinks, and bottled water, thick terry robes and slippers, and Bulgari soaps and toiletries. Glass-enclosed showers with twin showerheads make up for the tiny size of the bathrooms. No cabins have balconies; however, beds are next to a large picture window, and a curtain can be drawn between sleeping and sitting areas to create a space more conducive to entertaining. The level of service and attention to detail is unmatched. Waterskiing, windsurfing, and jet-skiing may be enjoyed directly from the ships' sterns—water-sports platforms are lowered when at anchor and sea conditions permit. No smoking is allowed indoors, which is unusual for a cruise ship. ⌖ *54 cabins, 108 passengers, 5 passenger decks* ♿ *Dining room, buffet, in-cabin safes, refrigerators, in-cabin DVDs, pool, fitness classes, gym, hair salon, hot tub, sauna, spa, 3 bars, casino, library, show-*

room, *dry cleaning, laundry service, computer room, no-smoking cab-ins* 🚢 *AE, D, MC, V.*

Silversea Cruise Line

High-quality features and personalization are Silversea maxims. Sil-versea ships have full-size showrooms, domed dining rooms, and a se-lection of bars and shops, yet all accommodations are spacious outside suites, most with private verandas. Silversea ships have large swimming pools in expansive Lidos—the space- and crew-to-passenger ratios are among the best at sea in the luxury small-ship category. Although their ships schedule more activities than other comparably sized luxury ves-sels, you can either take part or opt instead for a good book and any number of quiet spots to read or snooze in the shade. South Pacific–in-spired Mandara Spa offers numerous treatments, including exotic mas-sages, facials, and body wraps. A plus is that appointments for spa treatments and salon services can be made online from 60 days until 48 hours prior to sailing.

European service is personal—exacting and hospitable, yet discreet. A major selling point is the all-inclusive packaging, which includes gra-tuities, port charges, transfers, and all beverages. All packages include coach airfare to the port of embarkation and a complimentary pre-cruise hotel room. Perhaps more compelling is the line's flair for originality. The pasta chef's daily special is a passenger favorite, as is the galley brunch, held just once each cruise, when the galley is transformed into a buffet restaurant.

🏛 *Silversea Cruise Lines, 110 E. Broward Blvd., Fort Lauderdale, FL 33301* ☎ *954/522–4477 or 800/722–9955* 🌐 *www.silversea.com.*

THE SHIPS OF
SILVERSEA
CRUISE LINE

Silver Shadow, Silver Whisper. *Silver Shadow* and *Silver Whisper* extend the hospitality of a private yacht but with far more spaciousness, including larger public rooms and a multi-tier showroom with a movable stage. The clean modern decor is almost stark, but there is a notable empha-sis on comfort. Large expanses of glass afford sunshine and sea views. Crisp white tablecloths set with Cristofle silver, fine porcelain, and Eu-ropean crystal only hint at the fine dining experience to come. All cab-ins are outside suites with walk-in closets and marble baths, and most open onto a teak veranda with floor-to-ceiling glass doors. Creature com-forts include fine bedding (high-thread-count linens and down duvets and pillows), designer toiletries, stocked refrigerators, en suite bar setup, and a daily-replenished fruit basket. ⚓ *194 cabins, 388 passengers, 7 passenger decks* ♿ *2 specialty restaurants, dining room, buffet, in-cabin safes, refrigerators, in-cabin VCRs, pool, fitness classes, gym, hair salon, 2 hot tubs, sauna, spa, steam room, 3 bars, casino, dance club, library, showroom, dry cleaning, laundry facilities, laundry service, computer room* 🚢 *AE, D, MC, V.*

Windstar Cruises

Are they cruise ships with sails or sailing ships designed for cruises? Since 1986, the Windstar vessels have presented a conundrum. In ac-tuality they are masted sailing yachts, pioneers in the upscale sailing niche. Although the sails add speed, Windstar ships seldom depend on wind alone to sail—motors are necessary in order to maintain their sched-ules. However, if you are fortunate and conditions are perfect, the total silence of pure sailing is a thrill. Although the ships' design may be reminiscent of sailing vessels of yore, the amenities and shipboard service are among the best at sea. Life on board is unabashedly sybaritic, attracting a sophisticated, relatively young crowd happy to sacrifice bingo and pool games for the attractions of remote islands and water sports; even motorized water sports are included, and passengers pay extra only for scuba diving. A retractable marina at the stern allows water sports directly from the ship at anchor. These ships are especially popular with couples and honeymooners; you won't find many children aboard. Service is comprehensive, competent, and designed to create an elite and privileged atmosphere.

🕊 *Windstar Cruises, 300 Elliott Ave., Seattle, WA 98119* ☎ *206/281–3535 or 800/258–7245* 🖷 *206/281–7110* ⊕ *www.windstarcruises.com.*

THE SHIPS OF WINDSTAR CRUISES *Windspirit, Windsurf.* Inspired by the great sailing ships of a bygone era, Windstar ships are long, lean, and sparkling white with bow masts and brass-rimmed portholes. Though the hulls are steel, the interiors glow with wood paneling and teak trim—a look rare among modern cruise ships. Instead of the chrome-and-glass banisters so popular on other ships, the vessels feature iron banisters with teak handrails. Don't offer to help hoist the sails: they are operated from the bridge and unfurl in two minutes at the touch of a button. Every cabin is outside, appointed in burled maple veneer and outfitted with plentiful closet space and mirrors. Cabinetwork is accented with rich wood moldings and bathroom floors are teak. Refrigerators, entertainment centers, hair dryers, and terry robes are standard accoutrements in all staterooms. ↩ *74/152 cabins (Windspirit/Windsurf), 148/308 passengers, 4/6 passenger decks* ⚓ *Specialty restaurant (Windsurf), dining room, buffet, in-cabin safes, refrigerators, in-cabin DVDs, pool (2 on Windsurf), fitness classes, gym, hair salon, hot tub (2 on Windsurf), sauna, spa (Windsurf), 2 bars (3 on Windsurf), casino, dance club, library, laundry service, computer room* ▤ *AE, D, MC, V.*

Mainstream Cruise Lines

More than 85% of the Caribbean is covered by 10 mainstream cruise lines. They offer the advantage of something for everyone and nearly every available sports facility imaginable. Some ships even have ice-skating rinks, 18-hole miniature golf courses, and rock-climbing walls.

Generally speaking, the mainstream lines have two basic ship sizes—large cruise liner and mega-ship—in their fleets. Cruise liners have plentiful outdoor deck space, and many have a wraparound outdoor promenade deck that allows you to stroll or jog the ship's perimeter. In the newest cruise liners, traditional meets trendy. You'll find atrium lobbies and expansive sun and sports decks, picture windows instead of portholes, and cabins that open onto private verandas. For all their resort-style innovations, they still feature cruise ship classics—afternoon tea, complimentary room service, and lavish pampering. The smallest cruise liners carry 1,000 passengers or fewer, while the largest accommodate more than 3,000 passengers and are filled with diversions.

If you're into big, bold, brassy, and nonstop activity, these huge ships offer it all. The centerpiece of most mega-ships is a 3-, 5-, or even 11-story central atrium. However, these giant vessels are most readily distinguished by their profile: the boxy hull and superstructure rise as many as 14 stories out of the water and are capped by a huge sun or sports deck with a jogging track and one or more swimming pools. Some mega-ships have a traditional wraparound promenade deck. Picture windows are standard equipment, and cabins in the top categories have private verandas. From their casinos and discos to their fitness centers, everything is bigger and more extravagant than on other ships. You may want to rethink a cruise aboard one of these ships if you want a little downtime, since you'll be joined by 1,500 to 3,000 fellow passengers.

Carnival Cruise Lines

Carnival Cruise Lines is the largest and most successful cruise line in the world, carrying more passengers than any other. Today's Carnival is a vastly different company from the one launched in 1972 by entrepreneur Ted Arison, who made a vacation experience once reserved for the very rich widely accessible. From a "fleet" consisting of one refitted transatlantic ocean liner, Carnival became the standard by which lower-priced cruise lines are measured. Not even its critics can deny that the line delivers on its promises. Brash and always fun, Carnival throws a great party. Activities and entertainment are nonstop, beginning just after sunrise and continuing well into the night. Food has been upgraded in recent years, and it is plentiful and fairly diverse, better tasting and well presented, with healthful options.

Cabins are spacious and comfortable, often as much as 50% larger than other ships in this price category. Carnival's ships are like floating theme parks, though each one has a distinct personality. The effect is most exaggerated on the newer, bigger ships, including the Fantasy, Destiny, Spirit, and Conquest classes.

Carnival cruises are popular with young single cruisers as well as with those older than 55. The line's offerings also appeal to parents cruising with their children. A choice of flexible dining options and casual alternative restaurants are available on Carnival ships. Staggered dining room schedules, which include the selection of four set evening mealtimes (5:45 or 6:15 PM and 8 or 8:30 PM), means the ships' galleys serve fewer meals at any one time. The result is better service and higher-quality food preparation. All ships offer something for everyone at all hours, including pizza and 24-hour room service.

Gratuities of $10 per passenger, per day are automatically added to onboard accounts and are distributed to stewards and waitstaff. Passengers may adjust the amount based on the level of service experienced. A 15% gratuity is automatically added to bar and beverage tabs.

Carnival Cruise Lines, 3655 N.W. 87th Ave., Miami, FL 33178-2428 *305/599–2600, 800/438–6744, or 800/327–9501 www.carnival.com.*

Celebration, Holiday. Originally considered "superliners" when introduced in 1985, the Holiday-class ships are almost quaint by today's standards. These ships ushered in the age of boxy hulls and superstructures that rise straight out of the water. Inside, they have Carnival's trademark bold art, brightly colored decor, indoor promenades, and spectacularly lighted ceilings and floors. Cabins are more spacious than those on most lower-cost cruise ships. Outside cabins have picture windows, and all cabins are furnished with twin beds convertible to kings, as well as ample closet and drawer space. The lower-price Holiday-class ships have the same menus as other Carnival ships, with two dining rooms serving three meals and a Lido buffet for casual breakfasts and lunches. *743 cabins, 1,486 passengers (Celebration 1,896 at full occupancy, Holiday 1,800 at full occupancy), 9 passenger decks ⚓ 2 dining rooms, buffet, ice-cream parlor, pizzeria, in-cabin safes, Wi-Fi, 2 pools, children's pool, fitness classes, gym, hair salon, 2 hot tubs, sauna, spa, 5 bars, casino, 2 dance clubs, library, showroom, video game room, children's programs (ages 2–15), laundry facilities, laundry service, computer room 🖃 AE, D, MC, V.*

Fantasy, Fascination, Imagination, Inspiration, Sensation. The Fantasy-class ships based in the Caribbean are not unlike Las Vegas casino-hotels afloat. Identical in layout and bathed in light, they share vibrant marble, brass, and mirrored decor, though details differ. The *Sensation* is considered the most subtle in its design approach. A six-deck atrium is the centerpiece of each ship, and each has a bustling indoor promenade. Cabins are decorated in bright colors; each is fairly spacious, but only suites have private verandas. The Lido buffet is transformed nightly into Seaview Bistro for casual dining. A coffee bar, pizzeria, and poolside snack bars offer alternatives to the buffet. Activities tend to be high-spirited and nonstop. *1,022 cabins, 2,052 passengers (2,606 at full occupancy), 10 passenger decks ⚓ 2 dining rooms, buffet, ice-cream parlor, pizzeria, in-cabin safes, Wi-Fi, 2 pools, children's pool, fitness classes, gym, hair salon, 6 hot tubs, sauna, spa, steam room, 5 bars, casino, 2 dance clubs, library, 2 showrooms, video game room, children's programs (ages 2–15), laundry facilities, laundry service, computer room 🖃 AE, D, MC, V.*

Carnival Destiny, Carnival Triumph, Carnival Victory. Carnival's Destiny-class ships can carry a whopping 3,470 passengers when all their third and fourth berths are filled. In keeping with their size, everything on these ships is big: the atrium spans nine decks, the spa is on two levels, an outdoor waterslide stretches 200 feet, the casino covers 9,000 square feet, and there's a three-story showroom for the Las Vegas–style shows. The deck area has four swimming pools, two with swim-up bars, another with a retractable roof, and one reserved for children. More than half the cabins have ocean views, and 60% of the standard outside cabins and all suites have private verandas. Specially designed family staterooms, some with connecting cabins, are near the ship's children's facilities. Carnival has embraced the trend toward dining alternatives, and Italian and Chinese foods are featured, as well as pizza and pastries. The Lido buffet is transformed nightly into

Seaview Bistro for casual dining. ⟡ *1,321 cabins, 2,642 passengers (3,470 at full occupancy), 12 passenger decks ⚓ 2 dining rooms, buffet, ice-cream parlor, pizzeria, in-cabin safes, refrigerators, some in-cabin VCRs, Wi-Fi, 3 pools (1 indoor), children's pool, fitness classes, gym, hair salon, 7 hot tubs, sauna, spa, steam room, 7 bars, casino, 3 dance clubs, library, showroom, video game room, children's programs (ages 2–15), laundry facilities, laundry service, computer room ▭ AE, D, MC, V.*

⟲ ***Carnival Legend, Carnival Miracle.*** The first of Carnival's Spirit-class ships entered service in 2001 with notable design improvements over previous Carnival ships. For example, all staterooms aboard these superliners are above ocean level, making for a more comfortable cruise. Although the prototype *Carnival Spirit* spends time year-round on the West Coast, these sister ships sail regularly in the Caribbean. Cabins have ample drawer and closet space, and you can check your onboard account as well as select movies to view on the interactive in-cabin TV channels. Other innovations include eye-popping 11-story atriums, two-level indoor promenades, an outside promenade deck, shopping malls, and reservations-only supper clubs. Spirit-class ships are fast, cruising at 22 knots; their greater speed allows them to visit destinations in a week that would take other ships 10 days or more. Most staterooms have ocean views and, of those, 80% have balconies. Terrific children's facilities make these good ships for any family vacation. ⟡ *1,062 cabins, 2,124 passengers (2,667 at full occupancy), 13 passenger decks ⚓ Specialty restaurant, dining room, buffet, ice-cream parlor, pizzeria, in-cabin safes, refrigerators, some in-cabin VCRs, Wi-Fi, 3 pools (1 indoor), children's pool, fitness classes, gym, hair salon, 4 hot tubs, sauna, spa, steam room, 7 bars, casino, 2 dance clubs, library, showroom, video game room, children's programs (ages 2–15), laundry facilities, laundry service, computer room ▭ AE, D, MC, V.*

⟲ ***Carnival Conquest, Carnival Glory, Carnival Valor, Carnival Liberty.*** The 110,000-ton *Conquest*, the first in Carnival's Conquest class, debuted in 2002. Offering an enormous variety of entertainment areas, including an expanded kids' section and a teen club/video arcade, these huge ships expand upon the successful Destiny-class and set new standards for family travel. More than 60% of the cabins have an ocean view and more than 60% of those also feature a private balcony. Cabins are decorated in subdued peach tones and are among the largest offered in the cruise industry; standard interior cabins, the smallest, measure 185 square feet. Among the couple-pleasing settings is the romantic reservations-only supper club. ⟡ *1,487 cabins, 2,974 passengers (3,700 at full occupancy), 13 passenger decks ⚓ Specialty restaurant, 2 dining rooms, buffet, ice-cream parlor, pizzeria, in-cabin safes, refrigerators, some in-cabin VCRs, Wi-Fi, 3 pools (1 indoors), children's pool, fitness classes, gym, hair salon, 7 hot tubs, sauna, spa, steam room, 9 bars, casino, dance club, library, showroom, video game room, children's programs (ages 2–15), laundry facilities, laundry service, computer room ▭ AE, D, MC, V.*

Celebrity Cruises

Celebrity Cruises has based its reputation on sleek ships and superior food. Style and layout vary from ship to ship, lending each a unique personality. In terms of size and amenities, Celebrity's vessels rival almost any in cruising, but with a level of refinement rare on bigger ships. In less than a decade, Celebrity won the admiration of its passengers and its competitors—who have copied its nouvelle cuisine and cigar clubs and hired its personnel (a true compliment). Celebrity has risen above typical mass-market cruise cuisine by hiring chef Michel Roux as a consultant. Menus are creative; both familiar and exotic dishes have been customized to appeal to American palates. All food is prepared from scratch, using only fresh produce and herbs, aged beef, and fresh fish—even the ice cream on board is homemade. Entertainment choices range from Broadway-style productions, captivating shows, and lively discos to Monte Carlo–style casinos and specialty lounges. Multimillion-dollar art collections grace the entire fleet, which merged with Royal Caribbean International in 1997.

Celebrity attracts everyone from older couples to honeymooners. Summertime children's programs are as good as those on any cruise line. Service is friendly and first class, rapid and accurate in the dining rooms. Waiters, stewards, and bartenders are enthusiastic, take pride in their work, and try to please.

Tip your cabin steward/butlers $3.50 per day; chief housekeeper 50¢ per day; dining-room waiter $3.50 per day; assistant waiter $2 per day; and restaurant manager 75¢ per day, for a total of $10.25 per person, per day. Passengers may adjust the amount based on the level of service experienced. A 15% service charge is added to all beverage checks. For children under 12, or the third or fourth person in the stateroom, half the above amounts is recommended. Gratuities are typically handed out on the last night of the cruise, but they may be charged to your shipboard account as well.

📋 *Celebrity Cruises, 1050 Caribbean Way, Miami, FL 33132-2096* ☎ *305/539–6000 or 800/437–3111* 🖷 *800/437–5111* ⊕ *www. celebritycruises.com.*

THE SHIPS OF
CELEBRITY
CRUISES
🕓

Zenith. Big when she was introduced, but just midsize now, *Zenith* offers a somewhat more intimate alternative to the expansive mega-ships. Interiors are indisputably gracious, airy, and comfortable; the design makes the most of natural light through strategically placed, oversize windows. Wide corridors, broad staircases, seven elevators, and well-placed signs make it easy to get around. Nine passenger decks give ample breathing space. Cabins are modern and fairly roomy, with reasonably large closets and bathrooms. Food preparation receives as many accolades as presentation, and there are two seatings for breakfast, lunch, and dinner. Celebrity avoids theme nights for dinner—common on other lines. Since there is no midnight buffet, waiters circulate through lounges instead, offering late-night canapés and other finger food. ⇥ *687 cabins, 1,374 passengers, 9 passenger decks* ⛝ *Specialty restaurant, dining room, buffet, ice-cream parlor, pizzeria, in-cabin safes, some refrigerators, Wi-*

Fi, 2 pools, fitness classes, gym, hair salon, 4 hot tubs, sauna, spa, steam room, 8 bars, casino, cinema, dance club, library, showroom, video game room, children's programs (ages 3–17), dry cleaning, laundry service, computer room ▤ *AE, MC, V.*

🕙 ***Century, Galaxy.*** Celebrity's Century-class ships are larger than their predecessors, with modest atriums and contemporary art throughout. Impressive two-story dining rooms and large theaters with full-size stages are notable improvements over the earlier design of the *Zenith*. The elaborate Elemis spas, which have enormous thalassotherapy pools and the latest in treatments, are popular. The *Century* is high-tech and eclectically decorated, but the *Galaxy* is most impressive, with its aura of traditional elegance. With almost 50 additional feet in length, *Galaxy* has the advantage of a third swimming pool with a sliding roof for use in inclement weather. Standard cabins are intelligently appointed and apportioned, with few frills; space is well used, making for maximum elbow room in the bathrooms and good storage space in the closets. The *Century* has fewer private verandas than its sister ship. ↪ *875/ 935 cabins (Century/Galaxy), 1,750/1,870 passengers, 10/10 passenger decks ♿ Specialty restaurant, dining room, buffet, ice-cream parlor, pizzeria, in-cabin safes, refrigerators, some in-cabin VCRs, Wi-Fi, 2 pools (plus 2 indoor pools on Galaxy), children's pool, fitness classes, gym, hair salon, 4 hot tubs, sauna, spa, steam room, 7 bars (8 on Galaxy), casino, cinema, dance club, library, showroom, video game room, children's programs (ages 3–17), dry cleaning, laundry service, computer room* ▤ *AE, MC, V.*

🕙 ***Constellation, Millennium, Summit.*** Dramatic exterior glass elevators, a glass-domed pool area, and a window-wrapped ship-top observation lounge keep the magnificence of the Caribbean well within view aboard Millennium-class ships. These are the newest and largest in Celebrity's fleet, and each stocks plenty of premium amenities, including a flower-filled conservatory, music library, expansive spa, Internet café with 18 workstations, golf simulator, and brand-name boutiques. Cabins are bright, spacious, and well-appointed, and 80% have an ocean view (74% of those have private verandas). With a staff member for every two passengers, service is especially attentive for a mainstream line. ↪ *975 cabins, 1,950 passengers, 11 passenger decks ♿ Specialty restaurant, dining room, buffet, ice-cream parlor, pizzeria, in-cabin safes, refrigerators, some in-cabin DVDs, some in-cabin VCRs, in-cabin data ports (Constellation, Summit), Wi-Fi, 2 pools (1 indoors), children's pool, fitness classes, gym, hair salon, 4 hot tubs, sauna, spa, steam room, 7 bars, casino, cinema, dance club, library, showroom, video game room, children's programs (ages 3–17), dry cleaning, laundry service, computer room* ▤ *AE, MC, V.*

Costa Cruise Lines

The Genoa-based Costa Crociere, parent company of Costa Cruise Lines, had been in the shipping business for more than 100 years and in the passenger business for almost 50 years when it was bought by Airtours and Carnival Cruises in 1997; Carnival gained sole ownership of the line in 2000, but the ships retain their original flavor. Costa's Italian-inspired vessels bring the Mediterranean vitality of *La Dolce Vita* to far-flung regions of the Caribbean. The ships are a combination of classic and modern design. Passengers tend to be a little older—the average age is 54—and have an interest in all things Italian. You don't find a lot of first-time cruisers on Costa ships.

Suggested tipping guidelines are as follows: cabin steward, $3 per day; waiter, $3 per day; busboy, $1.50 per day; maître d' and head waiter, $1 per day. A 15% gratuity is added to beverage bills (including mineral water in the dining room). Gratuities are charged to your shipboard account for convenience but may be adjusted based on the level of service experienced.

⌂ *Costa Cruise Lines, 200 S. Park Rd., Suite 200, Hollywood, FL 33021-8541* ☎ *954/266–5600 or 800/462–6782* 🖷 *954/266–2100* ⊕ *www.costacruises.com.*

THE SHIPS OF **Costa Mediterranea.** These stylish ships embrace an atmosphere that is
COSTA CRUISE purely Italian, with marble floors and walls, wood cabinetry, and Ital-
LINES ian art throughout. Cooking classes, Roman-toga theme nights, pizza,
☾ bocce ball games, and tarantella dance lessons reinforce the Italian feel. Staterooms are cheerfully decorated and fairly comfortable; 78% have an ocean view, and more than half the cabins have private verandas, though some are small. The Costa Kids Club is good, and all cruises allow parents to enjoy two evenings alone while their children are supervised by youth counselors. Both ships have a "Golf Academy at Sea," with PGA onboard clinics and golf excursions in most ports. The ships have Internet service in cabins and in an Internet café. ⊏ *1,057 cabins, 2,114 passengers, 12 passenger decks* ♿ *Specialty restaurant, dining room, café, buffet, pizzeria, in-cabin safes, some in-cabin refrigerators, in-cabin data ports, 3 pools (1 indoors), children's pool, fitness classes, gym, hair salon, 4 hot tubs, sauna, spa, steam room, 6 bars, casino, cinema, 2 dance clubs, 2 showrooms, video game room, children's programs (ages 3–17), dry cleaning, computer room* ▭ *AE, D, MC, V.*

☾ **Costa Magica.** With a bit of interior alteration, *Costa Magica* is essentially a Euro-clone of parent company Carnival Cruise Line's *Carnival Triumph* and *Carnival Victory.* The mix and size of public rooms was determined to appeal to European as well as North American passengers sailing on Mediterranean itineraries as well as cruises the Caribbean region. Like Carnival ships designed by Joe Farcus, this Costa beauty has a theme running throughout—a sort of fantasy trip to the most widely known and beautiful holiday areas of Italy. Arches, murals, columns, and railings give the restaurants the feeling of al fresco dining in lovely courtyards. More than 60% of cabins have an ocean view and, of those, 60% have balconies outfitted with chairs and tables. Light wood cabinetry, soft pastel décor, Murano glass lighting fixtures, a hairdryer, and a sitting area with sofa, chair, and table are typical for ocean-view cabins and suites. Inside cabins have ample room, but sitting areas consist of a small table and chairs. Every cabin has adequate closet and drawer/shelf storage, as well as bathroom shelves. Suites have a whirlpool tub, double sinks, and a generous walk-in closet. In the style that Europeans favor, the casino is much smaller than those on comparably sized vessels, which made room for the huge Salento Grand Bar that houses the largest dance floor at sea. ➳ *1,358 cabins, 2,720 passengers, 13 passenger decks ⚓ Specialty restaurant, 2 dining rooms, café, buffet, pizzeria, in-cabin safes, refrigerators, in-cabin data ports, 3 pools (1 indoor), children's pool, fitness classes, gym, hair salon, 6 hot tubs, sauna, spa, steam room, 7 bars, casino, cinema, 2 dance clubs, showroom, video game room, children's programs (ages 3–17), dry cleaning, computer room ▭ AE, D, MC, V.*

Disney Cruise Line

Disney Cruise Line launched its first ship, *Disney Magic,* in 1998, followed by her sister ship, *Disney Wonder,* in 1999. Dozens of the best ship designers, industry veterans, and Disney creative minds planned intensely for three years to produce these vessels, which make a positive impression on adults and children alike. Exteriors are reminiscent of the great ocean liners of the early 20th century, but interiors are technologically up-to-the-minute and full of novel developments in dining, cabin, and entertainment facilities. Three- and four-night *Disney Wonder* cruises to the Bahamas can be coupled with a stay at Walt Disney World, or you can opt for a weeklong Caribbean cruise on *Disney Magic.* Passengers represent a cross-section of North Americans and Europeans of all ages, but there are certainly more kids on board than on many other cruise ships, and plenty of activities to keep them occupied.

Suggested gratuity amounts are calculated on a per-person/per-cruise rather than per-night basis and can be added to onboard accounts for convenience or offered in cash on the last night of the cruise. For the dining room server, assistant server, head server, and stateroom host/hostess, guidelines are $32.50 for three-night cruises, $43.75 for four-night cruises, and $76.25 for seven-night cruises. Tips for room service delivery and the dining manager are at your discretion. A 15% gratuity is added to bar service tabs.

🏠 *Disney Cruise Line, 210 Celebration Pl., Celebration, FL 34747* ☎ *407/566–3500 or 800/325–2500* ⊕ *www.disneycruise.com.*

THE SHIPS OF DISNEY CRUISE LINE ℭ **Disney Magic, Disney Wonder.** These sister ships offer family-friendly staterooms designed for maximum comfort. Cabins are among the largest in the industry. Most accommodate two adults and two children and have a unique bath-and-a-half arrangement—separating bathtub or shower and toilet in different rooms, each with a sink. More than 75% of all staterooms are outside, and 44% of those include private verandas. The Disney dining plan is novel in approach and inventive in its execution; passengers are rotated through three different theme restaurants, accompanied by their familiar waiters and tablemates. Adults also may opt to dine at Palo, an elegant, reservations-required northern Italian restaurant with sweeping views. With nearly an entire deck designed just for kids, Disney's age-specific, supervised group activities give parents plenty of downtime. Emphasis is placed on pure fun, but subtle educational themes pique children's imagination. An hourly fee is charged for child care in Flounder's Reef Nursery, which is open during select hours for infants as young as three months and toddlers as old as three years. The Stack is a teen coffeehouse-style club complete with music, dance floor, games, big-screen television, and Internet café.

877 cabins, 1,754 passengers (2,400 at full occupancy), 11 passenger decks ⚓ Specialty restaurant, 3 dining rooms, buffet, ice-cream parlor, pizzeria, in-cabin safes, refrigerators, 2 pools, children's pool, fitness classes, gym, hair salon, 4 hot tubs, sauna, spa, steam room, 6 bars, cinema, dance club, 2 showrooms, video game room, children's programs (ages 3–17), dry cleaning, laundry facilities, laundry service, computer room, no-smoking cabins, no infants under 12 wks.

Holland America Line

Founded in 1873, Holland America Line (HAL) is one of the oldest names in cruising. Steeped in the traditions of the transatlantic crossing, its cruises are classic, conservative affairs renowned for their grace and gentility. Service is taken seriously: the line maintains a school in Indonesia to train staff members. Food is very good by cruise ship standards and presentation on Rosenthal china is creative. In response to the challenge presented by its competitors, Holland America has introduced a lighter side to its menus, including many pastas and "heart-healthy" dishes. Holland America passengers tend to be older and less active than those traveling on the ships of its parent line, Carnival; however, despite an infusion of younger adults and families on board, they remain refined without being stuffy or stodgy. As its ships attract a more youthful clientele, Holland America has taken steps to shed its "old folks" image, now offering stops at a private island in the Bahamas, trendier cuisine, a culinary arts center, and an expanded "Club Hal" children's program. Still, these are not party cruises, and Holland America has managed to preserve the refined and relaxing qualities that have always been its hallmark, even on sailings that cater more to younger passengers and families.

In late 2003 HAL initiated the "Signature of Excellence" program to raise product and service standards throughout the fleet; upgrades to all ships are expected to be complete by the end of 2006. Pillow-top mattresses, 250-thread-count cotton bed linens, Egyptian-cotton towels, magnifying makeup mirrors, waffle and terry robes, fresh fruit baskets, flat-screen televisions, and DVD players will be features of all accommodations. In addition, all suites have duvets on beds, fully stocked mini-bars, personalized stationery, and access to the exclusive Neptune Lounge where beverages, breakfast pastries, afternoon snacks, and evening canapés are available. Dining is enhanced by the reservations-only Pinnacle Grill on every ship, one-on-one service in the main dining rooms, and table-side waiter service in the Lido casual dining room. The spas and salons will be revamped and an early-embarkation program implemented.

For convenience, $10 per passenger, per day is automatically added to onboard accounts, and these gratuities are distributed to stewards and waitstaff. Passengers may adjust the amount based on the level of service experienced. Tips for room service delivery are at passengers' discretion. A 15% gratuity is added to bar service tabs.

⌂ *Holland America Line, 300 Elliott Ave. W, Seattle, WA 98119* ☎ *206/281–3535 or 877/932–4259* 🖨 *206/281–7110* ⊕ *www.hollandamerica.com.*

THE SHIPS OF
HOLLAND
AMERICA LINE
🐧

Amsterdam. The *Amsterdam* reflects the highest attainments of the shipbuilders' art. Everywhere you look, there are priceless antiques and original works of art, burnished brass, and sweeping staircases; a promenade completely encircles the ship with sleek and inviting teak deck chairs. Passengers are pampered, savoring cuisine in their choice of dramatic venues—a two-tiered dining salon, whose windows soar above the sea, or a candlelit Venetian-style villa. Cabins were designed with world cruising in mind, so they are larger than average; many outside cabins have sitting areas. ⇨ *690 cabins, 1,380 passengers (1,776 at full occupancy), 10 passenger decks ⚐ 2 restaurants, dining room, food court, in-room safes, refrigerators, in-room VCRs, 2 pools (1 indoor), fitness classes, gym, hair salon, 2 outdoor hot tubs, sauna, spa, steam room, 6 bars, casino, cinema, dance club, showroom, video game room, children's programs (ages 5–17), laundry facilities, laundry service, computer room, no-smoking rooms* ▤ *AE, D, MC, V.*

🐧 **Maasdam, Ryndam, Veendam.** A stunning triple-deck atrium is just one of the welcoming public spaces; staterooms are restful, with understated elegance. From bow to stern, these ships are full of HAL's signature lounges—some cozy, some grand, and most with expansive floor-to-ceiling windows. Popular spaces include the Crow's Nest, a combined observation lounge and nightclub overlooking the bow; and the Lido Restaurant—the hallmark of every Holland America Line ship—which has an adjoining outdoor terrace and swimming pool. Routinely updated with innovations and features introduced on newer fleet mates, they nevertheless retain their charm. Priceless antiques and artwork line the public areas, as in all the line's ships. ⇨ *629 cabins, 1,258 passengers (1,627 at full occupancy), 10 passenger decks ⚐ Specialty restaurant, dining room, buffet, in-cabin safes, refrigerators, in-cabin DVDs, Wi-Fi, 2 pools (1 indoor), 2 children's pools, fitness classes, gym, hair salon, 2 hot tubs, sauna, spa, steam room, 9 bars, casino, cinema, dance club, library, showroom, video game room, children's programs (ages 3–17), dry cleaning, laundry facilities, laundry service, computer room* ▤ *AE, D, MC, V.*

🐧 **Volendam, Zaandam.** These ships are structurally similar to HAL's Statendam-class vessels, which no longer cruise in the Caribbean, with signature two-tier dining rooms and a retractable roof over the main pool, but they are newer, and their theme interior design elements inject elements of youthfulness. They are also slightly larger and have Internet cafés and practice-size tennis courts. Priceless antiques and artwork line the halls; huge bouquets of fresh, fragrant flowers are everywhere (a Holland America trademark); and each ship has a teak promenade completely encircling the ship, which means there will always be room for you at the rail to watch the sunset. All standard outside cabins come with a bathtub, and all suites and minisuites have private verandas. The "Passport to Fitness" program encourages a healthful diet and exercise. ⇨ *720 cabins, 1,440 passengers (1,848 at full occupancy), 10 passen-*

ger decks △ Specialty restaurant, dining room, buffet, in-cabin safes, refrigerators, in-cabin DVDs, Wi-Fi, 2 pools (1 indoors), 2 children's pools, fitness classes, gym, hair salon, 2 hot tubs, sauna, spa, steam room, 6 bars, casino, cinema, dance club, library, showroom, video game room, children's programs (ages 3–17), dry cleaning, laundry facilities, laundry service, computer room ⊟ AE, D, MC, V.

○ ***Zuiderdam, Oosterdam, Westerdam, Noordam.*** With the highest space-to-passenger ratio in the fleet, HAL's Vista-class ships—forward-looking both in design and spirit—launched in December 2002. Exterior panorama elevators provide expansive sea views and link the 10 passenger decks. The ships also offer a range of understated, spacious accommodation categories, 85% of which have ocean views, most with private verandas. The ships have all the hallmarks of the Holland America brand—extensive art collections, numerous dining options, a covered promenade deck encircling the entire ship, two interior promenades, and a large Lido pool with a retractable dome. In 2006 HAL will deploy Noordam for its inaugural Caribbean season on 10- and 11-night itineraries from New York City, the cruise line's former headquarters.
924 cabins, 1,848 passengers, (2,272 at full occupancy), 11 passenger decks △ Specialty restaurant, dining room, buffet, pizzeria, in-cabin safes, refrigerators, some in-cabin DVDs, in-cabin data ports, Wi-Fi, 2 pools (1 indoors), children's pool, fitness classes, gym, hair salon, 5 hot tubs, sauna, spa, steam room, 9 bars, casino, cinema, 2 dance clubs, library, showroom, video game room, children's programs (ages 3–17), dry cleaning, laundry service, computer room ⊟ AE, D, MC, V.

Mediterranean Shipping Cruises

With several seasons of Caribbean sailing behind them, Mediterranean Shipping Cruises (MSC) is poised to break out of "newcomer" status in the region. More widely known as one of the world's largest cargo shipping companies, MSC has operated cruises with an eclectic fleet since the late 1980s. Since introducing two graceful medium-size ships in 2003 and 2004, MSC's expansion plans include sailing from a year-round North American home port in 2005 and a larger new ship in the Caribbean for 2006. Prices are toward the low end of the mainstream premium category.

While sailing Caribbean itineraries, MSC cruises adopt activities that appeal to American passengers without abandoning those preferred by Europeans—prepare for announcements in Italian as well as English. In addition to guest lecturers, computer classes, and cooking lessons featured in the onboard enrichment program, a popular option is Italian language classes. Nightly shows accentuate MSC's Mediterranean heritage—there might be a flamenco show in the main showroom and live music for listening and dancing in the smaller lounges. Dinner on MSC ships is a traditional seven-course event centered around authentic Italian fare. Menus list Mediterranean regional specialties and classic favorites prepared from scratch the old-fashioned way. In a nod to American tastes, broiled chicken breast, grilled salmon, and Caesar salad are always available in addition to the regular dinner menu.

Tipping is not obligatory; however, passengers may reward staff members with a gratuity for exceptional service should they choose to do so. Guidelines are $3.50 to $5 per person, per day for waiters and stateroom attendants and $1 to $2 per person, per day for the dining room maître d'. Gratuities are incorporated into all bar purchases.

📬 *Mediterranean Shipping Cruises USA, 6750 N. Andrews Ave., Miami, FL 33309* ☎*954/662–6262 or 800/872–6400* ⊕*www.msccruises. com.*

THE SHIPS OF
MEDITERRANEAN
SHIPPING
CRUISES

MSC Lirica, MSC Opera. These two medium-size ships vary only slightly in basic layout, the number of staterooms, and passenger capacity. Light and bright by day, intimate and sophisticated by night, the contemporary design may not measure up to the sizzle expected by those North American passengers who don't appreciate European understatement. Extensive use of marble, brass, and wood reflect the best of Italian styling and design. Clean lines and bold colors set the modern sophisticated tone—no glitz, no clutter—elegant simplicity is the standard of MSC's interior decor. ⚓ *795/878 cabins (Lirica/Opera), 1,586/1,756 passengers, 12/12 passenger decks* ♿ *Specialty restaurant, 2 dining rooms, buffet, pizzeria, in-cabin safes, refrigerators, some in-cabin data ports, 2 pools, fitness classes, gym, hair salon, 2 hot tubs, sauna, spa, steam room, 8 bars, casino, dance club, library, showroom, video game room, children's programs (ages 3–17), laundry service, computer room.*

MSC Musica. MSC's largest and newest ship in the Caribbean blends authentic Italian design with elements of art deco, art nouveau, and contemporary styles for a fresh new look. Certainly the highlight of the decor is a three-deck waterfall in the central atrium, where a pianist tickles the ivories on a piano suspended on a transparent floor above a pool of water. Music plays a large role in the public rooms, many of which are equipped for jam sessions, classical duets, small orchestras, and even karaoke. In response to the preference of today's cruise passengers, 85% of accommodations have an ocean view and 65% of the total number of staterooms feature balconies. ⚓ *1,300 cabins, 2,550 passengers, 12 passenger decks* ♿ *Specialty restaurant, 2 dining rooms, buffet, pizzeria, in-cabin safes, refrigerators, some in-cabin data ports, 2 pools, fitness classes, gym, hair salon, 2 hot tubs, sauna, spa, steam room, 8 bars, casino, 2 dance clubs, library, showroom, video game room, children's programs (ages 3–17), laundry service, computer room.*

Norwegian Cruise Line

Norwegian Cruise Line (NCL) was established in 1966, when one of Norway's oldest and most respected shipping companies, Oslo-based Klosters Rederi A/S, acquired the *Sunward* and repositioned the ship from Europe to the then-obscure Port of Miami. With the formation of a company called Norwegian Caribbean Lines, the cruise industry was changed forever. NCL launched an entirely new concept with its regularly scheduled cruises to the Caribbean on a single-class ship, with an informal kind of luxury. No longer simply a means of transportation, the ship became a destination unto itself, offering guests an affordable alternative to land-based resorts. The *Sunward*'s popularity prompted other cruise lines to build ships to accommodate the burgeoning market, eventually turning Miami into the world's number one port of embarkation. NCL led the way with its fleet of sleek new ships. In another bold move, NCL purchased the former *France* in 1979 and rebuilt the grand ocean liner in Bremerhaven, Germany, for Caribbean cruising. Rechristened *Norway,* she assumed the honored position as flagship of the fleet. The late 1980s brought new ships and a new corporate name when Norwegian Caribbean Lines became Norwegian Cruise Line in 1987. NCL continued its expansion by acquiring other cruise lines, stretching and refurbishing older ships, and building new mega-ships, including the line's newest, two 2,400-berth "Freestyle Cruising" ships with delivery dates in time for the summer season of 2007.

Freestyle Cruising created a sensation in the industry when Asian shipping giant Star Cruises acquired NCL early in 2000—the new owners were confounded that Americans meekly conformed to rigid dining schedules and dress codes. All that changed with NCL's introduction of a host of flexible dining options that allow passengers to choose open seating in the main dining rooms or dine in any of a number of à la carte and specialty restaurants at any time and with whom they please. While the Freestyle Cruising concept now applies to all NCL ships, you'll still see fewer options on some of the smaller, older ships. The line has even loosened the dress code to resort casual at all times and relaxed the disembarkation process by inviting passengers to relax in their cabins until it's time to leave the ship (instead of gathering in a lounge to wait for their numbers to be called). NCL's passenger list usually includes a wide range of ages, including families and couples, mostly from the United States and Canada.

NCL applies a service charge to passengers' shipboard accounts: $10 per passenger, per day for those 13 and older and $5 per day for children ages 3–12. A 15% gratuity is added to bar tabs and spa bills.

Norwegian Cruise Line, 7665 Corporate Center Dr., Miami, FL 33126 ☎ *305/436–4000 or 800/327–7030* ⊕ *www.ncl.com.*

THE SHIPS OF **Norwegian Majesty.** The *Norwegian Majesty* was lengthened in 1999 with
NORWEGIAN the insertion of a prefab midsection that added 112 feet to its length and
CRUISE LINE 203 cabins; about 71% are outside. Other additions included a second
☾ pool, an additional dining room, a coffee bar, a casino, another outdoor bar, and NCL's hallmark Le Bistro premium restaurant offering French classics and nouvelle cuisine. There's also significantly more deck space. During the conversion, all interiors were spruced up and refurbished. Some of the standard cabins are fairly small, and all have a shower only. Most ocean-view staterooms have refrigerators. Lower beds in most staterooms can be combined to form a queen-size bed. ⇨ *731 cabins, 1,462 passengers, 9 passenger decks ☾ 2 specialty restaurants, 2 dining rooms, buffet, ice-cream parlor, pizzeria, in-cabin safes, some refrigerators, some in-cabin VCRs, Wi-Fi, 2 pools, children's pool, fitness classes, gym, hair salon, 2 hot tubs, sauna, spa, 8 bars, casino, dance club, library, showroom, video game room, children's programs (ages 2–17), dry cleaning, laundry service, computer room* ▭ *AE, D, MC, V.*

🐚 *Norwegian Dream.* Launched in 1992, *Norwegian Dream* gained something of a split personality in 1998 after being "stretched" when a 130-foot midsection was added to increase her size. Although 251 staterooms and a new reception area were added, unfortunately the size of most public rooms were not increased enough and can feel cramped when the ship is fully booked. Oddities are a way-too-small buffet restaurant and the passageways through the Four Seasons dining room and the show lounge to reach the forward staircase. Where *Norwegian Dream* shines is the abundance of outdoor forward-facing decks and a wraparound promenade deck. ↪ *874 cabins, 1,748 passengers, 10 passenger decks ⚓ 2 specialty restaurants, 2 dining rooms, buffet, ice-cream parlor, pizzeria, some in-cabin safes, some refrigerators, some in-cabin DVDs, Wi-Fi, 2 pools, fitness classes, gym, hair salon, 4 hot tubs, sauna, spa, 8 bars, casino, dance club, library, showroom, video game room, children's programs (ages 2–17), dry cleaning, laundry service, computer room ▤ AE, D, MC, V.*

🐚 *Norwegian Spirit.* East met West when parent-company Star Cruises moved the former *SuperStar Leo* to the NCL fleet and rechristened her *Norwegian Spirit.* While updates were made in 2004, the ship was designed for cruises in Asia and particular emphasis was placed on public areas that appeal to Eastern tastes. In addition to some stunning Asian artwork, the ship has a few quirky features—like a special mah-jongg room. With the exception of Disney ships, it would be difficult to find better children's facilities than the Buccaneer's Wet & Wild area—virtually a water park at sea with a viewing deck where parents can observe their children having fun. *Norwegian Spirit* is very family-friendly with many connecting staterooms and hidden, childproof locks on the sliding glass doors that open to private balconies. ↪ *983 cabins, 1,966 passengers, 10 passenger decks ⚓ 4 specialty restaurants, 2 dining rooms, café, buffet, ice-cream parlor, in-cabin safes, some refrigerators, Wi-Fi, 2 pools (1 indoors), children's pool, fitness classes, gym, hair salon, 4 hot tubs, sauna, spa, 8 bars, casino, dance club, library, showroom, video game room, children's programs (ages 2–17), dry cleaning, laundry service, computer room ▤ AE, D, MC, V.*

🐚 *Norwegian Sun.* This ship has all the bells and whistles, including a variety of dining options, specialty bars, and Internet access—both in a café and in cabins. A 24-hour health club has expansive ocean views, and the presence of the full-service Mandara Spa means you can turn your cruise into a spa vacation. Cabins are adequately laid out, with large windows and sitting areas, sufficient (but not generous) shelf and drawer space, and two lower beds that convert to a queen. But what makes this ship different from other large ships is its relaxed onboard atmosphere and Freestyle Cruising concept, which means main dining rooms are smaller but there are more dining venues (some with an additional cost). ↪ *1,001 cabins, 2,002 passengers (2,400 at full occupancy), 11 passenger decks ⚓ 7 specialty restaurants, 2 dining rooms, buffet, ice-cream parlor, pizzeria, in-cabin safes, refrigerators, Wi-Fi, 2 pools, fitness classes, gym, hair salon, 4 hot tubs, sauna, spa, steam room, 11 bars, casino, cinema, dance club, showroom, video game room, chil-*

dren's programs (ages 2–17), dry cleaning, laundry service, computer room ⊟ *AE, D, MC, V.*

🐧 ***Norwegian Dawn, Norwegian Jewel.*** Of the line's newest and largest ships, built specifically for Freestyle Cruising, *Norwegian Dawn* is based in New York City and comes bedecked with one of the largest art collections afloat. Andy Warhol prints are hung in stairwells and priceless originals by Matisse, Monet, and Renoir can be found in the Le Bistro premium restaurant. A top speed of 25 knots allows the ship to do seven-night round-trips to the Bahamas and Florida. Cabins are reasonably large, with stylish decor and nice-looking cherry-veneer cabinetry; minisuites with private verandas are especially nice. Most accommodations have compartmentalized bathrooms with toilet, sink, and shower separated by sliding glass doors; all cabins have coffeemakers. *Norwegian Jewel* is the "next generation" of Freestyle Cruising vessels with all the attributes of her near-twin, plus the advantage of 10 Courtyard Villas sporting private courtyards and sundecks. An extensive health club, wonderful children's facilities (including a children's pool), and separate teen disco are definite pluses, as is wireless Internet access throughout the ship. ↩ *1,112/ 1,200 cabins (Norwegian Dawn/Norwegian Jewel), 2,224/2,400 passengers, 11/11 passenger decks* ⚓ *4 restaurants, 3 dining rooms, café, buffet, ice-cream parlor, pizzeria, in-cabin safes, refrigerators, some in-cabin DVDs, in-cabin data ports, Wi-Fi, 3 pools (1 indoors), children's pool, fitness classes, gym, hair salon, 6 hot tubs, sauna, spa, steam room, 9 bars, casino, cinema, 2 dance clubs, library, showroom, video game room, children's programs (ages 2–17), dry cleaning, laundry facilities, laundry service, computer room* ⊟ *AE, D, MC, V.*

Oceania Cruises

This distinctive cruise line was founded by Frank Del Rio and Joe Watters, cruise industry veterans with the know-how to satisfy inquisitive passengers with interesting ports of call and upscale touches for fares much lower than you would expect. Oceania Cruises set sail in 2003 to carve a unique, almost "boutique" niche in the cruise industry by obtaining midsize "R-class" ships that made up the now-defunct Renaissance Cruises fleet.

Intimate and cozy public spaces reflect the importance of socializing on Oceania ships. Evening entertainment leans toward light cabaret, solo artists, music for dancing, and conversation with fellow passengers; however, you'll find lively karaoke sessions on the schedule as well. The sophisticated adult atmosphere is enhanced on sea days by a combo performing jazz or easy-listening melodies poolside.

Varied, destination-rich itineraries are an important characteristic of Oceania Cruises, and most Caribbean sailings are in the 10- to 12-night range, which means more interesting, less-visited ports. Before arrival in ports of call, lectures are presented on the historical background, culture, and traditions of the islands.

For convenience, $11.50 per person, per day is added to onboard accounts for distribution to stewards and waitstaff and an additional $3.50 per person, per day is added for suite occupants where butler service is provided. Passengers may adjust the amount based on the level of service experienced. Bar bills add an automatic 18% to all beverage tabs for bartenders and servers.

⌂ *Oceania Cruises, 8120 N.W. 53rd St., Suite 100, Miami, FL 33166* ☎ *305/514–2300 or 800/531–5658* ⊕ *www.oceaniacruises.com.*

THE SHIPS OF OCEANIA CRUISES

Regatta. Carefully furnished to impart the atmosphere of a private English country manor, this midsize ship is casual, yet elegant, with a sweeping central staircase, abundant flower arrangements, and rich fabrics covering the windows and overstuffed sofas and wing chairs. The feeling throughout is warm and intimate with cozy conversation areas surrounding faux fireplaces. Dark-wood cabinetry, soothing blue decor, mirrored accents, a vanity/desk, and a sitting area with sofa, chair, and table are typical stateroom features. Tranquility Beds pamper passengers in every stateroom with firm mattresses, 350-thread-count linens, goose-down pillows, and silk-cut duvets. These ships aren't really suited to children, and there are no facilities or programs dedicated to their entertainment. ⌁ *340 cabins, 680 passengers, 9 passenger decks ⚓ 2 specialty restaurants, dining room, buffet, pizzeria, in-cabin safes, some refrigerators, some in-cabin DVDs, in-cabin data ports, pool, fitness classes, gym, hair salon, 3 hot tubs, spa, steam room, 4 bars, casino, dance club, library, showroom, dry cleaning, laundry facilities, laundry service, computer room, no-smoking cabins.*

Princess Cruise Line

Rising from modest beginnings in 1965, when it began offering cruises to Mexico with a single ship, Princess has become one of the world's largest cruise lines. Its fleet sails to more destinations each year than any other major line, though many cruises depart from the West Coast of the United States rather than from the Caribbean. Princess was catapulted to stardom in 1977, when its flagship became the setting for *The Love Boat* television series, which introduced millions of viewers to the still-new concept of a seagoing vacation. The name and famous "sea-witch" logo have remained synonymous with cruising ever since. Nearly everything about Princess is big, but the line doesn't sacrifice quality for quantity when it comes to building beautiful vessels. Decor and materials are top-notch, and service, especially in the dining rooms, is of a high standard. In short, Princess is refined without being pretentious.

Princess ships plying the Caribbean feature the line's innovative "Personal Choice Cruising" program, an individualized, unstructured style of cruising that gives passengers choice and flexibility in customizing their cruise experience—multiple dining locations, flexible entertainment, and affordable private balconies are all highlights. Enrichment programs featuring guest lecturers and opportunities to learn new skills or crafts are welcome additions to a roster of adult activities, which still include staples such as bingo and art auctions. You can even earn PADI scuba diving certification in just one week by participating in the "Open Water Diver" program.

Princess passengers' average age is 45, and you see a mix of younger and older couples on board. The ships are some of the most accessible at sea, and passengers with disabilities can select from staterooms in a variety of categories that are tailored for their special needs.

Princess suggests tipping $10 per person, per day. Gratuities are automatically added to onboard accounts, which passengers can adjust at the purser's desk; 15% is added to bar bills.

🏛 *Princess Cruise Line, 24305 Town Center Dr., Santa Clarita, CA 91355-4999* ☎ *661/753–0000 or 800/774–6237* ⊕ *www.princess.com.*

THE SHIPS OF
PRINCESS CRUISE
LINE

☾ *Sun Princess, Sea Princess, Coral Princess.* The graceful Sun-class ships offer the range of choices attributed to larger Grand-class ships without sacrificing the small-ship atmosphere for which they are noted. Four-story atriums with circular marble floors, stained-glass domes, and magnificent floating staircases are ideal settings for relaxation, people-watching, and making a grand entrance. Many cabins have private balconies (more than 70% of outside cabins have them). All standard cabins are decorated in light colors and have a queen-size bed convertible to two singles, ample closet and bath space (with shower only), terry robes, mini-refrigerators, and hair dryers. Each subtly decorated vessel has two main showrooms and several dining rooms and restaurants (some with extra charges), from large to intimate. A wraparound teak promenade lined with canopied steamer chairs provides a peaceful setting for reading, napping, or daydreaming. ⇨ *975/987 cabins (Sun, Sea/Coral), 1,950/1,970 passengers, 10/11 passenger decks ♿ 1 specialty restaurant, 2 dining rooms, buffet, ice-cream parlor, pizzeria, in-cabin safes, refrigerators, Wi-Fi, 3 pools (1 indoors), children's pool, fitness classes, gym, hair salon, 5 hot tubs, sauna, spa, steam room, 7 bars, casino, 2 dance clubs, library, 2 showrooms, video game room, children's programs (ages 3–17), dry cleaning, laundry facilities, laundry service, computer room, no children under 6 months* ▭ *AE, D, MC, V.*

☾ *Grand Princess, Golden Princess, Star Princess.* Grand-class vessels have advanced the idea of floating resort to an entirely new level with more than 700 private-balcony staterooms. As in their predecessors, interiors are soothing pastel hues with splashes of glamour in the sweeping staircases and marble-floored atriums. Surprisingly intimate for such large ships, human scale in public lounges is achieved by judicious placement of furniture as unobtrusive room dividers. The casino, however, is massive and action-packed. Cabins, which are in a bewildering array of categories, have generous closet and shelf space but few drawers. Even the smallest standard cabins are adequate for two people, and all rooms have terry robes and hair dryers. A traditional touch is the Wheelhouse Bar, which evokes the long history of P. & O., Princess Cruise Line's parent company. ⇨ *1,300 cabins, 2,600 passengers, 14 passenger decks ♿ 2 specialty restaurants, 3 dining rooms, buffet, ice-cream parlor, pizzeria, in-cabin safes, refrigerators, Wi-Fi, 4 pools (1 indoor), children's pool, fitness classes, gym, hair salon, 9 hot tubs, sauna, spa, steam room, 9 bars, casino, outdoor cinema, 2 dance clubs, library, 2 showrooms, video game room, children's programs (ages 3–17), dry cleaning, laundry facilities, laundry service, computer room; no children under 6 months* ▭ *AE, D, MC, V.*

🕑 *Caribbean Princess, Crown Princess.* With dramatic atriums and Skywalker's Disco—the "spoiler" hovering 150 feet above the stern—*Caribbean Princess* is nearly identical to earlier Grand-class vessels with an additional deck of balcony staterooms. Not quite a "twin" ship, *Crown Princess* has more dining options and other redesigned or relocated signature public spaces—the atrium resembles an open piazza, Sabatini's Italian trattoria is found on a top deck with views on three sides, and Skywalker's Disco is located forward near the funnel, where it is topped with a sports court. As in the Grand-class vessels, a giant poolside LED screen shows up to seven movies or events daily. After dark, lounge chairs are covered with special cushions and blankets, and free popcorn plus a variety of drink specials and movie nibbles are available. Inside spaces are quietly neutral with sweeping staircases and marble-floored atriums. Surprising intimacy is achieved on these large ships by the number of public rooms and restaurants that swallow up passengers. Although the fleet's other spas are operated by Steiner Leisure, a departure for Princess is the in-house Lotus Spa on these ships. With a selection of treatments designed specifically for men and teens—and hair-care products by Carita of Paris—appointments for the private-label spa on these ships can be pre-reserved. ➪ *1,550 cabins, 3,100 passengers, 15 passenger decks & 2 specialty restaurants, 3 dining rooms, buffet, ice-cream parlor, pizzeria, in-cabin safes, refrigerators, Wi-Fi, 4 pools (1 indoors), children's pool, fitness classes, gym, hair salon, 7 hot tubs, sauna, spa, steam room, 9 bars, casino, outdoor cinema, 2 dance clubs, library, 2 showrooms, video game room, children's programs (ages 3–17), dry cleaning, laundry facilities, laundry service, computer room; no kids under 6 months* 🖃 *AE, D, MC, V.*

Royal Caribbean International

Imagine if the Mall of America were sent to sea. That's a fair approximation of what the mega-ships of Royal Caribbean International (RCI) are all about. These large-to-giant vessels are indoor-outdoor wonders, with every conceivable activity in a resortlike atmosphere, including atrium lobbies, shopping arcades, large spas, expansive sundecks, and rock-climbing walls. Several ships have such elaborate facilities as 18-hole miniature-golf courses, ice-skating rinks, and in-line skating tracks. These mammoth ships are quickly overshadowing the smaller vessels in Royal Caribbean's fleet, and passengers now have three generations of mega-ships to choose from, including the prototype, the *Sovereign of the Seas*, which was completely rejuvenated in late 2004.

The centerpiece of Royal Caribbean mega-ships is the multideck atrium, a hallmark that has been duplicated by many other cruise lines. The brilliance of this design is that all the major public rooms radiate from this central point, so you can learn your way around these huge ships within minutes of boarding. Ships in the Vision series (*Legend, Splendour, Enchantment, Grandeur,* and *Rhapsody of the Seas*) are especially bright and airy, with sea views almost anywhere you happen to be. The main problem with its otherwise well-conceived vessels is that, when booked to over 100% capacity, there are too many people on board, making for an exasperating experience at embarkation, when tendering, and at disembarkation. However, Royal Caribbean is one of the best-run and most popular cruise lines.

Although the line competes directly with Carnival for passengers—active couples and singles in their thirties to fifties, as well as a large family contingent—there are distinct differences of ambience and energy. Royal Caribbean is a bit more sophisticated and subdued than Carnival, even while delivering a good time on a grand scale.

Royal Caribbean suggests the following tips per passenger: stateroom attendant, $3.50 a day; dining-room waiter, $3.50 a day; assistant waiter, $2 a day. Gratuities for headwaiters and other service personnel are at your discretion. A 15% gratuity is automatically added to beverage and bar bills. All gratuities may be charged to your onboard account.

🖉 *Royal Caribbean International, 1050 Caribbean Way, Miami, FL 33132* ☎ *305/539–6000 or 800/327–6700* 🌐 *www.royalcaribbean.com.*

THE SHIPS OF
ROYAL
CARIBBEAN
CRUISE LINE

Empress of the Seas. Formerly christened *Nordic Empress,* this unique and distinctive-looking ship, with huge aft bay windows, was specifically designed for the short (3- to 4-day) cruise market and splits its year between 4- and 5-night Western Caribbean and 11-night Exotic Caribbean cruises. A simple design with a single main corridor makes it easy for passengers to learn their way about this medium-size vessel. The six-story atrium is dazzling and well lighted, with lots of glass, chrome, and a cascading waterfall. Interior spaces, updated in 2004, are filled with large and festive public rooms. Incorporated in the update were a Royal Caribbean signature, the Schooner Bar, and Boleros, a Latin-theme nightclub. Standard cabins are tight at 117 square feet to 139 square feet, and the bright decor can't make them feel any larger; balconies provide much-needed added space to suites and junior suites. ⟿ *801 cabins, 1,602 passengers (2,020 at full occupancy), 11 passenger decks* ♿ *Specialty restaurant, dining room, in-cabin safes, some refrigerators, in-cabin data ports, Wi-Fi, 2 pools, fitness classes, gym, hair salon, 4 hot tubs, sauna, spa, 5 bars, casino, dance club, showroom, video game room, children's programs (ages 3–17), dry cleaning, laundry service, computer room* ▭ *AE, D, MC, V.*

♻ ***Majesty of the Seas, Sovereign of the Seas.*** The first Sovereign-class ship entered service in 1988 and set the cruise industry abuzz. *Sovereign of the Seas* was the first of Royal Caribbean's floating-resort mega-ships—as tall as the Statue of Liberty and three football fields in length, with a multideck atrium and signature glass elevators. These ships now sail three- and four-night itineraries to the Bahamas and make a call at Royal Caribbean's private island, CocoCay. The two dining rooms serve a different international menu each evening and waiters dress accordingly. Relatively modest 112- and 119-square-foot standard cabins make the most of limited space. Each is fitted with twin beds convertible to a queen, a large dressing table, large wardrobe closet, chair, and full-length mirror. Upper category accommodations have safes and refrigerators. The 62 suites and junior suites on both ships have balconies. Extensively renovated in 2004, *Sovereign of the Seas* also has a Johnny Rockets diner and Boleros Latin-theme dance club. ✒ *1,175/1,146 cabins (Majesty/ Sovereign), 2,350/2,292 passengers (2,744/2,773 at full occupancy), 11/11 passenger decks* ⚓ *2 dining rooms, buffet, pizzeria, some in-cabin safes, some refrigerators, Wi-Fi, 2 pools, fitness classes, gym, hair salon, 2 hot tubs, sauna (Majesty only), spa, 7 bars, casino, 2 dance clubs, library, showroom, video game room, children's programs (ages 3–17), dry cleaning, laundry service, computer room* ▤ *AE, D, MC, V.*

Legend of the Seas, Splendour of the Seas, Enchantment of the Seas, Grandeur of the Seas, Rhapsody of the Seas. Conceived as three sets of twin sister ships, these vessels were the second Royal Caribbean class of large ships, although they almost seem petite next to the huge Voyager-class vessels. Namesake *Vision of the Seas* is the only vessel in the class permanently assigned to the Pacific. With seven-story atriums, bi-level health clubs, skylights, and acres of glass windows, all live up to their Vision-class designation with vast ocean views from most public areas. Solariums with retracting ceilings over one swimming pool on each ship were a first for Royal Caribbean. Accommodations are a bit larger than the Sovereign-class ships, and cabins on two entire decks have balconies. Royal Caribbean, living up to its reputation for renovating ships to incorporate new features, lengthened a Vision-ship in 2005, when *Enchantment of the Seas* went under the knife. By adding a 73-foot midsection, the ship gained 151 cabins, a specialty restaurant, and such innovations as top-deck suspension bridges and bungee trampolines, plus an interactive Splash Deck for children. ✒ *900/900/1,126/975/1,000 cabins (Legend/Splendour/Enchantment/Grandeur/Rhapsody), 1,800/ 1,800/2,252/2,252/2,000 passengers (2,076/2,076/2,446/2,748/2,435 at full occupancy), 11 passenger decks* ⚓ *Specialty restaurant (Enchantment only), dining room, buffet, ice-cream parlor, in-cabin safes, Wi-Fi, 2 pools (1 indoors), children's pool (Enchantment), fitness classes, gym, hair salon, 6 hot tubs, sauna, spa, 6 bars, casino, dance club, library, showroom, video game room, children's programs (ages 3–17), dry cleaning, laundry service, computer room* ▤ *AE, D, MC, V.*

⟳ **Brilliance of the Seas, Radiance of the Seas, Serenade of the Seas, Jewel of the Seas.** Royal Caribbean's Radiance-class ships aren't the largest in the fleet, but they offer great speed—allowing for longer itineraries to far-flung ports of call—and the line's highest percentage of outside cabins. They are also considered by many to be the fleet's most beautiful vessels, with central atriums spanning 10 decks and sea-facing elevators that offer panoramic ocean views while moving from deck to deck. The coffeehouse-bookstore combination is a novel touch. The solarium, filled with lush foliage and cascading waterfalls, has a retractable roof to convert it from indoor pool to an outdoor pool. All cabins have two twin beds convertible to a queen, computer jack, vanity table with an extendable working surface, and bedside reading lights. ✒ *1,050 cabins, 2,100 passengers (2,501 at full occupancy), 12 passenger decks* ⚓ *2 specialty restaurants, 2-deck dining room, buffet, pizzeria, in-cabin safes, refrigerators, some in-cabin VCRs, in-cabin data ports, Wi-Fi, 2 pools (1 indoors), children's pool, fitness classes, gym, hair salon, 3 hot tubs, sauna, spa, steam room, 11 bars, casino, cinema, dance club, li-*

brary, showroom, video game room, children's programs (ages 3–17), dry cleaning, laundry service, computer room ☰ *AE, D, MC, V.*

☾ ***Adventure of the Seas, Navigator of the Seas, Explorer of the Seas, Voyager of the Seas, Mariner of the Seas.*** Royal Caribbean's enormous Voyager-class vessels are among the world's largest cruise ships and represent the highest space-per-guest ratio in the RCL fleet. Innovative and amazing features include ice-skating rinks, basketball courts, shopping promenades, in-line skating tracks, 18-hole miniature-golf courses, and rock-climbing walls. Spectacular three-story dining rooms have two dinner seatings, but there are other options, both casual (a Johnny Rockets diner) and reservation-only (for an extra fee). As on all Royal Caribbean ships, accommodations are cheery; however, although cabins are larger than on earlier ships, the least expensive can be a tight squeeze for more than two occupants. Suites have the advantage of more floor space and larger closets; other cabins have twin beds convertible to a queen and bathrooms with hair dryers and sizable vanity areas; some inside staterooms have a view overlooking the gigantic atrium. Staterooms designed for families boast that they sleep up to eight. ⇨ *1,557 cabins, 3,114 passengers (3,835 to 3,844 at full occupancy), 14 passenger decks ⚓ 2 specialty restaurants, café, dining room, buffet, ice-cream parlor, pizzeria, in-cabin safes, refrigerators, some in-cabin VCRs, some in-cabin DVDs, in-cabin data ports, Wi-Fi, 3 pools, fitness classes, gym, hair salon, 7 hot tubs, sauna, spa, steam room, 12 bars, casino, cinema, 2 dance clubs, library, 3 showrooms, video game room, children's programs (ages 3–17), dry cleaning, laundry service, computer room, some no-smoking cabins* ☰ *AE, D, MC, V.*

☾ ***Freedom of the Seas.*** The world's largest cruise ship at this writing, the enormous *Freedom of the Seas* expands upon Voyager-class vessels with innovative and unexpected features, including an ice-skating rink, Royal Promenade, and rock-climbing wall. Spectacular three-story dining rooms have two dinner seatings, but there are other options as well, both casual and reservation-only (for an extra fee). The traditionally cheery cabins are also larger than on earlier Royal Caribbean ships, with larger balconies, too. Suites give you more floor space and larger closets; other cabins have twin beds convertible to a queen and bathrooms with hair dryers and sizable vanity areas; some inside staterooms have a view overlooking the gigantic atrium. Staterooms designed for families will sleep up to eight. ⇨ *1,800 cabins, 3,600 passengers (4,370 at full occupancy), 15 passenger decks ⚓ 2 specialty restaurants, dining room, buffet, ice-cream parlor, pizzeria, in-cabin safes, refrigerators, some in-cabin VCRs, some in-cabin DVDs, in-cabin data ports, Wi-Fi, 3 pools, fitness classes, gym, hair salon, 7 hot tubs, sauna, spa, steam room, 10 bars, casino, cinema, 2 dance clubs, library, showroom, video game room, children's programs (ages 3–17), dry cleaning, laundry service, computer room, some no-smoking cabins* ☰ *AE, D, MC, V.*

Other Cruise Lines

A few small cruise lines sail through the Caribbean and offer boutique to nearly bed-and-breakfast experiences. Notably, Clipper Cruise Line,

Star Clippers Cruise Line, and Windjammer Barefoot Cruises appeal to passengers who eschew mainstream cruises. Most of these niche vessels accommodate 200 or fewer passengers, and their focus is on soft adventure. Cruising between nearby ports and anchoring out so passengers can swim and snorkel directly from the ship, their itineraries usually leave plenty of time for exploring and other activities on- or offshore. Many of these cruises schedule casual enrichment talks that often continue on decks, at meals, and during trips ashore.

Clipper Cruise Line

The yachtlike *Nantucket Clipper* and *Yorktown Clipper* are small, American-built and U.S.-registered coastal cruisers. With their shallow drafts and inflatable, motorized landing craft, they are well suited to exploring remote and otherwise inaccessible tropical waters. Cruises are billed as soft adventure and educational, and include a naturalist, historian, or other expert to lead lectures and field trips. Itineraries include a full range of organized shore excursions, but there are few other organized activities: there are no discos, casinos, or musical reviews aboard Clipper ships, and reading, socializing, and board games are the most popular activities. Sometimes local entertainers perform on board, and there may be movies in the dining room after dinner, but often passengers go ashore for nightlife. These cruises don't sacrifice aesthetics, however, and the line emphasizes such shipboard refinements as fine dining in a single open seating, though service by the American staff is not of the white-glove variety. The line tries to maintain a sophisticated atmosphere, and there are two dressy evenings, where a jacket but no tie is appropriate for men. Passengers are typically older (often in their mid-sixties).

The line recommends $10 per day in gratuities, which are deposited in a box at the end of the cruise and divided equally among the crew. No service charges are added to wine or bar bills.

🗐 *Clipper Cruise Line, 11969 Westline Industrial Dr., St. Louis, MO 63146-3220 ☎ 314/655–6700 or 800/325–0010 ⊕ www.clippercruise. com.*

THE SHIPS OF **Nantucket Clipper, Yorktown Clipper.** The Clippers look more like boxy
CLIPPER CRUISE yachts than cruise ships. Their signature design is dominated by a large
LINE bridge and picture windows that ensure bright interior public spaces. In keeping with the small size of these ships, there are only two public rooms and deck space is limited. The glass-walled observation lounge does triple duty as the ship's bar, lecture room, and occasional movie "theater." You'll only find outside cabins, but most are small and have tiny bathrooms; small safes are in one of the drawers. Although the larger top-deck staterooms are quite spacious, there are only a handful of them. Most cabins have a picture window, but a few have portholes; none have televisions. A fleet of inflatable Zodiac landing craft takes passengers ashore for independent exploration. 🖢 *51/69 cabins (Nantucket/ Yorktown), 102/138 passengers, 3/4 passenger decks ৬ Dining room, in-cabin safes, bar, computer room, no-smoking cabins; no TV in cabins ▤ AE, MC, V.*

Star Clippers Cruise Line

In 1991 Star Clippers unveiled a new tall-ship alternative to sophisticated travelers whose wants included adventure at sea, but not on board a conventional cruise ship. Star Clippers vessels are the world's largest barkentine and full-rigged sailing ships—four- and five-masted sailing beauties filled with modern high-tech equipment as well as the amenities of private yachts. The ships rely on sail power while at sea unless conditions require the assistance of the engines. Old-fashioned sailing is the key to Star Clippers' appeal; minimum heeling, usually less than 6%, is achieved through judicious control of the sails. You can lounge on deck and simply soak in the nautical ambience or join crew members pitching the sails and steering the ship, as well as learn about navigational techniques from the captain. Although the line's laid-back philosophy is similar to Windjammer's, these vessels are geared toward more upscale passengers. Public rooms are larger than those aboard Windjammer ships, as are most cabins, which have hair dryers, televisions, and telephones. Star Clippers ships also have swimming pools. Other amenities fall somewhere between those of a true sailing yacht and the high-tech Windstar ships. The differences are more than just in the level of luxury—Star Clippers are true sailing vessels, albeit with motors, while Windstar ships are trim ocean liners with masts and sails. Prices, however, are a bit more affordable and often less than you would pay on a mass-market cruise ship.

Passengers are an international group: about half are European (mostly French, German, and Swedish), and nearly all are couples, from honeymooners to well-traveled retirees. This is not a cruise line for the physically challenged; there are no elevators and ramps or staterooms/bathrooms with wheelchair accessibility. Gangways and shore launches can be difficult to navigate.

Star Clippers recommends the following gratuities: room steward, $3 per day; dining-room staff, $5 per day. A 15% gratuity is added to bar bills. Gratuities may be charged to your shipboard account.

✑ *Star Clippers, Inc., 4101 Salzedo Ave., Coral Gables, FL 33146* ☎ *305/ 442–0550 or 800/442–0551* ⊕ *www.starclippers.com.*

THE SHIPS OF STAR CLIPPERS CRUISE LINE

Royal Clipper, Star Clipper. These sleek, white sailing ships have teak decks and tapered steel masts above, while belowdecks they gleam with abundant polished woods, brass fixtures, and nautical touches. *Royal Clipper* is only the second five-masted sailing ship in history and is rigged with an incredible 42 sails. In contrast, *Star Clipper*'s four masts are more traditionally rigged with 16 sails. Freshwater and saltwater swimming pools on both vessels are surrounded by sunning areas. The main swimming pool on *Royal Clipper* has an unusual glass bottom that enables patrons of the piano bar to view swimmers while seated beneath the pool. Each handsomely appointed cabin has a vanity and tiny sitting area and a handful on *Royal Clipper* have unexpected private verandas. But the smallest cabins are truly that (107 square feet on *Royal Clipper,* and only 97 square feet on *Star Clipper*). Think "yacht" and the cabin sizes make sense, especially when you consider the dress code is elegant casual and coats and ties are never required. Most outside cabins have portholes;

a few have picture windows. Dinner is served at one seating. A marina platform lowers at the stern of *Royal Clipper* for diving and water sports. *114/85 cabins (Royal Clipper/Star Clipper), 227/170 passengers, 5/4 passenger decks* *Dining room, in-cabin safes, 3/2 pools, fitness classes, gym (Royal Clipper), hair salon (Royal Clipper), 2 bars, library, computer room, no-smoking cabins* *AE, MC, V.*

Windjammer Barefoot Cruises

The world's largest fleet of tall ships evolved from a modest beginning—a single 19-foot sloop, *The Hangover,* on which Windjammer Barefoot Cruises founder Mike Burke sailed his friends from South Florida to the Bahamas. Or so the legend goes. The resulting fleet consists of four tall ships ranging in size from 327 tons to 1,740 tons, which carry between 64 and 119 passengers. Each vessel has a distinctive and unique heritage, usually as the private yacht of some legendary financial mogul or European royal or in the service of a government for oceanographic and meteorological research. Carefully restored, they sail affordable 6- and 13-day cruises year-round to out-of-the-way islands and anchor in pristine waters where traditional cruise ships can't go.

Windjammer cruises combine the adventure of a traditional sailing voyage with a nod to basic comforts. These are not frou-frou ships (translation: big, white cruise liners) and have no gyms, spas, or hair salons. Serious exercise is climbing the stairs (there are no elevators) and swimming, either at the beaches or sometimes right from the ship. Buccaneers at heart, many passengers join the crew to work the sails and participate in informal nautical games like crab racing contests and masquerading as pirates. Swizzle time comes late every afternoon when passengers need no encouragement to show up for their daily ration of complimentary grog. With a relatively small number of passengers, the ships provide a totally laid-back experience, and there are certainly no "formal" evenings. You might want to save a clean T-shirt for the Captain's Dinner—anyone dressing to impress should be prepared to walk the plank.

Though Windjammer offers singles-only and other specialty cruises, a typical sailing includes a diverse, unpretentious socioeconomic mix of shipmates who love the sea and the tall ships and wouldn't be caught dead on a traditional cruise ship. In summer months, Windjammer offers a supervised children's program called the "Junior Jammers Club," similar to a summer camp, so that parents can relax and enjoy their vacation time.

Windjammer recommends $60 per passenger/per week in optional gratuities, which are shared equally by the entire crew, though not by officers. Tips are usually extended in cash on the last day of the cruise.

Windjammer Cruises, Box 190120, Miami, FL 33119-0120 *305/672–6453 or 800/327–2601* *305/674–1219* *www.windjammer.com.*

THE SHIPS OF WINDJAMMER BAREFOOT CRUISES

Legacy. The flagship in the Windjammer fleet is a four-masted barkentine that was once a meteorological research and exploration vessel for the French government. She was acquired in 1989 by Windjammer and converted into a traditional tall ship. Expert craftsmanship is apparent in the hand-carved, exotic South American woods; custom-designed interiors; and relatively spacious accommodations. All cabins are air-conditioned and simply decorated and have either bunk, double, or twin beds; wooden wardrobes; and full-length mirrors. Baths have shower stalls. *Legacy* sails throughout the British and U.S. Virgin Islands during the winter and spring months, the ABC islands in fall, and the Bahamas during the summer season. ⤳ *61 cabins, 119 passengers, 4 passenger decks ⚓ Dining room, some in-cabin refrigerators, bar, some children's programs (ages 6–17), no-smoking cabins; no TV in cabins* 🖃 *D, DC, MC, V.*

Mandalay. Once considered the most luxurious yacht in the world and the dream boat of financier E. F. Hutton, the former *Hussar* is the queen of the Windjammer fleet. From 1953, the ship functioned as a floating laboratory for Columbia University's geological observation team; nearly half the existing knowledge of the ocean floor was gathered by the vessel. In 1982, she joined Windjammer and was renamed *Mandalay*. Although all cabins are air-conditioned and simply furnished, there are two larger cabins on the main deck—the Admiral Suite and the Captain's Cabin—that have large picture windows, refrigerators, and private sundecks. The *Mandalay* stops at unspoiled beaches with gentle waters as she sails the Windward and Leeward islands. ⤳ *36 cabins, 72 passengers, 3 passenger decks ⚓ Dining room, bar, no-smoking cabins; no TV in cabins* 🖃 *D, DC, MC, V.*

Polynesia. Built in Holland in 1938, this four-masted schooner, originally named *Argus*, was the swiftest fishing schooner in the Portuguese Grand Banks fishing fleet. She was bought and extensively renovated by Windjammer in 1975 and was renamed *Polynesia*. The refurbishment added modern plumbing, a teak deck, two main-deck admiral suites, 12 main-deck cabins, and 40 standard cabins. All the simply furnished, double-occupancy accommodations have air-conditioning, exotic wood paneling, and tile floors; bathrooms have only showers. *Polynesia* also has a specially designed family-style dining salon. It sails the Leeward and the Windward islands of the French West Indies. ⤳ *50 cabins, 112 passengers, 4 passenger decks ⚓ Dining room, bar, some children's programs (ages 6–17), no-smoking cabins; no TV in cabins* 🖃 *D, DC, MC, V.*

Yankee Clipper. Built in 1927 by industrialist Alfred Krup, the *Cressida* later became the *Pioneer* when she was acquired by the Vanderbilt family, who raced her from Newport Beach, California. Windjammer bought and rechristened her in 1984. Extensive refurbishments—conducted over a three-year period—restored some of her former majesty and beauty and also gave her three new masts of purpleheart and angelica woods, air-conditioned cabins, and a continuous upper deck. Passengers snorkel, scuba dive, sample exotic spices, and lounge on tranquil deserted beaches of the Grenadines. ⤳ *32 cabins, 64 passengers, 3 passenger decks ⚓ Dining room, bar, no-smoking cabins; no TV in cabins* 🖃 *D, DC, MC, V.*

Ports of
Embarkation

3

WORD OF MOUTH

"I want to go on a birthday cruise in Jan. with a friend and another couple. Charleston, S. C., is the best departure port for all of us. Any cruise lines leave from there?"

—Minette

"Any ideas for a few hours in the port area—restaurants/walks/shopping? We'll be in [New Orleans] for a few days pre-cruise also, so this will be our last chance to enjoy and say good-bye to the city."

—CaliNurse

"We are taking a cruise out of Miami and wanted to stay in Miami for a day or 2 before the cruise. How far is Miami (by the beach) from the Port? Does anybody have any recommendations for hotels?"

—AimeeNC

www.fodors.com/forums

MIAMI IS THE WORLD'S CRUISE CAPITAL, and more cruise ships are based here year-round than anywhere else. Caribbean cruises depart for their itineraries from several ports on either of Florida's coasts, as well as cities on the Gulf Coast and East Coast of the United States. Generally, if your cruise is on an Eastern Caribbean itinerary, you'll depart from Miami, Fort Lauderdale, or Port Canaveral; short 3- and 4-day cruises to the Bahamas also depart from these ports. Most cruises on Western Caribbean itineraries depart from Tampa, Mobile, New Orleans, or Galveston, though some depart from Miami as well. Cruises from ports farther up the East Coast of the United States, including such ports as Charleston, South Carolina, and even New York City, usually go to the Bahamas or Key West and often include a private-island stop or a stop elsewhere in Florida. Cruises to the Southern Caribbean might depart from Miami if they are 10 days or longer, but more likely, they will depart from San Juan, Puerto Rico, or some other port deeper in the Caribbean.

Regardless of which port you depart from, air connections may prevent you from leaving home on the morning of your cruise or going home the day you return to port. Or you may wish to arrive early simply to give yourself a bit more peace of mind, or you may just want to spend more time in one of these interesting port cities. Many people choose to depart from New Orleans just to have an excuse to spend a couple of days in the city before or after their cruise.

PORT ESSENTIALS

Car Rental

🚗 Major Agencies **Alamo** ☎ 800/327-9633 ⊕ www.alamo.com. **Avis** ☎ 800/331-1212, 800/879-2847 or 800/272-5871 in Canada, 0870/606-0100 in the U.K., 02/9353-9000 in Australia, 09/526-2847 in New Zealand ⊕ www.avis.com. **Budget** ☎ 800/527-0700 ⊕ www.budget.com. **Dollar** ☎ 800/800-4000, 0800/085-4578 in the U.K. ⊕ www.dollar.com. **Hertz** ☎ 800/654-3131, 800/263-0600 in Canada, 0870/844-8844 in the U.K., 02/9669-2444 in Australia, 09/256-8690 in New Zealand ⊕ www.hertz.com. **National Car Rental** ☎ 800/227-7368 ⊕ www.nationalcar.com.

SURCHARGES To avoid a hefty refueling fee, fill the tank just before you turn in the car, but be aware that gas stations near the rental outlet may overcharge. It's almost never a deal to buy the tank of gas that's in the car when you rent it; the understanding is that you'll return it empty, but some fuel usually remains. Surcharges may apply if you're under 25 or if you take the car outside the area approved by the rental agency. You'll pay extra for child seats (about $6 a day), which are compulsory for children under five, and usually for additional drivers (about $10 per day).

Dining

Unless otherwise noted, all prices are given in U.S. dollars. The following price categories are used in this book.

WHAT IT COSTS In US$					
	$$$$	$$$	$$	$	¢
AT DINNER	over $30	$20–$30	$12–$20	$8–$12	under $8

Prices are per person for a main course at dinner and do not include any service charges.

Lodging

Whether you are driving or flying into your port of embarkation, it is often more convenient to arrive the day before or to stay for a day after your cruise. Thus, we offer lodging suggestions for each port.

The lodgings we list are convenient to the cruise port and the cream of the crop in each price category. We always list the facilities that are available, but we don't specify whether they cost extra; when pricing accommodations, always ask what's included. Properties are assigned price categories based on the range between their least expensive standard double room at high season (excluding holidays) and the most expensive. But if you find everything sold out or wish to find a more predictable place to stay, there are chain hotels at almost all ports of embarkation.

Assume that hotels operate on the **European Plan** (EP, with no meals) unless we specify that they use either the **Continental Plan** (CP, with a Continental breakfast), **Breakfast Plan** (BP, with a full breakfast), or the **Modified American Plan** (MAP, with breakfast and dinner). The following price categories are used in this book.

WHAT IT COSTS In US$					
	$$$$	$$$	$$	$	¢
FOR 2 PEOPLE	over $250	$175–$250	$120–$175	$70–$120	under $70

Prices are for a double room, excluding service and taxes.

MAJOR CHAINS **Adam's Mark** (☎ 800/444–2326 ⊕ www.adamsmark.com). **Baymont Inns** (☎ 866/999–1111 or 800/428–3438 ⊕ www.baymontinns.com). **Best Western** (☎ 800/528–1234 ⊕ www.bestwestern.com). **Choice** (☎ 800/424–6423 ⊕ www.choicehotels.com). **Clarion** (☎ 800/424–6423 ⊕ www.choicehotels.com). **Comfort Inn** (☎ 800/424–6423 ⊕ www.choicehotels.com). **Days Inn** (☎ 800/325–2525 ⊕ www.daysinn.com). **Doubletree Hotels** (☎ 800/222–8733 ⊕ www.doubletree.com). **Embassy Suites** (☎ 800/362–2779 ⊕ www.embassysuites.com). **Fairfield Inn** (☎ 800/228–2800 ⊕ www.marriott.com). **Four Seasons** (☎ 800/332–3442 ⊕ www.fourseasons.com). **Hilton** (☎ 800/445–8667 ⊕ www.hilton.com). **Holiday Inn** (☎ 800/465–4329 ⊕ www.ichotelsgroup.com). **Howard Johnson** (☎ 800/446–4656 ⊕ www.hojo.com). **Hyatt Hotels & Resorts** (☎ 800/233–1234 ⊕ www.hyatt.com). **Inter-Continental** (☎ 800/327–0200 ⊕ www.ichotelsgroup.com). **La Quinta** (☎ 800/531–5900 ⊕ www.lq.com). **Le Meridien** (☎ 800/543–4300 ⊕ www.lemeridien.com). **Marriott** (☎ 800/228–9290 ⊕ www.marriott.com).

Omni (☎ 800/843–6664 ⊕ www.omnihotels.com). **Quality Inn** (☎ 800/424–6423 ⊕ www.choicehotels.com). **Radisson** (☎ 800/333–3333 ⊕ www.radisson.com). **Ramada** (☎ 800/228–2828, 800/854–7854 international reservations ⊕ www.ramada.com or www.ramadahotels.com). **Renaissance Hotels & Resorts** (☎ 800/468–3571 ⊕ www.marriott.com). **Ritz-Carlton** (☎ 800/241–3333 ⊕ www.ritzcarlton.com). **Sheraton** (☎ 800/325–3535 ⊕ www.starwood.com/sheraton). **Sleep Inn** (☎ 800/424–6423 ⊕ www.choicehotels.com). **Westin Hotels & Resorts** (☎ 800/228–3000 ⊕ www.starwood.com/westin). **Wyndham Hotels & Resorts** (☎ 800/822–4200 ⊕ www.wyndham.com).

CHARLESTON, SOUTH CAROLINA

At first glimpse, Charleston looks like an 18th-century etching come to life. The spires and steeples of more than 180 churches punctuate her low skyline, and tourists ride in horse-pulled carriages that pass grandiose, centuries-old mansions and antique gardens brimming with heirloom plants. First settled in 1670, immigrants flocked here initially for religious freedom and later for prosperity (compliments of the rice, indigo, and cotton plantation industries).

Preserved through the poverty following the Civil War, and natural disasters like fires, earthquakes, and hurricanes, many of Charleston's earliest public and private architecture still stands. And thanks to a rigorous preservation movement and strict Board of Architectural Review, the city's new structures blend with the old ones. In many cases, recycling is the name of the game—antique handmade bricks literally lay the foundation for new homes. But although locals do live—on some literal levels—in the past, the city is very much a town of today.

Charleston hosts a couple of cruise ships year-round, and if you are embarking here, it's worth coming in a few hours (or a day) ahead to explore the historic downtown area and eat in one of the many good restaurants.

The Cruise Port
Cruise ships embarking in Charleston leave from the Union Pier Terminal, which is in Charleston's historic district.

If you are driving, take the East Bay Street exit off the Cooper River Bridge on I–17 and follow the signs to the Charleston Aquarium. On ship embarkation days, police officers will direct you to the ship terminal from the intersection of Calhoun and Washington streets. Parking is near Union Pier (you can't park in the aquarium garage).

🚢 **Port of Charleston** ⊠ 196 Concord St., Market area, at foot of Market St. ☎ 843/577-8776 for Union Pier ⊕ www.port-of-charleston.com.

AIRPORT TRANSFERS
Several shuttle and cab companies service the airport. It costs about $19–$22 to travel downtown by taxi. Airport Ground Transportation arranges shuttles, which cost $10 per person to the downtown area.

PARKING
An outdoor parking lot is near the pier and patrolled 24 hours a day. Parking costs $12 per day ($72 per week) for regular vehicles, $25 per

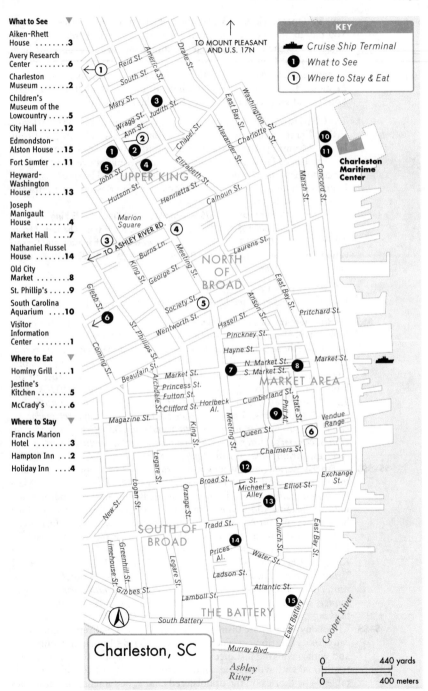

What to See ▼

Aiken-Rhett House **3**

Avery Research Center **6**

Charleston Museum **2**

Children's Museum of the Lowcountry **5**

City Hall **12**

Edmondston-Alston House . .**15**

Fort Sumter . . .**11**

Heyward-Washington House **13**

Joseph Manigault House **4**

Market Hall **7**

Nathaniel Russel House **14**

Old City Market **8**

St. Phillip's **9**

South Carolina Aquarium **10**

Visitor Information Center **1**

Where to Eat ▼

Hominy Grill **1**

Jestine's Kitchen **5**

McCrady's **6**

Where to Stay ▼

Francis Marion Hotel **3**

Hampton Inn . . .**2**

Holiday Inn **4**

KEY

⛴ *Cruise Ship Terminal*

1 *What to See*

① *Where to Stay & Eat*

Charleston Maritime Center

TO MOUNT PLEASANT AND U.S. 17N

Charleston, SC

| 0 | 440 yards |
| 0 | 400 meters |

Ashley River

Cooper River

day ($150 per week) for RVs or other vehicles more than 20 feet in length. You pay in advance (credit cards are not accepted). A free shuttle bus takes you to the cruise passenger terminal. Be sure to drop your large luggage off at Union Pier before you park your car; only carry-on size luggage is allowed on the shuttle bus, so if you have any bags larger than 22 inches by 14 inches, they will have to be checked before you park. You'll need your cruise tickets to board the shuttle bus.

VISITOR INFORMATION The Charleston Area Convention & Visitors Bureau runs the Charleston Visitor Center, which also has information on Kiawah Island, Seabrook Island, Mount Pleasant, North Charleston, Edisto Island, Summerville, and the Isle of Palms. You can pick up a schedule of events at the visitor center or at area hotels, inns, and restaurants. The Historic Charleston Foundation and the Preservation Society of Charleston have information on house tours.

🎏 **Charleston Visitor Center** ✉ 375 Meeting St., Upper King 🗂 423 King St., 29403 ☎ 843/853–8000 or 800/868–8118 ⊕ www.charlestoncvb.com. **Historic Charleston Foundation** 🗂 Box 1120, 29402 ☎ 843/723–1623 ⊕ www.historiccharleston.org. **Preservation Society of Charleston** 🗂 Box 521, 29402 ☎ 843/722–4630 ⊕ www. preservationsociety.org.

Where to Stay

For price categories, *see* Lodging at the beginning of this chapter.

$$$ 🏨 **Hampton Inn–Historic District.** Hardwood floors and a fireplace in the lobby of what was once an 1800s warehouse help elevate this chain hotel a bit above the standard. Spindle posts on the headboards give guest rooms a little personality, and there's a courtyard garden. The little perks of a chain—coffeemakers in your room, free coffee and newspaper in the lobby—are here, too. ✉ *373 Meeting St., Upper King, 29403* ☎ *843/ 723–4000 or 800/426–7866* 🖨 *843/722–3725* ⊕ *www.hamptoninn. com* 🛏 *166 rooms, 5 suites* ⚭ *Some microwaves, some refrigerators, cable TV with movies, in-room data ports, pool, babysitting, laundry facilities, concierge, Internet room, business services, meeting rooms, travel services, parking (fee), no-smoking rooms* 🚭 *AE, D, DC, MC, V* 🍽 *BP.*

$$–$$$ 🏨 **Francis Marion Hotel.** Wrought-iron railings, crown moldings, and decorative plasterwork speak of the elegance of 1924, when the Francis Marion was the largest hotel in the Carolinas. Bountiful throw pillows and billowy curtains add to the softness of the guest rooms, many of which have views of Marion Square and the harbor. Lowcountry cuisine can be had at Swamp Fox restaurant, where live jazz is played on weekends. Indulge in some self-care at the full-service day spa. ✉ *387 King St., Upper King, 29403* ☎ *843/722–0600 or 877/756–2121* 🖨 *843/723–4633* ⊕ *www.francismarioncharleston.com* 🛏 *193 rooms, 34 suites* ⚭ *Restaurant, coffee shop, room service, cable TV, in-room data ports, gym, spa, lounge, shop, concierge, Internet room, business services, meeting rooms, parking (fee), no-smoking rooms* 🚭 *AE, D, DC, MC, V.*

$–$$ 🏨 **Holiday Inn Historic District.** This hotel draws loyal repeat guests because of its location—a block from the Gaillard Municipal Auditorium and within walking distance of many must-see spots. Rooms are pretty traditional with wood-tone armoires, headboards, coffee table, and side tables. The fabrics on the upholstered chairs, bed linens, and draperies are hotel floral. Suites have a separate bedroom. ✉ *125 Calhoun St., Upper King, 29401* ☎ *843/805–7900 or 877/805–7900* 🖷 *843/805–7700* ⊕ *www.charlestonhotel.com* ⤴ *122 rooms, 4 suites* ♦ *Restaurant, cable TV, in-room data ports, pool, bar, concierge, concierge floor, Internet room, business services, meeting rooms, parking (fee), no-smoking rooms* ☰ *AE, D, DC, MC, V* ⦿| *BP.*

Where to Eat

For price categories, *see* Dining at the beginning of this chapter.

$$$ ✕ **McCrady's.** Locals rave over this 1778 tavern restaurant, with exposed beam ceilings and brick arches, tucked into a brick alleyway. Dishes are national caliber in look and taste: potato gnocchi, tuna tartare, grouper with a creamy leek sauce and truffle oil, and a rack of lamb flavored with thyme and other herbs, for example. Chocolate martinis for two appeal to those with a sweet tooth. The encyclopedia-size wine list birthed the adjoining McCrady's Wine Bar, a more casual rendition of the restaurant that sells the same amazing vinos, plus appetizers. ✉ *2 Unity Alley, Market area* ☎ *843/577–0025* ♣ *Reservations essential* ☰ *AE, MC, V* ◷ *No lunch.*

$–$$ ✕ **Hominy Grill.** The young chef's Southern upbringing shows in dishes from the vegetable plate (squash casserole, collard greens, black-eyed pea cakes with guacamole, and mushroom hominy) to the pimiento cheese sandwich and the turkey club with homemade french fries. The avocado and *wehani* (a clay-color brown variety) rice salad with grilled vegetables is a refreshing, don't-miss summer item. Leave room for the excellent buttermilk pie or bread pudding. This breezy café has a whitewashed wood floor, a pressed-tin ceiling, and chalkboard specials. Breakfast is served daily. ✉ *207 Rutledge Ave., Upper King* ☎ *843/937–0930* ☰ *AE, MC, V* ◷ *No dinner Sun.*

¢–$$ ✕ **Jestine's Kitchen.** Enjoy dishes made from passed-down family recipes—like sweet chicken with limas—at the last of the true down-home, blue-plate Southern restaurants in the historic district. This casual eatery is known for its fried everything: chicken, okra, shrimp, pork chops, green tomatoes, and more. The cola cake and coconut cream pie are divine. ✉ *251 Meeting St., Upper King* ☎ *843/722–7224* ☰ *MC, V* ◷ *Closed Mon.*

Shopping

The Market area is a complex of specialty shops and restaurants. **Old City Market** (✉ E. Bay and Market Sts., Market area) is a covered market. Sweetgrass basket weavers "sew" their creations here, and you can buy the resulting wares. **Shops at Charleston Place** (✉ 130 Market St., Market area) is home to Gucci, Caché, Benetton, Godiva, Limited Express, Brookstone, and more. **King Street** is the major shopping street in town. Lower King (from Broad to Market streets) is high-end antiques central. Middle King (from Market to Calhoun streets) is a mix of national chains like Banana Republic and Pottery Barn and local boutiques. Upper King (from Calhoun Street to Cannon Street) is the up-and-coming area where fashionistas search out one-of-a-kind deals. From May until September a festive **farmers' market** (✉ King St. at Calhoun St., Market area) takes place Saturday mornings (8–1) at Marion Square.

Nightlife

At **Mistral Restaurant** (⌧ 99 S. Market St., Market area ☎ 843/722–5709) there's a regular Dixieland jazz band Monday through Saturday, and a four-piece jazz band on Sunday.

Southend Brewery (⌧ 161 E. Bay St., Market area ☎ 843/853–4677) has a lively bar, and beer brewed on the premises; try the wood-oven pizzas.

Drinks and appetizers, with a view, draw young professionals to the covered rooftop at the **Terrace on Marion Square** (⌧ 145 Calhoun St., Market area ☎ 843/937–0314).

Listen to authentic Irish music at **Tommy Condon's Irish Pub & Restaurant** (⌧ 15 Beaufain St., Market area ☎ 843/577–5300).

Pop, hip-hop, and songs from the '70s and '80s alternate with a throbbing dance beat from DJ Amos at **213 Top of the Bay** (⌧ 213C E. Bay St., Market area ☎843/722–1311), a lively and lighthearted part of downtown's single scene.

Exploring Charleston

The heart of the city is on a peninsula, sometimes just called "downtown" by the nearly 100,000 residents who populate the area. Walking Charleston's peninsula is the best way to get to know the city. The main downtown historic district is roughly bounded by Calhoun Street to the north, the Cooper River to the east, the Battery to the south, and Lockwood Boulevard to the west. More than 2,000 historic homes and buildings occupy this fairly compact area divided into South of Broad (Street) and North of Broad. King Street, the main shopping street in town, cuts through Broad Street, and the most trafficked tourist area ends a few blocks south of the Crosstown, where U.S. 17 cuts across Upper King. Downtown you can explore most areas by foot. Otherwise, bikes, pedicab rickshaws, and cabs are the best way to get around, as the bus and shuttle system has been in flux for years, street parking is irksome, and tickets are given freely.

❸ **Aiken-Rhett House.** This stately 1819 mansion still has its original wallpaper, paint colors, and some of its furnishings. The kitchen, slave quarters, and work yard are much as they were when the original occupants lived here, making this one of the most complete examples of urban slave life of the period. Confederate general P. G. T. Beauregard made his headquarters here during his 1864 Civil War defense of Charleston. ⌧ *48 Elizabeth St., Upper King* ☎ *843/723–1159* ⊕ *www.historiccharleston. org* ⌦ *$8, combination ticket with Nathaniel Russell House $14* ☉ *Mon.–Sat. 10–5, Sun. 2–5.*

❻ **Avery Research Center for African-American History and Culture.** This center, part museum and part archives, was once a school for freed slaves. Collections include slavery artifacts (manacles, bills of sale, slave badges), old manuscripts, and African artifacts with ties to Lowcountry slaves. A riveting mural chronicles the Middle Passage—the journey slaves made from Africa to Charleston's shores. The free tours include a brief film. Although it's a short five-block walk from the Cistern quad, Avery Research Center is affiliated with the College of Charleston. ⌧ *125 Bull*

St., College of Charleston Campus ☎ *843/953–7609* ⊕ *www.cofc.edu* ☞ *Free* ⊙ *Weekdays noon–5, mornings by appointment.*

Charleston Museum. Founded in 1773, the country's oldest museum is now housed in a contemporary complex. The museum's decorative arts holdings and its permanent Civil War exhibit are extraordinary. There are more than 500,000 items in the collection. In addition to displaying Charleston silver, fashions, toys, snuffboxes, and the like, there are exhibits relating to natural history, archaeology, and ornithology. The 1803, federal-style ⇨ **Joseph Manigault House,** owned by the Charleston Museum, is across the street. George Washington once slept at the 1772 ⇨ **Heyward-Washington House,** which is seven blocks southeast of its parent, the Charleston Museum. ⊠ *360 Meeting St., Upper King* ☎ *843/ 722–2996* ⊕ *www.charlestonmuseum.org* ☞ *$9, museum and houses $18, 2 of 3 sights $12* ⊙ *Mon.–Sat. 9–5, Sun. 1–5.*

Children's Museum of the Lowcountry. Daily art projects and other exhibits promote hands-on science, culture, and creativity for toddlers up to 12-year-olds. Kids can climb on a replica of a local shrimp boat, play in exhibits that show how water evaporates from and returns to the Lowcountry, wander the inner workings of a medieval castle, and more. This top-notch museum opened in 2004. ⊠ *25 Ann St., Upper King* ☎ *843/ 853–8962* ⊕ *www.explorecml.org* ☞ *$5* ⊙ *Tues.–Sat. 10–5, Sun. 1–5.*

City Hall. The intersection of Meeting and Broad streets is known as the Four Corners of Law, representing the laws of nation, state, city, and church. On the northeast corner is the graceful, pale pink City Hall, dating from 1801. The second-floor council chambers double as a museum whose curator will explain the historical displays and portraits, including John Trumbull's 1791 satirical portrait of George Washington and Samuel F. B. Morse's likeness of James Monroe. ⊠ *80 Broad St., South of Broad* ☎ *843/577–6970 or 843/724–3799* ☞ *Free* ⊙ *Weekdays 8:30–5.*

Edmondston-Alston House. First built in 1825 in late-Federal style, the Edmondston-Alston House was transformed into the imposing Greek Revival structure you see today during the 1840s. Tours of the home—furnished with antiques, portraits, Piranesi prints, silver, and fine china—are informative and in-depth. The home commands an excellent view of Charleston Harbor. ⊠ *21 E. Battery, South of Broad* ☎ *843/ 722–7171* ⊕ *www.middletonplace.org* ☞ *$10, combination ticket with Middleton Place $36* ⊙ *Tues.–Sat. 10–4:30, Sun. and Mon. 1:30–4:30.*

Ft. Sumter National Monument. On a man-made island in Charleston Harbor, Confederate forces fired the first shot of the Civil War on April 12, 1861. After a 34-hour bombardment, Union forces surrendered and Confederate troops occupied Sumter, which became a symbol of Southern resistance. The Confederacy held the fort, despite almost continual bombardment, for nearly four years; when it was finally evacuated, the place was a heap of rubble. Today, the National Park Service oversees the Ft. Sumter National Monument complex. The **Ft. Sumter Liberty Square Visitor Center,** next to the South Carolina Aquarium, contains exhibits on the Civil War. This is one of the departure points for ferries headed to Ft. Sumter itself. ⊠ *340 Concord St., Upper King* ☎ *843/883–3123* ☜ *Free* ⊙ *Daily 8:30–5.*

Rangers conduct guided tours of the restored **Ft. Sumter,** which includes a museum with historical displays. Tours begin at 9:30, noon, and 2:30 from March through November and at 11 and 2:30 from December through February, with some variation during Christmastime. To access the island the fort occupies, you have to take a ferry; boats depart from Liberty Square Visitor Center and across from Cooper's River Bridge at Patriot's Point in Mount Pleasant. ⊠ *Charleston Harbor* ☎ *843/577–0242, 843/881–7337, 800/789–3678 for Ft. Sumter Tours Inc.* ⊕*www.fortsumtertours.com* ☜*Fort free, ferry ride $12* ⊙ *Apr.–early Sept., daily 10–5:30; early Sept.–Mar., daily 10–4. Park offices* ⊠ *1214 Middle St., Sullivan's Island* ☎ *843/883–3124* ⊕ *www.nps.gov/fosu* ⊙ *Weekdays 7:30–5:30.*

⑬ Heyward-Washington House. The area where rice planter Daniel Heyward built his home (1772) is believed to have been the inspiration for DuBose Heyward's book *Porgy,* and resulting folk opera *Porgy and Bess.* Once a mix of tenements and mansions known as Cabbage Row, the neighborhood is central to Charleston's African-American history. And the home has a history of its own: President George Washington stayed in the house during his 1791 visit. The fine period furnishings include those made by local craftsmen such as Thomas Elfe. The Holmes Bookcase (circa 1780) is one of the finest remaining American furniture pieces of its era because of its excellent condition and superb craftsmanship. Pay attention to the restored 18th-century kitchen, as it's the only one like it in Charleston open to the public. ⇨ **Charleston Museum** owns and runs the house museum. ⊠ *87 Church St., South of Broad* ☎ *843/ 722–2996* ⊕*www.charlestonmuseum.org* ☜*$8, combination ticket with Charleston Museum $14, with museum and Joseph Manigault House $18* ⊙ *Mon.–Sat. 10–5, Sun. 1–5.*

④ Joseph Manigault House. A National Historic Landmark and an outstanding example of Federal architecture, this home was designed by Charleston architect Gabriel Manigault in 1803 and is noted for its carved-wood mantels, elaborate plasterwork, and garden "folly." Furnishings are antiques from France, England, and Charleston; the pieces of rare tricolor Wedgwood are noteworthy. ⊠ *350 Meeting St., Upper King* ☎ *843/722–2996* ⊕ *www.charlestonmuseum.org* ☜ *$8, combination ticket with Charleston Museum $14, with museum and Heyward-Washington House $18* ⊙ *Mon.–Sat. 10–5, Sun. 1–5.*

⑦ Market Hall. Built in 1841, this imposing landmark was modeled after the Temple of Nike in Athens. The hall contains the **Confederate Museum,** in which the United Daughters of the Confederacy preserve and display flags, uniforms, swords, and other Civil War memorabilia. ⊠ *188 Meeting St., Market area* ☎ *843/723–1541* ☜*$5* ⊙ *Tues.–Sat. 11–3:30.*

⑭ Nathaniel Russell House. One of the nation's finest examples of Adam-style architecture, the Nathaniel Russell House was built in 1808. The interior is distinguished by its ornate detailing, its lavish period furnishings, and the "free-flying" circular staircase that spirals three stories with no visible support. The garden is well worth a stroll. ⊠ *51 Meeting St., South of Broad* ☎ *843/724–8481* ⊕ *www.historiccharleston.org* 🎫 *$8, garden free, combination ticket with Aiken-Rhett House $14* 🕐 *Mon.–Sat. 10–5, Sun. 2–5.*

🕐 **8** **Old City Market.** This area is often called the Slave Market because it's where house slaves once shopped for produce and fish. Today, stalls are lined with restaurants and shops selling children's toys, Charleston souvenirs, crafts, leather goods, and more. Local "basket ladies" weave and sell sweetgrass, pine-straw, and palmetto-leaf baskets—a craft passed down through generations from their West African ancestors. ⊠ *N. and S. Market Sts. between Meeting and E. Bay Sts., Market area* 🕐 *Daily 9–dusk.*

9 **St. Philip's (Episcopal) Church.** The namesake of Church Street, this graceful late-Georgian building is the second on its site: the congregation's first building burned down in 1835 and was rebuilt in 1838. During the Civil War, the steeple was a target for shelling; one Sunday a shell exploded in the churchyard—the minister continued his sermon. Afterward, the congregation gathered elsewhere for the duration of the war. Notable Charlestonians (like John C. Calhoun) can be found in the graveyard, which flanks the church and continues across the street. ⊠ *146 Church St., Market area* ☎ *843/722–7734* ⊕ *www.stphilipschurchsc. org* 🕐 *Church: weekdays 9–11 and 1–4; cemetery: daily 9–4.*

🕐 **10** **South Carolina Aquarium.** The 380,000-gallon Great Ocean Tank has the tallest aquarium window in North America. Exhibits display more than 10,000 living organisms, representing more than 500 species. You travel through the five major regions of the Southeast Appalachian Watershed as found in South Carolina: the Blue Ridge Mountains, the Piedmont, the coastal plain, the coast, and the ocean. Little ones can pet stingrays at one touch tank and horseshoe crabs and conchs at another. ⊠ *100 Aquarium Wharf, Upper King* ☎ *843/720–1990 or 800/722–6455* ⊕ *www.scaquarium.org* 🎫 *$15* 🕐 *Mid-Apr.–mid-Aug., Mon.–Sat. 9–5, Sun. noon–5; mid-Aug.–mid-Apr., Mon.–Sat. 9–4, Sun. noon–4.*

1 **Visitor Information Center.** The center's 20-minute film *Forever Charleston* is a fine introduction to the city. A $34.95 Charleston Heritage Passport, sold here, allows admission to the Gibbes Museum of Art, Nathaniel Russell House, Edmondston-Alston House, Aiken-Rhett House, Drayton Hall, and Middleton Place. The film starts on the half hour. Garage parking is $1 per hour. ⊠ *375 Meeting St., Upper King* ☎ *843/853–8000 or 800/868–8118* ⊕ *www.charlestoncvb.com.* 🎫 *Center free, film $2.50* 🕐 *Mar.–Oct., daily 8:30–5:30; Nov.–Feb., daily 8:30–5.*

FORT LAUDERDALE, FLORIDA

In the 1960s, Fort Lauderdale's beachfront was lined with T-shirt shops interspersed with quickie-food outlets, and downtown consisted of a lone office tower, some dilapidated government buildings, and motley other structures waiting to be razed. Today the beach is home to upscale shops and restaurants, including the popular Beach Place retail and dining complex, while downtown has exploded with new office and luxury residential development. The entertainment areas, Las Olas Riverfront and Himmarshee Village, are thriving. The airport is now one of Florida's busiest. And busy Port Everglades is giving Miami a run for its money in the cruise ship business.

A captivating shoreline with wide ribbons of sand for beachcombing and sunbathing makes Fort Lauderdale and Broward County a major draw for visitors and often tempts cruise ship passengers to spend an extra day or two in the sun. Fort Lauderdale's 2-mi (3-km) stretch of unobstructed beachfront has been further enhanced with a sparkling promenade designed more for the pleasure of pedestrians than vehicles.

The Cruise Port

Port Everglades, Fort Lauderdale's cruise port, is the second-largest in the world. The port is near downtown Fort Lauderdale, but it's spread out over a huge area.

If you are driving, to get to the main entrance take I–595 East straight into the Port (I–595 becomes Eller Drive once inside the Port). I–595 runs east–west with connections to the Fort Lauderdale–Hollywood International Airport, U.S. 1, I–95, State Road 7 (441), Florida's Turnpike, Sawgrass Expressway, and I–75.

🚺 **Port Everglades** ⊠ 1850 Eller Dr. ☎ 954/523-3404 ⊕ www.broward.org/port.htm.

AIRPORT TRANSFERS
Fort Lauderdale–Hollywood International Airport is 2 mi (3 km; 5 to 10 minutes) from the docks. If you haven't arranged an airport transfer with your cruise line, you'll have to take a taxi to the cruise ship port. The ride in a metered taxi costs about $10.

PARKING
There are two enclosed parking facilities, called Northport and Midport (the former for 2,500 cars, the latter for 2,000 cars), close to the terminals. Use the Northport garage if your cruise leaves from Pier 1, 2, or 4; use Midport if your cruise leaves from Pier 18, 19, 21, 22/24, 25, 26, 27, or 29. The cost is $12 per day for either garage ($15 for RVs).

VISITOR INFORMATION
🚺 **Chamber of Commerce of Greater Fort Lauderdale** ⊠ 512 N.E. 3rd Ave., Fort Lauderdale 33301 ☎ 954/462–6000 ⊕ www.ftlchamber.com. **Greater Fort Lauderdale Convention & Visitors Bureau** ⊠ 1850 Eller Dr., Suite 303, Fort Lauderdale 33316 ☎ 954/765–4466 ⊕ www.sunny.org. **Hollywood Chamber of Commerce** ⊠ 330 N. Federal Hwy., Hollywood 33020 ☎ 954/923–4000 ⊕ www.hollywoodchamber.org.

Where to Stay

Fort Lauderdale has a respectable variety of lodging options, from beachfront luxury suites to intimate B&Bs to chain hotels along the Intracoastal Waterway. If you want to be on the beach, be sure to mention this when booking your room, since many hotels advertise "waterfront" accommodations that are actually on the bay, not the beach.

For price categories, *see* Lodging at the beginning of this chapter.

$$–$$$$ 🏨 **Marriott's Harbor Beach Resort.** Look down from the upper stories (14 in all) at night, and this 16-acre property, on the secluded south end of Fort Lauderdale Beach, shimmers like a jewel. Spacious guest rooms have

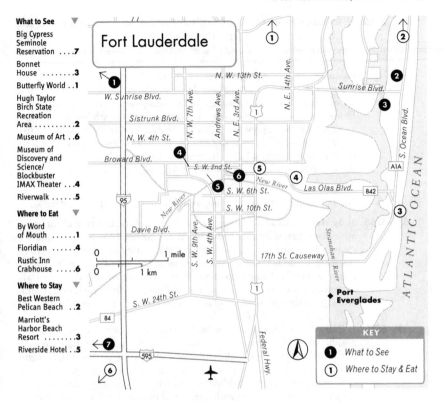

rich tropical colors, lively floral art prints, and warm woods. Part of the hotel's big-budget renovation is the addition of a European spa. No other hotel on the beach gives you so many activity options. ⊠ *3030 Holiday Dr., 33316* ☎ *954/525–4000 or 800/222–6543* 🖶 *954/766–6152* ⊕ *www.marriottharborbeach.com* 🛏 *602 rooms, 35 suites* ⚲ *3 restaurants, room TVs with movies and video games, in-room data ports, 5 tennis courts, 2 pools, gym, spa, beach, snorkeling, boating, parasailing, volleyball, 2 bars, children's programs (ages 5–12)* 🖃 *AE, D, DC, MC, V.*

$$–$$$ 🏨 **Best Western Pelican Beach.** On the beach and owned-managed by the hospitable Kruse family, this already lovely property has been transformed into an entirely new nonsmoking resort with a restaurant and lounge, an old-fashioned ice-cream parlor, and Fort Lauderdale's only Lazy River pool, allowing guests to float around a moatlike "river" via circulating current. For small fry, there's also a Funky Fish program. Rooms include 117 oceanfront suites. With the new building all aglow, the original Sun Tower is getting a makeover. ⊠ *2000 N. Atlantic Blvd., 33305* ☎ *954/568–9431 or 800/525–6232* 🖶 *954/565–2622* ⊕ *www.pelicanbeach.com* 🛏 *180 rooms* ⚲ *Restaurant, 2 pools, lounge* 🖃 *AE, DC, MC, V.*

$–$$ ⊞ **Riverside Hotel.** On Las Olas Boulevard, just steps from boutiques, restaurants, and art galleries, this charming hotel was built in 1936 and has taken on unprecedented luster with a $25 million renovation and expansion. Penthouse suites in the newer 12-story executive tower have balconies with sweeping views of Las Olas, New River, and the downtown skyline. Old Fort Lauderdale photos grace the hallways, and rooms are outfitted with antique oak furnishings and framed French prints. Enjoy afternoon tea in the lobby, and dine at Indigo, with Southeast Asian cooking, or the elegant Grill Room. ⊠ *620 E. Las Olas Blvd., 33301* ☎ *954/467–0671 or 800/325–3280* 🖷 *954/462–2148* ⊕ *www.riversidehotel.com* 🛏 *206 rooms, 11 suites* ♨ *2 restaurants, pool, dock, 2 bars, no-smoking rooms* ⊟ *AE, DC, MC, V.*

Where to Eat

For price categories, *see* Dining at the beginning of this chapter.

$$$–$$$$ ✕ **By Word of Mouth.** Unassuming but outstanding, this restaurant never advertises, hence its name. But word has sufficed for nearly a quarter century because locals consistently put this restaurant along the railroad tracks just off Oakland Park Boulevard at the top of "reader's choice" restaurant polls. There's no menu. Patrons are shown the day's specials to make their choice. Count on a solid lineup of fish, fowl, beef, pasta, and vegetarian entrées. A salad is served with each dinner entrée. ⊠ *3200 N.E. 12th Ave.* ☎ *954/564–3663* ⊟ *AE, MC, V.*

$$–$$$$ ✕ **Rustic Inn Crabhouse.** Wayne McDonald started with a cozy one-room roadhouse in 1955, when this stretch was a remote service road just west of the little airport. Now, the still-rustic place is huge. The ample menu includes a $24.95 garlic crab dinner, with patrons banging open the crabs with mallets directly on tables covered with newspapers, and peel-and-eat shrimp, served either with garlic and butter or spiced and steamed with Old Bay Seasoning. Finish with pie or cheesecake. ⊠ *4331 Ravenswood Rd.* ☎ *954/584–1637* ⊟ *AE, D, DC, MC, V.*

$–$$ ✕ **Floridian.** This Las Olas landmark with photos of Marilyn Monroe, Richard Nixon, and local notables past and present dishes up one of the best breakfasts around, with oversize omelets that come with biscuits, toast, or English muffins, plus a choice of grits or tomatoes. With sausage or bacon on the side, the feast will make you forget about eating again soon. Servers can be brisk, bordering on brusque, but chalk it up as part of the experience. Count on savory sandwiches and hot platters for lunch and dinner. It's open 24 hours every day—even during hurricanes. Feeling flush? For $229, try the Fat Cat Breakfast (New York strip steak, hash browns or grits, toast, and a worthy champagne) or, for $50, the Not-So-Fat-Cat, with the same grub and a lesser-quality vintage. ⊠ *1410 E. Las Olas Blvd.* ☎ *954/463–4041* ⊟ *No credit cards.*

Beaches

Fort Lauderdale's **beachfront** offers the best of all possible worlds, with easy access not only to a wide band of beige sand but also to restaurants and shops. For 2 mi (3 km) heading north, beginning at the Bahia Mar yacht basin, along Route A1A you'll have clear views, typically across rows of colorful beach umbrellas, to the sea and ships passing into and out of nearby Port Everglades. If you're on the beach, gaze back on an exceptionally graceful promenade.

Pedestrians rank above cars in Fort Lauderdale. Broad walkways line both sides of the beach road, and traffic has been trimmed to two gently curving northbound lanes, where in-line skaters skim past slow-moving cars. On the beach side, a low masonry wall doubles as an extended bench, separating sand from the promenade. At night the wall is accented with ribbons of fiber-optic color. The most crowded portion of beach is between Las Olas and Sunrise boulevards. Tackier aspects of this one-time strip—famous for the springtime madness spawned by the film *Where the Boys Are*—are now but a fading memory.

North of the redesigned beachfront are another 2 mi (3 km) of open and natural coastal landscape. Much of the way parallels the Hugh Taylor Birch State Recreation Area, preserving a patch of primeval Florida.

Shopping

When you're downtown, check out the **Las Olas Riverfront** (✉ 1 block west of Andrews Ave. on the New River), a shopping, dining, and entertainment complex. **Vogue Italia** (✉ Las Olas Riverfront, 300 S.W. 1st Ave. ☎ 954/527–4568) is packed with trendy fashions by D&G, Ferré, Versus, Moschino, and Iceberg, among others, at wholesale prices.

If only for a stroll and some window-shopping, don't miss **Las Olas Boulevard** (✉ 1 block off New River east of Andrews Ave.). The city's best boutiques plus top restaurants and art galleries line a beautifully landscaped street. **American Soul** (✉ 810 E. Las Olas Blvd. ☎ 954/462–4224) carries menswear from suits to socks, along with leather goods and gifts. **Casa Chameleon** (✉ 619 E. Las Olas Blvd. ☎ 954/763–2543) has antiques, linens, and beautiful things to top your table. **Giorgio** (✉ 825 E. Las Olas Blvd. ☎ 954/522–2479) focuses on sleek shoes, handbags, and belts. The sweet smell of waffle cones lures pedestrians to **Kilwin's of Las Olas** (✉ 809 E. Las Olas Blvd. ☎ 954/523–8338), an old-fashioned confectionery that also sells hand-paddled fudge and scoops of homemade ice cream. **Lily Pulitzer by Lauderdale Lifestyle** (✉ 819 E. Las Olas Blvd. ☎ 954/524–5459) specializes in the South Florida dress requisite—clothing and accessories in Lily Pulitzer's signature tropical colors and prints. **Seldom Seen** (✉ 817 E. Las Olas Blvd. ☎ 954/764–5590) is a gallery of contemporary and folk art including furniture, jewelry, ceramics, sculpture, and blown glass. **Zola Keller** (✉ 818 E. Las Olas Blvd. ☎ 954/462–3222) sells special-occasion dresses—cocktail dresses, evening gowns, bridal apparel, and, yes, Miss Florida and Mrs. America pageant dresses.

Nightlife

Café Iguana (✉ Beach Pl., 17 S. Fort Lauderdale Beach Blvd. ☎ 954/763–7222) has a nightly DJ to keep the dance floor hopping. **Howl at the Moon Saloon** (✉ Beach Pl., 17 S. Fort Lauderdale Beach Blvd. ☎ 954/522–5054) has dueling piano players and sing-alongs nightly. At the **Interlude Bar & Cabaret** (✉ 4 W. Las Olas Blvd. ☎ 954/779–3339) you can actually hear what companions have to say. **Maguire's Hill 16** (✉ 535 N. Andrews Ave. ☎ 954/764–4453) highlights excellent bands in classic Irish-pub surroundings. **O'Hara's Jazz Café** (✉ 722 E. Las Olas Blvd. ☎ 954/524–1764) belts out the live jazz, blues, R&B, and funk nightly. Its packed crowd spills onto this prettiest of downtown streets. **Rush Street** (✉ 220 S.W. 2nd St. ☎ 954/522–6900) is where hipsters line up around the corner to gain access to one of the best martini bar–dance clubs in Broward County. **Side Bar** (✉ 210 S.W. 2nd St. ☎ 954/524–1818) has a contemporary industrial feel and a polished professional crowd. **Tarpon Bend** (✉ 200 S.W. 2nd St. ☎ 954/523–3233) specialties—food, fishing gear and bait, and live bands playing current covers—draw a casual, beer-drinking crowd. **Tavern 213** (✉ 213 S.W. 2nd St. ☎ 954/463–6213) is a small, no-frills club where cover bands do classic rock nightly. **Voodoo Lounge** (✉ 111 S.W. 2nd Ave. ☎ 954/522–0733) plays the latest in club music inside the nightclub and high hip-hop on the elegant outside deck. The scene here doesn't start until close to midnight.

Exploring Fort Lauderdale

Like its southeast Florida neighbors, Fort Lauderdale has been busily revitalizing for several years. In a state where gaudy tourist zones often stand aloof from workaday downtowns, Fort Lauderdale is unusual in that the city exhibits consistency at both ends of the 2-mi (3 km) Las Olas corridor. The sparkling look results from efforts to thoroughly improve both beachfront and downtown. Matching the downtown's innovative arts district, cafés, and boutiques is an equally inventive beach area with its own share of cafés and shops facing an undeveloped shoreline.

Numbers in the margin refer to points of interest on the Fort Lauderdale map.

❼ Big Cypress Seminole Reservation. Some distance from Fort Lauderdale's tranquil beaches, but worth the one-hour drive, the reservation has two very different attractions. At the **Billie Swamp Safari,** experience the majesty of the Everglades firsthand. Daily tours of the wetlands and hammocks, where wildlife abounds, yield sightings of deer, water buffalo, bison, wild hogs, hawks, eagles, alligators, and occasionally the rare Florida panther. Animal and reptile shows are also offered. Eco-heritage tours are provided aboard motorized swamp buggies, and airboat rides are available, too. On the property is Swamp Water Café, which serves Seminole foods. ✉ *19 mi north of I–75 Exit 49* ☎ *863/983–6101 or 800/949–6101* ⊕ *www.seminoletribe.com* 🎫 *Free to visit reservation; combined ecotour, show, airboat ride $40* ⊙ *Daily 8–5.*

Not far from the Billie Swamp Safari is the **Ah-Tha-Thi-Ki Museum,** whose name means "a place to learn, a place to remember." It is just that. The museum documents and honors the culture and tradition of the Seminole Tribe of Florida through artifacts, exhibits, and reenactments of rituals and ceremonies. The site includes a living-history Seminole village, nature trails, and a boardwalk through a cypress swamp. ✉ *17 mi north of I–75 Exit 49* ☎ *863/902–1113* ⊕ *www.seminoletribe. com* 🎫 *$6* ⊙ *Tues.–Sun. 9–5.*

❸ Bonnet House. A 35-acre oasis in the heart of the beach area, this subtropical estate is a tribute to the history of Old South Florida. The charming home was the winter residence of the late Frederic and Eve-lyn Bartlett, artists whose personal touches and small surprises are evident throughout. Whether you're interested in architecture, artwork, or the natural environment, this is a special place. Be on the lookout for playful monkeys swinging from trees, a source of amusement at even some of the most solemn outdoor weddings on the grounds. Hours can vary, so call first. ✉ *900 N. Birch Rd.* ☎ *954/563–5393* ⊕ *www. bonnethouse.org* ✉ *House tours $10, grounds only $6* ⊙ *Wed.–Fri. 10–3, weekends noon–4.*

1 **Butterfly World.** As many as 80 butterfly species from South and Central America, the Philippines, Malaysia, Taiwan, and other Asian nations are typically found within this 3-acre site inside Tradewinds Park. A screened aviary called North American Butterflies is reserved for native species. The Tropical Rain Forest Aviary is a 30-foot-high construction, with observation decks, waterfalls, ponds, and tunnels where thousands of colorful butterflies flutter about. ✉ *3600 W. Sample Rd., Coconut Creek* ☎ *954/977–4400* ⊕ *www.butterflyworld.com* ✉ *$17.95* ⊙ *Mon.–Sat. 9–5, Sun. 1–5.*

2 **Hugh Taylor Birch State Recreation Area.** Amid the tropical greenery of this 180-acre park, stroll along a nature trail, visit the Birch House Museum, picnic, play volleyball, pitch horseshoes, and paddle a rented canoe. Since parking is limited on Route A1A, park here and take a walkway underpass to the beach (between 9 and 5). ✉ *3109 E. Sunrise Blvd.* ☎ *954/564–4521* ⊕ *www.abfla.com/parks* ✉ *$4 per vehicle with up to 8 people, $1 per pedestrian* ⊙ *Daily 8–sunset; ranger-guided nature walks Fri. at 10:30.*

5 **Museum of Art.** In an Edward Larrabee Barnes–designed building that's considered an architectural masterpiece, this museum's impressive permanent collection has 20th-century European and American art, including works by Picasso, Calder, Dalí, Mapplethorpe, Warhol, and Stella, as well as a notable collection of works by celebrated Ashcan School artist William Glackens. When its building opened in 1986, the museum helped launch revitalization of the downtown district and nearby Riverwalk area, and it since has become a magnet for special traveling exhibits (with higher admission fees) including "Tutankhamen and the Golden Age of the Pharaohs," which as of this writing is slated to run through spring 2006; this will mark the Egyptian king's first appearance in Florida and his first time in the United States in nearly 30 years. ✉ *1 E. Las Olas Blvd.* ☎ *954/763–6464* ⊕ *www.moafl.org* ✉ *$7 and up, depending on exhibit* ⊙ *Feb–mid-Dec., Fri.–Wed. 11–7, Thurs. 11–9; mid-Dec.–Jan., Fri.–Mon. and Wed. 11–7, Thurs. 11–9.*

4 **Museum of Discovery and Science/Blockbuster IMAX Theater.** The aim here is to show children—*and* adults—the wonders of science in an entertaining fashion. The 52-foot-tall Great Gravity Clock in the courtyard entrance lets arrivals know a cool experience awaits. Inside, exhibits include Choose Health, about healthful lifestyle choices; Kidscience, encouraging youngsters to explore the world around them; and Gizmo City, a look at how gadgets work. Florida Ecoscapes has a living coral reef as well as live bees, bats, frogs, turtles, and alligators. An IMAX theater, part of the complex, shows films (some 3-D) on a five-story-high screen. ✉ *401 S.W. 2nd St.* ☎ *954/467–6637 museum, 954/463–4629 IMAX* ⊕ *www.mods.org* 🎫 *Museum $14, includes 1 IMAX show* ⊙ *Mon.–Sat. 10–5, Sun. noon–6.*

❺ **Riverwalk.** Fantastic views and entertainment prevail on this lovely paved promenade on the New River's north bank. On the first Sunday of every month a jazz brunch attracts visitors. The walk has been extended 2 mi (3 km) on both sides of the beautiful urban stream, connecting the facilities of the Arts and Science District.

Boat Tours

Water Taxi was started by longtime resident Bob Bekoff, who decided to combine the need for transportation with one of the area's most appealing features: miles of waterways that make the city known as the Venice of America. The taxi will pick you up at any of several hotels along the Intracoastal Waterway, and you can stop off at attractions like Beach Place. For lunch, enjoy a restaurant on Las Olas Boulevard or Las Olas Riverfront. In the evening, water taxis are a great way to go out to dinner or bar-hop, without the worry of choosing a designated driver. Water Taxi and Broward County Mass Transit have partnered to create water buses. These environmentally friendly electric ferries can carry up to 70 passengers. Take unlimited rides on either the water taxi or water bus from 6:30 AM to 12:30 AM for $5 (one-way adult fare is $4). The best way to use the water taxi or bus is to call about 20 minutes ahead of your desired pickup time, or check the schedule on the company's Web site. ☎ *954/467–6677* ⊕ *www.watertaxi.com.*

GALVESTON, TEXAS

A thin strip of island in the Gulf of Mexico, Galveston is big sister Houston's beach playground—a year-round coastal destination just 50 mi (80 km) away. Many of the first public buildings in Texas, including a post office, bank, and hotel, were built here, but most were destroyed in the Great Storm of 1900. Those that endured have been well preserved, and the Victorian character of the Strand shopping district and the neighborhood surrounding Broadway is still evident. On the Galveston Bay side of the island (northeast), quaint shops and cafés in old buildings are near the Seaport Museum, harbor-front eateries, and the cruise ship terminal. On the Gulf of Mexico side (southwest), resorts and restaurants line coastal Seawall Boulevard. The 17-foot-high seawall abuts a long ribbon of sand and provides a place for rollerblading, bicycling, and going on the occasional surrey ride.

Galveston is a port of embarkation for cruises on Western Caribbean itineraries; some Panama Canal cruises leave from here as well. It's an especially popular port of embarkation for people living in the southeastern states who don't wish to fly to their cruise. Carnival, Royal Caribbean, and Princess have made Galveston the home port for their ships.

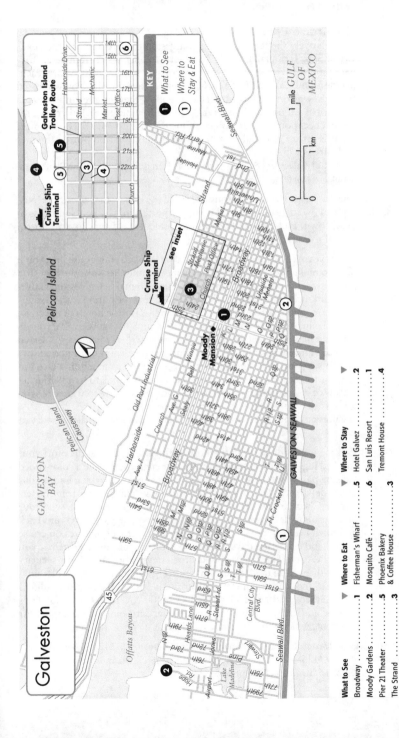

Galveston

KEY

▶ **What to See** 1

▷ **Where to Stay & Eat** ①

What to See

Broadway	...1
Moody Gardens	...2
Pier 21 Theater	...5
The Strand	...3
Texas Seaport Museum	...4

▶ **Where to Eat**

Fisherman's Wharf	...5
Mosquito Café	...6
Phoenix Bakery & Coffee House	...3

▶ **Where to Stay**

Hotel Galvez	...2
San Luis Resort	...1
Tremont House	...4

The Cruise Port

The relatively sheltered waters of Galveston Bay are home to the Texas Cruise Ship Terminal. It's only 30 minutes to open water from here. Driving south from Houston on I–45, you cross a long causeway before reaching the island. Take the first exit, Harborside Drive, left after you've crossed the causeway on to Galveston Island. Follow that for a few miles to the port. Turn left on 22nd Street (also called Kemper Street); there is a security checkpoint before you continue down a driveway. The drop-off point is set up much like an airport terminal, with pull-through lanes and curbside check-in.

🚢 **Port of Galveston** ✉ Harborside Dr. and 22nd St. ☎ 409/765–9321 ⊕ www.portofgalveston.com.

AIRPORT TRANSFERS

The closest airports are in Houston, 50 mi (80 km) from Galveston. Houston has two major airports: Hobby Airport, 9 mi (14 km) southeast of downtown, and George Bush Intercontinental, 15 mi (24 km) northeast of the city.

Unless you have arranged airport transfers through your cruise line, you'll have to make arrangements to navigate the miles between the Houston airport where you land and the cruise ship terminal in Galveston. Galveston Limousine Service provides scheduled transportation (return reservations required) between either airport and Galveston hotels or the cruise ship terminal. Hobby is a shorter ride (1 hour, $30 one-way, $50 round-trip), but Intercontinental (2 hours, $35 one-way, $60 round-trip) is served by more airlines, including international carriers. Taking a taxi allows you to set your own schedule but can cost twice as much (it's also important to note that there aren't always enough taxis to handle the demands of disembarking passengers, so you might have to wait after you leave your ship). Negotiate the price before you get in.

🚢 **Galveston Limousine Service** ☎ 800/640–4826 ⊕ www.galvestonlimousineservice.com.

PARKING

Parking is coordinated by the Port Authority. After you drop off your checked luggage and passengers at the terminal, you receive a color-coded parking pass from the attendant, with directions to a parking lot for your cruise departure. The lots are approximately ½ mi (1 km) from the terminal. Check-in, parking, and boarding are generally allowed four hours prior to departure. A shuttle bus (carry-on luggage only) runs back and forth between the lots and the ship every 7 to 12 minutes on cruise arrival and departure days (be sure to drop off your luggage *before* you park the car). The lot is closed other days. Port Authority security checks the well-lighted, fenced-in lots every two hours; there is also covered parking. Parking for a 5-day cruise is $50 ($60 covered), 7-day is $70 ($80 covered), and 11-day is $85 ($100 covered). Cash, traveler's checks, and credit cards (Visa and MasterCard only) are accepted for payment, which must be made in advance.

VISITOR INFORMATION

🚢 **Galveston Island Convention & Visitors Bureau** ✉ 2428 Seawall Blvd. ☎ 888/425–4753 ⊕ www.galveston.com ✉ Strand Visitors Center ✉ 2215 Strand ☎ No phone.

Where to Stay

For price categories, *see* Lodging at the beginning of this chapter.

$$–$$$$ 🏨 **San Luis Resort.** A long marble staircase alongside a slender fountain with sculpted dolphins welcomes you to the waterfront elegance of this resort. The upper-floor facade isn't much to look at, but don't let that fool you; inside, the colors of the cool, cream marble and taupe stone in the lobby are echoed in the guest rooms. The sculptural lines of pink granite on the headboards and armchairs say Italian villa. All rooms have balconies facing the gulf, and prices rise with the floor height. Back on ground level, step into the meandering (and heated) grotto pool with a rock waterfall set amid coconut palms and bougainvillea; then have a Balinese massage (or a wildflower compress) at the Spa San Luis. The resort offers free parking for the duration of a cruise as well as transportation to the cruise terminal. ⊠ *5222 Seawall Blvd., 77551* ☎ *409/744–1500 or 800/445–0090* 🖷 *409/744–8452* ⊕ *www.sanluisresort. com* 🛏 *246 rooms* 🍴 *Restaurant, café, room service, cable TV, in-room data ports, 2 tennis courts, 2 pools, health club, outdoor hot tub, spa, 2 bars, dry cleaning, business services, helipad, no-smoking rooms* 🖃 *AE, D, DC, MC, V.*

$$–$$$ 🏨 **Hotel Galvez.** This renovated six-story Spanish colonial hotel, built in 1911, was once called "Queen of the Gulf." Teddy Roosevelt and Howard Hughes were just two of the many well-known guests who have stayed here. Traditional dark wood and plush upholstery pieces furnish both the public and private areas. A pool, swim-up bar, and outdoor grill have been added to the tropical garden facing the sea. ⊠ *2024 Seawall Blvd., 77550* ☎*409/765–7721* 🖷*409/765–5780* ⊕*www.wyndham. com* 🛏 *231 rooms* 🍴 *Restaurant, cable TV, pool, health club, hot tub, Internet room, business services, meeting rooms, no-smoking rooms* 🖃 *AE, DC, MC, V.*

$–$$ 🏨 **Tremont House.** A four-story atrium lobby, with ironwork balconies and full-size palm trees, showcases an 1872 hand-carved rosewood bar in what was once a busy dry-goods warehouse. It is actually a historic place: Republic of Texas president Sam Houston presented his last speech at this hotel, both Confederate and Union soldiers bunked here, and Great Storm victims took refuge under this roof. Rooms have high ceilings and 11-foot windows. Period reproduction furniture and Victorian-pattern wallpapers add to the authenticity. It's the closest full-service lodging to the port, just a short walk from shopping on the Strand. ⊠ *2300 Ship's Mechanic Row, 77550* ☎ *409/763–0300* 🖷 *409/763–1539* ⊕ *www.wyndham.com* 🛏 *119 rooms* 🍴 *Restaurant, room service, cable TV with movies, golf privileges, bar, meeting rooms, no-smoking rooms* 🖃 *AE, D, DC, MC, V.*

Where to Eat

For price categories, *see* Dining at the beginning of this chapter.

$$–$$$ ✕ **Fisherman's Wharf.** New restaurants have sprung up to provide competition for the Landry's-owned harborside institution, but locals keep coming here for the reliably fresh seafood and reasonable prices. Dine indoors or watch the boat traffic (and waiting cruise ships) from the patio.

Start with a cold combo, like boiled shrimp and grilled rare tuna. The fried fish, shrimp, and oysters are hard to beat as an entrée. ⊠ *Pier 22, Harborside Dr. and 22nd St.* ☎ *409/765–5708* ⊟ *AE, D, DC, MC, V.*

$$–$$$ ✕ **Mosquito Café.** This chichi eatery in Galveston's historic East End serves fresh, contemporary food—some vegetarian—in a hip, high-ceilinged dining room and on an outdoor patio. Wake up to a fluffy egg frittata or a homemade scone topped with whipped cream, or try a large gourmet salad later on. The grilled snapper with Parmesan grits is a hit in the evening. ⊠ *628 14th St.* ☎ *409/763–1010* ⊟ *AE, D, DC, MC, V* ☉ *No dinner Sun.–Wed.*

¢–$ ✕ **Phoenix Bakery & Coffee House.** Every community needs a gathering place with the smell of fresh baked goods in the air. The New Orleans beignets, croissants, muffins, and other pastries at the Phoenix are impossible to resist. They also brew a flavorful cup of espresso and cook full breakfasts. Lunch is homemade soups, sandwiches, and maybe a slice of pie—old-fashioned apple, banana cream, bourbon pecan, or chocolate mousse, anyone? ⊠ *220 Tremont St., at 23rd St.* ☎ *409/763–4611* ⊟ *AE, D, DC, MC, V* ☉ *No dinner.*

Beaches

The **Seawall** (⊠ Seawall Blvd. from 61st St. to 25th St.) on the gulf-side waterfront attracts runners, cyclists, and rollerbladers. Just below it is a long, free beach near many big hotels and resorts. **Stewart Beach Park** (⊠ 6th St. and Seawall Blvd. ☎ 409/765–5023) has a bathhouse, amusement park, bumper boats, miniature-golf course, and a water coaster in addition to salt water and sand. It's open weekdays 9–5, weekends 8–6 from March to May; weekdays 8–6 and weekends 8–7 from June to September; and weekends 9–5 during the first two weekends of October. Admission is $5 per vehicle. **Galveston Island State Park** (⊠ 3 Mile Rd., 10 mi southwest on Seawall Blvd. ☎ 409/737–1222), on the western, unpopulated end of the island, is a 2,000-acre natural beach habitat ideal for birding, walking, and renewing your spirit. It's open daily from 8 AM to 10 PM; admission is $3.

Shopping

The **Strand** is the best place to shop in Galveston. Old storefronts are filled with gift shops, antiques stores, and one-of-a-kind boutiques. The area is bounded by Strand and Postoffice Street (running east–west) and 25th and 19th streets (running north–south). More than 50 antiques dealers are represented at **Eiband's Gallery** (⊠ 2001 Postoffice St. ☎ 409/763–5495), an upscale showroom filled with furniture, books, art, and jewelry. **Old Strand Emporium** (⊠ 2112 Strand ☎ 409/762–8566) is a charming deli and grocery reminiscent of an old-fashioned ice-cream parlor and sandwich shop, with candy bins, packaged nuts, and more.

Nightlife

For a relaxing evening, choose any of the harborside restaurant-bars on Piers 21 and 22 to sip a glass of wine or a frozen Hurricane as you watch the boats go by.

The **Grand 1894 Opera House** (⊠ 2020 Postoffice St. ☎ 409/765–1894 or 800/821–1894 ⊕ www.thegrand.com) stages musicals and hosts concerts year-round. It's worth visiting for the ornate architecture alone. Sarah Bernhardt and Anna Pavlova both performed on this storied stage.

Exploring Galveston

❶ Broadway. The late 1800s were the heyday of Galveston's port (before Houston's was dug out). Victorian splendor is evident in the meticulously restored homes of this historic district, some of which are now museums. **Moody Mansion** (✉ 2618 Broadway ☎ 409/762–7668), the residence of generations of one of Texas's most powerful families, was completed in 1895. Tour its interiors of exotic woods and gilded trim filled with family heirlooms and personal effects. **Ashton Villa** (✉ 2328 Broadway ☎ 409/762–3933), a formal Italianate villa, was built in 1859 of brick. Look for the curtains that shielded the more modest Victorian guests from the naked Cupids painted on one wall. If you're in town the first two weekends of May, don't miss the **Galveston Historic Homes Tour.** In addition to visiting the neighborhood's museums, you can walk through privately owned homes dating from the 1800s. For more information about area house museums or the tour, contact the Heritage Visitors Center. ✉ *2328 Broadway* ☎ *409/765–7834* 🖼 *Visitor center free, museums $6 each, tour $20* ⊙ *Mon.–Sat. 10–4, Sun. noon–4.*

☾ ❷ Moody Gardens is a multifaceted entertainment and educational complex inside pastel-color glass pyramid buildings. Attractions include the 13-story **Aquarium Pyramid,** showcasing marine life from four oceans in tanks and touch pools; **Rainforest Pyramid,** a 40,000-square-foot tropical habitat for exotic flora and fauna; **Discovery Pyramid,** a joint venture with NASA featuring more than 40 interactive exhibits; and two **IMAX theaters,** one of which has a space adventure ride. Outside, **Palm Beach** has white-sand beach, landscaped grounds, man-made lagoons, a kid-size waterslide and games, and beach chairs. ✉ *1 Hope Blvd.* ☎ *409/741–8484 or 800/582–4673* ⊕ *www.moodygardens.com* 🖼 *$7.95–$14.25 per venue, $31 day pass* ⊙ *Memorial Day–Labor Day, daily 10–9; Labor Day–Memorial Day, weekdays 10–6, weekends 10–8.*

❺ Pier 21 Theater. At this theater on the Strand, watch the Great Storm of 1900 come back to life in a multimedia presentation that includes video clips of archival drawings, still photos, and narrated accounts from survivors' diaries. Also playing is a film about the exploits of pirate Jean Lafitte, who used the island as a base. ✉ *Pier 21, Harborside Dr. and 21st St.* ☎ *409/763–8808* ⊕ *www.galvestonhistory.org/plc-pier21.htm* 🖼 *Great Storm $3.50, Pirate Island $2.50* ⊙ *Sun.–Thurs. 11–6, Fri. and Sat. 11–8.*

❸ The Strand. This shopping area is defined by the architecture of its 19th- and early-20th-century buildings, many of which survived the storm of 1900 and are on the National Register of Historic Places. When Galveston was still a powerful port city—before the Houston Ship Channel was dug, diverting most boat traffic inland—this stretch, formerly the site of stores, offices, and warehouses, was known as the Wall Street of the South. As you stroll up the Strand, you pass dozens of shops and cafés. ✉ *Between Strand and Postoffice St., 25th and 19th Sts.*

❹ **Texas Seaport Museum.** Aboard the restored 1877 tall ship *Elissa,* detailed interpretive signs provide information about the shipping trade in the 1800s, including the routes and cargoes this ship carried into Galveston. Inside the museum building is a replica of the historic wharf and information about the ethnic groups that immigrated through this U.S. point of entry after 1837. The tall ship *Elissa* was refurbished in 2004, reopening in mid-2005. ✉ *Pier 21* ☎ *409/763–1877* ⊕ *www.tsm-elissa.org* 🖾 *$6* ⊙ *Daily 10–5.*

JACKSONVILLE, FLORIDA

One of Florida's oldest cities and at 730 square mi (1,175 square km) the largest city in the continental United States, Jacksonville makes for an underrated vacation spot. It offers appealing downtown riverside areas, handsome residential neighborhoods, the region's only skyscrapers, a thriving arts scene, and, for football fans, the NFL Jaguars and the NCAA Gator Bowl. Remnants of the Old South flavor the city, especially in the Riverside/Avondale historic district where moss-draped oak trees frame prairie-style bungalows and Tudor Revival mansions, and palm trees, Spanish bayonet, and azaleas populate Jacksonville's landscape.

The Cruise Port

Cruise ships based in Jacksonville now use a temporary cruise facility that was constructed in 2003. It usually opens for passenger boarding at 10 AM on sailing dates. It's close to the airport (about 15 minutes away) but fairly sparse in terms of facilities, which basically consist of some vending machines and restrooms.

🛈 Jacksonville Port Authority ✉ 9810 August Dr., Jacksonville, FL ☎ 904/630–3006 ⊕ www.jaxport.com.

AIRPORT TRANSFERS The transfer from Jacksonville airport takes about 15 minutes and costs $16.50 for up to four passengers; if you use a shared minivan, the cost is $4 per passenger with a five-passenger minimum.

PARKING There is a guarded parking lot next to the cruise terminal within walking distance. Parking costs $10 per day for regular vehicles, $20 for RVs. You must pay in advance by cash or major credit card.

VISITOR INFORMATION 🛈 Jacksonville and The Beaches Convention & Visitors Bureau ✉ 550 Water St., Suite 1000, Jacksonville 32202 ☎ 904/798–9100 or 800/733–2668 ⊕ www.jaxcvb.com.

Where to Stay

A number of chain hotels around Jacksonville offer special cruise rates that include a one-night stay and free parking for the duration of your cruise with free or inexpensive transportation to the cruise port. Given the price of parking, such packages offer a good value. These can be booked through your travel agent.

For price categories, *see* Lodging at the beginning of this chapter.

$$–$$$ 🏨 **Embassy Suites Hotel.** The Baymeadows location makes Jacksonville's only full-service, all-suites hotel convenient to a number of restaurants,

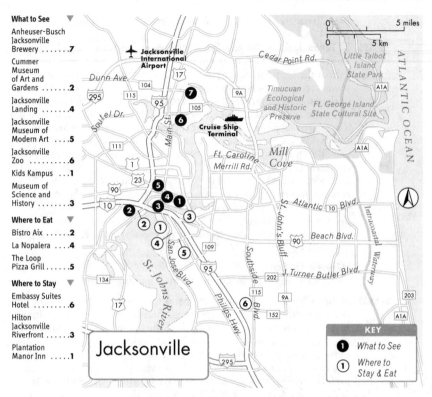

clubs, and shops. All units feature a balcony and overlook the six-story atrium. Each has a separate living room with a sleep sofa, a refrigerator, and a microwave. A cooked-to-order breakfast and a two-hour cocktail reception on weekdays are also included in the rate. ✉ *9300 Baymeadows Rd., 32256* ☎ *904/731–3555 or 800/362–2779* 📠 *904/ 731–4972* ⊕ *www.embassysuitesjax.com* 🛏 *277 suites* ⚐ *Restaurant, room service, kitchenettes, microwaves, refrigerators, cable TV with movies and video games, in-room data ports, indoor pool, gym, hot tub, sauna, steam room, bar, dry cleaning, laundry facilities, laundry service, business services, Internet room, meeting rooms, free parking, no-smoking floors* 🖃 *AE, DC, MC, V* ⦿ *BP.*

$$–$$$ 🏨 **Plantation Manor Inn.** Stately, yet cozy, this three-story Greek Revival plantation home has been divvied up into nine unique guest rooms, each with elegant antique furniture, Oriental rugs, and artwork. Authenticity aside, innkeepers Kathy and Jerry Ray understand the need for modern conveniences and equip each room with a private bath, hair dryer, iron and ironing board, and high-speed Internet access. The tranquil garden has a lap pool and hot tub. ✉ *1630 Copeland St., 32204* ☎ *904/384–4630* 📠 *904/387–0960* ⊕ *www.plantationmanorinn.com* 🛏 *9 rooms* ⚐ *Dining room, cable TV, some in-room VCRs, in-room data ports, pool, outdoor hot tub, Internet room, business services, meet-*

ing rooms, free parking; no kids under 12, no smoking ▭ *AE, DC, MC, V* ⓘ◎ⓘ *BP.*

$–$$$ ⊞ **Hilton Jacksonville Riverfront.** Sitting on the water, this handsome eight-story hotel has a commanding presence. Its location on the south side of the St. Johns River puts it within easy walking distance of museums, restaurants, and the water taxi; Ruth's Chris Steak House is one of the on-site restaurants. Spacious rooms have walk-out balconies and city or river views. Guests truly wanting to live like a king can book the San Marco (aka the Elvis Room), a premier suite, with Jacuzzi tub and two balconies, that Presley called home during numerous trips to Jacksonville. Or celebrate a special occasion aboard the hotel's private yacht, the *Jacksonville Princess*. ✉ *1201 Riverplace Blvd., 32207* ☏ *904/ 398–8800* 🖷 *904/398–9170* ⊕ *www.jacksonvillehilton.com* ⇥ *292 rooms, 30 suites* ⚐ *2 restaurants, room service, some kitchenettes, cable TV with movies and video games, in-room data ports, pool, gym, outdoor hot tub, massage, marina, 2 bars, shop, dry cleaning, laundry service, Internet room, business services, meeting rooms, parking (fee), no-smoking floors* ▭ *AE, D, DC, MC, V.*

Where to Eat

For price categories, *see* Dining at the beginning of this chapter.

$–$$$$ ✕ **Bistro Aix.** Locals head for the patio for a delightful candlelight dinner when the weather is nice; indoors, there are romantic velvet drapes, banquettes, and exposed brick walls. Grilled salmon or filet mignon are good choices. Crispy, thin-crust pizzas, baked in the wood-burning oven, pastas, and salads are among the lighter choices. Belgian chocolate cake, served warm and topped with vanilla whipped cream, caps a perfect evening. Call ahead for preferred seating. ✉ *1440 San Marco Blvd., San Marco* ☏ *904/398–1949* ⚑ *Reservations not accepted* ▭ *AE, D, DC, MC, V* ⊘ *No lunch weekends.*

¢–$ ✕ **La Nopalera.** For diners seeking authentic Mexican food in Jacksonville, this family-owned restaurant is numero uno. The menu is as standard—tacos, burritos, enchiladas, and fajitas with rice and beans as sides—as the decor, limited to serapes and neon beer signs on the walls and faded piñatas hanging from the ceiling. But huge and inexpensive portions keep customers loyal. ✉ *1621 Hendricks Ave., San Marco* ☏ *904/399–1768* ✉ *8818 Atlantic Blvd., Regency* ☏ *904/720–0106* ⚑ *Reservations not accepted* ▭ *AE, D, MC, V* ⊘ *Closed Sun.*

¢–$ ✕ **Loop Pizza Grill.** Standing in line to place their orders, first-time diners may think this Jacksonville-based chain is just another fast-food joint. But one look at the menu, chock-full of designer salads, specialty pizzas, and upscale sandwiches, not to mention the stylish dining room complete with upholstered booths, funky light fixtures, and tiled floors, and they'll think they're in McDreamland. The big sellers here are the burgers (the Loop 'N Cheddar and Loop 'N Blue, in particular) and pizzas (both California-thin and Chicago-thick), but sandwiches like the portobello mushroom and Cajun chicken merit special mention. The onion rings and milk shakes are among the best in town. ✉ *2014 San Marco Blvd., San Marco* ☏ *904/399–5667.*

Shopping

At **Five Points** (⊠ Intersection of Park, Margaret, and Lomax Sts., Riverside) you'll find a small but funky shopping district of new and vintage clothing boutiques, shoe stores, and antiques shops, as well as a handful of eateries and bars. The **Shoppes of Avondale** (⊠ St. Johns Ave.) highlight upscale clothing and accessories boutiques, art galleries, home-furnishing shops, a chocolatier, and trendy restaurants. **San Marco Square** (⊠ Intersection of San Marco and Atlantic Blvds.) has dozens of interesting apparel, home, and jewelry stores and restaurants in 1920s Mediterranean Revival–style buildings.

Nightlife

Buffalo Wild Wings (⊠ 9550 Baymeadows Rd., No. 26 ☎ 904/448–1293), or "BW3" to the locals, is *the* place to watch college and pro football. **57 Heaven** (⊠ 8136 Atlantic Blvd. ☎ 904/721–5757) draws a crowd in their forties and fifties with its selection of oldies but goodies and shag contests. **Harmonious Monks** (⊠ 10550 Old St. Augustine Rd. ☎ 904/880–3040) has the "world's most talented waitstaff" who perform throughout the night and encourage customers to dance on the bar. Fans of Christian music flock to the **Murray Hill Theatre** (⊠ 932 Edgewood Ave. S ☎ 904/388–7807), a no-smoking, no-alcohol club. **River City Brewing Company** (⊠ 835 Museum Circle ☎ 904/398–2299) showcases local bands or DJs Thursday through Saturday nights. Fronting on San Marco Boulevard, **Square One** (⊠ 1974 San Marco Blvd. ☎ 904/306–9004) is an upscale singles scene with live music on weekends.

Exploring Jacksonville

Because Jacksonville was settled along both sides of the twisting St. Johns River, a number of attractions are on or near a riverbank. Both sides of the river, which is spanned by myriad bridges, have downtown areas and waterfront complexes of shops, restaurants, parks, and museums; some attractions can be reached by water taxi or the Skyway Express monorail system—scenic alternatives to driving back and forth across the bridges—but a car is generally necessary.

⑦ Anheuser-Busch Jacksonville Brewery. If you're a beer connoisseur, don't miss a guided or self-guided tour here, which takes you through the entire brewing and bottling process. There are free beer tastings and logo-filled gift shops. You must be at least 18 to visit the brewery or shops. ⊠ *111 Busch Dr.* ☎ *904/696–8373* ⊕ *www.budweisertours.com* ☜ *Free* ☉ *Mon.–Sat. 10–4; guided tours Mon.–Sat. 10–3 on the half hr.*

② Cummer Museum of Art and Gardens. The world-famous Wark Collection of early-18th-century Meissen porcelain is just one reason to visit this former riverfront estate, which includes 12 permanent galleries with more than 5,000 items spanning more than 8,000 years and 3 acres of gardens reflecting northeast Florida's blooming seasons and indigenous varieties. For the kids, Art Connections allows them to "experience" art through hands-on, interactive exhibits. ⊠ *829 Riverside Ave.* ☎ *904/356–6857* ⊕ *www.cummer.org* ☜ *$6, free Tues. 4–9* ☉ *Tues. and Thurs. 10–9; Wed., Fri., and Sat. 10–5; Sun. noon–5.*

4 Jacksonville Landing. During the week, the riverfront festival marketplace here caters to locals and tourists alike, with more than 40 specialty shops with home furnishings, apparel, and toys, nine full-service restaurants—including a brewpub, Italian bistro, and steak house—and an international-flavor food court. On weekends the Landing hosts special events, including the American Cancer Society Duck Race, and the Florida–Georgia game after-party in the courtyard, directly on the St. Johns River. ⊠ *2 Independent Dr.* ☎ *904/353–1188* ⊕ *www.jacksonvillelanding.com* ✆ *Free* ⊙ *Mon.–Thurs. 10–8, Fri. and Sat. 10–9, Sun. noon–5:30; some restaurants open earlier and close later.*

5 Jacksonville Museum of Modern Art. In this loftlike, 14,000-square-foot building, the former headquarters of the Western Union Telegraph Company, a permanent collection of 20th-century art shares space with traveling exhibitions. The museum encompasses five galleries and ArtExplorium, a highly interactive educational exhibit for kids, as well as a funky gift shop and Cafe Nola, open for breakfast, lunch, and weekly wine-tasting events. JMOMA also hosts film series, lectures, and workshops. ⊠ *Hemming Plaza, 333 N. Laura St.* ☎ *904/366–6911* ⊕ *www.jmoma.org* ✆ *$6, free Wed. 5–9 and Sun.* ⊙ *Tues. and Fri. 11–5, Wed. and Thurs. 11–9, Sat. 11–4, Sun. noon–4; subject to change.*

6 Jacksonville Zoo. Among the zoo's outstanding exhibits is its collection of rare waterfowl and the Serona Overlook, which showcases some of the world's most venomous snakes. The Florida Wetlands is a 2½-acre area with black bears, bald eagles, white-tailed deer, and other animals native to Florida. The African Veldt has alligators, elephants, and white rhinos, among other species of African birds and mammals. Kids get a kick out of the petting zoo, and everyone goes bananas over Great Apes of the World. The zoo's newest exhibit, the Range of the Jaguar, includes 4 acres of exotic big cats as well as 20 other species of animals. ⊠ *8605 Zoo Pkwy., off Heckscher Dr. E* ☎ *904/757–4463* ⊕ *www.jaxzoo.org.* ✆ *$9.50* ⊙ *Daily 9–5.*

1 Kids Kampus. Directly on the St. Johns River adjacent to Metropolitan Park, this 10-acre recreational facility, developed by local educators, encourages children's natural curiosity with climbing and sliding apparatuses, engaging playscapes, mini-representations of Jacksonville landmarks, like Bay Street, Kings Road, and the main post office, and a splash park. The "kampus" also has a picnic pavilion and jogging trail. ⊠ *1410 Gator Bowl Blvd.* ☎ *904/630–5437* ✆ *Free* ⊙ *Mar.–Oct., Mon.–Sat. 8–8, Sun. 10–8; Nov.–Feb., Mon.–Sat. 8–6, Sun. 10–6.*

3 Museum of Science and History. Permanent exhibits here include Atlantic Tails, a hands-on exploration of whales, dolphins, and manatees; Currents of Time, chronicling 12,000 years of northeast Florida history; the Holo-Zone, a virtual-reality exhibit that puts guests right in the action; and the Universe of Science, a state-of-the-art center that investigates the world of science. The Alexander Brest Planetarium hosts daily shows on astronomy and, on weekends, Cosmic Concerts, 3-D laser shows set to pop music. ⊠ *1025 Museum Circle* ☎ *904/396–6674* ⊕ *www.themosh.com* ✆ *$7, Cosmic Concerts $3–$6* ⊙ *Weekdays 10–5, Sat. 10–6, Sun. 1–6.*

MIAMI, FLORIDA

Miami is the busiest of Florida's very busy cruise ports. Because there's so much going on here, you might want to schedule an extra day or two before and/or after your cruise to explore North America's most Latin city. Downtown is a convenient place to stay if you are meeting up with a cruise ship, but at night, except for Bayside Marketplace, the American Airlines Arena, and a few ever-changing clubs in warehouses, the area is deserted. Travelers spend little time here, since most tourist attractions are in other neighborhoods. Miami Beach, particularly the 1-square-mi Art Deco District in South Beach—the section below 24th to 28th streets—is the heart of Miami's vibrant nightlife and restaurant scene. But you may also want to explore beyond the beach, including the Little Havana, Coral Gables, and Coconut Grove sections of the city.

The Cruise Port

The Port of Miami, in downtown Miami near Bayside Marketplace and the MacArthur Causeway, bills itself as the Cruise Capital of the World. Home to 18 ships and the largest year-round cruise fleet in the world, the port accommodates more than 3 million passengers a year. It has 12 air-conditioned terminals, duty-free shopping, and limousine service. You can get taxis at all the terminals, and there is an Avis location at the port, while other car-rental agencies offer shuttles to off-site lots.

If you are driving, take I–95 north or south to I–395. Follow the directional signs to the Biscayne Boulevard exit. When you get to Biscayne Boulevard, make a right. Go to 5th Street, which becomes Port Boulevard (look for the American Airlines Basketball Arena); then make a left and go over the Port Bridge. Follow the directional signs to your terminal.

🚢 **Port of Miami** ✉ 1015 North American Way ☎ 305/371-7678 ⊕ www.co.miami-dade.fl.us/portofmiami.

AIRPORT
TRANSFERS

Miami International Airport (MIA), 6 mi (10 km) west of downtown Miami, is the only airport in Greater Miami. More than 1,400 daily flights make MIA one of the busiest passenger airports in the world. If you have not arranged an airport transfer through your cruise line, you have a couple of options to get to the cruise port. The first is a taxi, and the fares are reasonable. The fare between MIA and the Port of Miami is a flat fare of $20. This fare is per trip, not per passenger, and includes tolls and $1 airport surcharge but not tip.

SuperShuttle vans transport passengers between MIA and local hotels, as well as the Port of Miami. At MIA the vans pick up at the ground level of each concourse (look for clerks with yellow shirts, who will flag one down). Drivers provide narration en route. Service from MIA is available around the clock on demand; for the return it's best to make reservations 24 hours in advance, although SuperShuttle can sometimes arrange pickups on as little as four hours' notice. The cost from MIA to the cruise port is $10–$12. Additional members of a party pay a lower rate for many destinations, and children under three ride free.

🚢 **SuperShuttle** ☎ 305/871-2000 from MIA, 954/764-1700 from Broward [Fort Lauderdale], 800/874-8885 from elsewhere.

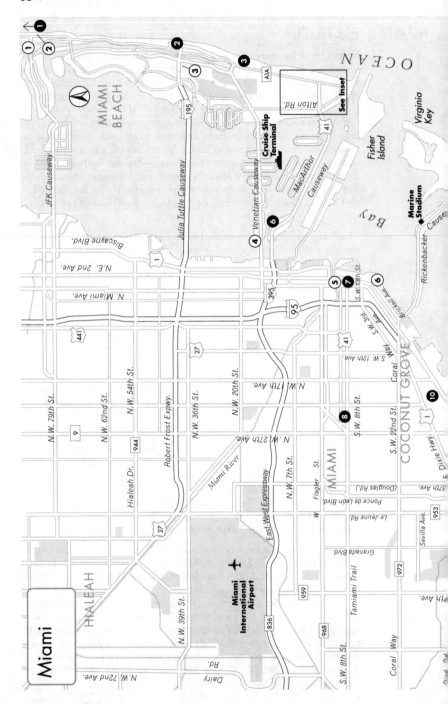

Miami

HIALEAH

Miami
International
Airport

MIAMI

MIAMI
BEACH

COCONUT GROVE

OCEAN

Bay

Virginia
Key

Fisher
Island

Marine
Stadium

Cruise Ship
Terminal

See Inset

JFK Causeway

Julia Tuttle Causeway

Venetian Causeway

MacArthur
Causeway

Rickenbacker Causeway

Biscayne Blvd.

N.E. 2nd Ave.

N. Miami Ave.

Biscayne Blvd.

Alton Rd.

Robert Frost Expwy.

Hialeah Dr.

N.W. 79th St.

N.W. 62nd St.

N.W. 54th St.

N.W. 36th St.

N.W. 20th St.

N.W. 27th Ave.

N.W. 17th Ave.

N.W. 7th Ave.

Miami River

East-West Expressway

W. Flagler St.

Ponce de León Blvd.

Le Jeune Rd.
(Douglas Rd.)

Granada Blvd.

Tamiami Trail

S.W. 8th St.

S.W. 22nd St.

Coral Way

S.W. 12th Ave.

S.W. 3rd Ave.

Brickell Ave.

S.W. 13th St.

S.W. 8th St.

37th Ave.

47th Ave.

Sevilla Ave.

Coral Way

Dairy Rd.

N.W. 39th St.

N.W. 72nd Ave.

S.W. 8th St.

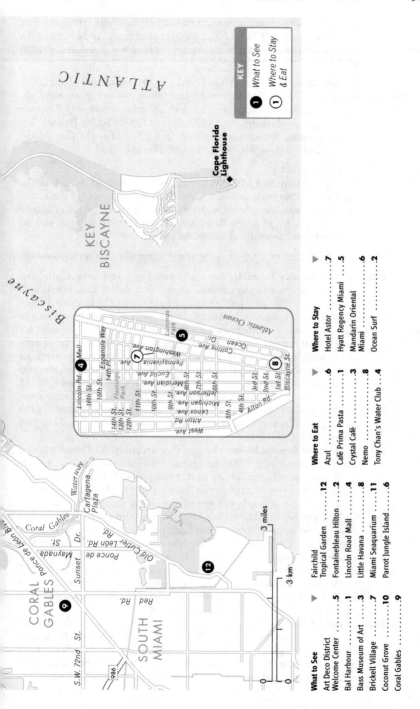

ATLANTIC

Cape Florida
Lighthouse

KEY
BISCAYNE

Biscayne

Lummus
Park

Lincoln Rd. Mall **4**
16th St.
15th St. Espanola Way
14th St.
14th Pl.

Pennsylvania Ave.
Washington Ave.
Euclid Ave. **7**
Flamingo
Park
11th St.
10th St.
9th St.
8th St.
7th St.
6th St.
5th St.
4th St.
3rd St.
2nd St.
1st St.

Collins Ave.
Ocean Dr.

Atlantic Ocean

Meridian Ave.
Jefferson Ave.
Michigan Ave.
Lenox Ave.
Alton Rd.
West Ave.
14th St.
13th St.
12th St.

8

5

Biscayne St.

KEY

① What to See

① Where to Stay
& Eat

Coral Gables

Watery
way

Cartagena
Plaza

Coral Gables
Maynada St.
Sunset Dr.
Ponce de León Rd.
Old Cutler Rd.
Red Rd.
Ponce de Leon Blvd.
S.W. 72nd St.
986

CORAL
GABLES **9**

SOUTH
MIAMI

12

0   3 km
0   3 miles

What to See

Art Deco District
Welcome Center **5**
Bal Harbour **1**
Bass Museum of Art ...**3**
Brickell Village **7**
Coconut Grove **10**
Coral Gables **9**
Fairchild
Tropical Garden **12**
Fontainebleau Hilton ..**2**
Lincoln Road Mall **4**
Little Havana **8**
Miami Seaquarium ...**11**
Parrot Jungle Island ...**6**

Where to Eat

Azul **6**
Café Prima Pasta **1**
Crystal Café **3**
Nemo **8**
Tony Chan's Water Club ..**4**

Where to Stay

Hotel Astor **7**
Hyatt Regency Miami ..**5**
Mandarin Oriental
Miami **6**
Ocean Surf **2**

PARKING   Street-level lots are right in front of each of the cruise terminals. The cost is $12 per day ($24 for RVs), payable in advance. You can pay with a credit card at most terminals (except for numbers 2 and 10), though it's MasterCard and Visa only.

VISITOR   ⑪ **Greater Miami Convention & Visitors Bureau** ⊠ 701 Brickell Ave., Suite 2700,
INFORMATION   Downtown, 33131 ☎ 305/539–3000 or 800/933–8448 ⊕ www.gmcvb. com ⊠ Bayside Marketplace tourist information center, 401 Biscayne Blvd., Bayside Marketplace, 33132 ☎ 305/539–2980 ⊠ Tropical Everglades Visitor Information Center, 160 U.S. 1, Florida City 33034 ☎ 305/245–9180 or 800/388–9669 🖷 305/247–4335.

Where to Stay

Staying in downtown Miami will put you close to the cruise terminals, but there is little to do at night. South Beach is the center of the action in Miami Beach, but it's fairly distant from the port. Staying in Miami Beach, but north of South Beach's Art Deco District, will put you on the beach but nominally closer to the port.

For price categories, *see* Lodging at the beginning of this chapter.

$$$$ 🏨 **Hyatt Regency Miami.** If your trip is based on boats, basketball, business, or bargains, you can't do much better than the Hyatt Regency, with its adjacent convention facilities and location near the Brickell Avenue business district, Bayside Marketplace, the American Airlines Arena, the Port of Miami, and downtown shopping. Distinctive public spaces are more colorful than businesslike, and guest rooms are a blend of avocado, beige, and blond. The James L. Knight International Center is accessible without stepping outside, as is the downtown Metromover and its Metrorail connection. ⊠ *400 S.E. 2nd Ave., Downtown, 33131* ☎ *305/358–1234 or 800/233–1234* 🖷 *305/358–0529* ⊕ *www.miami. hyatt.com* 🛏 *561 rooms, 51 suites* ⌂ *2 restaurants, cable TV, pool, health club, lounge, laundry service, concierge, business services, parking (fee)* ⊟ *AE, D, DC, MC, V.*

$$$$ 🏨 **Mandarin Oriental Miami.** Though it's a favorite of Wall Street tycoons and Latin American CEOs doing business with the Brickell Avenue banks, anyone who can afford to stay here, should. The location is excellent, at the tip of Brickell Key in Biscayne Bay; rooms facing west have a dazzling view of the downtown skyline, while those facing east overlook Miami Beach and the blue Atlantic. Everything is sheer perfection down to the smallest detail, from hand-painted room numbers on rice paper at check-in to the incredibly luxurious spa. ⊠ *500 Brickell Key Dr., Brickell Key, 33131* ☎ *305/913–8288 or 866/888–6780* 🖷 *305/ 913–8300* ⊕ *www.mandarinoriental.com* 🛏 *327 rooms, 31 suites* ⌂ *2 restaurants, in-room safes, cable TV, in-room data ports, pool, spa, 2 bars, dry cleaning, laundry service, concierge, business services, meeting rooms, parking (fee)* ⊟ *AE, D, DC, MC, V.*

$$–$$$$ 🏨 **Hotel Astor.** The Astor stands apart from the crowd by double-insulating walls against noise and offering such quiet luxuries as thick towels, down pillows, paddle fans, and a seductive pool. Rooms are built to recall deco ocean liner staterooms, with faux portholes, custom-milled French furniture, Roman shades, and sleek sound and video sys-

tems. A tasteful, muted color scheme and the most comfortable king beds imaginable make for eminently restful nights, and service is excellent. Metro Kitchen & Bar has exceptional fare and service. ⊠ *956 Washington Ave., South Beach, 33139* ☎ *305/531–8081 or 800/270–4981* 🖷 *305/531–3193* ⊕ *www.hotelastor.com* ↝ *24 rooms, 16 suites* ♻ *Restaurant, room service, in-room safes, minibars, in-room data ports, massage, bar, laundry service, concierge, Internet room, business services, meeting room, parking (fee)* ☰ *AE, DC, MC, V.*

¢–$ 🖻 **Ocean Surf.** For those who dig deco, this is a gem. Built in 1940 at the height of the art deco era, this three-story hotel looks like it's straight out of South Beach, with large porthole windows, ship-style railings, and wide ribbons of pink-and-white terrazzo swirling through the lobby. If one of the four oceanfront rooms is available, grab it—the view through the large porthole over the bed is remarkable. Rooms are smallish but impeccably clean. The tables on the front porch, with a great view of the beach across a quiet street, are perfect for enjoying breakfast. ⊠ *7436 Ocean Terr., 1 block east of Collins Ave., North Beach, 33141* ☎ *305/866–1648 or 800/555–0411* 🖷 *305/866–1649* ↝ *49 rooms* ♻ *Cable TV, beach* ☰ *AE, MC, V* ⑩ *CP.*

Where to Eat

Restaurants listed here have passed the test of time, but you might double-check by phone before you set out for the evening. At many of the hottest spots, you'll need a reservation to avoid a long wait for a table. And when you get your check, note whether a gratuity is included; most restaurants add 15% (ostensibly for the convenience of—and protection from—Latin-American and European tourists who are used to this practice in their homelands and would not normally tip), but you can reduce or supplement it depending on your opinion of the service.

For price categories, *see* Dining at the beginning of this chapter.

$$$–$$$$ ✕ **Azul.** This sumptuous eatery has truly conquered the devil in the details. In addition to chef Michelle Bernstein's exquisite French-Caribbean cuisine, the thoughtful touches in service graciously anticipate your needs. Does your sleeveless top mean your shoulders are too cold to properly appreciate the Swiss chard–stuffed pompano with caramelized pears? Ask for one of the house pashminas. Forgot your reading glasses and can't decipher the hanger steak with foie gras sauce? Request a pair from the host. Want to see how the other half lives? Descend the staircase to Cafe Sambal, the all-day casual restaurant. ⊠ *Mandarin Oriental Hotel, 500 Brickell Key Dr., Brickell Key* ☎ *305/913–8288* ♻ *Reservations essential* ☰ *AE, MC, V* ☉ *Closed Sun. No lunch Sat.*

$$$–$$$$ ✕ **Nemo.** The bright colors, copper fixtures, and tree-shaded courtyard lend Nemo casual comfort, but it's the menu that earns raves. Caribbean, Asian, Mediterranean, and Middle Eastern influences blend boldly, and succeed. Appetizers include garlic-cured salmon rolls with Tobiko caviar and wasabi mayo, and crispy prawns with spicy salsa *cruda*. Main courses might include wok-charred salmon or Indian-spice pork chop. Hedy Goldsmith's funky pastries are exquisite. ⊠ *100 Collins Ave., South Beach* ☎ *305/532–4550* ☰ *AE, DC, MC, V.*

$-$$$$ ✗ **Tony Chan's Water Club.** Off the lobby of the Doubletree Grand Hotel, this spot overlooks a bayside marina. On the menu of more than 200 appetizers and entrées are minced quail tossed with bamboo shoots and mushrooms wrapped in lettuce leaves. Indulge in a seafood spectacular of shrimp, conch, scallops, fish cakes, and crabmeat tossed with broccoli in a bird's nest, or go for pork chops sprinkled with green pepper in a black bean–garlic sauce. A lighter favorite is steamed sea bass with ginger and garlic. ⊠ *1717 N. Bayshore Dr., Downtown* ☎ *305/374–8888* ▤ *AE, D, DC, MC, V* ⊗ *No lunch weekends.*

$$-$$$ ✗ **Crystal Café.** Classic dishes like beef Stroganoff and chicken *paprikash* are updated and lightened up here; osso buco falls off the bone (there's also a seafood version with salmon). More contemporary items include chicken Kiev, stuffed with goat cheese and topped with a tricolor salad, and pan-seared duck breast with raspberry sauce. Multiple Golden Spoon award–winning Macedonian chef-proprietor Klime Kovaceski takes pride in serving more food than you can possibly manage, including home-baked rhubarb pie. ⊠ *726 41st St., Miami Beach* ☎ *305/673–8266* ▤ *AE, D, DC, MC, V* ⊗ *Closed Mon. No lunch.*

$-$$$ ✗ **Café Prima Pasta.** One of Miami's many signatures is this exemplary Argentine-Italian spot, which rules the emerging North Beach neighborhood. Service can be erratic, but you forget it all on delivery of fresh-made bread with a bowl of spiced olive oil. Tender carpaccio and plentiful antipasti are a delight to share, but the real treat here is the hand-rolled pasta, which can range from crab-stuffed ravioli to simple fettuccine with seafood. ⊠ *414 71st St., North Beach, Miami Beach* ☎ *305/867–0106* ▤ *MC, V.*

Beaches

The **beach on Ocean Drive from 1st to 22nd Street**—primarily the 10-block stretch from 5th to 15th Street—is one of the most talked-about beachfronts in America. The beach is wide, white, and bathed by warm aquamarine waves. Separating the sand from the traffic of Ocean Drive is palm-fringed Lummus Park, with its volleyball nets and chickee huts for shade. The beach also has some of the funkiest lifeguard stands you'll ever see, pop stars shooting music videos, and visitors from all over the world. Popular with gays is the beach at **12th Street.** Because much of South Beach has an adult flavor—women are often casually topless—many families prefer the beach's quieter southern reaches, especially **3rd Street Beach** (⊠ Ocean Dr. and 3rd St., South Beach). Unless you're parking south of 3rd Street, metered spaces near the waterfront are rarely empty. Instead, opt for a public garage and walk; you'll have lots of fun people-watching, too. ☎ *305/673–7714.*

Haulover Beach Park. At this county park, far from the action of SoBe (**South Beach**), you can see the Miami of 30 years ago. Pack a picnic, use the barbecue grills, or grab a snack at the concession stand. If you're into fitness, you may like the tennis and volleyball courts or paths designed for exercise, walking, and bicycling. The beach is nice for those who want water without long marches across hot sand, and a popular clothing-optional section at the north end of the beach lures people who want to tan every nook and cranny. Other offerings are kite rentals, kayak rentals, charter-fishing excursions, and a par-3, 9-hole golf course. ⌧ *10800 Collins Ave., Sunny Isles Beach, Miami Beach* ☎ *305/947–3525* ⊕ *www.metro-dade.com/parks* ⌑ *$4 per vehicle* ☉ *Daily dawn–dusk.*

North Shore Park Open Space. At this beach park between 79th and 87th streets on Collins Avenue, you'll find plenty of picnic tables, restrooms, and healthy dunes. An exercise trail, concrete walkways, a playground, and lifeguards compromise or enhance the otherwise natural scene, depending on your point of view. You can park at a meter or in one of the pay lots across Collins Avenue. ⌧ *7901 Collins Ave., south of Surfside, Miami Beach* ☎ *305/993–2032* ⌑ *$1* ☉ *Daily 7–6.*

Shopping

In Greater Miami you're never more than 15 minutes from a major commercial area that serves as both a shopping and entertainment venue for tourists and locals. The shopping is great on a two-block stretch of **Collins Avenue** between 6th and 8th Avenues. Club Monaco, Polo Sport, Intermix, Nike, Kenneth Cole, Sephora, Armani Exchange, and Banana Republic are among the high-profile tenants, and a parking garage is just a block away on 7th Avenue. The busy **Lincoln Road Mall** is just a few blocks from the beach and convention center, making it popular with locals and tourists. There's an energy to shopping here, especially on weekends, when the pedestrian mall is filled with locals. You'll find a Victoria's Secret, Pottery Barn, Gap, and a Williams-Sonoma, as well as smaller emporiums with unique personalities. Creative merchandise, galleries, and a Sunday-morning antiques market can be found among the art galleries and cool cafés. An 18-screen movie theater anchors the west end of the street.

Aventura Mall (⌧ 19501 Biscayne Blvd., Aventura, North Miami Beach) has more than 250 upscale shops anchored by Macy's, Lord & Taylor, JCPenney, Sears Roebuck, Burdines, and Bloomingdale's, along with a 24-screen theater with stadium seating and a Cheesecake Factory. In a tropical garden, **Bal Harbour Shops** (⌧ 9700 Collins Ave., Bal Harbour, Miami Beach) is a swank collection of 100 shops, boutiques, and department stores, such as Chanel, Gucci, Cartier, Gianfranco Ferré, Hermès, Neiman Marcus, and Saks Fifth Avenue. **Bayside Marketplace** (⌧ 401 Biscayne Blvd., Downtown), the 16-acre shopping complex on Biscayne Bay, has more than 100 specialty shops, live entertainment, tourboat docks, and a food court. It's open late (until 10 during the week, 11 on Friday and Saturday), but its restaurants stay open even later. Browse, buy, or simply relax by the bay with a tropical drink.

Nightlife

The best, most complete source is the *New Times,* a free weekly distributed throughout Miami–Dade County each Thursday. A good source of information on the performing arts and nightspots is the calendar in *Miami Today,* a free weekly newspaper available each Thursday in downtown Miami, Coconut Grove, and Coral Gables. Various tabloids reporting on Deco District entertainment and the Miami social scene come and go. *Wire* reports on the gay community. The **Greater Miami**

Convention & Visitors Bureau (☎ 305/539–3000 or 800/283–2707 ⊕ www.gmcvb.com) publishes a comprehensive list of dance venues, theaters, and museums.

If you're interested in high culture, the **Miami City Ballet** (✉ 2200 Liberty Ave., South Beach, Miami Beach ☎ 305/929–7000 ⊕ www.miamicityballet.org/mcbdev/index.shtml) is internationally renowned; its season runs from September to March. The **New World Symphony** (✉ 555 Lincoln Rd., South Beach, Miami Beach ☎ 305/673–3331 or 305/673–3330 ⊕ www.nws.org) performs in the Lincoln Theater in Lincoln Road Mall from October to May.

A gay club popular with locals is **crobar** (✉ 1445 Washington Ave., at 14th St., South Beach ☎ 305/531–5027), whose exterior is the historic Cameo Theater, while the interior is a *Blade Runner*–esque blend of high-tech marvels with some performance art thrown in. Dazzling and lots of fun, it's open Thursday through Monday. The Rose Bar at the **Delano** (✉ 1685 Collins Ave., South Beach ☎ 305/672–2000) is dramatic and chic, with long gauzy curtains and huge pillars creating private conversation nooks around the outdoor infinity pool. Inside, the cool, chic lounge area creates a glamorous space for the modelesque crowd. **Honey** (✉ 645 Washington Ave. ☎ 305/604–8222) has soft lighting, cozy couches, and chaise lounges, and vibey music every bit as smooth as their trademark honey-dipped apples. **Mansion** (✉ 1235 Washington Ave. ☎ 305/532–1525) is the hip-hop rebirth of a defunct club called Level. Mansion has lots of places to search out fun.

Offering more character than chic, the **Marlin** (✉ 1200 Collins Ave. ☎ 305/604–3595) gleams with the high-tech look of stainless steel. DJs spin different music every night for the 25-to-40 crowd. **Nikki Beach Club** (✉ 1 Ocean Dr., South Beach ☎ 305/538–1231) has seven bars in a beautiful beachfront location—complete with tepee cabanas—and includes Pearl Restaurant and Champagne Bar, a steadfast celeb hangout. Popular with casually chic twenty- and thirtysomethings, **Opium Garden** (✉ 136 Collins Ave., at 1st St., South Beach ☎ 305/674–8360) has a lush waterfall, an Asian temple motif with lots of candles, dragons and tapestries, and a restaurant next door. It's open 11 PM–6 AM Thursday through Sunday.

Want 24-hour partying? **Space** (✉ 34 N.E. 11th St., Downtown ☎ 305/375–0001), created from four warehouses downtown, has three dance rooms, an outdoor patio, a New York industrial look, and a 24-hour liquor license. It's open on Saturday only, and you'll need to look good to be allowed past the velvet ropes. The glass-top bar at the **Tides** (✉ 1220 Ocean Dr. ☎ 305/604–5000) is the place to go for martinis and piano jazz. **Tobacco Road** (✉ 626 S. Miami Ave., Downtown ☎ 305/374–1198), opened in 1912, holds Miami's oldest liquor license: Number 0001! Upstairs, in space occupied by a speakeasy during Prohibition, blues bands perform nightly, accompanied by single-malt Scotch and bourbon.

Exploring Miami

In the 1950s, Miami was best known for alligator wrestlers and you-pick strawberry fields or citrus groves. Well, things have changed. While

Disney sidetracked families in Orlando, Miami was developing a grown-up attitude, courtesy of *Miami Vice,* European fashion photographers, and historic preservationists. Today, the wildest ride is the city itself.

Climb aboard and check out the different sides of Greater Miami. Miami on the mainland is South Florida's commercial hub, while its sultry sister, Miami Beach (America's Riviera), encompasses 17 islands in Biscayne Bay. Seducing winter refugees with its sunshine, beaches, palms, and nightlife, this is what most people envision when planning a trip to what they think of as Miami. These same visitors fail to realize that there's more to Miami Beach than the bustle of South Beach and its Art Deco District. Indeed, there are quieter areas to the north like Sunny Isles Beach, Surfside, and Bal Harbour. During the day downtown Miami is the lively hub of the mainland city, now more accessible thanks to the Metromover extension, which connects downtown sights with Metrorail's Government Center and Brickell stations. Other major attractions include Coconut Grove, Coral Gables, Little Havana, and, of course, the South Beach/Art Deco District, but since these areas are spread out beyond the reach of public transportation, you'll have to drive.

⑤ Art Deco District Welcome Center. Run by the Miami Design Preservation League, the center provides information about the buildings in the district. A gift shop sells 1930s–1950s art deco memorabilia, posters, and books on Miami's history. Several tours—covering Lincoln Road, Espanola Way, North Beach, the entire Art Deco District—start here. Rent audiotapes for $15 per person for a self-guided tour, join the regular Wednesday-, Friday-, Saturday-, and Sunday-morning or Thursday-evening walking tours, or take a bicycle tour. Don't miss the special boat tours during Art Deco Weekend in early January. ⊠ *1001 Ocean Dr., at Barbara Capitman Way (10th St.), South Beach* ☎ *305/531–3484 or 305/672–2014* 🖾 *Tours $20* ☉ *Daily 10–7:30.*

① Bal Harbour. Known for its upscale shops, this affluent community has a stretch of prime beach real estate where wealthy condominium owners cluster in winter. Look close and you may spy Bob Dole sunning himself outside his condo. ⊠ *Collins Ave. between 96th and 103rd Sts., Bal Harbour.*

③ Bass Museum of Art. European art is the focus of this impressive museum in historic Collins Park, a short drive north of SoBe's key sights. Works on display include *The Holy Family,* a painting by Peter Paul Rubens; *The Tournament,* one of several 16th-century Flemish tapestries; and works by Albrecht Dürer and Henri de Toulouse-Lautrec. An $8 million, three-phase expansion by architect Arata Isozaki added another wing, cafeteria, and theater, doubling the museum's size to nearly 40,000 square feet. ⊠ *2121 Park Ave., South Beach* ☎ *305/673-7530* ⊕ *www.bassmuseum.org* 🖾 *$12* ☉ *Tues.–Sat. 10–5, Thurs. 10–9, Sun. 11–5.*

⑦ Brickell Village. Brickell (rhymes with fickle) is an up-and-coming downtown area with new low- and high-rise condos, a shopping area, Brickell Park, and plenty of popular restaurants. **Perricone's Marketplace and Café** (⊠ 15 S.E. 10th St., Brickell Village) is the biggest and most popular of the area's many Italian restaurants, in a 120-year-old Vermont barn. The cooking is simple and good. Buy your wine from the on-premises deli and bring it to your table for a small corking fee. ⊠ *Between Miami River and S.W. 15 St., Brickell Village.*

❿ Coconut Grove. South Florida's oldest settlement, the "Grove" was inhabited as early as 1834 and established by 1873, two decades before Miami. Its early settlers included Bahamian blacks, "Conchs" (white Key Westers, many originally from the Bahamas), and New England intellectuals, who built a community that attracted artists, writers, and scientists, who established winter homes. Coconut Grove still reflects its pioneers' eclectic origins. Posh estates mingle with rustic cottages, modest frame homes, and stark modern dwellings, often on the same block. The historic center of the Village of Coconut Grove went through a hippie period in the 1960s, a laid-back funkiness in the 1970s, and a teeny-bopper invasion in the early 1980s. Today the tone is upscale and urban, with a mix of galleries, boutiques, restaurants, bars, and sidewalk cafés. On weekends the Grove is jam-packed with both locals and tourists—especially teenagers—shopping at the Streets of Mayfair, CocoWalk, and small boutiques. Parking can be a problem, especially on weekend evenings, when police direct traffic and prohibit turns at some intersections to prevent gridlock.

Of the 10,000 people living in Miami between 1912 and 1916, about 1,000 of them were gainfully employed by Chicago industrialist James Deering to build the **Vizcaya Museum and Gardens** (⊠ 3251 S. Miami Ave., Coconut Grove ☎ 305/250–9133 ⊕ www.vizcayamuseum.com), a $20 million Italian Renaissance–style winter residence. Once comprising 180 acres, the grounds now cover a still-substantial 30-acre tract, including a native hammock and more than 10 acres of formal gardens and fountains overlooking Biscayne Bay. The house, open to the public, contains 70 rooms, 34 of which are filled with paintings, sculpture, antique furniture, and other decorative arts dating from the 15th through the 19th centuries and representing the Renaissance, baroque, rococo, and neoclassical styles. The house is open daily from 9:30 to 4:30, the garden from 9:30 to 5:30. Admission is $12.

❾ Coral Gables. If not for George E. Merrick, Coral Gables would be just another suburb. Merrick envisioned an American Venice, with canals and gracious homes spreading across the community. Today Coral Gables has a population of about 43,000. In its bustling downtown, more than 150 companies maintain headquarters or regional offices, and the University of Miami campus in the southern part of Coral Gables brings a youthful vibrancy: the median age of residents is 38. Like much of Miami, Coral Gables has realized the aesthetic and economic importance of historic preservation and has passed a Mediterranean design ordinance, rewarding businesses for maintaining their buildings' architectural styles. Even the street signs (ground-level markers that are hard to see in daylight, impossible at night) are preserved. They're worth the inconvenience, if only to honor the memory of Merrick. The upscale yet neighborly stretch of retail stores along the so-called **Miracle Mile** (⊠ Coral Way between S.W. 37th Ave. [Douglas Rd.] and S.W. 42nd Ave. [LeJeune Rd.], Coral Gables) is actually only ½ mi long. After years of neglect, it's been updated and upgraded and now offers a delightful mix of owner-operated shops and chain stores, bridal shops, art galleries and bistros, and enough late-night hot spots to keep things hopping.

⑫ Fairchild Tropical Garden. Comprising 83 acres, this is the largest tropical botanical garden in the continental United States. Eleven lakes, a rain forest, and lots of palm trees, cycads, and flowers, including orchids, mountain roses, bellflowers, coral trees, and bougainvillea make it a garden for the senses—and there's special assistance for the hearing impaired. Take the free guided tram tour, which leaves on the hour. Spicing up the social calendar are garden sales (don't miss the Ramble in November or the International Mango Festival in July), moonlight strolls, and symphony concerts. A gift shop in the visitor center is a popular source for books on gardening and horticulture, ordered by botanists the world over. ⊠ *10901 Old Cutler Rd., Coral Gables* ☎ *305/667–1651* ⊕ *www. fairchildgarden.org* ⊠ *$10* ☉ *Daily 9:30–4:30.*

❷ Fontainebleau Hilton Resort & Towers. For a sense of what Miami was like during the Fabulous '50s, take a drive north to see the finest example of Miami Beach's grandiose architecture. By the 1950s smaller deco-era hotels were passé, and architects like Morris Lapidus got busy designing free-flowing hotels that affirmed the American attitude of "bigger is better." Even if you're not a guest, wander through the lobby just to feel the energy generated by an army of bellhops, clerks, concierges, and travelers. ⊠ *4441 Collins Ave., between 44th and 45th Sts., South Beach* ☎ *305/538–2000* ⊕ *www.fontainebleau.hilton.com.*

❹ Lincoln Road Mall. The Morris Lapidus–renovated Lincoln Road, just a few blocks from the beach and convention center, is fun, lively, and friendly for people old, young, gay, and straight—and their dogs. Folks skate, scoot, bike, or jog here past the electronics stores at the Collins Avenue end toward the chichi boutiques and outdoor cafés heading west. An 18-screen movie theater anchors the west end of the street. The best times to hit the road are during Sunday-morning farmers' markets and on weekend evenings when cafés are bustling; art galleries, like Romero Britto's Britto Central, schedule openings; street performers take the stage; and bookstores, import shops, and clothing stores are open late. ⊠ *Lincoln Rd. between Collins Ave. and Alton Rd., South Beach.*

❽ Little Havana. More than 40 years ago the tidal wave of Cubans fleeing the Castro regime flooded into an older neighborhood west of downtown Miami. Don't expect a sparkling and lively reflection of 1950s Havana, however. What you will find are ramshackle motels and cluttered storefronts. With a million Cubans and other Latinos—who make up more than half the metropolitan population—dispersed throughout Greater Miami, Little Havana and neighboring East Little Havana remain magnets for Hispanics and Anglos alike, who come to experience the flavor of traditional Cuban culture. That culture, of course, functions in Spanish. Many Little Havana residents and shopkeepers speak little or no English. In Little Havana's commercial heart, **Calle Ocho** (⊠ *S.W. 8th St., Little Havana*), experience such Cuban favorites as hand-rolled cigars or sandwiches piled with meats and cheeses. Although the entire area deserves exploring, if time is limited, try the stretch from Southwest 14th to 11th Avenues. In **Plaza de la Cubanidad** (⊠ W. Flagler St. and S.W. 17th Ave., Little Havana) redbrick sidewalks surround a fountain and monument with the words of José Martí, a leader in Cuba's struggle for independence from Spain and a hero to Cuban refugees and immigrants in Miami. The quotation, LAS PALMAS SON NOVIAS QUE ESPERAN (The palm trees are waiting brides), counsels hope and fortitude to the Cubans.

🕒 ⓫ **Miami Seaquarium.** This old-fashioned attraction has six daily shows with sea lions, dolphins, and Lolita, a killer whale. (Lolita's tank is small for seaquariums—just three times her length—and so some wildlife advocates are trying to get her back to sea.) Exhibits include a shark pool, a 235,000-gallon tropical-reef aquarium, and manatees. Glass-bottom boats take tours of Biscayne Bay. Want to get your feet (and everything else) wet? The Water and Dolphin Exploration (WADE) program enables you to swim with dolphins during a two-hour session. Reservations are required. ⊠ *4400 Rickenbacker Causeway, Virginia Key* ☎ *305/361–5705* ⊕ *www.miamiseaquarium.com* ⊠ *$24.95, WADE $149, parking $5* ⊘ *Daily 9:30–6, last admission at 5; WADE daily at noon and 3:30.*

🕒 ❻ **Parrot Jungle Island.** One of South Florida's original tourist attractions, Parrot Jungle opened in 1936 and has relocated to Watson Island, linked by the MacArthur Causeway (I–395) to Miami and Miami Beach. In addition to a thousand exotic birds, the attraction includes a 17-foot Asian crocodile, a 9-foot albino alligator, a serpentarium filled with venomous snakes, a petting zoo, and a two-story-high aviary with more than 100 free-flying macaws. A restaurant with indoor and outdoor seating overlooks a lake where 60 postcard-perfect Caribbean flamingos hang out. Orchids and ferns and even trees from the original site were transplanted along a Disneyesque jungle river that meanders through the park. The Japanese garden that once stood on the new Parrot Jungle site is being reconstructed adjacent to the attraction. The original site on Southwest 57th Avenue at 111th Street has reopened as a park. The popular trails originally cut through coral rock and shaded by massive oaks and bald cypress remain a draw and showcase the region's natural flora. ⊠ *980 MacArthur Causeway, Watson Island* ☎ *305/258–6453* ⊕ *www.parrotjungle.com* ⊠ *$24.95 plus $6 parking* ⊘ *Daily 10–6; last admission 4:30.*

MOBILE, ALABAMA

Fort Condé was the name given by the French in 1711 to the site known today as Mobile; around it blossomed the first white settlement in what is now Alabama. For eight years it was the capital of the French colonial empire, and it remained under French control until 1763, long after the capital had moved to New Orleans.

Mobile, a busy international port, is noted for its tree-lined boulevards fanning westward from the riverfront. In the heart of busy downtown is Bienville Square, a park with an ornate cast-iron fountain and shaded by centuries-old live oaks. One of the city's main thoroughfares, Dauphin Street, has many thriving restaurants, bars, and shops.

The Cruise Port

Only one ship is based in Mobile at this writing, and it does shorter (four- and five-day) Western Caribbean itineraries. The cruise terminal is near the downtown area. It's a good home port to consider if you want to drive, but it's less convenient by air, with just a few airlines flying to the Mobile Regional Airport.

Mobile Alabama Cruise Terminal ✉ 201 S. Water St., Mobile, AL ☎ 251/338–7447 ⊕ www.shipmobile.com.

AIRPORT TRANSFERS Taxis are available to the cruise ship pier, or you can call the Mobile Regional Airport Shuttle, which will transport you for $20 ($30 round-trip).

Mobile Regional Airport Shuttle ☎ 251/633–0313 or 800/357–5373.

PARKING Parking is available in a garage next to the cruise ship pier. It costs $10 a day for cars, $20 for RVs. You can pay by cash or credit card.

VISITOR INFORMATION **Mobile Bay Convention & Visitor's Bureau** ✉ 1 S. Water St., Mobile, AL ☎ 251/208–2000 or 800/566–2453 ⊕ www.mobile.org.

Where to Stay

Several local hotels offer cruise packages that include lodging, parking for the duration of your cruise, and a shuttle to the cruise terminal.

For price categories, *see* Lodging at the beginning of this chapter.

$$ **Radisson Admiral Semmes Hotel.** This restored 1940 hotel in the historic district is a favorite with local politicians. It's also popular with partygoers, particularly during Mardi Gras, because of its excellent location directly on the parade route. The spacious, high-ceiling rooms have a burgundy-and-green color scheme and are furnished in Queen Anne and Chippendale styles. ✉ *251 Government St., 36602* ☎ *251/432–8000 or 800/333–3333* 🖶 *251/405–5942* ⊕ *www.radisson.com* 🛏 *148 rooms, 22 suites* ⚭ *Restaurant, pool, bar, business services* ▭ *AE, D, DC, MC, V.*

$–$$ **Malaga Inn.** A delightful, romantic getaway, this place comprises two town houses built by a wealthy landowner in 1862. The lobby is furnished with 19th-century antiques and opens onto a landscaped central courtyard with a fountain. The rooms are large, airy, and furnished with antiques. The Malaga is on a quiet street downtown, within walking distance of the Museum of Mobile and the Gulf Coast Exploreum, and offers a cruise package. ✉ *359 Church St., 36602* ☎ *251/438–4701 or 800/235–1586* 🖶 *251/438–4701 Ext. 123* ⊕ *www.malagainn.com* 🛏 *35 rooms, 3 suites* ⚭ *Cable TV, pool, lounge, business services* ▭ *AE, D, MC, V.*

$ **Holiday Inn Lafayette Plaza.** This hotel in the heart of downtown Mobile's business and historic districts is within walking distance of the Museum of Mobile, Phoenix Fire Museum, Gulf Coast Exploreum, and more. The rooftop lounge offers breathtaking views of the city and the waterfront. ✉ *301 Government St., 36602* ☎ *251/694–0100 or 800/692–6662* 🖶 *251/694–0160* ⊕ *www.lafayetteplazahotel.com* 🛏 *210 rooms*

♿ *Restaurant, cable TV, in-room data ports, pool, hair salon, bar, lounge, laundry service, business services, some pets allowed (fee), no-smoking rooms* ▭ *AE, D, DC, MC, V* ⍭ *BP.*

Where to Eat
For price categories, *see* Dining at the beginning of this chapter.

$-$$$ ✕ **Loretta's.** At a colorful corner a block off Dauphin Street, this place has its own dramatic flair. It's hidden behind a wall of glass covered in creeping fig, with a unique style—gleaming silver palm trees and whimsical, mismatched salt and pepper shakers. In the kitchen, owner-chef Christopher Hunter adds creative nuances to Southern favorites, such as sausage-stuffed pork loin and pan-seared sashimi tuna steak. ⊠ *19 S. Conception St.* ☎ *251/432–2200* ▭ *AE, D, DC, MC, V* ⊘ *Closed Sun.*

$-$$ ✕ **Roussos Restaurant & Catering.** With a nautical look created by lots of fishnets and scenes of ships at sea, this place serves seafood fried, broiled, or served Greek style (with a blend of spices and oils). Steaks and chicken are also available. The appetizers are big favorites—especially the baked oysters and seafood gumbo. ⊠ *Eastern Shore Centre, 30500 State Hwy. 181, at I–10 Exit 38, Spanish Fort* ☎ *251/625–3386* ▭ *AE, D, DC, MC, V* ⊘ *Closed Mon.*

¢-$ ✕ **Brick Pit.** It's "the best damn barbecue in the state of Alabama," owner Bill Armbrecht insists. Chicken, ribs, and pork are smoked for hours over a blend of hickory and pecan to achieve a distinct flavor. Barbecue sauce comes spicy or sweet, with soft white bread for dipping. Be sure to add your name to the graffiti scrawled in red marker all over the walls and ceiling. Try the smoked pulled-pork plate. ⊠ *5456 Old Shell Rd.* ☎ *251/343–0001* ▭ *MC, V* ⊘ *Closed Sun. and Mon.*

Shopping
Most shopping in Mobile is in malls and shopping centers in the suburbs. Stores are generally open Monday to Saturday 10–10, Sunday 1–6. Antiques buffs may be interested in Mobile's many antiques stores that are in the Loop area of midtown (where Government Street, Airport Boulevard, and Dauphin Island Parkway converge); several shops are within walking distance of each other.

Eastern Shore Centre (⊠ 30500 State Hwy. 181, at I–10, Spanish Fort ☎ 251/625–0060) is the newest shopping complex in Mobile, with 70 stores, including a large Dillard's. It's about 10 minutes from downtown. **Springdale Mall** (⊠ Airport Blvd. and I–65 ☎ 251/471–1945) has dozens of stores, including Best Buy, Linens & Things, and Barnes & Noble.

Nightlife
Most of Mobile's nightlife centers around the downtown's former commercial district, Dauphin Street, which today has a number of restaurants and nightspots spread out over several blocks. Mobilians have taken to calling the area LoDa, short for Lower Dauphin. In midtown Mobile, the **Double Olive** (⊠ 2033 Airport Blvd. ☎ 251/450–5001) is an artsy, urbane martini bar that draws hip crowds. **Monsoon's** (⊠ 210 Dauphin St. ☎ 251/433–3500) is one of several almost indistinguishable bars that host local bands as well as a few national ones, drawing crowds of twentysomethings on Friday and Saturday nights.

Exploring Mobile

Battleship Memorial Park. On Mobile Bay, east of downtown, is the site of the 155-acre park where the battleship USS *Alabama* is anchored. A self-guided tour gives a fascinating glimpse into the World War II vessel, which had a crew of 2,500. Anchored next to it is the USS *Drum*, a World War II submarine. Other exhibits include the B-52 bomber *Calamity Jane.* ⊠ *2703 Battleship Pkwy., Mobile* ☎ *251/433–2703 or 800/426–4929* ⊕ *www.ussalabama.com* ⌦ *$10* ⊙ *Apr.–Sept., daily 8–6; Oct.–Mar., daily 8–4.*

Bellingrath Gardens & Home. One of the most popular gardens in the South is Bellingrath, famous for its magnificent azaleas, which are part of 65 acres of gardens set amid a 905-acre semitropical landscape. Showtime for the azaleas is mid- to late-March, when some 250,000 plantings of 200 different species are ablaze with color. But Bellingrath is a year-round wonder, with more than 75 varieties of roses blooming in summer, 60,000 chrysanthemum plants cascading in fall, and red fields of poinsettias brightening winter. Countless species and flowering plants spring up along the Fowl River, surround streams, and a lake populated by ducks and swans. A free map lets you plan your own strolls along flagstone paths across charming bridges. In April and October, large numbers of migratory birds drop by. You can also visit the home of Coca-Cola bottling pioneer Walter D. Bellingrath. Forty-five-minute boat cruises on the Fowl River aboard the *Southern Belle* leave from the dock next to the home daily at 10, noon, and 2 from mid-February through Thanksgiving. Take I–10 West to Exit 15, then follow CR 59 South to Theodore. ⊠ *12401 Bellingrath Gardens Rd., Theodore* ☎ *251/973–2217, 800/ 247–8420, 251/973–1244 for boat cruises* ⊕ *www.bellingrath.org* ⌦ *Gardens $9; gardens and home $16.50; gardens, home, and cruise $25* ⊙ *Gardens daily 8–5, home daily 9–4.*

Ft. Condé. In 1711, France built this fort that would one day expand and become Mobile. The city's French origins endure in its creole cuisine. Now, 150 years after the fort was destroyed, its remains were discovered during construction of the I–10 interchange. A reconstructed portion houses the city's **visitor center,** as well as a museum. Costumed guides conduct tours. ⊠ *150 S. Royal St., Mobile* ☎ *251/208–7304* ⌦ *Free* ⊙ *Daily 8–5.*

☺ **Gulf Coast Exploreum Science Center.** Near Ft. Condé, Mobile's science museum for children hosts traveling exhibits and an IMAX dome theater. ⊠ *65 Government St., Mobile* ☎ *251/208–6883 or 877/625– 4386* ⊕ *www.exploreum.net* ⌦ *Museum $7.75, IMAX $7.75, both $12* ⊙ *Weekdays 9–5, Sat. 10–5, Sun. noon–5.*

Museum of Mobile. The museum opened in 2001 in the renovated circa-1857 Southern Market/Old City Hall building next to the Exploreum. Interactive exhibits and special collections of antique silver, weapons, and more tell the 300-year history of Mobile. ⊠ *111 S. Royal St., Mobile* ☎ *251/208–7569* ⊕ *www.museumofmobile.com* ⌦ *$5* ⊙ *Mon.–Sat. 9–5, Sun. 1–5.*

Oakleigh. About 1½ mi (2½ km) from Ft. Condé, in the heart of the historic Oakleigh Garden District, is an antebellum Greek Revival–style mansion, built between 1833 and 1838. Costumed guides give tours of the home, which has fine period furniture, portraits, silver, jewelry, kitchen implements, toys, and more. Tickets include a tour of neighboring **Cox-Deasy House,** an 1850s cottage furnished with simple 19th-century pieces, and the **Mardi Gras Cottage Museum,** devoted to exhibits on the history of the Mardi Gras celebration. ⊠ *350 Oakleigh Pl., Mobile* ☎ *251/432–1281* ⊕ *www.historicmobile.org* ✉ *$5* ⊗ *Oakleigh: Tues.–Sat., 9–3. Mardi Gras Cottage: Tues.–Sat., 10–2:30.*

NEW ORLEANS, LOUISIANA

Tucked beyond miles of marsh and isolated from the surrounding area, New Orleans sometimes seems closer in spirit to the Caribbean than to Our Town, U.S.A. The European, African, and Caribbean cultures that settled here are intact and even thriving—often, as during Mardi Gras, exuberantly. Creole cuisine, the continuing legacy of New Orleans jazz, and the unabashed prioritizing of pleasure that define life here are all part of a culture that is by geographical dictate self-contained. Visitors are treated to that oh-so-rare mixture of modernity and true individuality, found in the frank indifference of leisure-seeking locals no less than in the raucous revelry of the French Quarter. No wonder the city is a favorite of cruise goers, who enjoy strolling the narrow streets of the French Quarter and partaking in its culinary and atmospheric pleasures. Most who embark here on one of the Western Caribbean cruises that leave from the city's cruise ship terminal will spend a day or so either pre- or post-cruise taking it all in.

The Cruise Port

The Julia Street Cruise Terminal is at the end of Julia Street on the Mississippi River, in front of the Ernest M. Morial Convention Center. You can walk to the French Quarter from here in about 10 minutes; it's a short taxi ride to the Quarter or nearby hotels. Carnival, Norwegian, and Royal Caribbean base ships here at least part of the year, and the *Delta Queen, Mississippi Queen,* and *American Queen* river steamboats leave from the Robin Street Wharf, just south of the Julia Street terminals.

If you are driving, you'll probably approach New Orleans on I–10. Take the Business 90 West/Westbank exit, locally known as Pontchartrain Expressway, and proceed to the Tchoupitoulas Street/South Peters Street exit. Continue to Convention Center Boulevard, where you will take a right turn. Continue to Henderson Street, where you will turn left, and then continue to Port of New Orleans Place. Take a left on Port of New Orleans Place to Julia Street Terminals 1 and 2, or take a right to get to the Robin Street Wharf.

🚢 **Port of New Orleans** ⊠ Port of New Orleans Pl. at foot of Julia St. ☎ 504/522-2551 ⊕ www.portno.com.

AIRPORT TRANSFERS   Shuttle-bus service to and from the airport and the cruise port is available through New Orleans Tours Airport Shuttle. Buses leave regularly from the ground level near the baggage claim. Return trips to the airport need to be booked in advance. The cost one-way is $13 per person, and the trip takes about 40 minutes.

A cab ride to or from the airport from uptown or downtown New Orleans costs $28 for the first two passengers and $12 for each additional passenger. At the airport, pickup is on the lower level, outside the baggage claim area. There may be an additional charge for extra baggage. ⓘ **New Orleans Tours Airport Shuttle** ☎ 504/522-3500.

PARKING There is a lighted, outdoor parking lot on Tchoupitoulas Street, which is a few blocks from the cruise ship terminal and charges $12 a day ($84 for a one-week cruise); you will have to show your ticket and pay cash in advance. Cruisers can also park at the Fulton Street Garage at Convention Center Boulevard and North Diamond Street for the same $12 a day. Other nearby private lots and garages will accept cruise ship passengers. A shuttle operates from the port's parking lot to the terminal, but at this writing it didn't serve the private garages or lots. If you're going to park in one of the private lots, it's probably best to drop off your luggage first.

VISITOR You can get information about visiting New Orleans from the Louisiana
INFORMATION Office of Tourism and the New Orleans Convention & Visitors Bureau. ⓘ **Louisiana Office of Tourism** ✏ Box 94291, Baton Rouge, LA 70804-9291 ☎ 800/ 633-6970 ⎙ 225/342-8390 ⊕ www.louisianatravel.com. **New Orleans Convention & Visitors Bureau** ✉ 2020 St. Charles Ave., 70130 ☎ 504/566-5011 or 800/672-6124 ⎙ 504/ 566-5021 ⊕ www.visitneworleans.info ✉ in the U.K. ✉ 33 Market Pl., Hitchin, Hertfordshire SG5 1DY ☎ 146/245-8696 ⎙ 208/466-9205.

Where to Stay

You can stay in a large hotel near the cruise ship terminal or in more intimate places in the French Quarter. Hotel rates in New Orleans tend to be on the high end, though deals abound.

For price categories, *see* Lodging at the beginning of this chapter.

$$$$ ▦ **New Orleans Marriott Hotel.** The Marriott has a fabulous view of the Quarter, the Central Business District (CBD), and the river. It's an easy walk from Riverwalk, the Canal Place mall, and the convention center. The rooms are comfortable, the service is friendly, and nightly jazz enlivens the lobby and the Riverview Restaurant, which just happens to have one of the best views of New Orleans anywhere in the city, and possibly the best buffet Sunday brunch in the city. The Canal Street streetcar line makes transportation access to most parts of the city convenient. ✉ 555 Canal St., French Quarter, 70130 ☎ 504/581–1000 or 800/228-9290 ⎙ 504/523-6755 ⊕ www.neworleansmarriott.com ➘ 1,290 rooms, 54 suites ⚘ 3 restaurants, pool, health club, sauna, bar, lobby lounge, business services, meeting room, parking (fee) ▭ AE, D, DC, MC, V.

$-$$$$ ▦ **New Orleans Hilton Riverside.** This sprawling multilevel complex is smack on the Mississippi with superb river views. Guest rooms have French-provincial furnishings; the 180 rooms that share a concierge have fax machines. On Sunday the hotel's Kabby's Restaurant hosts a jazz brunch. The Riverfront streetcar stops out front. Adjacent to Riverwalk Shop-

New Orleans

Loyola St.
S. Rampart St.
University Pl.
Elk Pl.
Basin St.
N. Rampart St.
Perdido St.
O'Keefe St.
Penn St.
Baronne St.
Carroll St.
Union St.
Gravier St.
Common St.
Canal St.
Iberville St.
Bienville St.
Conti St.
St. Louis St.
Toulouse St.
Carondelet St.
Bourbon St.
Royal St.
Exchange Alley
Chartres St.
St. Charles Ave.
Commercial St.
Poydras St.
Camp St.
Natchez St.
North St.
Lafayette St.
Magazine St.
Constance St.
Tchoupitoulas St.
S. Peters St.
Dorsiere St.
Decatur St.
Clinton St.
N. Peters St.
Clay St.
N. Front St.
Commerce St.
Fulton St.
Girod St.
Wilk Row

Mississippi River

◆ Canal St.
Ferry Terminal

KEY
❶ What to See
① Where to Stay & Eat

SEE INSET

What to See ▼

Where to Eat ▼

Where to Stay ▼

ping Center and Aquarium of the Americas, and directly across the street from Harrah's New Orleans casino, the hotel has a resident golf pro and a 4-hole putting green. The recently remodeled health club is among the best in town. ⊠ *Poydras St. at the Mississippi River, CBD, 70140* ☎ *504/561–0500 or 800/445–8667* 🖷 *504/568–1721* ⊕ *www.hilton. com* ⟲ *1,600 rooms, 67 suites* ♨ *3 restaurants, Wi-Fi, putting green, 8 tennis courts, 2 pools, fitness classes, health club, hair salon, outdoor hot tub, massage, sauna, racquetball, squash, 7 lounges, business services, parking (fee), no-smoking floor* ▭ *AE, D, DC, MC, V.*

$$–$$$ 🏨 **Hilton Garden Inn New Orleans Convention Center.** The proximity to major attractions makes this hotel a popular draw for those who enjoy walking. Rooms are cheerfully appointed, and the private courtyard is one of the most charming in the area. Other comforts include a hot tub with a breathtaking view of the city skyline. ⊠ *1001 S. Peters St., Warehouse District, 70130* ☎ *504/525–0044* 🖷 *504/525–0035* ⊕ *www. neworleansconventioncenter.gardeninn.com* ⟲ *284 rooms* ♨ *Microwave, refrigerator, room TVs with movies and video games, in-room data ports, Wi-Fi, pool, gym, lounge, concierge, Internet room, business services* ▭ *AE, D, DC, MC, V.*

$–$$$ 🏨 **Ambassador Hotel.** Guest rooms at this hotel conveniently bordering the CBD and Warehouse District have real character. Four-poster iron beds, armoires, and local jazz prints are among the furnishings. Exposed brick walls, ceiling fans, and wood floors add to the ambience of the pre–Civil War building. This is a good alternative to huge convention hotels, but it's still just steps from all the major downtown attractions and the convention center. Bandito's Restaurant in the lobby level serves a tasty margarita and some stellar fajitas. ⊠ *535 Tchoupitoulas St., CBD, 70130* ☎ *504/527–5271 or 800/455–3417* 🖷 *504/599–2107* ⊕ *www. ahno.com* ⟲ *165 rooms* ♨ *Restaurant, lounge, meeting room, parking (fee)* ▭ *AE, D, DC, MC, V.*

Where to Eat

For price categories, *see* Dining at the beginning of this chapter.

$$$–$$$$ ✕ **Commander's Palace.** No restaurant captures New Orleans's gastronomic heritage and celebratory spirit as well as this one. The upstairs Garden Room's glass walls have marvelous views of the giant oak trees on the patio below, and other rooms promote conviviality with their bright pastels. The menu's classics include foie-gras-and-rabbit pie; a spicy and meaty turtle soup; terrific grilled veal chops with grits; and a wonderful sautéed gulf fish coated with crunchy pecans. Among the addictive desserts is the bread-pudding soufflé. Weekend brunches are less ambitious but also less costly. Jackets are preferred at dinner. ⊠ *1403 Washington Ave., Garden District* ☎ *504/899–8221* ♤ *Reservations essential* ▭ *AE, D, DC, MC, V.*

$$–$$$$ ✕ **Galatoire's.** Galatoire's has always epitomized the old-style French-creole bistro. Many of the recipes date to 1905. Fried oysters and bacon en brochette are worth every calorie, and the brick-red rémoulade sauce sets a high standard. Other winners include veal chops in béarnaise sauce, and seafood-stuffed eggplant. The setting downstairs is a single, narrow dining room lighted with glistening brass chandeliers; bentwood chairs and tables with white tablecloths add to its timelessness. You may reserve a table in the renovated upstairs rooms, though the action is on the first floor, where partying regulars inhibit conversation but provide good people-watching. ✉ *209 Bourbon St., French Quarter* ☎ *504/525–2021* 🎩 *Jacket required* 🚭 *AE, D, DC, MC, V* 🕙 *Closed Mon.*

$$–$$$ ✕ **Bayona.** "New World" is the label Louisiana native Susan Spicer applies to her cooking style, which results in such signature dishes as the goat-cheese crouton with mushrooms in Madeira cream, and crispy-fried smoked quail on a salad with bourbon-molasses vinaigrette. Vegetarian options include a farmers' market medley with cheddar spoon bread. These and other imaginative dishes are served in an early-19th-century creole cottage that fairly glows with flower arrangements, elegant photographs, and trompe l'oeil murals suggesting Mediterranean landscapes. Don't skimp on pastry chef Megan Roen's sweets, such as churros with chocolate mousse, and mint julep ice cream. ✉ *430 Dauphine St., French Quarter* ☎ *504/525–4455* 🍴 *Reservations essential* 🚭 *AE, DC, MC, V* 🕙 *Closed Sun. No lunch Sat.*

$$–$$$ ✕ **Herbsaint.** Upscale food and downscale prices are among Herbsaint's assets. Chef Donald Link turns out food that sparkles with robust flavors and top-grade ingredients. "Small plates" and side dishes such as charcuterie, a knock-'em-dead shrimp bisque, house-made pasta, and cheese- or nuts-studded salads are mainstays. More substantial appetites are courted with duck and dirty rice, rabbit fricassee, and pork belly. For dessert, the chocolate beignets filled with molten chocolate are deserving of love poems. The plates provide most of the color in the lighthearted, often noisy, rooms. The wine list is expertly compiled and reasonably priced. ✉ *701 St. Charles Ave., CBD* ☎ *504/524–4114* 🍴 *Reservations essential* 🚭 *AE, D, DC, MC, V* 🕙 *Closed Sun. No lunch Sat.*

¢–$$ ✕ **Central Grocery.** This old-fashioned Italian grocery store produces authentic muffulettas, one of the gastronomic gifts of the city's Italian immigrants. Good enough to challenge the po'boy as the local sandwich champs, they're made by filling round loaves of seeded bread with ham, salami, mozzarella, and a salad of marinated green olives. Each sandwich, about 10 inches in diameter, is sold in wholes and halves. You can eat your muffuletta at a counter, but some prefer to take theirs out to a bench on Jackson Square or the Moon Walk along the Mississippi riverfront. The Grocery closes at 5:30 PM. ✉ *923 Decatur St., French Quarter* ☎ *504/523–1620* 🚭 *D, MC, V.*

Shopping

The fun of shopping in New Orleans is in the regional items available throughout the city, in the smallest shops or the biggest department stores. You can take home some of the flavor of the city: its pralines (pecan candies), seafood (packaged to go), Louisiana red beans and rice, coffee (pure or with chicory), and creole and Cajun spices (cayenne pepper, chili, and garlic). There are even packaged mixes of such local favorites as jambalaya, gumbo, beignets, and the sweet red local cocktail called the Hurricane. Cookbooks also share the secrets of preparing distinctive New Orleans dishes. The French Quarter is well known for its fine antiques shops, located mainly on Royal and Chartres streets.

The main shopping areas in the city are the French Quarter, with its narrow streets lined with specialty, gift, and antiques shops and art galleries; the Central Business District (CBD), which has department stores and clothing, specialty, and jewelry shops; Magazine Street, known for its antiques shops and galleries; the Warehouse District, popular for Julia Street's contemporary arts galleries; and Uptown, with its neighborhood and specialty shops in several fashionable shopping areas.

Canal Place (✉ 333 Canal St., CBD ☎ 504/522–9200) draws fashionable shoppers to 60 shops that include Saks Fifth Avenue, Gucci, Williams-Sonoma, Pottery Barn, Laura Ashley, and Brooks Brothers. **Jax Brewery** (✉ 600 Decatur St., French Quarter ☎ 504/566–7245 ⊕ www. jacksonbrewery.com), a historic building that once was the factory for Jax beer, now is the anchor for three connected indoor malls with a mix of local shops and national chains. The Brewhouse, on Decatur Street across from Jackson Square, is home to a Virgin Megastore that is loaded with books and music and a number of other stores that sell locally inspired fashions and souvenirs. Adjacent to the Brewhouse, and connected by indoor and outdoor walkways, is the Millhouse. **New Orleans Centre** (✉ 1400 Poydras St., CBD ☎ 504/568–0000), a shopping complex between the Superdome and the Hyatt Regency hotel, houses Macy's and Lord & Taylor. **Riverwalk Marketplace** (✉ 1 Poydras St., Warehouse District ☎ 504/522–1555), along the riverfront, has a ½-mi-long marketplace with 180 local and nationally known shops and restaurants, including Café du Monde.

Nightlife

No American city places such a premium on pleasure as New Orleans. From the well-appointed lounges of swank hotels to raucous French Quarter bars and sweaty dance halls to funky dives and rocking clubs in far-flung neighborhoods, this city is serious about frivolity—and about its music.

Bars tend to open in the early afternoon and stay open into the morning hours; live music, though, follows a more restrained schedule. Some jazz spots and clubs in the French Quarter stage evening sets around 6 PM or 9 PM; at a few clubs, such as the Palm Court, the bands actually finish by 11 PM. But this is the exception: for the most part, gigs begin between 10 and 11 PM, and locals rarely emerge for an evening out before 10. Keep in mind that the lack of legal closing time means that shows advertised for 11 may not start until after midnight.

Commanding the foot of Canal Street, the beaux-arts-style **Harrah's New Orleans Casino** (✉ 4 Canal St., CBD ☎ 504/533–6000 or 800/427–7247 ⊕ www.harrahs.com) is the largest such facility in the South. Its 100,000 square feet hold 2,900 slots and 120 gaming tables. Valet parking is available.

Those partial to the cocktail, be it shaken or stirred, will appreciate the extensive selection of vodkas, single-malt scotches, ports, and cognacs at the **Bombay Club** (✉ 830 Conti St., French Quarter ☎ 504/586–0972), where the martinis approach high art. The plush, paneled interior creates a comfort zone for anyone nostalgic for the glory days of the British Empire. This bar in the Prince Conti Hotel features soft, live music nightly. This is one of the few places in the city that enforces a dress code, although it's not overly formal—no shorts, no jeans. The convivial **Crescent City Brewhouse** (✉ 527 Decatur St., French Quarter ☎ 504/522–0571) is known for its extensive menu of micro- and specialty brews; Abita Amber is a local favorite, but be sure to ask your server what's good—many of the selections are brewed on the premises. Live music is a dinnertime staple here. The river view from the second-floor balcony is worth a stop. **Pat O'Brien's** (✉ 718 St. Peter St., French Quarter ☎ 504/525–4823), one of the biggest tourist spots in town, is also the home of the oversize alcoholic beverage known as the Hurricane. Many people like to take their glass home as a souvenir; be wary of a deposit that is charged at the time of purchase and should be refunded if you don't take the glass with you. Actually five bars in one, Pat O's claims to sell more liquor than any other establishment in the world. The bar on the left through the entrance is popular with Quarterites, the patio in the rear draws the young (and young at heart) in temperate months, and the piano bar on the right side of the brick corridor packs in raucous celebrants year-round.

Across the street from the convention center, **Mulate's** (✉ 201 Julia St., Warehouse District ☎ 504/522–1492) seats 400, and the dance floor quickly fills with couples twirling and two-stepping to authentic Cajun bands. Regulars love to drag first-timers to the floor for impromptu lessons. The home-style Cajun cuisine is quite good, and the bands play until 10:30 or 11 PM. **Preservation Hall** (✉ 726 St. Peter St., French Quarter ☎ 504/522–2841 or 504/523–8939), the jazz tradition that flowered in the 1920s, is enshrined in this cultural landmark by a cadre of distinguished musicians, most of whom were schooled by an ever-dwindling group of elder statesmen who actually played with Louis Armstrong et al. There is limited seating on benches—many patrons end up squatting on the floor or standing in back—and no beverages are served or allowed. Nonetheless, legions of satisfied customers regard an evening here as an essential New Orleans experience. The original **Tipitina's** (✉ 501 Napoleon Ave., Uptown ☎ 504/895–8477) was founded in the mid-1970s as the home base for Professor Longhair, the pioneering rhythm-and-blues pianist and singer who died in 1980; the club takes its name from one of his most popular songs. A bust of "Fess" stands prominently near the front door; first-timers should place their hand upon his bald head upon entering, in a onetime homage. As the multitude of concert posters on the walls indicates, Tip's hosts a wide variety of local and global acts. For about a decade Bruce Daigrepont has played a weekly Cajun dance on Sunday 5 PM–9 PM; free red beans and rice are served.

Exploring New Orleans

The **French Quarter,** the oldest part of the city, lives up to all you've heard: it's alive with the sights, sounds, odors, and experiences of a major entertainment hub. At some point, ignore your better judgment and take a stroll down **Bourbon Street,** past the bars, restaurants, music clubs, and novelty shops that have given this strip its reputation as the playground of the South. Be sure to find time to stop at Café du Monde for chicory-laced coffee and beignets. With its beautifully landscaped gardens surrounding elegant antebellum homes, the **Garden District** is mostly residential, but most home owners do not mind your enjoying the sights from outside the cast-iron fences surrounding their magnificent properties.

🕐 ⓬ **Aquarium of the Americas.** In this marvelous family attraction more than 7,000 aquatic creatures swim in 60 displays ranging from 500 to 500,000 gallons of water. Each of the four major exhibit areas—the Amazon Rain Forest, the Caribbean Reef, the Mississippi River, and the Gulf Coast—has fish and animals native to that environment. A fun exhibit called Beyond Green houses more than 25 different frog species and includes informative displays. The aquarium's spectacular design allows you to feel part of the watery worlds by providing close-up encounters with the inhabitants. A gift shop and café are on the premises. You can get a combined ticket for the aquarium and the Audubon Zoo, including a round-trip cruise down the river. ✉ *1 Canal St., French Quarter* ☎ *504/ 581–4629 or 800/774–7394* ⊕ *www.auduboninstitute.org* ✉ *Aquarium $16; combination ticket with IMAX $20; combination ticket for aquarium, zoo, and round-trip cruise $38.25* ☉ *Aquarium: Sun.–Thurs. 9:30–6 (last ticket sold at 5), Fri. and Sat. 9:30–7 (last ticket sold at 6).*

❸ **Beauregard-Keyes House.** This stately 19th-century mansion with period furnishings was the temporary home of Confederate general P. G. T. Beauregard. The house and grounds had severely deteriorated by the 1940s, when the well-known novelist Frances Parkinson Keyes moved in and helped restore it. Her studio at the back of the large courtyard remains intact, complete with family photos, original manuscripts, and her doll and teapot collections. Keyes wrote 40 novels in this studio, all in longhand, among them the local favorite, *Dinner at Antoine's.* If you do not have time to tour the house, take a peek through the gates at the beautiful walled garden at the corner of Chartres and Ursulines streets, or enter the garden through the driveway alongside the house, where you will find the gate unlocked during open hours. Landscaped in the same sun pattern as Jackson Square, the garden is in bloom throughout the year. ✉ *1113 Chartres St., French Quarter* ☎ *504/523–7257* ✉ *$5* ☉ *Mon.–Sat. 10–3, tours on the hr.*

⓫ **Customs House.** From the time of its construction in 1849 until 2004, this massive building served as the customs house for the Port of New Orleans. It occupies an entire city block and replaces what had been Ft. St. Louis, which guarded the old French city. The building has identical entrances on all four sides, because at the time it was completed no decision had been made as to which side would be the main entrance. The building is currently closed for renovation, but in fall of 2005 it is scheduled to reopen as the home of the new **Audubon Insectarium,** planned to be the largest museum of its kind in the United States. Scheduled exhibits include displays of Louisiana swamp insects, prehistoric insect wonders, and even a cooking demonstration showcasing insect recipes from around the world. ✉ *423 Canal St., French Quarter.*

❿ **Garden District.** The Garden District is divided into two sections by Jackson Avenue. Upriver from Jackson is the wealthy **Upper Garden Dis-**

trict, where the homes are meticulously kept. Below Jackson, the **Lower Garden District** is considerably rougher. Though the homes here are often just as structurally beautiful, most of them lack the recent restorations of those of the Upper Garden District. The streets are also less well patrolled; wander cautiously. **Magazine Street,** lined with antiques shops and coffeehouses (ritzier along the Upper Garden District, hipper along the Lower Garden District), serves as a southern border to the Garden District. St. Charles Avenue forms the northern border, and the **St. Charles Avenue streetcar** is a convenient way to get here from downtown. Several companies offer walking tours.

❺ Gauche House. One of the most distinctive houses in the French Quarter, this mansion and its service buildings date from 1856. The cherub design of the effusive ironwork is the only one of its kind. It was once the estate of businessman John Gauche and is still privately owned. This house is not open to the public. ✉ *704 Esplanade Ave., French Quarter.*

❼ Hermann-Grima House. One of the largest and best-preserved examples of American architecture in the Quarter, this Georgian-style house has the only restored private stable and the only working 1830s creole kitchen in the Quarter. American architect William Brand built the house in 1831. Cooking demonstrations on the open hearth are held here all day Thursday from October through May. You'll want to check the gift shop, which has many local crafts and books. ✉ *820 St. Louis St., French Quarter* ☎ *504/525-5661* 💲 *$6, combination ticket with the Gallier House $10* ⊘ *Tours weekdays 10–4.*

❶ Jackson Square. Surrounded by historic buildings and filled with plenty of the city's atmospheric street life, the heart of the French Quarter is today a beautifully landscaped park. Originally called the Place d'Armes, the square was founded in 1718 as a military parade ground. It was also the site of public executions carried out in various styles, including burning at the stake, beheading, breaking on the wheel, and hanging. A **statue of Andrew Jackson,** victorious leader of the Battle of New Orleans in the War of 1812, commands the center of the square; the park was renamed for him in the 1850s. The words carved in the base on the cathedral side of the statue—"The Union must and shall be preserved"—are a lasting reminder of the federal troops who occupied New Orleans during the Civil War and who inscribed them.

Among the notable buildings around the square are **St. Louis Cathedral** and **Faulkner House.** Two Spanish colonial–style buildings, the **Cabildo** and the **Presbytère,** flank the cathedral. The handsome rows of brick apartments on each side of the square are the **Pontalba Buildings.** The park is landscaped in a sun pattern, with walkways set like rays streaming out from the center, a popular garden design in the royal court of King Louis XIV, the Sun King. In the daytime, dozens of artists hang their paintings on the park fence and set up outdoor studios where they work on canvases or offer to draw portraits of passersby. These artists are easy to engage in conversation and are knowledgeable about many aspects of the Quarter and New Orleans. You can also be entertained by musicians, mimes, tarot-card readers, and magicians who perform on the flagstone pedestrian mall surrounding the square, many of them day and night. ⊠ *French Quarter* ⊙ *Park daily 8–dusk; flagstone paths on park's periphery open 24 hrs.*

❻ Jean Lafitte National Park Visitor Center. This center has free visual and sound exhibits on the customs of various communities throughout the state, as well as information-rich daily history tours of the French Quarter. The one-hour tours leave at 9:30 AM and are free; tickets are handed out one per person (you must be present to get a ticket), beginning at 9 AM, for that day's tours only. Arrive at least 15 minutes before tour time to be sure of a spot. The office also supervises and provides information on Jean Lafitte National Park Barataria Unit across the river from New Orleans, and the Chalmette Battlefield, where the Battle of New Orleans was fought in the War of 1812. ⊠ *419 Decatur St., French Quarter* ☎ *504/589–2636* ⊙ *Daily 9–5.*

❾ Lafayette Cemetery No. 1. Begun around 1833, this was the first planned cemetery in the city, with symmetrical rows, roadways for funeral vehicles, and lavish aboveground vaults and tombs for the wealthy families who built the surrounding mansions. In 1852, 2,000 yellow fever victims were buried here. The cemetery and environs figure in Anne Rice's popular series *The Vampire Chronicles,* and movies such as *Interview with the Vampire* have used this walled cemetery for its eerie beauty. You can wander the grounds on your own or take an organized tour. One guided tour is arranged by **Save Our Cemeteries** (☎ 504/525–3377). ⊠ *1400 block of Washington Ave., Garden District* ☜ *Cemetery free, tour $6* ⊙ *Weekdays 7–2:30, Sat. 7–noon; tours Mon., Wed., Fri., and Sat. at 10:30.*

❹ Old Mint. Minting began in 1838 in this ambitious, Ionic structure, a project of President Andrew Jackson. The New Orleans mint was to provide currency for the South and the West, which it did until the Confederacy began minting its own currency here in 1861. When supplies ran out, the building served as a barracks, then a prison, for Confederate soldiers; the production of U.S. coins recommenced only in 1879. It stopped again, for good, in 1909. After years of neglect, the federal government handed the Old Mint over to Louisiana in 1966; the state now uses the quarters to exhibit collections of the Louisiana State Museum. The principal exhibit here is the **New Orleans Jazz Collection,** a brief but evocative tour through the history of traditional New Orleans jazz. In addition to informative written explanations, a wealth of artifacts movingly tells the story of the emergent art form. Among the gems are the soprano saxophone owned by Sidney Bechet, the trumpets of Pops Celestin and Dizzy Gillespie, and the cornet given to Louis Armstrong at the juvenile home where he spent much of his youth. Sheet music, biographies, personal effects, and photos round out the displays. Across the hall from the jazz exhibit are a few rooms filled with the beautiful and locally treasured Newcomb pottery. This school of pottery was developed by teachers and students at Newcomb Women's College in uptown New Orleans during the late 19th and early 20th centuries, and it subtly reflects the art-nouveau movement. The **Louisiana**

Historical Center, which holds the French and Spanish Louisiana archives, is open free to researchers by appointment. At the Barracks Street entrance, notice the one remaining sample of the mint's old walls—it'll give you an idea of the building's deterioration before its restoration. ⊠ *400 Esplanade Ave., French Quarter* ☎ *504/568–6968* 🖂 *$5* ◷ *Tues.–Sun. 9–5.*

❷ **St. Louis Cathedral.** The oldest active cathedral in the United States, this church at the heart of the Old City is named for the 13th-century French king who led two crusades. The current building, which replaced two former structures destroyed by fire, dates from 1794, although it was remodeled and enlarged in 1851. The austere interior is brightened by murals covering the ceiling and stained-glass windows along the first floor. A tour guide is on hand to answer questions and lead complete tours. ⊠ *615 Père Antoine Alley, French Quarter* ☎ *504/525–9585* 🖂 *Free* ◷ *Tours Mon.–Sat. 9–4:30, Sun. 1–4:30.*

❽ **St. Louis Cemetery No. 1.** New Orleans's "cities of the dead," with rows of crypts like little houses, are some of the city's most enduring images. This cemetery, the oldest in the city, is an example of the aboveground burial practices of the French and Spanish. Because of the high water table, it was difficult to bury bodies underground without having the coffin float to the surface after the first hard rain. Modern-day burial methods permit underground interment, but many people prefer these ornate family tombs and vaults, which have figured in several movies, among them *Easy Rider.* Buried here are such notables as Etienne Boré, father of the sugar industry; Homer Plessy of the *Plessy v. Ferguson* 1892 U.S. Supreme Court decision establishing the separate but equal "Jim Crow" laws for African-Americans and whites in the South (he was baptized and married in nearby St. Augustine Church); and Marie Laveau, voodoo queen. Her tomb is marked with Xs freshly chalked by those who still believe in her supernatural powers. **Save Our Cemeteries** leads tours every Sunday at 10 AM or by group appointment, departing from Royal Blend Coffee House at 621 Royal Street. Tickets are $12; reserve by Friday afternoon to be sure of a spot on the tour. ⊠ *Cemetery No. 1: Basin and Conti Sts., Tremé* ☎ *504/525–3377 for tour appointments (required)* ◷ *Mon.–Sat. 9–3, Sun. 9–noon.*

Sightseeing Tours

Several local tour companies give two- to four-hour city tours by bus that include the French Quarter, the Garden District, uptown New Orleans, and the lakefront. Prices range from $25 to $50 per person. Both Gray Line and New Orleans Tours offer a longer tour that combines a two-hour city tour by bus with a two-hour steamboat ride on the Mississippi River.

🗐 Tour Operators **Gray Line** ☎ 504/587-0861 or 800/535-7786 ⊕ www. graylineneworleans.com. **New Orleans Tours** ☎ 504/212-5925 or 866/596-2698 ⊕ www.notours.com. **Steppin' Out Tours** ☎ 888/557-7465 or 504/246-1006 ⊕ www. steppinouttours.com. **Tours by Isabelle** ☎ 504/391-3544 or 877/665-8687 ⊕ www. toursbyisabelle.com.

NEW YORK, NEW YORK

A few cruise lines now base Caribbean-bound ships in New York City year-round, though most of the market is made up of ships doing seasonal cruises to New England and Bermuda. If you're coming to the city from out of the immediate area, you can easily arrive the day before and do a bit of sightseeing and perhaps take in a Broadway show. The cruise port in Manhattan is fairly close to Times Square and Midtown hotels and theaters.

It's also now possible to leave from Cape Liberty Terminal in Bayonne, New Jersey, to cruise on a couple of Royal Caribbean ships. A new cruise-ship terminal will open in Brooklyn by late 2005 or early 2006.

The Cruise Port

The New York Passenger Ship Terminal is on the far west side of Manhattan, about five very long blocks from the Times Square area, between 48th and 52nd streets, but the vehicle entrance is at 55th Street. Traffic can be backed up in the area on days that cruise ships arrive and depart, so allow yourself enough time to check in and go through security. There are no nearby subway stops, though city buses do cross midtown at 50th and 42nd streets.

Cape Liberty Terminal in Bayonne is off Route 440. From the New Jersey Turnpike, take Exit 14A, then follow the signs for 440 South, and make a left turn into the Cape Liberty Terminal area (on Port Terminal Boulevard). If you are coming from Long Island, you cross Staten Island, and after crossing the Bayonne Bridge take 440 North, making a right into the terminal area. If you are coming from Manhattan, you can also reach the terminal on the New Jersey Transit light-rail line that connects to the PATH trains in Hoboken; get off at the Bayonne stop, and there will be a free shuttle bus to the terminal (about 3 mi [5 km] away) on sailing dates.

The forthcoming Brooklyn terminal in Red Hook will not be near subway lines, so you'll have to take a taxi. No further information was available at this writing.

🅵 **Cape Liberty Terminal** ✉ Off Rte. 440, Bayonne, NJ ☎ No phone. **New York Passenger Ship Terminal** ✉ 711 12th Ave., Midtown West, New York, NY ☎ 212/246-5450 ⊕ www.nypst.com.

AIRPORT TRANSFERS A cab from JFK to the passenger-ship terminal in Manhattan will cost $45 (a flat fare) plus toll and tip; expect to pay at least $35 on the meter if you are coming from LaGuardia and $45 or $50 from Newark.

From Newark Airport, it's approximately $35 to Cape Liberty, $65 from JFK (plus toll and tip), and $70 from La Guardia (plus toll and tip). Royal Caribbean offers free bus service from several Mid-Atlantic and Northeast cities.

PARKING You can park at the New York Passenger Ship Terminal for $24 a day; the fee is payable in advance in cash, traveler's checks, or by credit card (MasterCard and Visa only).

Parking at Cape Liberty Terminal in Bayonne is $12 per day, payable only in cash.

VISITOR INFORMATION 🏢 **NYC & Company Convention & Visitors Bureau** ✉ 810 7th Ave., between W. 52nd and W. 53rd Sts., 3rd fl., Midtown West ☎ 212/484–1222 ⊕ www.nycvisit.com. **Times Square Information Center** ✉ 1560 Broadway, between 46th and 47th Sts., Midtown West ☎ 212/768–1560 ⊕ www.timessquarenyc.org.

Where to Stay

There are no real bargains in the Manhattan hotel world, and you'll find it difficult to get a decent room for under $250. However, occasional weekend deals can be found. All the hotels we recommend for cruise passengers are in Midtown, on the west side, due to its relatively easy proximity to the cruise ship terminal.

For price categories, *see* Lodging at the beginning of this chapter.

$$$$ 🏨 **W Times Square.** Times Square finally goes hip on a grand scale with the opening of this super-sleek 57-floor monolith, the flagship of the white-hot W line. After passing through an entrance of cascading, glass-enclosed water, you alight to the seventh-floor lobby where Kenneth Cole–clad "welcome ambassadors" await. The Jetsons experience continues in the space-age, white-on-white lobby and the futuristic rooms with their glowing resin boxes and multiple shades of gray. The bi-level Blue Fin restaurant with its sushi bar and floor-to-ceiling windows caps the architectural wonderment. ✉ *1567 Broadway, at W. 47th St., Midtown West, 10036* ☎ *212/930–7400 or 877/946–8357* 🖷 *212/930–7500* ⊕ *www.whotels.com* 🛏 *466 rooms, 43 suites* ⚐ *Restaurant, café, room service, in-room safes, minibars, cable TV with movies, in-room DVDs, in-room data ports, exercise equipment, gym, massage, 4 bars, shop, dry cleaning, laundry service, concierge, Internet room, business services, parking (fee), some pets allowed (fee), no-smoking rooms, no-smoking floors* ☰ *AE, D, DC, MC, V* Ⓜ *Subway: 1, 2, 3, 7, S, N, Q, R, W to 42nd St./Times Sq.*

$$$$ 🏨 **Westin New York at Times Square.** The Westin changed the skyline of midtown with this soaring skyscraper that subtly mimics the flow of the city—look for subway patterns in the carpets and the city reflected on the building's exterior. A thoughtful staff helps make the cavernous lobby and throngs of guests tolerable. Exceptionally large rooms are blissfully quiet and built to give you optimal views—especially the light-filled corner rooms. The much-noted Heavenly Bed and double showerheads are indeed praiseworthy, but for even more comfort, spa-floor rooms come with massage chairs, aromatherapy candles, and other pampering pleasures. ✉ *270 W. 43rd St., at 8th Ave., Midtown West, 10036* ☎ *212/201–2700 or 866/837–4183* 🖷 *212/201–2701* ⊕ *www.westinny.com* 🛏 *737 rooms, 126 suites* ⚐ *Restaurant, café, room service, in-room fax, in-room safes, minibars, cable TV with movies, in-room data ports, Wi-Fi, gym, health club, massage, spa, 2 bars, babysitting, dry cleaning, laundry service, concierge, business services, meeting rooms, parking (fee), some pets allowed, no-smoking rooms, no-smoking floors.* ☰ *AE, D, DC, MC, V* Ⓜ *Subway: A, C, E to 42nd St./Times Sq.*

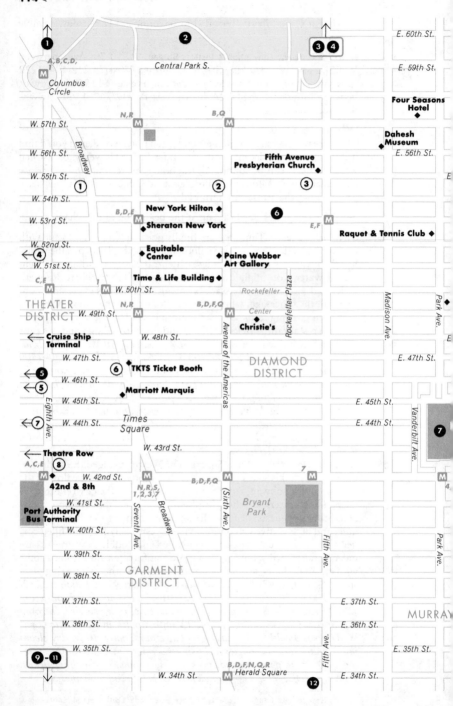

1

A,B,C,D,1 Ⓜ
Columbus
Circle

Central Park S.

E. 60th St.

3 **4**

E. 59th St.

N,R Ⓜ   B,Q Ⓜ

W. 57th St.

**Four Seasons
Hotel** ◆

W. 56th St.

**Dahesh
Museum** ◆

E. 56th St.

W. 55th St.

① **2** **3**

**Fifth Avenue
Presbyterian Church** ◆

Broadway

W. 54th St.

New York Hilton ◆

W. 53rd St.

B,D,E Ⓜ

6 ◆

Sheraton New York ◆

E,F Ⓜ

Raquet & Tennis Club ◆

W. 52nd St.

←**4**

**Equitable
Center** ◆

W. 51st St.

◆ **Paine Webber
Art Gallery**

C,E

Time & Life Building ◆

Ⓜ W. 50th St.

Rockefeller Plaza

Madison Ave.

Park Ave.

**THEATER
DISTRICT**   W. 49th St.

N,R Ⓜ   B,D,F,Q Ⓜ

Rockefeller
Center

← **Cruise Ship
Terminal**

W. 48th St.

◆ **Christie's**

**DIAMOND
DISTRICT**

E. 47th St.

W. 47th St.

Avenue of the Americas

←**5**

6 ◆ **TKTS Ticket Booth**

←**5**

W. 46th St.

Eighth Ave.

◆ **Marriott Marquis**

W. 45th St.

E. 45th St.

Vanderbilt Ave.

←**7**

W. 44th St.

*Times
Square*

E. 44th St.

7

W. 43rd St.

← **Theatre Row**

A,C,E **8**

Ⓜ ◆   W. 42nd St.

42nd & 8th

Ⓜ

N,R,S,
1,2,3,7

Ⓜ B,D,F,Q

7

Ⓜ

Ⓜ

Seventh Ave.

Broadway

(Sixth Ave.)

Fifth Ave.

Park Ave.

W. 41st St.

**Port Authority
Bus Terminal**

*Bryant
Park*

W. 40th St.

W. 39th St.

**GARMENT
DISTRICT**

W. 38th St.

W. 37th St.

E. 37th St.

W. 36th St.

E. 36th St.

MURRAY

9 – 11

W. 35th St.

E. 35th St.

↓

B,D,F,N,Q,R
Ⓜ *Herald Square*

W. 34th St.

12

E. 34th St.

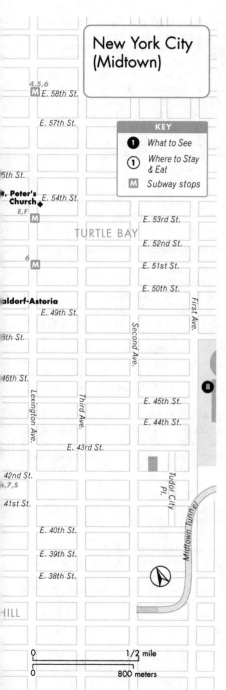

What to See ▼

American Museum of
Natural History 1

Central Park 2

Empire State Building ...12

Frick Collection 3

Grand Central Terminal ...7

Intrepid Sea-Air-Space
Museum 5

Metropolitan Museum
of Art 4

Museum of
Jewish Heritage 10

Museum of Modern Art ...6

Staten Island Ferry 9

Statue of Liberty
& Ellis Island 11

United Nations
Headquarters 8

Where to Eat ▼

Becco 5

Carnegie Deli 2

Island Burgers
and Shakes 4

Marseille 7

Osteria del Circo 3

Where to Stay ▼

Ameritania Hotel 1

W Times Square 6

Westin New York
at Times Square 8

$$$ 🖼 **Ameritania Hotel.** Guests at this busy crash pad just off Broadway are divided pretty evenly: half come for business, half for pleasure. Dimly lighted hallways create a feeling of perpetual nighttime—an impression that lingers in the bedrooms, where black metal furniture dominates. Rates may drop by as much as $100 a night off-season, depending on occupancy. ⊠ *230 W. 54th St., at Broadway, Midtown West, 10019* 🕾 *212/247–5000 or 888/664–6835* 🖷 *212/247–3316* ⊕ *www.nychotels. com/ameritania.html* ⤏ *207 rooms, 12 suites* ⌂ *Room service, some in-room safes, cable TV with movies, in-room data ports, bar, dry cleaning, laundry service, concierge, business services, parking (fee), no-smoking rooms* ⊟ *AE, D, DC, MC, V* ⍾⃝| *CP* Ⓜ *Subway: B, D, E to 7th Ave.*

Where to Eat

The restaurants we recommend below are all in Midtown West, near Broadway theaters and hotels. Make reservations at all but the most casual places or face a numbing wait.

For price categories, *see* Dining at the beginning of this chapter.

$$$–$$$$ ╳ **Osteria del Circo.** Opened by the sons of celebrity restaurateur Sirio Maccioni (Le Cirque 2000), this less-formal restaurant celebrates the Tuscan cooking of their Mamma Egi. The contemporary menu offers a wide selection and includes some traditional Tuscan specialties, such as Egi's ricotta-and-spinach-filled ravioli, tossed in butter and sage and gratinéed with imported Parmesan, and a stew of prawns, cuttlefish, octopus, monkfish, clams, and mussels. Don't miss the fanciful Circo desserts, especially the filled *bomboloncini* doughnuts. ⊠ *120 W. 55th St., between 6th and 7th Aves., Midtown West* 🕾 *212/265–3636* ⌂ *Reservations essential* ⊟ *AE, DC, MC, V* ⊙ *No lunch Sun.* Ⓜ *Subway: F, N, R, Q, W to 57th St.*

$$–$$$ ╳ **Becco.** An ingenious concept makes Becco a prime Restaurant Row choice for time-constrained theatergoers. There are two pricing scenarios: one includes an all-you-can-eat selection of antipasti and three pastas served hot out of pans that waiters circulate around the dining room; the other adds a generous entrée. The selection changes daily but often includes gnocchi, fresh ravioli, and something in a cream sauce. The entrées include braised veal shank, rack of lamb, and various fish. ⊠ *355 W. 46th St., between 8th and 9th Aves., Midtown West* 🕾 *212/397–7597* ⌂ *Reservations essential* ⊟ *AE, DC, MC, V* Ⓜ *Subway: A, C, E to 42nd St.*

$–$$$ ╳ **Marseille.** A fetching brasserie outfitted with dark cherry leather banquettes beautifully showcases the soulful Mediterranean/North African cooking of Andy D'Amico. Begin with mezes (think tapas), like juicy merguez sausages or white anchovies rolled into pinwheels with piquillo peppers. Grilled octopus is deeply flavored, and bouillabaisse is classically prepared, with four North Atlantic fillets and a nice garlicky rouille on the side. Service is skillful. The place is often mobbed before and after theater, usually restful from 8 to 10:30, but always intensely delicious. ⊠ *630 9th Ave., at W. 44th St., Midtown West* 🕾 *212/333–3410* ⌂ *Reservations essential* ⊟ *AE, D, MC, V* Ⓜ *Subway: A, C, E to 42nd St.*

$–$$ ✕**Carnegie Deli.** Although not what it once was, this no-nonsense deli is still a favorite with out-of-towners. The portions are so huge you feel like a child in some surreal culinary fairy tale. The matzo balls could eat Chicago, the knishes hang off the edge of the plates, and some combination sandwiches are so tall they have to be held together with bamboo skewers. Don't miss the cheesecake, to our palates the best (and, of course, biggest) in the city. ⊠ *854 7th Ave., at W. 55th St., Midtown West* ☎ *212/757–2245* ▭ *No credit cards* Ⓜ *Subway: B, D, C, E to 7th Ave.; N, R, Q, W to 57th St.*

¢–$ ✕**Island Burgers and Shakes.** Belly-busting burgers rule at this bright and cheery café with multicolor round tables and funky chairs. Every sandwich can be ordered with grilled chicken instead of the usual beef patty, but true believers stick to the real thing and choose from a staggering variety of toppings. If you're in the mood for even more calories, the tempting selection of shakes is extremely difficult to resist. The only drawback is that there are no french fries—you'll have to settle for "dirty potato chips." ⊠ *766 9th Ave., between W. 51st and W. 52nd Sts., Midtown West* ☎ *212/307–7934* ▭ *No credit cards* Ⓜ *Subway: C, E to 50th St.*

Shopping

You can find almost any major store from virtually any designer or chain in Manhattan. High-end designers tend to be along **Madison Avenue,** between 55th and 86th streets. Some are along **57th Street,** between Madison and 7th avenues. **Fifth Avenue,** starting at Saks Fifth Avenue (at 50th Street) and going up to 59th Street, is a hodgepodge of high-end stores and more accessible options, including the high-end department store Bergdorf-Goodman, at 58th Street. More interesting and individual stores can be found in **SoHo** (between Houston and Canal, West Broadway and Lafayette), the **East Village** (between 14th Street and Houston, Broadway and Avenue A). **Chinatown** is chock-full of designer knock-offs, crowded streets, and dim sum palaces; though frenetic during the day, it's a fun stop. The newest group of stores in Manhattan is at the **Time-Warner Center,** at Columbus Circle (at 8th Avenue and 59th Street); the high-rise mall has upscale stores and some of the city's best-reviewed and most expensive new restaurants.

Broadway Shows

Scoring tickets to Broadway shows is fairly easy except for the very top draws. The only way to ensure you will get the seats you want, on the day that you want, at the price you want, is to purchase tickets in advance—and that might be months ahead for a hit show. In general, you'll find that tickets are more readily available for evening performances from Tuesday through Thursday and matinees on Wednesday. Tickets for Friday and Saturday evenings and for weekend matinees are tougher to secure. For the most part, the top ticket price for Broadway musicals is about $110; the best seats for Broadway plays can run as high as $90.

For Broadway shows, off-Broadway shows, and other big-ticket events, you can order tickets well in advance through several agencies. You can also purchase tickets (even for same-day performances) at the theater box office, without any commission at all. Though these tickets aren't discounted, you won't have to pay the high fees the agencies charge. **Telecharge** (☎212/239–6200 ⊕ www.telecharge.com) sells tickets to most Broadway shows. **Ticketmaster** (☎212/307–4100 ⊕www.ticketmaster.com) sells a lot of Broadway tickets, but probably runs second to Telecharge.

For tickets at 25% to 50% off the usual price, head to **TKTS** (✉ Duffy Sq., W. 47th St. and Broadway, Midtown West Ⓜ Subway: N, R, W to 49th St.; 1 to 50th St. ✉ South St. Seaport at Front and John Sts., Lower Manhattan Ⓜ Subway: 2, 3 to Fulton St.). Run by the Theatre Development Fund, TKTS operates kiosks in Times Square and at the South Street Seaport. There's usually a good selection of shows available, but don't expect to see the latest hits. The kiosks accept cash and traveler's checks—no credit cards. The Times Square location is open Monday–Saturday 3–8 and Sunday 11–7:30, as well as Wednesday and Saturday at 10–2 for matinee shows. South Street Seaport hours are Monday–Saturday 11–6 and Sunday 11–3:30.

Top Attractions

There's no way to do justice to even the most popular tourist stops in New York in just a single day. Below is information about several top attractions. If you have only a day in the city, choose one or two attractions and buy a daily unlimited subway pass to get around.

❶ American Museum of Natural History. With 45 exhibition halls and more than 32 million artifacts and specimens, the world's largest and most important museum of natural history can easily occupy you for half a day. The dioramas might seem dated but are fun. The dinosaur exhibits are probably the highlight. Attached to the museum is the **Rose Center for Earth and Space** with various exhibits and housing the **Hayden Planetarium** and an **IMAX Theater.** ✉ *Central Park W at W. 79th St., Upper West Side* ☎ *212/769–5200* ⊕ *www.amnh.org* ✉ *$13 suggested donation, includes admission to Rose Center; museum and planetarium show combination ticket $22. Prices may vary for special exhibitions* ☼ *Daily 10–5:45* Ⓜ *Subway: B, C to 81st St.*

❷ Central Park. Without the Central Park's 843 acres of meandering paths, tranquil lakes, ponds, and open meadows, New Yorkers might be a lot less sane. You can drop by the zoo (near 64th Street, on the east side) or the famous Bethesda Fountain (mid-park, at around 72nd Street), but the main draw is just to wander the lanes. Central Park has one of the lowest crime rates in the city. Still, use common sense and stay within sight of other park visitors, and don't go into the park after dark. Directions, park maps, and event calendars can be obtained from volunteers at two 5th Avenue **information booths**, at East 60th Street and East 72nd Street. ☎ *212/408–0266 for schedule of park events, 212/360–2727 for schedule of walking tours* ⊕ *www.nycgovparks.org* Ⓜ *Subway: A, C or 1 to Columbus Circle.*

☾ ⓬ Empire State Building. It's no longer the world's tallest building (it currently ranks seventh), but it's one of the world's most recognizable landmarks, and still worth a visit. Its pencil-slim silhouette is an art-deco monument to progress, a symbol for New York City, and a star in some great romantic scenes, on and off-screen. Be prepared for long lines. The view late at night is sometimes more enchanting on a clear evening than during the day. Morning is the least crowded time. Unfortunately, the view is now horrendously overpriced. ⊠ *350 5th Ave., at E. 34th St., Murray Hill* ☎ *212/736–3100 or 877/692–8439* ⊕ *www.esbnyc.com* ☒ *$14* ◷ *Daily 9:30 AM–midnight; last elevator up leaves at 11:15 PM* Ⓜ *Subway: B, D, F, N, Q, R, V, W to 34th St./Herald Sq.*

❸ **Frick Collection.** Coke-and-steel baron Henry Clay Frick (1849–1919) amassed this superb art collection far from the soot and smoke of Pittsburgh, where he made his fortune. The mansion was designed by Thomas Hastings and built in 1913–14. It opened in 1935, but still resembles a gracious private home, albeit one with bona fide masterpieces in almost every room. This is the best small museum in town by a mile. ⊠ *1 E. 70th St., at 5th Ave., Upper East Side* ☎ *212/288–0700* ⊕ *www.frick. org* ☒ *$12* ☞ *Children under 10 not admitted; those under 16 must be accompanied by an adult* ◷ *Tues.–Thurs. 10–6, Fri. 10–9, Sat. 10–6, Sun. 1–6* Ⓜ *Subway: 6 to 68th St./Hunter College.*

❼ **Grand Central Terminal.** Grand Central is not only the world's largest railway station (76 acres) and the nation's busiest (500,000 commuters and subway riders use it daily), it's also one of the world's greatest public spaces, "justly famous," as critic Tony Hiss has said, "as a crossroads, a noble building . . . and an ingenious piece of engineering." A massive four-year renovation completed in October 1998 restored the 1913 landmark to its original splendor—and then some. *Main entrance* ⊠ *E. 42nd St. at Park Ave., Midtown East* ☎ *212/935–3960* ⊕ *www.grandcentralterminal. com* Ⓜ *Subway: 4, 5, 6, 7, S to 42nd St./Grand Central.*

❺ *Intrepid* **Sea-Air-Space Museum.** Formerly the USS *Intrepid,* this 900-foot aircraft carrier is serving out its retirement as the centerpiece of Manhattan's only floating museum. Best of all, it's within easy walking distance of all the passenger-ship piers. An A-12 Blackbird spy plane, a Concorde, lunar landing modules, helicopters, seaplanes, and two dozen other aircraft are on deck. Docked alongside, and also part of the museum, are the *Growler,* a strategic-missile submarine; the *Edson,* a Vietnam-era destroyer; and several other battle-scarred naval veterans. Children can explore the ships' skinny hallways and winding staircases, as well as manipulating countless knobs, buttons, and wheels. For an extra thrill (and an extra $8), they can try the Navy Flight Simulator and "land" an aircraft on board. ⊠ *Hudson River, Pier 86, 12th Ave. and W. 46th St., Midtown West* ☎ *212/245–0072* ⊕ *www.intrepidmuseum.org* ☒ *$17, free to active U.S. military personnel* ◷ *Apr.–Sept., weekdays 10–5, weekends 10–6; Oct.–Mar., Tues.–Sun. 10–5; last admission 1 hr before closing* Ⓜ *Subway: A, C, E to 42nd St.; M42 bus to pier.*

❹ **Metropolitan Museum of Art.** One of the world's greatest museums, the Met is also the largest art museum in the western hemisphere—spanning four blocks and encompassing 2 million square feet. Its permanent collection of nearly 3 million works of art from all over the world includes objects from the Paleolithic era to modern times. There's something for everyone here, but it's a bit overwhelming, so don't even try to see it all. ⊠ *5th Ave. at 82nd St., Upper East Side* ☎ *212/535–7710* ⊕ *www.metmuseum.org* ✉ *$15 suggested donation* ☉ *Tues.–Thurs. and Sun. 9:30–5:30, Fri. and Sat. 9:30–9* Ⓜ *Subway: 4, 5, 6 to 86th St.*

🔟 **Museum of Jewish Heritage—A Living Memorial to the Holocaust.** In a granite hexagon rising 85 feet above Robert F. Wagner Jr. Park at the southern end of Battery Park City, this museum pays tribute to the 6 million Jews who perished in the Holocaust. It's one of the best such museums in the country. ⊠ *36 Battery Pl., Battery Park City, Lower Manhattan* ☎ *646/437–4200* ⊕ *www.mjhnyc.org* ✉ *$10* ☉ *Thurs. and Sun.–Tues. 10–5:45; Wed. 10–8; Fri. and eve of Jewish holidays 10–3* Ⓜ *Subway: 4, 5 to Bowling Green.*

⑥ Museum of Modern Art (MoMA). The masterpieces—Monet's *Water Lilies,* Picasso's *Les Demoiselles d'Avignon,* Van Gogh's *Starry Night*—are still here, but for now the main draw at MoMA is, well, MoMA. A "modernist dream world" is how critics described the museum after its $425 million face-lift. Unfortunately, the museum was an instant success, which means lines are sometimes down the block. For the shortest wait, get here before the museum opens. Be prepared for sticker shock when you buy your ticket. ⊠ *11 W. 53rd St., between 5th and 6th Aves., Midtown East* ☎ *212/708–9400* ⊕ *www.moma.org* ✉ *$20* ☉ *Sat.–Mon. Wed., and Thurs. 10:30–5:30; Fri. 10:30–8* Ⓜ *Subway: E, V to 5th Ave./53rd St.; B, D, E to 7th Ave.; B, D, F, V to 47th–50th Sts./Rockefeller Center.*

⑨ Staten Island Ferry. The best transit deal in town is the Staten Island Ferry, a free 20- to 30-minute ride across New York Harbor providing great views of the Manhattan skyline, the Statue of Liberty, the Verrazano-Narrows Bridge, and the New Jersey coast. Ferries embark on various schedules: every 15 minutes during rush hours, every 20–30 minutes most other times, and every hour on weekend nights and mornings. If you can manage it, catch one of the older blue-and-orange ferries, which have outside decks. ⊠ *State and South Sts., Lower Manhattan* ☎ *718/390–5253* Ⓜ *Subway: 4, 5 to Bowling Green; 1 to South Ferry.*

⑪ Statue of Liberty & Ellis Island. Though you must endure a long wait and onerous security, it's worth the trouble to see one of the iconic images of New York. But the truth is there's not much to see in the statue itself. You can no longer climb up to the crown, just view the inside from the base. There's a small museum on-site. Much more interesting—and well worth exploring—is the Ellis Island museum, which traces the story of immigration in New York City with moving exhibits throughout the restored processing building. Other parts of the island are still ruins. Make reservations and go early if you want to see everything. The ferry stops first at the statue and then continues to Ellis Island. ⊠ *Castle Clinton, Battery Park, Lower Manhattan* ☎ *212/363–3200 for park service, 212/269–5755 for ferry information, 866/782–8834 for ticket reservations, 212/363–3200 for Ellis Island, 212/883–1986 for Wall of Honor information* ⊕ *www.nps.gov/stli, www.statuereservations.com for reservations* ✉ *Free, ferry $10 round-trip* ☉ *Daily 8:30–5; extended hrs in summer* Ⓜ *Subway: 5 to Bowling Green; 1 to South Ferry; or W to Whitehall.*

8 **United Nations Headquarters.** Officially an "international zone," not part of the United States, the U.N. Headquarters is a working symbol of global cooperation. A 45-minute-long guided tour (given in 20 languages) is the main attraction; it includes the **General Assembly,** the **Security Council Chamber,** the **Trustee Council Chamber,** and the **Economic and Social Council Chamber,** though some rooms may be closed on any given day. *Visitor entrance* ⊠ *1st Ave. and E. 46th St., Midtown East* ☎ *212/963–8687* ⊕ *www.un.org* 🎫 *Tour $11.50* 🍼 *Children under 5 not admitted* ⏱ *Tours weekdays 9:30–4:45, weekends 10–4:30 (no weekend tours Jan. and Feb.); tours in English leave General Assembly lobby every 30 mins* Ⓜ *Subway: 4, 5, 6, 7 to 42nd St./Grand Central.*

PORT CANAVERAL, FLORIDA

Port Canaveral is located at the top of the barrier island that includes Cocoa Beach, sister to the town of Cocoa, on the mainland. Cocoa Beach is a popular year-round escape for Central Floridians, and it's just 10 minutes from the Kennedy Space Center. It's a busy port, by some accounts even busier than Port Everglades in Fort Lauderdale, and the embarkation point for many three- and four-day cruises to the Bahamas, as well as a few seven-day cruises. Many cruisers combine a short cruise with a stay at one of Orlando's popular theme parks, which are about an hour away.

The Cruise Port

Port Canaveral has six cruise terminals and is the home port of the two Disney Cruise Line ships. Carnival and Royal Caribbean also base ships here, as do some smaller lines.

In Brevard County, Port Canaveral is on State Road (S.R.) 528, also known as the Beeline Expressway, which runs straight to Orlando, which has the nearest airport. To drive to Port Canaveral from there, take the north exit out of the airport, staying to the right, to S.R. 528 (Beeline Expressway) East. Take S.R. 528 directly to Port Canaveral; it's about a 45-minute drive.

🏳 **Canaveral Port Authority** ⊠ 9150 Christopher Columbus Dr., Cape Canaveral ☎ 321/783-7831 or 888/767-8226 ⊕ www.portcanaveral.org.

AIRPORT TRANSFERS The Orlando airport is 45 minutes away from the docks. If you have not arranged airport transfers with your cruise line, then you will need to make your own arrangements. Taxis are expensive, but many companies offer minivan and bus shuttles to Port Canaveral. They are all listed on the Canaveral Port Authority Web site. For example, you can rent an entire van from Art's Shuttle for your group (about $55 for up to three people and then $10 for each additional person). Other shuttle services include Busy Traveler Transport Service and Blue Dolphin Shuttle Lines. Some shuttles will charge a per-person rate, which can be cheaper if you are just a couple. Expect to pay at least $20 per person. But you will need to make a reservation in advance regardless of which service you use.

🏳 **Art's Shuttle** ☎ 371/783-2112 or 800/567-5099 ⊕ www.artsshuttle.com. **Blue Dolphin Shuttle Lines** ☎ 321/433-0011 or 888/361-0155 ⊕ www.gobluedolphin.com. **Busy Traveler Transport Service** ☎ 321/453-5278 or 800/496-7433 ⊕ www.abusytraveler.com.

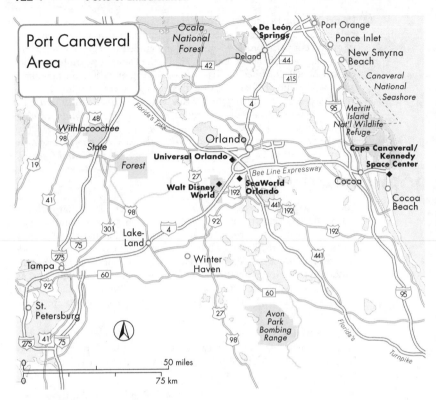

Port Canaveral Area

Ocala National Forest
De León Springs
Port Orange
Ponce Inlet
Deland
New Smyrna Beach
Canaveral National Seashore
Merritt Island Nat'l Wildlife Refuge
Withlacoochee State Forest
Orlando
Universal Orlando
Cape Canaveral/ Kennedy Space Center
Bee Line Expressway
SeaWorld Orlando
Cocoa
Walt Disney World
Cocoa Beach
Lake-Land
Tampa
Winter Haven
St. Petersburg
Avon Park Bombing Range
Florida's Turnpike

50 miles
75 km

PARKING Outdoor, gated lots and a six-story parking garage are near the termi-nals and cost $10 a day, which must be paid in advance, either in cash or by major credit card (MasterCard and Visa only).

VISITOR
INFORMATION 🔖 **Cocoa Beach Area Chamber of Commerce** ⊠ 400 Fortenberry Rd., Merritt Island 32952 ☎ 321/459–2200 ⊕ www.cocoabeachchamber.com.

Where to Stay

Many local hotels offer cruise packages that include one night's lodg-ing, parking for the duration of your cruise, and transportation to the cruise port.

For price categories, *see* Lodging at the beginning of this chapter.

$$–$$$$ 🏨 **Inn at Cocoa Beach.** One of the area's best, this charming oceanfront inn has spacious, individually decorated rooms with four-poster beds, upholstered chairs, and balconies or patios; most have ocean views. Deluxe rooms are much larger, with a king-size bed, sofa, and sitting area; most also have a dining table. Jacuzzi rooms are different sizes; several have fireplaces, and all have beautiful ocean views. Included in the rate are evening wine and cheese and a sumptuous Continental breakfast. ⊠ 4300 Ocean Beach Blvd., 32931 ☎ 321/799–3460, 800/343–5307

outside Florida ⊟ *321/784–8632* ⊕ *www.theinnatcocoabeach.com*
▭ *50 rooms* ⚭ *Dining room, in-room safes, some in-room hot tubs,
cable TV, in-room VCRs, pool, exercise equipment, gym, massage,
beach, bicycles, shuffleboard, dry cleaning, meeting rooms, free parking* ▭ *AE, D, MC, V* ⊙ *BP.*

$–$$$ 🏨 **Cocoa Beach Hilton Oceanfront.** At seven stories, this is one of the tallest
buildings in Cocoa Beach as well as one of the best hotels. Dense nat-
ural foliage separates the property from the roadway. Rooms are com-
fortably but not lavishly furnished. Most have ocean views, but for true
drama get a room on the east end, facing the water. The hotel's best fea-
ture is its location, right on the beach. In season, a band plays reggae
music poolside on weekends. ✉ *1550 N. Atlantic Ave., 32931* ☎ *321/
799–0003* ⊟ *321/799–0344* ⊕ *www.cocoabeachhilton.com* ▭ *296
rooms, 11 suites* ⚭ *2 restaurants, room service, cable TV with movies
and video games, in-room data ports, pool, exercise equipment, beach,
volleyball, bar, video game room, dry cleaning, laundry facilities, Internet
room, meeting rooms, free parking, no-smoking rooms* ▭ *AE, D, DC,
MC, V.*

$–$$$ 🏨 **Wakulla Suites Resort.** This two-story motel is clean and comfortable
and just off the beach. Some rooms are a block away from the water,
and a few are just a walk down the boardwalk. The bright rooms are
fairly ordinary, decorated in tropical prints. Completely furnished five-
room suites, designed to sleep six, are great for families; each includes
two bedrooms and a living room, dining room, and fully equipped
kitchen. ✉ *3550 N. Atlantic Ave., 32931* ☎ *321/783–2230 or 800/992–
5852* ⊟ *321/783–0980* ⊕ *www.wakulla-suites.com* ▭ *116 suites*
⚭ *Restaurant, kitchens, cable TV with movies, pool, shuffleboard, dry
cleaning, laundry facilities, business services, free parking, no-smoking
rooms* ▭ *AE, D, DC, MC, V.*

Where to Eat

For price categories, *see* Dining at the beginning of this chapter.

$$–$$$$ ✕ **Mango Tree Restaurant.** Candles, fresh flowers, and rattan basket
chairs set a romantic mood in the intimate dining room, designed to evoke
the feel of a South Pacific plantation. *Lobsterocki* (Maine lobster
wrapped in bacon with teriyaki cream sauce), baked Brie, or rare seared
tuna are good appetizer choices. For a main course, try Indian River crab
cakes, coq au vin, or veal française (scaloppine with mushroom sauce).
✉ *118 N. Atlantic Ave.* ☎ *321/799–0513* ▭ *AE, MC, V* ⊙ *Closed Mon.
No lunch.*

$–$$ ✕ **Atlantic Ocean Grille.** Jutting 500 feet out over the ocean on Cocoa
Beach Pier, this casual seafood restaurant has floor-to-ceiling windows
that overlook the water. Among the excellent fresh-fish options are
mahimahi and grouper, which you can order broiled, blackened, grilled,
or fried. ✉ *401 Meade Ave., Cocoa Beach Pier* ☎ *321/783–7549*
▭ *AE, D, DC, MC, V* ⊙ *No lunch.*

¢–$$ ✕ **Fischer's Bar and Grill.** This casual eatery, owned by the same family
that runs the more upscale Bernard's Surf, is a perfect spot for winding
down after a tough day at the beach. Although complete dinners are
available, people tend to come for the salads, pasta, burgers, and plat-

ters of tasty fried shrimp. The family's fleet of fishing boats brings in fresh seafood daily. Happy hour is from 4 to 7. ✉ *2 S. Atlantic Ave.* ☎ *321/783–2401* ▭ *AE, D, MC, V.*

Beaches

After crossing a long and high bridge just east of Cocoa Village, you'll be dropped down upon a barrier island. A few miles farther and you'll reach the Atlantic Ocean and picture-perfect **Cocoa Beach** at Route A1A. This is one of the Space Coast's nicest beaches, with many wide stretches that are excellent for biking, jogging, power walking, or strolling. In some places there are dressing rooms, showers, playgrounds, picnic areas with grills, snack shops, and surf-side parking lots. Beach vendors offer necessities, and guards are on duty in summer. Cocoa Beach is considered the capital of Florida's surfing community. North of Cocoa, **Playalinda Beach** (✉ Rte. 402, Titusville ☎ 321/267–1110), part of the **Canaveral National Seashore,** is the longest undeveloped stretch on Florida's Atlantic coast—hundreds of giant sea turtles come ashore here between May and August to lay their eggs. The park's extreme northern area is favored by nude sunbathers. There are no lifeguards, but park rangers patrol. Take Exit 80 from I–95 and follow Route 406 east across the Indian River, then Route 402 east for another 12 mi. It's open daily from 6 to 6, and admission is $5 per vehicle. **Sydney Fisher Park at Cocoa Beach** (✉ 2100 block of Rte. A1A) has showers, playgrounds, changing areas, picnic areas with grills, snack shops, and plenty of well-maintained, inexpensive, surf-side parking lots. Beach vendors carry necessities for sunning and swimming. The parking fee is $3 for cars and $5 for RVs.

Shopping

In downtown Cocoa, cobblestone walkways wend through **Olde Cocoa Village,** a cluster of restored turn-of-the-20th-century buildings now occupied by restaurants and specialty shops purveying crafts, fine art, and clothing. It's impossible to miss the **Ron Jon Surf Shop** (✉ 4151 N. Atlantic Ave., Rte. A1A ☎ 321/799–8888 ⊕ www.ronjons.com). With a giant surfboard and an aqua, teal, and pink art-deco facade, Ron Jon takes up nearly two blocks along Route A1A. What started in 1963 as a small T-shirt and bathing-suit shop has evolved into a 52,000-square-foot superstore that's open every day 'round the clock. The shop has water-sports gear as well as chairs and umbrellas for rent, and sells every kind of beachwear, surf wax, plus the requisite T-shirts and flip-flops. For up-to-the-minute surfing conditions, call the store and press 3 and then 7 for the **Ron Jon Surf and Weather Report.**

Exploring the Cape Canaveral Area

With the Kennedy Space Center just 10 minutes away, there is plenty to do in and around Cocoa Beach, though many folks opt to travel the extra hour into Orlando to visit the popular theme parks.

☾ The **Brevard Community College Planetarium and Observatory,** one of the largest public-access observatories in Florida, has a 24-inch telescope through which visitors can view objects in the solar system and deep space. On the campus of Brevard Community College, the planetarium has two theaters, one showing a changing roster of nature documentaries, the other hosting laser light shows as well as changing planetarium shows. Science Quest Exhibit Hall includes hands-on exhibits, including scales calibrated to other planets (on the moon, Vegas-era Elvis would have weighed just 62 pounds). The International Hall of Space Explorers displays exhibits on space travel. Show schedules and opening hours may vary, so it's best to call ahead. Travel 2½ mi east of I–95 Exit 75 on Route 520, and take Route 501 north for 1¾ mi. ⊠ *1519 Clearlake Rd.* ☎ *321/433–7373* ⊕ *www.brevardcc. edu/planet* ▣ *Observatory and exhibit hall free, film or planetarium show $6, both shows $10, laser show $6, triple combination $14* ☉ *Call for current schedule.*

To see what the local lay of the land looked like in other eras, check out the **Brevard Museum of History & Science.** Hands-on activities for children are the draw here. Not to be missed is the Windover Archaeological Exhibit of 7,000-year-old artifacts indigenous to the region. In 1984, a shallow pond revealed the burial ground for more than 200 Native Americans who lived in the area about 7,000 years ago. Preserved in the muck were bones and, to the archaeologists' surprise, the brains of these ancient people. Don't overlook the hands-on discovery rooms and the collection of Victoriana. The museum's nature center has 22 acres of trails encompassing three distinct ecosystems—sand pine hills, lake lands, and marshlands. ⊠ *2201 Michigan Ave.* ☎ *321/632–1830* ⊕ *www.brevardmuseum.com* ▣ *$5.50, trails free* ☉ *Mon.–Sat. 10–4, Sun. noon–4.*

The must-see **Kennedy Space Center Visitor Complex,** just southeast of Titusville, is one of Central Florida's most popular sights. Following the lead of the theme parks, they've switched to a one-price-covers-all admission. To get the most out of your visit to the space center, take the bus tour (included with admission), which makes stops at several facilities. Buses depart every 15 minutes, and you can get on and off any bus whenever you like. As you approach the Kennedy Space Center grounds, tune your car radio to AM1320 for attraction information.

The first stop on the tour is the **Launch Complex 39 Observation Gantry,** which has an unparalleled view of the twin space-shuttle launchpads. At the **Apollo Saturn V Center,** don't miss the presentation at the Firing Room Theatre, where the launch of America's first lunar mission, 1968's *Apollo VIII,* is re-created with a ground-shaking, window-rattling liftoff. At the **Lunar Surface Theatre,** recordings from *Apollo XI* offer an eerie and awe-inspiring reminder that when Armstrong and Aldrin landed, they had less than 30 seconds of fuel to spare. In the hall it's impossible to miss the 363-foot-long *Saturn V* rocket. A spare built for a moon mission that never took place, this 6.2-million-pound spacecraft has enough power to throw a fully loaded DC-3 all the way to the sun and back!

Exhibits near the center's entrance include the **Early Space Exploration** display, which highlights the rudimentary yet influential Mercury and Gemini space programs; **Robot Scouts,** a walk-through exhibit of unmanned planetary probes; and the **Exploration in the New Millennium** display, which offers you the opportunity to touch a piece of Mars (it fell to the Earth in the form of a meteorite). Don't miss the outdoor **Rocket Garden,** with walkways winding beside spare rockets from early Atlas spacecraft to a Saturn 1. Children love the space playground, with a one-fifth-scale space shuttle and a crawl-through, multilevel tower, about right for kids 3 and older. Also fun for kids is a full-scale reproduction of a space shuttle, *Explorer*: you can walk through the payload bay, cockpit, and crew quarters. Within the garden there's also a museum filled with exhibits on spacecraft that have explored the last frontier, and a theater showing several short films.

The most moving exhibit is the **Astronauts Memorial,** a tribute to those who have died while in pursuit of space exploration. A 42½-foot-high by 50-foot-wide "Space Mirror" tracks the movement of the sun throughout the day, using reflected sunlight to brilliantly illuminate the names of the 24 fallen astronauts that are carved into the monument's 70,400-pound polished granite surface.

During the **Astronaut Encounter,** in a pavilion near the center's entrance, an astronaut who's actually flown in space hosts a daily Q&A session to tell visitors about life in zero gravity, providing insights to an experience only a few hundred people have ever shared. If you'd like to have a closer encounter with an astronaut, you can purchase a special ticket option to **Lunch with an Astronaut** for $20—in addition to your regular KSC admission. For an added fee and a more in-depth experience ($22), take the **NASA Up Close** tour, which brings visitors to sights seldom accessible to the public, such as the NASA Press Site Launch Countdown Clock, the Vehicle Assembly Building, the shuttle landing strip, and the 6-million-pound crawler that transports the shuttle to its launchpad.

The only back-to-back twin **IMAX theater complex** in the world is in the complex, too. *The Dream Is Alive,* an awesome 40-minute film narrated by Walter Cronkite and shot mostly by the astronauts, takes you from astronaut training and a thundering shuttle launch to an astronaut's-eye view of life aboard the shuttle while in space. **Space Station IMAX 3-D** follows astronauts and cosmonauts on their missions, with the 3-D effects putting you in space with them. ⊠ *Rte. 405, Kennedy Space Center, Titusville* ☎ *321/449–4400, 800/572–4636 launch hotline* ⊕ *www.kennedyspacecenter.com* ✉ *General 1-day admission includes bus tour and IMAX movies, $30; Maximum Access Badge, valid for 2 days, includes bus tour, IMAX movies, and Astronaut Hall of Fame, $37; NASA Up Close Tour: $22 plus admission* ☉ *Space Center: daily 9 AM–5:30, last regular tour 3 hrs before closing; closed certain launch dates; IMAX I and II theaters: daily 10–5:40.*

If you prefer wading birds over waiting in line, don't miss the 140,000-acre **Merritt Island National Wildlife Refuge,** which adjoins the Canaveral National Seashore. It's an immense area dotted by brackish estuaries and marshes and patches of land consisting of coastal dunes, scrub oaks, pine forests and flat woods, and palm and oak hammocks. You can borrow field guides and binoculars at the visitor center to track down various types of falcons, osprey, eagles, turkeys, doves, cuckoos, loons, geese, skimmers, terns, warblers, wrens, thrushes, sparrows, owls, and woodpeckers. A 20-minute video about refuge wildlife and accessibility—only 10,000 acres are developed—can help orient you. You might take a self-guided tour along the 7-mi (11-km) **Black Point Wildlife Drive.** The dirt road takes you back in time, where there are no traces of encroaching malls or mankind and it's easy to visualize the Native American tribes who made this their home 7,000 years ago. On the **Oak Hammock Foot Trail,** you can see wintering migratory waterfowl and learn about the plants of a hammock community. If you exit the north end of the refuge, look for the **Manatee Observation Area** just north of the Haulover Canal (maps are at the visitor center). They usually show up in spring and fall. There are also fishing camps scattered throughout the area. The refuge is closed four days prior to a shuttle launch. ⊠ *Rte. 402 across Titusville Causeway, Titusville* ☎ *321/861–0667* ⊕ *merrittisland.fws.gov* ⊠ *Free* ☉ *Daily sunrise–sunset; visitor center open weekdays 8–4:30, Sat. 9–5.*

The original Mercury 7 team and the later Gemini, Apollo, Skylab, and shuttle astronauts contributed to make the **United States Astronaut Hall of Fame** the world's premium archive of astronauts' personal stories. Authentic memorabilia and equipment from their collections tell the story of human space exploration. You'll watch videotapes of historic moments in the space program and see one-of-a-kind items like Wally Schirra's relatively archaic Sigma 7 Mercury space capsule, Gus Grissom's space suit (silver color only because NASA thought silver looked more "spacey"), and a flag that made it to the moon. The exhibit **First on the Moon** focuses on crew selection for *Apollo 11* and the Soviet Union's role in the space race. Definitely don't miss the **Astronaut Adventure,** a hands-on discovery center with interactive exhibits that help you learn about space travel. One of the more challenging activities is a space-shuttle simulator that lets you try your hand at landing the craft—and afterward replays a side view of your rolling and pitching descent. ⊠ *6225 Vectorspace Blvd., off Rte. 405, Titusville* ☎ *321/452–2121 or 800/572–4636* ⊕ *www.kennedyspacecenter.com* ⊠ *Astronaut Hall of Fame only: $17; Maximum Access Pass, valid for 2 days, combines the Kennedy Space Center Visitor Complex and the Astronaut Hall of Fame, $37* ☉ *Daily 9–6.*

Orlando Theme Parks

☺ **SeaWorld Orlando.** In the world's largest marine adventure park, every attraction is devoted to demonstrating the ways that humans can protect the mammals, birds, fish, and reptiles that live in the ocean and its tributaries. The presentations are gentle reminders of our responsibility to safeguard the environment, and you'll find that SeaWorld's use of humor plays a major role in this education. The park is small enough that, armed with a map that lists show times, you can plan a chronological approach that flows easily from one attraction to the next. Near the intersection of I–4 and the Beeline Expressway; take I–4 to Exit 71 or 72 and follow signs. ⊠ *7007 Sea Harbor Dr., International Drive Area, Orlando* ☎ *407/351–3600 or 800/327–2424* ⊕ *www.seaworld.*

com ✉ *$59.75 for a 1-day ticket* ⊙ *Daily 9–6 or 7, until as late as 11 summer and holidays; educational programs daily, some beginning as early as 6:30* AM.

↻ **Universal Orlando.** The resort consists of **Universal Studios** (the original movie theme park), **Islands of Adventure** (the second theme park), and **CityWalk** (the dining-shopping-nightclub complex). Although it's bordered by residential neighborhoods and thickly trafficked International Drive, Universal Orlando is surprisingly expansive, intimate, and accessible, with two massive parking complexes, easy walks to all attractions, and a motor launch that cruises to the hotels. Universal Orlando emphasizes "two parks, two days, one great adventure," but you may find the presentation, creativity, and cutting-edge technology brings you back for more. ✉ *1000 Universal Studios Plaza, Orlando 32819-7610* ☎ *407/363–8000 or 888/331–9108* ⊕ *www.universalorlando.com* ✉ *1-day, 1-park ticket $59.75; 2-day pass $104.95* ⊙ *Usually daily 9–9, but hrs vary seasonally; CityWalk restaurants and bars have individual open hrs.*

↻ **Walt Disney World.** Walt Disney World is a huge complex of theme parks and attractions, each of which is worth a visit. Parks include the **Magic Kingdom,** a family favorite and the original here; **Epcot,** Disney's international, educational park; **Disney–MGM Studios,** a movie-oriented theme park; and **Disney's Animal Kingdom,** which is much more than a zoo. Beyond these, there are water parks, elaborate minigolf courses, a sports center, resorts, restaurants, and nightlife. If you have only one day, you'll have to concentrate on a single park; Disney–MGM Studios or Animal Kingdom are easiest to do in a day, but arrive early and expect to stay until park closing, which might be as early as 5 PM for Animal Kingdom or as late as 11 PM during busy seasons at the Magic Kingdom. The most direct route to the Disney Parks from Port Canaveral is S.R. 528 (the Beeline Expressway) to I–4; when you get through Orlando, follow the signs to Disney and expect traffic. ✉ *Lake Buena Vista* ☎ *407/824–4321* ⊕ *disneyworld.disney. go.com* ✉ *1-day, 1-park pass $59.75* ⊙ *Most parks open by 9* AM; *closing hrs vary, but usually 5* PM *for Animal Kingdom and 6–11* PM *for other parks, depending on season.*

SAN JUAN, PUERTO RICO

In addition to being a major port of call, San Juan is one of the preeminent ports of embarkation for cruises on Southern Caribbean itineraries. For information on dining, shopping, nightlife, and sightseeing *see* San Juan, Puerto Rico *in* Chapter 4.

The Cruise Port

Cruise ships dock within a couple of blocks of Old San Juan. The Paseo de la Princesa, a tree-lined promenade beneath the city wall, is a nice place for a stroll—you can admire the local crafts and stop at the refreshment kiosks. A tourist information booth is in the cruise terminal area. Major sights in the Old San Juan area are mere blocks from the piers, but be aware that the streets are narrow and steeply inclined in places. Even if you have only a few hours before your cruise, you'll have time to do a little sightseeing.

AIRPORT
TRANSFERS

The ride from the Luis Muñoz Marín International Airport, east of downtown San Juan, to the docks in Old San Juan takes about 20 minutes. The white "taxi turistico" cabs, marked by a logo on the door, have a fixed rate of $16 to the cruise ship piers; there is a small fee for luggage. Other taxi companies charge by the mile, which can cost a little more. Be sure the driver starts the meter, or agree on a fare beforehand.

VISITOR
INFORMATION

🚩 **Puerto Rico Tourism Company** ⊕ www.gotopuertorico.com 🖂 Box 902-3960, Old San Juan Station, San Juan, PR 00902-3960 ☎ 787/721-2400 or 800/223-6530 🖂 3575 W. Cahuenga Blvd., Suite 560, Los Angeles, CA 90068 ☎ 213/874-5991 🖂 901 Ponce de León Blvd., Suite 101, Coral Gables, FL 33134 ☎ 305/445-9112.

Where to Stay

If you are planning to spend one night in San Juan before your cruise departs, you'll probably find it easier to stay in Old San Juan, where the cruise ship terminals are. But if you want to spend a few extra days in the city, there are other possibilities near good beaches a bit farther out.

For price categories, *see* Lodging at the beginning of this chapter.

☪ **$$$$** 🏨 **Caribe Hilton San Juan.** This hotel's beach is the only private one in San Juan, and not many guests ever leave it. With one of the best developed children's programs to make vacation easy on the whole family, no wonder. The open-air lobby's sunken bar looks out over the gentle cascades of a tri-level pool, which is adjacent to a wading pool and an area with whirlpool tubs. Rooms have ocean or lagoon views, and those on the executive floor include such services as private check-in and check-out and free Continental breakfast and evening cocktails. Local businesspeople often frequent the on-site Morton's of Chicago restaurant. 🖂 *Calle Los Rosales, San Gerónimo Grounds, Puerta de Tierra, 00901* ☎ *787/721-0303 or 800/468-8585* 📠 *787/725-8849* ⊕ *www. hiltoncaribbean.com/sanjuan* 🛏 *602 rooms, 44 suites* ⚑ *6 restaurants, room service, in-room safes, minibars, cable TV, in-room data ports, 3 tennis courts, pool, wading pool, health club, hair salon, outdoor hot tub, spa, beach, bar, video game room, shops, children's programs (ages 4–12), dry cleaning, laundry service, concierge, business services, meeting rooms, parking (fee), no-smoking floors* 🚭 *AE, D, DC, MC, V.*

$$–$$$$ 🏨 **Sheraton Old San Juan Hotel.** This Sheraton serves primarily as a layover between the airport and the cruise ships. Its location in Old San Juan is also convenient for serial shoppers and businesspeople. The atmosphere in the Fogata bar—fire-red wall, torchlike lamps, and piano—is so entrancing that you forget the casino next to it. The rooms have been plushly renovated with custom-designed beds. With extra linen closets and other details on each floor, the hotel is designed to make it easy for the staff to cater to your every need. 🖂 *100 Calle Brumbaugh, Old San Juan, 00901* ☎ *787/721-5100 or 866/376-7577* 📠 *787/721-1111* ⊕ *www.sheratonoldsanjuan.com* 🛏 *200 rooms, 40 suites* ⚑ *Restaurant, room service, in-room safes, cable TV, in-room data ports, pool,* *gym, hot tub, bar, casino, dry cleaning, laundry service, concierge floor, business center, 2 meeting rooms, travel services, no-smoking floors, parking (fee)* ⊟ *AE, D, DC, MC, V.*

$–$$$ 🏠 **Numero Uno.** This inn is a peaceful and breezy oasis right on Ocean Park beach. It's at the end of the street in a quiet residential area, plus a walled-in patio provides privacy for sunning or hanging out by the small pool. Rooms are decorated in soothing whites and earth tones; three have ocean views. Two apartments come with kitchenettes. The inn is home to Pamela's restaurant ($$–$$$), which serves delicious Caribbean fare at teak, umbrella-shaded tables on the beach. Guests are provided with beach chairs and towels. ⊠ *1 Calle Santa Ana, Ocean Park, 00911* 🕾 *787/726–5010* 🖷 *787/727–5482* ⊕ *www. numero1guesthouse.com* 🛏 *11 rooms, 2 apartments* 🛆 *Restaurant, fans, cable TV, pool, beach, bar* ⊟ *AE, D, MC, V* ⦿ *CP.*

TAMPA, FLORIDA

Although glitzy Miami seems to hold the trendiness trump card and Orlando is the place your kids want to visit annually until they hit middle school, the Tampa Bay area has that elusive quality that many attribute to the "real Florida." The state's second-largest metro area is less fast-lane than its biggest (Miami), or even Orlando, but its strengths are just as varied, from broad cultural diversity to a sun-worshipping beach culture. Florida's third-busiest airport, a vibrant business community, world-class beaches, and superior hotels and resorts—many of them historic—make this an excellent place to spend a week or a lifetime. Carnival and Royal Caribbean base several ships in Tampa for cruises to the Western Caribbean, Holland America bases one ship, and several other lines base ships here seasonally.

The Cruise Port
Tampa is the largest shipping port in the state of Florida, and it's becoming ever more important to the cruise industry, now with three passenger terminals. In Tampa's downtown area, the port is linked to nearby Ybor City and the rest of the Tampa Bay Area by a new streetcar line.

To reach the port by car, take I–4 West to Exit 1 (Ybor City), and go south on 21st Street. To get to Terminals 2 and 6, turn right on Adamo Drive (Highway 60), then left on Channelside Drive. To get to Terminal 7, continue beyond Adamo Drive, where 21st Street merges with 22nd Street, and turn right on Maritime Boulevard, then left on Guy N. Verger to Hooker's Point.

🚢 **Tampa Port Authority** ⊠ 1101 Channelside Dr. 🕾 813/905–7678 or 800/741–2297 ⊕ www.tampaport.com.

AIRPORT TRANSFERS
Bay Shuttle provides van-shuttle service from Tampa International Airport to the cruise ship terminals for a fee of $10 for the first passenger, $8 for each additional passenger. You need to make a reservation.
🚢 **Bay Shuttle** 🕾 813/259–9998 ⊕ www.tampabayshuttle.com.

PARKING
Parking is available at the port directly across from the terminals. For Terminals 2 and 3 (Carnival and Royal Caribbean), parking is in a garage

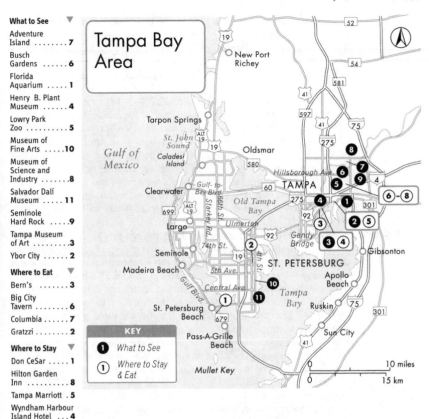

Tampa Bay Area

across the street. For Terminal 6 (Holland America), parking is outdoors in a guarded, enclosed lot. For Terminal 7, parking is available at the terminal building. The cost is $10 a day, payable in advance by credit card (MasterCard or Visa) or in cash.

VISITOR
INFORMATION

St. Petersburg/Clearwater Area Convention & Visitors Bureau ⊠ 14450 46th St. N, Suite 108, St. Petersburg 33762 ☎ 727/464–7200 or 877/352–3224 ⊕ www.floridasbeach.com. **Tampa Bay Convention and Visitors Bureau** ⊠ 400 N. Tampa St., Suite 2800, 33602 ☎ 813/223–1111 or 800/368–2672 ⊕ www.visittampabay.com.

Where to Stay in the Tampa Bay Area

If you want to be close to the cruise ship terminal, then you'll have to stay in Tampa, but if you want to spend more time in the area and perhaps stay on the beach, St. Petersburg and the beaches are close by.

For price categories, *see* Lodging at the beginning of this chapter.

$$$$ **Don CeSar Beach Resort, a Loews Hotel.** Once a favorite of Scott and Zelda Fitzgerald, this sprawling, sybaritic beachfront "Pink Palace," now part of the Loews hotel chain, has long been a Gulf Coast landmark because of its remarkable architecture. Steeped in turn-of-the-last-century elegance, the hotel claims a rich history, complete with a resident ghost. The restaurant, Maritana Grille, specializes in Florida seafood and is lined with huge fish tanks. The more casual Beach House Suites by the Don CeSar, less than ½ mi from the main building, has one-bedroom condos and a great little beach bar. The hotel now has Wi-Fi. ☒ *3400 Gulf Blvd., St. Pete Beach 33706* ☎ *727/360–1881 or 800/282–1116* 🖷 *727/363–5034* ⊕ *www.doncesar.com or www.loewshotels.com* 🛏 *Resort: 234 rooms, 43 suites; Beach House: 70 condos* ⚖ *3 restaurants, ice-cream parlor, room service, some in-room safes, some kitchens, cable TV, in-room data ports, Wi-Fi, 2 pools, health club, hair salon, massage, spa, beach, boating, jet skiing, parasailing, volleyball, 3 bars, lobby lounge, shops, babysitting, children's programs (ages 5–12), dry cleaning, laundry service, concierge, Internet room, business services, meeting rooms, parking (fee), some pets allowed, no-smoking rooms* ▤ *AE, D, DC, MC, V.*

$$$–$$$$ 🏨 **Wyndham Harbour Island Hotel.** Even though this 12-story hotel is on a 177-acre island in Tampa Bay, it's just an eight-minute walk and short drive from downtown Tampa. Many units have terrific views of the water or the downtown skyline. Service is attentive. There's a marina, and you may use the extensive health and fitness center and 20 tennis courts at the Harbour Island Athletic Club, next door, for a fee. Every room has high-speed Internet access. This is a good choice if you want to be downtown without actually being in the midst of the action, yet there's a trolley that takes you from the hotel to the convention center or to the electric street car (TECO) station where you can travel to Channelside, the Florida Aquarium, or Ybor City. ☒ *725 S. Harbour Island Blvd., Harbour Island, 33602* ☎ *813/229–5000* 🖷 *813/229–5322* ⊕ *www.wyndhamharbourisland.com* 🛏 *279 rooms, 20 suites* ⚖ *Restaurant, coffee shop, room service, minibars, some refrigerators, cable TV, in-room data ports, golf privileges, pool, dock, boating, fishing, bar, shop, laundry service, Internet room, business services, airport shuttle, parking (fee), no-smoking floors* ▤ *AE, DC, MC, V.*

$$–$$$$ 🏨 **Tampa Marriott Waterside.** Across from the Tampa Convention Center, this downtown hotel was built for conventioneers but is also convenient to popular tourist spots such as the Florida Aquarium, the St. Pete Times Forum hockey arena, and shopping and entertainment districts Channelside, Hyde Park, and Ybor City. At least half of the rooms and most of the suites overlook the channel to Tampa Bay; the bay itself is visible from the higher floors of the 27-story hotel. The lobby coffee bar overlooks the water. Il Terrazzo is the hotel's formal Italian dining room. ☒ *700 S. Florida Ave., Downtown, 33602* ☎ *813/221–4900* 🖷 *813/221–0923* ⊕ *www.tampawaterside.com* 🛏 *681 rooms, 36 suites* ⚖ *3 restaurants, room service, in-room safes, some kitchens, cable TV, in-room data ports, pool, gym, hair salon, spa, boating, marina, 2 bars, lobby lounge, shop, dry cleaning, laundry facilities, laundry service, concierge, concierge floor, Internet room, business services, meeting rooms, car rental, parking (fee), no-smoking floors* ▤ *AE, D, DC, MC, V.*

$$–$$$ 🏨 **Hilton Garden Inn Tampa Ybor Historic District.** Architecturally, this property pales when compared to the century-old classic structures around it in Ybor City. But it is convenient: it's across the street from the Centro Ybor complex, 3 mi from downtown Tampa, and 7 mi from Tampa International Airport. The hotel restaurant has a full breakfast buffet and doesn't try to compete with the culinary heavyweights in a six-block radius. Rooms are business traveler–friendly, with high-speed Internet access, dual phone lines, large desks, and ergonomic chairs. ⊠ *1700 E. 9th Ave., Ybor City, 33605* ☎ *813/769–9267* 🖷 *813/769– 3299* ⊕ *www.tampayborhistoricdistrict.gardeninn.com* ⇗ *84 rooms, 11 suites* ⚐ *Restaurant, microwaves, refrigerators, cable TV, in-room data ports, pool, exercise equipment, laundry facilities, laundry service, business services* ⊟ *AE, D, DC, MC, V.*

Where to Eat in the Tampa Bay Area

For price categories, *see* Dining at the beginning of this chapter.

$$$–$$$$ ✕ **Bern's Steak House.** Fine mahogany paneling and ornate chandeliers define the elegance at legendary Bern's, which many feel is Tampa's best restaurant. Owner David Laxer ages his own beef, grows his own organic vegetables, roasts his own coffee, and maintains his own saltwater fish tanks. Cuts of top-grade beef are sold by weight and thickness. The wine list includes some 6,500 selections (with 1,800 dessert wines). After dinner, tour the kitchen and wine cellar before having dessert upstairs in a cozy booth. ⊠ *1208 S. Howard Ave., Hyde Park* ☎ *813/251– 2421, 800/282–1547 in Florida* ⚐ *Reservations essential* ⊟ *AE, D, DC, MC, V* ☉ *No lunch.*

$$–$$$ ✕ **Big City Tavern.** The name makes the place sound like it's merely a bar, but it's far more than that. In the ballroom of the historic Cuban social club with an ornate tin ceiling and dark-wood furniture, this classy dining room serves many well-prepared dishes, from veal scaloppine with potato lasagna to a tasty shrimp pad thai. A great starter is the coconut shrimp. There's a good selection of wines by the glass and imported beers from Ireland to Australia and in between. The tavern is relatively quiet and removed from the frenzied crowds at street level. ⊠ *Centro Ybor, 1600 E. 8th Ave., 2nd fl., Ybor City* ☎ *813/247–3000* ⊟ *AE, D, DC, MC, V* ☉ *No lunch.*

$$–$$$ ✕ **Gratzzi.** This warm northern Italian eatery hits local critics' short lists of best restaurants, with tasty classics such as veal saltimbocca and osso buco with pan-seared polenta. Although the *zuppa di pesce* (fish soup) is a pricey dish at $18.99 a bowl, it's also one of the best, with expertly prepared mussels, clams, shrimp, scallops, and whitefish in a red sauce on pasta. Other dishes on the extensive menu are more affordable and include rotisserie-cooked meat and seafood. ⊠ *199 2nd Ave. N, BayWalk* ☎ *727/822–7769* ⊟ *AE, D, DC, MC, V* ☉ *No lunch Sun.*

$–$$$ ✕ **Columbia.** A fixture since 1905, this magnificent structure with spacious dining rooms and a sunny courtyard takes up an entire city block. The paella is possibly the best in Florida, and the Columbia 1905 salad—with ham, olives, cheese, and garlic—is legendary. The menu has Cuban classics such as *ropa vieja* (shredded beef with onions, peppers, and tomatoes) and *arroz con pollo* (chicken with yellow rice). There's flamenco dancing most nights. Buy hand-rolled cigars in the bar. ⊠ *2117 E. 7th Ave., Ybor City* ☎ *813/248–4961* ⊟ *AE, D, DC, MC, V.*

Beaches

Spread over six small islands, or keys, 900-acre **Fort De Soto Park** (✉ 3500 Pinellas Bayway S, Tierra Verde ☎ 727/582–2267) lies at the mouth of Tampa Bay. It has 7 mi of beaches, two fishing piers, picnic and camping grounds, and a historic fort. The fort was built on the southern end of Mullet Key to protect sea lanes in the gulf during the Spanish-American War. Roam the fort or wander the beaches and the islands. **Pass-A-Grille Beach** (✉ Off Gulf Blvd. [Rte. 699], St. Pete Beach), at the southern end of St. Pete Beach, has parking meters, a snack bar, restrooms, and showers. **St. Pete Beach** (✉ 11260 Gulf Blvd., St. Pete Beach) is a free beach on Treasure Island. There are dressing rooms, metered parking, and a snack bar.

Shopping

For bargains, stop at the **Big Top** (✉ 9250 E. Fowler Ave., Northeast Tampa ☎ 813/986–4004), open weekends 9 to 4:30, where vendors hawk new and used items at 1,000-plus booths. The **Channelside shopping and entertainment complex** (✉ 615 Channelside Dr., Downtown) offers movie theaters, shops, restaurants, and clubs; the official Tampa Bay visitors center is also here. If you want to grab something at Neiman-Marcus on your way to the airport, the upscale **International Plaza** (✉ 2223 N. Westshore Blvd., Airport Area) mall, which includes Betsey Johnson, J. Crew, L'Occitane, Louis Vuitton, Tiffany & Co., and many other shops, is immediately south of the airport. **Old Hyde Park Village** (✉ Swan Ave. near Bayshore Blvd., Hyde Park) is a gentrified shopping district like the ones you find in every major American city. Williams-Sonoma and Brooks Brothers are mixed in with bistros and sidewalk cafés. There are more than 120 shops, department stores, and eateries in one of the area's biggest market complexes, **Westfield Shopping Town at Brandon** (✉ Grand Regency and Rte. 60, Brandon), an attractively landscaped complex near I-75, about 20 minutes east of downtown by car. If you are shopping for hand-rolled cigars, head for 7th Avenue in **Ybor City,** where a few hand-rollers practice their craft in small shops.

Nightlife

The biggest concentration of nightclubs, as well as the widest variety, is found along 7th Avenue in Ybor City. It becomes a little like Bourbon Street in New Orleans after the sun goes down. Popular **Adobe Gilas** (✉ 1600 E. 8th Ave., Ybor City ☎ 813/241–8588) has live music every day but Monday, karaoke on Wednesday, and a balcony overlooking the crowds on 7th Avenue. There's a large selection of margaritas and more than 50 brands of tequila, and food is served until 2 AM. Considered something of a dive—but a lovable dive—by a loyal local following that ranges from esteemed jurists to nose ring–wearing night owls, the **Hub** (✉ 719 N. Franklin St., Downtown ☎ 813/229–1553) is known for one of Tampa's best martinis and one of its most eclectic jukeboxes.

Improv Comedy Theater & Restaurant (✉ Centro Ybor, 1600 E. 8th Ave., Ybor City ☎ 813/864–4000 ⊕ www.improvtampa.com) stars top comedians in performances Wednesday through Sunday. The bar **Legends** at the Wyndham Harbour Island Hotel (✉ 725 S. Harbour Island Blvd.,

Harbour Island ☏ 813/229–5000) has a great bay view, and two TVs behind the bar for viewing sports.

Metropolis (✉ 3447 W. Kennedy Blvd., Central Tampa ☏ 813/871–2410), a gay club near the University of Tampa, has DJs and male strippers. Catch live comedy Wednesday through Sunday nights at **Side Splitters** (✉ 12938 N. Dale Mabry Hwy., Central Tampa ☏ 813/960–1197 ⊕ www.sidesplitterscomedy.com). **Skippers Smokehouse** (✉ 910 Skipper Rd., Northeast Tampa ☏ 813/971–0666), a junkyard-style restaurant and oyster bar, has live reggae Wednesday, Grateful Dead night on Thursday, blues Friday through Sunday, and great smoked fish every night. **Stumps Supper Club** (✉ 615 Channelside Dr., Downtown ☏ 813/226–2261) serves Southern food, and has live dance music daily and a DJ on Friday and Saturday.

International Plaza's **Bay Street** (✉ 2223 N. Westshore Blvd., Airport Area) has become one of Tampa's dining and imbibing hot spots.

Exploring the Tampa Bay Area

Florida's west coast crown jewel as well as its business and commercial hub, Tampa has high-rises and heavy traffic. Amid the bustle is the region's greatest concentration of restaurants, nightlife, stores, and cultural events.

Numbers in the margin refer to points of interest on the Tampa Bay Area map.

🕐 ❼ **Adventure Island.** Waterslides, pools, and artificial-wave pools create a 30-acre wonderland at this water park, a corporate cousin of Busch Gardens. Rides such as the Key West Rapids and Tampa Typhoon are creative, if geographically incorrect. (There are no rapids in Key West and *typhoon* is a term used only in Pacific regions—Tampa Hurricane just wouldn't have had the same alliterative allure.) The park's planners took the younger kids into account, with offerings such as Fabian's Funport, which has a scaled-down wave pool and interactive water gym. Along with a championship volleyball complex and a surf pool, you'll find cafés, snack bars, changing rooms, and video games. ✉ *1001 Malcolm McKinley Dr., less than 1 mi north of Busch Gardens, Central Tampa* ☏ *813/987–5660 or 888/800–5447* ⊕ *www.adventureisland.com* 🎟 *$33* ⊙ *Mid-Mar.–late Oct., daily 10–5.*

🕐 ❻ **Busch Gardens.** More than 2,700 animals are just part of the attraction at this sprawling, carefully manicured theme park. Themed sections attempt to capture the spirit of 19th-century Africa, and the Skyride simulates an African safari—taking in free-roaming zebras, giraffes, rhinos, lions, and other animals. The 335-acre park also has live entertainment, animal exhibits, shops, restaurants, games, and thrill rides, including six roller coasters. The pulse-pumping lineup includes **Kumba** and **Montu,** both reaching speeds of more than 60 mph; **Gwazi,** a 7,000-foot-long wooden coaster; and **Python** and **Scorpion,** 360 degree–loop coasters with 60-foot drops. Passenger vans take you on a Serengeti safari in **Rhino Rally,** where you view Asian elephants, rhinos, and zebras. At one point, a bridge breaks away and passengers spend a few minutes on a rapids ride. You can also take a beer-tasting class—after all, Anheuser-Busch owns the park. Allow from six to eight hours to do Busch Gardens. This is not the ideal destination for small children. There are a few kid-oriented attractions, such as **Land of the Dragons,** a cool playground, and a children's ride area, but most of the park is geared toward teens or adults. ✉ *3000 E. Busch Blvd., 8 mi northeast of downtown Tampa and 2 mi east of I–275 Exit 50, Central Tampa* ☎ *813/987–5082 or 888/800–5447* ⊕ *www.buschgardens.com* 🎫 *$56* 🕐 *Daily 9–6; later in summer.*

❶ Florida Aquarium. The $84 million aquarium is no overpriced fishbowl; it's a dazzling architectural landmark with an 83-foot-high multitiered glass dome. It has more than 4,800 specimens of fish, other animals, and plants, representing 550 species native to Florida. Five major exhibit areas reflect the diversity of the state's natural habitats—wetlands, bays, beaches, and coral reefs. Creature-specific exhibits are the No Bone Zone (lovable invertebrates) and Sea Hunt, with predators ranging from sharks to exotic lionfish. The most impressive single exhibit is the living coral reef, in a 500,000-gallon tank ringed with viewing windows, including an awesome 43-foot-wide panoramic opening. Part of the tank is a walkable tunnel, almost giving the illusion of venturing into underwater depths. There you see a thicket of elk-horn coral teeming with tropical fish. A dark cave reveals sea life you would normally see only on night dives, and shark-feeding shows include divers chumming from the safety of a cage. If you have three hours, try the DolphinQuest Eco-Tour, which takes up to 50 passengers onto Tampa's bays in a 64-foot catamaran for an up-close look at bottlenose dolphins and other wildlife. ✉ *701 Channelside Dr., Downtown* ☎ *813/273–4000* ⊕ *www. flaquarium.org* 🎫 *Aquarium $17.95; Bay Spirit, Wild Dolphin Adventure $18.95* 🕐 *Daily 9:30–5.*

❹ Henry B. Plant Museum. This museum is one part architectural time capsule and one part magic-carpet ride to gilded-era America. Originally a luxury hotel, built by railroad magnate Henry B. Plant in 1891, the building is filled with the furnishings it held when Colonel Theodore Roosevelt made it his U.S. headquarters during the Spanish-American War. Plant spared no expense in constructing this classic Moorish Revival building. The museum displays the finer things of life from the 1890s, including 19th-century artwork and furniture brought from Europe when the hotel opened. On Sunday afternoons, get a glimpse into the time period through "Upstairs/Downstairs," in which actors play the parts of hotel staff and guests. At periodic Saturday antiques appraisals, you can bring up to three personal treasures for expert evaluation. ✉ *401 W. Kennedy Blvd., off I–275 Exit 44, Downtown* ☎ *813/254–1891* ⊕ *www. plantmuseum.com* 🎫 *$5* 🕐 *Tues.–Sat. 10–4, Sun. noon–4.*

❺ Lowry Park Zoo. In Tampa's 24-acre zoo, exotic creatures from four continents live in their natural habitats. Check out the Asian Domain and its primates, from chimpanzees to woolly monkeys. Spot some fancy flying in the free-flight bird aviary, and come face to face with alligators, panthers, bears, and red wolves at the Florida Wildlife Center, a sanctuary for indigenous animals. There's also a walk-in lorikeet aviary where you can feed and pet the colorful birds, as well as a stringray touch tank, and Manatee and Aquatic Center, one of the most extensive in the state. Gentle animals such as sheep and goats are the primary residents of the children's petting zoo. To get a look at a gentle creature that is quintessentially part of Florida, visit the Manatee Amphitheater. This zoo is particularly attuned to night events: parties range from food and beer tastings for adults to chaperoned sleepovers for children ages 6–14. Adjacent to the zoo, the Fun Forest at Lowry Park has rides and an arcade. ✉ *1101 W. Sligh Ave., Central Tampa* ☎ *813/935–8552* ⊕ *www. lowryparkzoo.com* 💲 *$14.95* ⊙ *Daily 9:30–5.*

⑩ Museum of Fine Arts. Outstanding examples of European, American, pre-Columbian, and Far Eastern art are at St. Petersburg's major art museum. There are also photographic exhibits. Staff members give narrated gallery tours two to five times a day. ✉ *255 Beach Dr. NE* ☎ *727/896–2667* ⊕ *www.fine-arts.org* 💲 *$8* ⊙ *Tues.–Sat. 10–5, Sun. 1–5.*

⑧ Museum of Science & Industry (MOSI). This fun and stimulating scientific playground is a place where you learn about Florida weather, anatomy, flight, and space by seeing *and* by doing. At the Gulf Coast Hurricane Exhibit you can experience what a hurricane and its 74-mph winds feel like (and live to write home about it). The Bank of America BioWorks Butterfly Garden is a 6,400-square-foot engineered ecosystem project that not only serves as a home for free-flying butterflies but also demonstrates how wetlands can clean water. The Verizon *Challenger* Learning Center gives simulated flights, and the 100-seat Saunders Planetarium—Tampa Bay's only planetarium—has afternoon and evening shows, one of them a trek through the universe. For adventurous spirits, there's a high-wire bicycle ride 30 feet above the floor. Don't worry, you're strapped to the bike, which is attached to the wire and can't fall. There's also an IMAX theater, where films are projected on a hemispherical 82-foot dome. ✉ *4801 E. Fowler Ave., 1 mi north of Busch Gardens, Northeast Tampa* ☎ *813/987–6300 or 800/995–6674* ⊕ *www.mosi.org* 💲 *$15.95* ⊙ *Weekdays 9–5, weekends 9–7.*

⑪ Salvador Dalí Museum. The world's most extensive collection of originals by the Spanish surrealist Salvador Dalí is found here. Valued at more than $125 million, the collection includes 94 oils, more than 100 watercolors and drawings, and 1,300 graphics, sculptures, photographs, and objets d'art, including floor-to-ceiling murals. Frequent tours are led by well-informed docents. How did the collection end up here? A rich northern industrialist and friend of Dalí, Ohio magnate A. Reynolds Morse, was looking for a museum site after his huge personal Dalí collection began to overflow his mansion. The people of St. Petersburg vied admirably for the collection, and the museum was established here as a result. ✉ *1000 3rd St. S* ☎ *727/823–3767 or 800/442–3254* ⊕ *www. salvadordalimuseum.org* 💲 *$14* ⊙ *Mon.–Wed., Fri., and Sat. 9:30–5:30; Thurs. 9:30–8; Sun. noon–5:30.*

⑨ Seminole Hard Rock Hotel & Casino. If you've brought your body to Tampa but your heart's in Vegas, you can satisfy that urge to hang around a poker table at 4 AM here. The casino has poker tables, high-stakes bingo, and gaming machines. Coffee and doughnuts are free for gamblers, and the casino lounge serves drinks until 2:15 AM. ⊠ *5223 N. Orient Rd., off I–4 at N. Orient Rd. Exit* ☎ *813/627–7625 or 866/762–5463* ⊕ *www.seminolehardrock.com* ☒ *Free* ⊙ *Daily 24 hrs.*

❸ **Tampa Museum of Art.** The 35,000-square-foot museum has an impressive permanent collection of Greek and Roman antiquities, along with five galleries that host traveling exhibits. A 124,000-square-foot space, designed by internationally renowned architect Rafael Viñoly, is still under construction at this writing; until then, the museum will remain open at its current location next to the new building. It will close for a short time when exhibits are moved. ⊠ *600 N. Ashley Dr., Downtown* ☎ *813/274–8130* ⊕ *www.tampamuseum.com* ☒ *$7* ⊙ *Tues.–Sat. 10–5, Sun. 11–5; 3rd Thurs. of month open until 9 PM.*

❷ **Ybor City.** One of only three National Historic Landmark districts in Florida, Tampa's lively Cuban enclave has brick streets and wrought-iron balconies. Cubans brought their cigar-making industry to Ybor (pronounced *ee*-bore) City in 1866, and the smell of cigars—hand-rolled by Cuban immigrants—still wafts through the heart of this east Tampa area, along with the strong aroma of roasting coffee. These days the neighborhood is emerging as Tampa's hot spot as empty cigar factories and social clubs are transformed into boutiques, galleries, restaurants, and nightclubs that rival those in Miami's sizzling South Beach. Take a stroll past the ornately tiled **Columbia** restaurant and the stores lining 7th Avenue. Guided walking tours of the area ($5) enable you to see artisans hand-roll cigars following time-honored methods. Step back into the past at **Centennial Park** (⊠ 8th Ave. and 18th St.), which re-creates a period streetscape and hosts ℃ the Fresh Market every Saturday. Ybor City's destination within a destination is the dining and entertainment palace **Centro Ybor** (⊠ 1600 E. 7th Ave.). It has shops, trendy bars and restaurants, a 20-screen movie theater, and GameWorks, an interactive playground developed by Steven Spielberg. The **Ybor City Museum State Park** provides a look at the history of the cigar industry. Admission includes a tour of La Casita, one of the shotgun houses occupied by cigar workers and their families in the late 1890s. ⊠ *1818 E. 9th Ave., between Nuccio Pkwy. and 22nd St., from 7th to 9th Ave.* ☎ *813/247–6323* ⊕ *www.ybormuseum.org* ☒ *$3* ⊙ *Daily 9–5; tours Sat. 10:30.*

Ports of Call

WORD OF MOUTH

"I love planning a trip and seeing the island on my own terms . . . and not with hordes of other people. . . . It takes a little more work to research and make arrangements, but it is always worth it to me."
—Cathy

"[T]hese excursion companies depend on the cruise industry for their living, and they are all very much aware of the sailing times. Don't be scared off from arranging your own tours because of the threat of [the ship] leaving without you."
—PumpkinEater

"There are times when it is a good idea to book with the ship. Last year we did a tour that let us swim with the dolphins then it took us to the ship's private beach."

—toontown

NOWHERE IN THE WORLD are conditions better suited to cruising than in the Caribbean Sea. Tiny island nations, within easy sailing distance of one another, form a chain of tropical enchantment that curves from Cuba in the north all the way down to the coast of Venezuela. There's far more to life here than sand and coconuts, however. The islands are vastly different, with a variety of cultures, topographies, and languages represented. Colonialism has left its mark, and the presence of the Spanish, French, Dutch, Danish, and British is still felt. Slavery, too, has left its cultural legacy, blending African overtones into the colonial/Indian amalgam. The one constant, however, is the weather. Despite the islands' southerly latitude, the climate is surprisingly gentle, due in large part to the cooling influence of the trade winds.

The Caribbean is made up of the Greater Antilles and the Lesser Antilles. The former consist of those islands closest to the United States: Cuba, Jamaica, Hispaniola (Haiti and the Dominican Republic), and Puerto Rico. (The Cayman Islands lie south of Cuba.) The Lesser Antilles, including the Virgin, Windward, and Leeward islands and others, are greater in number but smaller in size, and constitute the southern half of the Caribbean chain.

GOING ASHORE

Traveling by cruise ship presents an opportunity to visit many places in a short time. The flip side is that your stay in each port of call will be brief. For this reason cruise lines offer shore excursions, which maximize passengers' time. There are a number of advantages to shore excursions arranged by your ship: in some destinations, transportation may be unreliable, and a ship-packaged tour is the best way to see distant sights. Also, you don't have to worry about missing the ship. The disadvantage of a shore excursion is the cost—you usually pay more for the convenience of having the ship do the legwork for you, but it's not always a lot more. Of course, you can always book a tour independently, hire a taxi, or use foot power to explore on your own. For each port of call included in this guide, we've provided some suggestions for the best shore excursions—in terms of both quality of experience and price—as well as some suggestions for what to do if you want to explore on your own.

Arriving in Port

When your ship arrives in a port, it will tie up alongside a dock or anchor out in a harbor. If the ship is docked, passengers walk down the gangway to go ashore. Docking makes it easy to move between the shore and the ship.

Tendering

If your ship anchors in the harbor, you will have to take a small boat—called a launch or tender—to get ashore. Tendering is a nuisance. Passengers wishing to disembark may be required to gather in a public room, get sequenced boarding passes, and wait until their numbers are called. The ride to shore may take as long as 20 minutes. If you don't like waiting, plan to go ashore an hour or so after the ship drops its anchor. On a very large ship, the wait for a tender can be quite long and frustrating.

Because tenders can be difficult to board, passengers with mobility problems may not be able to visit certain ports. The larger ships are more likely to use tenders. It is usually possible to learn before booking a cruise whether the ship will dock or anchor at its ports of call.

Before anyone is allowed to walk down the gangway or board a tender, the ship must be cleared for landing. Immigration and customs officials board the vessel to examine passports and sort through red tape. It may be more than an hour before you're allowed ashore. You will be issued a boarding pass, which you'll need to get back on board.

Returning to the Ship

Cruise lines are strict about sailing times, which are posted at the gangway and elsewhere and announced in the daily schedule of activities. Be sure to be back on board (not on the dock waiting to get a tender back to the ship) at least a half hour before the announced sailing time or you may be stranded. If you are on a shore excursion that was sold by the cruise line, however, the captain will wait for your group before casting off. That is one reason many passengers prefer ship-packaged tours.

If you're not on one of the ship's tours and the ship sails without you, immediately contact the cruise line's port representative, whose phone number is often listed on the daily schedule of activities. You may be able to hitch a ride on a pilot boat, although that is unlikely. Passengers who miss the boat must pay their own way to the next port.

CARIBBEAN ESSENTIALS

Currency

The U.S. dollar is the official currency on Puerto Rico and in the USVI, as well as the British Virgin Islands. On Grand Cayman you will usually have a choice of Cayman or U.S. dollars when you take money out of an ATM, and you may even be able to get change in U.S. dollars. On most other islands, U.S. paper currency (not coins) is usually accepted, but you may need to change a few dollars into local currency for phone calls, tips, and taxis. When you pay in dollars you'll almost always get change in local currency, so it's best to carry bills in small denominations. Canadian dollars and British pounds are occasionally accepted. If you need local currency (say, for a trip to one of the French islands), change money at a local bank or use an ATM for the best rate. Most major credit cards are accepted all over the Caribbean, except at local market stalls and small establishments. Euros are now the currency on the French islands of St. Barths, Guadeloupe, and Martinique; while the euro is the official currency on St. Martin as well, dollars are more widely accepted, often with a favorable exchange rate.

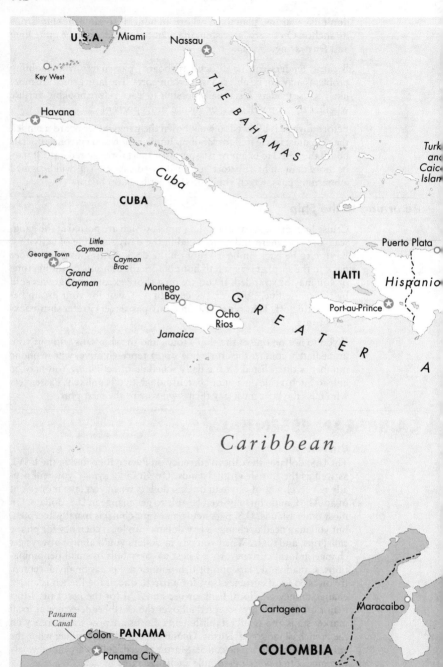

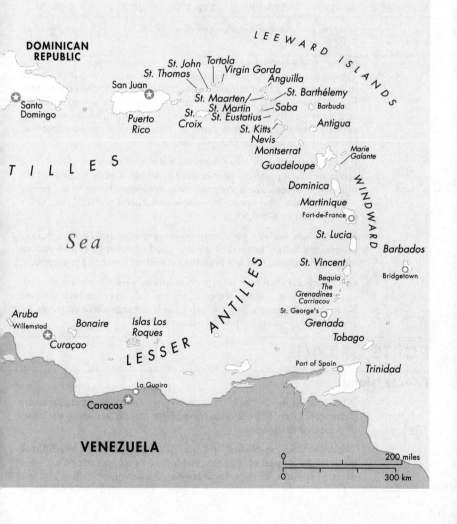

Caribbean

ATLANTIC OCEAN

DOMINICAN REPUBLIC

Santo Domingo

LEEWARD ISLANDS

St. John Tortola
St. Thomas   Virgin Gorda
San Juan   Anguilla
   St. Barthélemy
Puerto   St. Maarten/
Rico   St. Martin   Saba   Barbuda
St.   St. Eustatius
Croix   St. Kitts   Antigua
   Nevis
   Montserrat   Marie
   Guadeloupe   Galante

TILLES

Sea

Dominica
Martinique
Fort-de-France
St. Lucia   Barbados

WINDWARD

St. Vincent   Bridgetown
Bequia
The
Grenadines
Aruba   Carriacou
Willemstad   Bonaire   Islas Los   St. George's
   Roques   Grenada
Curaçao   Tobago

LESSER ANTILLES

Port of Spain   Trinidad

La Guaira

Caracas

VENEZUELA

0   200 miles
0   300 km

Where to Eat

Cuisine on the Caribbean's islands is as varied as the islands themselves. The region's history as a colonial battleground and ethnic melting pot creates plenty of variety and adds lots of unusual tropical fruit and spices. In fact, the one quality that defines most Caribbean cooking is its spiciness, acquired from nutmeg, mace, allspice, peppers, saffron, and many other seasonings grown in the islands. Dress is generally casual, although throughout the islands, beachwear is inappropriate most anywhere except on the beach. Unless otherwise noted, prices are given in U.S. dollars. The following price categories are used in this book.

WHAT IT COSTS In US$				
	$$$$	$$$	$$	$	¢
AT DINNER	over $30	$20–$30	$12–$20	$8–$12	under $8

Prices are per person for a main course at dinner and do not include any service charges.

Shore Excursions

Typical excursions include an island or town bus tour, a visit to a beach or rum factory, a boat trip, snorkeling or diving trip, and charter fishing. In recent years, however, shore excursions have gotten more adventurous with mild river rafting, parasailing, jet skiing, hiking, and biking added to the mix. It's often easier to take a ship-arranged excursion, but it's almost never the cheapest option.

If you prefer to break away from the pack, find a knowledgeable taxi driver or tour operator—they're usually within a stone's throw of the pier—or wander around on your own. A group of four to six people will usually find this option more economical and practical than will a single person or a couple.

Renting a car is also a good option on many islands—again, the more people, the better the deal. But get a good island map before you set off, and be sure to find out how long it will take you to get around.

Conditions are ideal for water sports of all kinds—scuba diving, snorkeling, windsurfing, sailing, waterskiing, and fishing excursions abound. Your shore-excursion director can usually arrange these activities for you if the ship offers no formal excursion.

PORTS OF CALL

Private Islands

When evaluating the "best" Caribbean ports of call, many repeat cruise passengers often add the cruise lines' own private islands to their lists of preferred destinations.

The cruise lines established "private" islands to provide a beach break on an island (or part of one) reserved for their exclusive use. While most passengers don't select an itinerary based solely upon calling at a private island, they usually consider them a highlight of their cruise vacation. The very least you can expect of your private island is lush foliage and a wide swath of beach surrounded by azure water. Facilities vary, but a beach barbeque, water-sports equipment rental, lounge chairs, hammocks, and restrooms are standard. Youth counselors come ashore to conduct sand castle building competitions and lead junior pirates on swashbuckling island treasure hunts, but Disney Cruise Line is the only one to offer extensive facilities and activities for different age groups.

The use of strollers and wheelchairs equipped with all-terrain wheels may be offered on a complimentary first-come, first-served basis. However, with the exception of some participation sports on the beach, plan to pay for most water toys and activities. Costs associated with private island fun and recreation can range from $6 to use of a snorkel vest (you may use your own snorkel equipment; however, in the event that a flotation vest is required, you must rent one) to $30 for rental of an entire snorkeling outfit for the day (mask, fins, snorkel vest, a mesh bag, fish identification card, and fish food). You can often take a banana boat ride for $16 to $19 (15-minute ride), sail a small boat or catamaran for $30 to $50 (one hour), paddle a kayak for $18 to $30 (half-hour), ride a jet ski for $59 to $95 (45 minutes to one hour), or parasail for a hefty $69 to $79 (10 minutes or less). Floating mats are a relative bargain at $10 for all day lounging in the water. You might also find open-air massage cabanas with pricing comparable to the spa on board.

There is no charge for food or basic beverages, such as those served on board ship. While soft drinks and tropical cocktails can be charged to your shipboard account, you might want to bring a small amount of cash ashore for souvenir shopping, which is usually possible from vendors set up on or near the beach. You will also want to bring beach towels ashore and return them to the ship at the end of the day because, as Princess Cruises reminds passengers, "Although locals may offer to do this for you, unfortunately we seldom see the towels again!"

Even if you do nothing more than lie in a shaded hammock and sip fruity tropical concoctions, the day can be one of the most fun and relaxing of your entire cruise.

Islands by Cruise Line

At this writing, Carnival is the only major cruise line without any sort of private-island experience.

COSTA CRUISES An unspoiled island paradise, Costa's **Catalina Island** is located just off the coast of the Dominican Republic. Passengers can participate in Costa's "Beach Olympics," schedule a seaside massage, or just kick back on a chaise lounge or water float. Water toy rentals, banana boat rides, and sailing tours are available from independent concessionaires. Local vendors set up souvenir shops offering crafts and T-shirts. The ship provides the food for a lunch barbeque and tropical beverages at the beach bar.

Activities: Snorkeling, sailing, jet skiing, waterskiing, hiking, volleyball, organized games, massages, shopping.

DISNEY CRUISE LINE   Unique among private islands, Disney's **Castaway Cay** has a dock, so passengers simply step ashore (rather than tendering, as is required to reach all other private islands). Like everything associated with Disney, the line's private island is almost too good to be true. In the Abacos, a chain in the Bahamas, only 10% of Castaway Cay is developed, leaving plenty of unspoiled area to explore in Robinson Crusoe fashion. Trams are provided to reach separate beaches designated for children, teens, families, and adults, and Disney is the only line to offer age-specific activities and extensive, well-planned children's activities. In addition to barbeque fare and several beverage stations, beach games, island-style music, and a shaded game pavilion, there are shops and even a post office.

Activities: Snorkeling, kayaking, parasailing, sailing, fishing, bicycles, basketball, billiards, hiking, Ping-Pong, shuffleboard, soccer, volleyball, organized games, massages, shopping.

HOLLAND AMERICA LINE   Little San Salvador, one of the Bahamian out-islands, was renamed **Half Moon Cay** by Holland America Line to honor Henry Hudson's ship (depicted on the cruise line's logo) as well as to reflect the beach's crescent shape. Even after development, the island is still so unspoiled that it has been named a Wild Bird Preserve by the Bahamian National Trust. Passengers, who are welcomed ashore at a West Indies Village complete with shops and straw market, find Half Moon Cay easily accessible—all facilities are connected by hard-surfaced and packed sand pathways and meet and exceed ADA requirements. In addition to the beach area for lazing in the sun or shade, the island has a post office, Bahamian-style chapel, and a water park for family fun.

Activities: Scuba diving, snorkeling, windsurfing, jet skiing, kayaking, parasailing, sailing, fishing, bicycles, basketball, hiking, horseback riding, shuffleboard, volleyball, massages, shopping.

NORWEGIAN CRUISE LINE   Only 120 miles east of Fort Lauderdale in the Berry Island chain of the Bahamas, much of **Great Stirrup Cay** looks as it did when it was acquired by Norwegian Cruise Line in 1977. The first uninhabited island purchased to offer cruise ship passengers a private beach day, Great Stirrup Cay's white sand beaches are fringed by coral and ideal for snorkeling. Permanent facilities have been added to and improved in the intervening years, but bougainvillea, sea grape, and coconut palms are still as abundant as the colorful tropical fish that inhabit the reef. To reduce beach erosion and preserve the environment, a sea wall was erected. A straw market, water sports centers, bars, volleyball courts, and food pavilion round out the facilities.

Activities: Snorkeling, kayaking, parasailing, sailing, Ping-Pong, hiking, volleyball, massages, shopping.

PRINCESS CRUISES   **Princess Cays** is a 40-acre haven on the southern tip of Eleuthera Island in the Bahamas. Not quite an uninhabited island, it nevertheless offers a wide ribbon of beach, long enough for passengers to splash in the surf, relax in a hammock, or limbo to the beat of local music and never feel crowded. In a similar fashion to booking shore excursions, water-sports equipment can be reserved ahead of time, either on board the ship or through the Princess website. Permanent facilities include small shops that sell island crafts and trinkets, but if you head around the back and through the fence, independent vendors sell similar goods for lower prices.

Activities: Snorkeling, kayaking, parasailing, sailing, hiking, shopping.

ROYAL CARIBBEAN & CELEBRITY CRUISES

Royal Caribbean and Celebrity Cruises passengers have twice as many opportunities to visit a private island. The lines share two, and many Caribbean itineraries include one or the other.

Coco Cay is a 140-acre island in the Berry Island chain between Nassau and Freeport. Originally known as Little Stirrup Cay, it's within view of Great Stirrup Cay (NCL's private island) and the snorkeling is just as good, especially around a sunken airplane and a replica of Blackbeard's flagship, *Queen Anne's Revenge*. In addition to activities and games ashore, Coco Cay boasts the largest Aqua Park in the Caribbean, where children and adults alike can jump on an in-water trampoline or climb a floating sand castle before they dig into a beach barbeque or explore a nature trail.

Activities: Scuba diving, snorkeling, jet skiing, kayaking, parasailing, hiking, volleyball, shopping.

Labadee is a 260-acre peninsula approximately six miles (10 km) from Cap Haitien on the secluded north coast of Hispaniola. In addition to swimming, water sports, an Aqua Park, and nature trails to explore, bonuses on Labadee are an authentic folkloric show presented by island performers and a market featuring work of local artists and crafters, where you might find an interesting painting or unique wood carving. Due to the proximity of Labadee to mainland Haiti, it is sometimes necessary to cancel calls there due to political unrest. In that event, an alternate port is usually scheduled.

Activities: Snorkeling, jet skiing, kayaking, parasailing, hiking, volleyball, shopping.

Antigua

Some say Antigua has so many beaches that you could visit a different one every day for a year. Most have snow-white sand, and many are backed by lavish resorts that offer sailing, diving, windsurfing, and snorkeling.

The larger of the British Leeward islands, Antigua was the headquarters from which Lord Horatio Nelson (then a mere captain) made his forays against the French and pirates in the late 18th century. You may wish to explore English Harbour and its carefully restored Nelson's Dockyard, as well as tour old forts, historic churches, and tiny villages. Appealing aspects of the island's interior include a small tropical rain forest ideal for hiking, ancient Native American archaeological digs, and restored sugar mills. Due to time constraints, it's best to make trips this far from port with an experienced tour operator. But you can easily take a taxi to any number of fine beaches on your own and escape from the hordes descending from the ship.

About 4,000 years ago Antigua was home to a people called the Ciboney. They disappeared mysteriously, and the island remained uninhabited for about 1,000 years. When Columbus sighted the 108-square-mi (173-square-km) island in 1493, the Arawaks had already set up housekeeping. The English moved in 130 years later, in 1623. Then a sequence of bloody battles involving the Caribs, the Dutch, the French, and the English began. Africans had been captured as slaves to work the sugar plantations by the time the French ceded the island to the English in 1667. On November 1, 1981, Antigua, with Barbuda, its sister island 30 mi (48 km) to the north, achieved full independence. The combined population of the two islands is about 70,000, only 1,200 of whom live on Barbuda.

CURRENCY   Antigua uses the Eastern Caribbean (E.C.) dollar. Figure about EC$2.70 to US$1. Although U.S. dollars are generally accepted, you may get your change in beewees. Prices given below are in U.S. dollars unless otherwise indicated.

TELEPHONES   You can use the Caribbean Phone Card (available in $5, $10, and $20 denominations in most hotels and post offices) for local and long-distance calls. To call the United States and Canada, dial 1 + the area code + the seven-digit number, or use the phone card or one of the "CALL USA" phones, which are available at several locations, including the airport departure lounge, the cruise terminal at St. John's, and the English Harbour Marina. These take credit cards and, supposedly, calling cards (though Cable & Wireless tacks on a fee).

SHORE EXCURSIONS   The following are good choices in Antigua. They may not be offered by all cruise lines. Times and prices are approximate.

Hiking Safari. Hike approximately 2 mi (3 km) through the rain forest to the top of Signal Hill, one of the island's highest points. The view is always splendid and includes Guadeloupe and Nevis on a clear day. ⊙ 3–4 hrs 🖭 $42–$59.

Historical Tour. Antigua's British-colonial heritage and great views of the island are highlighted on the drive to Nelson's Dockyard. The Georgian British maritime architecture is a must-see for history buffs and Anglophiles. Tours usually include a stop for refreshments. ⊙ 3–4 hrs 🖭 $40.

Island Jeep Safari. Get an insider's look of the countryside via four-wheel drive over dirt tracks passing deserted plantation houses, rain forest trails, sugar mill ruins, and forts. Some tours visit Fort George and most include a stop for a swim at one of the island's many beaches. Most tours include soft drinks. ⊙ 3 hrs 🖭 $52-$69.

Jolly Roger Pirate Cruise. Cruise along the coast on a replica pirate ship with an open bar, dancing, and sometimes live music; then take a swim when the ship anchors. The tour ends with a West Indian jump-up. ⊙ 3 hrs 🖭 $39–$45.

Coming Ashore

Though some ships dock at the deep-water harbor in downtown St. John's, most use Heritage Quay, a multimillion-dollar complex with shops, condominiums, a casino, and a food court. Most St. John's attractions are

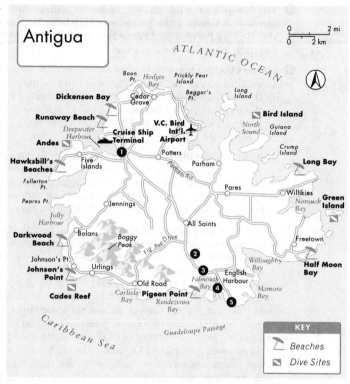

an easy walk from Heritage Quay; the older part of the city is eight blocks away. A tourist information booth is in the main docking building.

If you intend to explore beyond St. John's, consider hiring a taxi driver-guide. Taxis meet every cruise ship. They're unmetered; fares are fixed, and drivers are required to carry a rate card. Agree on the fare before setting off, and plan to tip drivers 10%. Some cabbies may take you from St. John's to English Harbour and wait for a "reasonable" amount of time (about a half hour) while you look around, for about $40; you can usually arrange an island tour for around $25 per hour. Renting your own car isn't usually practical, since you must purchase a $19 temporary driving permit in addition to the car-rental fee, which is usually about $50 per day in the high season.

Exploring Antigua
Numbers in the margin correspond to points of interest on the Antigua map.

❸ Falmouth. This town sits on a lovely bay backed by former sugar plantations and sugar mills. The most important historic site here is St. Paul's Church, which was rebuilt on the site of a church once used by troops during the Nelson period.

❷ Fort George. East of Liberta—one of the first settlements founded by freed slaves—on Monk's Hill, this fort was built from 1689 to 1720. Among the ruins are the sites for 32 cannons, water cisterns, the base of the old flagstaff, and some of the original buildings.

❹ Nelson's Dockyard. Antigua's most famous attraction is the world's only Georgian dockyard still in use, a treasure trove for history buffs and nautical nuts alike. In 1671 the governor of the Leeward Islands wrote to the Council for Foreign Plantations in London, pointing out the advantages of this landlocked harbor. By 1704 English Harbour was in regular use as a garrisoned station.

In 1784 26-year-old Horatio Nelson sailed in on the HMS *Boreas* to serve as captain and second-in-command of the Leeward Island Station. Under him was the captain of the HMS *Pegasus*, Prince William Henry, duke of Clarence, who was later crowned King William IV. The prince acted as best man when Nelson married Fannie Nisbet on Nevis in 1787.

When the Royal Navy abandoned the station at English Harbour in 1889, it fell into a state of decay, though adventuresome yachties still lived there in near-primitive conditions. The Society of the Friends of English Harbour began restoring it in 1951; it reopened with great fanfare as Nelson's Dockyard, November 14, 1961. Within the compound are crafts shops, restaurants, and two splendidly restored 18th-century hotels, the Admiral's Inn and the Copper & Lumber Store Hotel, worth peeking into. (The latter, occupying a supply store for Nelson's Caribbean fleet, is a particularly fine example of Georgian architecture and has an interior courtyard evoking Old England.) The Dockyard is a hub for ocean-going yachts and serves as headquarters for the annual Sailing Week Regatta. Water taxis will ferry you between points for EC$5. The Dockyard National Park also includes serene nature trails accessing beaches, rock pools, and crumbling plantation ruins and hilltop forts.

The **Dockyard Museum,** in the original Naval Officer's House, displays ship models, mock-ups of English Harbour, displays on the people who worked there, and typical ships that docked, silver regatta trophies, maps, prints, and Nelson's very own telescope and tea caddy. ⊠ *English Harbour* ☎ *268/481–5022, 268/481–5028 for the National Parks Department* ⊕ *www.antiguamuseums.org* 🖃 *$2, suggested donation* ☉ *Daily 8–5.*

❶ St. John's. Antigua's capital, with some 45,000 inhabitants (approximately half the island's population), lies at sea level at the inland end of a sheltered northwestern bay. Although it has seen better days, a couple of notable historic sights and some good waterfront shopping areas and restaurants make it worth a visit. Signs at the **Museum of Antigua & Barbuda** say PLEASE TOUCH, encouraging you to explore Antigua's past. Try your hand at the educational video games or squeeze a cassava through a *matapi* (a grass sieve). Exhibits interpret the nation's history, from its geological birth to its political independence in 1981. There are fossil and coral remains from some 34 million years ago; models of a sugar plantation and a wattle-and-daub house; an Arawak canoe; and a wildly eclectic assortment of objects from cannonballs to 1920s telephone exchanges. The museum occupies the former courthouse, which dates from 1750. The superlative museum gift shop carries such unusual items as calabash purses, seed earrings, and lignum vitae pipes, as well as historic maps and local books (including engrossing, detailed monographs on varied subjects by longtime resident, Desmond Nicholson). ⊠ *Church and Market Sts.* ☎ *268/462–1469* ⊕ *www.antiguamuseums. org* ⊑ *$2, suggested donation* ☉ *Weekdays 8:30–4, Sat. 10–1.*

At the south gate of the **Anglican Cathedral of St. John the Divine** are figures of St. John the Baptist and St. John the Divine said to have been taken from one of Napoléon's ships and brought to Antigua. The original church was built in 1681, replaced by a stone building in 1745, and destroyed by an earthquake in 1843. The present neo-Baroque building dates from 1845; the parishioners had the interior completely encased in pitch pine, hoping to forestall future earthquake damage. The church attained cathedral status in 1848. Tombstones bear eerily eloquent testament to the colonial days. ⊠ *Between Long and Newgate Sts.* ☎ *268/461–0082.*

Redcliffe Quay, at the water's edge just south of Heritage Quay, is the most appealing part of St. John's. Attractively restored (and superbly re-created) buildings in a riot of cotton-candy colors house shops, restaurants, and boutiques and are linked by courtyards and landscaped walkways.

❺ Shirley Heights. This bluff affords a spectacular view of English Harbour. The heights are named for Sir Thomas Shirley, the governor who fortified the harbor in 1787. At the top is Shirley Heights Lookout, a restaurant built into the remnants of the 18th-century fortifications. Most notable for its boisterous Sunday barbecues that continue into the night with live music and dancing, it serves dependable burgers, pumpkin soup, grilled meats, and rum punches. Not far from Shirley Heights is the **Dows Hill Interpretation Centre,** where observation platforms provide still more sensational vistas of the English Harbour area. A multimedia sound-and-light presentation on island history and culture, spotlighting lifelike figures and colorful tableaux accompanied by running commentary and music, results in a cheery, if bland, portrait of Antiguan life from Amerindian times to the present. ☎ *268/460–2777 for National Parks Authority* ⊑ *EC$15* ☉ *Daily 9–5.*

Shopping

Redcliffe Quay, on the waterfront at the south edge of St. John's, is by far the most appealing shopping area. Several restaurants and more than 30 boutiques, many with one-of-a-kind wares, are set around landscaped courtyards shaded by colorful trees. **Heritage Quay,** in St. John's, has 35 shops—including many that are duty-free—that cater to the cruise-ship crowd, which docks almost at its doorstep. Outlets here include Benetton, the Body Shop, Sunglass Hut, Dolce and Gabbana, and Oshkosh B'Gosh. There are also shops along **St. John's, St. Mary's, High,** and **Long streets.** The tangerine-and-lilac-hue four-story **Vendor's Mall** at the intersection of Redcliffe and Thames streets gathers the pushy, pesky vendors that once clogged the narrow streets. It's jammed with stalls; air-conditioned indoor shops sell some higher-price, if not higher-quality merchandise. On the west coast the Mediterranean-style, arcaded **Jolly Harbour Villa Resort & Marina** holds some interesting galleries and shops.

The **Goldsmitty** (⊠ Redcliffe Quay, St. John's ☎ 268/462–4601) is Hans Smit, an expert goldsmith who turns gold, black coral, and precious and semiprecious stones into one-of-a-kind works of art. **Isis** (⊠ Redcliffe Quay, St. John's ☎ 268/462–4602) sells island and international bric-a-brac, such as antique jewelry, hand-carved walking sticks, and glazed pottery. **Jacaranda** (⊠ Redcliffe Quay, St. John's ☎ 268/462–1888) sells batik, sarongs, and swimwear, as well as Caribbean food, perfumes, soaps, and artwork. **Noreen Phillips** (⊠ Redcliffe Quay, St. John's ☎ 268/462–3127) creates glitzy appliquéd and beaded evening wear—inspired by the colors of the sea and sunset—in sensuous fabrics ranging from chiffon and silk to Italian lace and Indian brocade.

Map Shop (⊠ St. Mary's St., St. John's ☎ 268/462–3993) has a "must" buy for those interested in Antiguan life: the paperback *To Shoot Hard Labour: The Life and Times of Samuel Smith, an Antiguan Working-man*. Also check out any of the books of Jamaica Kincaid, whose writing about her native Antigua has won international acclaim. The shop also offers a fine assortment of books on Caribbean cuisine, flora, fauna, and history.

Abbott's (⊠ Heritage Quay, St. John's ☎ 268/462–3108) sells pricey items from Baume & Mercier watches to Belleek china to Kosta Boda art glass in a luxurious, air-conditioned showroom.

Sports & Activities

DIVING   With all the wrecks and reefs, there are lots of undersea sights to explore, from coral canyons to sea caves. The most accessible wreck is the schooner **Andes,** not far out in Deep Bay, off the Five Islands Peninsula. Among the favorite sites are **Green Island, Cades Reef,** and **Bird Island** (a national park). **Big John's Dive Antigua** (⊠ Rex Halcyon Cove Beach Resort, Dickenson Bay ☎ 268/462–3483 ⊕ www.diveantigua.com) offers certification courses and day and night dives. Advantages include the central location, knowledgeable crew, satellite technology sounding the day's best dive sites, free drinks after dives, and exceptionally priced packages. Drawbacks include generally noisy groups and inconsistent maintenance (less safety than hygiene concerns) now that John doesn't personally supervise trips. **Dockyard Divers** (⊠ Nelson's Dockyard, English Harbour ☎ 268/460–1178), owned by British ex-merchant seaman Captain A. G. "Tony" Fincham, is one of the island's most established outfits and offers diving and snorkeling trips, PADI courses, and dive packages with accommodations. They're geared to seasoned divers, but work patiently with novices.

GOLF   **Cedar Valley Golf Club** (⊠ Friar's Hill ☎ 268/462–0161), northeast of St. John's, has a par-70, 6,157-yard, 18-hole course. The bland, not terribly well-maintained terrain offers some challenge with tight hilly fairways and numerous doglegs. The 5th hole has exceptional vistas from the top of the tee, while the 9th offers the trickiest design. Greens fees are $35; carts are $30.

Beaches

Antigua's beaches are public, and many are dotted with resorts that have water-sports outfitters and beach bars. Most hotels have taxi stands, so getting back to the ship isn't usually a problem. Sunbathing topless or in the buff is strictly illegal except on one of the small beaches at Hawksbill Beach Hotel on the Five Islands Peninsula. Most cruise-ship beach excursions go to the beaches on the west coast.

Dickenson Bay is a lengthy stretch of powder-soft white sand and exceptionally calm water, where you'll find small and large hotels, water sports, concessions, and beachfront restaurants. **Half Moon Bay,** a ¾-mi (1-km) crescent, is a prime snorkeling and windsurfing area. On the Atlantic side of the island the water can be quite rough (the eastern end is calmer). **Johnson's Point** is a series of connected, deliciously deserted beaches of bleached white sand on the southwest coast overlooking Montserrat. You can explore a ruined fort at one end; notable beach bars are OJ's (try the snapper) and Turner's. **Pigeon Point,** near Falmouth Harbour, has two fine white-sand beaches; the leeward side is calmer, while the windward side is rockier, with sensational views and snorkeling around the point. Several restaurants and bars are nearby. **Runaway Beach,** a stretch of glittering sand, is still rebuilding after years of hurricane erosion. Both the water and the scene are relatively calm, and beach bars such as Lashings and Amigo's (the surprisingly good Mexican restaurant at Barrymore Beach Hotel) offer cool shade and cold beer.

Where to Eat

In restaurants, a 10% service charge and 7% tax are usually added to the bill.

$$–$$$ ✕ **Catherine's Café.** This little deck café overlooking English Harbour marina brims with Gallic verve thanks to ebullient hostess Catherine Ricard, whose definition of table-hopping sometimes includes strangers' laps. The food is simple: zucchini-Roquefort quiche, a proper *salade niçoise,* and lovely brochettes. Evening delights might include *moules marinéres* (marinated mussels) or *gratin de cèpes* (wild mushrooms in a cheese sauce). There's a fairly priced, extensive wine list highlighted by Catherine's pert comments. This delightful place always percolates with life and good strong espresso. ⊠ *English Harbour* ☎ *268/460–5050* ▭ *MC, V* ☺ *Closed Tues. and Sept. No dinner Mon.*

$–$$ ✕ **Big Banana–Pizzas in Paradise.** This tiny, often crowded spot is tucked into one side of a restored 18th-century rum warehouse with broad plank floors, wood beams, and stone archways. Cool Benetton-style photos of locals and jamming musicians adorn the brick walls. It serves some of the island's best pizza—try the lobster or the seafood variety—as well as such tasty specials as conch salad, fresh fruit crushes, and sub sandwiches bursting at the seams. There's live entertainment Thursday night, and sports nuts congregate at the bar's huge satellite TV. ⊠ *Redcliffe Quay, St. John's* ☎ *268/480–6985* ▭ *AE, MC, V* ☺ *Closed Sun.*

Aruba

Though the "A" in the ABC (Aruba, Bonaire, Curaçao) Islands is small—only 19 mi (31 km) long and 6 mi (10 km) at its widest—the island's national anthem proclaims "the greatness of our people is their great cordiality," and this is no exaggeration. Once a member of the Netherlands Antilles, Aruba became a quasi-independent "separate entity within the Kingdom of the Netherlands" in 1986, with its own royally appointed governor, a democratic government, and a 21-member elected parliament. Long secure in a solid economy—with good education, housing, and health care—the island's population of nearly 95,000 treats visitors as welcome guests. English is spoken everywhere.

The island's distinctive beauty lies in the stark contrast between the sea and the countryside: rocky deserts, cactus jungles, secluded coves, and aquamarine panoramas with crashing waves. But it's best-known for its duty-free shops, the glorious 7-mi (11-km) strand of Palm and Eagle beaches, and casinos.

CURRENCY   Arubans accept U.S. dollars readily, so you need only acquire Aruban florins (AFl) for pocket change. Note that the Netherlands Antilles florin used on Bonaire and Curaçao is not accepted on Aruba.

TELEPHONES   When making calls to anywhere in Aruba, simply dial the seven-digit number. AT&T customers can dial 800–8000 from special phones at the cruise dock and in the airport's arrival and departure halls. Otherwise dial 121 to contact the international operator to place an international call.

SHORE   The following are good choices on Aruba. They may not be offered by
EXCURSIONS   all cruise lines. Times and prices are approximate.

Aruba Town & Countryside Drive. A comprehensive bus tour takes in the major island sights, including the popular limestone Natural Bridge, California Lighthouse, desolate Alto Vista Chapel, sculptural boulder formations, and caves stippled with petroglyphs, stalactites, and stalagmites. The bus will drop you either in town or at the cruise-ship terminal. ⊙ 3 hrs 🖼 $34–$36.

Atlantis Submarine Tour. Dive 95 to 150 feet (29 to 46 meters) below the surface along Barcadera Reef to explore an underwater sanctuary teeming with colorful marine life without getting wet. The 65-foot air-conditioned sub, *Atlantis VI* accommodates 48 people and, during the 30-minute cruise to the dive site, drinks are available on deck; the dive itself is approximately an hour in duration. ⊙ 2 hrs 🖼 $84–$89.

***Kukoo Kunuku* Bar Hop & Dinner Tour.** Board an Aruba institution, the psychedelically painted 1957 Chevy bus called the *Kukoo Kunuku,* for a champagne toast followed by dinner and a lively evening of bar hopping. Included is dinner, your first drink at each bar stop, and transportation. The price is a $15 premium over what you'd pay otherwise. ⊙ 4–5 hrs 🖼 $69.

Sailing & Snorkeling Tour. A motorized catamaran takes you to a shallow coral reef and the wreck of the German freighter *Antilla*, which was sunk during World War II. Tours include equipment and beverages;

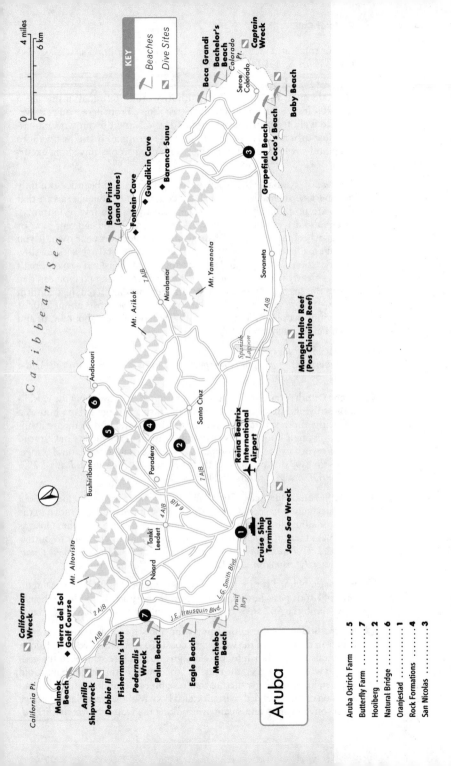

Aruba

Caribbean Sea

California Pt.

Californian Wreck

Malmok Beach
Antilla Shipwreck
Debbie II
Mt. Altovista
Tierra del Sol Golf Course
♦

Bushiribana

Andicouri

6
5
4
2

Pedernalis Wreck
Fisherman's Hut
Palm Beach

Noord

Eagle Beach

7

Manchebo Beach

J.E. Irausquin Blvd.
L.G. Smith Blvd.
Druif Bay

Tanki Leendert

4 A/B
6 A/B
2 A/B
1 A/B

Paradera

Santa Cruz

Mt. Arikok

Miralamar

Mt. Yamanota

7 A/B

1 A/B

Savaneta

Spanish Lagoon

Reina Beatrix International Airport ✈

Cruise Ship Terminal

1

Jane Sea Wreck

Mangel Halto Reef (Pos Chiquito Reef)

Boca Prins (sand dunes)
Fontein Cave ♦
Guadikin Cave ♦
Baranca Sunu ♦

Boca Grandi
Bachelor's Beach
Seroe Colorado
Colorado Pt.
Captain Wreck

Grapefield Beach
Coco's Beach
Baby Beach

3

KEY
Beaches
Dive Sites

N

0 | 4 miles
0 | 6 km

Aruba Ostrich Farm **5**
Butterfly Farm **7**
Hooiberg **2**
Natural Bridge **6**
Oranjestad **1**
Rock Formations **4**
San Nicolas **3**

5-hour tours also include morning brunch or afternoon snacks. ⊙ *3–5 hrs* ⊙ *3 hrs $38–$44, 5 hrs $69.*

Coming Ashore

Ships tie up at the Aruba Port Authority cruise terminal; inside are a tourist information booth and duty-free shops. From here, you're a five-minute walk from various shopping districts and downtown Oranjestad. Just turn right as you leave the cruise terminal. If you just want to shop and stroll around town, there's no need to buy any shore excursions or even hire a cab.

The "real" Aruba—what's left of its wild, untamed beauty—can only be experienced on a drive through the countryside (though be aware that there are no public bathrooms except for those in a few restaurants). Your valid driver's license will work in Aruba, so you can rent a car or a four-wheel-drive vehicle if you want to explore on your own. If you haven't made reservations, be aware that the car rental agencies are slow at processing walk-up rental applications. And the island's roads aren't always clearly marked. Your best bet may be to hire a taxi (you can flag one in the street). There are no meters, but rates are fixed; just confirm the fare before setting off. An hour-long island tour costs about $40 for up to four people. Rides to and from Eagle Beach run about $5; to and from Palm Beach, about $8.

Exploring Aruba

Numbers in the margin correspond to points of interest on the Aruba map.

❺ Aruba Ostrich Farm. Everything you ever wanted to know about the world's largest living birds can be found at the farm. A large palapa houses a gift shop and restaurant (popular with bus tours) and tours are available every half-hour. This is virtually identical to the facility in Curaçao and is owned by the same company. It's on the road to the natural bridge, so it's an easy stop on the way there or back. ⊠ *Makividiri Rd.* ☎ *297/ 585–9630* ☞ *$10 adults* ⊙ *Daily 9–5.*

❼ Butterfly Farm. Hundreds of butterflies from around the world flutter about this spectacular garden. Guided 20- to 30-minute tours (included in the price of admission) provide an entertaining look into how these insects complete their life cycle: from egg to caterpillar to chrysalis to butterfly. ⊠ *J. E. Irausquin Blvd., Palm Beach* ☎ *297/586–3656* ⊕ *www.thebutterflyfarm.com* ☞ *$12* ⊙ *Daily 9–4:30; last tour at 4.*

❷ Hooiberg. Named for its shape (*hooiberg* means "haystack" in Dutch), this 541-foot peak lies inland just past the airport. If you have the energy, climb the 562 steps to the top for an impressive view of the city.

❻ Natural Bridge. Centuries of raging wind and sea sculpted this coral-rock bridge in the center of the windward coast. To reach it, drive inland along Hospitalstraat and then follow the signs. Just before you reach the geological wonder, you pass the massive stone ruins of the Bushiribana Gold Smelter, an intriguing structure that resembles a crumbling fortress, and a section of surf-pounded coastline called Boca Mahos. Near Natural Bridge are a souvenir shop and a café overlooking the water. ⊠ *Makividiri Rd.*

① **Oranjestad.** Aruba's charming capital is best explored on foot. The palm-lined thoroughfare in the center of town runs between pastel-painted buildings, old and new, of typical Dutch design. There are many malls with boutiques and shops.

At the **Archaeological Museum of Aruba** you can find two rooms chock-full of fascinating artifacts from the indigenous Arawak people, including farm and domestic utensils dating back hundreds of years. ✉ *J. E. Irausquinplein 2A* ☎ *297/582–8979* 🎫 *Free* ☉ *Weekdays 8–noon and 1–4.*

Learn all about aloe—its cultivation, processing, and production—at **Aruba Aloe,** Aruba's own aloe farm and factory. Guided tours lasting about a half hour will show you how the gel—revered for its skin-soothing properties—is extracted from the aloe vera plant and used in a variety of products, including after-sun creams, soaps, and shampoos. You can purchase the finished goods in the gift shop. ✉ *Pitastraat 115, Oranjestad* ☎ *297/588-3222* 🎫 *$6* ☉ *Weekdays 8:30–4:30, Sat. 9–2.*

One of the island's oldest edifices, **Fort Zoutman** was built in 1796 and played an important role in skirmishes between British and Curaçao troops in 1803. The Willem III Tower, named for the Dutch monarch of that time, was added in 1868 to serve as a lighthouse. Over time, the fort has been put to use as a government office building, a police station, and a prison. Now its historical museum displays Aruban artifacts in an 18th-century house. ✉ *Zoutmanstraat* ☎ *297/582-6099* 🎫 *Free* ☉ *Weekdays 8–noon and 1–4.*

The **Numismatic Museum** displays more than 40,000 historic coins and paper money from around the world. A few pieces were salvaged from shipwrecks in the region. Some of the coins circulated during the Roman Empire, the Byzantine Empire, and the ancient Chinese dynasties; the oldest dates to the 3rd century BC. The museum—which moved in 2003 to a new, larger location next to the central bus station—had its start as the private collection of one Aruban who dug up some old coins in his garden. It's now run by his granddaughter. ✉ *Westraat* ☎ *297/ 582-8831* 🎫 *$5* ☉ *Mon.–Thurs. 9–4, Fri. 9–1, Sat. 9–noon.*

④ **Rock Formations.** The massive boulders at Ayo and Casibari are a mystery, as they don't match the island's geological makeup. You can climb to the top for fine views of the arid countryside. On the way you'll doubtless pass Aruba whip-tail lizards—the males are cobalt blue, the females blue with dots. The main path to Casibari has steps and handrails (except on one side), and you must move through tunnels and along narrow steps and ledges to reach the top. At Ayo you can find ancient pictographs in a small cave (the entrance has iron bars to protect the drawings from vandalism). You may also encounter a boulder climber, one of many who are increasingly drawn to Ayo's smooth surfaces. Access to Casibari is via Tanki Highway 4A to Ayo via Route 6A; watch carefully for the turnoff signs near the center of the island on the way to the windward side.

❸ San Nicolas. During the heyday of the oil refineries, Aruba's oldest village was a bustling port; now its primary purpose is tourism. *The* institution in town is Charlie's Restaurant & Bar. Stop in for a drink and advice on what to see and do in this little town.

Shopping

Caya G. F. Betico Croes in Oranjestad is Aruba's chief shopping street. Several malls—gabled, pastel-hued re-creations of traditional Dutch colonial architecture—house branches of such top names as Tommy Hilfiger, Little Switzerland, Nautica, and Benetton; the ritziest are the **Royal Plaza** and **Renaissance Mall,** both right near the cruise-ship pier. The stores are full of Dutch porcelains and figurines. Also consider the Dutch cheeses (you're allowed to bring up to 10 pounds of hard cheese through U.S. Customs), hand-embroidered linens, and any product made from the native aloe vera plant. There's no sales tax, and Arubans consider it rude to haggle.

Art & Tradition Handicrafts (✉ Caya G. F. Betico Croes 30, Oranjestad ☎ 297/583–6534 ✉ Royal Plaza Mall, L. G. Smith Blvd. 94, Oranjestad ☎ 297/582–7862) sells intriguing souvenirs. Buds from the *mopa mopa* tree are boiled to form a resin colored by vegetable dyes. Artists then stretch the resin by hand and mouth. Tiny pieces are cut and layered to form intricate designs—truly unusual gifts. For perfumes, cosmetics, men's and women's clothing, and leather goods (including Bally shoes), stop in at **Aruba Trading Company** (✉ Caya G. F. Betico Croes 12, Oranjestad ☎ 297/582–2602), which has been in business since the 1930s. Filling 6,000 square feet of space, **Boolchand's** (✉ Renaissance Mall, L. G. Smith Blvd. 82, Oranjestad ☎ 297/583–0147) sells jewelry and watches. It also stocks leather goods, cameras, and electronics. **Wulfsen & Wulfsen** (✉ Caya G. F. Betico Croes 52, Oranjestad ☎ 297/58–23823) has been one of the most highly regarded clothing stores in the Netherlands Antilles since the 1970s.

Sports & Activities

FISHING Captain Kenny of **Teaser Charters** (✉ St. Vincentweg 5, Oranjestad ☎ 297/582–5088 ⊕ www.teasercharters.com) runs a thrilling expedition. The expertise of the crew is matched by a commitment to sensible fishing practices, making this an excellent as well as enjoyable choice. The company's two boats are fully equipped, and the crew seem to have an uncanny ability to locate the best fishing spots.

GOLF **The Links at Divi Aruba** (✉ J. E. Irasquin Blvd. 93, Oranjestad ☎ 297/581–4653), a 9-hole course designed by Karl Litten and Lorie Viola, opened in 2004. The par-36 course on paspalum grass (best for seaside courses) takes you past beautiful lagoons. Amenities include a golf school with professional instruction, a swing analysis station, a driving range, and a two-story golf clubhouse with a pro shop. Two restaurants serving contemporary American cuisine with Caribbean accents are par for the course. Greens fees are $70 for 9 holes, $105 for 18 (high season). **Tierra del Sol** (✉ Malmokweg ☎ 297/586–0978), a stunning course, is on the northwest coast near the California Lighthouse. Designed by Robert Trent Jones, Jr., this 18-hole championship course combines Aruba's native beauty—cacti and rock formations—with the lush greens of the world's best courses. The $145 greens fee includes a golf cart equipped with a communications system that allows you to order drinks for your return to the clubhouse. Half-day golf clinics (Monday, Tuesday, and Thursday), a bargain at $45, include lunch in the clubhouse. The pro shop is one of the Caribbean's most elegant, with an extremely attentive staff.

HORSEBACK RIDING **Rancho Daimari** (✉ Tanki Leendert 249, San Nicholas ☎ 297/587–5674 ⊕ www.visitaruba.com/ranchodaimari) will lead your horse to water—either at Natural Bridge or Natural Pool—in the morning or afternoon for $55 per person. The "Junior Dudes" program is tailored for young riders. They even have ATV trips. **Rancho Notorious** (✉ Boroncana, Noord ☎ 297/586–0508 ⊕ www.ranchonotorious.com) will take you on a tour of the countryside for $50, to the beach to snorkel for $55, or on a three-hour ride up to the California Lighthouse for $65. The company also organizes ATV and mountain-biking trips.

KAYAKING Kayaking is a popular sport on Aruba, especially along the south coast, where the waters are calm. It's a great way to explore a stretch of coastline. **Aruba Kayak Adventure** (✉ Ponton 90, Oranjestad ☎ 297/587–7722 ⊕ www.arubawavedancer.com/arubakayak) has excellent half-day kayak trips, which start with a quick lesson before you begin paddling through caves and mangroves, and along the scenic coastline. The tour makes a lunch stop at De Palm Island, where snorkeling is included as part of the $77 package.

WATER SPORTS **De Palm Tours** (✉ L. G. Smith Blvd. 142, Oranjestad ☎ 297/582–4400 or 800/766–6016 ⊕ www.depalm.com) is one of the best options for novice divers who don't want to be certified. Don a helmet and walk along the ocean floor near De Palm Island, home of huge blue parrot fish. Have your picture taken at an underwater table loaded with champagne and roses. Try Snuba—like scuba diving but without the heavy air tanks—either from a boat or from an island. Rates are $79 to $99, including meals. **Pelican Tours & Watersports** (✉ Pelican Pier, near the Holiday Inn and Playa Linda hotels, Palm Beach ☎ 297/586–3271 ⊕ www.pelican-aruba.com) has snorkeling tours for around $30, brunch tours or sunset cruises for around $50. **Red Sail Sports** (✉ Renaissance Mall, L. G. Smith Blvd. 83, Oranjestad ☎ 297/586–1603, 877/733–7245 in U.S. ⊕ www.aruba-redsail.com), with courses for children and others new to scuba diving, is especially good for beginners. It also offers snorkeling tours.

Beaches

Beaches in Aruba are beautiful and clean. On the north side the water is too choppy for swimming, but the views are great. **Baby Beach,** on the island's eastern tip, is a semicircle bordering a bay that's as placid and just about as deep as a wading pool—perfect for tots and terrible swimmers. Thatched shaded areas are good for cooling off. Just down the road is the island's unusual pet cemetery. You may see some shore divers here. Stop by the nearby snack shop for chicken legs, burgers, hot dogs, beer, and soda. **Eagle Beach,** on the southwestern coast, is across the highway from what is known as Time-Share Lane. This beach, which is more than a mile long is one of the best in the Caribbean, if not the world. **Manchebo Beach (Punta Brabo)** is impressively wide. The shoreline in front of the Manchebo Beach Resort is where officials turn a blind eye to the occasional topless sunbather. **Palm Beach,** the center of Aruban tourism, offers the best in swimming, sailing, and other water sports. It runs from the Wyndham Aruba Beach Resort to the Aruba Marriott Resort.

Where to Eat

Restaurants usually add a 10% to 15% service charge.

$$–$$$$ ✕ **Hostaria Da' Vittorio.** Part of the fun at this family-oriented spot is watching chef Vittorio Muscariello prepare authentic Italian regional specialties in the open kitchen. Rising above the decibel level of the crowd, the staff helps you choose wines from the extensive list and recommends portions of hot-and-cold antipasti, risottos, and pastas. As you leave, pick up some limoncello or olive oil at the gourmet shop. This is one of the few restaurants in Aruba that has a stringent dress code, so avoid jeans. A 15% gratuity is automatically added to your bill. AGA VIP member. ⊠ *L. G. Smith Blvd. 380, Palm Beach* ☎ *297/586–3838* ☱ *AE, D, MC, V.*

$$–$$$ ✕ **Qué Pasa?** The exterior of this funky eatery is lemon yellow and the interior serves as something of an art gallery. Despite the name, there isn't a Mexican dish to be seen: the menu includes everything from sashimi to ribs, but everything is done with Aruban flair. The fish dishes are especially good. The bar area is lively and friendly. ⊠ *Wilheminastraat 2, Oranjestad* ☎ *297/583–4888* ☱ *D, MC, V.*

Barbados

Barbadians (Bajans) are a warm, friendly, and hospitable people, who are genuinely proud of their country and culture. Tourism is the island's number one industry; but with a sophisticated business community and stable government, life here doesn't skip a beat after passengers return to the ship. A resort island since the 1700s, Barbados has cultivated a civilized attitude toward tourists.

Under uninterrupted British rule for 340 years—until independence in 1966—Barbados retains a very British atmosphere. Afternoon tea is a ritual, and cricket is the national sport. The atmosphere, though, is hardly stuffy. This is still the Caribbean, after all.

Beaches along the island's south and west coasts are picture-perfect, and all are open to cruise passengers. On the rugged east coast, where Bajans have their vacation homes, the Atlantic Ocean attracts world-class surfers. The northeast is dominated by rolling hills and valleys; the interior of the island is covered by acres of sugarcane and dotted with small villages. Historic plantations, a stalactite-studded cave, a wildlife preserve, rum factories, and tropical gardens are among the island's attractions. Bridgetown, the capital, is a busy city with more traffic than charm.

CURRENCY   The currency of Barbados is the Barbados dollar (BDS$), and the exchange rate is set at about two Barbados dollars to one U.S. dollar. Either currency is accepted almost everywhere on the island, as are major credit cards and traveler's checks, so you may not need to exchange money. Always ask which currency is being quoted. Prices given below are in U.S. dollars unless otherwise indicated.

TELEPHONES You can purchase phone cards at the cruise-ship terminal. Direct-dialing to the United States, Canada, and other countries is efficient and reasonable, but always check with your hotel to see if a surcharge is added. Some toll-free numbers cannot be accessed in Barbados. To charge your overseas call on a major credit card without incurring a surcharge, dial 800/744–2000 from any phone.

SHORE The following are popular choices on Barbados. They may not be of-
EXCURSIONS fered by all cruise lines. Times and prices are approximate.

Atlantis Submarine. Dive as deep as 150 feet below the surface on a 50-foot mini-submarine. You will view profuse marine life without getting wet. ☉ 2½ hrs ⊠ $89–$99.

Island Tour and Harrison's Cave. Drive through Holetown, the interior of the island, and along the rugged Atlantic coast before arriving at Barbados' famous Harrison Cave. A highlight of the one-hour tram ride through the limestone cave is a 40-foot underground waterfall. The tour usually includes a visit to the Flower Forest, Orchid World, or Andromeda Gardens. ☉ 4 hrs ⊠ $58–$69.

Kayak and Turtle Encounter. After a boat ride along the west coast, you will paddle kayaks for approximately 45 minutes to reach the snorkeling site, where the guides feed the turtles while you swim among them. Beverages are included on the boat ride back to the ship; snorkel equipment is also provided. ☉ 3½ hrs ⊠ $69–$79.

Malibu Beach Break. Sample a rum drink and tour the Malibu Rum Distillery before relaxing at the beach, where there are changing rooms, showers, lockers, and beach chairs. ☉ 4 hrs ⊠ $25.

Coming Ashore

Up to eight ships at a time can dock at Bridgetown's Deep Water Harbour, on the northwest side of Carlisle Bay. The cruise-ship terminal has duty-free shops, handicraft vendors, a post office, a telephone station, a tourist information desk, and a taxi stand. To get downtown, follow the shoreline to the Careenage. It's a 15-minute walk or a $3–$5 cab ride.

Taxis await ships at the pier. Drivers accept U.S. dollars and appreciate a 10% tip. Taxis are unmetered and operate at a fixed hourly rate of $25 per carload (up to three passengers). Most drivers will cheerfully narrate an island tour. You can rent a car with a valid driver's license, but rates are steep—during the high season, up to $125 per day.

Exploring Barbados

Numbers in the margin correspond to points of interest on the Barbados map.

BRIDGETOWN This bustling capital city is a major duty-free port with a compact shopping area. The principal thoroughfare is Broad Street, which leads west from National Heroes Square. Bridgetown, surprisingly enough, has both rush hours and traffic congestion.

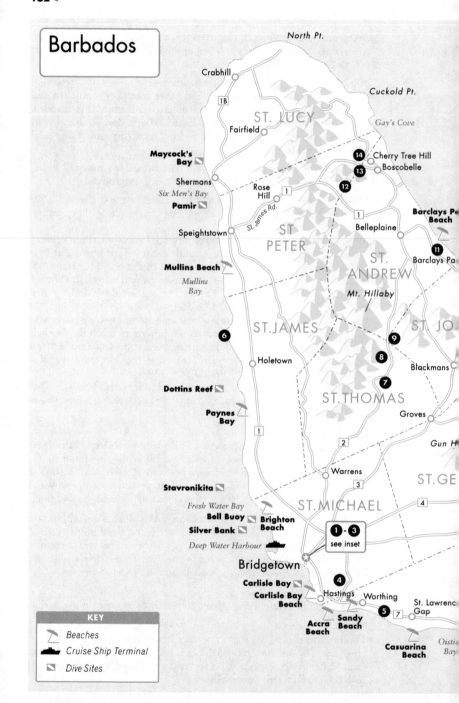

Barbados

North Pt.

Crabhill

Cuckold Pt.

1B

ST. LUCY

Gay's Cove

Fairfield

Maycock's Bay

14 Cherry Tree Hill
13 Boscobelle
12

Shermans
Six Men's Bay
Pamir

Rose Hill
1

St. James Rd.

Belleplaine

Speightstown

ST PETER

Barclays P Beach

11 Barclays Pa

ST. ANDREW

Mullins Beach

Mullins Bay

Mt. Hillaby

6

ST.JAMES

9

ST JO

Holetown

8

Dottins Reef

7

Blackmans

Paynes Bay

1

ST.THOMAS

Groves

Gun H

2

Stavronikita

Warrens

3

ST.GE

Fresh Water Bay

ST.MICHAEL

4

Bell Buoy Brighton Beach
Silver Bank

Deep Water Harbour

1 - 3
see inset

Bridgetown

4

Carlisle Bay
Carlisle Bay Beach

Hastings Worthing

St. Lawrenc Gap

5 7

Accra Beach

Sandy Beach

Oisti Bay

Casuarina Beach

KEY

Beaches

Cruise Ship Terminal

Dive Sites

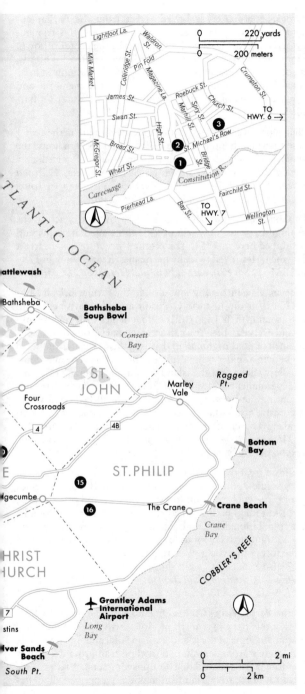

1 **National Heroes Square.** Across Broad Street from the Parliament Buildings and bordered by High and Trafalgar streets, this triangular area (formerly called Trafalgar Square) marks the center of town. Its monument to Lord Horatio Nelson—who was in Barbados briefly, as a 19-year-old navy lieutenant—predates Nelson's Column in London's Trafalgar Square by 36 years. Also here are a war memorial and a fountain that commemorates the advent of running water on Barbados in 1865.

2 **Parliament Buildings.** Overlooking National Heroes Square in the center of town, these Victorian buildings were built around 1870 to house the British Commonwealth's third-oldest parliament. A series of stained-glass windows depicts British monarchs from James I to Victoria. ⊠ *Broad St., St. Michael* ☎ *246/427–2019* ✏ *Donations welcome* ⊘ *Tours weekdays at 11 and 2, when parliament isn't in session.*

3 **St. Michael's Cathedral.** Although no one has proved it conclusively, George Washington, on his only trip outside the United States, is said to have worshipped here in 1751. The original structure was nearly a century old by then. Destroyed twice by hurricanes, it was rebuilt in 1784 and again in 1831. ⊠ *Spry St., east of National Heroes Sq., St. Michael.*

CENTRAL & WEST **Barbados Museum.** This intriguing museum, in the former British Military Prison (1815) in the historic Garrison area, has artifacts from Arawak days (around 400 BC) and galleries that depict 19th-century military history and everyday life. You can see cane-harvesting tools, wedding dresses, ancient (and frightening) dentistry instruments, and slave sale accounts kept in a spidery copperplate handwriting. The museum's Harewood Gallery showcases the island's flora and fauna; its Cunard Gallery has a permanent collection of 20th-century Barbadian and Caribbean paintings and engravings; and its Connell Gallery features European decorative arts. Additional galleries include one for children; the museum also has a gift shop and a café. ⊠ *Hwy. 7, Garrison Savannah, St. Michael* ☎ *246/427–0201 or 246/436–1956* ⊕ *www.barbmuse.org.bb* ✏ *$4* ⊘ *Mon.–Sat. 9–5, Sun. 2–6.*

9 **Flower Forest.** It's a treat to meander among fragrant flowering bushes, canna and ginger lilies, puffball trees, and more than 100 other species of tropical flora in a cool, tranquil forest of flowers and other plants. A ½-mi-long (1-km-long) path winds through the 50 acres of grounds, a former sugar plantation; it takes about 30 to 45 minutes to follow the path, or you can wander freely for as long as you wish. Benches located throughout the forest give you a place to pause, sit down for a bit, and reflect. There's also a snack bar, a gift shop, and a beautiful view of Mt. Hillaby. ⊠ *Hwy. 2, Richmond Plantation, St. Joseph* ☎ *246/433–8152* ✏ *$7* ⊘ *Daily 9–5.*

6 **Folkestone Marine Park & Visitor Centre.** On land and offshore, the whole family will enjoy this park just north of Holetown. The museum and aquarium illuminate some of the island's marine life; and for some firsthand viewing, there's an underwater snorkeling trail around Dottin's Reef (glass-bottom boats are available for nonswimmers). A barge sunk in shallow water is home to myriad fish, making it a popular dive site.

✉ *Church Point, Holetown, St. James* ☎ *246/422–2871* 🎫 *Free* ⊙ *Weekdays 9–5.*

⟲ ⑩ **Gun Hill Signal Station.** The 360-degree view from Gun Hill, 700 feet above sea level, was what made this location of strategic importance to the 18th-century British army. Using lanterns and semaphore, soldiers based here could communicate with their counterparts at The Garrison, on the south coast, and at Grenade Hill in the north. Time moved slowly in 1868, and Captain Henry Wilkinson whiled away his off-duty hours by carving a huge lion from a single rock—which is on the hillside just below the tower. Come for a short history lesson but mainly for the view; it's so gorgeous, military invalids were once sent here to convalesce. ✉ *Gun Hill, St. George* ☎ *246/429–1358* 🎫 *$4.60* ⊙ *Weekdays 9–5.*

⟲ ⑦ **Harrison's Cave.** This limestone cavern, complete with stalactites, stalagmites, subterranean streams, and a 40-foot waterfall, is a rare find in the Caribbean—and one of Barbados's most popular attractions. The one-hour tours are conducted via electric trams, which fill up fast; reserve ahead of time. Hard hats are required and provided, but all that may fall on you is a little dripping water. ✉ *Hwy. 2, Welchman Hall, St. Thomas* ☎ *246/438–6640* 🎫 *$13* ⊙ *Daily 9–6; last tour at 4.*

⟲ ⑤ **Tyrol Cot Heritage Village.** This interesting coral-stone cottage just south of Bridgetown was constructed in 1854 and has been preserved as an example of period architecture. In 1929 it became the home of Sir Grantley Adams, the first premier of Barbados and the namesake of its international airport. Part of the Barbados National Trust, the cottage is now filled with antiques and memorabilia of the late Sir Grantley and Lady Adams. It's also the centerpiece of an outdoor "living museum," where artisans and craftsmen have their workshops in a cluster of traditional chattel houses. The crafts are for sale, and refreshments are available at the "rum shop." ✉ *Rte. 2, Codrington Hill, St. Michael* ☎ *246/424–2074 or 246/436–9033* 🎫 *$6* ⊙ *Weekdays 9–5.*

⑧ **Welchman Hall Gully.** This 1-mi-long (2-km-long) natural gully is really a collapsed limestone cavern, once part of the same underground network as Harrison's Cave. The Barbados National Trust protects the peace and quiet here, making it a beautiful place to hike past acres of labeled flowers and stands of trees. You can see and hear some interesting birds—and, with luck, a native green monkey. ✉ *Welchman Hall, St. Thomas* ☎ *246/438–6671* 🎫 *$5.75* ⊙ *Daily 9–5.*

NORTH & EAST ⑪ **Andromeda Gardens.** Beautiful and unusual plant specimens from around the world are cultivated in 6 acres of gardens that are nestled among streams, ponds, and rocky outcroppings overlooking the sea above the Bathsheba coastline. The gardens were created in 1954 with flowering plants collected by the late horticulturist Iris Bannochie. They're now administered by the Barbados National Trust. The Hibiscus Café serves snacks and drinks. ✉ *Bathsheba, St. Joseph* ☎ *246/433–9261* 🎫 *$6* ⊙ *Daily 9–5.*

⟲ ⑬ **Barbados Wildlife Reserve.** The reserve is the habitat of herons, innumerable land turtles, screeching peacocks, shy deer, elusive green monkeys, brilliantly colored parrots (in a large walk-in aviary), a snake, and a caiman. Except for the snake and the caiman, the animals run or fly freely—so step carefully and keep your hands to yourself. Late afternoon is your best chance to catch a glimpse of a green monkey. ⊠ *Farley Hill, St. Peter* ☎ *246/422–8826* ☜ *$11.50* ☉ *Daily 10–5.*

⑫ **Farley Hill.** At this national park in northern St. Peter, across the road from the Barbados Wildlife Reserve, the imposing ruins of a plantation greathouse are surrounded by gardens and lawns, along with an avenue of towering royal palms and gigantic mahogany, whitewood, and casuarina trees. Partially rebuilt for the filming of *Island in the Sun,* the classic 1957 film starring Harry Belafonte and Dorothy Dandridge, the structure was later destroyed by fire. Behind the estate, there's a sweeping view of the region called Scotland for its rugged landscape. ⊠ *Farley Hill, St. Peter* ☎ *246/422–3555* ☜ *$2 per car, pedestrians free* ☉ *Daily 8:30–6.*

⑭ **St. Nicholas Abbey.** There's no religious connection here at all. The island's oldest greathouse (circa 1650) was named after the British owner's hometown, St. Nicholas parish near Bristol, and Bath Abbey nearby. Its stone-and-wood architecture makes it one of only three original Jacobean-style houses still standing in the Western Hemisphere. It has Dutch gables, finials of coral stone, and beautiful grounds. The first floor, fully furnished with period furniture and portraits of family members, is open to the public. Fascinating home movies, shot by the current owner's father, record Bajan life in the 1930s. The Calabash Café, in the rear, serves snacks, lunch, and afternoon tea. ⊠ *Cherry Tree Hill, St. Lucy* ☎ *246/422–8725* ☜ *$5* ☉ *Weekdays 10–3:30.*

SOUTH **Foursquare Rum Distillery & Heritage Park.** A long road bisecting acres of
♻ ⑯ cane fields brings you to the newest rum distillery built in Barbados. Situated on a 19th-century sugar plantation, the spotless, environmentally friendly, high-tech distillery produces ESA Field white rum and premium Alleyne Arthur varieties. Adjacent is the 7-acre Heritage Park, which showcases Bajan skills and talents in its Art Foundry and Cane Pit Amphitheatre; a row of shops and vendor carts has a diverse selection of local products, crafts, and foods. ⊠ *Foursquare Plantation, St. Philip* ☎ *246/420–1977* ☜ *$7.50* ☉ *Daily 9–5.*

⑮ **Sunbury Plantation House & Museum.** Lovingly rebuilt after a 1995 fire destroyed everything but the thick flint-and-stone walls, Sunbury offers an elegant glimpse of the 18th and 19th centuries on a Barbadian sugar estate. Period furniture, old prints, and a collection of horse-drawn carriages have been donated to lend an air of authenticity. Luncheon is served in the back garden. ⊠ *Off Hwy. 5, Six Cross Roads, St. Philip* ☎ *246/ 423–6270* ⊕ *www.barbadosgreathouse.com* ☜ *$7.50* ☉ *Daily 10–5.*

Shopping

Duty-free shopping is found in Bridgetown's Broad Street department stores and their branches in Holetown and at the cruise-ship terminal. (Note that to purchase items duty-free, you must show your passport). Stores are generally open weekdays 8:30–4:30 and Saturdays 8:30–1.

Best of Barbados (✉ Worthing, Christ Church ☎ 246/421–6900), which has a total of seven locations, offers high-quality artwork and crafts in both "native" style and modern designs; everything is made or designed on Barbados. **Earthworks Pottery** (✉ No. 2, Edgehill Heights, St. Thomas ☎ 246/425–0223) is a family-owned and -operated pottery where you can purchase anything from a dish or knickknack to a complete dinner service or one-of-a-kind art piece. You can find the characteristically blue or green pottery decorating hotel rooms or for sale in gift shops throughout the island, but the biggest selection (including some "seconds") is at the pottery, where you also can watch the potters work. **Greenwich House Antiques** (✉ Greenwich Village, Trents Hill, St. James ☎ 246/432–1169) fills an entire plantation house with Barbadian mahogany furniture, crystal, silver, china, books, and pictures; it's open daily from 10:30 to 5:30. **Pelican Craft Centre** (✉ Princess Alice Hwy., Bridgetown, St. Michael ☎ 246/427–5350) is a cluster of workshops halfway between the Cruise Ship Terminal and downtown Bridgetown, where craftspeople create and sell locally made leather goods, batik, basketry, carvings, jewelry, glass art, paintings, pottery, and other items. It's open weekdays 9 to 5 and Saturday 9 to 2, with extended hours during holidays or to accommodate cruise-ship arrivals.

Sports & Activities

FISHING **Billfisher II** (☎ 246/431–0741), a 40-foot Pacemaker, accommodates up to six passengers with three fishing chairs and five rods. Captain Winston ("The Colonel") White has been fishing these waters since 1975. His full-day charters include a full lunch and guaranteed fish (or a 25% refund); all trips include drinks and transportation to and from the boat. **Blue Jay** (☎ 246/429–2326 ⊕ www.bluemarlinbarbados.com) is a spacious, fully equipped, 45-foot Sport Fisherman with a crew that knows the denizens of blue marlin, sailfish, barracuda, and kingfish. Four to six people can be accommodated—it's the only charter boat on the island with four chairs. Most fishing is done by trolling. Drinks, snacks, bait, tackle, and transfers are provided.

GOLF **Barbados Golf Club** (✉ Hwy. 7, Durants, Christ Church ☎ 246/428–8463 ⊕ www.barbadosgolfclub.com), the first public golf course on Barbados, is an 18-hole championship course (6,805 yards, par 72) redesigned in 2000 by golf course architect Ron Kirby. Greens fees are $119 for 18 holes, plus a $13 per person cart fee. Unlimited three-day and seven-day golf passes are available. Several hotels offer preferential tee-time reservations and reduced rates. Club and shoe rentals are available. At the prestigious **Country Club at Sandy Lane** (✉ Hwy. 1, Paynes Bay, St. James ☎ 246/432–2829 ⊕ www.sandylane.com/golf), golfers can play on the Old Nine or on either of two 18-hole championship courses: the Tom Fazio–designed Country Club Course or the spectacular Green Monkey Course, which opened in October 2004 and is reserved for hotel guests and club members only. Greens fees in high season are $85 for 9 holes ($75 for hotel guests) or $200 for 18 holes ($150 for hotel guests). Golf carts are equipped with GPS, which alerts you to upcoming traps and hazards, provides tips on how to play the hole, and allows you to order refreshments! **Rockley Golf & Country Club** (✉ Golf Club Rd., Worthing, Christ Church ☎ 246/435–7873), on the southeast coast, has a challenging 9-hole (2,800 yards, par 35) course that can be played as 18 from varying tee positions. Club and cart rentals are available. Greens fees on weekdays are $40 for 18 holes and $30 for 9 holes; on weekends, $56 for 18 holes and $38 for 9 holes. The **Royal Westmoreland Golf Club** (⊠ Westmoreland, St. James ☎246/422–4653) has a world-class Robert Trent Jones, Jr., 18-hole championship course (6,870 yards, par 72) that meanders through the former 500-acre Westmoreland Sugar Estate. The course is restricted to villa renters in high season (Nov. 15 to April 30 each year); greens fees are $175 for 18 holes, $87.50 for 9 holes. In the off-season, greens fees for visitors are $125 for 18 holes and, for villa renters, $75 for either 18 or 9 holes. Greens fees include use of an electric cart; club rental is available.

WATER SPORTS Waterskiing, snorkeling, and parasailing are available on most beaches along the west and south coasts. Windsurfing is best at Silver Sand–Silver Rock Beach near the southern tip of the island, where the winds are strongest. For scuba divers, Barbados is a rich and varied underwater destination. On the south coast, **The Dive Shop, Ltd** (⊠ Bay St., Aquatic Gap, St. Michael ☎ 246/426–9947, 888/898–3483 in U.S., 888/575–3483 in Canada ⊕ www.divebds.com), the island's oldest dive shop, offers daily reef and wreck dives, plus beginner classes, certification courses, and underwater photography instruction. Underwater cameras are available for rent.

On the west coast, **Dive Barbados** (⊠ Mount Standfast, St. James ☎ 246/422–3133 ⊕ www.divebarbados.net), on the beach next to the Lone Star Hotel, offers all levels of PADI instruction, two- or three-reef and wreck dives daily for up to six divers each time, snorkeling with Hawksbill turtles just offshore, as well as underwater camera rental and free transportation. **Hightide Watersports** (⊠ Coral Reef Club, Holetown, St. James ☎ 246/432–0931 or 800/513–5761 ⊕ www.divehightide.com) offers three dive trips—one- and two-tank dives and night reef/wreck/drift dives—daily for up to 8 divers, along with PADI instruction, equipment rental, and free transportation.

Beaches

All beaches in Barbados are open to cruise-ship passengers. The west coast has the stunning coves and white-sand beaches dear to the hearts of postcard publishers, plus calm, clear water for snorkeling, scuba diving, and swimming. Popular **Accra Beach,** in Rockley, has gentle surf and a lifeguard. There are plenty of places to eat and drink and to rent water-sports equipment. There's also a convenient parking lot. The exquisite crescent of pink sand at **Crane Beach** is protected by steep cliffs. As attractive as this location is now, it was named not for the elegant long-legged wading birds but for the crane used for hauling and loading cargo when this area was a busy port. Protected by a reef, the rolling surf is great for bodysurfing. A lifeguard is usually on duty. Changing rooms are available at Crane Beach Hotel for a small fee (which you can apply toward drinks or a meal at the restaurant). Beach access is through the hotel and down about 200 steps. Picturesque **Mullins Beach,** just south of Speightstown, is a perfect place to spend the day.

The water is safe for swimming and snorkeling, there's easy parking on the main road, and Suga Suga Restaurant serves snacks, meals, and drinks—and rents chairs and umbrellas. South of Holetown, **Paynes Bay** is lined with luxury hotels. It's a very pretty area, with plenty of beach to go around and good snorkeling. Parking areas and public access are available opposite the Coach House. You can grab a bite to eat or a cold drink at Bomba's Beach Bar. Close to the southernmost tip of the island, **Silver Sands/Silver Rock Beach** is a beautiful strand of white sand that always has a stiff breeze, which attracts intermediate and advanced windsurfers.

Where to Eat

A 15% V.A.T. (value-added tax) is in effect in Barbados. Most restaurant prices are V.A.T.-inclusive. A 10% service charge is added to most restaurant bills; if no service charge is added, tip waiters 10% to 15%.

$$–$$$ ✕ **Atlantis Hotel Restaurant.** People have enjoyed lunch with a view here for more than 40 years—especially on Wednesday and Sunday, when an enormous Bajan buffet includes pumpkin fritters, rice and peas, breadfruit casserole, steamed fish creole, oven-barbecued chicken, pepper pot, macaroni pie, ratatouille, and more. Homemade coconut pie tops the dessert list. The Atlantis is a lunch stop for several organized day tours, so it can get crowded. ⊠ *Atlantis Hotel, Tent Bay, Bathsheba, St. Joseph* ☎ *246/433–9445* ☐ *AE, D, MC, V.*

$$ ✕ **Waterfront Cafe.** This friendly bistro alongside the Careenage is the perfect place to enjoy a drink, snack, or meal—and to people-watch. Locals and tourists alike gather for all-day alfresco dining on sandwiches, salads, fish, pasta, pepper pot stew, and tasty Bajan snacks such as buljol, fish cakes, or plantation pork (plantains stuffed with spicy minced pork). The pan-fried flying fish sandwich is especially popular. In the evening you can gaze through the arched windows while savoring nouvelle Caribbean cuisine, enjoying cool trade winds, and listening to live jazz. There's a special Caribbean buffet and steel-pan music on Tuesday night from 7 to 9. ⊠ *The Careenage, Bridgetown, St. Michael* ☎ *246/427–0093* ☐ *AE, D, DC, MC, V* ☉ *Closed Sun.*

☽ $–$$ ✕ **Baku Beach Bar.** Whether you're going to the beach, coming from the beach, or just wanting to be near the beach, this is a great place for lunch or an informal dinner. Tables spill into the courtyard, through tropical gardens, and onto a boardwalk by the sea. Try a Caesar salad, a burger, spareribs, or grilled fish served with the salsa of your choice: fruit, pesto, herb lemon, or ginger soy. On the side, have garlic bread, sautéed onions, rice pilaf, or spicy potato wedges. Got room for crème brûlée, lemon tart, or a brownie with ice cream? Maybe dawdling over cappuccino is enough. ⊠ *Hwy. 1, Holetown, St. James* ☎ *246/432–2258* ☐ *AE, D, MC, V.*

Belize

A sliver of land wedged between Guatemala and the Caribbean Sea, Belize is only 68 mi (109 km) wide at its broadest point. Belize probably has the greatest variety of flora and fauna of any country of its size in the world. Because Belize is so small, even if you are in port only a few hours, with careful planning you can experience a good deal of its glorious diversity. Until 1973, the country was known as British Honduras, so English, the official language here, aligns the nation more with the British Caribbean than with the rest of Central America.

Belize City, the country's business, cultural, and transportation hub, has a population of around 50,000, but it is not really representative of the rest of the country. Where Belize City is crowded and uncharming, elsewhere in Belize you'll often find more iguanas or howler monkeys than humans. A few miles off the mainland is the Belize Barrier Reef, a great wall of coral stretching the entire 200 mi (333 km) length of the coast. Dotting the reef like punctuation marks are more than 200 cayes (pronounced keys), and farther out to sea are three coral atolls—all superb for diving and snorkeling. Many, like Ambergris Caye (pronounced Am-*bur*-griss Key) and Caye Caulker, which are jolly resort islands with ample supplies of bars, restaurants, and inns, are reachable on day trips from Belize City.

The main choice you'll have to make is whether to stay in Belize City for a little shopping, a little walking, and perhaps lunch or a dram at one of the Fort George hotels or restaurants, or alternatively to head out by boat, rental car, taxi, or tour on a more active adventure. Alas, poor Belize's tourist infrastructure, used to handling small numbers of international visitors, is not always up to the task of dealing with 2,000-some cruise-ship passengers at one time. Some popular spots, such as Belize Zoo or cave tubing sites, are swamped on cruise-ship days. Even the nurse sharks at Shark-Ray Alley in Hol Chan Marine Reserve get stuffed with chum by early afternoon and often disappear for a little shark nap.

CURRENCY The Belize dollar ($) is the official currency of Belize. For years, it's been pegged to the United States dollar at a rate of 2 to 1. Since the U.S. dollar is universally accepted, there's no need to acquire Belize currency. Prices quoted throughout this chapter are in U.S. dollars unless otherwise indicated.

TELEPHONES Calling locally or internationally is easy, but rates are high; around 90¢ a minute for calls to the U.S. To call the United States, dial 001 plus the area code and number. Pay phones accept only pre-paid phone cards, available in shops in denominations from $2.50 to $25. To place a call using your own calling card, use your long-distance carrier's access code or call the operator by dialing 114.

SHORE EXCURSIONS The following are good choices in Belize. They may not be offered by all cruise lines. Times and prices are approximate.

Cave Tubing and Jungle Walk. Your inner tube will be issued after a one-hour ride to the jungle, where you will then walk 45 minutes to the entrance of the caves on the Branch River. After an hour of tubing through the underground caves, lunch is served and you can then either rest or explore. ⊙ 6½ hrs 🚌 $79–$96.

Maya Ruins at Altun Ha. An hour by bus from Belize City, these are the country's most thoroughly excavated ruins. After a one-hour walking tour, there is time for lunch on your own or to explore the Belize Tourism Village. ⊙ *4 hrs* ⌷ *$45–$50.*

Shark-Ray Alley Snorkel and Sightseeing. A speedboat delivers you to one of the offshore cays, where you snorkel among stingrays and nurse sharks, with a barbeque on the beach afterward. Snorkel equipment is provided. ⌷ *6–7½ hrs* ⌷ *$69–$92.*

Wildlife Adventure Tour. Lunch is served after a motor-launch trip up the Belize River. Then you are taken to the Belize Zoo, where you will see animals only indigenous to Belize. ⊙ *6 hrs* ⌷ *$81.*

Coming Ashore

Because Belize City's harbor is shallow, passengers are tendered in. If you're going the independent route, try to get in line early for the tenders, as it sometimes takes an hour and a half or more for all the passengers to be brought ashore. The Fort Pointe Tourist Village, which opened in 2002, is a clean but antiseptic collection of gift shops, restaurants, and tour operators nicely situated along the harbor.

Taxis, tour guides, and car rental desks are readily available. Taxi trips—official taxis have green license plates—within Belize City's small downtown area are supposed to be set at BZ$5 plus BZ$1 for each additional passenger, although drivers meeting the cruise ships try to charge whatever the traffic will bear. Taxis don't have meters, so settle on the fare in advance; you shouldn't have to pay more than BZ$10 to go anywhere in the city. By the hour, expect to pay BZ$80–BZ$100. There's no need to tip cab drivers.

It's also possible to rent a car and explore on your own. Crystal, a local company, has a branch at the Tourist Village, but rates can be high (around $65 per day). Downtown streets are narrow and often one-way. You can take two major roads out of Belize City—the Northern Highway, which leads to the Mexican border, 102 mi (164 km) away, and the Western Highway, which runs 81 mi (130 km) to Guatemala. Both are paved and in good condition. Recently installed signs point you to nearby destinations such as the Belize Zoo.

By and large, Belizeans are among the friendliest folks you'll meet in any port in the Caribbean. Give them respect rather than just a tip, a smile rather than a command, and you'll enjoy a delightful side of the Caribbean that's long lost in many other destinations.

Belize City

Numbers in the margins correspond to points of interest on the Belize map.

Many Belize hands will tell you the best way to see Belize City is through a rear-view window. But, with an open mind to its peculiarities, and with a little caution (the city has a crime problem, though this rarely affects visitors since the areas usually frequented by cruise-ship passengers are closely watched by tourist police), you may decide Belize City has a raffish, atmospheric charm rarely found in other Caribbean ports of call. You might even see the ghost of Graham Greene at a hotel bar.

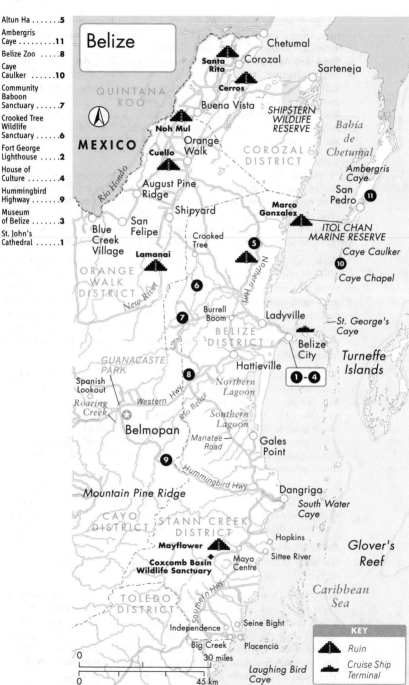

Belize

Chetumal

Santa
Rita

Corozal

Sarteneja

Cerros

QUINTANA
ROO

Buena Vista

SHIPSTERN
WILDLIFE
RESERVE

Bahía
de
Chetumal

Noh Mul

Orange
Walk

COROZAL
DISTRICT

MEXICO

Cuello

Ambergris
Caye

San
Pedro

11

Río Hondo

August Pine
Ridge

Marco
Gonzalez

San
Felipe

Shipyard

ITOL CHAN
MARINE RESERVE

Blue
Creek
Village

Crooked
Tree

5

Caye Caulker

Lamanai

10

ORANGE
WALK
DISTRICT

New River

6

Caye Chapel

Burrell
Boom

Ladyville

St. George's
Caye

7

BELIZE
DISTRICT

Belize
City

Turneffe
Islands

GUANACASTE
PARK

Spanish
Lookout

8

Hattieville

1 - 4

Roaring
Creek

Western Hwy.

Río Belize

Northern
Lagoon

Belmopan

Southern
Lagoon

Manatee
Road

Gales
Point

9

Hummingbird Hwy.

Dangriga

Mountain Pine Ridge

South Water
Caye

CAYO
DISTRICT

STANN CREEK
DISTRICT

Hopkins

Glover's
Reef

Mayflower

Coxcomb Basin
Wildlife Sanctuary

Maya
Centre

Sittee River

Southern Hwy.

Caribbean
Sea

TOLEDO
DISTRICT

Independence

Seine Bight

0

30 miles

Big Creek

Placencia

0

45 km

Laughing Bird
Caye

KEY

Ruin

Cruise Ship
Terminal

A 5- to 10-minute stroll from the perky Tourist Village brings you into the other worlds of Belize City. On the north side of Haulover Creek is the colonial-style world of the Fort George section, where large old homes, stately but sometimes down at the heels, take the breezes off the sea and share their space with hotels and restaurants. On the south side is the bustling world of Albert Street, the main commercial thoroughfare. But don't stroll too far. Parts of Belize City are unsafe by night or day. During the daylight hours, as long as you stay within the main commercial district and the Fort George area—and ignore the street hustlers—you should have no problem. Nearly all the sights worth seeing in Belize City are in this part of town.

❷ **Fort George Lighthouse.** Towering over the entrance to Belize Harbor, this lighthouse stands guard on the tip of Fort George Point. It was designed and funded by the country's greatest benefactor, Baron Bliss, to whom a memorial stands nearby. The lighthouse is for photo ops only—you can't enter it. ⊠ *Fort St.*

❹ **House of Culture.** Formerly called Government House, the city's finest colonial structure is said to have been designed by the illustrious British architect Sir Christopher Wren. Built in 1812 it was once the residence of the governor general, the queen's representative in Belize. Following Hurricane Hattie, he and the rest of the government moved to Belmopan, and the house became a venue for social functions and a guesthouse for visiting VIPs. (Queen Elizabeth stayed here in 1985, Prince Philip in 1988.) Now it's open to the public, and you can peruse its archival records, silver, glassware, and furniture or mingle with the tropical birds that frequent the gardens. ⊠ *Regent St. at Southern Foreshore* ☎ 227/3050 ⬚ *BZ$5* ⊙ *Weekdays 8:30–4:30.*

❸ **Museum of Belize.** Debuting in 2002, this small but interesting museum was a Belize City jail from the 1850s until 1993. Displays on Belize history and culture include ancient Mayan artifacts and an actual jail cell. ⊠ *Gabourel La.* ☎ 223/4524 ⬚ *BZ$10* ⊙ *Tues.–Fri. 10–6, Sat. 10–3.*

❶ **St. John's Cathedral.** On Albert Street's south end is the oldest Anglican church in Central America and the only one outside England where kings were crowned. From 1815 to 1845 four kings of the Mosquito Coast (a British protectorate along the coast of Honduras and Nicaragua) were crowned here. ⊠ *Albert St.* ☎ 227/2137.

INDEPENDENT TOURS Several Belize City–based tour guides and operators offer custom trips for ship passengers. Tour guide Reginald Tripp, of **Reggie's Tours** (⊠ 29 Clinic Rd., Ladyville ☎ 501/225–2195), has carved out a profitable niche running independent trips for cruise passengers to Sibun River for cave tubing, to Goff Caye for snorkeling, and elsewhere. Katie Valk of **Maya Travel Services** (⊠ 42 Cleghorn St. ☎ 501/223–1623 ⊕ www.mayatravelservices.com), a New Yorker with attitude (softened by some 15 years' residency in Belize), can organize a custom trip to just about anywhere in the country.

Shopping

Belize does not have the crafts tradition of its neighbors, Guatemala and Mexico, and imported goods are expensive due to high duties, but hand-carved items of Zircote or other local woods make good souvenirs. The **Fort Pointe Tourist Village,** where the ship tenders come in, is a collection of bright and clean gift shops selling T-shirts and Belizean and Guatemalan crafts. Beside the Tourist Village is an informal **Street Vendor Market,** with funkier goods and performances by a "Brukdown" band or a group of Garifuna drummers.

The **Image Factory** (⊠ 91 N. Front St. ☎ 501/223–4151) is a gallery featuring Belize's hippest artists. **National Handicraft Center** (⊠ 2 South Park St. ☎ 223/3636) has Belizean souvenir items, including hand-carved figurines, hand-made furniture, pottery, and woven baskets.

Sports & Activities

GOLF **Caye Chapel Island Resort** (⊠ Caye Chapel, 16 mi northeast of Belize City ☎ 501/226–8250) has a beautiful 18-hole seaside course occupying much of Caye Chapel, a privately owned island. Some water taxis to Caye Caulker will drop you here, or you can fly the 12 minutes to the island's private airstrip, by prior arrangement with the resort, for $100 round-trip. Challenges include brisk prevailing winds and the occasional crocodile. Unlimited golf, with clubs and cart rental and a poolside lunch, costs $200. Reservations are required.

Beaches

There are no beaches of note within easy driving distance of Belize City. For beaches, you'll have to pop over to Ambergris Caye or Caye Caulker.

Where to Eat

Whether it's local creole fare like stew chicken or a succulent spiny lobster (in season mid-June through mid-February), you can enjoy Belizean cuisine in Belize City and on the islands. Tap water (pipe water as it's called here) is safe to drink in Belize City and San Pedro; on Caye Caulker, it's best to drink bottled water.

$$–$$$ ✕🏠 **The Smoky Mermaid.** On the ground floor of the Great House is one of the best restaurants in the city. In a large courtyard shaded by breadfruit and sapodilla trees, amiable servers bring Caribbean-influenced seafood dishes, inventive pasta, and savory barbecues. At lunch, a shrimp burger costs $9 and the piña colada pie is $6. ⊠ *The Great House, 13 Cork St.* ☎ *501/223–4759* ▤ *AE, MC, V.*

¢–$$ ✕ **Macy's.** Stewed iguana, known locally as bamboo chicken, is available on request here, but you can also try armadillo, brocket deer, and gibnut. Macy, the Jamaican-born proprietor, says iguana is tough to prepare—it has to be scalded, then washed in lime juice and vinegar—but delicious to eat. On display are a letter from the bishop of Belize congratulating the staff on its catering feats and a photo of Harrison Ford, who commandeered the table by the door during the making of *The Mosquito Coast.* ⊠ *18 Bishop St.* ☎ *207/3419* ▤ *No credit cards.*

Side Trips by Road from Belize City
Numbers in the margins correspond to points of interest on the Belize map.

⑤ **Altun Ha.** If you've never visited an ancient Maya site, make a trip to Altun Ha, 28 mi (45 km) north of Belize City. It's not the most dramatic site in the country, but it is the most thoroughly excavated and the most accessible from Belize City. The first inhabitants settled here before 900 BC, and their descendants abandoned the site around AD 900. At its height the city was home to 10,000 people. ☎ *No phone* ➲ *BZ$10* ⊙ *Daily 9–5.*

⑧ **Belize Zoo.** One of the smallest, but arguably one of the best, zoos in the world, this park houses only animals native to Belize. As you stroll the trails on a self-guided tour, you visit several Belizean ecosystems—rain forest, lagoons, and riverine forest—and spot more than 125 species. Besides spotted and rare black jaguars, you'll also see the country's four other wild cats; the puma, margay, ocelot, and jaguarondi. Probably the most famous resident of the zoo is named April. She's a Baird's tapir, the national animal of Belize. This relative of the horse and rhino is known to locals as the mountain cow. ✉ *Western Hwy., 30 mi (48 km) west of Belize City* ☎ *501/220–8004* ⊕ *www.belizezoo.org* ➲ *BZ$15* ⊙ *Daily 9–4:30.*

⑦ **Community Baboon Sanctuary.** One of the country's most interesting wildlife conservation projects, the Community Baboon Sanctuary is actually a haven for black howler monkeys, agile bundles of black fur with deafening roars. The reserve, encompassing a 20 mi (35 km) stretch of the Belize River, was established in 1985 by a group of local farmers. Today there are nearly 1,000 black howler monkeys in the sanctuary, as well as numerous other species of birds and mammals. Exploring the sanctuary is made easy by about 3 mi (5 km) of trails that start near a small museum. ✉ *Bermudian Landing Village, 28 mi (45 km) northwest of Belize City—turn left off Northern Hwy. at Mile 14* ☎ *501/220–2181* ➲ *BZ$10* ⊙ *Daily 8–5.*

⑥ **Crooked Tree Wildlife Sanctuary.** A paradise for animal lovers, this sanctuary encompasses a chain of inland waterways covering more than 3,000 acres. You're likely to see iguanas, crocodiles, coatis, and turtles. The sanctuary's most prestigious visitor, however, is the jabiru stork. With a wingspan of up to 9 feet, it is the largest flying bird in the Americas. At the center of the reserve is Crooked Tree, one of the oldest inland villages in Belize. There are a number of excellent guides in the village, including Sam Tillet. ✉ *Turn west off Northern Hwy. at Mile 30.8, then drive 2 mi (3 km)* ☎ *501/223–4987 for Belize Audubon Society* ➲ *BZ$8.*

⑨ **Hummingbird Highway.** Belmopan, Belize's little capital, a town of 8,000 civil servants and their families and nondescript government buildings about 50 mi (80 km) southwest of Belize City, isn't really worth a special trip. But the road that begins near Belmopan, the Hummingbird Highway, is. Once a potholed nightmare, this 49-mi (78-km) paved two-lane, which turns south off the Western Highway, is now the best road in Belize, if not in all of Central America. It's also the country's most scenic route. As you go south toward Dangriga Town, on your right rise the jungle-covered Maya Mountains, largely free of signs of human habitation except for the occasional field of corn or beans. Closer to Dangriga are large citrus groves and banana plantations.

Less than half an hour south of Belmopan on the Hummingbird is the **Blue Hole,** a natural turquoise pool surrounded by mosses and lush vegetation, excellent for a cool dip. The Blue Hole is actually part of an underground river system. On the other side of the hill is St. Herman's Cave, once inhabited by the Maya. A path leads up from the highway, near the Blue Hole. To explore the cave, it's best to wear sturdy shoes and bring a flashlight. Some years ago there were some unfortunate incidents at the site, with tourists robbed and, in one case, sexually assaulted. Subsequently, a full-time attendant has been appointed to patrol the area. ⊠ *Hummingbird Hwy.* 🖃 *BZ$8.*

Ambergris Caye & Caye Caulker

If you would rather spend your time in Belize on an island instead of the mainland, you have two main choices: Ambergris Caye or Caye Caulker.

Ambergris Caye, also known as San Pedro, after its only town, is a laid-back Caribbean-style resort island that's the most popular tourist destination in Belize. Once a sleepy fishing village, San Pedro still has streets of sand, and the tallest building is only three stories high. Caye Caulker is Ambergris Caye's little-sister island—smaller, less developed, and cheaper.

Once on Ambergris or Caulker, you can laze on a beach, shop, ride around on a golf cart (there are no rental cars on the islands, but golf carts rent for around BZ$80 for eight hours), have lunch in a seaside bistro, or take a boat out to the barrier reef for some of the Caribbean's best snorkeling.

It's usually possible to get to either island (but not both) during the typical ship's stop, either by scheduled water taxi or by puddle-jumper airplane.

GETTING TO AMBERGRIS CAYE & CAYE CAULKER **Air Travel:** Especially if you are going to Ambergris Caye, you may prefer to fly, or you can water taxi over and fly back. There are hourly flights on two airlines. The flight to Caulker takes about 15 minutes and that to San Pedro about 25 minutes. The cost is $BZ104 round-trip to either island. A taxi between the Tourist Village and the Municipal Airport is around $3. On Ambergris, the airstrip is at the south end of town, within easy walking distance of restaurants and shops. Be sure you fly out of Belize City's Municipal, not out of the international airport north of the city. Flights from International are about twice as costly, plus you'll have a BZ$40 cab fare each way to the airport. **Maya Island Airways** (☎ 501/223–1140, 800/225–6732 in U.S. ⊕ www.mayaislandair.com) has hourly flights, and you can make a reservation on the company Web site. **Tropic Air** (☎ 501/226–2012 or 800/422–3435 in the U.S. ⊕ www.tropicair.com) has frequent flights, and you can make reservations by e-mail.

Boat & Ferry Travel: To go by water taxi—fast open boats with twin outboard engines—turn left from the Tourist Village and walk about five minutes to the Marine Terminal, which is next to the Swing Bridge. Boats to both islands are operated by the Caye Caulker Water Taxi Association. There are at least six trips a day to each island, beginning at 8 AM. The trip to or from Caulker takes 45 minutes and costs BZ$18 one-way. The trip to or from San Pedro takes 75 minutes and costs BZ$28 one-way. In San Pedro, these water taxis dock at Shark's Pier in the middle of town. For information on schedules, contact the **Caye Caulker Water Taxi Association** (☎ 501/223–1969 ⊕ www.gocayecaulker.com).

EXPLORING   *Numbers in the margins correspond to points of interest on the Belize map.*

⓫ Ambergris Caye. Ambergris is the queen of the cayes. With a population around 4,400, the island's only town, San Pedro, remains a small, friendly, and prosperous village. It has one of the highest literacy rates in the country and an admirable level of awareness about the fragility of the reef. The large number of substantial private houses being built on the edges of town is proof of how much tourism has enriched San Pedro.

Hol Chan Marine Reserve (Maya for "little channel"), 4 mi (6 km) from San Pedro at the southern tip of Ambergris, is a 20-minute boat ride from the island. Hol Chan is a break in the reef about 100 feet wide and 20 feet to 35 feet deep, through which tremendous volumes of water pass with the tides. Varying in depth from 50 feet to 100 feet, Hol Chan's canyons lie between buttresses of coral running perpendicular to the reef, separated by white, sandy channels. Because fishing is forbidden, snorkelers and divers can see teeming marine life, including spotted eagle rays, squirrel fish, butterfly fish, parrot fish, and queen angelfish as well as Nassau groupers, barracuda, and large shoals of yellowtail snappers. Shark-Ray Alley, a sandbar where you can snorkel with nurse sharks and rays (which gather here to be fed) and even larger numbers of day-trippers, was added to the reserve in 1999. Sliding into the water is a feat of personal bravery, as the sight of the sharks and rays brushing past you is daunting yet spectacular. You need above-average swimming skills, as the current is often strong. ✉ *Southern tip, Ambergris Caye* 🖼 *BZ$10.*

⓾ Caye Caulker. On Caye Caulker, where the one village is home to around 800 people, brightly painted houses on stilts line the coral sand streets. Although the island is being developed more each year, flowers still outnumber cars 10 to 1 (golf carts, bicycles, and bare feet are the preferred means of transportation). The living is easy, as you might guess from all the NO SHIRT, NO SHOES, NO PROBLEM signs at the bars. This is the kind of place where most of the listings in the telephone directory give addresses like "near football field."

SHOPPING   At **Belizean Arts** (✉ Fido's Courtyard off Barrier Reef Dr., Ambergris Caye 🖼 226/3019) you'll find works by local painters as well as handicrafts from Belize, Guatemala, and Mexico. The owner of **Sea Gal Boutique** (✉ Barrier Reef Dr., in Holiday Hotel, Ambergris Caye

☎ 226/2431) has an artist's eye for beauty: everything here is stunning, even the T-shirts. **Annie's Boutique** (✉ North end of island, near the Split at Chocolate's, Caye Caulker ☎ 226/0151) has some of Belize's best clothing for women and children. Here you'll find dresses and sarongs made with fabrics from Bali, unique silver jewelry, and Guatemalan bags.

Scuba Diving and Snorkeling: If you get to Ambergris Caye early enough, you'll have time for a quick dive or snorkel trip out to the reef. More than a dozen dive and snorkel shops line the beachfront downtown, offering about the same trips at similar prices. Speedboats take divers and snorkelers out to their destinations, usually to Hol Chan Marine Reserve south of Ambergris or Mexico Rocks off North Ambergris. Dives off Ambergris are usually single tank at depths of 50 feet–80 feet, allowing about 35 minutes of bottom time. Most companies offer two single-tank dives per day, one in the morning and one in the afternoon. Snorkeling generally costs BZ$40–BZ$60 per person for two or three hours or BZ$90–BZ$200 for a day trip, including lunch. Diving trips run BZ$70–BZ$80 for a single-tank dive, BZ$100–BZ$130 for a double-tank dive, and BZ$340–BZ$400 for day trips with dives to Turneffe Atoll or Lighthouse Reef.

Dive and snorkeling trips to Hol Chan that originate in Caye Caulker are a bit cheaper. Plan on spending about BZ$30–BZ$50 for a snorkeling trip around the island or to Hol Chan Marine Reserve. If you arrive on the island after the first wave of boats go to the reef, usually around 10:30 AM, you may have to pay more for a "custom" trip. Diving trips run around BZ$70 for a single-tank dive, BZ$90–BZ$120 for a double-tank dive, plus equipment rental.

Amigos del Mar (✉ off Barrier Reef Dr., near Mayan Princess Hotel, Ambergris Caye ☎ 501/226–2706 ⊕ amigosdive.com) is probably the most consistently recommended dive operation on the island. It offers a range of local dives and snorkel trips. The well-regarded **Gaz Cooper's Dive Belize** (✉ 5 mi [8 km] north of town at Playa Blanca Resort, Ambergris Caye ☎ 501/226–3202 ⊕ www.divebelize.com) boasts about having the smallest dive operation on the island.

On Caye Caulker, if you're looking for someone to take you out to the reef, **Frenchie's Diving Services** (✉ Front St., Caye Caulker ☎ 501/226–0234) is a well-regarded local operator. For trips to the Blue Hole and local dives, **Paradise Down** (✉ Front St. north of the public pier, Caye Caulker ☎ 226/0437) has three well-equipped dive boats.

Although the barrier reef just offshore limits the wave action, which, over eons, builds classic wide sandy beaches, and there is a good deal of seagrass on the shore bottom, Ambergris Caye's beaches are among the best in Belize. All beaches in Belize are public. **Mar de Tumbo**, 1½ mi (3 km) south of town near Tropica Hotel, is the best beach on the south end of the island. **North Ambergris**, accessible by water taxi from San Pedro or via a hand-pulled ferry across a river channel, has miles of narrow beaches and few people. **Ramon's Village's beach**, right across from the airstrip, is the best in the town area.

The beaches on Caulker are not as good as those on Ambergris. Along the front side of the island is a narrow strip of sand, but the water is shallow and swimming conditions poor. **The Split,** on the north end of the village (turn to your right from the main public pier), is the best place on Caye Caulker for swimming.

WHERE TO EAT ✕ **JamBel Jerk Pit.** In the middle of town next door to Big Daddy's is this

$$ casual eatery, which blends Jamaican and Belizean cuisines (hence the name) to produce spicy jerk-style dishes. You can relax in the main dining room, where reggae is always playing, or upstairs on the roof, where it's often so windy you need to hang on to your napkin. The ocean views make it worth the trouble. ⊠ *Barrier Reef Dr., next to Central Park and Big Daddy's, Ambergris Caye* ☎ *501/226–3303* ▤ *AE, MC, V.*

$$ ✕ **Rasta Pasta.** This is the third reincarnation of Rasta Pasta in Belize: the first, in San Pedro, lost its lease, and the second, in Placencia, was destroyed by Hurricane Iris. The third time's a charm, though, and people line up salivating for owner Maralyn Gill's conch fritters, chicken tostadas, giant English muffins, and scrumptious coconut macaroons. ⊠ *Front St., Caye Caulker* ☎ *501/206–0356* ▤ *MC, V* ☯ *Closed Wed.*

$$ ✕ **The Sandbox.** Whether outside under the palms or indoors under the lazily turning ceiling fans, you'll always have your feet in the sand here. The names of regulars are carved on the backs of the chairs. Open from 7 AM to 10 PM, the Sandbox serves lobster omelet for breakfast, ceviche or seafood salad for lunch, and red snapper in mango sauce for dinner. The chowders are also very good. Prices are reasonable, and portions are large. ⊠ *Front St., near the public pier, Caye Caulker* ☎ *501/226–0200* ▤ *AE, MC, V.*

$–$$ ✕ **Papi's Diner.** Atmosphere is in short supply at Papi's, as are views of the sea. Little more than a screened porch with a few wooden tables, the unpretentious diner is tucked away at San Pedro's north end. The seafood and other dishes are expertly prepared at some of the town's most reasonable prices. Grilled fish is served with multiple side dishes. ⊠ *Pescador Dr. at north end of town behind Seven Seas Resort, Ambergris Caye* ☎ *501/226–2047* ▤ *No credit cards.*

British Virgin Islands

The British Virgin Islands (BVI) consist of about 50 mostly volcanic islands, islets, and cays; most are remarkably hilly. The BVI are serene, seductive, spectacularly beautiful, and still remarkably laid-back. Their pleasures are mostly understated, and overall, there is a sense of a Caribbean you don't see much anymore. Several factors have enabled the BVI to retain these qualities: no building can rise higher than the surrounding palms, and there are no direct flights from the mainland United States, so the tourism tide is held back. In fact, things only get crowded when a big cruise ship docks off Road Town, Tortola.

Sailing has always been a popular activity in the BVI. The first arrivals here were a seafaring tribe, the Ciboney Indians. They were followed (circa AD 900) by the Arawaks, who sailed from South America, established settlements, and farmed and fished. Still later came the mighty Caribs.

British Virgin Islands

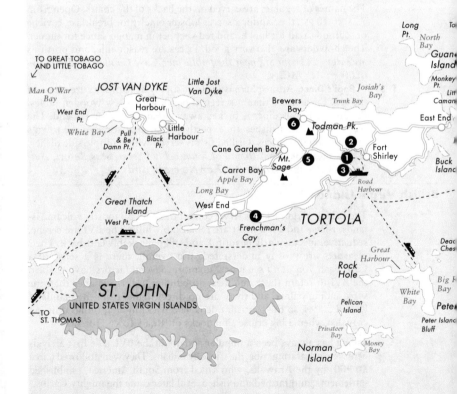

ATLANTIC

TO GREAT TOBAGO
AND LITTLE TOBAGO

JOST VAN DYKE

Man O'War
Bay

West End
Pt.

White Bay

Great
Harbour

Little Jost
Van Dyke

Little
Harbour

*Black
Pt.*

Pull
& Be
Damn Pt.

Brewers
Bay

*Josiah's
Bay*

Trunk Bay

Long
Pt.

*North
Bay*

*Guana
Island*

*Monkey
Pt.*

*Litt
Caman*

East End

Cane Garden Bay

⑥

Todman Pk.

Carrot Bay

*Mt.
Sage*

Apple Bay

Long Bay

West End

②

⑤

①

③

Fort
Shirley

Buck
Island

*Road
Harbour*

④

*Frenchman's
Cay*

TORTOLA

Great Thatch
Island

West Pt.

ST. JOHN
UNITED STATES VIRGIN ISLANDS

TO
ST. THOMAS

Rock
Hole

*Great
Harbour*

*White
Bay*

*Pelican
Island*

*Privateer
Bay*

Norman
Island

*Money
Bay*

Dead
Chest

*Big H
Bay*

Peter

Peter Island
Bluff

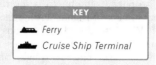

KEY
🚤 Ferry
🚢 Cruise Ship Terminal

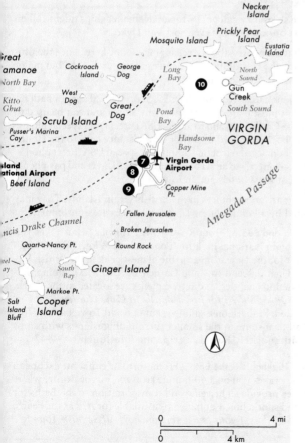

0   4 mi

0   4 km

In 1493 Christopher Columbus was the first European visitor. Impressed by the number of islands dotting the horizon, he named them *Las Once Mil Virgines*—the 11,000 Virgins—in honor of the 11,000 virgin companions of St. Ursula, martyred in the 4th century. In the ensuing years, the Spaniards passed through, fruitlessly seeking gold. Then came pirates and buccaneers, who found the islands' hidden coves and treacherous reefs ideal bases from which to prey on passing galleons crammed with gold, silver, and spices. It was the British who established a plantation economy and for 150 years developed the sugar industry. When slavery was abolished in 1838 the plantation economy faltered, and the majority of the white population left for Europe.

The islands are still politically tied to Britain. The governor, appointed by the queen of England, has limited powers, and these are concentrated on external affairs and local security. Although tourism is the number one industry, there's little doubt that BVIers—who so love their unspoiled tropical home—will maintain their islands' easygoing charms for both themselves and their guests.

Larger cruise ships may call on Tortola, but smaller ships might call on Virgin Gorda or occasionally even Jost Van Dyke.

CURRENCY   You won't have to worry about exchanging money here, since the official currency is the U.S. dollar. Some places accept cash only, but major credit cards are widely accepted.

TELEPHONES   Caribbean phone cards are available in $5, $10, and $20 denominations. They're sold at most major hotels and many stores and can be used to call all over the Caribbean, and to access USADirect from special phonecard phones. For credit-card or collect long-distance calls to the United States, use a phone-card telephone or look for special USADirect phones, which are linked directly to an AT&T operator. USADirect and pay phones can be found at most hotels and in towns.

SHORE EXCURSIONS   The following are good choices in the British Virgin Islands. They may not be offered by all cruise lines. Times and prices are approximate.

Sage Mountain and Beach. From Road Town, Tortola, a bus takes you to Sage Mountain National Park for a one-mile (1 ½ km) hike through the rain forest for the view from atop the highest peak in the British Virgin Islands. Then descend to Cane Garden Beach for swimming. Restrooms, changing facilities, and refreshments are located at the beach. ⊙ *4 hrs* ▣ *$39–$45 ($24 for just a shuttle to Cane Garden Bay).*

Sailing Excursion. Embark on a sailing yacht in Road Town harbor, Tortola, and sail past some of the smaller surrounding islands with stops to swim and snorkel. Full-day trips include lunch. ⊙ *4–7 hrs* ▣ *$54–$90.*

Virgin Gorda Highlights & the Baths. From Tortola, either an excursion launch or ferry takes you on a 40-minute cruise to Virgin Gorda, where open-air buses provide sightseeing and transportation to the Baths for swimming and snorkeling. Equipment is available for rent at the beach. ⊙ *4 hrs* ▣ *$54 (less if your cruise ship anchors off Spanish Town).*

Coming Ashore

Large cruise ships usually anchor in Road Town Harbor and bring passengers ashore by tender. Small ships can sometimes tie up at Wickham's Cay dock. Either way, it's a short stroll to Road Town. If your ship isn't going to Virgin Gorda, you can make the 12-mi (19-km) trip by ferry from the dock in Road Town in about 30 minutes for about $25 round-trip, but you'll still have to take a taxi to get to The Baths for swimming and snorkeling, so it's not necessarily a bad deal to go on the shore excursion.

There are taxi stands at Wickham's Cay and in Road Town. Taxis are unmetered, and there are minimums for travel throughout the island, so it's usually cheaper to travel in groups. Negotiate to get the best fares, as there is no set fee schedule. If you are in the islands for just a day, it's usually more cost-effective to share a taxi with a small group than to rent a car, since you'd have to pay an agency at Wickham's Cay or in Road Town $10 for a temporary license and car-rental charges of at least $60 a day.

On Virgin Gorda, ships often dock off Spanish Town or Leverick Bay and tender passengers to the ferry dock. A few taxis will be available at Leverick Bay—you can set up an island tour for about $40—but Leverick Bay is far away from The Baths, the island's must-see beach, so a shore excursion is often the best choice. If you are tendered to Spanish Town, then it's possible to take a shuttle taxi to The Baths for as little as $5 per person.

If your ship calls on Jost Van Dyke, you'll probably be tendered ashore at Great Harbour, where you can easily walk from one informal bar to another.

Exploring Tortola

Tortola doesn't have many historic sights, but it does have abundant natural beauty. Beware of the roads, which are extraordinarily steep and twisting, making driving demanding. The best beaches are on the north shore.

Numbers in the margin correspond to points of interest on the British Virgin Islands map.

② **Fort Burt.** The most intact historic ruin on Tortola was built by the Dutch in the early 17th century to safeguard Road Harbour. It sits on a hill at the western edge of Road Town and is now the site of a small hotel and restaurant. The foundations and magazine remain, and the structure offers a commanding view of the harbor. ⊠ *Waterfront Dr., Road Town* ☎ *No phone* ☜ *Free* ☾ *Daily dawn–dusk.*

④ **Fort Recovery.** The unrestored ruins of a 17th-century Dutch fort, 30 feet in diameter, sit amid a profusion of tropical greenery on the Villas of Fort Recovery Estates grounds. There's not much to see here, and there are no guided tours, but you're welcome to stop by and poke around. ⊠ *Waterfront Dr., Road Town* ☎ *284/485–4467* ☜ *Free.*

③ **J. R. O'Neal Botanic Gardens.** Take a walk through this 4-acre showcase of lush plant life. There are sections devoted to prickly cacti and succulents, hothouses for ferns and orchids, gardens of medicinal herbs, and plants and trees indigenous to the seashore. From the Tourist Board office in Road Town, cross Waterfront Drive and walk one block over to Main Street and turn right. Keep walking until you see the high school. The gardens are on your left. ⊠ *Botanic Station, Road Town* 📞 *284/494–3904* 💲 *Free* 🕐 *Mon.–Sat. 9–4:30.*

❶ Road Town. The laid-back capital of the BVI looks out over Road Town Harbour. It takes only an hour or so to stroll down Main Street and along the waterfront, checking out the traditional West Indian buildings, painted in pastel colors and sporting high-pitched, corrugated-tin roofs; bright shutters; and delicate fretwork trim. For hotel and sightseeing brochures and the latest information on everything from taxi rates to ferry-boat schedules, visit the BVI Tourist Board office. Or just choose a seat on one of the benches in Sir Olva Georges Square, on Waterfront Drive, and watch the people come and go from the ferry dock and customs office across the street.

❺ Sage Mountain National Park. At 1,716 feet, Sage Mountain is the highest peak in the BVI. From the parking area, a trail leads you in a loop not only to the peak itself (and extraordinary views) but also to a small rain forest, sometimes shrouded in mist. Most of the forest was cut down over the centuries to clear land for sugarcane, cotton, and other crops; to create pastureland; or to simply utilize the stands of timber. In 1964 this park was established to preserve what remained. Up here you can see mahogany trees, white cedars, mountain guavas, elephant-ear vines, mamey trees, and giant bullet woods, to say nothing of such birds as mountain doves and thrushes. Take a taxi from Road Town or drive up Joe's Hill Road and make a left onto Ridge Road toward Chalwell and Doty villages. The road dead-ends at the park. ⊠ *Ridge Rd., Sage Mountain* 📞 *284/494–3904* 💲 *$3* 🕐 *Daily dawn–dusk.*

❻ Skyworld. Drive up here and climb the observation tower for a stunning 360-degree view of numerous islands and cays. On a clear day you can even see St. Croix (40 mi [64½ km] away) and Anegada (20 mi [32 km] away). ⊠ *Ridge Rd., Joe's Hill* 📞 *No phone* 💲 *Free.*

Exploring Virgin Gorda

There are few roads on Virgin Gorda, and most byways don't follow the scalloped shoreline. The main route sticks resolutely to the center of the island, linking The Baths at the tip of the southern extremity with Gun Creek and Leverick Bay at North Sound and providing exhilarating views. The craggy coast, scissored with grottos and fringed by palms and boulders, has a primitive beauty. If you drive, you can hit all the sights in one day. Stop to climb Gorda Peak, in the island's center.

Numbers in the margin correspond to points of interest on the British Virgin Islands map.

❾ The Baths. At Virgin Gorda's most celebrated sight, giant boulders are scattered about the beach and in the water. Some are almost as large as houses and form remarkable grottos. Climb between these rocks to swim in the many pools. Early morning and late afternoon are the best times to visit if you want to avoid crowds. If it's privacy you crave, follow the shore northward to quieter bays—Spring Bay, the Crawl, Little Trunk, and Valley Trunk—or head south to Devil's Bay. ⊠ *Off Tower Rd., The Baths* ☎ *284/494–3904* ☜ *$3* ☽ *Daily dawn–dusk.*

❽ Little Fort National Park. This 36-acre wildlife sanctuary has the ruins of an old Spanish fort. Giant boulders like those at The Baths are scattered throughout the park. ⊠ *Spanish Town Rd.* ☎ *No phone* ☜ *Free.*

❼ Spanish Town. Virgin Gorda's peaceful main settlement, on the island's southern wing, is so tiny that it barely qualifies as a town at all. Also known as The Valley, Spanish Town has a marina, some shops, and a couple of car-rental agencies. Just north of town is the ferry slip. At the Virgin Gorda Yacht Harbour you can stroll along the dock and do a little shopping.

❿ Virgin Gorda Peak National Park. There are two trails at this 265-acre park, which contains the island's highest point, at 1,359 feet. Small signs on North Sound Road mark both entrances; sometimes, however, the signs are missing, so keep your eyes open for a set of stairs that disappears into the trees. It's about a 15-minute hike from either entrance up to a small clearing, where you can climb a ladder to the platform of a wooden observation tower and a spectacular 360-degree view. ⊠ *North Sound Rd., Gorda Peak* ☎ *No phone* ☜ *Free.*

Shopping

TORTOLA Many shops and boutiques are clustered along and just off Road Town's **Main Street.** You can shop in Road Town's **Wickham's Cay I** area adjacent to the marina, where cruise ships tender their passengers in. Don't be put off by an informal shop entrance; some of the best finds in the BVI lie behind shabby doors.

The **BVI Post Office** (⊠ Main St., Road Town ☎ 284/494–3701) is a philatelist's dream. It has a worldwide reputation for exquisite stamps in all sorts of designs. Although the stamps carry U.S. monetary designations, they can be used for postage only in the BVI. **Caribbean Fine Arts Ltd.** (⊠ Main St., Road Town ☎ 284/494–4240) carries Caribbean art, including original watercolors, oils, and acrylics, as well as signed prints, limited-edition serigraphs, and turn-of-the-20th-century sepia photographs. **Pusser's Company Store** (⊠ Main St. at Waterfront Rd., Road Town ☎ 284/494–2467 ⊠ Soper's Hole Marina, West End ☎ 284/495–4599) sells nautical memorabilia, ship models, marine paintings, an entire line of clothes (for both men and women), and gift items bearing the Pusser's logo, handsome decorator bottles of Pusser's rum, Caribbean books, Cuban cigars, and luggage. **Samarkand** (⊠ Main St., Road Town ☎ 284/494–6415) crafts charming gold-and-silver pendants, earrings, bracelets, and pins—many with an island theme: seashells, lizards, pelicans, and palm trees. There are also reproduction Spanish pieces of eight (coins—old Spanish pesos worth eight reals—from sunken galleons).

Sunny Caribbee (⊠ Main St., Road Town ☎ 284/494–2178), in a brightly painted West Indian house, packages its own herbs, teas, coffees, vinegars, hot sauces, soaps, skin and suntan lotions, and exotic concoctions—

Arawak Love Potion and Island Hangover Cure, for example. There are also Caribbean books and art and hand-painted decorative accessories.

VIRGIN GORDA Most boutiques are within hotel complexes—one of the best is at Little Dix Bay. There is a respectable and diverse scattering of shops in the bustling yacht harbor complex in Spanish Town.

Thee Artistic Gallery (✉ Virgin Gorda Yacht Harbour, Spanish Town ☎ 284/495–5104) has Caribbean-made jewelry, 14-karat-gold nautical jewelry, maps, collectible coins, crystal, and Christmas tree ornaments with tropical themes. **Margo's Boutique** (✉ Virgin Gorda Yacht Harbour, Spanish Town ☎ 284/495–5237) is the place to buy breezy, boldly printed sarongs and hand-made accessories like shell and pearl jewelry. **Next Wave** (✉ Virgin Gorda Yacht Harbour, Spanish Town ☎ 284/495–5623) sells bathing suits, T-shirts, canvas tote bags, and locally made jewelry.

Sports & Activities

TORTOLA **Diving & Snorkeling:** Clear waters and numerous reefs afford some wonderful opportunities for underwater exploration. In 1867 the RMS *Rhone*, a 310-foot-long royal mail steamer, split in two when it sank in a devastating hurricane. It's so well preserved that it was used in the movie *The Deep*. You can see the crow's nest and bowsprit, the cargo hold in the bow, and the engine and enormous propeller shaft in the stern. Every dive outfit in the BVI runs superlative scuba and snorkel tours here. Rates start at around $50 for a one-tank dive and $80 for a two-tank dive. **Blue Waters Divers** (✉ Nanny Cay ☎ 284/494–2847 ✉ Sopers Hole, West End ☎ 284/294–1200 ⊕ www.bluewaterdiversbvi.com) teaches resort, open-water, rescue, and advanced diving courses and also makes daily trips. If you're chartering a sailboat, the company's boat will meet your boat at Peter, Salt, or Cooper Islands for a rendezvous dive. Rates include all equipment as well as instruction. Make arrangements two days in advance. **Dive Tortola** (✉ Prospect Reef ☎ 284/494–3311 ⊕ www.divetortola.com) offers beginner and advanced diving courses and daily trips. Trainers teach open-water, rescue, advanced diving, and resort courses. Dive Tortola also offers a rendezvous diving option for folks on charter sailboats.

Fishing: Most of the boats that take you deep-sea fishing for bluefish, wahoo, swordfish, and shark leave from nearby St. Thomas, but local anglers like to fish the shallower water for bonefish. A half-day of bone fishing runs about $450, a full day around $850. Call **Caribbean Fly Fishing** (✉ Nanny Cay ☎ 284/499–4797).

Sailing: The BVI are among the world's most popular sailing destinations. They're close together and surrounded by calm waters, so it's fairly easy to sail from one anchorage to the next. **Aristocat Charters** (✉ West End ☎ 284/499–1249 ⊕ www.aristocatcharters.com) sets sail daily to the Indians and Peter Island aboard a 48-foot catamaran. **White Squall II** (✉ Village Cay Marina, Road Town ☎ 284/495–2564 ⊕ www.whitesquall2.com) takes you on regularly scheduled daysails to The Baths at Virgin Gorda, Jost Van Dyke, or the Caves at Norman Island on an 80-foot schooner.

VIRGIN GORDA **Diving & Snorkeling:** There are some terrific snorkel and dive sites off Virgin Gorda, including areas around The Baths, North Sound, and The Dogs. The ☺ **Bitter End Yacht Club** (✉ North Sound ☎ 284/494–2746 ⊕ www.beyc.com) offers a number of snorkeling trips day and night. **Dive BVI** (✉ Virgin Gorda Yacht Harbour, Spanish Town ☎ 284/495–5513 or 800/848–7078 ⊕ www.divebvi.com) offers expert instruction, certification, and day trips. **Sunchaser Scuba** (✉ Bitter End Yacht Harbor, North Sound ☎ 284/495–9638 ⊕ www.sunchaserscuba.com) offers resort, advanced, and rescue courses, offering the second scuba operation at the Bitter End Yacht Club—in addition to that of the resort's own dive shop.

Fishing: The sport fishing here is so good that anglers come from all over the world. **Charter Virgin Gorda** (✉ Leverick Bay, North Sound ☎ 284/495–7421 ⊕ www.chartervirgingorda.com) offers a choice of trips aboard its 46-foot Hatteras, the *Mahoe Bay,* for full-day marlin hunting. Plan to spend $800 to $1,200.

Sailing: The BVI waters are calm, and terrific places to learn to sail. The ☺ **Bitter End Sailing & Windsurfing School** (✉ Bitter End Yacht Club, North Sound ☎ 284/494–2746 ⊕ www.beyc.com) offers classroom, dockside, and on-the-water lessons for sailors of all levels. Private lessons are $70 per hour. If you just want to sit back, relax, and let the captain take the helm, choose a sailing or power yacht from **Double "D" Charters** (✉ Virgin Gorda Yacht Harbour, Spanish Town ☎ 284/495–6510 ⊕ www.doubledbvi.com). Rates range from $55 to $90 for a half-day and full-day island-hopping trip, respectively. Private full-day cruises or sails for up to eight people range from $750 to $850.

Beaches

TORTOLA Tortola's north side has several perfect palm-fringed white-sand beaches that curl around turquoise bays and coves. Nearly all are accessible by car (preferably one with four-wheel-drive), albeit down bumpy roads that corkscrew precipitously. Facilities run the gamut from absolutely none to a number of beachside bars and restaurants as well as places to rent water-sports equipment. The water at **Brewers Bay** (✉ Brewers Bay Rd. W or Brewers Bay Rd. E) is good for snorkeling, and there is a campground and beach bar here. The beach and its old sugar-mill and rum-distillery ruins are north of Cane Garden Bay, just past Luck Hill. There's another entrance just east of the Skyworld restaurant. Enticing **Cane Garden Bay** (✉ Cane Garden Bay Rd.) has exceptionally calm, crystalline waters and a silky stretch of sand. It's the closest beach to Road Town—one steep uphill and downhill drive—and one of the BVI's best-known anchorages, and it's where cruise ships send their passengers for beach excursions. You can rent sailboards and such, stargaze from the bow of a boat, and nosh or sip at several beachside restaurants, including Quito's Gazebo. Have your camera ready for snapping the breathtaking approach to the 1-mi (2-km) stretch of white sand at **Long Bay West** (✉ Long Bay Rd.). Although Long Bay Resort sprawls along part of it, the entire beach is open to the public. The water isn't as calm here as at Cane Garden or Brewers Bay, but it's still swimmable.

VIRGIN GORDA The best beaches are easily reached by water, although they're also accessible on foot, usually after a moderately strenuous 10- to 15-minute hike. Anybody going to Virgin Gorda should experience swimming or snorkeling among its unique boulder formations, which can be visited at several beaches along Lee Road. The most popular of these spots is The Baths, but there are several others nearby that are easily reached. Featuring a stunning maze of huge granite boulders that extend into the sea, **The Baths** is usually crowded mid-day with day-trippers and cruise-ship passengers. Beach lockers are available to keep belongings safe. There's an entry fee of $3. For a wonderfully private beach close to Spanish Town, try **Savannah Bay.** It may not always be completely deserted, but it's a lovely, long stretch of white sand. Bring your mask, fins, and snorkel. From The Baths you can walk on Lee Road or swim north to the less-populated **Spring Bay Beach,** where the snorkeling is excellent.

Where to Eat

TORTOLA ✕ **Capriccio di Mare.** The owners of the well-known Brandywine Bay
¢–$$ restaurant also run this authentic little Italian outdoor café. Stop by for an espresso, fresh pastry, toast Italiano (a grilled ham and Swiss cheese sandwich), a bowl of perfectly cooked linguine, or a crispy tomato and mozzarella pizza. Drink specialties include a mango Bellini, an adaptation of the famous cocktail served at Harry's Bar in Venice. ⊠ *Waterfront Dr.* ☏ *284/494–5369* ⬧ *Reservations not accepted* 🖃 D, MC, V ⊙ *Closed Sun.*

☺ ¢–$$ ✕ **Pusser's Road Town Pub.** Almost everyone who visits Tortola stops here at least once to have a bite to eat and to sample the famous Pusser's Rum Painkiller (fruit juices and rum). The nonthreatening menu includes cheesy pizza, shepherd's pie, fish-and-chips, and hamburgers. Dine inside in air-conditioned comfort or outside on the verandah, which looks out on the harbor. Thursday is nickel beer night. ⊠ *Waterfront Dr., Road Town* ☏ *284/494–3897* 🖃 AE, D, MC, V.

VIRGIN GORDA ✕ **The Restaurant at Leverick Bay.** This bi-level restaurant at the Leverick
$$$–$$$$ Bay Hotel looks out over North Sound. The upstairs is slightly less casual and more expensive, with a menu that includes steaks, pork chops, chicken, and fresh fish. There's a prime rib special on Saturday nights. Below, the bar offers light fare all day—starting with breakfast and moving on to hamburgers, salads, and pizzas until well into the evening. There's also a children's menu downstairs. ⊠ *Leverick Bay Resort & Marina, Leverick Bay* ☏ *284/495–7154* 🖃 MC, V.

$$–$$$ ✕ **The Bath and Turtle.** You can really sit back and relax at this informal patio tavern with a friendly staff—although the TV noise can be a bit much. Burgers, well-stuffed sandwiches, homemade pizzas, pasta dishes, and daily specials like conch gumbo round out the casual menu. Live entertainers perform Saturday nights. ⊠ *Virgin Gorda Yacht Harbour, Spanish Town* ☏ *284/495–5239* 🖃 AE, MC, V.

☺ ¢–$ ✕ **Mad Dog's.** Piña coladas are *the* thing at this breezy bar just outside the entrance to The Baths. The menu includes great triple-decker sandwiches and hot dogs. It's significantly cheaper than the more popular Top of the Baths, nearby. ⊠ *The Valley* ☏ *284/495–5830* 🖃 *No credit cards* ⊙ *No dinner.*

Costa Maya, Mexico

The newest cruise-ship destination on Mexico's Caribbean Coast, Puerto Costa Maya is something of an anomaly. Unlike other, already-established tourist attractions in the area (the island of Cozumel being the primary Yucatan cruise port), this port of call near the town of Majahual has been created exclusively for cruise-ship passengers. The shops, restaurants, activities, and entertainment you'll find here aren't open to the general public.

At first glance, the port complex itself may seem to be little more than an outdoor mall. The docking pier (which can accommodate three ships at once) leads to a bazaar-type compound, where shops selling local crafts—jewelry, pottery, woven straw hats and bags, and embroidered dresses—are interspersed with duty-free stores and souvenir shops. There are two alfresco restaurants, which serve seafood, American-friendly Mexican dishes like tacos and quesadillas, and cocktails at shaded tables. An outdoor amphitheater stages eight daily performances of traditional music and dance.

The strip of beach edging the complex has been outfitted with colorful lounge chairs and *hamacas* (hammocks), and may tempt you to linger and sunbathe. If you want to have a truly authentic Mexican experience, though, you'll take advantage of the day tours Puerto Costa Maya offers to outlying areas. These give you a chance to see some of the really spectacular sights in this part of Mexico, many of which are rarely visited. This is one port where the shore excursion is the point, and there are no options except to purchase what your ship offers.

Among the best tours are those that let you explore the gorgeous (and usually deserted) Maya ruin sites of Kohunlich, Dzibanche, and Chaccoben. The ancient pyramids and temples at these sites, surrounded by jungle that's protected them for thousands of years, are still dazzling to behold. Since the sites are some distance from the port complex, and require some road travel in one of the port's air-conditioned vans, these tours are all-day affairs.

CURRENCY In Mexico the currency is the peso, designated as MX$. U.S. dollars and credit cards are accepted by everyone at the port. There is no advantage to paying in dollars, but there may be an advantage to paying in cash.

TELEPHONES Most pay phones accept prepaid Ladatel cards, sold in 30-, 50-, or 100-peso denominations. To use the card, insert it in the pay phone's slot, dial 001 (for calls to the U.S.) or 01 (for calls within Mexico), followed by the area code and number. Credit is deleted from the card as you use it, and the balance is displayed on a small screen on the phone.

SHORE EXCURSIONS The following are good choices in Costa Maya. They may not be offered by all cruise lines. Times and prices are approximate.

Coral Reef Snorkel. If you prefer your adventures on—or under—the water, an excellent tour choice is the catamaran and snorkeling trips to the nearby reef at Banco Chinchorro. The largest coral atoll in Mexico, and a protected nature reserve, Chinchorro is home to a wild profusion of sealife, including conches, anemones, sea rods, moray eels, rare black corals, and some 500 varieties of fish. Parts of the reef are also scattered with shipwrecks—although most of these date from long ago, when ship travel was a riskier undertaking than it is today. ☉ *3 hrs* 🚌 *$54.*

Chacchoben Mayan Ruins. An air-conditioned bus transports you to a secluded jungle setting near the border with Belize. Your guide will explain the significance of the excavated portion of the 10-acre site, which includes detailed Mayan temples and the remains of the Mayan village. Afterwards, you have time for more exploration or to shop for crafts. Walking and climbing is over uneven surfaces. ☉ *4 hrs* 🚌 *$59–$69.*

Kohunlich & Dzibanche Mayan Ruins. An air-conditioned bus takes you to an isolated site near the Belize border where, spread over a wide area, the ruins include a variety of architectural styles, from the wide lawns of the ball courts and public plazas to the great temples with sculpted masks. Considerable walking and climbing is over uneven surfaces. A snack is included. Some tours visit only Kohunlich. ☉ *6½–8 hrs* 🚌 *$89–$98.*

Unimog 4X4 Expedition. Board a vintage World War II-era Class S Mercedes Benz Unimog truck and ride across the countryside to La Palapa beach, where you can swim, play volleyball, or simply relax. Kayaks, floats, and hammocks are available; basic facilities include freshwater showers. Complimentary soft drinks, beer, water, chips and salsa are served, and there's also a Mexican buffet lunch. The return route to the ship travels through the fishing village of Majahual. ☉ *3½ hrs* 🚌 *$79–$85.*

Jungle Beach Break. Spend the day relaxing after a short transfer to Uvero Beach. Included are an open bar and use of beach chairs, hammocks, and non-motorized water sports. Freshwater showers, rest rooms, and changing rooms are available. There's a restaurant, but you must pay for the food here. ☉ *5 hrs* 🚌 *$34–$40.*

Cozumel, Mexico

Cozumel, with its sun-drenched ivory beaches fringed with coral reefs, fulfills the tourist's vision of a tropical Caribbean island. Smaller than Cancún, Cozumel surpasses its fancier neighbor in many ways. It has more history and ruins, superior diving and snorkeling, more authentic cuisine, and a greater diversity of handicrafts at better prices.

The island is a heady mix of the natural and the commercial. Although Cozumel's sole city, San Miguel, is busy and expanding, there are still wild pockets scattered throughout the island where flora and fauna flourish. The numerous coral reefs, particularly the world-renowned Palancar Reef, attract divers from around the world. Cozumel is also the mainstay for ships sailing on western Caribbean itineraries, and as a result the island has grown very commercial. Shops stay open as long as a ship is in town, and most of the salespeople speak English. Wednesdays are the most hectic days, when it seems all the cruise ships land.

Cozumel's main road is Avenida Rafael E. Melgar, which runs along the island's western shore. South of San Miguel, the road is known as Carretera Chankanaab or Carretera Sur; it runs past hotels, shops, and the international cruise-ship terminals. Alongside Avenida Rafael E. Melgar in San Miguel is the 9-mi (14-km) walkway called the *malecón.* The sidewalk by the water is relatively uncrowded; the other side, packed with shops and restaurants, gets clogged with crowds when cruise ships are in port. Plaza Central, or *la plaza,* the heart of San Miguel, is directly across from the docks.

Cruise ships visiting for one day normally call only at Cozumel; ships staying for two days typically spend the second anchored off Playa del Carmen, across the channel on the Yucatán Peninsula. From there, excursions go to Cancún or to the Maya ruins at Tulum, Cobá, and Chichén Itzá.

CURRENCY In Mexico the currency is the peso, designated as MX$. U.S. dollars and credit cards are eagerly accepted by everyone on the island, including taxi drivers. There is no advantage to paying in dollars, but there may be an advantage to paying in cash. To avoid having unused pesos, change just enough to cover public transportation, refreshments, phones, and tips. Most prices given below are in U.S. dollars.

TELEPHONES Most pay phones accept prepaid Ladatel cards, sold in 30-, 50-, or 100-peso denominations. To use the card, insert it in the pay phone's slot, dial 001 (for calls to the U.S.) or 01 (for calls within Mexico), followed by the area code and number. Credit is deleted from the card as you use it, and the balance is displayed on a small screen on the phone.

Shore Excursions

Cozumel offers more worthwhile shore excursions than most Caribbean ports. The following are among the good choices. They may not be offered by all cruise lines. Times and prices are approximate. In general, you are better off using shore excursions from your ship if you want to see the Maya ruins. Many ships will stop briefly off Playa del Carmen to discharge passengers for Chichén Itzá and Tulum, saving a great deal of travel time.

Atlantis Submarine Trip. Dive 100 feet below the surface on a mini-submarine to reach one of the world's best dive sites and view marine life and coral reefs without getting wet. ⊘ *2 hrs* ⌂ *$75–$94.*

Chichén Itzá. Either a 45-minute flight from Cozumel, or an eleven- to twelve-hour tour (including 45-minute, each way ferry transfers to Playa Del Carmen where busses take over), takes you to the ruins at Chichén-Itzá, some of the world's largest and best examples of Mayan civilization. Approximately two hours are spent exploring the ruins. Lunch is included. Excursions that include a flight are almost double the cost. ⊘ *11–12 hrs* ⌂ *$129.*

Passion Island. After a short ride from the ship, you arrive at Bahia Ciega Pier, where you cross over to Passion Island by canoe or motorized tender. The offshore island has white sand beaches where you can play beach volleyball, lie in the water on an ocean float, or swing in a hammock. A traditional lunch of Mexican fare, including chicken and fish, as well as an open bar are provided. ⊘ *5 hrs* ⌂ *$69–$72.*

San Gervasio & Playa Sol Beach. After a guided tour of the San Gervasio archaeological site, once an important pilgrimage center for the Mayans, you will have time to swim and snorkel at Playa Sol beach. Equipment rental, restrooms, showers, and refreshments are located at the beach. This is your best option if you want to see some Mayan ruins without taking a day-long trip. ☉ *4–4½ hrs* ▦ *$52–$59.*

Snorkel Tours. Popularized by Jacques Cousteau, Cozumel's coral reefs are considered to be some of the world's finest. Most ships offer snorkeling excursions, some with lessons and equipment provided. Locales and tour lengths vary by cruise line. ☉ *Approx. 3 hrs* ▦ *$45–$55.*

Tulum Ruins and Xel-ha Lagoon. The only Mayan settlement built on a cliff overlooking the sea, Tulum was dedicated to the setting sun. A 45-minute ferry transfer takes you to Playa Del Carmen, where buses transport you to your guided tour of the ruins and a stop for swimming and snorkeling in the crystal clear waters of Xel-ha. ☉ *7–8 hrs* ▦ *$90–$129.*

Coming Ashore

As many as six ships call at Cozumel on a busy day, tendering passengers to the downtown pier in the center of San Miguel or docking at the two international piers 4 mi (6 km) away. From the downtown pier you can walk into town or catch the ferry to Playa del Carmen. Taxi tours are also available. An island tour, including the ruins and other sights, costs about $50 to $70. The international pier is close to many beaches, but you'll need a taxi to get into town. There's rarely a wait for a taxi, but prices are high, and drivers are often aggressive, asking double or triple the reasonable fare. Expect to pay $10 for the ride into San Miguel from the pier. Tipping is not necessary.

Passenger ferries to Playa del Carmen leave Cozumel's main pier approximately every hour on the hour from 5 AM to 10 PM (no ferries at 11 AM, 1, 7, and 9 PM). They also leave Playa del Carmen's dock about every hour on the hour, from 6 AM to 11 PM (no service at 7 AM, noon, 2 PM, and 9 PM). The trip takes 45 minutes. Call, or better yet, stop by the ferry pier, to verify the times since schedules change frequently and you don't want to miss your ship's departure.

Exploring Cozumel

Numbers in the margin correspond to points of interest on the Cozumel map.

San Miguel is tiny—you cannot get lost—and is best explored on foot. The main attractions are the small eateries and shops that line the streets, and the activity centers at the main square, where the locals congregate in the evenings.

⑤ Castillo Real. A Maya site on the coast near the island's northern end, the "royal castle" includes a lookout tower, the base of a pyramid, and a temple with two chambers capped by a false arch. The waters here harbor several shipwrecks, and it's a fine spot for snorkeling because there are few visitors to disturb the fish. Note, however, that you can't get here by rental car; plan to explore the area on a guided tour.

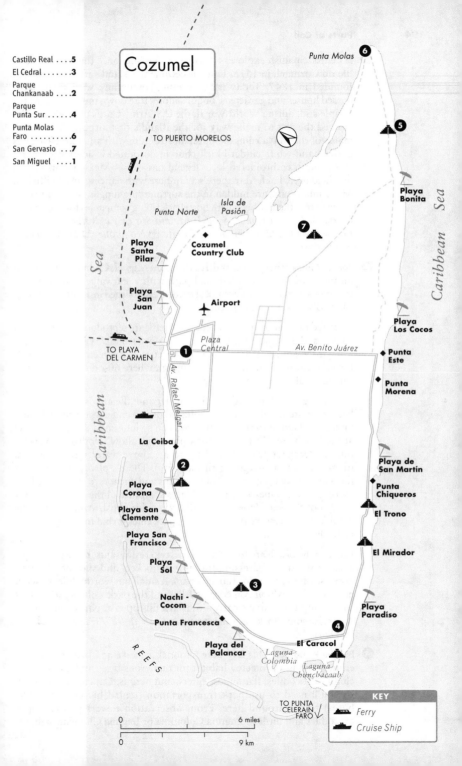

Cozumel

TO PUERTO MORELOS

Punta Molas   **6**

                                     5

Punta Norte   Isla de
                   Pasión

                                     Playa
                                     Bonita

Playa   **7**
Santa   Cozumel
Pilar   Country Club

Playa
San
Juan   Airport

                                     Playa
                                     Los Cocos

TO PLAYA   Plaza
DEL CARMEN   Central   Av. Benito Juárez   Punta
              1   Este

                                                    Punta
                                                    Morena

La Ceiba

                                                    Playa de
                                                    San Martín
Playa   **2**
Corona   Punta
                                                    Chiqueros
Playa San
Clemente   El Trono

Playa San
Francisco   El Mirador

Playa
Sol
                     3
Nachi-   Playa
Cocom   Paradíso

Punta Francesca   **4**

Playa del   El Caracol
Palancar   Laguna
                    Colombia
        R E E F S   Laguna
                             Chimchacaab

                   TO PUNTA
                   CELERAIN
                   FARO ↓

Sea

Caribbean Sea

Caribbean Sea

Av. Rafael Melgar

KEY
🚢 Ferry
🛳 Cruise Ship

0 ————— 6 miles

0 ————— 9 km

❸ El Cedral. Spanish explorers discovered this site, once the hub of Maya life on Cozumel, in 1518. Later, it became the island's first official city, founded in 1847. Today it's a farming community with small well-tended houses and gardens. Conquistadores tore down much of the Maya temple and, during World War II, the U.S. Army Corps of Engineers destroyed the rest to make way for the island's first airport. All that remains of the Maya ruins is one small structure with an arch. Nearby is a green-and-white cinder-block church, decorated inside with crosses shrouded in embroidered lace; legend has it that Mexico's first Mass was held here. Each May there's a fair here with dancing and bullfights. More small ruins are hidden in the surrounding jungle, but you need a guide to find them. Check with horseback riding companies for specialized tours. ⊠ *Turn at Km 17.5 off Carretera Sur or Av. Rafael E. Melgar, then drive 3 km (2 mi) inland to the site* ☎ *No phone* ☞ *Free* ☉ *Daily dawn–dusk.*

☟ ❷ Parque Chankanaab. A short drive from San Miguel, Chankanaab (which means "small sea") is a national park with a saltwater lagoon, an archaeological park, and a botanical garden. Established in 1980, it's among Mexico's oldest marine parks.

Scattered throughout the archaeological park are reproductions of a Maya village, and of Olmec, Toltec, Aztec, and Maya stone carvings. The botanical garden has more than 350 plant species. You can enjoy a cool walk through pathways leading to the lagoon, where 60-odd species of marine life make their home.

Swimming is no longer allowed in the lagoon; the area's ecosystem has become quite fragile since the collapse of the underwater tunnels that linked the lagoon to the sea. But you can swim, scuba dive, or snorkel at the beach. Sea Trek and Snuba programs allow nondivers to spend time underwater while linked up to an above-water oxygen system (there's an extra charge for this activity). There's plenty to see under the sea: a sunken ship, crusty old cannons and anchors, a statue of Chacmool (the Maya messenger god), and a sculpture of the Virgin del Mar (Virgin of the Sea). Hordes of brilliantly colored fish swim around the coral reef. To preserve the ecosystem, park rules forbid touching the reef or feeding the fish.

Close to the beach are four dive shops, two restaurants, three gift shops, a snack stand, and dressing rooms with lockers and showers. There's also a sea-lion enclosure and an aviary. A small but worthwhile museum nearby offers exhibits on coral, shells, and the park's history as well as some sculptures. Arrive early—the park fills up fast, particularly when the cruise ships dock. ⊠ *Carretera Sur, Km 9* ☎ *987/872–2940* ☞ *$10* ☉ *Daily 7–5.*

❹ Parque Punta Sur. This 247-acre national preserve at Cozumel's southernmost tip is a protected habitat for numerous birds and animals, including crocodiles, flamingos, egrets, and herons. Cars aren't allowed, so you'll need to use park transportation (rented bicycles or public buses) to get around here. From observation towers you can spot crocodiles and birds in **Laguna Colombia** or **Laguna Chunchacaab.** Or visit the ancient Maya lighthouse, **El Caracol,** constructed to whistle when the wind blows in a certain direction. At the park's (and the island's) southernmost point is the **Faro de Celarain,** a lighthouse that is now a museum of navigation. Climb the 134 steps to the top; it's a steamy effort, but the views are incredible. Beaches here are wide and deserted, and there's great snorkeling offshore. Snorkeling equipment is available for rent, as are kayaks. The park also has an excellent restaurant (it's prohibited to bring food and drinks to the park), an information center, a small souvenir shop, and restrooms. Without a rental car, expect to pay about $40 for a round-trip taxi ride from San Miguel. ⊠ *Southernmost point in Punta Sur Park and the coastal Road* ☎ *987/872–2940 or 987/872–8462* ⌨ *$10* ⊙ *Daily 9–5.*

❻ Punta Molas Faro (Molas Point Lighthouse). The lighthouse, at Cozumel's northernmost point, is an excellent destination for exploring the island's wild side. The jagged shoreline and open sea offer magnificent views, making it well worth the cost of a guided tour. Even tour Jeeps and dune buggies may not be able to make it all the way to the lighthouse if storms have completely destroyed the road, but the scenery is still awesome. Most tours include stops at Maya sites and plenty of time for snorkeling at Hanan Reef, about a 10-minute swim off the coast.

When booking a tour, ask about the size of the group. Some companies work with the cruise ships and lead large groups on limited schedules. If you're taking young children along you may want to book a Jeep tour, as the bumps along the road could bounce the kids right out of the vehicle.

❼ San Gervasio. Surrounded by a forest, these temples comprise Cozumel's largest remaining Maya and Toltec site. San Gervasio was once the island's capital and ceremonial center, dedicated to the fertility goddess Ixchel. The Classic- and Postclassic-style buildings were continuously occupied from AD 300 to AD 1500. Typical architectural features include limestone plazas and arches atop stepped platforms, as well as stelae and bas-reliefs. Be sure to see the "Las Manitas" temple with red handprints all over its altar. Plaques clearly describe each structure in Maya, Spanish, and English. At the entrance there are craft shops and a snack bar. ⊠ *From San Miguel, take the cross-island road (follow signs to the airport) east to San Gervasio access road; turn left and follow road for 7 km (4½ mi)* ⌨ *$5.50* ⊙ *Daily 8–5.*

❶ San Miguel. Cozumel's only town feels more traditional the farther you walk away from the water; the waterfront has been taken over by large shops selling jewelry, imported rugs, leather boots, and souvenirs to cruise ship passengers. Head inland to the pedestrian streets around the plaza, where family-owned restaurants and shops cater to locals and savvy travelers.

Shopping

San Miguel's biggest industry—even bigger than diving—is selling souvenirs to cruise-ship passengers. The primary items are ceramics, onyx, brass, wood carvings, colorful blankets and hammocks, reproductions of Maya artifacts, shells, silver, gold, sportswear, T-shirts, perfume, and liquor. Look for Mexican pewter; it's unusual, affordable, and attractive. Almost all stores take U.S. dollars. If your ship docks at International Pier, you can shop dockside for T-shirts, crafts, and more.

Before you spend any serious cash, though, keep in mind the following tips. Don't pay attention to written or verbal offers of "20% discount, today only" or "only for cruise-ship passengers"—they're nothing but bait to get you inside. Similarly, many of the larger stores advertise "duty-free" wares, but prices tend to be higher than retail prices in the United States. Avoid buying from street vendors, as the quality of their merchandise can be questionable, which may not be apparent until it's too late. Don't buy anything from the black coral "factories." The items are overpriced, and black coral is an endangered species.

The center of the shopping district is the main square off Avenida Melgar, across from the ferry terminal. The district extends north along Avenida Melgar and Calles 5 Sur and Norte. As a general rule, the newer, trendier shops line the waterfront, and the better crafts shops can be found around Avenida 5a. Other plazas include Plaza del Sol (on the east side of the main plaza), Villa Mar (on the north side of the main plaza), and the Plaza Confetti (on the south side of the main plaza).

Forum Shops (⊠ Av. Rafael E. Melgar and Calle 10 Norte ☎ 987/ 869–1687) is a flashy marble-and-glass mall with jewels glistening in glass cases and an overabundance of eager salesclerks. Diamonds International and Tanzanite International have shops in the Forum and all over Avenida Rafael E. Melgar, as does Roger's Boots, a leather store. There's a Havana Club restaurant and bar upstairs, where shoppers select expensive cigars. **Puerto Maya** (⊠ Carretera Sur at the southern cruise dock) is a mall geared toward cruise-ship passengers. It's close to the ships at the end of a huge parking lot. **Punta Langosta** (⊠ Av. Rafael E. Melgar 551, at Calle 7), a fancy multilevel shopping mall, is across the street from the cruise-ship dock. An enclosed pedestrian walkway leads over the street from the ships to the center, which houses several jewelry and sportswear stores. The center is designed to lure cruise-ship passengers into shopping in air-conditioned comfort and has decreased traffic for local businesses.

Bugambilias (⊠ Av. 10 Sur, between Calles Adolfo Rosado Salas and 1 Sur ☎ 987/872–6282) sells handmade Mexican linens. **Los Cinco Soles** (⊠ Av. Rafael E. Melgar at Calle 8 Norte ☎ 987/872–0132) is a good one-stop shop for crafts from around Mexico. The **Hammock House** (⊠ Av. 5 and Calle 4 ☎ No phone) has long been a local curiosity thanks to its bright-blue exterior and the inventory that hangs out front. Manuel Azueta Vivas has been selling hammocks here for more than four decades.

Sports & Activities

DIVING & SNORKELING
Cozumel is famous for its reefs. In addition to Chankanaab Nature Park, a great dive site is La Ceiba Reef, in the waters off La Ceiba and Sol Caribe hotels. Here lies the wreckage of a sunken airplane blown up for a Mexican disaster movie. Cozumel has plenty of dive shops to choose from. **Aqua Safari** (⊠ Av. Rafael E. Melgar 429, between Calles 5 and 7 Sur ☎ 987/872–0101) is one of the oldest and most professional

shops and offers PADI certification. Formerly at the La Ceiba Hotel, **Del Mar Aquatics** (✉ Carretera Sur, Km 4 ☎ 987/872–5949) has an ideal location for both boat and shore dives. **Dive Cozumel-Yellow Rose** (✉ Calle Adolfo Rosado Salas 72, between Avs. Rafael E. Melgar and 5 Sur ☎ 987/872–4167) specializes in cave diving for experienced divers. Dive magazines regularly rate **Scuba Du** (✉ at the Presidente InterContinental Hotel ☎ 987/872–9505) among the best dive shops in the Caribbean. Along with the requisite Cozumel dives, the company offers an advanced divers' trip searching for eagle rays and a wreck dive to a minesweeper sunk in 2000. **Fury Catamarans** (✉ Carretera Sur beside Casa del Mar hotel ☎ 987/872–5145) runs snorkeling tours from its 45-foot catamarans. Rates begin at about $58 per day and include equipment, a guide, soft drinks, beer, and margaritas and a beach party with lunch.

FISHING Regulations forbid commercial fishing, sportfishing, spear fishing, and collecting any marine life in certain areas around Cozumel. It's illegal to kill some species within marine reserves, including billfish, so be prepared to return prize catches to the sea. You can charter high-speed fishing boats for about $420 per half-day or $600 per day (with a maximum of six people). Your hotel can help arrange daily charters—some offer special deals, with boats leaving from their own docks. **Albatross Deep Sea Fishing** (☎ 987/872–7904 or 888/333–4643) offers full-day rates that include boat and crew, tackle and bait, and lunch with beer and soda. All equipment and tackle, lunch with beer, and the boat and crew are also included in **Marathon Fishing & Leisure Charters'** full-day rates (☎ 987/872–1986). **3 Hermanos** (☎ 987/872–6417 or 987/876–8931) specializes in deep-sea and fly-fishing trips. Their rates for a half-day deep-sea fishing trip start at $350. They also offer scuba diving trips.

Beaches

Cozumel's beaches vary from sandy treeless stretches to isolated coves to rocky shores. Most of the development on the island is on the leeward (western) side, where the coast is relatively sheltered by the mainland. Beach clubs sometimes charge admission, but it will often be waived if you buy food and drinks. Cruise ship excursions tend to bus passengers to larger clubs, so avoid those if you want to avoid huge crowds. A cab ride from San Miguel to most of the beach clubs costs about $15 each way. Reaching beaches on the windward (eastern) side is more difficult, but the solitude is worth the effort.

There's no charge to enter **Mr. Sancho's Beach Club** (✉ Carretera Sur, Km 15 ☎ 987/876–1629 ⊕ www.mrsanchos.com), but there's always a party going on: scores of holidaymakers come here to swim, snorkel, and drink. Seemingly every water toy known to man is here; kids shriek happily as they hang onto banana boats dragged behind speedboats. Guides lead horseback and ATV rides into the jungle and along the beach, and the restaurant holds a lively, informative tequila seminar at lunchtime. Showers and lockers are available. Mr. Sancho's is one of the few Cozumel beaches whose lifeguard tower sometimes actually houses a lifeguard.

Punta Chiqueros, a half-moon-shaped cove sheltered by an offshore reef, is the first popular swimming area on the windward side as you drive north on the coastal road (it's about 8 mi [12 km] north of Parque Punta Sur). Part of a longer beach that some locals call Playa Bonita, it has fine sand, clear water, and moderate waves. This is a great place to swim, watch the sunset, and eat fresh fish at the restaurant, also called Playa Bonita.

South of the resorts lies the mostly ignored (and therefore serene) **Playa Palancar** (⊠ Carretera Sur ☎ 987/878–5238). Offshore is the famous Palancar Reef, easily accessed by the on-site dive shop. There's also a water-sports center, a bar-café, and a long beach with hammocks hanging under coconut palms. The aroma of grilled fish with garlic butter is tantalizing. Playa del Palancar keeps prices low and rarely feels crowded.

Usually one of the calmer beach clubs, **Nachi-Cocom** (⊠ Carretera Sur, Km 16.5 ☎ 987/872–0555 ⊕ www.cozumelnachicocom.net), south of Playa Sol, has a wide, uncluttered, and shallow beach, a freshwater pool, lounge chairs, a dive shop, a restaurant, and a beach bar. It gets around charging an admission by having a food-or-beer minimum of $10 per adult and $5 per child.

Where to Eat

Some restaurants serving large groups may add a 10% to 15% service charge to the bill. Otherwise, a 15% to 20% tip is customary.

$–$$ ✕ **Las Tortugas.** "Delicious seafood at accessible prices" is the motto at this simple eatery. The menu consists primarily of fish, lobster, and conch caught by local fishermen, and changes according to what's available. Fajitas and other traditional Mexican dishes are also options. Don't look for Las Tortugas on Avenida 10—that location closed several years ago. ⊠ *Av. Pedro Joaquin Coldwell (also called Av. 30) and Calle 19 Sur* ☎ *987/872–1242* ▭ *MC, V* ⊘ *Closed Mon.*

$–$$ ✕ **Plaza Leza.** The outdoor tables here are a wonderful place to linger; you can watch the crowds in the square while savoring Mexican dishes like *poc chuc* (tender pork loin in a sour orange sauce), enchiladas, and lime soup. Breakfast is available here as well. For more privacy, there's also a somewhat secluded, cozy inner patio. ⊠ *Calle 1 Sur, south side of Plaza Central* ☎ *987/872–1041* ▭ *MC, V.*

Curaçao

Try to be on deck as your ship sails into Curaçao. The tiny Queen Emma Floating Bridge swings aside to allow ships to pass through the narrow channel. Pastel gingerbread buildings on shore look like dollhouses, especially from a large cruise ship. Although the gabled roofs and red tiles show a Dutch influence, the gleeful colors of the facades are peculiar to Curaçao. It's said that an early governor of the island suffered from migraines that were aggravated by the color white, so all the houses were painted in hues from magenta to mauve.

Thirty-five miles (56 km) north of Venezuela and 42 mi (67 km) east of Aruba, Curaçao is, at 38 mi (61 km) long and 3 to 7½ mi (5 to 12 km) wide, the largest of the Netherlands Antilles. Although always sunny, it's never stiflingly hot here because of the constant trade winds. Water sports attract enthusiasts from all over the world, and the reef diving is excellent.

History books still don't agree as to whether Alonzo de Ojeda or Amerigo Vespucci discovered Curaçao, only that it happened around 1499. In 1634 the Dutch came and promptly shipped off the Spanish settlers and the few remaining Indians to Venezuela. To defend itself against French and British invasions, the city built massive ramparts, many of which now house unusual restaurants and hotels.

Curaçao's population, which comprises more than 50 nationalities, is one of the best educated in the Caribbean. The island is known for its religious tolerance, and tourists are warmly received. Although there's plenty to see and do in Willemstad, the rest of the island features rugged natural beauty in the form of rocky coves shadowed by gunmetal cliffs and a remarkable, beautifully preserved collection of *landhuisen*, or plantation land houses, many of which are open to the public.

CURRENCY U.S. dollars are accepted everywhere except pay phones. The local currency is the Netherlands Antilles guilder or florin, indicated by "fl" or "NAf" on price tags.

TELEPHONES The telephone system is reliable. To place a local call, dial the seven-digit number. A local call costs NAf.50 from a pay phone. You can use the AT&T calling center at the cruise ship terminal and at the mega pier in Otrobanda to call the U.S. From other public phones, use phones marked "Lenso." You can also call direct from the air-conditioned Curaçao Telecom (CT) center using a prepaid phone card (open 8 AM–5:30 PM Monday–Saturday; the center also offers Internet access).

SHORE EXCURSIONS The following are good choices in Curaçao. They may not be offered by all cruise lines. Times and prices are approximate.

Country Drive. This is a good tour if you'd like to see Westpunt and Mt. Christoffel but don't want to drive an hour there yourself. Other stops are made at a land house, Hato Caves, and the Curaçao Museum. ☉ 3 hrs ☜ $40–$42.

Sharks, Stingrays & Shipwrecks. You visit the Curaçao Seaquarium, a marine park, and view two sunken ships as you take a 30-minute trip by semi-submersible. ☉ 3 hrs ☜ $39–$49.

Willemstad Trolley Train. Although there are several walking tours of the charming capital, Willemstad, they're lengthy and detailed. The trolley visits such highlights as the Floating Market, the Synagogue, Fort Amsterdam, and Waterloo Arches. ☉ 1½ hrs ☜ $29–$31.

Coming Ashore

Ships dock at the terminal just beyond the Queen Emma Bridge, which leads to the floating market and the shopping district. The walk to downtown takes less than 10 minutes. Easy-to-read maps are posted dockside and in the shopping area. The terminal has a duty-free shop, telephones, and a taxi stand. Taxis, which meet every ship, now have

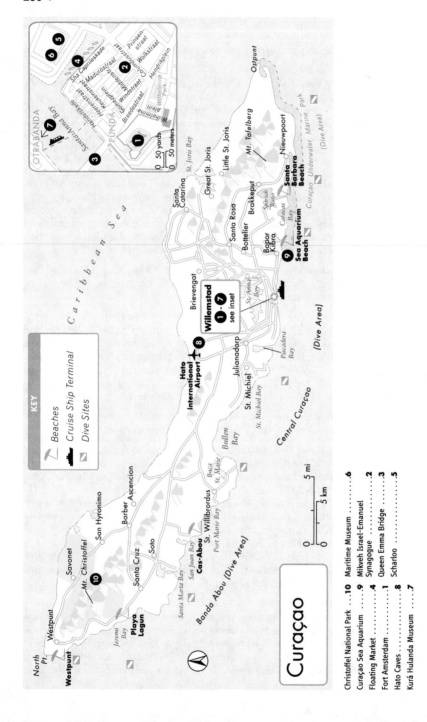

Curaçao

KEY

⌐ Beaches

⚓ Cruise Ship Terminal

◪ Dive Sites

Christoffel National Park ...**10**
Curaçao Sea Aquarium **9**
Floating Market **4**
Fort Amsterdam **1**
Hato Caves **8**
Kurá Hulanda Museum **7**

Maritime Museum **6**
Mikveh Israel-Emanuel
Synagogue **2**
Queen Emma Bridge **3**
Scharloo **5**

meters but they still aren't always used; be sure you agree on a fare before you leave. It's easy to see the sights on Curaçao without going on an organized shore excursion. Downtown can be walked, and a taxi for up to four people will cost about $30 an hour. Car rentals are available but are not cheap (about $60 per day, plus $10 compulsory insurance).

Exploring Curaçao
Numbers in the margin correspond to points of interest on the Curaçao map.

WILLEMSTAD Willemstad is small and navigable on foot. You needn't spend more than two or three hours wandering around here, although the narrow alleys and various architectural styles are enchanting. English, Spanish, and Dutch are widely spoken. Narrow Santa Anna Bay divides the city into two sides: Punda, where you'll find the main shopping district, and Otrabanda (literally, the "other side"), where the cruise ships dock. Punda is crammed with shops, restaurants, monuments, and markets. Otrabanda has narrow winding streets full of colonial homes notable for their gables and Dutch-influenced designs.

You can cross from Otrabanda to Punda in one of three ways: walk over the Queen Emma Bridge; ride the free ferry, which runs when the bridge swings open to let seagoing vessels pass; or take a cab across the Juliana Bridge (about $7). On the Punda side of the city, Handelskade is where you'll find Willemstad's most famous sights—the colorful colonial buildings that line the waterfront. The original red roof tiles came from Europe on trade ships as ballast.

❸ The **Queen Emma Bridge** is affectionately called the Swinging Old Lady by the locals, and connects the two sides of Willemstad—Punda and Otrobanda—across the Santa Anna Bay. The bridge swings open at least 30 times a day to allow passage of ships to and from sea. The original bridge, built in 1888, was the brainchild of the American consul Leonard Burlington Smith, who made a mint off the tolls he charged for using it: 2¢ per person for those wearing shoes, free to those crossing barefoot. Today it's free to everyone.

❹ Each morning dozens of Venezuelan schooners laden with tropical fruits and vegetables arrive at the bustling **Floating Market** (⊠ Sha Caprileskade, Punda) on the Punda side of the city. Mangoes, papayas, and exotic vegetables vie for space with freshly caught fish and herbs and spices. The buying is best at 6:30 AM—too early for most cruise-ship visitors—but there's plenty of action throughout the afternoon. Any produce bought here, however, should be thoroughly washed or peeled before being eaten.

❺ The Wilhelmina Drawbridge connects Punda with the once-flourishing district of **Scharloo**, where the early Jewish merchants built stately homes. The end of the district closest to Kleine Werf is now a run-down red-light district, but the rest of the area is well worth a visit. The architecture along Scharlooweg (much of it from the 17th century) is intriguing, and many of the structures that had become dilapidated have been meticulously renovated.

❼ Opened in 1999, the **Kurá Hulanda Museum** features exhibits on African history and is the largest of its kind in the Caribbean. Displays include a full-size reconstruction of a slave ship's hold and gut-wrenching first-hand accounts of the slave-trade era. ⊠ *Klipstraat, Otrobanda* ☎ *5999/462–1400* ⊕ *www.kurahulanda.com* 🖃 *$6* ⊙ *Daily 10–5.*

❷ The **Mikveh Israel-Emanuel Synagogue** was founded in 1651 and is the oldest temple still in use in the Western Hemisphere. It draws 20,000 visitors a year. Enter through the gates around the corner on Hanchi Di Snoa. The Jewish Cultural Museum in the back displays antiques and fine Judaica. ⊠ *Hanchi Snoa 29, Punda* ☎ *5999/461–1067* ⊕ *www.snoa.com* 🖃 *Synagogue free, donations accepted; Jewish Cultural Museum $2* ⊙ *Weekdays 9–11:45 and 2:30–4:45.*

❻ The 40-odd chronological exhibits at the **Maritime Museum** truly give you a sense of Curaçao's maritime history, using ship models, maps, nautical charts, navigational equipment, and audiovisual displays. Topics explored along the way include the development of Willemstad as a trading city, Curaçao's role as a contraband hub, the explosion of *De Alphen* in 1778, the slave trade, the development of steam navigation, the rise of cruise tourism, and the role of the Dutch navy on the island. The third floor hosts temporary exhibits, and the museum also offers a two-hour guided tour on its "water bus" through Curaçao's harbor—a route familiar to traders, smugglers, and pirates. When you're ready for a break, drop anchor at the Harbor Café or browse through the souvenir shop. ⊠ *Van der Brandhofstraat 7, Scharloo* ☎ *5999/465–2327* 🖃 *$6 museum only; $12 museum and harbor tour* ⊙ *Tues.–Sat. 10–5.*

❶ Step through the archway of **Fort Amsterdam** and enter another century. The entire structure dates from the 1700s, when it was the center of the city and the island's most important fort. Now it houses the governor's residence, the Fort Church, the Council of Ministers, and government offices. Outside the entrance, a series of majestic gnarled wayaka trees are fancifully carved with human forms—the work of local artist Mac Alberto. ⊠ *Foot of Queen Emma Bridge, Punda* ☎ *5999/461–1139* 🖃 *$1.75, to church museum only* ⊙ *Weekdays 9–noon and 2–5, Sun. service at 10.*

ELSEWHERE ON CURAÇAO   The road that leads to the northwest tip of the island winds through landscape resembling a Georgia O'Keeffe painting—towering cacti, flamboyant dried shrubbery, aluminum-roof houses. You may see fishermen hauling in their nets, women pounding cornmeal, and donkeys blocking traffic. You can often glimpse land houses from the road.

❿ **Christoffel Park** is a good hour from Willemstad but worth a visit. This 4,450-acre garden and wildlife preserve with Mt. Christoffel at its center consists of three former plantations. As you drive through the park, watch for deer, goats, and smaller wildlife that might suddenly dart in front of your car. If you skip everything else on the island, it's possible to drive to the park and climb 1,239-foot Mt. Christoffel, which takes two to three strenuous hours. On a clear day you can then see the mountain ranges of Venezuela, Bonaire, and Aruba. ⊠ *Savonet* ☎ *5999/*

864–0363 for information and tour reservations ⊠ *$10* ◐ *Mon.–Sat. 8–4, Sun. 6–3; last admission 1 hr before closing.*

9 At the **Curaçao Sea Aquarium** more than 400 varieties of exotic fish and vegetation are displayed. Outside is a 1,623-foot-long artificial beach of white sand, well suited to novice swimmers and children. There's also a platform overlooking the wreck of the steamship S.S. *Oranje Nassau* and an underwater observatory where you can watch divers and snorkelers swimming with stingrays and feeding sharks.

At the **Dolphin Academy** (☎ 5999/465–8900 ⊕ www.dolphin-academy. com), you can watch a fanciful dolphin show (included in the price of Sea Aquarium admission). For more up-close interaction, you may choose from several special programs (extra charges apply and reservations are essential) to encounter the dolphins in shallow water, or to swim, snorkel, or dive with them. ⊠ *Bapor Kibra* ☎ *5999/461–6666* ⊕ *www.curacao-sea-aquarium.com* ⊠ *$15; animal encounters $54 for divers, $34 for snorkelers; sea lion programs $39–$149; Dolphin Academy $64–$179* ◐ *Sea aquarium daily 8:30–5:30; Dolphin Academy daily 8:30–4:30.*

8 Hour-long guided tours of the **Hato Caves** wind down into various chambers to the water pools, a "voodoo" chamber, a wishing well, fruit bats' sleeping quarters, and Curaçao Falls, guarded by a limestone "dragon." Hidden lights illuminate the limestone formations and gravel walkways. This is one of the better Caribbean caves open to the public, but keep in mind that there are 49 steep steps to reach the entrance, and the cave itself is dank and hot (though they've put electric fans in some areas to provide relief). To reach the caves, head northwest toward the airport, take a right onto Gosieweg, follow the loop right onto Schottegatweg, take another right onto Jan Norduynweg, a final right onto Rooseveltweg, and follow signs. ⊠ *Rooseveltweg, Hato* ☎ *5999/ 868–0379* ⊠ *$6.50* ◐ *Tues.–Sun. 10–5.*

Shopping
Curaçao has some of the best shops in the Caribbean, but in many cases the prices are no lower than in U.S. discount stores. Hours are usually Monday–Saturday 8–noon and 2–6. Most shops are within the six-block area of Willemstad described above. The main shopping streets are Heerenstraat, Breedestraat, and Madurostraat. **Bamali** (⊠ Breedestraat, Punda, Willemstad ☎ 5999/461–2258) sells Indonesian batik clothing, leather bags, and charming handicrafts. **Boolchand's** (⊠ Heerenstraat 4B, Willemstad ☎ 5999/461–6233) sells electronics, jewelry, Swarovski crystal, Swiss watches, and cameras behind a facade of red-and-white-checkered tiles. The sweet smell of success permeates **Cigar Emporium** (⊠ Gomezplein, Willemstad ☎ 5999/465–3955), where you can find the largest selection of Cuban cigars on the island, including H. Upmann, Romeo & Julieta, and Montecristo. Visit the climate-controlled cedar cigar room. However, remember that Cubans cannot be taken back to the United States legally. **Freeport** (⊠ Heerenstraat 13, Willemstad ☎ 5999/461–9500) has a fine selection of watches and jewelry (lines include David Yurman, Movado, and Maurice Lacroix). **Julius L.**

Penha & Sons (⊠ Heerenstraat 1, Willemstad ☎ 5999/461–2266), in front of the Pontoon Bridge, sells French perfumes and cosmetics, clothing, and accessories, in a baroque-style building that dates from 1708. At **Little Switzerland** (⊠ Breedestraat 44, Willemstad ☎ 5999/461–2111) you can find jewelry, watches, crystal, china, and leather goods at significant savings. **New Amsterdam** (⊠ Gomezplein 14, Willemstad ☎ 5999/461–2437 ⊠ Breedestraat 29, Willemstad ☎ 5999/461–3239) is the place to price hand-embroidered tablecloths, napkins, and pillowcases, as well as blue Delft.

Sports & Activities

BIKING &
KAYAKING

Dutch Dream Adventures (☎ 5999/864–7377 ⊕ www.dutchdreamcuracao.com) targets the action-seeker with guided canoe and kayak safaris, mountain bike excursions through Christoffel Park for groups of 10 or more, or custom-designed tours to suit your group's interests.

DIVING &
SNORKELING

The **Curaçao Underwater Marine Park** is about 12½ mi (21 km) of untouched coral reef that has national park status. Mooring buoys mark the most interesting dive sites. **Easy Divers** (⊠ Habitat Curaçao, Coral Estates, Rif St. Marie ☎ 5999/864–8800 ⊕ www.habitatcuracao.com) offers everything from introductory dives to advanced open-water courses. You are free to dive any time, night or day, in addition to the regularly scheduled dives, because the abundance of marine life at the house reef makes for easily accessible shore dives right from the resort. **Ocean Encounters** (⊠ Lions Dive & Beach Resort, Bapor Kibra ☎ 5999/461–8131 ⊕ www.oceanencounters.com) is the largest dive operator on the island, with several outlets under its umbrella, including Toucan Diving at Kontiki Beach, which caters to walk-ins. These operations cover the popular east side dive sites including the *Superior Producer* wreck, where barracudas hang out, and the tug boat wreck.

Beaches

Curaçao doesn't have long, powdery stretches of sand. Instead you'll discover the joy of inlets: tiny bays marked by craggy cliffs, exotic trees, and scads of interesting pebbles, and coral that has washed up on the beaches. **Cas Abou** is a white-sand gem with the brightest blue water in Curaçao. Divers and snorkelers will appreciate the on-site dive shop, and sunbathers can make use of the small snack bar. The rest rooms and showers are immaculate. Entry is $3. You'll pay a fee ($3 per person) to enter **Sea Aquarium Beach,** but the amenities (rest rooms, showers, boutiques, water-sports center, snack bar, restaurants with beach bars, thatched shelters and palm trees for shade, security patrols) on this 1,600-foot (490-m) man-made sandy beach and the calm waters protected by a carefully placed breakwater are well worth it. Two protected covers offer crystal-clear, turquoise water at **Playa Knip,** an expanse of alluring white sand, perfect for swimming and snorkeling. You can rent beach chairs and hang out under the palapas, or cool off with ice cream at the snack bar. There are restrooms here, but no showers. Best of all, there's no fee, but that means it's popular with locals and particularly crowded on Sunday.

Where to Eat

Restaurants usually add a 10% to 15% service charge.

☾ **$$** ✕ **Mambo Beach.** Spread over the sand, this open-air bar and grill serves hearty sandwiches and burgers for lunch. Steaks, fresh seafood, and pasta fill the dinner menu. There's an excellent fish buffet on Friday. ✉ *Sea Aquarium Beach, Bapor Kibra* ☎ *5999/461–8999* ☰ *MC, V.*

¢–**$$** ✕ **Time Out Café.** Tucked into an alley in the shopping heartland of Punda, this outdoor spot serves up light bites like tuna sandwiches and grilled cheese, as well as heartier fare, including chicken shwarma. You can also connect to friends and family via the Internet at reasonable rates. From Breedestraat facing Little Switzerland, take the alley to the left of the store (Kaya A. M. Prince) and walk about 20 yards, or look for the sign in Gomezplein square and follow the arrow. ✉ *Keukenplein 8, Punda, Willemstad* ☎ *5999/524–5071* ☰ *AE, MC, V* ☾ *Closed Sun.*

Dominica

In the center of the Caribbean archipelago, wedged between the two French islands of Guadeloupe, to the north, and Martinique, to the south, Dominica is a wild place. All over the island, orchids, anthurium lilies, ferns, heliconias, and fruit trees sprout profusely. Water chutes cascade down cliff faces by the roadside. So unyielding is the terrain that colonists surrendered efforts at colonization, and the last survivors of the Caribbean's original people, the Carib Indians, have made her rugged northeast their home. From the elfin woodlands and dense, luxuriant rain forest to the therapeutic geothermal springs and world-class dive sites that mirror her terrestrial terrain, to experience Dominica is really to know the earth as it was created.

Dominica—just 29 mi (47 km) long and 16 mi (26 km) wide—is an independent country with a seat in the United Nations and the region's only natural World Heritage Site. Its capital is Roseau (pronounced rose-*oh*), its official language is English, and driving is on the left. Family and place names are a mélange of French, English, and Carib.

With a population of just 70,000, and the National Forestry Division preserving and designating more national forest and marine reserves and parks per capita than almost anywhere else on earth, Dominica is the alternative Caribbean. So if you've had enough of casinos, crowds, and swim-up bars and want to take leave of everyday life—to hike, bike, trek, spot birds and butterflies in the rain forest, explore waterfalls; discover a boiling lake; kayak, dive, snorkel, or sail in marine reserves; or go out in search of the many resident whale and dolphin species—this is the place to do it.

CURRENCY The official currency is the Eastern Caribbean dollar (EC$). Figure about EC$2.70 to the US$1. U.S. currency is readily accepted, but you will usually get change in E.C. dollars. Most major credit cards are accepted, as are traveler's checks. Prices throughout this chapter are quoted in U.S. dollars unless otherwise indicated.

TELEPHONES   The island has a very advanced telecommunication system and accordingly efficient direct-dial international service. All pay phones are equipped for local and overseas dialing, accepting either EC coins, credit cards, or phone cards, which you can buy at many island stores and at the airports. To call Dominica from the United States, dial the area code (767) and the local access code (44), followed by the five-digit local number. On the island, dial only the seven-digit number that follows the area code.

SHORE EXCURSIONS   The following are good choices in Dominica. They may not be offered by all cruise lines. Times and prices are approximate.

Champagne Reef Snorkel. A catamaran ride takes you to the most popular snorkeling spot in Dominica, where bubbling underwater geothermal vents create the sensation of swimming in a flute of warm champagne. ☾ *3 hrs* ✉ *$39–$55.*

Dominica Favorites. From Roseau, travel through the Botanic Gardens and village of Trafalgar before starting on the trail to the double cascades of Trafalgar Falls. Then head to the Emerald Pool in Morne Trois Pitons World Heritage Site to swim in the refreshing (but chilly) pools at the base of the falls. ☾ *4½ hrs* ✉ *$49–$52.*

River Tubing. Travel down the Layou River by inner tube, passing unspoiled vegetation and the soaring cliffs above. ☾ *3 hrs* ✉ *$64–$69.*

Whale & Dolphin Watching. Dominica is one of the best whale-watching destinations in the Caribbean, so if you have the opportunity to go whale-watching here, take it. On a catamaran, you'll have a good chance of spotting dolphins or whales in one of their favorite breeding grounds. ☾ *4 hrs* ✉ *$69–$79.*

Coming Ashore

In Roseau, most ships dock along the Bayfront. Across the street from the pier, in the Old Post Office, is a visitor information center.

Taxis, minibuses, and tour operators are available at the berths. If you do decide to tour with one of them, choose one who is certified, and be explicit when discussing where you will go and how much you will pay—don't be afraid to ask questions. The drivers usually quote a fixed fare, which is regulated by the Division of Tourism and the National Taxi Association. Drivers also offer their services for tours anywhere on the island beginning at $20 an hour for up to four persons; a 3½-hour island tour will cost approximately $80.

Some ships berth at the Cabrits National Park, just north of Portsmouth. Portsmouth is quieter than Roseau and in close proximity to some of Dominica's best nature sites, hikes, and river and beach bathing. The cruise-ship facility offers a cooperative crafts shop, a continuously screened film about Fort Shirley, and the occasional dance or music performance. As in Roseau, taxi and minibus drivers meet arriving cruisers near the dock. Prices are comparable to those in Roseau.

You can rent a car in Roseau for about $39, not including insurance and a mandatory EC$20 driving permit.

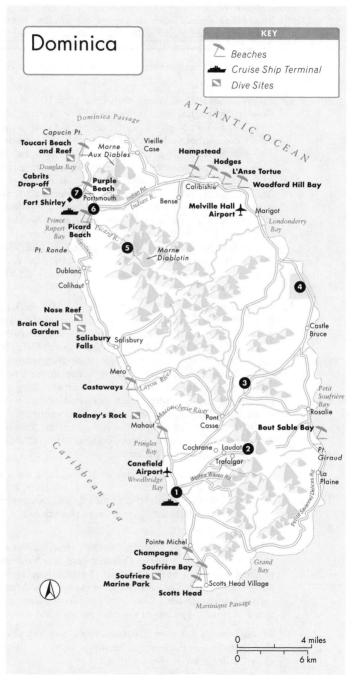

Dominica

Exploring Dominica

Most of Dominica's roads are narrow and winding, so you'll need a few hours to take in the sights. Be adventurous, whether you prefer sightseeing or hiking—you'll be amply rewarded.

Numbers in the margin correspond to points of interest on the Dominica map.

❼ Cabrits National Park. Along with Brimstone Hill in St. Kitts, Shirley Heights in Antigua, and Ft. Charlotte in St. Vincent, the Cabrits National Park's Fort Shirley ruins are among the most significant historic sites in the Caribbean. Just north of the town of Portsmouth, this 1,300-acre park includes a marine park and herbaceous swamps, which are an important environment for several species of rare birds and plants. At the heart of the park is the Ft. Shirley military complex. Built by the British between 1770 and 1815, it once comprised 50 major structures, including storehouses that were also quarters for 700 men. With the help of the Royal Navy (which sends sailors ashore to work on the site each time a ship is in port) and local volunteers, historian Dr. Lennox Honychurch restored the fort and its surroundings, incorporating a small museum that highlights the natural and historic aspects of the park, and an open canteen-style restaurant. ⊠ *Portsmouth* ☎ *No phone* 🖃 *$2* ☽ *Museum daily 8–4.*

❹ Carib Indian Territory. In 1903, after centuries of conflict, the Caribbean's first settlers, the Kalinago, were granted a portion of land (approximately 3,700 acres) on the island's northeast coast, on which to establish a reservation with their own chief. Today it's known as Carib Territory, clinging to the northeasterly corner of Dominica, where a group of just over 3,000 Caribs, who resemble native South Americans, live like most other people in rural Caribbean communities. Many are farmers and fishermen; others are entrepreneurs who have opened restaurants, guesthouses, and little shops where you can buy exquisite Carib baskets and other handcrafted items. The craftspeople retain knowledge of basket weaving, wood carving, and canoe building, which has been passed down from one generation to the next.

The Caribs' long, elegant canoes are created from the trunk of a single *gommier* tree. If you're lucky, you may catch canoe builders at work. The reservation's Catholic church in Salybia has a canoe as its unique altar, which was designed by Dr. Lennox Honychurch, a local historian, author, and artist.

L'Escalier Tête Chien (literally "Snake's Staircase," it's the name of a snake whose head resembles that of a dog), is a hardened lava formation that runs down into the Atlantic. The ocean here is particularly fierce, and the shore is full of countless coves and inlets. According to Carib legend, at night the nearby Londonderry Islets metamorphose into grand canoes to take the spirits of the dead out to sea.

Though there's not currently much in the territory that demonstrates the Caribs' ancient culture and customs, plans for a museum showing early Carib life are in the works.

3 Emerald Pool. Quite possibly the most-visited nature attraction on the island, this emerald-green pool fed by a 50-foot waterfall is an easy trip to make. To reach this spot in the vast Morne Trois Pitons National Park, you follow a trail that starts at the side of the road near the reception center (it's an easy 20-minute walk). Along the way you can pass lookout points with views of the windward (Atlantic) coast and the forested interior.

6 Indian River. The mouth of the Indian River, which flows into the ocean in Portsmouth, was once a Carib Indian settlement. A gentle rowboat ride for wildlife spotting along this river lined with *terra carpus officinalis* trees, whose buttress roots spread up to 20 feet, is not only a relaxing treat but educational and most times entertaining. To arrange such a trip, stop by the visitor center in Portsmouth and ask for one of the "Indian River boys." These young, knowledgeable men are members of the Portsmouth Indian River Tour Guides Association (PIRTGA) and have for years protected and promoted one of Dominica's special areas. Most boat trips take you up as far as Rahjah's Jungle Bar. You can usually do an optional guided walking tour of the swamplands and the remnants of one of Dominica's oldest plantations. Tours last one to three hours and cost $15 to $30 per person.

5 Morne Diablotin National Park. The park is named after one of the region's highest mountains, Morne Diablotin—at 4,747 feet, Dominica's highest peak. The peak takes its name, in turn, from a bird, known in English as the black-capped petrel, which was prized by hunters in the 18th century. Though the mountain's namesake bird is now extinct on the island, Dominica is still a major birding destination. Of the island's many exotic—and endangered—species, the green-and-purple Sisserou parrot (*Amazona imperialis*) and the Jaco, or red-neck, parrot (*Amazona arausiaca*) are found here in greater numbers than anywhere else in Dominica. Before the national park was established, the Syndicate Nature Trail was protected with the help of some 6,000 schoolchildren, each of whom donated 25¢ to protect the habitat of the flying pride of Dominica, as well as countless other species of birds and other wildlife. The west coast road (at the bend near Dublanc) runs through three types of forest and leads into the park. The trail offers a casual walk; just bring a sweater and binoculars. The five- to eight-hour hike up Morne Diablotin isn't for everyone. You need a guide, sturdy hiking shoes, warm clothing, and a backpack with refreshments and a change of clothes (including socks) that are wrapped in plastic to keep them dry. A good guide for Morne Diablotin is local ornithology expert **Betrand Jno Baptiste** (☎ 767/446–6358).

2 Morne Trois Pitons National Park. A UNESCO World Heritage Site, this 17,000-acre swath of lush, mountainous land in the south-central interior (covering 9% of Dominica) is the island's crown jewel. Named after one of the highest 4,600-foot mountains on the island, it contains the island's famous boiling lake, majestic waterfalls, and cool mountain lakes. There are four types of vegetation zones here. Ferns grow 30 feet tall, wild orchids sprout from trees, sunlight leaks through green canopies, and a gentle mist rises over the jungle floor. A system of trails has been developed in the park, and the Division of Forestry and Wildlife works hard to maintain it—with no help from the excessive rainfall and the profusion of vegetation that seems to grow right before your eyes. Access to the park is possible from most points of the compass, though the easiest approaches are via the small mountaintop villages of Laudat (pronounced low-*dah*) and Cochrane.

The undisputed highlight of the park is **Boiling Lake.** The world's largest such lake, it's a cauldron of gurgling gray-blue water, 70 yards wide and of unknown depth, with water temperatures from 180°F to 197°F. Although generally believed to be a volcanic crater, the lake is actually a flooded fumarole—a crack through which gases escape from the molten lava below. As many visitors discovered in late 2004, the "lake" can sometimes dry up, though it fills again within a few months and, shortly after that, once more starts to boil. The two- to four-hour (one-way) hike up to the lake is challenging (on a very rainy day, be prepared to slip and slide the whole way up and back). You'll need attire appropriate for a strenuous hike, and a guide is a must. Most guided trips start early (no later than 8:30 AM) for this all-day, 7-mi (11-km) round-trip trek. On your way to Boiling Lake you pass through the **Valley of Desolation,** a sight that definitely lives up to its name. Harsh sulfuric fumes have destroyed virtually all the vegetation in what must once have been a lush forested area. Small hot and cold streams with water of various colors— black, purple, red, orange—web the valley. Stay on the trail to avoid breaking through the crust that covers the hot lava. During this hike you'll pass rivers where you can refresh yourself with a dip (a particular treat is a soak in a hot-water stream on the way back). At the beginning of the Valley of Desolation trail is the **TiTou Gorge,** where you can swim in the pool or relax in the hot-water springs along one side. If you're a strong swimmer, you can head up the gorge to a cave (it's about a five-minute swim) that has a magnificent waterfall; a crack in the cave about 50 feet above permits a stream of sunlight to penetrate the cavern.

Also in the national park are some of the island's most spectacular waterfalls. The 45-minute hike to **Sari Sari Falls,** accessible through the east-coast village of La Plaine, can be hair-raising. But the sight of water cascading some 150 feet into a large pool is awesome. So large are these falls that you feel the spray from hundreds of yards away. Just beyond the village of Trafalgar and up a short hill, there's the reception facility, where you can purchase passes to the national park and find guides to take you on a rain-forest trek to the twin **Trafalgar Falls.** If you like a little challenge, let your guide take you up the riverbed to the cool pools at the base of the falls. Guides for these hikes are available at the trailheads; still, it's best to arrange a tour before even setting out.

❶ Roseau. Although it's one of the smallest capitals in the Caribbean, Roseau has the highest concentration of inhabitants of any town in the eastern Caribbean. Caribbean vernacular architecture and a bustling marketplace transport visitors back in time. Although you can walk the entire town in about an hour, you'll get a much better feel for the place on a leisurely stroll.

For some years now, the Society for Historical Architectural Preservation & Enhancement (SHAPE) has organized programs and projects to preserve the city's architectural heritage. Several interesting buildings have already been restored. **Lilac House,** on Kennedy Avenue, has three types of gingerbread fretwork, latticed veranda railings, and heavy hurricane shutters. The **J. W. Edwards Building,** at the corner of Old and King George V streets, has a stone base and a wooden second-floor gallery; it's now the cozy Cornerhouse Cafe. **The old market plaza** is the center of Roseau's historic district, which was laid out by the French on a radial plan rather than a grid, so streets such as Hanover, King George V, and Old radiate from this area. South of the marketplace is the Fort Young Hotel, built as a British fort in the 18th century; the nearby state house, public library, and Anglican cathedral are also worth a visit. New developments at bayfront on Dame M. E. Charles Boulevard have brightened up the waterfront.

The 40-acre **Botanical Gardens,** founded in 1891 as an annex of London's Kew Gardens, is a great place to relax, stroll, or watch a cricket match. In addition to the extensive collection of tropical plants and trees, there's also a parrot aviary. At the Forestry Division office, which is also on the garden grounds, you can find numerous publications on the island's flora, fauna, and national parks. The forestry officers are particularly knowledgeable on these subjects and can also recommend good hiking guides. ⊠ *Between Bath Rd. and Valley Rd.* ☎ *767/448–2401 Ext. 3417* 🖃 *$2* ⊘ *Mon. 8–1 and 2–5, Tues.–Fri. 8–1 and 2–4.*

The old post office now houses the **Dominica Museum.** This labor of love by local writer and historian Dr. Lennox Honychurch contains furnishings, documents, prints, and maps that date back hundreds of years; you can also find an entire Carib hut as well as Carib canoes, baskets, and other artifacts. ⊠ *Dame M. E. Charles Blvd., opposite cruise ship berth* ☎ *767/448–8923* 🖃 *$2* ⊘ *Weekdays 9–4 and Sat. 9–noon.*

Shopping

Dominicans produce distinctive handicrafts, with communities specializing in materials-at-hand: *vertivert* straw rugs, screwpine tableware, *larouma* basketware, and wood carvings are just some. Also notable are local herbs, spices, condiments, and herb teas. Café Dominique, the local equivalent of Jamaican Blue Mountain coffee, is an excellent buy, as are the Dominican rums Macoucherie and Soca. Proof that the old ways live on in Dominica can be found in the number of herbal remedies available. One stimulating memento of your visit is rum steeped with *bois bandé* (bark of a tree), which is reputed to have aphrodisiacal properties. These drinks are sold at shops, vendors' stalls, and supermarkets all over the island. There are a few options for duty-free shopping in Roseau.

Stores are generally open from 8 until 4 or 5 on weekdays and from 8 to 1 on Saturdays. Most are closed on Sundays. Vendors are almost always out when a ship's in port.

One of the easiest places to pick up a souvenir is the Old Market Plaza. Slaves were once sold here, but today it's the scene of happier trading: key rings, magnets, dolls, baskets, handcrafted jewelry, T-shirts, spices, souvenirs, and batiks are available from a select group of entrepreneurs in open-air booths set up on the cobblestones.

The Crazy Banana (✉ 17 Castle St., Roseau ☎ 767/449–8091) purveys everything from earthenware to doorstops, as well as other Caribbean-made crafts, rums, cigars, jewelry, and local art. **Dominica Pottery** (✉ Bayfront St. and Kennedy Ave., Roseau ☎ No phone) is run by a local priest, whose products are fashioned with various local clays and glazes. **Tropicrafts** (✉ At Queen Mary St. and Turkey La., Roseau ☎ 767/448–2747) has a back room where you can watch local ladies weave grass mats. You can also find arts and crafts from around the Caribbean, local wood carvings, rum, hot sauces, perfumes, and traditional Carib baskets, hats, and woven mats.

Sports & Activities

DIVING & SNORKELING

Dominica's dive sites are awesome. There are numerous highlights all along the west coast of the island, but the best are those in the southwest—within and around **Soufrière/Scotts Head Marine Reserve**. This bay is the site of a submerged volcanic crater. Within a ½ mi (1 km) of the shore, there are vertical drops of 800 feet (240 m) to more than 1,500 feet (450 m), with visibility frequently extending to 100 feet (30 m). Shoals of boga fish, creole wrasse, and blue cromis are common, and you might even see a spotted moray eel or a honeycomb cowfish. Crinoids (rare elsewhere) are also abundant here, as are giant barrel sponges. Other noteworthy dive sites outside this reserve are **Salisbury Falls, Nose Reef, Brain Coral Garden,** and—even farther north—**Cabrits Drop-Off** and **Toucari Reef.** The conditions for underwater photography, particularly macrophotography, are unparalleled. The going rate is between $65 and $75 for a two-tank dive or $100 for a resort course with an open-water dive. All scuba-diving operators also offer snorkeling; equipment rents for $10 to $20 a day.

The **Anchorage Dive & Whale Watch Center** (✉ Anchorage Hotel, Castle Comfort ☎ 767/448–2639 ⊕ www.anchoragehotel.dm) has two dive boats that can take you out day or night. They also offer PADI instruction (all skill levels), snorkeling and whale-watching trips, and shore diving. One of the island's first dive operations, it offers many of the same trips as Dive Dominica. **Cabrits Dive Center** (✉ Portsmouth ☎ 767/445–3010 ⊕ www.cabritsdive.com) is the only PADI five-star dive center in Dominica. Since Cabrits is the sole operator on the northwest coast, its dive boats have the pristine reefs almost to themselves, unlike other operations whose underwater territories may overlap. **Dive Dominica** (✉ Castle Comfort Lodge, Castle Comfort ☎ 767/448–2188 ⊕ www. divedominica.com) conducts NAUI, PADI, and SSI courses as well as Nitrox certification. With four boats, they offer diving, snorkeling, and whale-watching trips and packages including accommodation at the Castle Comfort Lodge. One of the island's dive pioneers, its trips are similar to Anchorage. **Fort Young Dive Centre** (✉ Fort Young Hotel, Victoria St., Roseau ☎ 767/448–5000 Ext. 333 ⊕ www.divefortyoung.com) conducts snorkeling, diving, and whale-watching trips departing from the hotel's own dock. **Nature Island Dive** (✉ Soufrière ☎ 767/449–8181 ⊕ www.natureislanddive.com) is run by an enthusiastic crew. Some of the island's best dive sites are right outside their door, and they offer diving, snorkeling, kayaking, and mountain biking as well as resort and full PADI courses.

HIKING Dominica's majestic mountains, clear rivers, and lush vegetation conspire to create adventurous hiking trails. The island is crisscrossed by ancient footpaths of the Arawak and Carib Indians and the Nègres Maroons, escaped slaves who established camps in the mountains. Existing trails range from easygoing to arduous. To make the most of your excursion, you'll need sturdy hiking boots, insect repellent, a change of clothes (kept dry), and a guide. Hikes and tours run $25 to $50 per person, depending on destinations and duration. Some of the natural attractions within the island's National Parks require visitors to purchase a site pass. These are sold for varying numbers of visits. A single-entry site pass costs $2, a day pass $5, and a week pass $10. Local bird and forestry expert **Bertrand Jno Baptiste** (☎ 767/446–6358) leads hikes up Morne Diablotin and along the Syndicate Nature Trail; if he's not available, ask him to recommend another guide. Hiking guides can be arranged through the **Dominican Tourist Office** (✉ Valley Rd., Roseau ☎ 767/448–2045 ⊕ www.dominica.dm). The **Forestry Division** (✉ Dominica Botanical Gardens, between Bath Rd. and Valley Rd., Roseau ☎ 767/448–2401) is responsible for the management of forests and wildlife and has numerous publications on Dominica as well as a wealth of information on reputable guides.

Beaches

On Dominica you'll find mostly black-sand beaches, evidence of the island's volcanic origins, or secluded white- or brown-sand beaches along the northeast coast. The best sandy beaches are around Portsmouth, but swimming off the rocky shores has its pleasures, too: the water is deeper and bluer, and the snorkeling is far more interesting. The beaches of the southwest coast are mostly rocks and black sand. On the west coast, just south of the village of Pointe Michel, **Champagne**, a stony beach, is hailed as one of the best spots for swimming, snorkeling, and diving. It gets its name from volcanic vents that constantly puff steam into the sea, which makes you feel as if you are swimming in warm champagne. Extravagantly shaped, red-sandstone boulders surround the beautiful **Pointe Baptiste** in Calibishi. Access is a 15-minute walk, entering through private property, so the beach is quiet and unpopulated. Come here to relax, tan, take dips in the ocean, and climb these incredible rock formations. There are no facilities, but this is one of the nicest beaches on the island. It's near the Pointe Baptiste Guest House.

Where to Eat

There is a 5% sales tax added to all bills. Some restaurants include a 10% service charge in the final tab; otherwise tip 10% for good service.

$$–$$$ ✕ **Guiyave.** This popular lunchtime restaurant in a quaint Caribbean town house also has a shop downstairs serving a scrumptious selection of sweet and savory pastries, tarts, and cakes. These can also be ordered upstairs, along with more elaborate fare such as fish court bouillon or chicken in a sweet-and-sour sauce. Choose to dine either in the airy dining room or on the sunny balcony perched above Roseau's colorful streets—the perfect spot to indulge in one of the fresh-squeezed tropical juices. ☒ *15 Cork St., Roseau* ☎ *767/448–2930* ▭ *AE, D, MC, V* ☉ *Closed Sun. No dinner.*

¢–$$ ✕ **Cornerhouse Café.** Just off the Old Market Plaza in a historic three-story stone-and-wood town house is Dominica's only true Internet café; the sign on the lattice verandah reads DOMINICA'S INFORMATION CAFÉ. Here an eclectic menu of meals and other treats is on offer: bagels with an assortment of toppings, delicious soups, sandwiches, salads, cakes, and coffee. Computers are rented by the half-hour; relax on soft chairs and flip through books and magazines while you wait. ☒ *At Old and King George V Sts., Roseau* ☎ *767/449–9000* ▭ *No credit cards* ☉ *Closed Sun.*

Freeport-Lucaya, Bahamas

Grand Bahama Island, the fourth-largest island in the Bahamas, lies only 52 mi off Palm Beach, Florida. In 1492, when Columbus first set foot in the Bahamas, Grand Bahama was already populated. Skulls found in caves attest to the existence of the peaceable Lucayans, who were constantly fleeing the more bellicose Caribs. But it was not until the 1950s, when the harvesting of Caribbean yellow pine trees (now protected by Bahamian environmental law) was the island's major industry, that American financier Wallace Groves envisioned Grand Bahama's grandiose future as a tax-free port for the shipment of goods to the United States.

On August 5, 1955, largely due to Groves's efforts, the government signed an agreement to develop a planned city and administer a 200-square-mi tax-free area near the island's center. Developers built a port, an airport, a power plant, roads, waterways, and utilities. They also promoted tourism and industrial development.

From that agreement, the city of Freeport and later Lucaya evolved. They are separated by a 4-mi (6 km) stretch of East Sunrise Highway, although few can tell you where one community ends and the other begins. Most of Grand Bahama's commercial activity is concentrated in Freeport, the Bahamas's second-largest city. Lucaya, with its sprawling shopping complex and water-sports reputation, stepped up to the role of island tourism capital. Resorts, beaches, casinos, and golf courses make both cities popular with visitors. Hurricane Frances caused a great deal of damage in 2004, though at this writing, most business and resorts were reopened, even those that were substantially damaged.

CURRENCY   The Bahamian dollar is the official currency of the Bahamas. But since the U.S. dollar is universally accepted, there's no need to acquire any Bahamian currency. Prices quoted throughout this chapter are in U.S. dollars unless otherwise indicated.

TELEPHONES   Calling locally or internationally is easy in the Bahamas. To place a local call, dial the seven-digit phone number. To call the United States, dial 1 plus the area code. Pay phones cost 25¢ per call; Bahamian and U.S. quarters are accepted, as are BATELCO phone cards. To place a call using a calling card, use your long-distance carrier's access code or dial 0 for the operator.

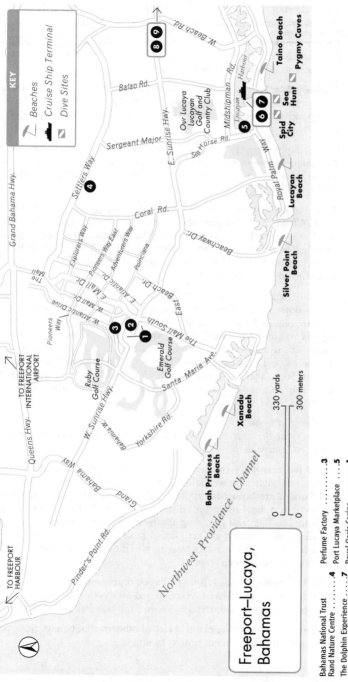

Freeport–Lucaya, Bahamas

Bahamas National Trust
Rand Nature Centre **4**

The Dolphin Experience **7**

International Bazaar **2**

Lucayan National Park **9**

Parrot Jungle's
Garden of the Groves **8**

Perfume Factory **3**

Port Lucaya Marketplace **5**

Royal Oasis Casino **1**

Underwater Explorers
Society (UNEXSO) **6**

KEY

Beaches

Cruise Ship Terminal

Dive Sites

SHORE
EXCURSIONS The following are good choices in Freeport-Lucaya. They may not be offered by all cruise lines. Times and prices are approximate.

Dolphin Encounter. Travel by ferry to Sanctuary Bay where, after an informative introduction, you observe the bottle-nosed dolphins and enter the water to interact with them. ☼ *3 hrs* 🎫 *$79–$89.*

Snorkeling Tour. Board a 72-foot catamaran and sail to Lucaya Beach where you anchor near an offshore reef and snorkel among the colorful fish. Rum punch is served on the return sail to the dock. ☼ *3 hrs* 🎫 *$38–$49.*

Coming Ashore

Cruise-ship passengers arrive at Lucayan Harbour, which has a clever Bahamian-style look, extensive cruise-passenger terminal facilities, and an entertainment-shopping village. The harbor lies about 10 minutes west of Freeport.

Taxis and limos meet all cruise ships. Two passengers are charged $16 and $24 for trips to Freeport and Lucaya, respectively. Fare to Xanadu Beach is $17; it's $24 to Taino Beach. The price per person drops with larger groups. It's customary to tip taxi drivers 15%. A three-hour sightseeing tour of the Freeport-Lucaya area costs $25–$35. Four-hour West End trips cost about $40.

Grand Bahama's flat terrain and straight, well-paved roads make for good scooter riding. Rentals run $35 a day (about $15 an hour). Helmets are required and provided. Look for small rental stands in parking lots and along the road in Freeport and Lucaya and at the larger resorts. It's usually cheaper to rent a car than to hire a taxi. Automobiles, jeeps, and vans can be rented at the Grand Bahama International Airport. Some agencies provide free pickup and delivery service to the cruise-ship port and Freeport and Lucaya, but prices are still not cheap; cars run $50–$100 per day.

Exploring Freeport-Lucaya

Numbers in the text correspond to numbers in the margin on the Freeport-Lucaya map.

Grand Bahama is the only planned island in the Bahamas. Its towns, villages, and sights are well laid out but far apart. Downtown Freeport and Lucaya are both best appreciated on foot. Buses and taxis can transport you the 4-mi (6 km) distance between the two. In Freeport, shopping, golfing, and gambling are the main attractions. Bolstered by the Westin & Sheraton at Our Lucaya resort complex, Lucaya has its beautiful beach and water-sports scene, plus more shopping and a casino that is expected to open soon.

Outside of town, isolated fishing villages, beaches, natural attractions, and the once-rowdy town of West End make it worthwhile to hire a tour or rent a car. The island stretches 96 mi from one end to the other.

EXPLORING
FREEPORT Freeport is an attractive, planned city of modern shopping centers, resorts, and other convenient tourist facilities.

❹ **Bahamas National Trust Rand Nature Centre.** On 100 acres just minutes from downtown Freeport, a ½ mi (1 km) of trails show off 130 types of native plants, including many orchid species. The center is the island's birding hot spot, where you might spy a red-tailed hawk or a Cuban emerald hummingbird sipping hibiscus nectar. Don't miss the Flamingo Pond. From its observation deck you'll spot graceful pink flamingos. The reserve is named for philanthropist James H. Rand, the former president of Remington Rand, who donated a hospital and library to the island. ✉ *E. Settlers Way, Freeport* ☎ *242/352–5438* 💲 *$5* ⊙ *Weekdays 9–4.*

❷ **International Bazaar.** If the cobbled lanes and jumble of shops and restaurants in this 10-acre complex look like something from a Hollywood soundstage, that's not surprising: It was designed by special-effects artist Charles Perrin in 1967. Having undergone a recent face-lift, it once again exudes the energy and exotica it did when it opened. Sections themed Africa, Greece, China, France, and beyond sell clothing, T-shirts, and tacky souvenirs, along with the island's widest selection of duty-free goods. A new straw market sits behind the stores complex and at the entrance stands a 35-foot *torii* arch, a red-lacquered gate that is a traditional symbol of welcome in Japan. ✉ *W. Sunrise Hwy. and Mall Dr.* ☎ *242/352–2828* 💲 *Free* ⊙ *Mon.–Sat. 10–6.*

❸ **Perfume Factory.** The quiet and elegant Perfume Factory is in a replica 19th-century Bahamian mansion—the kind built by Loyalists who settled in the Bahamas after the American Revolution. The interior resembles a tasteful drawing room. This is the home of Fragrance of the Bahamas, a company that produces perfumes, colognes, and lotions using the scents of jasmine, cinnamon, gardenia, spice, and ginger. Take a free five-minute tour of the mixology laboratory. For $30 an ounce, you can blend your own perfume using any of the 35 scents ($15 for 1.5 ounces of blend-it-yourself body lotion). Sniff mixtures until they hit the right combination, then bottle, name, and take home the personalized potion. ✉ *Behind International Bazaar, on access road* ☎ *242/352–9391* ⊕ *www.perfumefactory.com* 💲 *Free* ⊙ *Weekdays 10–5:30, Sat. 11–3.*

❶ **Royal Oasis Casino.** Completely renovated with new games and contemporary entertainment, this longstanding Freeport landmark now has a Mediterranean look and feel, with a bell tower replacing the erstwhile trademark onion domes. Gamblers come in droves to try their hand at about 700 slot machines, blackjack, and other gambling temptations. Place a bet on your favorite NFL, NBA, NHL, and NCAA contenders at the digitized Sports Book, surrounded by 18 sports-tuned TVs. The casino is part of the Royal Oasis Golf Resort and adjacent to the International Bazaar. ✉ *W. Sunrise Hwy.* ☎ *242/350–7000, 800/422–2294 in the U.S.* ⊙ *Daily 8:30 AM–3 AM.*

EXPLORING LUCAYA Lucaya, on Grand Bahama's southern coast and just east of Freeport, was developed as the island's resort center. These days, it's booming with the megaresort complex called the Westin & Sheraton at Our Lucaya, a fine sandy beach, championship golf courses, a first-class dive operation, and Port Lucaya's marina facilities.

❼ The Dolphin Experience. Encounter Atlantic bottle-nosed dolphins in Sanctuary Bay at one of the world's first and largest dolphin facilities, about 2 mi (3 km) east of Port Lucaya. A ferry takes you from Port Lucaya to the bay to observe and photograph the animals. If you don't mind getting wet, you can sit on a partially submerged dock or stand waist deep in the water, and one of these friendly creatures will swim up and touch you. You can also engage in one of several swim-with-the-dolphins programs. The Dolphin Experience began in 1987, when it trained five dolphins to interact with people. Later, the animals learned to head out to sea and swim with scuba divers on the open reef. A two-hour dive program is available. Buy tickets for The Dolphin Experience at the Underwater Explorers Society (UNEXSO) in Port Lucaya. Make reservations as early as possible. ⊠ *The Dolphin Experience, Port Lucaya* ☎ *242/373–1244 or 800/992–3483* ⊕ *www.unexso.com* ⊠ *2-hr interaction program $75, 2-hr swim program $169, open ocean experience $199* ⊙ *Daily 9–5; dolphin programs by reservation only.*

❺ Port Lucaya Marketplace. Lucaya's capacious and lively shopping complex—a dozen low-rise, pastel-painted colonial buildings whose style was influenced by traditional island homes—is on the waterfront 4 mi (6 km) east of Freeport and across the street from a massive resort compound. The shopping center, whose walkways are lined with hibiscus, bougainvillea, and croton, has about 100 well-kept establishments, among them waterfront restaurants and bars, and shops that sell clothes, crystal and china, watches, jewelry, and perfumes. Vendors display crafts in small, brightly painted wooden stalls. A straw market embraces the complex at both ends. ⊠ *Sea Horse Rd., Port Lucaya* ☎ *242/373–8446* ⊕ *www.portlucaya.com* ⊙ *Mon.–Sat. 10–6.*

❻ Underwater Explorers Society (UNEXSO). One of the world's most respected diving facilities, UNEXSO welcomes more than 50,000 individuals each year and trains hundreds of them in scuba diving. UNEXSO's facilities include an 18-foot-deep training pool with windows that look out on the harbor, changing rooms and showers, docks, equipment rental, and an air-tank filling station. There are several programs for divers with little or no experience. ⊠ *On the wharf at Port Lucaya Marketplace, Port Lucaya* ☎ *242/373–1244 or 800/992–3483* ⊕ *www.unexso.com* ⊠ *Beginner dives $25–$79, experienced dives $35–$159* ⊙ *Daily 8–5.*

BEYOND FREEPORT-LUCAYA   Grand Bahama Island narrows at picturesque West End, once Grand Bahama's capital and still home to descendants of the island's first settlers.

Seaside villages, with concrete block houses painted in bright blue and pastel yellow, fill in the landscape between Freeport and West End. The East End is Grand Bahama's "back-to-nature" side. The road east from Lucaya is long, flat, and mostly straight. It cuts through vast pine forest to reach McLean's Town, the end of the road.

❾ Lucayan National Park. In this 40-acre seaside land preserve, trails and elevated walkways wind through a natural forest of wild tamarind and gumbo-limbo trees, past an observation platform, a mangrove swamp, sheltered pools containing rare marine species, and what is believed to be the largest explored underwater cave system in the world (7 mi [11 km] long). You can enter the caves at two access points. One is closed during bat nursing season (June and July). Just 20 mi (32 km) east of Lucaya, the park contains examples of the island's five ecosystems: beach, sandy or whiteland coppice (hardwood forest), mangroves, rocky coppice, and pine forest. Across the road, trails and boardwalks lead through pine forest and mangrove swamp to Gold Rock Beach, a beautiful, lightly populated strand of white sand, aquamarine sea, and coral reef. Signs along the trail detail the park's distinctive features. ⊠ *Grand Bahama Hwy.* 🕾 *242/352–5438* 🖃 *$3 (tickets must be purchased in advance at Rand Nature Centre)* ⊙ *Daily 8:30–4:30.*

🐚 ❽ **Parrot Jungle's Garden of the Groves.** Some 10,000 varieties of tropical flora, including fruit trees, ferns, bougainvillea, oleander, and chenille plant, flourish at this 12-acre botanical paradise. Birds, alligators, Bahamian raccoons, a playground, and a petting zoo add family appeal. Follow the Main Waterfall Trail to a picture-perfect church on a hill. It is a full-size replica of the chapel at Pine Ridge, one of Grand Bahama's earliest settlements. A small café serves breakfast and dinner daily. The garden was renovated after the hurricane of 2004 and reopened in Spring 2005. ⊠ *Midshipman Rd. and Magellan Dr.* 🕾 *242/373–5668* ⊕ *www.gardenofthegroves.com* 🖃 *$9.95* ⊙ *Daily 9–4.*

Shopping

Best known for duty-free bargains in perfume and jewelry, the shopping centers of Freeport and Lucaya also harbor straw markets, a Bahamian folk tradition where visitors will find not only the baskets that give them their name but jewelry, clothing, carvings, and other souvenir trinkets. Shops in Freeport and Lucaya are open Monday–Saturday from 9 or 10 to 6. Stores may stay open later in Port Lucaya. Most accept major credit cards. The two main shopping centers are the International Bazaar in Freeport and Port Lucaya Marketplace in Port Lucaya.

Sports & Activities

FISHING Fishing charters for up to four people cost $250–$500 for a half day and $350 and up for all day; many fishing outfitters charge by the person, about $85. In deep waters, anglers pull up dolphinfish, kingfish, or wahoo. Along the flats, the elusive bonefish is the catch of fishing aficionados. **Reef Tours Ltd.** (⊠ Port Lucaya MarketPl. 🕾 242/373–5880) offers sportfishing for four to six people on custom boats. Equipment and bait are provided free.

GOLF Because Grand Bahama is such a large island, it can afford long fairways puddled with lots of water and fraught with challenge. Four championship golf courses (two at the Crown Plaza Royal Oasis, two at the Westin & Sheraton at Our Lucaya) and one 9-hole course constitute a major island attraction. The Butch Harmon School of Golf at Our Lucaya is one of three in the world. At this writing, the courses at the Crowne Plaza had still not reopened after damage from Hurricane Frances in 2004; if you want to play either course, definitely call ahead. **Fortune Hills Golf & Country Club** (⊠ E. Sunrise Hwy., Lucaya 🕾 242/373–2222), a 3,453-yard, 9-hole, par-36 course, was designed by Dick Wilson and Joe Lee. **Lucayan Course** (⊠ Our Lucaya Beach & Golf Resort, Lucaya ☎ 242/373–1066, 242/373–1333, 877/687–2474 for Butch Harmon golf school)—6,824-yards, par-72—is a dramatic 18-hole course. The 18th hole has a double lake and a dramatic Balancing Boulders feature. Home to Butch Harmon School of Golf, it also has the Arawak Dining Room, a cocktail lounge, and a pro shop. **Reef Course** (⊠ West & Steraton at Our Lucaya Beach & Golf Resort, Lucaya ☎ 242/373–2002), a 6,920-yard, par-72 course, was designed by Robert Trent Jones, Jr. It has lots of water and a tricky dog-leg left on the 18th hole. **Crowne Plaza Golf Resort & Casino at the Royal Oasis** (⊠ W. Sunrise Hwy., Freeport ☎ 242/350–7000) has two 18-hole, par-72 championship courses refashioned by the Fazio Design Group: the 7,000-yard Ruby and the 6,679-yard Emerald.

HORSEBACK RIDING **Pinetree Stables** (⊠ Beachway Dr., Freeport ☎ 242/373–3600) runs trail and beach rides twice a day for $75; it's closed on Monday. All two-hour trail rides are accompanied by an experienced guide. Rides for expert equestrians are also available. Reservations are essential.

Beaches

Some 60 mi (96 km) of pristine stretches of sand extend between Freeport-Lucaya and the island's eastern end. Most are used only by people who live in adjacent settlements. The beaches have no public facilities, so beachgoers often headquarter at one of the local beach bars, which often provide free transportation. **Lucayan Beach** is readily accessible from the town's main drag and is always lively and lovely. **Taíno Beach**, near Freeport, is fun for families, water-sports enthusiasts, and partyers. Near Freeport, **Xanadu Beach** provides a mile of white sand.

Where to Eat

★ $–$$ ✕**Pier One.** Observe Lucayan Harbour's cruise-ship activity over lunch, sunset over cocktails, or the frenzied feeding of sharks over dinner. Shark—prepared blackened, curried with bananas, panfried, and in spicy fritters—is the specialty of the house. Steak, grouper, and lobster also star on the extensive menu. In season, call ahead to reserve an outdoor table, or dine inside, surrounded by aquariums and nautical paraphernalia. Swarms of fish and sharks frenzy for handouts at 7, 8, and 9 PM. ⊠ *Lucayan Harbour* ☎ 242/352–6674 ▤ AE, D, MC, V ☉ *No lunch Sun.*

★ ¢–$$ ✕**Becky's Restaurant & Lounge.** This popular eatery opens at 7 AM and may be the best place in town to fuel up before a full day of gambling or shopping. Its diner-style booths provide a comfortable backdrop for the inexpensive menu of traditional Bahamian and American food, from conch salad and steamed mutton to steak or a BLT. Pancakes, eggs, and special Bahamian breakfasts—"stew" fish, "boil" fish, or chicken souse (the latter two are both lime-seasoned soups), with johnnycake or grits—are served all day. ⊠ *E. Beach Dr. and E. Sunrise Hwy.* ☎ 242/352–5247 ▤ D, MC, V.

¢–$ ✕**Club Caribe.** Small and very casual, this beachside haunt is an ideal place to headquarter your day at the beach. Unwind with a Bahama Mama and try the local fare, such as conch fritters, grilled grouper, or barbecued ribs. You can also get American burgers and sandwiches. Free transportation is provided to and from your hotel (reservations are essential). ⊠ *Mather Town, off Doubloon Rd. on Spanish Main Dr.* ☎ *242/ 373–6866* ⊟ *AE, D, MC, V* ☺ *Closed Mon.*

Nightlife

If your ship doesn't depart until late at night, look to the big resorts— particularly the Westin & Sheraton at Our Lucaya in Lucaya—for shows and lively nightclubs. **Bahama Mama Cruises** (⊠ Superior Watersports ☎ 242/373–7863) offers some of the best nightlife in Grand Bahama. In addition to sunset "booze cruises," Bahama Mama serves a surf-and-turf dinner and has a colorful native show. Reservations are essential. The dinner cruise and sunset cruise with show are offered Monday, Wednesday, and Friday. **Port Lucaya Marketplace** (⊠ Sea Horse Rd. ☎ 242/373–8446) has a stage that becomes lively after dark, with calypso music and other performers at Count Basie Square (ringed by three popular hangouts: the Corner Bar, Pusser's Daiquiri Bar, and the Pub at Port Lucaya).

Grand Cayman, Cayman Islands

The largest and most populous of the Cayman Islands, Grand Cayman is also one of the most popular cruise destinations in the Western Caribbean, largely because it doesn't suffer from the ailments afflicting many larger ports: panhandlers, hasslers, and crime. Instead, the Cayman economy is a study in stability, and residents are renowned for their courteous behavior. Though cacti and scrub fill the dusty landscape, Grand Cayman is a diver's paradise, with pristine waters and a colorful variety of marine life.

Compared with other Caribbean ports, there are few things to see on land here; instead, the island's most impressive sights are underwater. Snorkeling, diving, and glass-bottom boat and submarine rides top every ship's shore-excursion list and can also be arranged at major aquatic shops. Grand Cayman is also famous for the 554 offshore banks in George Town; not surprisingly, the standard of living is high, and nothing is cheap. The island sustained substantial damage from Hurricane Ivan in 2004, but at this writing, most businesses and facilities were back in operation.

CURRENCY The Cayman Island dollar (CI$) is worth about US$1.20. The U.S. dollar is accepted everywhere and ATMs often dispense cash in both currencies, though you may receive change in Cayman dollars. Prices are often quoted in Cayman dollars, so make sure you know which currency you're dealing with. Prices given below are in U.S. dollars unless otherwise indicated.

TELEPHONES To call the United States, dial 01 followed by the area code and telephone number. To place a credit-card call, dial 110; credit-card and calling-card calls can be made from any public phone.

SHORE EXCURSIONS The following are good choices in Grand Cayman. They may not be offered by all cruise lines. Times and prices are approximate.

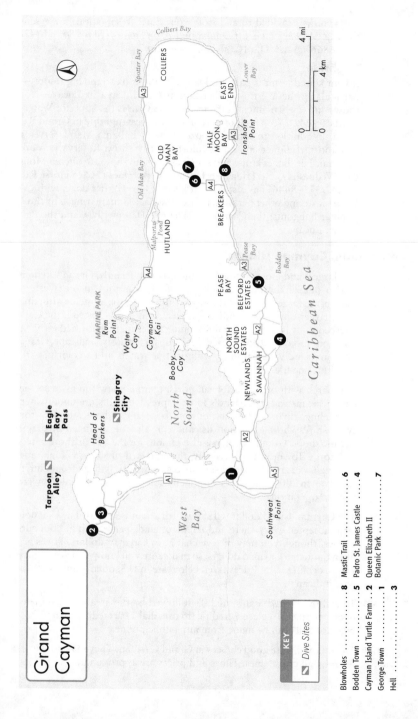

Grand Cayman

KEY

☑ *Dive Sites*

Blowholes **8**
Bodden Town **5**
Cayman Island Turtle Farm . . **2**
George Town **1**
Hell **3**

Mastic Trail **6**
Padro St. James Castle **4**
Queen Elizabeth II
Botanic Park **7**

Atlantis Submarine. Your real submarine dives beneath the waters off Grand Cayman to reveal marine life and an underwater vista usually only visible to scuba divers. ⊙ *2 hrs* ▤ *$75–$89.*

Island Tour. Drives around the island may include the Turtle Farm, "Hell" (a touristy stop with a post office and souvenir shop at the site of a formerly underwater coral reef), the blowholes, Seven Mile Beach, Pedro St. James Castle, and the rum cake factory. ⊙ *2 hrs* ▤ *$27–$34.*

***Seaworld Explorer* Cruise.** A glass bottom boat with seating five feet below the water's surface takes you on an air-conditioned, narrated voyage to view sunken ships, tropical fish, and coral reefs. ⊙ *1 hr* ▤ *$24–$39; 2 hrs, $52.*

Sting Ray City Snorkel Tour. A boat brings you offshore to a shallow sandbar inside the North Sound reef where guides feed the waiting stingrays as you swim and play with the gentle creatures. This is by far the most popular water excursion for non-divers. ⊙ *3 hrs.* ▤ *$45; an additional land tour increases price to $59–$69.*

Wetland Kayak Safari & Snorkel. Paddle your two-person kayak along the ecologically sensitive coastal mangroves, secluded inlets, and bird nesting areas while your guide points out interesting sights and explains the importance of the delicate eco-system. Snorkel and swim before returning to the pier in Georgetown. Snorkel equipment is provided. ⊙ *3–4 hrs* ▤ *$62–$69.*

Coming Ashore

Ships anchor in George Town Harbour and tender passengers onto Harbour Drive, the center of the shopping district. If you just want to walk around town and ship or visit Seven Mile Beach, you're probably better off on your own, but the Stingray Sandbar snorkeling trip is a highlight of many Caribbean vacations and fills up quickly on cruise-ship days, so it's better to order that excursion from your ship. A tourist information booth is on the pier, and taxis cue for disembarking passengers. Taxi fares are determined by an elaborate structure set by the government, and although rates may seem high, cabbies rarely try to rip off tourists. Ask to see the chart if you want to check a quoted fare. Taxi drivers won't usually do hourly rates for small-group tours; you must arrange a sightseeing tour with a company. Car rentals start at $45 a day (plus a $7.50 driving permit), so they are a good option if you want to do some exploring.

Exploring Grand Cayman

Numbers in the margin correspond to points of interest on the Grand Cayman map.

❽ Blowholes. When the trade winds blow hard, crashing waves force water into caverns and send geysers shooting up through the ironshore. ✉ *Frank Sound Rd., near East End.*

❺ Bodden Town. In the island's original south-shore capital you can find an old cemetery on the shore side of the road. Graves with A-frame structures are said to contain the remains of pirates. There are also the ruins of a fort and a wall erected by slaves in the 19th century. A curio shop serves as the entrance to what's called the Pirate's Caves, partially underground natural formations that are more hokey (decked out with fake treasure chests and mannequins in pirate garb) than spooky.

🐢 ❷ **Cayman Island Turtle Farm.** You can tour ponds with thousands of turtles in various stages of growth, and some can be picked up from the tanks—a real treat for children and adults. Future development plans are extensive but were still undecided at this writing. ⊠ *West Bay Rd.* ☎ *345/949–3893* ⊕ *www.turtle.ky* ☎ *$6* ⊙ *Daily 8:30–5.*

❶ **George Town.** Begin exploring the capital by strolling along the waterfront, Harbour Drive to **Elmslie Memorial United Church,** named after the first Presbyterian missionary to serve in the Caymans. Its vaulted ceiling, wooden arches, and sedate nave reflect the religious nature of island residents. In front of the court building, in the center of town, names of influential Caymanians are inscribed on the **Wall of History,** which commemorates the islands' quincentennial in 2003. Across the street is the Cayman Islands Legislative Assembly Building, next door to the 1919 Peace Memorial Building.

In the middle of the financial district is the **General Post Office,** built in 1939. Let the kids pet the big blue iguana statues.

🐢 Built in 1833, the home of the **Cayman Islands National Museum** has had several different incarnations over the years, including that of courthouse, jail (now the gift shop), post office, and dance hall. It's small but fascinating, with excellent displays and videos that illustrate local geology, flora, and fauna, and island history. Pick up a walking-tour map of George Town at the museum gift shop before leaving. ⊠ *Harbour Dr., George Town* ☎ *345/949–8368* ☎ *$5* ⊙ *Weekdays 9–5, Sat. 10–2.*

❸ **Hell.** The touristy stopover in West Bay is little more than a patch of incredibly jagged black rock formations. The attractions are the small post office and a gift shop, where you can get cards and letters postmarked from Hell.

❻ **Mastic Trail.** In the 1800s this woodland trail was used as a shortcut to and from the North Side. Much of the foliage was destroyed by Hurricane Ivan, and a comfortable walk depends on season and weather, winter being better. Call the National Trust to determine suitability and to book a guide for $45; tours are run daily from 9 to 5 by appointment only. The trip takes 2½ to 3 hours. ⊠ *Frank Sound Rd., entrance by the fire station and across from the Botanic Park* ☎ *345/949–0121 for guide reservations.*

🐢 ❹ **Pedro St. James Castle.** Built in 1780, the great house is Cayman's oldest stone structure and the only remaining late-18th-century residence on the island. The buildings are surrounded by 8 acres of natural parks and woodlands, struggling to grow back after Hurricane Ivan. You can stroll through landscaping of native Caymanian flora and experience one of the most spectacular views on the island from atop the dramatic Great Pedro Bluff. Don't miss the impressive multimedia theater show complete with smoking pots, misting rains, and two film screens where the story of Pedro's Castle is presented. The show plays on the hour; see it before you tour the site. On Sundays there is an extra-special brunch serving all local cuisine. ⊠ *S. Sound Rd., Savannah* ☎ *345/947–3329* 🍽 *$8.*

❼ Queen Elizabeth II Botanic Park. This 65-acre wilderness preserve showcases a wide range of indigenous and nonindigenous tropical vegetation. Rare blue iguanas are bred and released in the gardens. Hurricane Ivan destroyed a lot of the foliage, but it's being replanted and rapidly growing back. If you're lucky, you'll see the brilliant green Cayman parrot—not just here but virtually anywhere in Cayman. ⊠ *Frank Sound Rd., Frank Sound* ☎ *345/947–9462, 345/947–3558 info line* 🍽 *$3* ☉ *Daily 9–6:30; last admission 5:30.*

Shopping

The **Anchorage Center** across from the cruise ship North Terminal has 10 of the most affordable stores and boutiques selling duty-free goods from such great brand names as John Hardy, Movado, and Concord, as well as designer ammolite jewelry. Downtown is the **Kirk Freeport Plaza,** known for its boutiques selling fine watches, duty-free china, Gucci goods, perfumes, and cosmetics. Just keep walking—there's plenty of shopping in all directions. Stores in the **Landmark** sell perfumes, treasure coins, and upscale beachwear; Breezes by the Bay restaurant is upstairs. The **Heritage Crafts Shop** (⊠ George Town ☎ 345/945–6041), near the harbor, sells local crafts and gifts. **Cathy Church's Underwater Photo Centre & Gallery** (⊠ S. Church St., George Town ☎ 345/949–7415) has a collection of underwater photos by the famed photographer Cathy Church. Debbie van der Bol runs the arts-and-crafts shop **Pure Art** (⊠ S. Church St., George Town ☎ 345/949–9133), which sells watercolors, wood carvings, and lacework by local artists, as well as her own paintings and cards. This is a great place to browse even if you weren't planning a purchase. The **Tortuga Rum Company** (⊠ N. Sound Rd., George Town ☎ 345/949–7701 or 345/949–7867) has scrumptious rum cake (sealed fresh) that's sweet and moist and makes a great gift to take back to those who stayed behind. Buy all sizes and flavors at the airport on the way home, fresh, at the same prices.

Sports & Activities

DIVING & SNORKELING Pristine water (visibility often exceeding 100 feet [30 m]), breathtaking coral formations, and plentiful and exotic marine life mark the **Great Wall**—a world-renowned dive site just off the north side of Grand Cayman. A must-see for adventurous souls is **Stingray City** in the North Sound, noted as the best 12-foot (3½-m) dive in the world, where dozens of stingrays congregate, tame enough to suction squid from your outstretched palm. Nondivers gravitate to **Stingray Sandbar,** a shallower part of the North Sound, which has become a popular snorkeling spot; it is also a popular spot for the stingrays. **Don Foster's Dive Cayman Islands** (⊠ 218 South Church St., George Town ☎ 345/949–5679 or 800/833–4837 ⊕ www.donfosters.com) has a pool with a shower and also snorkeling along the ironshore. The shore diving includes a few interesting swim-throughs, or you can book a boat dive. **Eden Rock Diving Center** (⊠ 124 South Church St., George Town ☎ 345/949–7243 ⊕ www.edenrockdive.com), south of George Town, provides easy access to one of the best shore dives on the island—Eden Rock and Devil's

Grotto. If someone tells you that the minnows are in, drop everything and make a scuba dive here. ☺ **Red Sail Sports** (☎ 345/949–8745 or 877/733–7245 ⊕ www.redsailcayman.com) offers daily trips from most of the major hotels along Seven Mile Beach and Rum Point. Their dives are run as guided tours only, but if you're a beginner this would be a perfect option.

FISHING Cayman waters are abundant with blue and white marlin, yellowfin tuna, sailfish, dolphinfish, bonefish, and wahoo. Two dozen boats are available for charter. **Burton's Tourist Information & Activity Services** (☎ 345/949–6598 or 345/926–8294) can hook you up with a number of different charters and tours.

Beaches

The west coast, the island's most developed area, is where you'll find the famous **Seven Mile Beach.** This white, powdery, 5½-mi-long strand is Grand Cayman's busiest vacation center, and most of the island's resorts, restaurants, and shopping centers are along this strip. At the public beach toward the north end you can find chairs for rent ($10 for the day, including a beverage) and plenty of water toys, two beach bars, restrooms, and showers.

Where to Eat

Many restaurants add a 10% to 15% service charge. If a service charge is not added, tip 15% of the total bill.

$$–$$$$ ╳ **Cracked Conch by the Sea.** Visiting here is like taking a trip to a nautical museum, so don't be shy about asking for the story behind the hatches-cum-table tops, or the mirror frames in the ladies' room. The rustic, family-friendly restaurant has a huge menu that includes a heavenly turtle steak in coconut rum sauce, not to mention the island's best conch fritters. The Sunday brunch is also a justifiably popular crowd-pleaser. ⊠ *N. West Point Rd., next door to Turtle Farm, West Bay* ☎ 345/945–5217 ▱ AE, MC, V.

$–$$$ ╳ **Breezes by the Bay.** This cheerful restaurant overlooks the busy George Town harbor from across Harbor Drive, so go to the second floor to avoid traffic noise. Prices are a bargain, especially for peel-and-eat shrimp. The desserts are huge. The bar mixes great specialty drinks. Inside is no-smoking. ⊠ *Harbor Dr., George Town* ☎ 345/943–8469 ▱ AE, MC, V.

¢–$ ╳ **Ye Old English Bakery.** This bakery is a fine place to stop for breakfast, lunch, or snacks. The menu of specialty breads, pastries, and scones is for sale, as is good coffee. There's Internet service, too. ⊠ *Harbour Dr., George Town* ☎ 345/945–2420 ▱ *No credit cards* ⊗ *No dinner.*

Grenada & Carriacou

Nutmeg, cinnamon, cloves, cocoa . . . those heady aromas fill the air in Grenada (pronounced gruh-*nay*-da). Only 21 mi (33½ km) long and 12 mi (19½ km) wide, the Isle of Spice is a tropical gem of lush rain forests, white-sand beaches, secluded coves, exotic flowers, and enough locally grown spices to fill anyone's kitchen cabinet.

Grenada is a safe and secure vacation spot with friendly, hospitable people and enough good shopping, restaurants, historic sites, and natural wonders to make it a popular port of call. About one-third of Grenada's visitors arrive by cruise ship, and that number continues to grow each year. Hurricane Ivan crippled island tourism for several months after its landfall in September 2004, but cruise ships brought the first tourists back to the island and have helped with the recovery since.

Nearby Carriacou (pronounced carry-a-*coo*), which was not seriously affected by Ivan, is visited mostly by smaller sailing ships since its port is simply not prepared for the infusion of thousands of passengers from a large liner. Part of the three-island nation of Grenada, which also includes tiny Petite Martinique (pronounced pitty mar-ti-*neek*) 3 km (2 mi) north of Carriacou, the 13-square-mi (21-square-km) island is 23 mi (37 km) north of the island of Grenada. Carriacou is the largest and southernmost island of the Grenadines, an archipelago of 32 small islands and cays that stretch northward from Grenada to St. Vincent.

The colonial history of Carriacou parallels Grenada's, but the island's small size has restricted its role in the nation's political history. Carriacou is hilly and not lush like Grenada. In fact, it's quite arid in some areas. A chain of hills cuts a wide swath through the center, from Gun Point in the north to Tyrrel Bay in the south. The island's greatest attractions for cruise passengers are diving and snorkeling.

CURRENCY Grenada uses the Eastern Caribbean dollar (EC$). The exchange rate is EC$2.70 to US$1, although taxi drivers, stores, and vendors will frequently calculate at a rate of EC$2.50. U.S. dollars, major credit cards, and traveler's checks are readily accepted, but always ask which currency is being referenced when asking prices. Prices given below are in U.S. dollars unless otherwise indicated.

TELEPHONES Prepaid phone cards, which can be used in special card phones throughout the Caribbean for local or international calls, are sold in denominations of EC$20 ($7.50), EC$30 ($12), EC$50 ($20), and EC$75 ($28) at shops, attractions, transportation centers, and other convenient outlets. For international calls using a major credit card, dial 111; to place a collect call or use a calling card, dial 800/225–5872 from any telephone. Pay phones are available at the airport, the cruise-ship welcome center, or the Cable & Wireless office on the Carenage in St. George's, shopping centers, and other convenient locations.

SHORE EXCURSIONS The following are good choices in Grenada. They may not be offered by all cruise lines. Times and prices are approximate.

Island Drive & Annandale Falls. Ride north along the west coast, through small villages and past lush greenery, to the Gouyave Nutmeg Cooperative in Grenville for a fascinating look at how Grenada's most famous export is processed. From Grenville, drive to the National Park Nature Center and climb to Annandale Falls before returning to the ship. ⊙ *3 hrs* 🚌 *$46–$49.*

Island Jeep Tour. After driving through St. George Parish, travel north, stopping at a sulphur spring and pond, then through Grenada's central

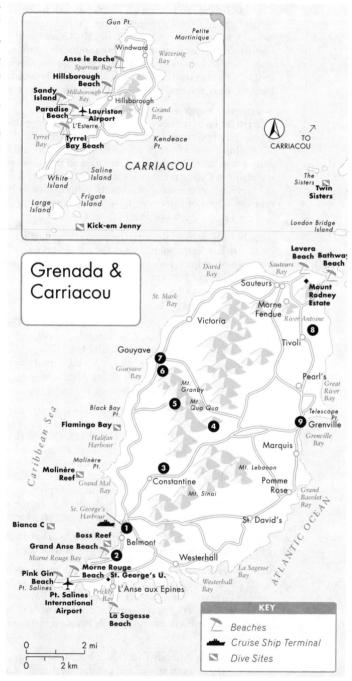

mountain range to the rain forest, Crater Lake, and Grand Étang National Park. ⊙ *4 hrs* ⌫ *$69–$75.*

Nature Walk. You travel to an undisturbed rain forest, which is an important island watershed. There, you'll climb to the summit of the hill (1,420 feet) and get a panoramic view of Port Salines in the south, all the way to Grand Étang forest. Then it's back to St. George. ⊙ *2 hrs* ⌫ *$32–$39.*

Coming Ashore

A new cruise-ship pier opened in 2005. Although it was damaged by Hurricane Ivan, it was expected to be fully operational by Fall 2005 and will allow larger ships to anchor at the pier near the Carenage instead of in the harbor. You can easily tour the capital on foot, but be prepared to climb up and down steep hills. Taxis often wait for fares at the welcome center at the Cruise Ship Terminal on the north side of St. George's.

If you don't want to walk into town, you can find a taxi to take you around The Carenage to Market Square ($3 or $4 each way), or a water taxi across the harbor ($1 each way).

To explore areas outside St. George's, hiring a taxi or arranging a guided tour is more sensible than renting a car. Taxis are plentiful, and fixed rates to popular island destinations are posted at the welcome center.

A taxi ride from the welcome center to the beach will cost $10, but water taxis are a less expensive and more picturesque way to get there; the one-way fare is $4 to Grand Anse and $8 to Morne Rouge. Minibuses are the least expensive (and most crowded) way to travel between St. George's and Grand Anse; pay EC$1.50 (55¢), but hold on to your hat. Taxis, water taxis, and minibuses are all available at the pier.

If you want to rent a car and explore on your own, be prepared to pay $12 for a temporary driving permit and about $55 to $75 for a day's car rental.

Exploring Grenada & Carriacou

Numbers in the margin correspond to points of interest on the Grenada and Carriacou map.

GRENADA
❸ **Annandale Falls.** A mountain stream cascades 40 feet into a pool surrounded by exotic vines, such as liana and elephant ear. A paved path leads to the bottom of the falls, and a trail leads to the top. This is a lovely, cool spot for swimming and picnicking. ✉ *Main interior road, 15 min northeast of St. George's, St. George* ☎ *473/440-2452* ⌫ *$1* ⊙ *Daily 9–5.*

❺ **Concord Falls.** About 8 mi (13 km) north of St. George's, a turnoff from the West Coast Road leads to Concord Falls—actually three separate waterfalls. The first is at the end of the road; when the currents aren't too strong, you can take a dip under the cascade. Reaching the two other waterfalls requires an hour's hike into the forest reserve. The third and most spectacular waterfall, at Fountainbleu, thunders 65 feet over huge boulders and creates a small pool. It's smart to hire a guide. The path is clear, but slippery boulders toward the end can be treacherous without assistance. ⊠ *Off West Coast Rd., St. John* ☎ *$2 for changing room.*

🐾 ❻ **Dougaldston Spice Estate.** Just south of Gouyave, this historic plantation, now primarily a living museum, still grows and processes spices the old-fashioned way. You can see cocoa, nutmeg, mace, cloves, and other spices laid out on giant racks to dry in the sun. A worker will be glad to explain the process (and will appreciate a small donation). You can buy spices for about $2 a bag. ⊠ *Gouyave, St. John* ☎ *No phone* ☎ *Free* ☺ *Weekdays 9–4.*

🐾 ❼ **Gouyave Nutmeg Processing Cooperative.** Touring the nutmeg processing coop, in the center of the west coast fishing village of Gouyave (pronounced *gwahve*), is a fragrant, fascinating way to spend half an hour. You can learn all about nutmeg and its uses, see the nutmegs laid out in bins, and watch the workers sort them by hand and pack them into burlap bags for shipping worldwide. The three-story plant turned out 3 million pounds of Grenada's most famous export each year prior to Hurricane Ivan's devastating effect on the crop in 2004. It will take a few more years for the nutmeg industry to get back to that level. ⊠ *Gouyave, St. John* ☎ *473/444–8337* ☎ *$1* ☺ *Weekdays 10–1 and 2–4.*

🐾 ❷ **Grand Anse.** A residential and commercial area about 5 mi (8 km) south of downtown St. George's, Grand Anse is named for the world-renowned beach it surrounds. Most of Grenada's tourist facilities—resorts, restaurants, some shopping, and most nightlife—are in this general area, although a couple of the beachfront resorts were among those most heavily damaged by Hurricane Ivan in 2004. **Grand Anse Beach** is a 2-mi (3-km) crescent of sand shaded by coconut palms and sea grape trees, with gentle turquoise surf. A public entrance is at Camerhogne Park, just a few steps from the main road. Water taxis from the Carenage in St. George's pull up to a jetty on the beach. **St. George's University,** which for years held classes at its enviable beachfront location in Grand Anse, has a sprawling campus in True Blue, a nearby residential community. The university's Grand Anse property, from which the evacuation of U.S. medical students was a high priority of the U.S. Marines during the 1983 intervention, is currently used for administrative purposes. ⊠ *St. George.*

🐾 ❹ **Grand Étang National Park and Forest Reserve.** Deep in the mountainous interior of Grenada is a bird sanctuary and forest reserve with miles of hiking trails, lookouts, and fishing streams. **Grand Étang Lake** is a 36-acre expanse of cobalt-blue water that fills the crater of an extinct volcano 1,740 feet above sea level. Although legend has it the lake is bottomless, maximum soundings are recorded at 18 feet. The informative **Grand Étang Forest Center** has displays on the local wildlife and vegetation. A forest manager is on hand to answer questions. A small snack bar and souvenir stands are nearby. ⊠ *Main interior road, between Grenville and St. George's, St. Andrew* ☎ *473/440–6160* ☎ *$1* ☺ *Daily 8:30–4.*

🐾 ❾ **Grenville Cooperative Nutmeg Association.** Like its counterpart in Gouyave, this nutmeg processing plant is open to the public for guided tours. You can see and learn about the entire process of receiving, drying, sorting, and packing nutmegs. ✉ *Grenville, St. Andrew* ☎ *473/442–7241* 💲 *$1* 🕙 *Weekdays 10–1 and 2–4.*

8 River Antoine Rum Distillery. At this rustic operation, kept open primarily as a museum, a limited quantity of Rivers rum is produced by the same methods used since the distillery opened in 1785. The process begins with the crushing of sugarcane from adjacent fields in the River Antoine (pronounced an-*twine*) Estate. The result is a potent overproof rum, sold only in Grenada, that will knock your socks off. ✉ *River Antoine Estate, St. Patrick, St. Patrick* ☎ *473/442–7109* 💲 *$2* 🕙 *Guided tours daily 9–4.*

1 St. George's. Grenada's capital is a busy West Indian city, most of which remains unchanged from colonial days. Narrow streets lined with shops wind up, down, and across steep hills. Pastel-painted warehouses cling to the waterfront, while small rainbow-hue houses rise from the waterfront and disappear into steep green hills.

St. George's Harbour is the center of town. Schooners, ferries, and tour boats tie up along the seawall or at the small dinghy dock. On weekends a tall ship is likely to be anchored in the middle of the harbor, giving the scene a 19th-century flavor. **The Carenage** (pronounced car-a-*nahzh*), which surrounds horseshoe-shape St. George's Harbour, is the capital's main thoroughfare. Warehouses, shops, and restaurants line the waterfront. At the south end of the Carenage, the Grenada Board of Tourism has its offices. At the center of The Carenage, on the pedestrian plaza, sits the *Christ of the Deep* statue. It was presented to Grenada by Costa Cruise Line in remembrance of its ship *Bianca C*, which burned and sank in the harbor in 1961 and is now a favorite dive site.

The **Grenada National Museum** (✉ Young and Monckton Sts. ☎ 473/440–3725 💲 $1 🕙 Weekdays 9–4:30, Sat. 10–1), a block from the Carenage, is built on the foundation of a French army barracks and prison that was originally built in 1704. The small museum has exhibitions of news items, photos, and proclamations relating to the 1983 intervention, along with Empress Josephine's childhood bathtub and other memorabilia from earlier historical periods.

Fodor'sChoice **Ft. George** (✉ Church St.) is high on the hill at the entrance to St. ★ George's Harbour. It's Grenada's oldest fort—built by the French in 1705 to protect the harbor. No shots were ever fired here until October 1983, when Prime Minister Maurice Bishop and some of his followers were assassinated in the courtyard. The fort now houses police headquarters, but is open to the public daily; admission is free. The 360-degree view of the capital city, St. George's Harbour, and the open sea is spectacular. An engineering feat for its time, the 340-foot-long **Sendall Tunnel** was built in 1895 and named for an early governor. It separates the harborside of St. George's from the Esplanade on the bay side of town, where you can find the markets (produce, meat, and fish), the cruise-ship terminal, and the public bus station.

Don't miss St. George's picturesque **Market Square** (✉ Granby St.), a block from the Esplanade. It's open every weekday morning, but really comes alive on Saturday from 8 to noon. Vendors sell baskets, spices, brooms, clothing, knickknacks, coconut water, and heaps of fresh produce. Market Square is historically where parades and political rallies take place—and the beginning of the minibus routes to all areas of the island.

St. Andrew's Presbyterian Church (✉ At Halifax and Church Sts.), also known as Scots' Kirk, was constructed with the help of the Freemasons in 1830. It was heavily damaged by Hurricane Ivan in 2004 and now resembles the bombed-out buildings common throughout Europe following World War II. Its future is unclear at this point. Built in 1825, the beautiful stone-and-pink-stucco **St. George's Anglican Church** (✉ Church St.) is filled with statues and plaques depicting Grenada in the 18th and 19th centuries. **St. George's Methodist Church** (✉ Green St., near Herbert Blaize St.) was built in 1820 and is the oldest original church in the city. The Gothic tower of **St. George's Roman Catholic Church** (✉ Church St.) dates from 1818, but the current structure was built in 1884; the tower is the city's most visible landmark. **York House** (✉ Church St.), dating from 1801, is home to Grenada's Houses of Parliament and Supreme Court. It, the neighboring Registry Building (1780), and Government House (1802) are fine examples of early Georgian architecture.

Overlooking the city of St. George's and the inland side of the harbor, historic **Ft. Frederick** (✉ Richmond Hill) provides a panoramic view of two-thirds of Grenada. The fort was started by the French and completed in 1791 by the British; it was also the headquarters of the People's Revolutionary Government during the 1983 coup. Today you can get a bird's-eye view of much of Grenada from here.

CARRIACOU Carriacou, the land of many reefs, is a hilly island and (unlike its lush sister island of Grenada) has neither lakes nor rivers, so its drinking water comes from the falling rain, which is caught in cisterns and purified with bleach. It gets quite arid during the dry season (January through May). Nevertheless, pigeon peas, corn, and fruit are grown here, and the climate seems to suit the mahogany trees used for furniture-making and the white cedar critical to the boatbuilding that has made Carriacou famous.

Hillsborough is Carriacou's main town. Just offshore, Sandy Island is one of the nicest beaches around (although the natural phenomenon of a gradually rising sea is taking its toll on this tiny spit of land). Almost anyone with a boat can give you a ride out to the island for a small fee (about $10 round-trip), and you can leave your cares on the dock. Rolling hills cut a wide swath through the middle of Carriacou, from Gun Point in the north to Tyrrel Bay in the south.

Interestingly, tiny Carriacou has several distinct cultures. Hillsborough is decidedly English; the southern region, around L'Esterre, reflects French roots; and the northern town of Windward has Scottish ties. African culture, of course, is the overarching influence. The high-speed power catamaran *Osprey Express* makes two round-trip voyages daily from Grenada to Carriacou and on to Petite Martinique. The fare for the 90-minute one-way trip between Grenada and Carriacou is $19 per person, $35 round-trip. The boat leaves Grenada from The Carenage in St. George's.

Shopping

Granada's best souvenirs or gifts for friends back home are spice baskets filled with cinnamon, nutmeg, mace, bay leaves, cloves, turmeric, and ginger. You can buy them for as little as $2 in practically every shop, at the open-air produce market at **Market Square** in St. George's, at the vendor stalls near the pier, and at the Craft & Spice Market on Grand Anse Beach. Vendors also sell handmade fabric dolls, coral jewelry, seashells, and hats and baskets handwoven from green palm fronds. Bargaining is not appropriate in the shops, and it isn't customary with vendors—although most will offer you "a good price."

Art Fabrik (⊠ 9 Young St., St. George's, St. George ☎ 473/440–0568) is a studio where you can watch artisans create batik before turning it into clothing or accessories. In the shop you can find fabric by the yard or fashioned into dresses, shirts, shorts, hats, and scarves. **Art Grenada** (⊠ Grand Anse Shopping Centre, Suite 7, Grand Anse, St. George ☎473/444–2317) displays and sells paintings, drawings, and watercolors exclusively by Grenadian artists, among them Canute Caliste, Lyndon Bedeau, and Susan Mains. Exhibitions change monthly, and you can have your purchases shipped. **Tikal** (⊠ Young St., St. George's, St. George ☎ 473/440–2310) is known for its exquisite baskets, artwork, jewelry, batik items, and fashions, both locally made and imported from Africa and Latin America.

Sports & Activities

FISHING Deep-sea fishing around Grenada is excellent, with marlin, sailfish, yellowfin tuna, and dolphinfish topping the list of good catches. You can arrange half- or full-day sportfishing trips for $250 to $500, depending on the type of boat, number of people, and length of trip. **Bezo Charters** (☎ 473/443–5477 or 473/443–5021 ⊕ www.ultimateangling.com) has a tournament-equipped Bertram 31 Flybridge Sport Fisherman, called *Bezo,* with an air-conditioned cabin, fighting chair, and an experienced crew just waiting to take you blue-water fishing. Charters can be customized; equipment and beverages are included. **Evans Fishing Charters** (☎ 473/444–4422 or 473/444–4217) has a Bertram 35 Sport Fisherman, *Xiphias Seeker,* with an air-conditioned cabin; equipment includes Penn International and Shimano reels. **True Blue Sportfishing** (☎ 473/444–2048) offers big-game charters on its "purpose-built" 31-foot Sport Fisherman, *Yes Aye.* It has an enclosed cabin, fighting chair, and professional tackle. Refreshments and courtesy transport are included.

WATER SPORTS Hotels on Grand Anse Beach have water-sports centers where you can rent small sailboats, Windsurfers, and Sunfish (as well as beach chairs). **Aquanauts Grenada** (⊠ Grenada Grand Beach Resort, Grand Anse ☎ 473/444–1126 ⊕ www.aquanautgrenada.com ⊠ True Blue Bay Resort, True Blue ☎ 473/439–2500) has a multilingual staff, so instruction is available in English, German, Dutch, French, and Spanish. Two-tank dive trips, accommodating no more than eight divers, are offered each morning to both the Caribbean and Atlantic sides of Grenada. **Dive Grenada** (✉ Flamboyant Hotel, Morne Rouge, St. George ☎ 473/444–1092 ⊕ www.divegrenada.net) offers dive trips twice daily (at 10 AM and 2 PM), specializing in diving the *Bianca C*. **EcoDive** (✉ Grenada Grand Beach Resort, Grand Anse, St. George ☎ 473/444–7777 ⊕ www.ecodiveandtrek.com) offers two dive trips daily, both drift and wreck dives, as well as weekly day trips to dive Isle de Rhonde. The company also runs Grenada's marine conservation and education center, which conducts coral-reef monitoring and turtle projects. **ScubaTech Grenada** (✉ Calabash Hotel, L'anse aux Épines ☎ 473/439–4346 ⊕ www.scubatech-grenada.com) has two full-time diving instructors and, in addition to daily dive trips, offers the complete range of PADI programs, from discover scuba to divemaster.

Arawak Divers (✉ Tyrrel Bay, Carriacou ☎ 473/443–6906 ⊕ www.arawak.de) has its own jetty at Tyrrel Bay; it takes small groups on daily dive trips and night dives, offers courses in German and English, and provides pickup service from yachts.

Carriacou Silver Diving (✉ Main St., Hillsborough, Carriacou ☎ 473/443–7882 ⊕ www.scubamax.com) accommodates up to 12 divers on one of its dive boats and up to six on another. The center operates two guided single-tank dives daily, as well as individually scheduled excursions. **Tanki's Watersport Paradise Ltd** (✉ Paradise Beach, Carriacou ☎ 473/443–8406) offers dive trips to nearby reefs and snorkeling trips to Sandy Island.

Beaches

Bathway Beach, a broad strip of sand with a natural reef that protects swimmers from the rough Atlantic surf on Grenada's far northern shore, has changing rooms at the Levera National Park headquarters.

Grand Anse Beach, in the southwest about 3 mi (5 km) south of St. George's, is Grenada's loveliest and most popular beach. It's a gleaming 2-mi (3-km) semicircle of white sand lapped by clear, gentle surf. Sea grape trees and coconut palms provide shady escapes from the sun. Brilliant rainbows frequently spill into the sea from the high green mountains that frame St. George's Harbour to the north. The Grand Anse Craft & Spice Market is at the midpoint of the beach.

Sandy Island, just off the shore of Carriacou, is a truly deserted island off Hillsborough—just a strip of white sand with a few palm trees, surrounded by a reef and crystal-clear waters. Anyone hanging around the jetty with a motorboat will provide transportation for about $10 per person, round-trip. Bring your snorkeling gear and, if you want, a picnic—and leave all your cares behind.

Where to Eat

Restaurants add an 8% government tax to your bill and usually add a 10% service charge; if not, tip 10% to 15% for a job well done.

GRENADA ¢–$$ ✗ **Tropicana.** The chef-owner here hails from Trinidad and specializes in both Chinese and West Indian cuisine. Local businesspeople seem to be the best customers for the extensive menu of Chinese food, the tantalizing aroma of barbecued chicken notwithstanding. Eat in or take out—

it's open from 7:30 AM to midnight. Tropicana is right at the Lagoon Road traffic circle, overlooking the marina. ⊠ *Lagoon Rd., St. George's, St. George* ☎ *473/440–1586* ⊟ *AE, DC, MC, V.*

¢–$ ✕ **The Nutmeg.** Fresh seafood, homemade West Indian dishes, great hamburgers, and the waterfront view make this a favorite with locals and visitors alike. It's upstairs on the Carenage (above Sea Change bookstore), with large, open windows from which you can watch the harbor activity as you eat. Try the callaloo soup, curried lambi, fresh seafood or a steak—or just stop by for a rum punch and a roti, a fish sandwich and a Carib beer, or a hamburger and a Coke. ⊠ *The Carenage, St. George's, St. George* ☎ *473/440–2539* ⊟ *AE, D, MC, V.*

CARRIACOU ✕ **Scraper's.** Scraper's serves up lobster, conch, and the fresh catch of ¢–$ the day. It's a simple spot seasoned with occasional calypsonian serenades (by owner Steven "Scraper" Gay, who's a pro). Order a rum punch to really enjoy yourself. ⊠ *Tyrrel Bay* ☎ *473/443–7403* ⊟ *AE, D, MC, V.*

Jamaica

The third-largest island in the Caribbean, the English-speaking nation of Jamaica enjoys considerable self-sufficiency thanks to tourism, agriculture, and mining. Its physical attractions include jungle-covered mountains, clear waterfalls, and unforgettable beaches, yet the country's greatest resource may be its people. Although 95% of Jamaicans trace their bloodlines to Africa, their national origins also lie in Great Britain, the Middle East, India, China, Germany, Portugal, and South America, as well as in many other islands in the Caribbean. Their cultural life is a rich one—the music, art, and cuisine of Jamaica are vibrant with a spirit easy to sense but as hard to describe as the rhythms of reggae or the streetwise patois.

Don't let Jamaica's beauty cause you to relax the good sense you would use at home. Resist the promise of adventure should any odd character offer to show you the "real" Jamaica. Jamaica on the beaten track is wonderful enough, so don't take chances by wandering too far off it.

CURRENCY Currency-exchange booths are set up on the docks at Montego Bay and Ocho Rios whenever a ship is in port. The U.S. dollar is accepted virtually everywhere, but change is made in Jamaican dollars (J$). At this writing the exchange rate was J$49.85 to US$1. Prices given below are in U.S. dollars unless otherwise indicated.

TELEPHONES Direct telephone services are available in communication stations at the ports. Because of recent fraud problems, some U.S. phone companies (such as MCI) will not accept credit card calls placed from Jamaica. Phones take only Jamaican phone cards, available from kiosks or variety shops.

SHORE EXCURSIONS The following are good choices in Jamaica. They may not be offered by all cruise lines. Times and prices are approximate.
Appleton Estate Rum Tour. Usually offered on Montego Bay port calls. You travel by bus to the Appleton Estate Rum Distillery for a tour followed by a Jamaican buffet lunch. ⏱ *7 hrs* 🎫 *$65–$84.*

Croydon Estate Trip. Usually offered on Montego Bay port calls. You travel by bus to Jamaica's scenic interior to Croydon Estate to tour a working rural plantation, have a barbeque lunch, and stop in Montego Bay for shopping on the way back to the ship. ⊙ *6 hrs* 🚌 *$54–$65.*

Prospect Plantation & Dunn's River Falls. Usually offered on Ocho Rios port calls but often from Montego Bay as well. You travel by bus to the gardens of Prospect Plantation and then climb uphill in the rushing water of Dunn's River Falls, one of Jamaica's most popular attractions. ⊙ *4 hrs* 🚌 *$59–$62; excursions to Dunn's River Falls alone are approximately $35–$40.*

Rafting on the Martha Brae River. Pass the verdant plant life as you glide down the river on a 30-foot, two seat bamboo raft. Usually offered for ships stopping in Ocho Rios or Montego Bay. ⊙ *5 hrs* 🚌 *$53–$69 from Ocho Rios, $49 from Montego Bay.*

Coming Ashore

Jamaica is one place in the Caribbean where it's usually to your advantage to take an organized shore excursion offered by your ship unless you just want to do a bit of shopping in town. Taxis aren't particularly cheap, and a full-day tour for a small group will run $150 to $180 (because of road conditions and the distances in Jamaica, most tours take a full day).

Some of Jamaica's taxis are metered; rates are per car, not per passenger. You can flag cabs on the street. All licensed and properly insured taxis display red Public Passenger Vehicle (PPV) plates. Licensed minivans also bear the red PPV plates. If you hire a taxi driver as a tour guide, be sure to agree on a price before the vehicle is put into gear. Because of the cost of insurance, which you must buy since most credit cards offering coverage exclude Jamaica, it's expensive to rent a car; you may also find it difficult to arrange a rental on-island. It's far easier to arrange a taxi.

IN MONTEGO BAY   Some ships use Montego Bay, 67 mi (108 km) west of Ocho Rios, as their Jamaican port of call. The cruise port in Montego Bay is a $10 taxi ride from town; however, there's one shopping center within walking distance of the docks. If you just want to visit a beach, then Doctor's Cave, a public beach, is a very good nearby alternative, and it's right in town.

IN OCHO RIOS   Most cruise ships dock at this port on Jamaica's north coast, near Dunn's River Falls. Less than 1 mi (2 km) from the Ocho Rios pier are the Taj Mahal Duty-Free Shopping Center and the Ocean Village Shopping Center. Getting anywhere else in Ocho Rios will require a taxi.

Exploring Jamaica

Numbers in the margin correspond to points of interest on the Jamaica map.

MONTEGO BAY   **Greenwood Great House.** Although this historic home has no spooky legend to titillate, it's much better than Rose Hall at evoking life on a sugar plantation. The Barrett family, from whom the English poet Elizabeth Barrett Browning descended, once owned all the land from Rose Hall to Falmouth; they built this and several other great houses on it. (The

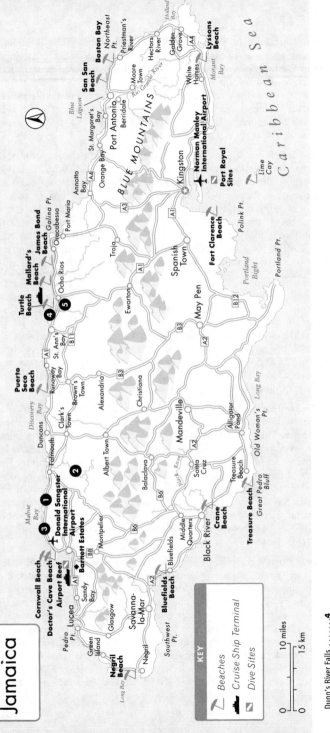

Jamaica

San San Beach
Boston Bay
Lyssons Beach
Puerto Seco Beach
Mallard's Beach
James Bond Beach
Turtle Beach
Cornwall Beach
Doctor's Cave Beach
Airport Reef
Negril Beach
Bluefields Beach
Crane Beach
Treasure Beach
Fort Clarence Beach

Northeast Pt.
Priestman's River
Hectors River
Golden Grove
A4
White Horses
Morant Bay
Holland Bay

Blue Lagoon
St. Margaret's Bay
Port Antonio
Berridale
Moore Town
Rio Grande River

Orange Bay
Annotto Bay
A4
Kingston
Norman Manley International Airport
Port Royal Sites
Lime Cay

BLUE MOUNTAINS

A3
Port Maria
Galina Pt.
Oracabessa
Ocho Rios
St. Ann's Bay
B11
A1
Runaway Bay
Brown's Town
A1
Spanish Town
A1
Troja
Ewarton
May Pen
B12
Polink Pt.
Portland Bight
Portland Pt.

Discovery Bay
Duncans
Clark's Town
Falmouth
A1
Alexandria
B3
Christiana
Mandeville
A2
Santa Cruz
Alligator Pond
Old Woman's Pt.
Long Bay
Treasure Beach
Great Pedro Bluff

Mahoe Bay
Donald Sangster International Airport
Barnett Estates
Montpelier
B6
Albert Town
Balaclava
B6
Middle Quarters
Bluefields
Black River
Black River
B3
A2

Pedro Pt.
Lucea
Green Island
Sandy Bay
Glasgow
Savanna-la-Mar
Negril
Southwest Pt.
Long Bay
Caribbean Sea

KEY

⌐ Beaches
▰ Cruise Ship Terminal
◩ Dive Sites

0 ___ 10 miles
0 ___ 15 km

Dunn's River Falls **4**
Greenwood Great House . .**1**
Martha Brae River **2**
Prospect Plantation **5**
Rose Hall **3**

poet's father, Edward Moulton Barrett, "the Tyrant of Wimpole Street," was born at nearby Cinnamon Hill, the estate of the late country singer Johnny Cash.) Highlights of Greenwood include oil paintings of the Barretts, china made for the family by Wedgwood, a library filled with rare books from as early as 1697, fine antique furniture, and a collection of exotic musical instruments. There's a pub on-site as well. It's 15 mi (24 km) east of Montego Bay. ⊠ *Greenwood* ☎ *876/953–1077* ⊕ *www. greenwoodgreathouse.com* ✉ *$12* ⊙ *Daily 9–6.*

❷ Martha Brae River. A gentle waterway about 25 mi (40 km) southeast of Montego Bay, it takes its name from an Arawak Indian who killed herself because she refused to reveal the whereabouts of a local gold mine to the Spanish. According to legend, she agreed to take them there and, on reaching the river, used magic to change its course, drowning herself and the greedy Spaniards with her. Her *duppy* (ghost) is said to guard the mine's entrance. Rafting on this river is a very popular activity. Martha Brae River Rafting arranges trips downriver. Near the rafting company ticket office you'll find gift shops, a bar and restaurant, and a swimming pool.

❸ Rose Hall. In the 1700s, Rose Hall may have been the greatest of great houses in the West Indies. Today it's popular less for its architecture than for the legend surrounding its second mistress: Annie Palmer was credited with murdering three husbands and a *busha* (plantation overseer) who was her lover. The story is told in a novel that's sold everywhere in Jamaica: *The White Witch of Rose Hall.* There's a pub on-site. The house is across the highway from the Wyndham Rose Hall resort. ⊠ *North Coast Hwy.* ☎ *876/953–2341* ✉ *$15* ⊙ *Daily 9–6.*

OCHO RIOS

❹ Dunn's River Falls. The falls are an eye-catching sight: 600 feet of cold, clear mountain water splashing over a series of stone steps to the warm Caribbean. The best way to enjoy the falls is to climb the slippery steps: don a swimsuit, take the hand of the person ahead of you, and trust that the chain of hands and bodies leads to an experienced guide. The leaders of the climbs are personable fellows who reel off bits of local lore while telling you where to step; you can hire a guide's service for a tip of a few dollars. After the climb, you exit through a crowded market, another reminder that this is one of Jamaica's top tourist attractions. ⊠ *Off A1, between St. Ann's and Ocho Rios* ☎ *876/974–2857* ✉ *$10* ⊙ *Daily 8:30–5.*

❺ Prospect Plantation. To learn about Jamaica's former agricultural economy, a trip to this working plantation, just west of town, is a must. But it's not just a place for history lovers or farming aficionados; everyone seems to enjoy the views over the White River Gorge and the tour by jitney (a canopied open-air cart pulled by a tractor). The grounds are full of exotic fruits and tropical trees, some planted over the years by such celebrities as Winston Churchill and Charlie Chaplin. You can also go horseback riding on the plantation's 900 acres or play miniature golf, grab a drink in the bar, or buy souvenirs in the gift shop. ⊠ *Hwy. A1, west of Ocho Rios* ☎ *876/994–1058* ✉ *$29* ⊙ *Daily 8–5; tours Mon.–Sat. 10:30, 2, and 3:30.*

Shopping

Jamaican artisans express themselves in silk-screening, wood carvings, resort wear, hand-loomed fabrics, and paintings. Jamaican rum makes a great gift, as do Tia Maria (the famous coffee liqueur) and Blue Mountain coffee.

Before visiting the crafts markets in Montego Bay and Ocho Rios, consider how much tolerance you have for pandemonium and price haggling. If you're looking to spend money, head for City Centre Plaza, Half Moon Village, Holiday Inn Shopping Centre, Montego Bay Shopping Center, St. James's Place, or Westgate Plaza in Montego Bay; in Ocho Rios, go to Pineapple Place, Ocean Village, the Taj Mahal, Coconut Grove, and Island Plaza. Some cruise lines run shore excursions that focus on shopping.

Gallery of West Indian Art (⊠ 11 Fairfield Rd., Montego Bay ☎ 876/952–4547) is the place to find Jamaican and Haitian paintings. A corner of the gallery is devoted to hand-turned pottery (some painted) and beautifully carved and painted birds and animals. **Harmony Hall** (⊠ Hwy. A1, Ocho Rios ☎ 876/975–4222), an eight-minute drive east of the main part of town, is a restored greathouse, where Annabella Proudlock sells her unique wooden boxes (their covers are decorated with reproductions of Jamaican paintings). Also on sale—and magnificently displayed—are larger reproductions of paintings, lithographs, and signed prints of Jamaican scenes and hand-carved wooden combs. In addition, Harmony Hall is well-known for its shows by local artists.

Sports & Activities

GOLF Montego Bay has more good options for golf than Ocho Rios, but there are a couple of courses in Ocho Rios that are easily accessible and worth the effort. The 18-hole course at **Breezes Runaway Bay** (⊠ North Coast Hwy., Runaway Bay ☎ 876/973–7319) has hosted many championship events (greens fees are $80). **Half Moon Golf, Tennis & Beach Club** (⊠ Montego Bay ☎ 876/953–3105), a Robert Trent Jones–designed 18-hole course 7 mi (11 km) east of town, is the home of the Red Stripe Pro Am (greens fees are $130). In 2004 the course received an upgrade and once again draws international attention. **Ironshore** (⊠ Montego Bay ☎ 876/953–2800), 3 mi (5 km) east of the airport, is an 18-hole links-style course (the greens fees are $50). The golf course at **Sandals Golf & Country Club** (⊠ Ocho Rios ☎ 876/975–0119) is 700 feet (214 m) above sea level (greens fees for 18 holes are $100, or $70 for 9 holes for nonguests). **Tryall Golf, Tennis & Beach Club** (⊠ North Coast Hwy., Sandy Bay ☎ 876/956–5681), 15 mi (24 km) west of Montego Bay, has an 18-hole championship course on the site of a 19th-century sugar plantation (greens fees are $125).

HORSEBACK RIDING Ocho Rios has excellent horseback riding, but the best of the operations is **Chukka Cove Adventure Tours** (⊠ Llandovery, St. Ann's Bay ☎ 876/972–2506 ⊕ www.chukkacaribbean.com), which is adjacent to the polo field, just west of town. The trainers here originally exercised the polo ponies by taking them for therapeutic rides in the sea; soon there were requests from visitors to ride the horses in the water. The company now offers a three-hour beach ride that ends with a bareback swim on the horses in the sea from a private beach. It's a highlight of many trips to Jamaica. Rather than be part of a guided group ride, you can opt to rent a horse by the hour at **Prospect Plantation** (⊠ Ocho Rios ☎ 876/994–1058), which offers horseback riding for $48 per hour, but advance reservations are required.

Beaches

There are several good beaches near Montego Bay. **Doctor's Cave Beach** has been spotlighted in so many travel articles and brochures that it often resembles Florida during spring break. On the bright side, the 5-mi (8-km) strand has much to offer beyond sugary sand, including changing rooms, water sports, colorful if overly insistent vendors, and plenty of places to grab a snack.There is an admission fee. Near the center of town, there's protection from the surf on a windy day and therefore unusually fine swimming at **Walter Fletcher Beach;** the calm waters make it a good bet for children, though it's not as pretty or as tidy as Doctor's Cave.

East of Ocho Rios in the village of Oracabessa is **James Bond Beach,** which is popular because of the reggae performances that take place on its bandstand. There's a $5 admission fee. **Turtle Beach,** stretching behind the Sunset Jamaica Grande, is the busiest beach in Ocho Rios (where the islanders come to swim). Though much more convenient for cruise-ship passengers, it's not nearly as pretty as James Bond Beach.

Where to Eat

Many restaurants add a 10% service charge to the bill. Otherwise, a tip of 10% to 20% is customary.

$$–$$$ ✕ **Evita's Italian Restaurant.** Just about every celebrity who has visited Ocho Rios has dined at this hilltop restaurant, and Evita has the pictures to prove it. Guests feel like stars themselves with attentive waitstaff helping to guide them through a list of about 30 kinds of pasta, ranging from lasagna Rastafari (vegetarian) and fiery jerk spaghetti to *rotelle colombo* (crabmeat with white sauce and noodles). Kids under 12 eat for half-price, and light eaters will appreciate half portions. ⊠ *Eden Bower Rd., Ocho Rios* ☎ 876/974–2333 ▭ *AE, D, MC, V.*

¢–$$ ✕ **The Native.** Shaded by a large poinciana tree and overlooking Gloucester Avenue, this open-air stone terrace serves Jamaican and international dishes. To go native, start with smoked marlin, move on to the *boonoonoonoos* platter (a sampler of local dishes), and round out with coconut pie or *duckanoo* (a sweet dumpling of cornmeal, coconut, and banana wrapped in a banana leaf and steamed). Live entertainment and candlelight tables make this a romantic choice for dinner on weekends. ⊠ *29 Gloucester Ave., Montego Bay* ☎ 876/979–2769 ⌲ *Reservations essential* ▭ *AE, MC, V.*

¢ ✕ **Ocho Rios Village Jerk Centre.** This blue-canopied, open-air eatery is a good place to park yourself for frosty Red Stripe beer and fiery jerk pork, chicken, or seafood. Milder barbecued meats, also sold by weight (typically, ¼ or ½ pound makes a good serving), turn up on the fresh daily chalkboard menu posted on the wall. It's lively at lunch, especially when passengers from cruise ships swamp the place. ⊠ *DaCosta Dr., Ocho Rios* ☎ *876/974–2549* ▭ *D, MC, V.*

¢ ✕ **The Pork Pit.** A favorite with many MoBay locals, this no-frills eatery serves Jamaican specialties including some fiery jerk, which we must warn is spiced to local tastes, not watered down for tourist palates. Many get their food to go but you can also find picnic tables just outside. ⊠ *27 Gloucester Ave., Montego Bay* ☎ *876/952–3663.*

Key West, Florida

The southernmost city in the continental United States was originally a Spanish possession. Along with the rest of Florida, Key West became part of American territory in 1821. In the late 19th century, Key West was Florida's wealthiest city per capita. The locals made their fortunes from "wrecking"—rescuing people and salvaging cargo from ships that foundered on nearby reefs. Cigar making, fishing, shrimping, and sponge gathering also became important industries.

Capital of the self-proclaimed "Conch Republic," Key West today makes for a unique port of call for the 10 or so ships that visit each week. A genuinely American town, it nevertheless exudes the relaxed atmosphere and pace of a typical Caribbean island. Major attractions for cruise passengers are the home of the Conch Republic's most famous citizen, Ernest Hemingway; the imposing Key West Museum of Art & History, a former U.S. Customs House and site of the military inquest of the USS *Maine*; and, if your cruise ship stays in port late enough, the island's renowned sunset celebrations.

CURRENCY   The U.S. dollar is the only currency accepted in Key West.

TELEPHONES   Public phones are found at the pier and on street corners.

SHORE EXCURSIONS   The following are good choices in Key West. They may not be offered by all cruise lines. Times and prices are approximate.

Historic Key West Walking Tour. During the guided walk through the historic district, you will pass the Harry S. Truman Little White House, the Hemingway House, and the Audubon House and Gardens. ⊙ *1½ hrs* ⊡ *$19.*

Old Town Trolley or Conch Tour Train. Choose either the one-hour narrated tour by trolley bus or the unique conch train for an introduction to Key West and the "Conch Republic" while you pass the Harry S. Truman Little White House, the Hemingway House, the Audubon House, and other highlights. Buying the ticket from your ship adds a $4 premium to the cost of either tour. ⊙ *1 hr* ⊡ *$26.*

Reef Snorkeling. Your catamaran sails to the last living coral reefs in the continental United States. Changing facilities, snorkeling equipment, and beverages are provided. ⊙ *3 hrs* ⊡ *$44–$49.*

Coming Ashore

Cruise ships dock at Mallory Square or near the Truman Annex. Both are within walking distance of Duval and Whitehead streets, the two main tourist thoroughfares. Because Key West is so easily explored on foot, there is rarely a need to hire a cab. If you plan to venture beyond the main tourist district, a fun way to get around is by bicycle or scooter. Key West is a cycling town. In fact, there are so many bikes around that cyclists must watch out for one another as much as for cars.

For maps and other tourist information, drop by the **Greater Key West Chamber of Commerce** (✉ 402 Wall St., Key West 33040 ☎ 305/294–2587 or 800/527–8539), which is just off Mallory Square.

BICYCLE & MOPED RENTALS **Keys Moped & Scooter** (✉ 523 Truman Ave. ☎ 305/294–0399) rents beach cruisers with large baskets as well as scooters. Rates for scooters start at $15 for three hours. Look for the huge American flag on the roof. **Moped Hospital** (✉ 601 Truman Ave. ☎ 305/296–3344) supplies balloon-tire bikes with yellow safety baskets for adults and kids, as well as mopeds and double-seater scooters for adults.

GUIDED TOURS The **Conch Tour Train** (☎ 305/294–5161) is a 90-minute narrated tour of Key West, traveling 14 mi through Old Town and around the island. Board at Mallory Square and Flagler Station (901 Caroline St.) every half hour (9–4:30 from Mallory Square, later at other stops). The cost is $22. **Old Town Trolley** (✉ 6631 Maloney Ave., Key West ☎ 305/296–6688) operates trackless trolley-style buses, departing from the Mallory Square and Roosevelt Boulevard depots every 30 minutes (9:15–4:30 from Mallory Square, later at other stops), for 90-minute narrated tours of Key West. The smaller trolleys go places the train won't fit. You may disembark at any of 10 stops and reboard a later trolley. The cost is $22.

Exploring Key West
Numbers in the margin correspond to points of interest on the Key West map.

6 **Audubon House & Gardens.** If you've ever seen an engraving by ornithologist John James Audubon, you'll understand why his name is synonymous with birds. See his work in this three-story house, which was built in the 1840s for Captain John Geiger but now commemorates Audubon's 1832 stop in Key West while he was traveling through Florida to study birds. Several rooms of period antiques and a children's room are also of interest. Admission includes an audiotape (in English, French, German, or Spanish) for a self-guided tour of the house and tropical gardens, complemented by an informational booklet and signs that identify the rare indigenous plants and trees. ✉ 205 Whitehead St. ☎ 305/294–2116 ⊕ www.audubonhouse.com ☞ $10 ☉ Daily 9:30–4:30, last tour starts at 4.

7 **Duval Street Wreckers Museum.** Most of Key West's early wealthy residents made their fortunes from the sea. Among them was Francis Watlington, a sea captain and wrecker, who in 1829 built this house, alleged to be the oldest house in South Florida. Six rooms are open, furnished with 18th- and 19th-century antiques and providing exhibits on the island's wrecking industry of the 1800s, which made Key West one of the most affluent towns in the country. ✉ 322 Duval St. ☎ 305/294–9502 ☞ $5 ☉ Daily 10–4.

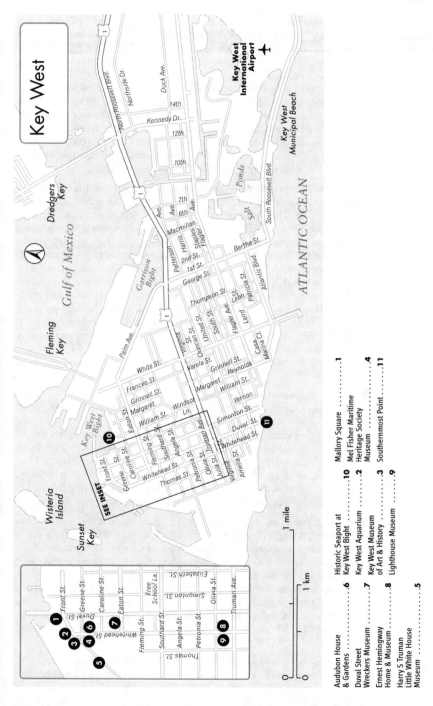

Key West

Gulf of Mexico

Dredgers Key

Fleming Key

Wisteria Island

Sunset Key

Garrison Bight

Key West Bight

ATLANTIC OCEAN

Key West Municipal Beach

Key West International Airport

North Roosevelt Blvd.

Northside Dr.

Duck Ave.

Kennedy Dr.

14th

12th

10th

7th

Ave.

6th Ave.

Macmillan Ave.

Staples

Flagler

Harris

Patterson

2nd St.

1st St.

George St.

Thompson St.

South St.

United St.

Duncan St.

Varela St.

Grinnell St.

Reynolds

Margaret

William St.

Vernon

Simonton St.

Duval St.

Whitehead St.

Bertha St.

South Roosevelt Blvd.

Ponds

Salt

Leon

Patricia St.

Atlantic Blvd.

Flagler Ave.

Laird

Casa Marina Ct.

Palm Ave.

White St.

Frances St.

Grinnell St.

Margaret

Eaton St.

William St.

Windsor Ln.

Greene St.

Caroline St.

Fleming St.

Whitehead St.

Thomas St.

Southard St.

Angela St.

Front St.

Petronia St.

Olivia St.

Julia St.

Truman Ave.

Virginia

Amelia St.

SEE INSET

10

11

1 mile

1 km

0

0

Front St.

Duval St.

Greene St.

Caroline St.

Whitehead St.

Fleming St.

Eaton St.

Free School La.

Simonton St.

Elizabeth St.

Southard St.

Thomas St.

Angela St.

Petronia St.

Olivia St.

Truman Ave.

1

2

3

4

6

7

5

9

8

8 **Ernest Hemingway Home & Museum.** Guided tours of Ernest Hemingway's home are full of anecdotes about the author's life in the community and his household quarrels with wife Pauline. While living here between 1931 and 1942, Hemingway wrote about 70% of his life's work, including *For Whom the Bell Tolls*. Few of the family's belongings remain, but photographs help illustrate his life, and scores of descendants of Hemingway's cats have free reign of the property. Literary buffs should be aware that there are no curated exhibits from which to gain much insight into Hemingway's writing career. Tours begin every 10 minutes and take 25–30 minutes; then you're free to explore on your own. ⊠ *907 Whitehead St.* ☎ *305/294–1136* ⊕ *www.hemingwayhome.com* 🎫 *$10* ⊙ *Daily 9–5.*

5 **Harry S. Truman Little White House Museum.** In a letter to his wife during one of his visits, President Harry S Truman wrote, "Dear Bess, you should see the house. The place is all redecorated, new furniture and everything." If he visited today, he'd write something similar. There's a photographic review of visiting dignitaries and permanent audiovisual and artifact exhibits on the Florida Keys as a presidential retreat; Ulysses S. Grant, John F. Kennedy, and Jimmy Carter are among the chief executives who passed through here. Tours lasting 45 minutes begin every 15 minutes. On the grounds of **Truman Annex**, a 103-acre former military parade grounds and barracks, the home served as a winter White House for presidents Truman, Eisenhower, and Kennedy. The two-bedroom Presidential Suite, with a veranda and sundeck, is available for a novelty overnight stay. ⊠ *111 Front St.* ☎ *305/294–9911* ⊕ *www. trumanlittlewhitehouse.com* 🎫 *$11* ⊙ *Daily 9–5, grounds 8–sunset; last tour at 4:30.*

10 **Historic Seaport at Key West Bight.** What used to be a funky—in some places even seedy—part of town is now an 8½-acre historic restoration project of 100 businesses, including waterfront restaurants, open-air people- and dog-friendly bars, museums, clothing stores, bait shops, docks, a marina, a wedding chapel, the Waterfront Market, the Key West Rowing Club, and dive shops. It's all linked by the 2-mi waterfront **Harborwalk,** which runs between Front and Grinnell streets, passing big ships, schooners, sunset cruises, fishing charters, and glass-bottom boats. Additional construction continues on outlying projects.

2 **Key West Aquarium.** Explore the fascinating underwater realm of the Keys without getting wet at this kid-friendly aquarium. Hundreds of tropical fish and sea creatures live here. A touch tank enables you to handle starfish, sea cucumbers, horseshoe and hermit crabs, even horse and queen conchs—living totems of the Conch Republic. Built in 1934 by the Works Progress Administration as the world's first open-air aquarium, most of the building has been enclosed for all-weather viewing. Guided tours include shark petting and feedings. Tickets are good for the entire day. ⊠ *1 Whitehead St.* ☎ *305/296–2051* ⊕ *www.keywestaquarium. com* 🎫 *$10* ⊙ *Daily 10–6; tours at 11, 1, 3, and 4:30.*

3 **Key West Museum of Art & History.** When Key West was designated a U.S. port of entry in the early 1820s, a custom house was established. Salvaged cargoes from ships wrecked on the reefs could legally enter here, thus setting the stage for Key West to become the richest city in Florida. Following a $9-million restoration, the imposing redbrick-and-terra-cotta Richardsonian Romanesque–style U.S. Custom House reopened as a museum. Its main gallery displays major rotating exhibits. Smaller galleries have long-term and changing exhibits about the history of Key West, such as *Remember the Maine.* ⊠ *281 Front St.* ☎ *305/295–6616* ⊕ *www.kwahs.com* ⊠ *$7* ☉ *Daily 9–5.*

❾ Lighthouse Museum. For the best view in town and a history lesson at the same time, climb the 88 steps to the top of this 92-foot lighthouse. It was built in 1847. About 15 years later, a Fresnel lens was installed at a cost of $1 million. The keeper lived in the adjacent 1887 clapboard house, which now exhibits vintage photographs, ship models, nautical charts, and lighthouse artifacts from all along the Key reefs. ⊠ *938 Whitehead St.* ☎ *305/294–0012* ⊠ *$8* ☉ *Daily 9:30–4:30; last admission at 4:15.*

❶ Mallory Square. The central meeting point in old Key West is named for Stephen Mallory, secretary of the Confederate Navy, who later owned the Mallory Steamship Line. On nearby Mallory Dock, a nightly sunset celebration draws street performers, food vendors, and thousands of onlookers.

❹ Mel Fisher Maritime Heritage Society Museum. In 1622 two Spanish galleons loaded with riches from South America foundered in a hurricane 40 mi (64 km) west of the Keys. In 1985 Mel Fisher recovered the treasures from the lost ships, the *Nuestra Señora de Atocha* and the *Santa Margarita.* In this museum, see, touch, and learn about some of the artifacts, including a gold bar weighing 6.3 troy pounds and a 77.76-carat natural emerald crystal worth almost $250,000. Exhibits on the second floor rotate and might cover slave ships, including the excavated 17th-century *Henrietta Marie,* or the evolution of Florida maritime history. ⊠ *200 Greene St.* ☎ *305/294–2633* ⊕ *www.melfisher.org* ⊠ *$10* ☉ *Daily 9:30–5.*

⓫ Southernmost Point. At the foot of Whitehead Street, a huge concrete marker proclaims this spot to be the southernmost point in the continental United States. Turn left on South Street. To your right are two dwellings that both claim to be the Southernmost House. Take a right onto Duval Street, which ends at the Atlantic Ocean, and you will be at the Southernmost Beach.

Shopping

Passengers looking for T-shirts, trinkets, and other souvenirs will find them along Duval Street and around the cruise-ship piers. **Fast Buck Freddie's** (⊠ 500 Duval St. ☎ 305/294–2007) sells a classy, hip selection of crystal, furniture, tropical clothing, and every flamingo item imaginable. It also carries such imaginative items as a noise-activated rat in a trap and a raccoon tail in a bag. **Key West Aloe** (⊠ 540 Greene St., at Simonton St. ☎ 305/294–5592 or 800/445–2563) was founded in a garage in 1971; today it produces some 300 perfume, sunscreen, and skin-care products for men and women. After years downtown on Front Street, in April 2004 it moved back to a new showroom at the original factory location.

The **Key West Island Bookstore** (⌧ 513 Fleming St. ☎ 305/294–2904) is the literary bookstore of the large Key West writers' community. It carries new, used, and rare titles and specializes in Hemingway, Tennessee Williams, and South Florida mystery writers. **Lucky Street Gallery** (⌧ 1120 White St. ☎ 305/294–3973) sells high-end contemporary paintings, watercolors, and a few pieces of jewelry by internationally recognized Key West–based artists.

Sports & Activities

BOAT TOURS   **M/V Discovery** (⌧ Land's End Marina, 251 Margaret St., Key West 33040 ☎ 305/293–0099) glass-bottom boats have submerged viewing rooms for 360-degree marine watching and cost $30. **Mosquito Coast Island Outfitters & Kayak Guides** (⌧ 310 Duval St., Key West 33040 ☎ 305/294–7178 ⊕ www.mosquitocoast.net) runs full-day guided sea-kayak natural-history tours around the mangrove islands just east of Key West. The $55 charge covers transportation, bottled water, a snack, and supplies, including snorkeling gear.

DIVING &   **Adventure Charters & Tours** (⌧ 6810 Front St., 33040 ☎ 305/296–0362
SNORKELING   or 888/817–0841) has sail-and-snorkel coral reef adventure tours ($35) aboard the 42-foot trimaran sailboat *Fantasea,* with a maximum of 16 people. There are two daily departures. **Captain's Corner** (⌧ Corner of Greene and Elizabeth ☎ 305/296–8865), a PADI five-star shop, has dive classes in several languages and twice-daily snorkel and dive trips to reefs and wrecks aboard the 60-foot dive boat *Sea Eagle.*

FISHING   Captain Steven Impallomeni works as a flats-fishing guide, specializing in ultralight and fly-fishing for tarpon, permit, and bonefish, as well as near-shore and light-tackle fishing. Charters on the *Gallopin' Ghost* leave from **Murray's Marina** (⌧ MM 5, Stock Island ☎ 305/292–9837). **Key West Bait and Tackle** (⌧ 241 Margaret St. ☎ 305/292–1961) carries live bait, frozen rigged and unrigged bait, and fishing and rigging equipment. It also has the Live Bait Lounge; unwind and sip ice-cold beer while telling tall tales after fishing.

Beaches

Key West doesn't have any great swimming beaches, but there are a few that might be worth a visit. **Fort Zachary Taylor State Historic Site** (⌧ end of Southard St., through Truman Annex) has an uncrowded beach, which is the best in Key West. There is an adjoining picnic area with barbecue grills and shade trees. **Smathers Beach** (⌧ S. Roosevelt Blvd.) has nearly 2 mi of sand, rest rooms, picnic areas, and volleyball courts, all of which make it popular with the spring-break crowd. Trucks along the road rent rafts, Windsurfers, and other beach "toys."

Where to Eat

$$–$$$ ✕ **Alice's Key West Restaurant.** There's a current of excitement in the air here, generated by the enthusiasm that chef-owner Alice Weingarten exudes. Nothing is plain. Everything has to have color, zing, or spice. Take the tuna tartar tower: it's spiced with a garlic-chili paste, topped with tomato ginger jam, and served between crisp wonton wafers. Many restaurants in the Keys serve coconut shrimp; few come close to giving it the spicy tang and aroma that Alice has perfected. The secret is the honey wasabi and papaya ginger chutney. She still serves Aunt Alice's magic meat loaf with a mushroom sauce. You may never eat strawberry short-cake again after trying Alice's tropical fruit shortcake dessert. The feel is calm and cool, the service exemplary. You can end your Duval Crawl here for a breakfast of eggs, fries, and toast for as little as $4. ⊠ *1114 Duval St.* ☎ *305/292–5733* ⊟ *AE, D, MC, V* ⊘ *No lunch.*

¢–$$ ✕ **Crabby Bill's.** The scene is a warehouse-size room with beer flags, a concrete floor, old surfboards, and a large bar, but what Bill lacks in decorating skills he makes up for in cooking seafood, lots of it—there are nine popular Crabby Bill's in Florida. Oysters and soft-shell crabs are best sellers. Bring the kids: there's lots of space, a pinball machine, free soda refills, and a few dishes just for the 12-and-under set. ⊠ *511 Greene St.* ☎ *305/292–0802* ⊟ *AE, D, DC, MC, V.*

Nightlife

Three spots stand out for first-timers among the saloons frequented by Key West denizens. All are within easy walking distance of the cruise-ship piers. In its earliest incarnation, back in 1851, **Capt. Tony's Saloon** (⊠ 428 Greene St. ☎ 305/294–1838) was a morgue and icehouse, then Key West's first telegraph station. It became the original Sloppy Joe's in the mid-1930s, when Hemingway was a regular. Later, a young Jimmy Buffett sang here. Bands play nightly. The **Schooner Wharf Bar** (⊠ 202 William St. ☎ 305/292–9520), an open-air waterfront bar and grill in the historic seaport district, retains its funky Key West charm. There's live island music all day, plus happy hour, and special events. There's more history and good times at **Sloppy Joe's** (⊠ 201 Duval St. ☎ 305/294–5717), the successor to a famous 1937 speakeasy named for its founder, Captain Joe Russell. Ernest Hemingway came here to gamble and tell stories. Decorated with Hemingway memorabilia and marine flags, the bar is popular with travelers and is full and noisy all the time. Live entertainment plays daily 10 AM–2 AM.

Martinique

Martinique is lush with wild orchids, frangipani, anthurium, jade vines, flamingo flowers, and hundreds of hibiscus varieties. Trees bend under the weight of tropical fruits such as mangoes, papayas, lemons, limes, and bright-red West Indian cherries. Acres of banana plantations, pineap-ple fields, and waving sugarcane stretch to the horizon.

The towering mountains and verdant rain forest in the north lure hik-ers, while underwater sights and sunken treasures attract snorkelers and scuba divers. Martinique is also wonderful if your idea of exercise is turn-ing over every 10 minutes to get an even tan and your taste in adven-ture runs to duty-free shopping.

The largest of the Windward Islands, Martinique is 4,261 mi (6,817 km) from Paris, but its spirit and language are decidedly French, with more than a soupçon of West Indian spice. Tangible, edible evidence of the fact is the island's cuisine, a superb blend of French and creole.

Fort-de-France is the capital, but at the turn of the 20th century, St-Pierre, farther up the coast, was Martinique's premier city. In 1902, volcanic

Martinique

Mont Pelée blanketed the city in ash, killing all its residents except a condemned prisoner. Today, the ruins are a popular excursion for cruise passengers.

CURRENCY   The French franc is no longer. It has been replaced by the euro (€). You won't be able to use dollars in shops, though most restaurants take credit cards. Banks usually give the best exchange rates. A currency exchange service that also offers a favorable rate is Change Caraïbes. If you are cashing less than $100, it is usually better to go to the exchange or to use your ATM card. Local prices given below are in euros unless otherwise indicated.

TELEPHONES   There are no coin-operated phone booths. Public phones now use a *télé-carte,* which you can buy at post offices, café-tabacs, hotels, and at *bureaux de change.* To call the States from Martinique, dial 00 + 1, the area code, and the local number. You can now make collect calls to Canada through the Bell operator; you can get the AT&T or MCI operators from blue special service phones at the cruise ports and in town, such as at the Super Sumo snack bar, on rue de la Liberté, near the library.

Shore Excursions

The following are good choices but may not be offered by all cruise lines. Times and prices are approximate. Given the weakness of the U.S. dollar and traffic around Fort-de-France, it's usually to your advantage to take an organized shore excursion if you want to see a bit of the island.

Bat Caves & Snorkel. After your catamaran sail to the bat caves, you will have an opportunity to snorkel near a colorful coral reef. Snorkel equipment is included. ⊙ *3 hrs* ▣ *$45–$49.*

Island Tour with St-Pierre. Ride along the coastal road to St-Pierre, which was once the capital of Martinique. The ruined city is a museum of devastated houses, monuments, and industries destroyed by the volcanic eruption of Mt. Pelée in 1902. Return to the ship over an inland road through the rain forest. ⊙ *4 hrs* ▣ *$65–69.*

Rain Forest & Plantations 4-Wheel Drive Safari. Your driver takes you in an off-road vehicle through sugarcane plantations, tropical forests, and banana plantations where you'll stop for a tour and also to taste sugarcane. Before heading back to the port you'll also tour a distillery. ⊙ *4 hrs* ▣ *$84.*

Coming Ashore

Cruise ships call at the Maritime Terminal east of Fort-de-France. The only practical way to get into town is by cab (approximately €15 round-trip). To reach the Maritime Terminal tourist information office, turn right and walk along the waterfront. Large ships that anchor in the Baie des Flamands tender passengers to the Fort-de-France waterfront. It is always advisable to check in with the tourist office, which is staffed with friendly, helpful, English-speaking personnel and is just across the street from the landing pier, in the Air France building. Ask about the guided walking tours that can be arranged at the nearby open-air market.

Taxis are metered, and there's no extra charge for extra passengers; however, rates are expensive. A journey of any distance can cost €25 or more, and traffic in Fort-de-France can be nightmarish (your driver may also not speak English). If you want to go to the beach, a much cheaper option is to take a ferry from Fort-de-France. *Vedettes* (ferries) operate daily between Quai d'Ensnambuc in Fort-de-France and the marina in Pointe du Bout, Anse-Mitan, and Anse-à-l'Ane. Any of the three trips takes about 15 minutes, and the ferries operate about every 30 minutes on weekdays. Two companies, Madinina and Somatour, operate these ferries. If you buy a round-trip you must use the return ticket for the same ferry company.

Renting a car in Fort-de-France is possible, but the heavy traffic can be forbidding. Rates start at €60 per day for a car with manual transmission; those with automatic transmissions are substantially more expensive and rarely available.

Exploring Martinique

Numbers in the margin correspond to points of interest on the Martinique map.

If you want to see the lush island interior and St-Pierre, take the N3, which snakes through dense rain forests, north through the mountains to Le Morne Rouge, then take the coastal N2 back to Fort-de-France via St-Pierre. You can do the 40-mi (64-km) round-trip in half a day—that is if you don't get lost, can comprehend the road signs, avoid collisions in the roundabouts, drive as fast as the flow of frenetic traffic, and can ask directions in French (probably of someone on the street who only speaks a creole patois). But your best option is to hire an English-speaking driver.

❼ Ajoupa-Bouillon. This flower-filled 17th-century village amid pineapple fields is the jumping-off point for several sights. The Saut Babin is a 40-foot waterfall, a half-hour walk from Ajoupa-Bouillon. The Gorges de la Falaise is a river gorge where you can swim. **Les Ombrages** botanical gardens has marked trails through the rain forest. ⊠ *Ajoupa-Bouillon* 🖼 *€4* ⊙ *Daily 9–5:30.*

❸ Aqualand. This U.S.-style water park is a great place for families to have a wet, happy day. The large wave pool is well-tended; little ones love it, as they do the pirate's galleon in their own watery playground. Older kids may prefer to get their thrill from the slides, including the hairpin turns of the Giant Slalom, the Colorado slide, and the Black Hole, which winds around in total darkness. In the best French tradition, fast-food options are attractive, including crêpes, salads, and even beer. ⊠ *Route des Pitons, Carbet* 🕾 *0596/78–40–00* ⊕ *www.aqualand-martinique.fr* 🖼 *€16* ⊙ *Daily 10–6.*

❷ Balata. This quiet little town has two sights worth visiting. Built in 1923 to commemorate those who died in World War I, **Balata Church** is an exact replica of Paris's Sacré-Coeur Basilica. The **Jardin de Balata** (Balata Gardens), has thousands of varieties of tropical flowers and plants. There are shaded benches from which to take in the mountain view. You can order anthurium and other tropical flowers to be delivered to the airport. ⊠ *Rte. de Balata, Balata* 🕾 *0596/64–48–73* 🖼 *€7* ⊙ *Daily 9–5.*

❶ Fort-de-France. With its historic fort and superb location beneath the towering Pitons du Carbet on the Baie des Flamands, Martinique's capital—home to about one-third of the island's 360,000 inhabitants—should be a grand place. It isn't. The most pleasant districts, such as Didier, Bellevue, and Schoelcher, are on the hillside, and you need a car to reach them. Traffic is especially bad on cruise-ship days. There are some good shops with Parisian wares (at Parisian prices) and lively street markets. Near the harbor is a marketplace where local crafts and souvenirs are sold. Going to town can be fun, but the heat, exhaust fumes, and litter tend to make exploring here a chore rather than a pleasure.

The heart of Fort-de-France is **La Savane**, a 12½-acre park filled with trees, fountains, and benches. It's a popular gathering place and the scene of promenades, parades, and impromptu soccer matches. Along the east side are numerous snack wagons. Alas, it's no longer a desirable oasis, what with a lot of litter and other negatives often found in urban parks. A statue of Pierre Belain d'Esnambuc, leader of the island's first settlers, is unintentionally upstaged by Vital Dubray's vandalized—now headless—white Carrara marble statue of the empress Joséphine, Napoléon's first wife. Across from La Savane, you can catch the ferry *La Vedette* for the beaches at Anse-Mitan and Anse-à-l'Ane and for the 20-minute run across the bay to Pointe du Bout. It's relatively cheap as well as stress-free—much safer, more pleasant, and faster than by car.

The most imposing historic site in La Savane (and in Fort-de-France) is **Fort St-Louis**, which runs along the east side of La Savane. It's open Monday through Saturday from 9 to 3, and admission is €4.

The **Bibliothèque Schoelcher** is the wildly elaborate Romanesque public library. It was named after Victor Schoelcher, who led the fight to free the slaves in the French West Indies in the 19th century. The eye-popping structure was built for the 1889 Paris Exposition, after which it was dismantled, shipped to Martinique, and reassembled piece by ornate piece. ⊠ *At rue de la Liberté, runs along west side of La Savane, and rue Perrinon* ☎ *0596/70–26–67* ☒ *Free* ☉ *Mon. 1–5:30, Tues.–Fri. 8:30–5:30, Sat. 8:30–noon.*

★ **Le Musée Régional d'Histoire et d'Ethnographie** is a learning experience that is best undertaken at the beginning of your vacation, so you can better understand the history, background, and people of the island. Housed in an elaborate former residence (circa 1888) with balconies and fretwork, it has everything from displays of the garish gold jewelry that prostitutes wore after emancipation to reconstructed rooms of a home of proper, middle-class Martinicans. There's even a display of madras, creole headdresses with details of how they were tied to indicate if a woman was single, married, or otherwise occupied. ⊠ *10 bd. General de Gaulle* ☎ *0596/72–81–87* ☒ *€3* ☉ *Mon. and Wed.–Fri. 8:30–5, Tues. 2–5, Sat. 8:30–noon.*

Rue Victor Schoelcher runs through the center of the capital's primary shopping district, a six-block area bounded by rue de la République, rue de la Liberté, rue de Victor Severe, and rue Victor Hugo. Stores sell Paris fashions and French perfume, china, crystal, and liqueurs, as well as local handicrafts. The Romanesque **St-Louis Cathedral** (⊠ Rue Victor Schoelcher) with its lovely stained-glass windows, was built in 1878, the sixth church on this site (the others were destroyed by fire, hurricane, and earthquake).

The Galerie de Biologie et de Géologie at the **Parc Floral et Culturel,** in the northeastern corner of the city center, will acquaint you with the island's exotic flora. There's also an aquarium. The park contains the island's official cultural center, where there are sometimes free evening concerts. ⊠ *Pl. José-Marti, Sermac* ☎ *0596/71–66–25* ☒ *Grounds free; aquarium €5.60; botanical and geological gallery €1.12* ☉ *Park daily dawn–10 PM; aquarium daily 9–7; gallery Tues.–Fri. 9:30–12:30 and 3:30–5:30, Sat. 9–1 and 3–5.*

❽ Macouba. Named after the Carib word for "fish," this village was a prosperous tobacco town in the 17th century. Today its clifftop location affords magnificent views of the sea, the mountains, and—on clear days—the neighboring island of Dominica. The **JM Distillery** (☎ 0596/78–92–55) produces some of the best *vieux rhum* on the island here, though it's now owned by Habitation Clément. A tour and samples are free. Macouba is the starting point for a spectacular drive, the 6-mi (9½-

km) **route to Grand'Rivière** on the northernmost point. This is Martinique at its greenest: groves of giant bamboo, cliffs hung with curtains of vines, and 7-foot tree ferns that seem to grow as you watch them. Literally, at the end of the road, is Grand' Rivière, a colorful sprawling fishing village at the foot of high cliffs.

❻ Le Morne Rouge. This town sits on the southern slopes of the volcano that destroyed it in 1902. Today it's a popular resort spot and offers hikers some fantastic mountain scenery. From Le Morne Rouge you can start the climb up the 4,600-foot **Mont Pelée** volcano. But don't try it without a guide unless you want to get buried alive under pumice stones. Instead, drive up to the Refuge de l'Aileron. From the parking lot it's a mile (1½ km) up a well-marked trail to the summit. Bring a sweatshirt, because there's often a mist that makes the air damp and chilly. From the summit follow the route de la Trace (Route N3), which winds south of Le Morne Rouge to St-Pierre. It's steep and winding, but that didn't stop the *porteuses* of old: balancing a tray, these women would carry up to 100 pounds of provisions on their heads for the 15-hour trek to the Atlantic coast.

❹ Musée Gauguin. Martinique was a brief station in Paul Gauguin's wanderings but a decisive moment in the evolution of his art. He arrived from Panama in 1887 with friend and fellow painter Charles Laval and, having pawned his watch at the docks, rented a wooden shack on a hill above the village of Carbet. Dazzled by the tropical colors and vegetation, Gauguin developed a style, his Martinique period, that directly anticipated his Tahitian paintings. Disappointingly, this modest museum has no originals, only reproductions. There's an exhibit of original letters and documents relating to the painter. Also remembered here is the writer Lafcadio Hearn. In his endearing book *Two Years in the West Indies* he provides the most extensive description of the island before St-Pierre was buried in ash and lava. ⊠ *Anse-Turin, Carbet* ☎ *0596/78–22–66* 🎫 *€4* 🕐 *Daily 9–5:30.*

❺ St-Pierre. The rise and fall of St-Pierre is one of the most remarkable stories in the Caribbean. Martinique's modern history began here in 1635. By the turn of the 20th century St-Pierre was a flourishing city of 30,000, known as the Paris of the West Indies. As many as 30 ships at a time stood at anchor. By 1902 it was the most modern town in the Caribbean, with electricity, phones, and a tram. On May 8, 1902, two thunderous explosions rent the air. As the nearby volcano erupted, Mont Pelée split in half, belching forth a cloud of burning ash, poisonous gas, and lava that raced down the mountain at 250 mph. At 3,600°F, it instantly vaporized everything in its path; 30,000 people were killed in two minutes. Only one man, a prisoner in an underground cell in the town jail, survived. An Office du Tourisme is on the *moderne* seafront promenade. Stroll the main streets and check the blackboards at the sidewalk cafés, before deciding where to lunch. Like stage sets for a dramatic opera, there are the ruins of the island's first church (built in 1640), the imposing theater, the toppled statues. This city, situated on its naturally beautiful harbor and with its narrow, winding streets, has the feel of a European seaside hill town. Although many of the historic buildings need work, stark modernism has not invaded this burg. As much potential as it has, this is one town in Martinique where real estate is cheap—for obvious reasons. The **Cyparis Express,** a small tourist train, will take you around to the main sights with running narrative (in French) for €9.

⟲ For those interested in the eruption of 1902, the **Musée Vulcanologique Frank Perret** is a must. Established in 1932, it houses photographs of the old town, documents, and a number of relics—some gruesome—excavated from the ruins, including molten glass, melted iron, and contorted clocks stopped at 8 AM. ⊠ *Rue de Victor Hugo* ☎ *0596/78–15–16* 🖼 *€3* ⊙ *Daily 9–5.*

An excursion to **Depaz Distillery** is one of the island's nicest treats. For four centuries it has been at the foot of the volcano. In 1902 the great house was destroyed in the eruption, but soon after it was courageously rebuilt and the fields replanted. A self-guided tour includes the workers' gingerbread cottages, and an exhibit of art and sculpture made from wooden casks and parts of distillery machinery. The tasting room sells their rums, including golden and aged rum (notably Rhum Dore) and distinctive liqueurs made from ginger and basil. ⊠ *Mt. Pelée Plantation* ☎ *0596/78–13–14* 🖼 *Free* ⊙ *Mon.–Sat. 9–5.*

Shopping

French products, such as perfume, wines, liquors, designer scarves (Hermès, for example), leather goods, and crystal, are good buys in Fort-de-France. Luxury goods are discounted 20% when paid for with traveler's checks or major credit cards. Look for creole gold jewelry; white, dark, flavored, and aged rums; and handcrafted straw goods, pottery, madras fabric, and tapestries. Shops that sell luxury items are abundant around the cathedral in Fort-de-France, particularly on rue Victor Hugo, rue Moreau de Jones, rue Antoine Siger, and rue Lamartine. The work of **Antan Lontan** (⊠ 213 rte. de Balata, Fort-de-France ☎ 0596/64–52–72) has to be seen. Sculptures, busts, statuettes, and artistic lamps portray the Creole women and the story of the Martiniquequaise culture.

Cadet Daniel (⊠ 72 rue Antoine Siger, Fort-de-France ☎ 0596/71–41–48) sells Lalique, Limoges, and Baccarat. **Centre des Métiers d'Art** (⊠ Rue Ernest Deproge, Fort-de-France ☎ 0596/70–25–01) exhibits authentic local arts and crafts. **Roger Albert** (⊠ 7 rue Victor Hugo, Fort-de-France ☎ 0596/71–71–71) carries designer crystal.

Sports & Activities

FISHING Fish cruising these waters include tuna, barracuda, dolphinfish, kingfish, bonito, and the big game—white and blue marlins. The **Limited Edition** (⊠ Marina du Marin, Le Marin ☎ 0596/76–24–20 or 0696/28–80–58), a fully loaded Davis 47-foot fishing boat, is like a sportsfisherman's dream. It goes out with a minimum of five anglers for €150 per person for a half day, or €260 per person for a full day, including lunch. Nonanglers can come for the ride for €70 and €130, respectively. Captain Yves speaks English fluently and is a fun guy.

GOLF The **Golf Country Club de la Martinique** (⊠ Les Trois-Ilets ☎ 0596/68–32–81) has a par-71, 18-hole Robert Trent Jones course with an English-speaking pro, a pro shop, bar, and restaurant. The club offers special greens fees to cruise-ship passengers. Normal greens fees are €46; an electric cart costs another €46. For those who don't mind walking while admiring the Caribbean view between the palm trees, club trolleys are €6. There are no caddies.

HIKING The island has 31 marked hiking trails. At the beginning of each, a notice is posted advising on the level of difficulty, the duration of a hike, and any interesting points to note. The **Parc Naturel Régional de la Martinique** (⌧ 9 bd. Général de Gaulle, Fort-de-France ☎ 0596/73–19–30) organizes inexpensive guided excursions year-round. If there have been heavy rains, though, give it up. The tangle of ferns, bamboo trees, and llanai vines is dramatic, but during rainy season, the springs and waterfalls and wet, muddy trails will negate any enthusiasm.

HORSEBACK At **Black Horse Ranch** (⌧ Les Trois-Ilets ☎ 0596/68–37–80), one-hour
RIDING trail rides (€22) go into the countryside and across waving cane fields; two hours on the trail (€35) brings riders near a river. Only western saddles are used. Semi-private lessons (€35 a person) are in French and English. ☾ **Ranch Jack** (⌧ Anse-d'Arlets ☎ 0596/68–37–69) has trail rides (English saddle) across the countryside for €22 an hour; half-day excursions (€43) go through the country and forests to the beach, beverages included. And the lessons for kids are recommendable. Some guides are English-speaking at **Ranch de Caps** (⌧ Cap Macré, Le Marin ☎ 0596/74–70–65 or 0696/23–18–18), where you can take a half-day ride (western) on the wild southern beaches and across the countryside for €45. Rides go out in the morning (8:30 to noon) and afternoon (1:30 to 5) every day but Monday. If you can manage a full day in the saddle, it costs €75. A real memory is the full-moon ride. Most of the mounts are Anglo-Arabs. Riders are encouraged to help cool and wash their horses at day's end. Reserve in advance. Riders of all levels are welcomed.

Beaches

All of Martinique's beaches are open to the public, but hotels charge a fee for nonguests to use changing rooms and facilities. Topless bathing is prevalent at the large resort hotels. Unless you're an expert swimmer, steer clear of the Atlantic waters, except in the area of Cap Chevalier and the Caravelle Peninsula—an incredibly beautiful area, with cliffs that stagger down to the sea. You'll find golden sand and excellent snorkeling at **Anse-Mitan.** Family-owned bistros are half hidden among palm trees nearby. You can rent a chaise lounge from a hotel for about €5. **Pointe du Bout** has small, man-made beaches that are lined with luxury resorts. Across from the main pedestrian entrance to the marina, if you take a left—between the taxi stand and the Kalenda Hotel (you could always use the beach here, if you are having lunch)—then go left again, you will reach the Sofitel beach, which has especially nice facilities. **Les Salines,** a cove of soft white sand lined with coconut palms, is a short drive south of Ste-Anne, which is about an hour from Fort-de-France. Les Salines is awash with families and children during holidays and on weekends, but quiet and uncrowded during the week—even at the height of the winter season. This beach, especially the far end, is most appealing.

Where to Eat

All restaurants include a 15% service charge in their prices. Leaving a little extra gives Americans a good name.

$$ ✕ **Le Grange Inn.** Nearly every item is cooked over the open grill: top-quality meats, fresh jumbo crayfish (fresh and salt water), scallops (Ste-Jacque), and fresh fish, with a choice of sauces, from *chien* to roquefort, and *provencale* available. It's also about terrace dining and innovative salads like camembert with bacon and honey, greens, cucumbers, and green papaya, or smoked fish with avocado sauce. Grilled gingerbread with coconut dressing is an original dessert. Owner Phillipe loves kids, and their menu is fun. If you don't want to dine, just order a glass of champagne and listen to the hip music. ✉ *Village Créole, Pointe du Bout, Les Trois-Ilets* ☎ *0596/66–01–66* 🖃 *AE, MC, V.*

$$ ✕ **Mille Et Une Brindilles.** At this trendy salon, aromatic pots of tea come in flavors like vanilla, cherry, apricot, rose, mango, and orange. You'll find a litany of tapenades, olive cakes, flans, couscous, and other items for lunch. Fred, the cute, bubbly Parisian who is both chef and proprietress, is the queen of terrines and can make a delicious paté out of any vegetable or fish. Saturday brunch is very social and even includes a beverage. The best-ever desserts, like the *moelleux au chocolat* (a rich chocolate and coffee pudding) are what you would want after your last supper on earth. ✉ *27 rte. de Didier, Didier, Fort-de-France* ☎ *0596/71–75–61* 🖃 *No credit cards* ☺ *Closed Sun. and Mon. No dinner.*

Nassau, Bahamas

Nassau, the capital of the Bahamas, has witnessed Spanish invasions and hosted pirates, who made it their headquarters for raids along the Spanish Main. The American navy seized Fort Montagu here in 1776, when it won a victory without firing a shot. The heritage of old Nassau blends the Southern charm of British loyalists from the Carolinas, the African tribal traditions of freed slaves, and a bawdy history of blockade-running during the Civil War and rum-running in the Roaring '20s. Over it all is a subtle layer of civility and sophistication, derived from three centuries of British rule.

Reminders of the island's British heritage are everywhere in Nassau. Court justices sport wigs and scarlet robes. The police wear colonial garb: starched white jackets, red-striped navy trousers, and tropical pith helmets. Traffic keeps to the left, and the spoken language has a British-colonial lilt, softened by a slight drawl. Nassau's charm, however, is often lost in its commercialism. There's excellent shopping, but if you look past the duty-free shops, you'll also find sights of historical significance that are worth seeing.

CURRENCY The Bahamian dollar ($ or B$) is the official currency. Since the U.S. dollar is universally accepted, however, there's no need to acquire Bahamian money. Prices quoted throughout this chapter are in U.S. dollars unless otherwise indicated.

Nassau, Bahamas

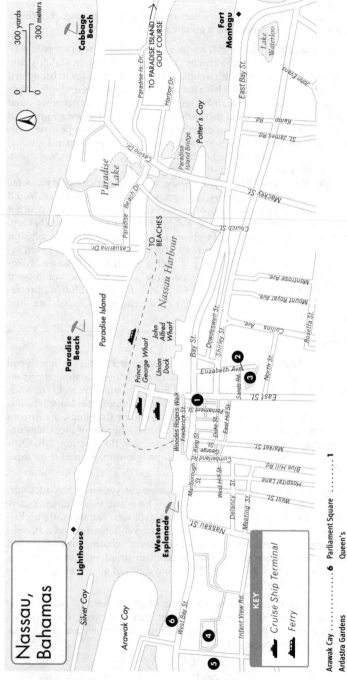

300 yards
300 meters

Silver Cay
Lighthouse ◆
Arawak Cay
Paradise Beach ⊤
Paradise Island
Western Esplanade ⊤
Cabbage Beach ⊤

Paradise Lake
Casino Dr.
Paradise Beach Dr.
Casuarina Dr.
TO BEACHES
Paradise Is. Dr.
TO PARADISE ISLAND GOLF COURSE
Harbor Dr.
Paradise Island Bridge
Potter's Cay
Fort Montagu ◆

Nassau Harbour
Prince George Wharf
John Alfred Wharf
Union Dock
Woodes Rogers Walk

Lake Waterloo
John Evans

East Bay St.
Kemp Rd.
St. James Rd.
Mackey St.
Church St.
Montrose Ave.
Mount Royal Ave.
Collins Ave.
Rosetta St.
Dowdeswell St.
Shirley St.
North St.
Elizabeth Ave.
Sands Rd.
East St.
Bay St.
Frederick St.
Parliament St.
East Hill St.
Duke St.
King St.
George St.
Cumberland Rd.
Market St.
Blue Hill Rd.
Hospital Lane
West Hill St.
Marlborough St.
Delancy St.
West St.
Meeting St.
Nassau St.
West Bay Rd.
Infant View Rd.

① ② ③ ⑥ ④ ⑤

KEY

🚢 Cruise Ship Terminal
⛴ Ferry

Arawak Cay 6
Ardastra Gardens
and Conservation Centre 5
Fort Charlotte 4
Fort Fincastle and the
Water Tower 3
Parliament Square 1
Queen's
Staircase 2

TELEPHONES Calling locally or internationally is easy in the Bahamas. To place a local call, dial the seven-digit phone number. To call the United States, dial 1 plus the area code. Pay phones cost 25¢ per call; Bahamian and U.S. quarters are accepted, as are BATELCO phone cards. To place a call using a calling card, use your long-distance carrier's access code or dial 0 for the operator.

Shore Excursions

The following are good choices in Nassau, but these excursions may not be offered by all cruise lines. Times and prices are approximate.

Harbor Tour & Discover Atlantis. After a half-hour harbor tour, your boat docks near the Atlantis Resort on Paradise Island, where you will be admitted to tour the world famous "Atlantis Dig" aquarium, receive a coupon for lunch at the beach snack bar, and have the use of a beach chair and towel for the afternoon. Changing rooms and lockers are not available. ⊘ 3–6 hrs ▧ $78 ($42 for the tour without lunch and/or use of the beach facilities).

Dolphin Encounter. A thirty-minute boat ride delivers you to Blue Lagoon Island (Salt Cay), the home of sixteen bottlenose dolphins. After an informative briefing, you observe the dolphins and enter the water to swim, touch, and interact with them. ⊘ 3½ hrs ▧ $110–$119.

Nassau & Ardastra Gardens. Your tour takes in the major points of interest in Nassau, such as the Queen's Staircase and Fort Fincastle as well as Ardastra Gardens, a tropical zoo featuring pink flamingos, the national bird. ⊘ 2–3 hrs ▧ $33–$39.

Sailing & Snorkeling. Numerous sail and snorkel excursions to nearby islands are available on a variety of motor or sailing yachts. Especially satisfying are those to Blue Lagoon Island that include snorkeling among the stingrays. Most tours include equipment and rum punch or other beverages after snorkeling. ⊘ 3–5 hrs ▧ $42–$55.

Coming Ashore

Cruise ships dock at one of three piers on Prince George's Wharf. Taxi drivers who meet the ships may offer you a $2 "ride into town," but the historic government buildings and duty-free shops lie just steps from the dock area. As you leave the pier, look for a tall pink tower—diagonally across from here is the tourist information office. Stop in for maps of the island and downtown Nassau. On most days you can join a one-hour walking tour ($10 per person) conducted by a well-trained guide. Tours generally start every hour on the hour from 10 AM to 4 PM; confirm the day's schedule in the office. Just outside, an ATM dispenses U.S. dollars.

As you disembark from your ship, you will find a row of taxis and air-conditioned limousines. Fares are fixed by the government by zones. The fare is $6 for trips within downtown Nassau and around Paradise Island; $9 from downtown Nassau to Paradise Island (which includes the bridge toll); $8 from Paradise Island to downtown Nassau; and $18 from Cable Beach to Paradise Island, including toll ($17 for the return trip). Fares cover two passengers; each additional passenger is $3, regardless of destination. It is customary to tip taxi drivers 15%. You can also hire a car or small van for sightseeing for $45 to $60 per hour or about $13 per person.

Beautifully painted horse-drawn carriages will take as many as four people around Nassau at a rate of $10 per adult and $5 per child for a 30-minute ride; don't hesitate to bargain. Most drivers give a comprehensive tour of the Bay Street area, including an extensive history lesson. Look for the carriages on Woodes Rogers Walk, in the center of Rawson Square.

Two people can ride around the island on a motor scooter for about $40 for a half day, $50 for a full day. Helmets and insurance for both driver and passenger are mandatory and are included in the rental price. Many hotels have scooters on the premises. You can also try Knowles, on West Bay Street, in the British Colonial Hilton parking lot, or check out the stands in Rawson Square. Remember to drive on the left.

The cheapest way to get to Paradise Island on your own is to take the ferry from the dock area ($3 each way).

Exploring Nassau

Numbers in the margins correspond to points of interest on the Nassau map.

Nassau's sheltered harbor bustles with cruise-ship hubbub, while a block away, broad, palm-lined Bay Street is alive with commercial activity. Shops angle for tourist dollars with fine imported goods at duty-free prices, yet you will find a handful of stores overflowing with authentic Bahamian crafts, foods, and other delights. Most of Nassau's historic sites are centered around downtown.

With its thoroughly revitalized downtown—the revamped British Colonial Hilton lead the way—Nassau is recapturing some of its glamour. Nevertheless, modern influence is apparent: fancy restaurants, suave clubs, and trendy coffeehouses have popped up everywhere. This trend comes partly in response to the burgeoning upper-crust crowds that now supplement the spring-breakers and cruise passengers who have traditionally flocked to Nassau.

Today the seedy air of the town's not-so-distant past is almost unrecognizable. Petty crime is no greater than in other towns of this size, and the streets not only look cleaner but feel safer. You can still find a wild club or a rowdy bar, but you can also sip cappuccino while viewing contemporary Bahamian art or dine by candlelight beneath prints of old Nassau, serenaded by soft, island-inspired calypso music.

6 Arawak Cay. For a literal taste of Bahamian culture throughout the island chain, take the slightly long walk west on Bay Street to this cluster of eateries and shops. You can buy crafts and food, especially squeaky-fresh conch salad, often made before your very eyes. An ice-cold Kalik beer makes the perfect foil. ⊠ *W. Bay St.* 🖼 *Free* ☉ *Daily.*

5 Ardastra Gardens & Conservation Centre. Marching flamingos? These national birds of the Bahamas give a parading performance at Ardastra daily at 10:30, 2, and 4. The zoo, with more than 5 acres of tropical greenery and flowering shrubs, also has an aviary of rare tropical birds, native Bahamian creatures such as rock iguanas, and a global collection of small animals. ⊠ *Chippingham Rd., south of W. Bay St.* ☎ *242/323–5806* ⊕ *www.ardastra.com* ⊠ *$12* ⊙ *Daily 9–5.*

❹ **Fort Charlotte.** Built in the late 18th century, this imposing fort comes complete with a waterless moat, drawbridge, ramparts, and dungeons. Lord Dunmore, who built it, named the massive structure in honor of George III's wife. At the time, some called it Dunmore's Folly because of the staggering expense of its construction. It cost eight times more than was originally planned. (Dunmore's superiors in London were less than ecstatic with the high costs, but he managed to survive unscathed.) Ironically, no shots were ever fired in battle from the fort. It is about 1 mi (1½ km) west of central Nassau. ⊠ *W. Bay St. at Chippingham Rd.* ⊠ *Free* ⊙ *Local guides conduct tours daily 8–4.*

❸ **Fort Fincastle** and **the Water Tower.** Shaped like a paddle-wheel steamer and perched near the top of the **Queen's Staircase,** Fort Fincastle—named for Royal Governor Lord Dunmore (Viscount Fincastle)—was completed in 1793 to serve as a lookout post for marauders trying to sneak into the harbor. It served as a lighthouse in the early 19th century. The fort's 126-foot-tall water tower, which is more than 200 feet above sea level, is the island's highest point. From here, the panorama of Nassau and its harbor is spectacular. ⊠ *Top of Elizabeth Ave. hill, south of Shirley St., Nassau* ⊠ *Water Tower 50¢* ⊙ *Daily 8–5.*

❶ **Parliament Square.** Nassau is the seat of the national government. The Bahamian Parliament comprises two houses—a 16-member Senate (Upper House) and a 40-member House of Assembly (Lower House)—and a ministerial cabinet headed by a prime minister. Parliament Square's pink, colonnaded government buildings were constructed in the early 1800s by Loyalists who came to the Bahamas from North Carolina. The square is dominated by a statue of a slim young Queen Victoria that was erected on her birthday, May 24, in 1905. In the immediate area are a half dozen magistrates' courts (open to the public; obtain a pass at the door to view a session). Behind the House of Assembly is the **Supreme Court.** Its four-times-a-year opening ceremonies (held the first weeks of January, April, July, and October) recall the wigs and mace-bearing pageantry of the Houses of Parliament in London. The Royal Bahamas Police Force Band is usually on hand for the event. ⊠ *Bay St., Nassau* ☎ *242/322–7500 for information on Supreme Court ceremonies* ⊠ *Free* ⊙ *Weekdays 10–4.*

❷ **Queen's Staircase.** These 65 steps are thought to have been carved out of a solid limestone cliff by slaves in the 1790s. The staircase was later named to honor Queen Victoria's 65-year reign. Recent innovations include a waterfall cascading from the top, and an ad hoc straw market along the narrow road that leads to the site. ⊠ *Top of Elizabeth Ave. hill, south of Shirley St.*

Shopping

Duty-free shopping is a major pastime in Nassau, and there are plenty of bargains to be found. Most of the stores selling duty-free items are clustered along an eight-block stretch of Bay Street in Old Nassau and on a few downtown side streets. Most stores are open Monday–Saturday 9–5 and accept credit cards.

On Bay Street at Market Street, the **Straw Market** has convened for hundreds of years. After a disastrous fire in 2001, it relocated to a nearby concrete structure. Its counterpart on Paradise Island, **BahamaCraft Centre**, is set up in a collection of colorful kiosks. The straw markets carry inexpensive straw and carved items, plus T-shirts and other souvenir apparel and jewelry.

Doongalik Studios Gallery (✉ 18 Village Rd., Paradise Island ☎ 242/394–1886) showcases Bahamian fine art, crafts, and culture in an old-Bahamian setting with a focus on the islands' annual Junkanoo festival.

Sports & Activities

FISHING   The waters here are generally smooth and alive with many species of game fish, which is one of the reasons why the Bahamas has more than 20 fishing tournaments open to visitors every year. A favorite spot just west of Nassau is the Tongue of the Ocean, so called because it looks like that part of the body when viewed from the air. The channel stretches for 100 mi. For boat rentals, parties of two to six will pay $300 or so for a half day, $600 for a full day.

Born Free Charters (☎ 242/393–4144 ⊕ www.bornfreefishing.com/) has three boats and guarantees a catch on full-day charters—if you don't get a fish, you don't pay. **Brown's Charters** (☎ 242/324–2061) specializes in 24-hour shark fishing trips, as well as reef and deep-sea fishing. **Chubasco Charters** (☎ 242/324–3474 ⊕ www.chubascocharters.com) has four boats for sportfishing and shark fishing charters.

GOLF   **Cable Beach Golf Club** (✉ Cable Beach ☎ 800/214–4281 ⊕ www.radisson-cablebeach.com), at 7,040 yards and with a par of 72, is the oldest golf course in the Bahamas. The links are owned by the Radisson Cable Beach Casino & Golf Resort. **Ocean Club Golf Course** (✉ Paradise Island Dr., Paradise Island ☎ 242/363–6682 800/321–3000 in the U.S. ⊕ www.oceanclub.com) was designed by Tom Weiskopf. The par-72 championship course is surrounded by the ocean on three sides, which means that winds can get stiff. Tee times can be reserved 60 days in advance.

WATER SPORTS   A number of outfitters rent jet skis and do parasailing in front of the Atlantis resort on Paradise Island.

Beaches

New Providence is blessed with stretches of white sand studded with palm and sea grape trees. Some of the beaches are small and crescent-shaped; others stretch for miles. On the north side of the island lies Paradise Island's showpiece, **Cabbage Beach**, which is popular with locals and tourists and is the home of most of the island's resorts. The beach rims the north coast from the Atlantis lagoon to Snorkeler's Cove. At the north end you can rent Jet Skis and nonmotorized pedal boats and go parasailing. **Cable Beach** is on New Providence's north shore, about 3 mi (5 km) west of downtown Nassau. Resorts line much of this beautiful, broad swath of white sand, but there is public access. Jet-skiers and beach vendors abound, so don't expect quiet isolation. Just west of Cable Beach is a rambling pink house on the Rock Point promontory, where much of the 1965 James Bond movie *Thunderball* was filmed. Downtown, the **Western Esplanade** sweeps westward from the British Colonial Hotel on Bay Street (a 10-minute walk from the cruise-ship pier). It's just across the street from shops and restaurants, and it has rest rooms, a snack bar, and changing facilities. **Paradise Beach** stretches for more than 1 mi (1½ km) on the western end of Paradise Island.

Where to Eat

$–$$$ ✕ **Anthony's Caribbean Grill.** Color is the standout feature of Anthony's: bright red, yellow, and blue tablecloths spiked with multihued squiggles; yellow-and-green walls with jaunty cloths hanging from the ceilings; booths printed with bright sea themes; and buoyant striped curtains. The lively spirit is reflected in the bouncy, often live music, and cheery service. The food is standard Caribbean fare: jerk chicken, rib eye seasoned with "Rasta" spices, or ribs served a multitude of ways—jerk, barbecue, or coconut-mango style. There's also a good selection of burgers, pasta, and salads. ⊠ *Paradise Village Shopping Centre* ☎ *242/ 363–3152* ▭ *AE, D, MC, V.*

¢–$$$ ✕ **Conch Fritters Bar & Grill.** A favorite in downtown Nassau, this lively, tropically themed restaurant is best known for conch. You can sample this Bahamian specialty in chowders, salads, and, of course, fritters. That said, conch-phobes need not worry. You'll find a diverse menu brimming with burgers, sandwiches, and pasta; the selection of steaks includes a serious 24-ounce porterhouse. There's a live band 7 to midnight nightly except Monday and a festive Junkanoo celebration on Saturday from 8 to 11 PM. ⊠ *Marlborough St., across from the British Colonial Hilton* ☎ *242/323–8778* ▭ *AE, D, MC, V* ☺ *Breakfast also served.*

¢–$ ✕ **Mama Lyddy's Place.** Just off the beaten tourist track, this old house is the place for true Bahamian cooking. Start with a local-style breakfast of souse or "boil fish" and watch Nassau residents stream in for takeout or sit-down meals. For lunch and dinner try fried snapper, cracked conch, minced or broiled crawfish, pork chops, and chicken. All are served with peas 'n' rice or peas 'n' grits and other typical Bahamian side dishes. ⊠ *Market St. at Cockburn St.* ☎ *242/328–6849* ▭ *No credit cards.*

Nightlife

Some ships stay late into the night or until the next day so that passengers can enjoy Nassau's nightlife. You'll find nonstop entertainment nightly along Cable Beach and on Paradise Island. All the larger hotels offer lounges with island combos for listening or dancing and restaurants with soft guitar or piano music.

CASINOS   At 50,000 square feet (100,000 if you include the dining and drinking areas), the **Atlantis Casino** (⊠ Atlantis Resort, Paradise Island ☎ 242/ 363–3000 ⊕ www.atlantis.com) is the Caribbean's largest gambling hall. Ringed with restaurants, it offers more than 1,000 slot machines, baccarat, blackjack, roulette, craps tables, and such local specialties as Caribbean stud poker. There's a high-limit table area, additional games available at most of the eateries within its walls, and a spectacularly open and airy design. Tables are open from 10 AM to 4 AM daily; slots, 24 hours daily. At the **Crystal Palace Casino** (⊠ Nassau Marriott Resort, Cable Beach ☎ 242/327–6200), slots, craps, baccarat, blackjack, roulette, Big Six, and face-up 21 are among the games in the 35,000-square-foot space. There's a Sports Book facility for sports betting, equipped with big-screen TVs, which air ongoing sporting events. Both VIPs and low-limit bettors have their own areas. Casino gaming lessons are available for beginners. Tables and slots are open 24 hours daily.

NIGHTCLUBS **Club Waterloo** (⊠ E. Bay St., Nassau ☎ 242/393–7324) claims to be Nassau's largest indoor-outdoor nightclub, with five bars and nonstop dancing Monday through Saturday until 4 AM (with bands on weekends). Try the spring-break-special Waterloo Hurricane, a mixture of rums and punches. Nassau's largest indoor nightclub, **Club Eclipse** (⊠ Bay St. ☎ 242/322–3041) is a large club aimed directly at tourists. There is a cover, though women are admitted free until 11 PM. It's closed Monday through Wednesday.

Panama Canal

Transit of the Panama Canal takes only one day. The rest of your cruise will be spent on islands in the Caribbean or at ports along the Mexican Riviera. Increasingly, Panama Canal itineraries include stops in Central America; some may also call along the northern coast of South America. Most Panama Canal cruises are one-way trips, part of a 10- to 14-day cruise between the Atlantic and Pacific oceans. Shorter loop cruises enter the canal from the Caribbean, sail around Gatún Lake for a few hours, and return to the Caribbean.

The Panama Canal is best described as a water bridge that raises ships up and over Central America and then lets them down, using a series of locks or water steps. Artificially created Gatún Lake, 85 feet above sea level, is the canal's highest point. The route is approximately 50 mi (80 km) long, and the crossing takes from 8 to 10 hours. Cruise ships pay more than $100,000 for each transit, which is less than half of what it would cost them to sail around Cape Horn, at the southern tip of South America.

Just before dawn, your ship will line up with dozens of other vessels to await its turn to enter the canal. Before it can proceed, two pilots and a narrator will come on board. The sight of a massive cruise ship being raised dozens of feet into the air by water is so fascinating that passengers will crowd all the forward decks at the first lock. If you can't see, go to the rear decks, where there is usually more room and the view is just as intriguing. Later in the day you won't find as many people up front.

On and off throughout the day, commentary is broadcast over the ship's loudspeakers, imparting facts and figures as well as anecdotes about the history of the canal. The canal stands where it does not because it's the best route but because the railroad was built there first, making access to the area relatively easy. The railway had followed an old Spanish mule trail that had been there for more than 300 years.

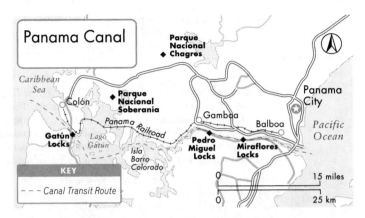

These days, ships in transit through the Canal Zone increasingly make stops at Cristobal Pier in Colón and also Fuerte Amador Island.

SHORE
EXCURSIONS
If you wish to see a bit of Panama during your canal transit, you'll almost certainly need to book a shore excursion. This is one of the few cruise destinations where that is the case. The following are good choices for Panama excursions. Times and prices are approximate.

Authentic Embera Indian Village. Travel by dugout canoe to an Embera village in the Chagres National Park. The village chief greets guests with a traditional welcome and his people perform native song, dance, and music and display their crafts. ⏲ *3½–6½ hrs* 🎫 *$75–$110.*

Caribbean Rain Forest Nature & Wildlife Hike. Explore remote jungle trails on the western shore of the canal during your guided nature hike through Fort Sherman, site of the former United States Army elite jungle-training school. You may see toucans, sloths, anteaters, and howler monkeys in the intricate jungle eco-system. ⏲ *4½–5 hrs* 🎫 *$59.*

Gatún Locks & Eco Cruise. Transfer to your tour by boat from your cruise ship at anchor in Gatún Lake. Guides will point out wildlife as you cruise through the rain forest along the Chagres River. Afterward, you will trade in your tour boat for a bus and stop at the Gatún Locks Observation Area to watch ships traverse the locks. The observation platform has 80 steps; an alternate viewing sight is available at ground level. ⏲ *4 hrs* 🎫 *$65.*

"Old Panama" City Tour. Drive from the Atlantic to the Pacific through the rain forest from Colón to Panama City, where you will tour the city's highlights. A snack and beverages are served before returning to Colón. ⏲ *5½–6 hrs* 🎫 *$72–$80.*

Panama Canal Railway Journey. Travel Panama's transcontinental railroad from Colón to Panama City, where you will then take a scenic drive and stop at Amador Causeway before returning to Colón by air-conditioned bus. Snacks and beverages are served on the train. ⏲ *5½ hrs* 🎫 *$138–$159.*

Panama's Rain Forest Aerial Tram. Transfer by bus from Colón to Gamboa Rain Forest Resort, where the aerial tram ride begins. After your narrated ascent through the forest canopy, you can walk to the observation platform before stopping for a picnic lunch on the way back to Colón. ⊙ *5–6 hrs* ▨ *$94–$98*.

St. Barthélemy

Hilly St. Barthélemy, popularly known as St. Barths or St. Barts, is just 8 square mi (21 square km), but the island has at least 20 good beaches, one reason it is a favorite with well-to-do travelers. The island was always a free port, building its wealth on trading commercial goods rather than on agriculture. What has drawn visitors is its sophisticated but unstudied approach to relaxation: the finest food, excellent wine, high-end shopping, and lack of large-scale commercial development.

A favorite among upscale cruise-ship passengers, who appreciate the shopping opportunities, fine dining, and beautiful beaches, St. Barths isn't really equipped for large-scale cruise-ship visits, which is why most ships calling here are smaller premium lines. This is one place where you don't need to take the ship's shore excursions to have a good time. Just hail a cab or rent a car and go to one of the many wonderful beaches, or linger in Gustavia, shopping and eating. It's the best way to relax on this most relaxing of islands.

CURRENCY   The official currency in St. Barths is the euro (€). However, U.S. dollars are accepted in almost all shops and in many restaurants, though you will probably receive euros in change. All credit-card transactions are charged in euros.

TELEPHONES   MCI and AT&T services are available. Public telephones do not accept coins; they accept *télécartes,* prepaid calling cards that you can buy at the gas station next to the airport and at post offices in Lorient, St-Jean, and Gustavia. Making an international call using a télécarte is the best way to go. To call the United States from St. Barths, dial 001 + the area code + the local seven-digit number.

SHORE EXCURSIONS   The following are good choices in St. Barths. They may not be offered by all cruise lines. Times and prices are approximate.

Catamaran Cruise. Superb coral reefs are only a short sail from Gustavia Harbor, where you board your catamaran at the pier and head for your snorkel site. Equipment and instructions are provided and refreshments are served during the sail back to the pier. ⊙ *2 hrs* ▨ *$53–$59*.

Horseback Riding. Ride along narrow trails in the rugged northwest part of the island where there are dramatic views from the cliffs to the ocean below. ⊙ *4 hrs* ▨ *$80*.

Coming Ashore

Even medium-size ships must anchor in Gustavia Harbor and bring passengers ashore on tenders. The tiny harbor area is right in Gustavia, which is best explored on foot at your leisure. Taxis, which meet all cruise ships, can be expensive. Technically, there's a flat rate for rides up to five minutes long. Each additional three minutes is an additional amount. In reality, however, cabbies usually name a fixed rate—and will not budge. Fares are 50% higher from 8 PM to 6 AM and on Sunday and holidays. St. Barths is one port where it's really worth it to arrange a car rental,

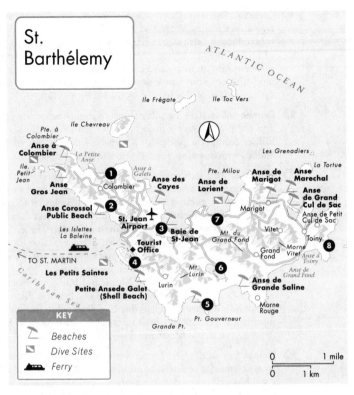

since this will give you the freedom to explore some of the island's out-of-the-way beaches. But be aware that during high season there is often a three-day minimum, so this may not be possible. Most car-rental firms operate at the airport; expect to pay about $55 a day.

Exploring St. Barths

With a little practice, negotiating St. Barths' narrow, steep roads soon becomes fun. Free maps are everywhere, roads are well marked, and painted signs will point you where you want to be. Take along a towel, sandals, and a bottle of water, and you will surely find a beach upon which to linger.

Numbers in the margin correspond to points of interest on the St. Barthélemy map.

① Anse des Flamands. From this wide, white-sand, hotel-lined beach you can take a brisk hike to the top of the now-extinct volcano believed to have given birth to St. Barths.

⑤ Anse du Gouverneur. Legend has it that pirates' treasure is buried at this beautiful beach. The road from Gustavia offers spectacular vistas. If the weather is clear you'll be able to see the islands of Saba, St. Eustatius, and St. Kitts from the beach.

❷ **Corossol.** The island's French-provincial origins are most evident in this two-street fishing village with a little rocky beach. Older local women weave lantana straw into handbags, baskets, hats, and delicate strings of birds. Ingenu Magras's **Inter Oceans Museum** has more than 9,000 seashells and an intriguing collection of sand samples from around the world. You can buy souvenir shells. ✉ *Corossol* ☎ *0590/27–62–97* 🖾 €3 ⊙ *Tues.–Sun. 9–12:30 and 2–5.*

❻ **Grande Saline.** The big salt ponds of Grande Saline are no longer in use, and the place looks a little desolate. Still, you should climb the short hillock behind the ponds for a surprise—the long arc of Anse de Grande Saline, which is almost everyone's favorite beach.

❹ **Gustavia.** You can easily explore all of Gustavia during a two-hour stroll. Street signs in both French and Swedish illustrate the island's history. Most shops close from noon to 2, so plan lunch accordingly. A good spot to park your car is rue de la République, where catamarans, yachts, and sailboats are moored. The **tourist office** (☎ 0590/27–87–27) on the pier can provide maps and a wealth of information. It's open Monday from 8:30 to 12:30, Tuesday through Friday from 8 to noon and 2 to 5, and Saturday from 9 to noon. On the far side of the harbor known as La Pointe is the charming **Municipal Museum,** where you can find watercolors, portraits, photographs, and historic documents detailing the island's history as well as displays of the island's flowers, plants, and marine life. ☎ *599/29–71–55* 🖾 €2 ⊙ *Mon.–Thurs. 8:30–12:30 and 2:30–6, Fri. 8:30–12:30 and 3–6, Sat. 9–11.*

❼ **Lorient.** Site of the first French settlement, Lorient is one of the island's two parishes; a restored church, a school, and a post office mark the spot. Note the gaily decorated graves in the cemetery. One of St. Barths' secrets is **Le Manoir** (☎ 0590/27–79–27), a 1610 Norman manor, now a guesthouse, which was painstakingly shipped from France and reconstructed in Lorient in 1984. Look for the entrance by the Ligne St. Barth building.

❸ **St-Jean.** The ½-mi (¾-km) crescent of sand at St-Jean is the island's most popular beach. Windsurfers skim along the water here, catching the strong trade winds. A popular activity is watching and photographing the hair-raising airplane landings. You'll also find some of the best shopping on the island here, as well as several restaurants.

❽ **Toiny Coast.** Over the hills beyond Grand Cul de Sac is this much-photographed coastline. Stone fences crisscross the steep slopes of Morne Vitet, one of many small mountains on St. Barths, along a rocky shore that resembles the rugged coast of Normandy. It's one island beach that's been nicknamed the "washing machine" because of its turbulent surf. Even expert swimmers should beware of the strong undertow here; swimming is generally not recommended.

Shopping

St. Barths is a duty-free port, and with its sophisticated crowd of visitors, shopping in the island's 200-plus boutiques is a definite delight, especially for beachwear, accessories, jewelry, and casual wear. Note that stores often close from noon to 2, and many are shuttered all Wednesday afternoon, but most are open until about 7 PM.

In Gustavia, boutiques line the two major shopping streets, and the Carré d'Or plaza is great fun to explore. Shops are also clustered in **La Villa Créole** (in St-Jean) and **Espace Neptune** (on the road to Lorient). It's worth working your way from one end to the other at these shopping complexes—just to see or, perhaps, be seen. Boutiques in all areas carry the latest in French and Italian sportswear and some haute couture. Prices, although on the high side, are often well below those for comparable merchandise in France or the United States.

Look for Fabienne Miot's unusual gold jewelry at **L'Atelier de Fabienne** (⊠ Rue de la République, Gustavia ☎ 0590/27–63–31). **Black Swan** (⊠ Le Carré d'Or, Gustavia ☎ 0590/27–65–16 ⊠ La Villa Créole, St-Jean) has an unparalleled selection of bathing suits. The wide range of styles and sizes is appreciated. **Le Comptoir du Cigare** (⊠ Rue de Général-de-Gaulle, Gustavia ☎ 0590/27–50–62), run by Jannick and Patrick Gerthofer, is a top purveyor of cigars. The walk-in humidor has an extraordinary selection. Try the Cubans while you are on the island, and take home the Davidoffs. Refills can be shipped stateside. Be sure to try on the genuine Panama hats. A good selection of watches, including Patek Phillippe and Chanel, can be found at **Diamond Genesis** (⊠ Rue Général-de-Gaulle, Gustavia). Fans of Longchamp handbags and leather goods will find a good selection at about 20% off stateside prices at **Elysée Caraïbes** (⊠ Le Carré d'Or, Gustavia ☎ 0590/52–00–94). The **Hermès** (⊠ Rue de la République, Gustavia ☎ 0590/27–66–15) store in St. Barths is an independently owned franchise, and prices are slightly below those in the States. Don't miss the superb skin-care products made on-site from local tropical plants by **Ligne de St. Barths** (⊠ Rte. de Saline, Lorient ☎ 0590/27–82–63). Don't miss **Lolita Jaca** (⊠ Le Carré d'Or, Gustavia ☎ 0590/27–59–98) for trendy tailored sportswear by Paul & Joe and other fresh names from Paris. Local works of art, including paintings, are sold in the bright **Made in St-Barth La Boutique** (⊠ La Villa Créole, St-Jean ☎ 0590/27–56–57). **Pati de Saint Barth** (⊠ Passage de la Crémaillière, Gustavia ☎ 0590/29–78–04) is the largest of the three shops that stock the chic, locally made T-shirts that have practically become the "logo" of St. Barths. The newest styles have hand-done graffiti lettering. **Stéphane & Bernard** (⊠ Rue de la République, Gustavia ☎ 0590/27–69–13) stocks a large selection of French fashion designers, including Rykiel, Tarlazzi, Kenzo, Feraud, and Mugler. **SUD SUD.ETC** (⊠ Galerie du Commerce, St-Jean ☎ 0590/27–98–75) stocks hippie-chic styles from Betty Boom, and shell and mother-of-pearl jewelry. Cute sandals and raffia accessories complete the look.

Sports & Activities

BOATING St. Barths is a popular yachting and sailing center, thanks to its location midway between Antigua and St. Thomas. Gustavia's harbor, 13- to 16-feet deep, has mooring and docking facilities for 40 yachts. There are also good anchorages available at Public, Corossol, and Colombier. **Marine Service** (⊠ Gustavia ☎ 0590/27–70–34 ⊕ www.st-barths.com/

marine.service) offers full-day outings on a 40-foot catamaran to the un-inhabited Ile Fourchue for swimming, snorkeling, cocktails, and lunch; the cost is $100 per person. The company also arranges deep-sea fishing trips, with a full-day charter of a 30-foot crewed cabin cruiser running $800; an unskippered motor rental runs about $260 a day. Marine Service can also arrange an hour's cruise ($32) on the glass-bottom boat *L'Aquascope*.

HORSEBACK RIDING   Two-hour horseback trail-ride excursions in the morning or the afternoon led by Coralie Fournier are about $40 per person at **St. Barth Equitation** (✉ Ranch des Flamands, Anse des Flamands ☎ 0690/62–99–30). Instruction is also available.

WINDSURFING   You can rent boards for about $20 an hour at water-sports centers along Baie de St-Jean and Grand Cul de Sac beaches. Lessons are offered for about $40 an hour at **Eden Rock Sea Sport Club** (✉ Eden Rock Hotel, Baie de St-Jean ☎ 0590/29–79–93), which also rents boards. **Wind Wave Power** (✉ St. Barth Beach Hotel, Grand Cul de Sac ☎ 0590/27–82–57) offers an extensive, six-hour training course. For €60, you can have a one-hour introductory lesson, along with the use of the windsurfer for as long as you can stand up.

Beaches

There are many *anses* (coves) and nearly 20 *plages* (beaches) scattered around the island, each with a distinctive personality and each open to the general public. Even in season you can find a nearly empty beach. Topless sunbathing is common, but nudism is technically forbidden—although both Saline and Gouverneur are de facto nude beaches. Because **Anse du Gouverneur** is so secluded, nude sunbathing is popular here; the beach is truly beautiful, with blissful swimming and views of St. Kitts, Saba, and St. Eustatius. Like a mini Côte d'Azur—beachside bistros, bungalow hotels, bronzed bodies, windsurfing, and lots of day-trippers—the reef-protected strip along **Baie de St-Jean** is divided by Eden Rock promontory, and there's good snorkeling west of the rock. **Anse des Flamands** is the most beautiful of the hotel beaches—a roomy strip of silken sand. The shallow, reef-protected beach at **Anse de Grand Cul de Sac** is especially nice for small children, fly fishermen, and windsurfers; it has excellent lunch spots and lots of pelicans. Secluded, with a sandy ocean bottom, **Anse de Grande Saline** is just about everyone's favorite beach and a great place for swimmers. In spite of the prohibition, young and old alike go nude. It can get windy here, so go on a calm day. **Anse de Lorient** beach is popular with St. Barths families and surfers, who like its rolling waves. Be aware of the level of the tide, which can come in very fast. Hikers and avid surfers like the walk over the hill to Point Milou in the late afternoon sun when the waves roll in.

Where to Eat

Check restaurant bills carefully. A service charge is always added by law, but you should leave the server 5% to 10% extra. It is generally advisable to charge restaurant meals on a credit card, as the issuer will offer a better exchange rate than the restaurant.

$$–$$$ ✕ **La Marine.** In-the-know islanders and returning friends settle at the popular dockside tables for mussels that arrive straight from France and are available only on Thursday and Friday. Be sure to reserve in advance for these. The menu also includes fish, oysters, hamburgers, steaks, and omelets. Many think that meals here are the best buys on the island. ✉ *Rue Jeanne d'Arc, Gustavia* ☎ *0590/27–68–91* ▤ *AE, MC, V.*

$$–$$$ ✕ **Le Repaire.** This friendly brasserie overlooks Gustavia's harbor and is a popular spot from its early-morning opening at 7 AM to its late-night closing at midnight. Grab a cappuccino, pull a captain's chair to the street-side rail, and watch the pretty girls. The menu ranges from cheeseburgers, which are served only at lunch along with the island's best fries, to simply grilled fish and meat. The composed salads always please. Try your hand at the billiards table or show up on weekends for live music. ✉ *Quai de la République, Gustavia* ☎ *0590/27–72–48* ▤ *MC, V.*

$$ ✕ **Bar B. Q.** New on the St. Barths restaurant scene in 2004, this friendly restaurant combines real Spanish-style tapas starters, such as coriander-garlic shrimp, and a generous Serrano ham and chorizo plate, followed by huge wood platters heaped with real American-style barbecue ribs and other grilled meats. If you're hungry, go for the mixed grill platter—literally a sword-full of grilled chicken, beef, lamb, and more. A plasma TV in the bar, which mixes the best mojitos in the immediate vicinity, is usually tuned to satellite sports. ✉ *Rue du Roi Oscar II, Gustavia* ☎ *0590/51–00–05* ▤ *AE, MC, V.*

St. Kitts & Nevis

Mountainous St. Kitts, the first English settlement in the Leeward Islands, crams some stunning scenery into its 65 square mi (168 square km). Vast, brilliant green fields of sugarcane run to the shore. The fertile, lush island has some fascinating natural and historical attractions: a rain forest replete with waterfalls, thick vines, and secret trails; a central mountain range, dominated by the 3,792-foot Mt. Liamuiga, whose crater has long been dormant; and Brimstone Hill, known in the 17th century as the Gibraltar of the West Indies.

In 1493, when Columbus spied a cloud-crowned volcanic isle during his second voyage to the New World, he named it Nieves—the Spanish word for "snows"—because it reminded him of the peaks of the Pyrenees. Nevis rises from the water in an almost perfect cone, the tip of its 3,232-foot central mountain hidden by clouds. Even less developed than St. Kitts, Nevis is known for its long beaches with white and black sand, its lush greenery, and its restored sugar plantations that now house charming inns.

St. Kitts and Nevis, along with Anguilla, achieved self-government as an Associated State of Great Britain in 1967. In 1983, St. Kitts & Nevis became an independent nation. English with a strong West Indian lilt is spoken here. People are friendly but shy; always ask before you take photographs. Also, be sure to wear wraps or shorts over beach attire when you're in public places.

CURRENCY Legal tender is the Eastern Caribbean (E.C.) dollar. At this writing, the rate of exchange was EC$2.70 to US$1. U.S. dollars are accepted practically everywhere, but you'll usually get change in E.C. currency. Prices quoted throughout this chapter are in U.S. dollars unless otherwise noted.

TELEPHONES Phone cards, which you can buy in denominations of $5, $10, and $20, are handy for making local phone calls, calling other islands, and accessing U.S. direct lines. To make a local call, dial the seven-digit number. To call St. Kitts and Nevis from the United States, dial the area code 869, then access code 465, 466, 468, or 469 and the local four-digit number.

SHORE The following are good choices in St. Kitts and Nevis. They may not be
EXCURSIONS offered by all cruise lines. Times and prices are approximate.

Brimstone Hill Fortress & Gardens. You will visit Brimstone Hill, a 300-year old fortress and World Heritage Site before going to Romney Gardens, where you can browse through the wares of Caribelle Batik Studio. Your tour ends after a drive through Basseterre. ☉ 3 hrs 🖃 $56–$59.

Catamaran Sail & Snorkeling Adventure. Sail to Ballast Bay to snorkel and view the tropical fish and coral. ☉ 3 hrs 🖃 $59–$70.

Nevis Catamaran Getaway. Sail from St. Kitts to the island of Nevis for a day of snorkeling and a beach barbeque. Some tours also include a bus trip to Alexander Hamilton Museum and the Botanical Garden. ☉ 7 hrs 🖃 $120–$150.

Ocean Kayaking. Board your ocean kayak in White House Bay to paddle into secluded coves along the shore, making stops for snorkeling. ☉ 3 hrs 🖃 $69.

St. Kitts Scenic Railway. After a bus trip to the rail station, you board a double-decker, narrow-gauge railway car for a trip partway around the island. Each passenger gets a comfortable downstairs air-conditioned seat fronting vaulted picture windows and an upstairs open-air observation spot. The conductor's running discourse embraces not only the history of sugar cultivation but the railway's construction, island folklore, island geography, even other agricultural mainstays from papayas and pineapples to pigs. Refreshments are provided. ☉ 3½ hrs 🖃 $92.

Coming Ashore

Cruise ships calling at St. Kitts dock at Port Zante, which is a new deepwater port directly in Basseterre, the capital of St. Kitts. The cruise-ship terminal is right in the downtown area, two minutes' walk from sights and shops. Taxi rates on St. Kitts are fixed and should be posted right at the dock. The same is true in Nevis, where taxi rates are posted at the dock in Charlestown.

Rates are fairly expensive, and you may have to pay $32 for a ride to Brimstone Hill (for one to four passengers). A three-hour driving tour of Nevis costs about $60; a four-hour tour of St. Kitts about $70. It's often cheaper to arrange an island tour with one of the local companies. On both islands, several restored great-house plantations are known for their lunches; your driver can provide information and arrange drop-off and pickup. Before setting off in a cab, be sure to clarify whether the rate quoted is in E.C. or U.S. dollars.

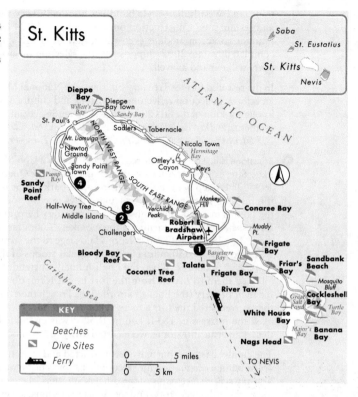

Exploring St. Kitts

Numbers in the margin correspond to points of interest on the St. Kitts map.

❶ Basseterre. On the south coast, St. Kitts's walkable capital is graced with tall palms, and although many of the buildings appear run-down, there are interesting shops, excellent art galleries, and some beautifully maintained houses. Duty-free shops and boutiques line the streets and courtyards radiating from the octagonal **Circus**, built in the style of London's famous Piccadilly Circus. There are lovely gardens on the site of a former slave market at **Independence Square** (⊠ Off Bank St.). The square is surrounded on three sides by 18th-century Georgian buildings. **St. George's Anglican Church** (⊠ Cayon St.) is a handsome stone building with a crenellated tower originally built by the French in 1670 and called Nôtre-Dame. The British burned it down in 1706 and rebuilt it four years later, naming it after the patron saint of England. Since then it has suffered a fire, an earthquake, and hurricanes, and was once again rebuilt in 1869. **Port Zante** (⊠ Waterfront, behind the Circus) is an ambitious 27-acre cruise-ship pier and marina in an area that has been reclaimed from the sea. The domed welcome center is an imposing neoclassical hodgepodge, with columns and stone arches, shops, walkways, fountains, and West Indian–style buildings housing luxury shops, galleries, and restaurants. Construction on a second pier, 1,434 feet long with a draught to accommodate even the leviathan cruise ships, should be completed by late 2005. Supposedly, the selection of shops and restaurants will expand as well.

In the restored former Treasury Building, the **National Museum** presents an eclectic collection reflecting the history and culture of the island—as a collaboration of the St. Christopher Heritage Society and the island government. ⊠ *Bay Rd., Basseterre* ☎ *869/465–5584* ✉ *EC$1 residents, U.S.$1 nonresidents* ☉ *Mon. and Sat. 9:30–2, Tues.–Fri. 9–1 and 2–5.*

❹ Brimstone Hill. The well-restored 38-acre fortress, a UNESCO World Heritage Site, is part of a national park dedicated by Queen Elizabeth in 1985. The steep walk up the hill from the parking lot is well worth it if military history and/or spectacular views interest you. After routing the French in 1690, the English erected a battery here, and by 1736 the fortress held 49 guns, earning it the moniker "Gibraltar of the West Indies." In 1782, 8,000 French troops laid siege to the stronghold, which was defended by 350 militia and 600 regular troops of the Royal Scots and East Yorkshires. When the English finally surrendered, the French allowed them to march from the fort in full formation out of respect for their bravery (the English afforded the French the same honor when they surrendered the fort a mere year later). A hurricane severely damaged the fortress in 1834, and in 1852 it was evacuated and dismantled. The beautiful stones were carted away to build houses.

The citadel has been partially reconstructed and its guns remounted. A seven-minute orientation film recounts the fort's history and restoration. You can see what remains of the officers' quarters, the redoubts, the barracks, the ordinance store, and the cemetery. Its museum collections were depleted by hurricanes, but some pre-Columbian artifacts, objects pertaining to the African heritage of the island's slaves (masks, ceremonial tools, etc.), weaponry, uniforms, photographs, and old newspapers remain. The view from here includes Montserrat and Nevis to the southeast; Saba and St. Eustatius to the northwest; and St. Barths and St. Maarten to the north. Nature trails snake through the tangle of surrounding hardwood forest and savanna (a fine spot to catch the green vervet monkeys—inexplicably brought by the French and now outnumbering the residents—skittering about). ⊠ *Main Rd., Brimstone Hill* ☎ *869/465–2609* ⊕ *www.brimstonehillfortress.org* ✉ *$8* ☉ *Daily 9:30–5:30.*

❷ Old Road Town. This site marks the first permanent English settlement in the West Indies, founded in 1624 by Thomas Warner. Take the side road toward the interior to find some Carib petroglyphs, testimony of even earlier habitation. The largest depicts a female figure on black volcanic rock, presumably a fertility goddess. Less than a mile east of Old Road along Main Road is **Bloody Point,** where French and British soldiers joined forces in 1629 to repel a mass Carib attack; reputedly so many Caribs were massacred that the stream ran red for three days. ⊠ *Main Rd., west of Challengers.*

❸ **Romney Manor.** The ruins of this partially restored house and surrounding cottages that duplicate the old chattel-house style are set in 6 acres of gardens, with exotic flowers, an old bell tower, and an enormous, gnarled, 350-year-old *samaan* tree (sometimes called a rain tree). Inside, at **Caribelle Batik,** you can watch artisans hand-printing fabrics. Look for signs indicating a turnoff for Romney Manor near Old Road.

Exploring Nevis

Numbers in the margin correspond to points of interest on the Nevis map.

Nevis is a 45-minute ferry ride from Basseterre. You can tour Charlestown, the capital, in a half hour or so, but you'll need three to four hours to explore the entire island. There are ample rewards if you decide to explore Nevis independently, but whether this is an option for you will depend largely on your ship's schedule. Most cruise ships arrive in port at around 8 AM, and the ferry schedule can be irregular and infrequent, so many passengers sign up for a cruise line–run shore excursion. If you travel independently, confirm departure times with the tourist office to be sure you'll make it back to your ship on time.

There are three services between St. Kitts and Nevis, all with byzantine schedules that are subject to change. Call the ferry information lines for the most up-to-date schedules. The 150-passenger government-operated ferry M/V *Caribe Queen* makes the 45-minute crossing between St. Kitts and Nevis two to three times daily, except Thursday and Sunday. The former cargo ship *Sea Hustler* is larger and makes the trip twice-daily. Round-trip fare for either is $10. The faster, air-conditioned, 110-passenger ferry M/V *Caribe Breeze* makes the run twice-daily Thursday and Sunday, more frequently other days. The fare is $12 ($15 first class) round-trip.

Sea-taxi service between the two islands is operated by Kenneth Samuel, Nevis Water Sports, Leeward Island Charters, and Austin Macleod of Pro-Divers for $20 one-way in summer, $25 in winter; discounts can be negotiated for small groups. There's an additional EC$1 tax for port security, paid separately upon departure.

❷ **Bath Springs.** The Caribbean's first hotel, the Bath Hotel, built by businessmann Joh Huggins in 1778, was so popular in the 19th century that visitors, including such dignitaries as Samuel Taylor Coleridge and Prince William Henry, traveled two months by ship to "take the waters" in the property's hot thermal springs. It suffered extensive hurricane and probably earthquake damage over the years and languished in disrepair until recently. Local volunteers have cleaned up the spring, built a stone pool and steps to enter the waters, and now residents and visitors enjoy the springs, which range from 104°F to 108°F, though signs still caution that you bathe at your own risk, especially if you have heart problems. Upon completion, this promising development will house the Nevis Island Administration offices, massage huts and changing rooms, a restaurant, and a cultural center and historic exhibit on the original hotel property. Follow Main Street south from Charlestown. ⊠ *Charlestown outskirts.*

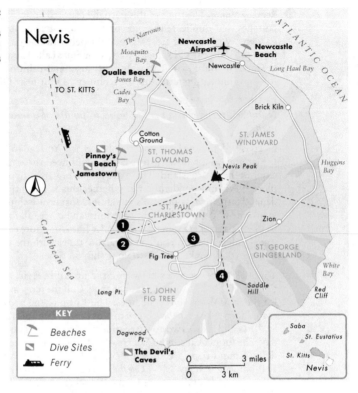

Nevis

The Narrows

Mosquito Bay

Newcastle Airport

Newcastle Beach

Newcastle

Long Haul Bay

Oualie Beach
Jones Bay

TO ST. KITTS

Cades Bay

Brick Kiln

Cotton Ground

ST. JAMES WINDWARD

Pinney's Beach
Jamestown

ST. THOMAS LOWLAND

Nevis Peak

Huggins Bay

Caribbean Sea

ST. PAUL CHARLESTOWN

❶
❷

Zion

❸

Fig Tree

ST. GEORGE GINGERLAND

White Bay

❹

Long Pt.

ST. JOHN FIG TREE

Saddle Hill

Red Cliff

KEY

⌇ Beaches
◼ Dive Sites
🚢 Ferry

Dogwood Pt.

◼ The Devil's Caves

0   3 miles
0   3 km

Saba
St. Eustatius

St. Kitts

Nevis

❹ **Botanical Gardens of Nevis.** In addition to terraced gardens and arbors, this remarkable 7.8-acre site in the glowering shadow of Mt. Nevis has natural lagoons, streams, and waterfalls, superlative bronze mermaids, egrets and herons, and extravagant fountains. You can find a proper rose garden, sections devoted to orchids and bromeliads, cacti, and flowering trees and shrubs—even a bamboo garden. The entrance to the Rain Forest Conservatory—which attempts to include every conceivable Caribbean ecosystem and then some—duplicates an imposing Mayan temple. A splendid re-creation of a plantation-style great house contains a tearoom with sweeping sea views and a souvenir shop. ⊠ Montpelier Estate ☎ 869/469–3509 ⊡ $9 ⊗ Mon.–Sat. 9–4:30.

❶ **Charlestown.** About 1,200 of Nevis's 10,000 inhabitants live in the capital. The town faces the Caribbean, about 12½ mi (20 km) south of Basseterre on St. Kitts. If you arrive by ferry, as most people do, you'll walk smack onto Main Street from the pier. It's easy to imagine how tiny Charlestown, founded in 1660, must have looked in its heyday. The weathered buildings still have their fanciful galleries, elaborate gingerbread fretwork, wooden shutters, and hanging plants. The stonework building with the clock tower (1825) houses the courthouse and the second-floor **library** (a cool respite on sultry days). A fire in 1873 damaged the building and destroyed valuable records; much of the present building dates from the turn of the 20th century. The little park next to the library is Memorial Square, dedicated to the fallen of World Wars I and II. Down the street from the square, archaeologists have discovered the remains of a Jewish cemetery and synagogue (Nevis reputedly had the Caribbean's second-oldest congregation), but there's little to see. The **Alexander Hamilton Birthplace,** which contains the Museum of Nevis History, is on the waterfront, covered in bougainvillea and hibiscus. This Georgian-style house is a reconstruction of what is believed to have been the American patriot's original home, built in 1680 and thought to have been destroyed during an earthquake in the mid-19th century. Hamilton was born here in 1755 and moved to St. Croix when he was about 12. A few years later, at 17, he moved to the American colonies to continue his education; he became Secretary of the Treasury to George Washington and died in a duel with political rival Aaron Burr. The Nevis House of Assembly occupies the second floor of this building, and the museum downstairs contains Hamilton memorabilia, documents pertaining to the island's history, and displays on island geology, politics, architecture, culture, and cuisine. The gift shop is a wonderful source for historic maps, crafts, and books on Nevis. ⊠ *Low St., Charlestown* ☎ *869/ 469–5786* ⊕ *www.nevis-nhcs.org* ▧ *$5, includes admission to Nelson Museum* ☉ *Weekdays 9–4, Sat. 9–noon.*

❸ **Nelson Museum.** This collection merits a visit for its memorabilia of Lord Horatio Nelson, including letters, documents, paintings, and even furniture from his flagship. Historical archives of the Nevis Historical and Conservation Society are housed here and are available for public viewing. Nelson was based in Antigua but on military patrol came to Nevis, where he met and eventually married Frances Nisbet, who lived on a 64-acre plantation here. Half the space is devoted to often provocative displays on island life, from leading families to vernacular architecture to the adaptation of traditional African customs, from cuisine to Carnival. ⊠ *Bath Rd., outside Charlestown* ☎ *869/469–0408* ⊕ *www.nevis-nhcs.org* ▧ *$5, includes admission to Museum of Nevis History* ☉ *Weekdays 9–4, Sat. 9–noon.*

Shopping

Shops used to close for lunch from noon to 1, but more and more establishments are remaining open Monday–Saturday 8–4. Some shops close earlier on Thursday.

ST. KITTS St. Kitts has limited shopping, but there are a few duty-free shops with good deals on jewelry, perfume, china, and crystal. Don't forget to pick up some CSR, a "new cane spirit drink" that's distilled from fresh sugarcane right on St. Kitts.

Most shopping plazas are in downtown Basseterre—try the **Shoreline Plaza,** next to the Treasury Building; the **Pelican Mall,** across the street from Port Zante (which has a tourism office); and **Port Zante,** which has about 25 shops of its own.

Caribelle Batik (⊠ Romney Manor, Old Road ☎ 869/465–6253) sells batik wraps, kimonos, kaftans, T-shirts, dresses, wall hangings, and the like. **Kate Design** (✉ Bank St., Basseterre ☎ 869/465–5265) showcases the highly individual style of Kate Spencer, whose original paintings, serigraphs, note cards, and other pieces that she regularly introduces, are also available from her studio outside the Rawlins Plantation. **Spencer Cameron Art Gallery** (✉ 10 N. Independence Sq., Basseterre ☎ 869/465–1617) has historical reproductions of Caribbean island charts and prints, in addition to owner Rosey Cameron's popular Carnevale clown prints and a wide selection of exceptional artwork by Caribbean artists. They will mail anywhere. **Stonewall's Tropical Boutique** (✉ Stonewall's, 5 Princes St., Basseterre ☎ 869/465–5248) carries top-of-the-line products from around the Caribbean: hand-painted Jamaican pottery, West Indian photos and artworks, brass jewelry, hand-painted T-shirts, and flowing resort wear by leading Caribbean designer John Warden. It's open evenings only, accessible through the restaurant.

NEVIS Nevis is certainly not the place for a shopping spree, but there are some wonderful surprises, notably the island's stamps, fragrant honey, and batik and hand-embroidered clothing. Other than a few hotel boutiques and isolated galleries, virtually all shopping is concentrated on or just off Main Street in Charlestown. The lovely old stonework and wood floors of the waterfront Cotton Ginnery Complex make an appropriate setting for stalls of local artisans.

Cheryl "Cherrianne" Liburd's **Bocane Ceramics** (✉ Main St., Stoney Grove ☎ 869/469–5437) stocks beautifully designed and glazed local pottery, such as platters painted with marine life, pineapple tea sets, and coffee tables topped with mosaic depictions of chattel houses. Nevis has produced one artist of some international repute, the late Dame Eva Wilkin, who for more than 50 years painted island people, flowers, and landscapes in an evocative art naïf style. Her originals are now quite valuable, but prints are available in some local shops. The **Eva Wilkin Gallery** (✉ Clay Ghaut, Gingerland ☎ 869/469–2673) occupies her former atelier. If the paintings, drawings, and prints are out of your price range, consider buying the lovely note cards based on her designs. **Island Fever** (✉ Main St., Charlestown ☎ 869/469–0867) has become the island's classiest boutique, with an excellent selection of everything from bathing suits and dresses to straw bags and jewelry. **Knick Knacks** (✉ Main St., Hanfield Bldg. near Ferry Dock, Charlestown ☎ 869/469–5784) showcases top local artisans, including Marvin Chapman (stone-and-wood carvings) and Jeannie Rigby (exquisite dolls). The **Nevis Handicraft Co-op Society** (✉ Main St., Charlestown ☎ 869/469–1746), next to the tourist office, offers works by local artisans (clothing, ceramic ware, woven goods) and locally produced honey, hot sauces, and jellies (try the guava and soursop).

Sports & Activities

ST. KITTS **Diving & Snorkeling:** St. Kitts has more than a dozen excellent dive sites. **Dive St. Kitts** (✉ Frigate Bay, 2 mi [3 km] east of Basseterre ☎ 869/465–1189 ⊕ www.divestkitts.com), a PADI–NAUI facility, offers competitive prices; friendly, laid-back dive masters; and a more international clientele. The Bird Rock location features superb beach diving: common sightings 20 feet to 30 feet out include octopi, nurse sharks, manta, spotted eagle rays, and seahorses. Shore dives are unlimited when you book packages. Kenneth Samuel of **Kenneth's Dive Centre** (☎ 869/465–2670) is a PADI-certified dive master who takes small groups of divers with C cards to nearby reefs. Rates average $50 for single-tank dives, $75 for double-tank dives; add $10 for equipment. Night dives, including lights, are $50, and snorkeling trips (four-person minimum) are $35, drinks included. After 25 years' experience, Samuel is considered an old pro and strives to keep groups small and prices reasonable. Austin Macleod, a PADI-certified dive master–instructor and owner of **Pro-Divers** (✉ Ocean Terrace Inn, Basseterre ☎ 869/466–3483 ⊕ www. prodiversstkitts.com), offers resort and certification courses. His prices for an open-water certification course and dive package prices are the lowest on the island. He also takes groups to snorkeling sites accessible only by boat.

Golf: The Royal St. Kitts Golf Club (✉ St. Kitts Marriott Resort, Frigate Bay ☎ 869/466–2700 ⊕ www.royalstkittsgolfclub.com) is an 18-hole, par-71 links-style championship course that underwent a complete re-design by Thomas McBroom to maximize Caribbean and Atlantic views and increase the challenge (there are now 12 lakes, and 83 bunkers). Holes 15 through 17 actually skirt the Atlantic in their entirety, lending new meaning to the term sand trap. The sudden gusts and extremely hilly terrain demand pinpoint accuracy and finesse, yet holes such as 18 require your power game. Greens fees are $160 for nonguests. The development includes practice bunkers, putting green, and a short-game chipping area.

Hiking: Trails in the central mountains of St. Kitts vary from easy to don't-try-it-by-yourself. Monkey Hill and Verchild's Peak aren't difficult, although the Verchild's climb will take the better part of a day. Don't attempt Mt. Liamuiga without a guide. Tour rates range from $35 for a rain-forest walk to $65 for a volcano expedition. Addy of **Addy's Nature Tours** (☎ 869/465–8069) offers a picnic lunch and cold tropical juices during treks through the rain forest; she also discusses the history and folklore relating to native plants, including their supposed healing properties. Earl of **Duke of Earl's Adventures** (☎ 869/465–1899) is as entertaining as his nickname suggests—and his prices are slightly cheaper. He genuinely loves his island and conveys that enthusiasm, encouraging hikers to swing on vines or sample unusual-looking fruits during his rainforest trip. He also conducts a thorough volcano tour to the crater's rim. Greg Pereira of **Greg's Safaris** (☎ 869/465–4121 ⊕ www.gregssafaris.com), whose family has lived on St. Kitts since the early 19th century, takes groups on half-day trips into the rain forest and on full-day hikes up the volcano and through the grounds of a private 18th-century greathouse. The first includes visits to sacred Carib sites, abandoned sugar mills, and an excursion down a 100-foot coastal canyon containing a wealth of Amerindian petroglyphs. The Sugar Plantation Heritage Tour provides a thorough explanation of the role sugar and rum played in the Caribbean economy and colonial wars. He and his staff relate fascinating histori-cal, folkloric, and botanical information.

Horseback Riding: Guides from **Trinity Stables** (☎ 869/465–3226) offer beach rides ($35) and trips into the rain forest ($45). The latter is intriguing as guides discuss plants' medicinal properties along the way (such as sugarcane to stanch bleeding) and pick oranges right off a tree to squeeze fresh juice. Otherwise, the staffers are cordial but shy, and this isn't a place for beginners' instruction.

NEVIS **Golf:** Duffers doff their hats to the beautiful, impeccably maintained Robert Trent Jones, Jr.–designed 18-hole, par-72, 6,766-yard championship course at the **Four Seasons Resort Nevis** (✉ Pinney's Beach, Nevis ☎ 869/469–1111). The signature hole is the 15th, a 660-yard monster that encompasses a deep ravine; other holes include bridges, steep drops, rolling pitches, and fierce doglegs. The virtual botanical gardens surrounding the fairways almost qualify as a hazard themselves. Greens fees are $110 per person for 9 holes, $175 for 18.

Hiking: Herbert Heights Village Experience (☎ 869/469–2856 ⊕ www. herbertheights.com) is run by the Herbert family, who have fashioned their own unique activities. They lead four-hour nature hikes up to panoramic Herbert Heights, where you drink in fresh local juices and the views of Montserrat; the powerful telescope makes you feel as if you're staring right into that island's simmering volcano. The trail formed part of an escape route for runaway slaves. Numerous hummingbirds, doves, and butterflies flit and flutter through the rain forest. The Herberts painstakingly reconstructed thatched cottages that offer a glimpse of village life a century ago at Nelson's Lookout. The price is $15, for $35 you can ride one of their donkeys. The festive activities include crab races, refreshments, rock climbing, and whale-watching in season through a telescope donated by Greenpeace. **Sunrise Tours** (☎ 869/469–3512 ⊕ www.nevisnaturetours.com), run by Lynell and Earla Liburd, offers a range of hiking tours, but their most popular is Devil's Copper, a rock configuration full of ghostly legends. Local people gave it its name because at one time the water was hot—a volcanic thermal stream. The area features pristine waterfalls and splendid bird-watching. They also do a Nevis village walk, a Hamilton Estate Walk, an Amerindian walk along the wild southeast Atlantic coast, and trips to the rain forest and Nevis Peak. They love highlighting Nevisian heritage, explaining time-honored cooking techniques, the many uses of dried grasses, and medicinal plants. Hikes range from $20 to $40 per person, and you receive a certificate of achievement. **Top to Bottom** (☎ 869/469–9080), run by Jim and Nikki Johnston, offers ecorambles (slower tours) and hikes that emphasize Nevis's volcanic and horticultural heritage (including pointing out folkloric herbal medicines). The Johnstons are also keen star- and bird-watchers (their Nevis Nights magically explain nocturnal biology, astronomy, even astrology). Three-hour rambles or hikes are $20 per person (snacks and juice included); it's $30–$35 for more strenuous climbs (two offered) up Mount Nevis.

Horseback Riding: The **Hermitage Stables** (✉ Gingerland ☎ 869/469–3477) arrange everything from horseback riding to jaunts in hand-carved mahogany carriages. The **Nevis Equestrian Centre** (⊠ Clifton Estate, Pinney's Beach ☎ 869/469–8118) offers leisurely beach rides, as well as more demanding canters through the lush hills.

Beaches

ST. KITTS   The powdery white-sand beaches of St. Kitts, free and open to the public (even those occupied by hotels), are in the Frigate Bay area or on the lower peninsula. **Banana Bay,** one of the island's loveliest beaches, stretches over a mile (1½ km) at the southeastern tip of the island. Several large hotels were abandoned in the early stages of development; their skeletal structures mar an otherwise idyllic scene. **Cockleshell Bay,** Banana Bay's twin beach, is another eyebrow of glittering sand backed by lush vegetation and reachable on foot. Locals consider the Caribbean (southern) side of **Friar's Bay** the island's finest beach. It has two hopping beach bars, Monkey and Sunset, which serve excellent inexpensive grilled and barbecued food. You can haggle with fishermen here to take you snorkeling off the eastern point. The waters on the Atlantic (northern) side are rougher, but the beach has a wild, desolate beauty. On the Caribbean side of **Frigate Bay** you'll find talcum powder–fine sand, while on the Atlantic side, the 4-mi-wide (6½-km-wide) stretch is a favorite with horseback riders.

NEVIS   On Nevis all the beaches are free to the public, but there are no changing facilities, so wear a swimsuit under your clothes. **Oualie Beach,** south of Mosquito Bay and north of Cades and Jones bays, is a beige-sand beach where the folks at Oualie Beach Hotel can mix you a drink and fix you up with water-sports equipment. **Pinney's Beach,** the island's showpiece, has almost 4 mi (6½ km) of soft, golden sand on the calm Caribbean, lined with a magnificent grove of palm trees. The Four Seasons Resort is here, as are the private cabanas and pavilions of several mountain inns and casual beach bars.

Where to Eat

Restaurants occasionally add a 10% service charge to your bill; if this information isn't printed on the menu, ask about it. When there's no service charge, a tip of 15% is appropriate.

ST. KITTS   ✕ **Ballahoo.** This second-floor terrace restaurant draws a crowd for
$–$$$ breakfast, lunch, and dinner, primarily due to the lack of other viable options. Lilting calypso and reggae on the sound system, and whirring ceiling fans, potted palms, and colorful island prints are appropriately tropical. Specialties include chili shrimp, conch simmered in garlic butter, Madras beef curry, and a toasted rum-and-banana sandwich topped with ice cream. Go at lunchtime, when you can watch the bustle of the Circus, and specials such as rotis bursting with curried chicken or vegetables slash prices nearly in half. Grab fresh local juices (tamarind, guava) if you can. Though the service is lackadaisical bordering on rude, the food is at least plentiful, the daiquiris killer, and the people-watching delightful. ⊠ *Fort St., Basseterre* ☎ *869/465–4197* ▭ *AE, MC, V* ☉ *Closed Sun.*

$–$$ ✕ **Turtle Beach Bar & Grill.** Treats at this popular daytime watering hole at the south end of S.E. Peninsula Road include honey-mustard ribs, coconut-shrimp salad, grilled lobster, decadent bread pudding with rum sauce, and an array of tempting tropical libations. Business cards and pennants from around the world plaster the bar; the room is decorated with a variety of nautical accoutrements. You can snorkel here, spot hawksbill turtles, feed the tame monkeys that boldly belly-up to the bar (they adore green bananas and peaches), serve Wilbur the pig a beer, laze in a palm-shaded hammock, or rent a kayak or snorkel gear. Locals come Sunday afternoons for dancing to live bands, and volleyball. Friday nights have developed a following for a seafood and mixed grill buffet, while live music accompanies Saturday evening's Caribbean buffet and bonfire party. If you don't mind the day traffic, two two-bedroom air-conditioned apartments with full kitchen and cable TV rent for just $150. ☒ *S.E. Peninsula Rd., Turtle Beach* ☎ *869/469–9086* ▭ *AE, D, MC, V* ☺ *No dinner Mon.–Thurs.*

NEVIS ✕ **Unella's.** It's nothing fancy here—just tables on a second-floor porch
$–$$$ overlooking Charlestown's waterfront. Stop for exceptional lobster (more expensive than the rest of the menu), curried lamb, island-style spareribs, and steamed conch, all served with local vegetables, rice, and peas. Unella opens shop around 9 AM, when locals and boaters appear eager for their breakfast, and stays open all day, as island ladies stop by in curlers, and cops and cabbies flirt shyly with the waitresses. ☒ *Waterfront, Charlestown* ☎ *869/469–5574* ▭ *No credit cards.*

¢–$$ ✕ **Sunshine's.** Everything about this beach shack is larger than life, including the Rasta man Llewelyn "Sunshine" Caines himself. Flags from around the world drape the lean-to and complement the international patrons (including an occasional movie star), who wander over from the adjacent Four Seasons. Picnic tables are splashed with bright sunrise-to-sunset colors; even the palm trees are painted. Fishermen cruise up with their catch—you might savor lobster rolls or snapper creole. Don't miss the lethal house specialty, Killer Bee rum punch. As Sunshine boasts, "One and you're stung, two you're stunned, three it's a knockout." ☒ *Pinney's Beach* ☎ *869/469–1089* ▭ *No credit cards.*

St. Lucia

Magnificent St. Lucia—with towering mountains, dense rain forest, fertile green valleys, and acres of banana plantations—lies in the middle of the Windward Islands. Nicknamed "the Helen of the West Indies" because of its natural beauty, St. Lucia is distinguished from its neighbors by its distinctive geological landmarks, the Pitons, twin peaks on the southwest coast that have become a symbol of this island, soar nearly ½ mi (1 km) above the ocean floor. Nearby, outside the French colonial town of Soufrière, is a "drive-in" volcano, with neighboring sulfur springs that have rejuvenated bathers for nearly three centuries.

A century and a half of battles between the French and English resulted in St. Lucia's changing hands 14 times before 1814, when England established possession. In 1979 the island became an independent state within the British Commonwealth of Nations. The official language is English, although most people also speak a French-creole patois.

CURRENCY St. Lucia uses the Eastern Caribbean (E.C.) dollar. The exchange rate is EC$2.70 to US$1. Although U.S. dollars are readily accepted, you'll often get change in E.C. currency. Credit cards and traveler's checks are widely accepted. Prices given below are in U.S. dollars unless otherwise indicated.

TELEPHONES You can make direct-dial overseas and interisland calls from St. Lucia, and the connections are excellent. You can charge an overseas call to a major credit card with no surcharge by dialing 811. Phone cards can be purchased at many retail outlets and used from any touch-tone telephone (including pay phones) in St. Lucia.

SHORE EXCURSIONS The following are good choices in St. Lucia. They may not be offered by all cruise lines. Times and prices are approximate.

La Soufrière & the Pitons. Travel the winding mountainous West Coast Road for spectacular views of the Pitons on the way to La Soufrière volcano, the sulfur springs, nearby Diamond Falls and Mineral Baths, and the Botanical Gardens. A creole lunch buffet is included in longer tours. ⏱ 4–6 hrs 🖃 $50–$76.

Northern Highlights. Drive along the tropical northern part of the island, going to Morne Fortune, Rodney Bay, Pigeon Island, and Reduit Beach for swimming and snorkeling. ⏱ 4 hrs 🖃 $34–$38.

Pitons by Land & Sea. Sail along the coast by catamaran to La Soufrière volcano, Diamond Botanical Gardens, and Soufrière Estate, with a stop for snorkeling. ⏱ 7 hrs 🖃 $60–$82.

Rain-forest Biking Adventure. Travel into the island's rain forest by bus and then bike along a fairly level path through a private banana plantation to Errard Falls for an invigorating swim. ⏱ 4 hrs 🖃 $59–$64.

Coming Ashore

Most cruise ships call at the capital city of Castries, on the island's northwest coast. Either of two docking areas is used: Pointe Seraphine, a port of entry and duty-free shopping complex, or Port Castries, a commercial dock across the harbor. Ferry service connects the two piers.

Smaller vessels can call at Soufrière, on the island's southwest coast. Ships calling at Soufrière must usually anchor offshore and transport passengers to the wharf via launch.

Tourist information offices are at Pointe Seraphine in Castries and along the waterfront on Bay Street in Soufrière. Downtown Castries is within walking distance of the pier, and the produce market and adjacent crafts and vendors' markets are the main attractions. Soufrière is a sleepy West Indian town, but it's worth a short walk around the central square to view the French colonial architecture. Most of St. Lucia's sightseeing attractions are in or near Soufrière.

Taxis are available at the docks. Although they are unmetered, the government has issued a list of standard fares that are posted at the entrance to Pointe Seraphine. Taxi drivers are well informed and can give you a full tour—often an excellent one, thanks to government-sponsored training programs. From the Castries area, full-day island tours cost about $140 for up to four people; sightseeing trips to Soufrière, around $120.

If you plan your own day, expect to pay the driver at least $20 per hour plus a 10% tip. Whatever your destination, negotiate the price with the driver before you depart—and be sure that you both understand whether the rate is in E.C. or U.S. dollars.

Exploring St. Lucia

Numbers in the margin correspond to points of interest on the St. Lucia map.

CASTRIES AREA
❸

Castries. The capital, a busy commercial city of about 65,000 people, wraps around a sheltered bay. Morne Fortune rises sharply to the south of town, creating a dramatic green backdrop. The charm of Castries lies almost entirely in its liveliness, since most of the colonial buildings were destroyed by four fires that occurred between 1796 and 1948. Freighters (exporting bananas, coconut, cocoa, mace, nutmeg, and citrus fruits) and cruise ships come and go daily, making Castries Harbour one of the Caribbean's busiest ports. **Pointe Seraphine** is a duty-free shopping complex on the north side of the harbor, about a 20-minute walk or 2-minute cab ride from the city center; a launch ferries passengers across the harbor when ships are in port. Pointe Seraphine's attractive Spanish-style architecture houses more than 20 upscale duty-free shops, a tourist information kiosk, a taxi stand, and car-rental agencies. **Derek Walcott Square** is a green oasis bordered by Brazil, Laborie, Micoud, and Bourbon streets. Formerly Columbus Square, it was renamed to honor the hometown poet who won the 1992 Nobel prize for literature—one of two Nobel laureates from St. Lucia (the late Sir W. Arthur Lewis won the 1979 Nobel prize in economics). Some of the 19th-century buildings that have survived fire, wind, and rain can be seen on Brazil Street, the square's southern border. On the Laborie Street side, there's a huge, 400-year-old *samaan* tree with leafy branches that shade a good portion of the square. Directly across Laborie Street from Derek Walcott Square is the Roman Catholic **Cathedral of the Immaculate Conception,** which was built in 1897. Though it's rather somber on the outside, its interior walls are decorated with colorful murals reworked by St. Lucian artist Dunstan St. Omer in 1985, just prior to the pope's visit. This church has an active parish and is open daily for both public viewing and religious services. At the corner of Jeremie and Peynier streets, spreading beyond its brilliant orange roof, is the **Castries Market.** Full of excitement and bustle, the market is open every day except Sunday. It's liveliest on Saturday morning, when farmers bring their fresh produce and spices to town, as they have for more than a century. Next door to the produce market is the **Craft Market,** where you can buy pottery, wood carvings, and handwoven straw articles. Across Peynier Street from the Craft Market, at the **Vendor's Arcade,** there are still more handicrafts and souvenirs.

❹ Fort Charlotte. Begun in 1764 by the French as the Citadelle du Morne Fortune, Fort Charlotte was completed after 20 years of battling and changing hands. Its old barracks and batteries are now government buildings and local educational facilities, but you can drive around and look at the remains, including redoubts, a guardroom, stables, and cells. You can also walk up to the Inniskilling Monument, a tribute to the 1796

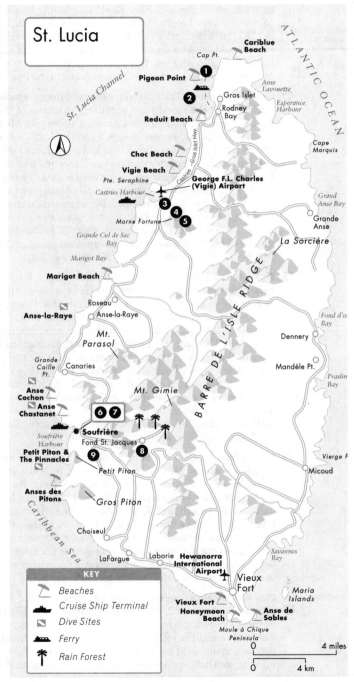

battle in which the 27th Foot Royal Inniskilling Fusiliers wrested the Morne from the French. At the military cemetery, which was first used in 1782, faint inscriptions on the tombstones tell the tales of French and English soldiers who died here. Six former governors of the island are buried here as well. From this point atop Morne Fortune you can view Martinique to the north and the twin peaks of the Pitons to the south.

5 **Government House.** The official residence of the governor-general of St. Lucia, one of the island's few remaining examples of Victorian architecture is perched high above Castries, half-way up Morne Fortune—the "Hill of Good Fortune"—which forms a backdrop for the capital city. Morne Fortune has also overlooked more than its share of *bad* luck of the years, including devastating hurricanes and four fires that leveled Castries. Within Government House itself is the **Le Pavillion Royal Museum,** which houses important historical photographs and documents, artifacts, crockery, silverware, medals, and awards; original architectural drawings of Government House are displayed on the walls. However, you must make an appointment to visit. ⊠ *Morne Fortune, Castries* ☎ *758/452–2481* ⊕ *www.stluciagovernmenthouse.com* ➲ *Free* ☉ *Tues. and Thurs. 10–noon and 2–4, by appointment only.*

1 **Pigeon Island.** Jutting out from the northwest coast, Pigeon Island is connected to the mainland by a causeway. Tales are told of the pirate Jambe de Bois (Wooden Leg), who once hid out on this 44-acre hilltop islet—a strategic point during the struggles for control of St. Lucia. Now, it's a national landmark and a venue for concerts, festivals, and family gatherings. There are two small beaches with calm waters for swimming and snorkeling, a restaurant, and picnic areas. Scattered around the grounds are ruins of barracks, batteries, and garrisons that date from 18th-century French and English battles. In the Museum and Interpretative Centre, housed in the restored British officers' mess, a multimedia display explains the island's ecological and historical significance. ⊠ *Pigeon Island, St. Lucia National Trust, Rodney Bay* ☎ *758/452–5005* ⊕ *www.slunatrust.or* ➲ *$4* ☉ *Daily 9–5.*

2 **Rodney Bay.** About 15 minutes north of Castries, the natural bay and an 80-acre man-made lagoon—surrounded by hotels and many popular restaurants—are named for British admiral George Rodney, who sailed the English Navy out of Gros Islet Bay in 1780 to attack and ultimately decimate the French fleet. Rodney Bay Marina is one of the Caribbean's premier yachting centers and the destination of the Atlantic Rally for Cruisers (trans-Atlantic yacht crossing) each December. Yacht charters and sightseeing day trips can be arranged at the marina. The Rodney Bay Ferry makes hourly crossings between the marina and the shopping complex, as well as daily excursions to Pigeon Island.

SOUFRIÈRE AREA **Diamond Botanical Gardens & Waterfall.** These splendid gardens are part
7 of Soufrière Estate, a 2,000-acre land grant made in 1713 by Louis XIV to three Devaux brothers from Normandy in recognition of their services to France. The estate is still owned by their descendants; the gardens are maintained by Joan Du Bouley Devaux. Bushes and shrubs bursting with brilliant flowers grow beneath towering trees and line path-

ways that lead to a natural gorge. Water bubbling to the surface from underground sulfur springs streams downhill in rivulets to become Diamond Waterfall, deep within the botanical gardens. Through the centuries, the rocks over which the cascade spills have become encrusted with minerals and tinted yellow, green, and purple. Adjacent to the falls, curative mineral baths are fed by the underground springs. For a small fee you can slip into your swimsuit and bathe for 30 minutes in one of the outside pools; a private bath costs slightly more. King Louis XVI of France provided funds in 1784 for the construction of a building with a dozen large stone baths to fortify his troops against the St. Lucian climate. It's claimed that Joséphine Bonaparte bathed here as a young girl while visiting her father's plantation nearby. During the Brigand's War, just after the French Revolution, the bathhouse was destroyed. In 1930 the site was excavated by André Du Boulay, and two of the original stone baths were restored for his use. The outside baths were added later. ⊠ *Soufrière Estate, Soufrière* 🕾 *758/452–4759 or 758/454–7565* 💷 *$2.75, outside bath $2.50, private bath $3.75* ☉ *Mon.–Sat. 10–5, Sun. and holidays 10–3.*

❾ Fond Doux Estate. One of the earliest French estates established by land grant (1745 and 1763), 135 hilly acres of this old plantation still produce cocoa, citrus, bananas, coconut, and vegetables; the restored 1864 plantation house is still in use as well. A 30-minute walking tour begins at the cocoa fermentary, where you can see the drying process underway. You then follow a trail through the lush cultivated area, where a guide points out the various fruit- or spice-bearing trees and tropical flowers. Additional trails lead to old military ruins, a religious shrine, and another vantage point for the spectacular Pitons. Cool drinks and a creole buffet lunch are available at the restaurant. Souvenirs, including just-made chocolate balls, are sold at the boutique. ⊠ *Chateaubelair, Soufrière* 🕾 *758/459–7545* ⊕ *www.fonddouxestate.com* 💷 *$6, buffet lunch $14* ☉ *Daily 9–4.*

☾ ❽ La Soufrière Drive-In Volcano. As you approach, your nose will pick up the strong scent of the sulfur springs—more than 20 belching pools of muddy water, multicolor sulfur deposits, and other assorted minerals baking and steaming on the surface. Actually, you don't drive in. You drive up within a few hundred feet of the gurgling, steaming mass, then walk behind your guide—whose service is included in the admission price—around a fault in the substratum rock. It's a fascinating, educational half hour that can also be pretty stinky on a hot day. ⊠ *Bay St., Soufrière* 🕾 *758/459–5500* 💷 *$1.25* ☉ *Daily 9–5.*

❻ Soufrière. It's a 1½-hour drive on the winding West Coast Road (or a 45-minute boat ride) from Castries to Soufrière, the oldest town in St. Lucia and the former French colonial capital. The town was founded in 1746 and named for its proximity to the volcano. The wharf is the center of activity in this sleepy town (which has a population of about 9,000), particularly when a cruise ship is moored in pretty Soufrière Bay. French-colonial influences can be noticed in the architecture of the wooden buildings, with second-story verandahs and gingerbread trim, that surround the market square. The market building is decorated with colorful murals. The **Soufrière Tourist Information Centre** (✉ Bay St., Soufrière ☎ 758/459–7200) provides information about area attractions.

Shopping

Soufrière is not much of a shopping port, although a small arts-and-crafts center is adjacent to the wharf. The island's best-known products are: artwork and wood carvings; clothing and household articles made from batik and silk-screen fabrics, designed and printed in island workshops; and clay pottery. You can also take home straw hats and baskets and locally grown cocoa, coffee, and spices. The only duty-free shopping is at **Pointe Seraphine** or **La Place Carenage,** on opposite sides of the harbor. You must show your cabin key to get duty-free prices. You'll want to experience the **Castries Market** and scour the adjacent **Vendor's Arcade** and **Craft Market** for handicrafts and souvenirs at bargain prices.

Artsibit Gallery (✉ Brazil and Mongiraud Sts., Castries ☎ 758/452–7865) exhibits and sells moderately priced pieces by St. Lucian painters and sculptors. **Bagshaw Studios** (✉ La Toc Rd., La Toc Bay, Castries ☎ 758/452–2139 or 758/451–9249) sells clothing and table linens in colorful tropical patterns using Stanley Bagshaw's original designs. The fabrics are silk-screened by hand in the adjacent workroom. You can also find Bagshaw boutiques at Pointe Seraphine, La Place Carenage, and Rodney Bay, and a selection of items in gift shops at Hewanorra Airport. Visit the workshop to see how designs are turned into colorful silk-screen fabrics, which are then fashioned into clothing and household articles. It's open weekdays from 8:30 to 5, Saturday 8:30 to 4, and Sunday 10 to 1. Weekend hours may be extended if a cruise ship is in port. At **Caribelle Batik** (✉ La Toc Rd., Morne Fortune, Castries ☎ 758/452–3785), craftspeople demonstrate the art of batik and silk-screen printing. Meanwhile, seamstresses create clothing and wall hangings, which you can purchase in the shop. The studio is in an old Victorian mansion, high atop the Morne overlooking Castries. There's a terrace where you can have a cool drink, and there's a garden full of tropical orchids and lilies. Caribelle Batik creations are featured in many gift shops throughout St. Lucia. **Eudovic Art Studio** (✉ Morne Fortune, Castries ☎ 758/452–2747) is a workshop and studio where you can buy trays, masks, and figures sculpted from local mahogany, red cedar, and eucalyptus wood. **Noah's Arkade** (✉ Jeremie St., Castries ☎ 758/452–2523 ✉ Pointe Seraphine, Castries ☎ 758/452–7488) has hammocks, wood carvings, straw mats, T-shirts, books, and other regional goods.

Sports & Activities

BIKING Although the terrain can get pretty rugged, two tour operators have put together fascinating bicycle and combination bicycle-hiking tours that appeal to novice riders as well as those who enjoy a good workout. Prices range from $60 to $100 per person. **Bike St. Lucia** (✉ Anse Chastanet, Soufrière ☎ 758/451–2453 ⊕ www.bikestlucia.com) takes small groups of bikers on Jungle Biking™ tours along trails that meander through the remnants of an 18th-century plantation near Soufrière. Stops are made to explore the French colonial ruins, study the beautiful tropical plants and fruit trees, enjoy a picnic lunch, and take a dip in a river swimming hole or a swim at the beach. If you're staying in the north, you can get a tour that includes transportation to the Soufrière area. **Island Bike Hikes** (✉ Castries ☎ 758/458–0908 ⊕ www.cyclestlucia.com) is suitable for all fitness levels. Jeep or bus transportation is provided across the central mountains to Dennery, on the east coast. After a 3-mi (5-km) ride through the countryside, bikes are exchanged for shoe leather. The short hike into the rain forest ends with a picnic and a refreshing swim next to a sparkling waterfall—then the return leg to Dennery. All gear is supplied.

DIVING The coral reefs at Anse Cochon and Anse Chastanet, on the southwest coast, are popular beach-entry dive sites. In the north, Pigeon Island is the most convenient site. **Buddies** (✉ Rodney Bay Marina, Rodney Bay ☎ 758/452–8406) offers wall, wreck, reef, and deep dives; resort courses and open-water certification with advanced and specialty courses are taught by PADI-certified instructors. **Dive Fair Helen** (✉ Vigie Marina, Castries ☎ 758/451–7716 or 888/855–2206 in U.S. and Canada ⊕ www.divefairhelen.com) is a PADI center that offers half- and full-day excursions to wreck, wall, and marine reserve areas, as well as night dives. **Scuba St. Lucia** (✉ Anse Chastanet, Soufrière ☎ 758/459–7755 ⊕ www.scubastlucia.com) is a PADI five-star training facility. Daily beach and boat dives and resort and certification courses are offered; underwater photography and snorkeling equipment are available. Day-trips from the north of the island include round-trip speedboat transportation.

FISHING Among the deep-sea creatures you can find in St. Lucia's waters are dolphin (also called dorado or mahimahi), barracuda, mackerel, wahoo, kingfish, sailfish, and white or blue marlin. Sportfishing is generally done on a catch-and-release basis. Neither spearfishing nor collecting live fish in coastal waters is permitted. Half- or full-day deep-sea fishing excursions can be arranged at either Vigie Cove or Rodney Bay Marina. A half-day of fishing on a scheduled trip runs about $80 per person. Beginners are welcome. **Captain Mike's** (✉ Vigie Cove ☎ 758/452–1216 or 758/452–7044 ⊕ www.captmikes.com) has a fleet of Bertram power boats (31- to 38-feet) that accommodate as many as eight passengers; tackle and cold drinks are supplied. **Mako Watersports** (✉ Rodney Bay Marina, Rodney Bay ☎ 758/452–0412) takes fishing enthusiasts out on the well-equipped six-passenger *Annie Baby.*

HIKING The island is laced with trails, but you shouldn't attempt the more challenging ones on your own. The **St. Lucia National Trust** (☎ 758/452–5005 ⊕ www.slunatrust.org) maintains two trails: one is at Anse La Liberté, near Canaries on the Caribbean coast; the other is on the Atlantic coast, from Mandélé Point to the Frégate Islands Nature Reserve. Full-day excursions with lunch cost about $50 to $85 per person and can be arranged through hotels or tour operators. The **St. Lucia Forest & Lands Department** (☎ 758/450–2231 or 758/450–2078) manages trails throughout the rain forest and provides guides who explain the plants and trees you'll encounter and keep you on the right track for a small fee.

HORSEBACK Creole horses, an indigenous breed, are fairly small, fast, sturdy, and
RIDING even-tempered animals suitable for beginners. Established stables can accommodate all skill levels and offer countryside trail rides, beach rides

with picnic lunches, plantation tours, carriage rides, and lengthy treks. Prices run about $40 for one hour, $50 for two hours, and $70 for a three-hour beach ride and barbecue. Transportation is usually provided between the stables and nearby hotels. People sometimes appear on beaches with their steeds and offer 30-minute rides for $10; ride at your own risk. **Country Saddles** (⊠ Marquis Estate, Babonneau ☎ 758/450–5467), 45 minutes east of Castries, guides beginners and advanced riders through banana plantations, forest trails, and along the Atlantic coast. **International Riding Stables** (⊠ Beauséjour Estate, Gros Islet ☎ 758/452–8139 or 758/450–8665) offers either English- or western-style riding. Their beach-picnic ride includes time for a swim—with or without your horse. **Trim's National Riding Stable** (⊠ Cas-en-Bas, Gros Islet ☎ 758/452–8273 or 758/450–9971), the island's oldest establishment, offers four riding sessions per day, plus beach tours, trail rides, and carriage tours to Pigeon Island.

Beaches

All of St. Lucia's beaches are open to the public, but resorts are sometimes less than welcoming to large groups of cruise-ship passengers. **Anse Chastanet,** in front of the resort of the same name, is just north of Soufrière. This palm-studded dark-sand beach has a backdrop of green hills, brightly painted fishing skiffs bobbing at anchor, and the island's best reefs for snorkeling and diving. The resort's wooden gazebos are nestled among the palms; its dive shop, restaurant, and bar are on the beach and open to the public, but unless you are with a group, a taxi ride may be prohibitively expensive. At **Pigeon Point,** a small beach within Pigeon Island National Historic Park, a restaurant serves snacks and drinks, but this is also a perfect spot for picnicking. It's about a 30-minute taxi ride ($20) from Pointe Seraphine. **Reduit Beach,** a long stretch of golden sand, is next to Rodney Bay. The Rex St. Lucian Hotel, which faces the beach, has a water-sports center. Many feel that Reduit (pronounced red-*wee*) is the island's finest beach.

Where to Eat

An 8% government tax is applicable to your bill, and most restaurants add a 10% service charge in lieu of tip.

$$ ✕ **The Coal Pot.** Popular since the early 1960s, this tiny (only 10 tables) waterfront restaurant overlooking pretty Vigie Cove is managed by Michelle Elliott, noted artist and daughter of the original owner, and her French husband, Chef Xavier. For a light lunch opt for Greek or shrimp salad, or broiled fresh fish with creole sauce. Dinner might start with divine lobster bisque, followed by fresh seafood accompanied by one (or more) of the chef's fabulous sauces—ginger, coconut-curry, lemon–garlic butter, or wild mushroom. Hearty eaters may prefer duck, lamb, beef, or chicken laced with peppercorns, red wine, and onion or Roquefort sauce. ⊠ Vigie Marina, Castries ☎ 758/452–5566 ⚏ Reservations essential ▭ AE, D, MC, V ☉ Closed Sun. No lunch Sat.

$–$$ ✕ **Lifeline Restaurant at The Hummingbird.** Cajou, the chef at this cheerful restaurant-bar in the Hummingbird Beach Resort, specializes in French creole cuisine, starting with fresh seafood or chicken seasoned with local herbs and accompanied by a medley of vegetables just picked from the Hummingbird's garden. Sandwiches and salads are also available. If you stop for lunch, be sure to visit the batik studio and art gallery of proprietor Joan Alexander and her son, adjacent to the dining room. ⊠ *Hummingbird Beach Resort, Anse Chastanet Rd., Soufrière* ☎ *758/ 459–7232* ⊟ *AE, D, MC, V.*

St. Martin/St. Maarten

St. Martin/St. Maarten: one tiny island, just 37 square mi (59 square km), with two different accents, and ruled by two sovereign nations. Here French and Dutch have lived side by side for hundreds of years, and when you cross from one country to the next there are no border patrols, no customs. In fact, the only indication that you have crossed a border at all is a small sign and a change in road surface.

St. Martin/St. Maarten epitomizes tourist islands in the sun, where services are well developed but there's still some Caribbean flavor. The Dutch side is ideal for people who like plenty to do. The French side has a more genteel ambience, more fashionable shopping, and a Continental flair. The combination makes an almost ideal port. On the negative side, the island has been completely developed. There's gambling, but table limits are so low that high rollers will have a better time gamboling on the beach. It can be fun to shop, and you'll find an occasional bargain, but many goods are cheaper in the United States.

Though Dutch is the official language of St. Maarten, and French of St. Martin, almost everyone speaks English. If you hear a language you can't quite place, it's most likely Papiamento, a Spanish-based Creole.

CURRENCY Legal tender on the Dutch side is the Netherlands Antilles florin (guilder), written NAf; on the French side, the official currency is the euro (€). There's little need to exchange money. On the Dutch side, prices are usually given in both NAf and U.S. dollars, and dollars are accepted all over the island. On the French side, you may get your change in euros, but the island is very popular with Americans, so you'll sometimes even get dollars in return.

TELEPHONES To phone from the Dutch side to the French, you first must dial (00–590–590) for local numbers, or (00–590–690) for cell phones, then the six-digit local number. To call from the French side to the Dutch, dial "00–599" then the seven-digit local number. Remember that a call from one side to the other is an international call.

At the Landsradio in Philipsburg, there are facilities for overseas calls and a USADirect phone, where you're directly in touch with an operator who will accept collect or credit-card calls. To call direct with an AT&T credit card or operator, dial 001–800/872–2881. On the French side, AT&T can be accessed by calling 080–099–00–11. If you need to use public phones, go to the special desk at Marigot's post office and buy a *télécarte*. There's a public phone at the tourist office in Marigot where you can make credit-card calls: the operator takes your card number (any major card) and assigns you a PIN (Personal Identification Number), which you then use to charge calls to your card.

The following are good choices in St. Martin/St. Maarten. They may not be offered by all cruise lines. Times and prices are approximate.

Beach Sojourn. A short bus ride takes you from the pier on the Dutch side of St. Martin to Orient Beach on the island's French side. Often referred to as the French Riviera of the Caribbean, it's a lively beach where you will find restaurants, bars, lounge chairs, and umbrellas. Lunch and drinks are included. ☉ *4½ hrs* ▭ *$45–$60.*

America's Cup Sailing Regatta. Join your crew aboard an authentic 12-meter, multi-million dollar America's Cup yacht and participate in a race around an "America's Cup" course. Either sit back and watch or join in to grind a winch, trim the sails, or take the helm after instructions from the crew. This is one of the most popular shore excursions, so book it as far in advance as possible. ☉ *3 hrs* ▭ *$69–$89.*

Butterfly Farm. Tour the island's butterfly farm and stop in Marigot on the French side for shopping and a stroll along the waterfront. ☉ *3½ hrs* ▭ *$32–$39.*

Under Two Flags. This bus tour includes the island's highlights from the Dutch capital of Philipsburg to the French side's capital of Marigot with a stop at Hope Hill for the view and a drink. ☉ *3½ hrs* ▭ *$20–$29.*

Coming Ashore

Most cruise ships drop anchor off the Dutch capital of Philipsburg or dock in the marina at the southern tip of the Philipsburg harbor. If your ship anchors, tenders will ferry you to the town pier in the middle of town, where taxis await passengers. If your ship docks at the marina, downtown is a 15-minute taxi ride away. The walk is not recommended. To get to major sights outside of Philipsburg or Marigot, your best bet is a tour via taxi; negotiate the rate before you get in. A 2½-hour to 3-hour tour of the island for two people should be about $30, plus $10 per additional person. No place on the island is more than a 30-minute drive from Marigot or Philipsburg. Car-rental rates are moderate, starting at as little as $25 a day during the low season, and you do not need a temporary driving permit.

Taxis are government-regulated and fairly costly. Authorized taxis display stickers of the St. Maarten Taxi Association. Taxis are also available at Marigot.

Exploring St. Martin/St. Maarten

Numbers in the margin correspond to points of interest on the St. Martin/St. Maarten map.

❹ Butterfly Farm. Visitors enter a serene, tropical environment when they walk through the terrariumlike Butterfly Sphere amid dozens of colorful butterfly varieties at the farm. At any given time, some 40 species of butterflies, numbering as many as 600, flutter inside the garden under a tented net. Butterfly art and memorabilia are for sale in the gift shop. In case you want to come back, your ticket, which includes a guided tour, is good for your entire stay. ⊠ *Rte. de Le Galion, Quartier d'Orleans* ☎ *590/87–31–21* ⊕ *www.thebutterflyfarm.com* ▭ *$12* ☉ *Daily 9–3:30.*

❻ French Cul de Sac. North of Orient Bay Beach, the French-colonial mansion of St. Martin's mayor is nestled in the hills. Little red-roof houses

St. Martin/
St. Maarten

TO ANGUILLA

TO ST. BARTHÉLEMY →

KEY

Beaches
Cruise Ship Terminal
Dive Sites
Ferry

look like open umbrellas tumbling down the green hillside. The area is peaceful and good for hiking. There's construction, however, as the surroundings are slowly being developed. From the beach here, shuttle boats make the five-minute trip to **Ilet Pinel,** an uninhabited island that's fine for picnicking, sunning, and swimming.

❼ Grand Case. The island's most picturesque town is set in the heart of the French side on a beach at the foot of green hills and pastures. Though it has only a 1-mi-long (1½-km-long) main street, it's known as the "restaurant capital of the Caribbean." More than 27 restaurants serve French, Italian, Indonesian, and Vietnamese fare here. The budget-minded love the half-dozen *lolos*—kiosks at the far end of town that sell savory barbecue and seafood. Grand Case Beach Club is at the end of this road and has two beaches where you can take a dip.

❷ Guana Bay Point. On the rugged, windswept east coast about 10 minutes north of Philipsburg, Guana Bay Point offers isolated, untended beaches and a spectacular view of St. Barths. However, because of the undercurrent this should be more of a turf than a surf destination.

❽ Le Fort Louis. Though not much remains of the structure itself, the fort, completed by the French in 1789, commands a sweeping view of

Marigot, its harbor, and the English island of Anguilla, which alone makes it worth the climb. There are few signs to show the way, so the best way to find the fort is to go to Marigot and look up. ⊠ *Marigot.*

❾ Marigot. This town has a southern European flavor, especially its beautiful harborfront, with shopping stalls, open-air cafés, and fresh-food vendors. It's well worth a few hours to explore if you're a shopper, a gourmand, or just a Francophile. Marina Royale is the shopping complex at the port, but rue de la République and rue de la Liberté, which border the bay, are also filled with duty-free shops, boutiques, and bistros. The West Indies Mall offers a deluxe shopping experience. There's less bustle here than in Philipsburg, and the open-air cafés are tempting places to sit and people-watch. Marigot doesn't die at night, so you might wish to stay here into the evening—particularly on Wednesday, when the market opens its art, crafts, and souvenir stalls, and on Thursday, when the shops of Marina Royale remain open until 10 and shoppers enjoy live music. From the harborfront you can catch the ferry for Anguilla or St. Barths. Overlooking the town is Le Fort Louis, from which you get a breathtaking, panoramic view of Marigot and the surrounding area. Every Wednesday and Saturday at the foot of Le Fort Louis, there's an open-air food market where fresh fish, produce, fruits, and spices are sold and crowds sample the goods. Parking can be a real challenge during the business day and even at night during the high season. The small, ambitious **Musée de Saint-Martin** (St. Martin Museum), south of town is a treasure for anyone interested in the history and archaeology of the island. It has artifacts from the island's pre-Columbian days. Included are pottery exhibits, rock carvings, and petroglyphs, a 1,500-year-old burial, pictures of early-20th-century St. Martin as well as displays from colonial and sugar-plantation days. Upstairs is a small art gallery, where you can find locally produced art, including lithographs and posters. ⊠ *Terres-Basses Rd., Marigot* ☎ *590/29–48–36* ☜ *$5* ⊙ *Mon.–Sat. 9–1 and 3–6.*

❸ Orléans. North of Oyster Pond and the Étang aux Poissons (Fish Lake) is the island's oldest settlement, also known as the French Quarter. You can find classic, vibrantly painted West Indian–style homes with elaborate gingerbread fretwork.

❶ Philipsburg. The capital of Dutch St. Maarten stretches about a mile (1½ km) along an isthmus between Great Bay and the Salt Pond and has five parallel streets. Most of the village's dozens of shops and restaurants are on Front Street, narrow and cobblestoned, closest to Great Bay. It's generally congested when cruise ships are in port. It features many duty-free shops and several casinos. Little lanes called *steegjes* connect Front Street with Back Street, which has fewer shops and considerably less congestion.

Wathey Square (pronounced watty), is in the heart of the village. Directly across from the square are the town hall and the courthouse, in the striking white building with the cupola. The structure was built in 1793 and has served as the commander's home, a fire station, a jail, and a post office. The streets surrounding the square are lined with hotels, duty-free shops, fine restaurants, and cafés. The **Captain Hodge Pier,**

just off the square, is a good spot to view Great Bay and the beach that stretches alongside. The **Sint Maarten Museum** hosts rotating cultural exhibits and a permanent historical display called Forts of St. Maarten–St. Martin. The artifacts range from Arawak pottery shards to objects salvaged from the wreck of the HMS *Proselyte*. ⊠ *7 Front St., Philipsburg* ☎ *599/542–4917* ✆ *Free* ☉ *Weekdays 10–4, Sat. 10–2.*

❺ **Pic du Paradis.** From Friar's Bay Beach, a bumpy, tree-canopied road leads inland to this peak. At 1,492 feet, it's the island's highest point. There are two observation areas. From them, the tropical forest unfolds below and the vistas are breathtaking. The road is quite isolated, so it's best to travel in groups. It's also quite steep and not in particularly good shape, becoming a single lane as you near the summit; if you don't have a four-wheel-drive vehicle, you will not make it. Parking at the top is iffy, and it's best if you turn around before you park. It may not be so easy later. Near the bottom of Pic du Paradis is **Loterie Farm,** a peaceful 150-acre private nature preserve opened to the public in 1999 by American expat B. J. Welch. Designed to preserve island habitats, Loterie Farm offers a rare glimpse of Caribbean forest and mountain land. Welch has renovated an old farmhouse and welcomes visitors for horseback riding, hiking, mountain biking, ecotours, or less-strenuous activities, such as meditation and yoga. The Hidden Forest Café is open for lunch and dinner Tuesday through Sunday. ⊠ *Rte. de Pic du Paradis* ☎ *590/87–86–16* ⊕ *www.loteriefarm.com* ✆ *$5, 1½-hr tour $25, 4-hr tour $45* ☉ *Daily sunrise–sunset.*

Shopping

It's true that the island sparkles with its myriad outdoor activities—diving, snorkeling, sailing, swimming, and sunning—but shopaholics are drawn to sparkle within the jewelry stores. The huge array of such stores is almost unrivaled in the Caribbean. In addition, duty-free shops offer substantial savings—about 15% to 30% below U.S. and Canadian prices—on cameras, watches, liquor, cigars, and designer clothing. It's no wonder that each year 500 cruise ships make Philipsburg a port of call. On both sides of the island, be alert for idlers. They can snatch unwatched purses.

Philipsburg's **Front Street** has reinvented itself. Now it's mall-like, with redbrick walk and streets, palm trees lining the sleek boutiques, jewelry stores, souvenir shops, outdoor restaurants, and the old reliables—including McDonald's and Burger King. Here and there a school or a church appears to remind visitors there's more to the island than shopping. On Back Street is the **Philipsburg Market Place,** an open-air market where you can haggle for bargains on items such as handicrafts, souvenirs, and cover-ups. **Old Street,** near the end of Front Street, has stores, boutiques, and open-air cafés offering French crêpes, rich chocolates, and island mementos. You can find an outlet mall amid the more upscale shops at the **Maho** shopping plaza. The **Plaza del Lago** at the Simpson Bay Yacht Club complex has an excellent choice of restaurants as well as shops.

On the French side, wrought-iron balconies, colorful awnings, and gingerbread trim decorate Marigot's smart shops, tiny boutiques, and bistros in the **Marina Royale** complex and on the main streets, **rue de la Liberté** and **rue de la République**. Also in Marigot is the pricey **West Indies Mall** and the **Plaza Caraibes,** which houses designer shops like Hermès and Ralph Lauren.

Sports & Activities

DIVING & SNORKELING Although St. Maarten is not known as a dive destination, the water temperature here is rarely below 70°F, and visibility is usually excellent, averaging about 100 feet (30 m). For snorkelers, the area around Orient Bay, Caye Verte (Green Key), Ilet Pinel, and Flat Island is especially lovely and is officially classified, and protected, as a regional underwater nature reserve. You can take a half-day snorkeling trip for around $25. On the Dutch side, **Dive Safaris** (⊠ Bobby's Marina, Yrausquin Blvd., Philipsburg ☎ 599/544–9001 ⊕ www.thescubashop.net) is a full-service outfit for divers. SSI- (Scuba Schools International) and PADI-certified dive centers include **Ocean Explorers Dive Shop** (⊠ 113 Welfare Rd., Simpson Bay ☎ 599/544–5252 ⊕ www.stmaartendiving.com).

On the French side, **Blue Ocean** (⊠ Sandy Ground Rd., Baie Nettlé ☎ 590/87–89–73) is a PADI-certified dive center that also offers regularly scheduled snorkeling trips. Arrange equipment rentals and snorkeling trips through **Kontiki Watersports** (⊠ Northern beach entrance, Baie Orientale ☎ 590/87–46–89 ⊕ www.sxm-game.com). **Octoplus** (⊠ Bd. de Grand Case, Grand Case ☎ 590/87–20–62) is a complete PADI-certified dive center. **O2 Limits** (⊠ Blvd. de Grand Case, Grand Case ☎ 690/50–04–00 ⊕ www.o2limits.com), in the Grand Case Beach Club, is PADI-certified.

FISHING You can angle for yellowtail snapper, grouper, marlin, tuna, and wahoo on deep-sea excursions. Costs (for four people) range from $425 for a half day, a full day from $750. Prices usually include bait and tackle, instruction for novices, and refreshments. Ask about licensing and insurance. **Big Sailfish Too** (⊠ Marigot waterfront ☎ 690/27–11–12) is your best bet on the French side of the island. **Lee's Deepsea Fishing** (⊠ 84 Welfare Rd., Simpson Bay ☎ 599/544–4233 or 599/544–4234) organizes excursions, and when you return, Lee's Roadside Grill will cook your catch: tuna, wahoo, or whatever. **Rudy's Deep Sea Fishing** (⊠ 14 Airport Rd., Simpson Bay ☎ 599/545–2177 ⊕ www.rudysdeepseafishing.com) has been around for years and is one of the more experienced sport angling outfits.

GOLF St. Maarten is not a golf destination. Although **Mullet Bay Golf Course** (⊠ Airport Rd., north of the airport ☎ 599/545–3069), on the Dutch side, is an 18-hole course—the island's *only* one, it's in very poor shape and not worth the trouble or cost.

Beaches

The island's 10 mi (16 km) of beaches are all open to cruise-ship passengers. On beaches owned by resorts, you might be charged a small fee (about $3) for access to changing facilities. Water-sports equipment can be rented at most hotels. Topless bathing is common on the French side. If you take a cab to a remote beach, be sure to arrange a specific time for the driver to return for you. Don't leave valuables unattended on the beach or in a rental car, even in the trunk.

The nice, well-maintained beach at **Baie des Friars** is at the end of a poorly maintained dirt road. On a small, picturesque cove between Marigot and Grand Case, it attracts a casual crowd of locals and a couple of good beachside restaurants. Getting to secluded **Baie Longue**, a mile-long curve of white sand on the island's westernmost tip, requires a bumpy, 10-minute, we-must-be-lost drive off the main road, with just one small, unmarked entry down to the water. Though the beach is gravelly in places, this is a good place for snorkeling and swimming, but beware of a strong undertow when the waters are rough. If you want privacy, visit this isolated spot. There are no facilities or vendors. By far the most beautiful beach on the island, mile-long **Baie Orientale** has something for everyone, with its clean white sand, clear blue water, and an assortment of beach bars serving Mexican, Caribbean, American, and even kosher fare. There are plenty of places to rent equipment for water activities. The north end tends to be conservative and family oriented, while the far south is almost exclusively for nudists. A protected nature reserve, kid-friendly **Ilet Pinel** is a five-minute ferry ride from French Cul de Sac ($5 per person round-trip). The water is clear and shallow, and the shore is sheltered. If you like snorkeling, don your gear and swim along both sides of the coasts of this pencil-shape speck in the ocean. Food is available at the isle's two restaurants.

Where to Eat

Restaurants on the French side often figure a service charge into the menu prices. On the Dutch side, most restaurants add 10% to 15% to the bill. You can, if so moved by exceptional service, leave a tip.

$$–$$$$ ✕ **Claude Mini-Club.** This brightly decorated upstairs restaurant, with a sweeping view of Marigot Harbor, has served traditional creole and French cuisine since the 1970s. The chairs and madras tablecloths are a mélange of sun-yellow and orange, and the whole place is built (tree house–style) around the trunks of coconut trees. It's the place to be on Wednesday and Saturday nights, when the dinner buffet includes roast pig, lobster, roast beef, and all the trimmings. ⊠ *Front de Mer, Marigot* ☎ *590/87-50-69* ▤ *AE, MC, V* ☉ *No lunch Sun.*

$$ ✕ **Chesterfield's.** On the Great Bay waterfront, a five-minute walk from the ship pier in Philipsburg, nautically themed "Chesty's" serves breakfast, lunch, and dinner at reasonable prices. The main fare is steak and seafood, though the dinner menu includes French onion soup, roast duckling with fresh pineapple and banana sauce, and several different shrimp dishes. The Mermaid Bar is popular with yachties. ⊠ *Great Bay Marina, Philipsburg* ☎ *599/542–3484* ▤ *MC, V.*

St. Thomas & St. John, U.S. Virgin Islands

St. Thomas is the busiest cruise port of call in the world. Up to eight giant ships may visit in a single day. Don't expect an exotic island experience: one of the three U.S. Virgin Islands (with St. Croix and St. John), St. Thomas is as American as any place on the mainland, complete with McDonald's and HBO. The positive side of all this development is that there are more tours here than anywhere else in the Caribbean, and every year the excursions get better. Of course, shopping is the big draw in Charlotte Amalie, but experienced travelers remember the days of "real" bargains. Today, so many passengers fill the stores that it's a seller's market. One of St. Thomas's best tourist attractions is its neighboring island, St. John, with its beautiful Virgin Islands National Park and beaches.

CURRENCY   The U.S. dollar is the official currency of St. Thomas and St. John.

TELEPHONES   It's as easy to call home from St. Thomas and St. John as from any city in the United States. On St. Thomas, public phones are easily found, and AT&T has a telecommunications center across from the Havensight Mall. On St. John, public phones are in front of the post office, east of the tender landing, and at the ferry dock.

SHORE
EXCURSIONS   The following are good choices on St. Thomas and St. John. They may not be offered by all cruise lines. Times and prices are approximate.

Helmet Dive. This is a unique diving opportunity for non-divers at Coral World Marine Park, using helmets that provide oxygen as you walk along the bottom of the sea. Afterwards, you can also visit the aquarium. ⊙ 3 hrs. ▭ $99.

Kayaking & Snorkeling Tour. Paddle your kayak through a marine sanctuary as your guide narrates both the above- and underwater scenery. ⊙ 3½ hrs ▭ $60–$79.

Sailing the Virgin Islands. Sail aboard a private yacht with a small group to Turtle Cove on St. Thomas's own Buck Island for snorkeling and swimming to view a sunken ship, tropical fish, and coral. ⊙ 4 hrs ▭ $50–$60.

St. John Eco Hike. After a ferry ride to St. John, you hike approximately 1¼ mi (3 km) to Linde Point and then to Honeymoon Beach for a swim. Continue on to Caneel Bay to visit some ruins before returning to the ferry landing by safari van. ⊙ 5 hrs ▭ $59–$64.

St. John Island Tour. Either your ship tenders you to St. John before docking in St. Thomas or you are transferred to the St. Thomas ferry dock in for the ride to St. John. On St. John, an open-air safari bus winds through the national park to a beach for snorkeling, swimming, and sunbathing. (If you have the option, you might avoid the often-crowded beach at Trunk Bay.) ⊙ 4½ hrs ▭ $39–$49.

Coming Ashore

Depending on how many ships are in port, cruise ships drop anchor in the harbor at Charlotte Amalie and tender passengers directly to the waterfront duty-free shops, dock at the Havensight Mall at the eastern end of the crescent-shaped bay, or dock at Crown Bay Marina a few miles west of town. The distance from Havensight to the duty-free shops is 1½ mi (3 km), which can be walked in less than half an hour, or a taxi costs $3 per person (all taxis are per-person and hold multiple passengers). Tourist information offices are at the Havensight Mall (across from Building No. 1) for docking passengers and downtown near Fort Christian (at the eastern end of the waterfront shopping area) for those coming ashore by tender. Both offices distribute free maps. From Crown Bay, it's also a half-hour walk or a $3 per person cab ride.

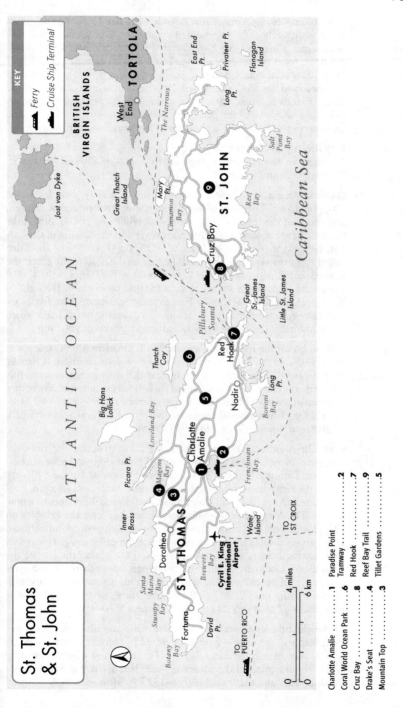

St. Thomas & St. John

KEY

🚢 Ferry
🚢 Cruise Ship Terminal

ATLANTIC OCEAN

BRITISH VIRGIN ISLANDS

Jost van Dyke

Great Thatch Island

TORTOLA

West End

The Narrows

East End Pt.

Long Pt.

Privateer Pt.

Flanagan Island

ST. JOHN

Mary Pt.

Cinnamon Bay

Reef Bay

Salt Pond Bay

❾

Cruz Bay

❽

Caribbean Sea

Pillsbury Sound

Great St. James Island

Little St. James Island

❼ Red Hook

Thatch Cay

❻

❺

Nadir

Boron Bay

Long Pt.

Loveland Bay

Big Hans Lollick

Picara Pt.

Magens Bay

❹

❸

Charlotte Amalie

❷

❶

Frenchman Bay

Inner Brass

Dorothea

ST. THOMAS

Water Island

Cyril E. King International Airport

TO ST CROIX

Santa Maria Bay

Stumpy Bay

David Pt.

Fortuna

Brewers Bay

Botany Bay

TO PUERTO RICO

0 ⊢⎯⎯⎯⎯⎯⊣ 4 miles
0 ⊢⎯⎯⎯⎯⎯⊣ 6 km

In St. John, your ship may pause outside Cruz Bay Harbor to drop you off or drop anchor if it's spending the day. You'll be tendered to shore at the main town of Cruz Bay. The shopping district starts just across the street from the tender landing. You'll find an eclectic collection of shops, cozy restaurants, and places where you can just sit and take it all in. The island has few sights to see. Your best bet is to take a tour of the Virgin Islands National Park. (If your ship doesn't offer such a tour, arrange one with one of the taxi drivers who will meet your tender.) The drive takes you past luscious beaches to a restored sugar plantation.

Exploring St. Thomas

Numbers in the margin correspond to points of interest on the St. Thomas & St. John map.

❶ Charlotte Amalie. St. Thomas's major burg is a hilly, overdeveloped shopping town. There are plenty of interesting historic sights, though, and much of the town is quite pretty—so while you're shopping, take the time to see at least a few. For a great view of the town and the harbor, begin at the Spanish-style Hotel 1829, on Government Hill (also called Kongens Gade). A few yards farther up the road to the east is the base of the 99 Steps, a staircase "street" built by the Danes in the 1700s. Go up the steps (there are more than 99) and continue to the right to Blackbeard's Castle, originally Fort Skytsborg. The massive five-story watchtower was built in 1679. It's now a dramatic perch from which to sip a drink, admire the harbor, and snap a photo of your ship.

Built to honor the freeing of slaves in 1848, **Emancipation Garden** was the site of a 150th anniversary celebration of emancipation. A bronze bust of a freed slave blowing a symbolic conch shell commemorates this anniversary. The gazebo here is used for official ceremonies. Two other monuments show the island's Danish-American tie—a bust of Denmark's King Christian and a scaled-down model of the U.S. Liberty Bell. ⊠ *Between Tolbod Gade and Fort Christian.*

Fort Christian, St. Thomas's oldest standing structure, anchors the shopping district. It was built between 1672 and 1680 and now has U.S. National Landmark status. The clock tower was added in the 19th century. This remarkable building has, over time, been used as a jail, governor's residence, town hall, courthouse, and church. Fort Christian now houses **The Virgin Islands Museum,** where you can see exhibits on USVI history, natural history, and turn-of-the-20th-century furnishings. Local artists display their works monthly in the gallery. A gift shop sells local crafts, books, and other souvenirs. This is also the site of the Chamber of Commerce's Hospitality Lounge, where there are public restrooms, and brochures. The fort is closed for a year-long renovation at this writing until 2006. ⊠ *Waterfront Hwy., east of shopping district* ☎ *340/776–4566* ⊠ *Free* ⊙ *Weekdays 8:30–4:30.*

Frederick Lutheran Church has a massive mahogany altar, and its pews—each with its own door—were once rented to families of the congregation. Lutheranism is the state religion of Denmark, and when the territory was without a minister the governor—who had his own elevated pew—filled in. ⊠ *Norre Gade* ☎ *340/776–1315* ⊙ *Mon.–Sat. 9–4.*

Built in 1867, **Government House,** a neoclassical white brick-and-wood structure, houses the offices for the governor of the Virgin Islands. Inside, the staircases are of native mahogany, as are the plaques hand-lettered in gold with the names of the governors appointed and, since 1970, elected. Brochures detailing the history of the building are available, but you may have to ask for them. ⊠ *Government Hill* ☎ *340/774–0294* 🖀 *Free* ⊙ *Weekdays 8–5.*

The pastoral-looking lime-green exterior of the **Legislature Building** conceals the vociferous political wrangling of the Virgin Islands Senate going on inside. Constructed originally by the Danish as a police barracks, the building was later used to billet U.S. Marines, and much later it housed a public school. You're welcome to sit in on sessions in the upstairs chambers. ⊠ *Waterfront Hwy., across from Fort Christian* ☎ *340/774–0880* ⊙ *Daily 8–5.*

❻ Coral World Ocean Park. Coral World has an offshore underwater observatory that houses the Predator Tank, one of the world's largest coral-reef tanks, and an aquarium with more than 20 portholes providing close-ups of Caribbean sea life. *Sea Trekkin'* lets you tour the reef outside the park at a depth of 15 feet, thanks to specialized high-tech headgear and a continuous air supply that's based on the surface. A guide leads the ½-hour tour and the narration is piped through a specialized microphone inside each trekker's helmet; the minimum age to participate is eight years. The park also has several outdoor pools where you can touch starfish, pet a baby shark, feed stingrays, and view endangered sea turtles. In addition there's a mangrove lagoon and a nature trail full of lush tropical flora. Daily feedings and talks take place at most every exhibit. ⊠ *Coki Point, turn north off Rte. 38 at sign, Estate Frydendal* ☎ *340/775–1555* ⊕ *www.coralworldvi.com* 🖀 *$18, Sea Trekkin' $50* ⊙ *Daily 9–5.*

❹ Drake's Seat. Sir Francis Drake was supposed to have kept watch over his fleet and looked for enemy ships from this vantage point. The panorama is especially breathtaking (and romantic) at dusk, and if you arrive late in the day you can miss the hordes of day-trippers on taxi tours who stop here to take a picture and buy a T-shirt from one of the many vendors. ⊠ *Rte. 40, Estate Zufriedenheit.*

❸ Mountain Top. Stop here for a banana daiquiri and spectacular views from the observation deck more than 1,500 feet above sea level. There are also shops that sell everything from Caribbean art to nautical antiques, ship models, and T-shirts. Kids will like talking to the parrots—and hearing them answer back. ⊠ *Head north off Rte. 33, look for signs* ⊕ *www. greathouse-mountaintop.com.*

❷ Paradise Point Tramway. Fly skyward in a gondola to Paradise Point, an overlook with breathtaking views of Charlotte Amalie and the harbor. There are several shops, a bar, restaurant, and a wedding gazebo; kids enjoy the tropical bird show held daily at 10:30 AM and 1:30 PM. A ¼-mi (½-km) hiking trail leads to spectacular views of St. Croix to the south. Wear sturdy shoes; the trail is steep and rocky. ⊠ *Rte. 30 across from*

Havensight Mall, Charlotte Amalie ☎ 340/774–9809 ⊕ *www. paradisepointtramway.com* 🎫 *$16* ⊘ *Thurs.–Tues. 9–5, Wed. 9–9.*

❼ Red Hook. In this nautical center there are fishing and sailing charter boats, dive shops, and powerboat-rental agencies at the American Yacht Harbor marina. There are also several bars and restaurants, including Molly Molone's, Duffy's Love Shack, and Off the Hook. One grocery store and two delis offer picnic fixings—from sliced meats and cheeses to rotisserie-cooked chickens, prepared salads, and freshly baked breads.

❺ Tillett Gardens. East of Charlotte Amalie, Tillett Gardens is an oasis of artistic endeavor across from the Tutu Park Shopping Mall. The late Jim Tillett and then-wife Rhoda converted this old Danish farm into an artists' retreat in 1959. Today you can watch artisans produce silk-screen fabrics, pottery, candles, watercolors, jewelry, and other handicrafts. Something special is often happening in the gardens: there's a Classics in the Gardens music series, and the Pistarckle Theater performs here. ✉ *Rte. 38.*

Exploring St. John

St. John's best sights are preserved in the sprawling Virgin Islands National Park, which covers most of the island. Stunning vistas and beaches can be reached by taxi tour or car. If you want to spend a relaxing day, head for Cinnamon Bay, which is a bit less frantic than the more popular Trunk Bay. This National Park Service campground has a beach with water-sports equipment for rent, hiking, a modest restaurant, and cool showers.

❽ Cruz Bay. St. John's main town may be compact (it consists of only several blocks), but it's definitely a hub: the ferries from St. Thomas and the BVI pull in here, and it's where you can get a taxi or rent a car to travel around the island. There are plenty of shops in which to browse, a number of watering holes where you can stop for a breather, many restaurants, and a grassy square with benches where you can sit back and take everything in. Look for the current edition of the handy, amusing "St. John Map" featuring Max the Mongoose. To pick up a handy guide to St. John's hiking trails, see various large maps of the island, and find out about current park service programs, including guided walks and cultural demonstrations, stop by the **V. I. National Park Visitors Center** (✉ In an area known as the Creek, near Cruz Bay bulkhead and baseball field, Cruz Bay ☎ 340/776–6201 ⊕ www.nps.gov/viis). It's open daily from 8 to 4:30.

❾ Reef Bay Trail. Although this is one of the most interesting hikes on St. John, unless you're a rugged individualist who wants a physical challenge (and that describes a lot of people who stay on St. John), you can probably get the most out of the trip if you join a hike led by a park service ranger, who can identify the trees and plants on the hike down, fill you in on the history of the Reef Bay Plantation, and tell you about the petroglyphs on the rocks at the bottom of the trail. A side trail takes you to the Reef Bay Plantation greathouse, a gutted, but mostly intact structure that maintains vestiges of its former beauty. If you're without a car, take a taxi or the public Vitran bus from the Cruz Bay ferry dock to the trailhead on Route 10, where you can meet a ranger for the hike downhill. A boat will take you to Cruz Bay, saving you the uphill return climb. ⊠ *Rte. 10, Reef Bay* ☎ *340/776–6201 Ext. 238 reservations* ⊕ *www.nps.gov/viis* 🖂 *Free, return boat trip to Cruz Bay $15* ⊙ *Tours at 10* AM, *days change seasonally.*

Shopping

ST. THOMAS The prime shopping area in **Charlotte Amalie** is between Post Office and Market squares; it consists of three parallel streets that run east–west (Waterfront Highway, Main Street, and Back Street) and the alleyways that connect them. Particularly attractive are the historic **A. H. Riise Alley, Royal Dane Mall, Palm Passage,** and pastel-painted **International Plaza**—quaint alleys between Main Street and the Waterfront.

Vendors Plaza, on the waterfront side of Emancipation Gardens in Charlotte Amalie, is a central location for vendors selling handmade earrings, necklaces, and bracelets; straw baskets and handbags; T-shirts; fabrics; African artifacts; and local fruits. Look for the many brightly colored umbrellas.

West of Charlotte Amalie, the pink-stucco **Nisky Center,** on Harwood Highway about ½ mi (¾ km) east of the airport, is more of a hometown shopping center than a tourist area, but there's a bank, pharmacy, record shop, and Radio Shack.

Havensight Mall, next to the cruise-ship dock, may not be as charming as downtown Charlotte Amalie, but it does have more than 60 shops. It has an excellent bookstore, a bank, a pharmacy, a gourmet grocery, and smaller branches of many downtown stores. The shops at **Port of Sale,** which adjoins the Havensight Mall (its buildings are pink instead of the brown of the Havensight shops), sell discount goods.

Don't forget **St. John.** A ferry ride (an hour from Charlotte Amalie or 20 minutes from Red Hook) will take you to the charming shops of **Mongoose Junction** and **Wharfside Village,** which specialize in unusual, often island-made articles.

Shopping maps are available at the tourist offices and often from your ship's shore-excursion desk. U.S. citizens can carry back a gallon, or six "fifths," of liquor duty-free.

A. H. Riise Liquors (⊠ 37 Main St., at Riise's Alley, Charlotte Amalie ☎ 340/776–2303 ⊠ Havensight Mall, Bldg. I, Rte. 30, Charlotte Amalie ☎ 340/776–7713) offers a large selection of tobacco (including imported cigars), as well as cordials, wines, and rare vintage Armagnacs, cognacs, ports, and Madeiras. It also stocks fruits in brandy and barware from England. Enjoy rum samples at the tasting bar. The wine selection is large at warehouse-style **Al Cohen's Discount Liquor** (⊠ Rte. 30 across from Havensight Mall, Charlotte Amalie ☎ 340/774–3690).

Caribbean Marketplace (⊠ Havensight Mall, Rte. 30, Charlotte Amalie ☎ 340/776–5400) is a great place to buy handicrafts from the Caribbean and elsewhere. Also look for Sunny Caribee spices, soaps, coffee, and teas from Tortola, and coffee from Trinidad. **Down Island Traders** (⊠ Waterfront Hwy. at Post Office Alley, Charlotte Amalie ☎ 340/776–4641) carries hand-painted calabash bowls; finely printed Caribbean note cards; jams, jellies, spices, hot sauces, and herbs; teas made of lemongrass, passion fruit, and mango; coffee from Jamaica; and handicrafts from throughout the Caribbean.

Little Switzerland (✉ 5 Dronningens Gade, across from Emancipation Garden, Charlotte Amalie ☎ 340/776–2010 ✉ 3B Main St., Charlotte Amalie ☎ 340/776–2010 ✉ Havensight Mall, Bldg. II, Rte. 30, Charlotte Amalie ☎ 340/776–2198) carries crystal from Baccarat, Waterford, and Orrefors; china from Kosta Boda, Rosenthal, Wedgwood, and others; Swarovski cut-crystal animals; Lladró and other porcelain figurines; gemstone globes; and many other affordable collectibles. It also does a booming mail-order business; ask for a catalog. Men, women, and children will find something to choose from at **Local Color** (✉ Royal Dane Mall, at Waterfront, Charlotte Amalie ☎ 340/774–2280), among brand-name wear like Jams World and Urban Safari, and St. John artist Sloop Jones's colorful, hand-painted island designs on cool dresses, T-shirts, and sweaters. There are also tropically oriented accessories like big-brimmed straw hats, bold-color bags, and casual jewelry. More than 40 local artists—including schoolchildren, senior citizens, and people with disabilities—create the handcrafted items for sale at **Native Arts & Crafts Cooperative** (✉ Tolbod Gade, across from Emancipation Garden and next to visitor center, Charlotte Amalie ☎ 340/777–1153). Here you'll find African-style jewelry, quilts, calabash bowls, dolls, carved-wood figures, woven baskets, straw brooms, note cards, and cookbooks.

Royal Caribbean (✉ 23 Main St., Charlotte Amalie ☎ 340/776–5449 ✉ 33 Main St., Charlotte Amalie ☎ 340/776–4110 ✉ Havensight Mall, Bldg. I, Rte. 30, Charlotte Amalie ☎ 340/776–8890), which has no affiliation with the cruise line, has cameras, camcorders, stereos, watches, and clocks.

ST. JOHN   In St. John, the small shopping district runs from Wharfside Village near the ferry landing to Mongoose Junction, just up the street from the cruise-ship dock and tender landing, with lots of shops tucked in between. The owner of **Bamboula** (✉ Mongoose Junction, N. Shore Rd., Cruz Bay ☎ 340/693–8699), Jo Sterling, travels the Caribbean and beyond to find unusual housewares, art, rugs, bedspreads, accessories, shoes, and men's and women's clothes for this multicultural boutique. If you want to look like you stepped out of the pages of the resort-wear spread in an upscale travel magazine, try **Bougainvillea Boutique** (✉ Mongoose Junction, N. Shore Rd., Cruz Bay ☎ 340/693–7190). Owner Susan Stair carries chic men's and women's clothes, straw hats, leather handbags, and fine gifts. Owner Radha Speer of **Caravan Gallery** (✉ Mongoose Junction, N. Shore Rd., Cruz Bay ☎ 340/779–4566) travels the world to find much of the unusual jewelry she sells here. And the more you look, the more you see—folk art, tribal art, and masks cover the walls and tables, making this a great place to browse.

Pink Papaya (✉ Lemon Tree Mall, King St., Cruz Bay ☎ 340/693–8535) is the home of longtime Virgin Islands resident M. L. Etre's well-known artwork, plus a huge collection of one-of-a-kind gifts, including bright tablecloths, unusual trays, dinnerware, and unique tropical jewelry. **St. John Editions** (⊠ N. Shore Rd., Cruz Bay ☎ 340/693–8444) has nifty cotton dresses that go from beach to dinner with a change of shoes and accessories. Owner Ann Soper also carries attractive straw hats and inexpensive jewelry.

Sports & Activities

ST. THOMAS **Diving & Snorkeling: Aqua Adventures** (⊠ Crown Bay Marina, Rte. 304, Charlotte Amalie ☎ 340/715–0348 ⊕ www.bobusvi.com) offers an alternative to traditional diving in the form of an underwater motor scooter called BOB, or Breathing Observation Bubble. A half-day tour, including snorkel equipment, guided BOB excursion, rum punch, and towels is $99 per person. **Chris Sawyer Diving Center** (☎ 340/775–7320 or 877/929–3483 ⊕ www.sawyerdive.vi) is a PADI five-star outfit that specializes in dives to the 310-foot-long *Rhone,* in the British Virgin Islands. Hotel–dive packages are offered through the Wyndham Sugar Bay Beach Club & Resort. **Snuba of St. Thomas** (⊠ Rte. 388, at Coki Point, Estate Smith Bay ☎ 340/693–8063 ⊕ www.visnuba.com) offers something for nondivers, a cross between snorkeling and scuba diving: a 20-foot air hose connects you to the surface. The cost is $60. Children must be eight years or older to participate.

Fishing: Fishing here is synonymous with blue marlin angling. If you're not into marlin fishing, try hooking sailfish in the winter, dolphinfish come spring, and wahoo in the fall. To really find the trip that will best suit you, walk down the docks at either American Yacht Harbor or Sapphire Beach Marina in the late afternoon and chat with the captains and crews. The **Charter Boat Center** (⊠ 6300 Red Hook Plaza, Red Hook ☎ 340/775–7990 ⊕ www.charterboat.vi) is a major source for sportfishing charters, both marlin and inshore. For inshore trips, *Peanut Gallery Charters* at the **Crown Bay Marina** (⊠ Rte. 304, Estate Contant ☎ 340/775–5274 ⊕ www.fishingstthomas.com) offers trips on its 18-foot *Dauntless* or 28-foot custom sportfishing catamaran.

Golf: The **Mahogany Run Golf Course** (⊠ Rte. 42, Estate Lovenlund ☎ 340/777–6006 or 800/253–7103 ⊕ www.mahoganyrungolf.com) attracts golfers for its spectacular view of the British Virgin Islands and the challenging 3-hole Devil's Triangle on this Tom and George Fazio–designed par-70, 18-hole course. Greens and half-cart fees for 18 holes are $130. There's a fully stocked pro shop, snack bar, and open-air club house. The course is open daily and there are frequently informal weekend tournaments. It's the only course on St. Thomas but one of the Caribbean's best.

ST. JOHN **Diving & Snorkeling: Cruz Bay Watersports** (☎ 340/776–6234 ⊕ www.divestjohn.com) has two locations: in Cruz Bay at the Lumberyard Shopping Complex and at the Westin Resort, St. John. Owners Marcus and Patty Johnston offer regular reef, wreck, and night dives and USVI and BVI snorkel tours. The company holds PADI five-star facility and NAUI Dream Resort status. **Low Key Watersports** (☎ 340/693–8999 or 800/835–7718 ⊕ www.divelowkey.com) at Wharfside Village, offers one- and two-tank dives, and specialty courses. It's certified as a PADI five-star training facility.

Fishing: Well-kept charter boats—approved by the U.S. Coast Guard—head out to the north and south drops or troll along the inshore reefs, depending on the season and what's biting. The captains usually provide bait, drinks, and lunch, but you need to bring your own hat and sunscreen. Fishing charters run around $500 per half day for the boat. **Captain Bryon Oliver** (☎ 340/693–8339), takes you out to the north and south drops or closer in to St. John. **Gone Ketchin'** (☎ 340/714–1175 ⊕ www.goneketchin.com), in St. John, arranges trips with old salt Captain Griz.

Hiking: Although it's fun to go hiking with a Virgin Islands National Park guide, don't be afraid to head out on your own. To find a hike that suits your ability, stop by the park's visitor center in Cruz Bay and pick up the free trail guide; it details points of interest, dangers, trail lengths, and estimated hiking times. Although the park staff recommends long pants to protect against thorns and insects, most people hike in shorts because it can get very hot. Wear sturdy shoes or hiking boots even if you're hiking to the beach. Don't forget to bring water and insect repellent. The **Virgin Islands National Park** (☎ 340/776–6201 ⊕ www.nps.gov/viis) maintains more than 20 trails on the north and south shores and offers guided hikes along popular routes. A full-day trip to Reef Bay is a must; it's an easy hike through lush and dry forest, past the ruins of an old plantation, and to a sugar factory adjacent to the beach, but it can be a bit arduous for young kids. Take the public Vitran bus or a taxi to the trailhead, where you can meet a ranger who'll serve as your guide. The park provides a boat ride back to Cruz Bay for $15 to save you the walk back up the mountain. The schedule changes from season to season; call for times and reservations, which are essential.

Beaches

ST. THOMAS   All beaches in the USVI are public, but occasionally you'll need to stroll through a resort to reach the sand. **Coki Beach,** next to Coral World (turn north off Route 38), is the island's best snorkeling spot. It's popular for cruise-ship excursions, though there's no reason why you can't go there on your own. Colorful beachside shops rent water-sports equipment. Some also sell snack foods, cold drinks, and even fish food (dry dog food). On Route 35, **Magens Bay** is usually lively because of its spectacular crescent of white sand, more than ½ mi (¾ km) long, and its calm waters, which are protected by two peninsulas. It's often listed among the world's most beautiful beaches. (If you arrive between 8 AM and 5 PM, you have to pay an entrance fee of $3 per person, $1 per vehicle, and 25¢ per child under age 12.) The bottom is flat and sandy, so this is a place for sunning and swimming rather than snorkeling. There's also a bar, snack bar, and bathhouses with toilets and saltwater showers. Close to Charlotte Amalie and fronting the Marriott Frenchman's Reef Hotel, pretty **Morning Star Beach** is where many young locals bodysurf or play volleyball. Snorkeling is good near the rocks when the current doesn't affect visibility. There's a fine view of St. John and other islands from **Sapphire Beach.** The snorkeling is excellent at the reef to the right, or east, near Pettyklip Point. The constant breeze makes this a great spot for windsurfing. The condo resort at **Secret Harbor** doesn't detract from the attractiveness of the cove-like beach. Not only is this East End spot pretty, it also has superb snorkeling—head out to the left, near the rocks.

ST. JOHN Long, sandy **Cinnamon Bay** faces beautiful cays and abuts the national park campground. Facilities are open to the public and include cool showers, toilets, a commissary, and a restaurant. You can rent water-sports equipment here. There's excellent snorkeling off the point to the right; look for the big angelfish and large schools of purple triggerfish. Afternoons on Cinnamon Bay can be windy, so arrive early to beat the gusts. **Hawksnest Beach** is the closet beach to Cruz Bay, so it's often crowded. Sea grape trees line this narrow beach, and there are rest rooms, cooking grills, and a covered shed for picnicking. **Trunk Bay**, St. John's most-photographed beach, is also the preferred spot for beginning snorkelers because of its underwater trail, but if you're looking for seclusion, don't come here because it's the island's busiest. Crowded or not, this stunning beach is still beautiful. There are changing rooms, a snack bar, picnic tables, a gift shop, phones, lockers, and snorkeling-equipment rentals. You have to pay an entrance fee of $4 if you don't have a National Park Pass.

Where to Eat

Some restaurants add a 10% to 15% service charge. If not, leave a 15% tip.

ST. THOMAS ✕ **Cuzzin's Caribbean Restaurant & Bar.** The top picks in this restaurant
$$ in a 19th-century livery stage are Virgin Islands' staples. For lunch, order tender slivers of conch stewed in a rich onion butter sauce, savory braised oxtail, or curried chicken. At dinner, the island-style mutton served in a thick gravy and seasoned with locally grown herbs offers a taste treat that's deliciously different. Side dishes include peas and rice, boiled green bananas, fried plantains, and potato stuffing. ⊠ 7 *Wimmelskafts Gade, also called Back St.* ☎ 340/777–4711 ⊟ AE, MC, V.

$–$$ ✕ **Gladys' Cafe.** Even if the local specialties—conch in butter sauce, saltfish and dumplings, hearty red bean soup—didn't make this a recommended café, it would be worth coming for Gladys's smile. While you're here, pick up a $5 or $10 bottle of her hot sauce. There are mustard-, oil and vinegar-, and tomato-based versions; the latter is the hottest. ⊠ *Waterfront, at Royal Dane Mall* ☎ 340/774–6604 ⊟ AE ⊗ No dinner.

ST. JOHN ✕ **Sun Dog Cafe.** There's an unusual assortment of dishes at this charm-
$ ing alfresco restaurant, which is tucked into a courtyard in the upper reaches of the Mongoose Junction shopping center. Kudos to the white artichoke pizza with roasted garlic, artichoke hearts, mozzarella cheese, and capers. The Jamaican jerk chicken sub or the black-bean quesadilla are also good choices. ⊠ *Mongoose Junction, N. Shore Rd.* ☎ 340/693–8340 ⊟ AE, MC, V ⊗ No dinner.

☾ $ ✕ **Uncle Joe's Barbecue.** Juicy ribs and tasty chicken legs dripping with the house barbecue sauce make for one of St. John's best dining deals. An ear of corn, rice, and a generous scoop of macaroni salad or coleslaw round out the plate. This casual spot crowds the edge of a busy sidewalk in the heart of Cruz Bay. Even though there are a few open-air tables for dining "in," the ambience is more than a tad on the pedestrian side, so take-out is a better bet. ⊠ *N. Shore Rd., across from post office* ☎ *340/693–8806* ▭ *No credit cards.*

St. Vincent & Bequia

You won't find glitzy resorts or flashy discos in St. Vincent or Bequia. Rather, you'll be dazzled by picturesque villages, secluded beaches, and fine sailing waters. St. Vincent is the largest and northernmost island in the Grenadines archipelago; Kingstown, the capital city, is the government and business center and major port. Except for one barren area on the island's northeast coast—remnants of the 1979 eruption of La Soufrière, one of the last active volcanoes in the Caribbean—the countryside is mountainous, lush, and green.

The Grenadines extend in a 45-mi (73-km) arc from St. Vincent to Grenada. As similar as they may appear, each inhabited island has its own personality. Just south of St. Vincent is Bequia (pronounced *beck*-way), one of the most popular anchorages in the Caribbean for smaller cruise ships. Next is Mustique, getaway of the glitterati. Making up the southern Grenadines are sleepy Canouan (*can*-oo-wan), pastoral Mayreau (*my*-row), and busy Union, along with tiny Palm Island and Petit St. Vincent.

St. Vincent's mountains and forests thwarted European settlement for many years. As colonization advanced elsewhere in the Caribbean, in fact, the island became a refuge for Carib Indians—descendants of whom still live in northeastern St. Vincent. Eventually, British troops prevailed, overpowering the French and banishing Carib warriors to Central America. Independent since 1979, St. Vincent and the Grenadines remains a member of the British Commonwealth. The official language is English.

CURRENCY St. Vincent and the Grenadines uses the Eastern Caribbean (E.C.) dollar. The exchange rate is EC$2.70 to US$1. U.S. dollars are generally accepted, although E.C. currency is preferred. Large U.S. bills may be difficult to change in small shops. Hotels and many restaurants and shops accept credit cards and traveler's checks. Prices given below are in U.S. dollars unless otherwise indicated.

TELEPHONES Pay phones are readily available and best operated with the prepaid phone cards that are sold at many stores and can be used on many Caribbean islands. Telephone services are available at the cruise ship terminal in Kingstown, St. Vincent, and near the jetty in Port Elizabeth, Bequia. For an international operator, dial 115; to charge your call to a credit card, call 117. To make an international call using your credit card, dial 800/877–8000.

SHORE EXCURSIONS The following are good choices in St. Vincent and Bequia. They may not be offered by all cruise lines. Times and prices are approximate. Note that the St. Vincent shore excursions are often offered by ships that dock in Bequia but will include a ferry to St. Vincent.

Falls of Baleine. After a bus ride to Villa Beach, you board a boat for the trip north along St. Vincent's leeward coast. The arrival at the Falls of Baleine is a wet-landing, where you will wade through shallow water to the beach for a five-minute trek to the falls. Wear a bathing suit and protective foot covering. Complimentary soft drinks and rum punch are served. ⊙ *4 hrs* 🖼 *$99.*

Island History & Natural Beauty. A bus first takes you to Dorsetshire Hill for a view of Kingstown Harbour and the Grenadines, then to 18th-century Fort Charlotte, where murals depict the turbulent history of St. Vincent. On a walk through the Botanical Gardens, the oldest in the western hemisphere, your guide will describe the various trees and shrubs. ⊙ *4 hrs* 🖼 *$49.*

Coming Ashore

Some cruise ships call at Kingstown, St. Vincent's capital city. Its berth accommodates two cruise ships; additional vessels anchor outside the harbor and bring passengers to the jetty by launch. The facility has about two dozen shops that sell duty-free items and handicrafts. There's a communications center, post office, tourist information desk, restaurant, and food court. Buses and taxis are available at the wharf. Taxi drivers are well equipped to take you on an island tour; expect to pay $25 per hour for up to four passengers. The ferry to Bequia (1 hour each way) is at the adjacent pier. Renting a car for just one day isn't advisable, since car rentals are expensive (at least $55 per day) and require a $28 temporary driving permit on top of that.

Smaller cruise ships sometimes call directly at Port Elizabeth, on Bequia. They anchor offshore and bring passengers ashore by launch. Shops, restaurants, and a tourist information office are all just steps from the jetty. Taxis are available for island tours and transportation to the beach; taxi drivers charge about $15 per hour for up to four passengers. Water taxis are also available for beach transport; the cost is a couple of dollars.

Exploring St. Vincent & Bequia

Numbers in the margin correspond to points of interest on the St. Vincent and Bequia map.

ST. VINCENT **Botanical Garden.** A few minutes north of downtown by taxi is the oldest
❷ botanical garden in the Western Hemisphere, founded in 1765. Captain Bligh—of *Bounty* fame—brought the first breadfruit tree to this island for landowners to propagate. The prolific bounty of the breadfruit tree was used to feed the slaves. You can see a direct descendant of this original tree among the specimen mahogany, rubber, teak, and other tropical trees and shrubs in the 20 acres of gardens. Two dozen rare St. Vincent parrots live in the small aviary. Guides explain all the medicinal and ornamental trees and shrubs; they also appreciate a tip at the end of the tour. ✉ *Off Leeward Hwy., Montrose* ☎ *784/457–1003* 🖼 *$3* ⊙ *Daily 6–6.*

❺ **Falls of Baleine.** The falls are impossible to reach by car, so book an escorted, all-day boat trip from Villa Beach or the Lagoon Marina. The boat ride along the coast offers scenic island views. When you arrive, you have to wade through shallow water to get to the beach. Then local guides help you make the easy five-minute trek to the 60-foot falls and the rock-enclosed freshwater pool the falls create—plan to take a dip.

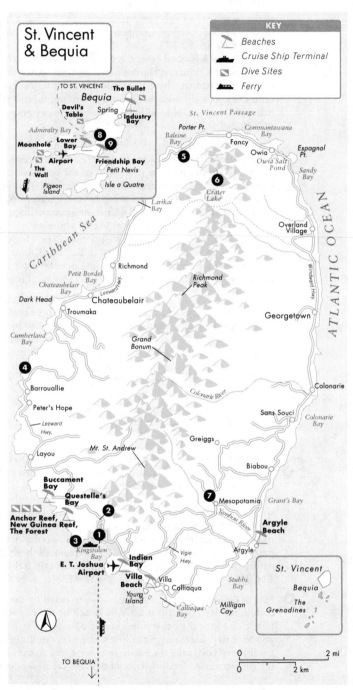

St. Vincent
& Bequia

KEY

Beaches

Cruise Ship Terminal

Dive Sites

Ferry

TO ST. VINCENT

Bequia

The Bullet

Devil's Table   Spring

Industry Bay

Admiralty Bay

Moonhole

Lower Bay

8 **9**

Airport

Friendship Bay

The Wall

Petit Nevis

Pigeon Island

Isle a Quatre

St. Vincent Passage

Porter Pt.   Commantawana Bay

Baleine Bay   Fancy

5

Owia   Espagnol Pt.

Owia Salt Pond   Sandy Bay

6

Crater Lake

Overland Village

Larikai Bay

Caribbean Sea

Petit Bordel Bay   Richmond

Chateaubelair Bay

Dark Head

Chateaubelair

Troumaka

Richmond Peak

Georgetown

Cumberland Bay

Grand Bonum

4

Barrouallie

Peter's Hope

Colonarie River

Colonarie

Leeward Hwy.

Sans Souci   Colonarie Bay

Layou

Mt. St. Andrew

Greiggs

Biabou

Buccament Bay

Questelle's Bay

2

7 Mesopotamia   Grant's Bay

Yambou River

Anchor Reef, New Guinea Reef, The Forest

3 **1**

Argyle Beach

Kingstown Bay

E. T. Joshua Airport

Indian Bay

Argyle

Vigie Hwy.

Villa Beach   Villa

Calliaqua

Young Island

Calliaqua Bay

Stubbs Bay

Milligan Cay

St. Vincent

Bequia

The Grenadines

ATLANTIC OCEAN

Windward Hwy.

TO BEQUIA

0   2 mi

0   2 km

🐚 ❸ **Fort Charlotte.** Started by the French in 1786 and completed by the British in 1806, the fort was named for King George III's wife. It sits on Berkshire Hill, a dramatic promontory 636 feet above sea level, with a stunning view of Kingstown and the Grenadines. Interestingly, cannons face inward—the fear of attack by native peoples was far greater than any threat approaching from the sea, though, truth be told, the fort saw no action. Nowadays the fort serves as a signal station for ships; its ancient cells house paintings, by Lindsay Prescott, depicting early island history.

❶ **Kingstown.** The capital city of St. Vincent and the Grenadines is on the island's southwestern coast. The town of 13,500 residents wraps around Kingstown Bay; a ring of green hills and ridges, studded with homes, forms a backdrop for the city. This is very much a working city, with a busy harbor and few concessions to tourists. Kingstown Harbour is the only deepwater port on the island.

What few gift shops there are can be found on and around **Bay Street,** near the harbor. Upper Bay Street, which stretches along the bayfront, bustles with daytime activity—workers going about their business and housewives doing their shopping. Many of Kingstown's downtown buildings are built of stone or brick brought to the island in the holds of 18th-century ships as ballast (and replaced with sugar and spices for the return trip to Europe). The Georgian-style stone arches and second-floor overhangs on former warehouses create shelter from midday sun and the brief, cooling showers common to the tropics.

Grenadines Wharf, at the south end of Bay Street, is busy with schooners loading supplies and ferries loading people bound for the Grenadines. The **Cruise Ship Complex,** south of the commercial wharf, has a mall with a dozen or more shops, plus restaurants, a post office, communications facilities, and a taxi–minibus stand.

An almost infinite selection of produce fills the **Kingstown Produce Market,** a three-story building that takes up a whole city block on Upper Bay, Hillsboro, and Bedford streets in the center of town. It's noisy, colorful, and open Monday through Saturday—but the busiest times (and the best times to go) are Friday and Saturday mornings. In the courtyard, vendors sell local arts and crafts. On the upper floors, merchants sell clothing, household items, gifts, and other products.

Little Tokyo, so called because funding for the project was a gift from Japan, is a waterfront shopping area with a bustling indoor fish market and dozens of stalls where you can buy inexpensive homemade meals, drinks, ice cream, bread and cookies, clothing, and trinkets, and even get a haircut.

St. George's Cathedral, on Grenville Street, is a pristine, creamy-yellow Anglican church built in 1820. The dignified Georgian architecture includes simple wooden pews, an ornate chandelier, and beautiful stained-glass windows; one was a gift from Queen Victoria, who actually commissioned it for London's St. Paul's Cathedral in honor of her first grandson. When the artist created an angel with a red robe, she was horrified and sent it abroad. The markers in the cathedral's graveyard recount the history of the island. Across the street is **St. Mary's Cathedral of the Assumption** (Roman Catholic), built in stages beginning in 1823. The strangely appealing design is a blend of Moorish, Georgian, and Romanesque styles applied to black brick. Nearby, freed slaves built the **Kingstown Methodist Church** in 1841. The exterior is brick, simply decorated with quoins (solid blocks that form the corners), and the roof is held together by metal straps, bolts, and wooden pins. **Scots Kirk** (1839–80) was built by and for Scottish settlers but became a Seventh-Day Adventist church in 1952.

❻ La Soufrière. The volcano, which last erupted in 1979, is 4,000 feet high and so huge in area that it covers virtually the entire northern third of the island. The eastern trail to the rim of the crater, a two-hour ascent, begins at Rabacca Dry River.

❼ Mesopotamia Valley. The rugged, ocean-lashed scenery along St. Vincent's windward coast is the perfect counterpoint to the lush, calm west coast. The fertile Mesopotamia Valley (nicknamed "Mespo") offers a panoramic view of dense rain forests, streams, and endless banana and coconut plantations. Breadfruit, sweet corn, peanuts, and arrowroot also grow in the rich soil here. The valley is surrounded by mountain ridges, including 3,181-foot Grand Bonhomme Mountain, and overlooks the Caribbean.

❹ Wallilabou Bay. You can sunbathe, swim, picnic, or buy your lunch at Wallilabou (pronounced wally-la-*boo*) Anchorage, on the bay. This is a favorite stop for day-trippers returning from the Falls of Baleine and boaters anchoring for the evening. Nearby there's a river with a small waterfall where you can take a freshwater plunge.

BEQUIA Bequia is the Carib word for "island of the cloud." Hilly and green, with several gold-sand beaches, Bequia is just 9 mi (14½ km) south of St. Vincent's southwestern shore; with 5,000 inhabitants, it's the most populous of the Grenadines.

❾ Mount Pleasant. Bequia's highest point (an elevation of 881 feet) is a reasonable goal for a hiking trek. Alternatively, it's a pleasant drive. The reward is a stunning view of the island and surrounding Grenadines.

❽ Port Elizabeth. Bequia's capital is on the northeast side of Admiralty Bay. The ferry from St. Vincent docks at the jetty, in the center of the tiny town that's only a few blocks long and a couple of blocks deep. Walk north along Front Street, which faces the water, to the open-air market, where you can buy local fruits and vegetables and some handicrafts; farther along, you can find the model-boat builders' workshops for which Bequia is renowned. Walk south along Belmont Walkway, which meanders along the bay front past shops, cafés, restaurants, bars, and hotels.

Shopping

The 12 blocks that hug the waterfront in **downtown Kingstown** comprise St. Vincent's main shopping district. Among the shops that sell goods to fulfill household needs are a few that sell local crafts, gifts, and souvenirs. Bargaining is neither expected nor appreciated. The **Cruise Ship Complex,** on the waterfront in Kingstown, has a collection of a dozen or so boutiques, shops, and restaurants that cater primarily to cruise-ship passengers but welcome all shoppers.

Stores are generally open weekdays from 8 to 4 or 4:30, Saturday 8–1, and are closed on Sunday. St. Vincent is not a major duty-free shopping port, although several shops at the cruise-ship terminal and a few stores in town sell duty-free items.

ST. VINCENT At **FranPaul's Selections** (✉ 2nd fl., Bonadie's Plaza, Bay St., Kingstown ☎ 784/456–2662), Francelia St. John fashions dresses, pants, and shirts from colorful fabrics she selects in Trinidad. The emphasis is on African, Afro-Caribbean, and casual wear. At **Gonsalves Duty-Free Liquor** (✉ Airport Departure Lounge, Arnos Vale ☎ 784/456–4781), spirits and liqueurs are available at discounts of up to 40%. **Nzimbu Browne** (✉ Bay St., in front of Cobblestone Inn, Kingstown ☎ 784/457–1677) creates original art from dried banana leaves, carefully selecting and snipping bits and arranging them on pieces of wood to depict local scenes. He often sets up shop on Bay Street, near the Cobblestone Inn. **St. Vincent Craftsmen's Centre** (✉ Frenches St., Kingstown ☎ 784/457–2516), three blocks from the wharf, sells locally made grass floor mats, place mats, and other straw articles, as well as batik cloth, handmade West Indian dolls, hand-painted calabashes, and framed artwork. The large grass mats can be rolled and folded for easy transport home. No credit cards are accepted.

BEQUIA Bequia's shops are mostly on Front Street and Belmont Walkway, its waterfront extension, just steps from the jetty where the ferry arrives in Port Elizabeth. North of the jetty there's an open-air market and farther along the road are the model-boat builders' shops. Opposite the jetty, at Bayshore Mall, shops sell ice cream, baked goods, stationery, gifts, and clothing; a liquor store, pharmacy, travel agent, and bank are also here. On Belmont Walkway, south of the jetty, shops and studios showcase gifts and handmade articles. Shops here are open weekdays from 8 to 5, Saturday 8 to noon. **Mauvin's Model Boat Shop** (✉ Front St., Port Elizabeth ☎ 784/458–3344) is where you can purchase the handmade model boats for which Bequia is known. You can even special-order a replica of your own yacht. They're incredibly detailed and quite expensive—from a few hundred to several thousand dollars. The simplest models take about a week to make. **Sargeant Brothers Model Boat Shop** (✉ Front St., Port Elizabeth ☎ 758/458–3344) sells handmade model boats and will build special requests on commission. Housed in the ruins of an old sugar mill, **Spring Pottery & Studios** (✉ Spring ☎ 784/457–3757) is the working pottery of Mike Goddard and Maggie Overal, with gallery exhibits of ceramics, paintings, and crafts—their own and those of other local artists. All works are for sale.

Sports & Activities

ST. VINCENT **Boating, Fishing & Sailing:** From St. Vincent you can charter a monohull or catamaran (bareboat or complete with captain, crew, and cook) to weave you through the Grenadines for a day or a week of sailing—or a full-day fishing trip. Boats of all sizes and degrees of luxury are available. Charter rates run about $250 per day and up for sailing yachts;

$120 per person for a fishing trip. **Barefoot Yacht Charters** (✉ Blue Lagoon, Ratho Mill ☎ 784/456–9526 🖷 785/456–9238 ⊕ www. barefootyachts.com) has a fleet of catamarans and monohulls in the 32- to 50-foot range. **Crystal Blue Charters** (✉ Indian Bay ☎ 784/457–4532 🖷 784/456–2232) offers sportfishing charters on a 34-foot pirogue for amateur and serious fishermen. **Sunsail St. Vincent** (✉ Blue Lagoon, Ratho Mill ☎ 784/458–4308 ⊕ www.sunsail.com) charters bareboat and crewed yachts ranging from 30 feet to 50 feet.

Diving & Snorkeling: Novices and advanced divers alike will be impressed by the marine life in St. Vincent's waters—brilliant sponges, huge deep-water coral trees, and shallow reefs teeming with colorful fish. The best dive spots on St. Vincent are in the small bays along the coast between Kingstown and Layou; many are within 20 yards of shore and only 20 feet to 30 feet down. About 35 dive sites around Bequia and nearby islands are accessible within 15 minutes by boat. The leeward side of the 7-mi (11-km) reef that fringes Bequia has been designated a marine park.

Anchor Reef has excellent visibility for viewing a deep-black coral garden, schools of squid, seahorses, and maybe a small octopus. **The Forest,** a shallow dive, is still dramatic, with soft corals in pastel colors and schools of small fish. **New Guinea Reef** slopes to 90 feet (28 m) and can't be matched for its quantity of corals and sponges. **Young Island** is also a good place for snorkeling, but you need to phone for permission to take the ferry from Villa Beach over to the island and rent snorkeling equipment from the resort's water-sports center. The pristine waters surrounding the **Tobago Cays,** in the Southern Grenadines, will give you a world-class diving experience.

Dive Fantasea (✉ Villa Beach ☎ 784/457–5560 or 784/457–5577) offers dive and snorkeling trips to the St. Vincent coast and the Tobago Cays. **Dive St. Vincent** (✉ Young Island Dock, Villa Beach ☎ 784/457–4714 or 784/547–4928 ⊕ www.divestvincent.com) is where NAUI- and PADI-certified instructor Bill Tewes and his staff offer beginner and certification courses and dive trips to the St. Vincent coast and the southern Grenadines.

Hiking: St. Vincent offers hikers and trekkers a choice of experiences: easy, picturesque walks near Kingstown; moderate-effort nature trails in the central valleys; and exhilarating climbs through a rain forest to the rim of an active volcano. Bring a hat, long pants, and insect repellent if you plan to hike in the bush.

La Soufrière, the queen of climbs, is St. Vincent's active volcano (which last erupted, appropriately enough, on Friday, April 13, 1979). Approachable from either the windward or leeward coast, this is *not* a casual excursion for inexperienced walkers—the massive mountain covers nearly the entire northern third of the island. Climbs are all-day excursions. You'll need stamina and sturdy shoes to reach the top and peep into the mile-wide (1½-km-wide) crater at just over 4,000 feet. Be sure to check the weather before you leave; hikers have been sorely disappointed to find a cloud-obscured view at the summit. A guide ($25 to $30) can be arranged through the Ministry of Tourism & Culture or tour operators. The eastern approach is more popular. In a four-wheel-drive vehicle you pass through Rabacca Dry River, north of Georgetown, and the Bamboo Forest; then it's a two-hour, 3½-mi (5½-km) hike to the summit. Approaching from the west, near Châteaubelair, the climb is longer—10 to 12 mi (6 to 7 km)—and rougher, but even more scenic. If you hike up one side and down the other, arrangements must be made in advance to pick you up at the end.

Trinity Falls, in the north, requires a trip by a four-wheel-drive vehicle from Richmond to the interior, then a steep two-hour climb to a crystal-clear river and three waterfalls, one of which forms a whirlpool where you can take a refreshing swim.

Vermont Nature Trails are two hiking trails that start near the top of the Buccament Valley, 5 mi (8 km) north of Kingstown. A network of 1½-mi (2½-km) loops passes through bamboo, evergreen forest, and rain forest. In the late afternoon you may be lucky enough to see the rare St. Vincent parrot, *Amazona guildingii.*

BEQUIA **Boating & Sailing:** With regular trade winds, visibility for 30 mi (48 km), and generally calm seas, Bequia is a center for some of the best blue-water sailing you'll find anywhere in the world, with all kinds of options: day sails or weekly charters, bareboat or fully crewed, monohulls or catamarans—whatever's your pleasure. Prices for day trips run $50 to $75 per person, depending on the destination.

Friendship Rose (✉ Port Elizabeth ☎ 784/458–3373), an 80-foot schooner that spent its first 25 years as a mail boat, was subsequently refitted to take passengers on day trips from Bequia to Mustique and the Tobago Cays. The 65-foot catamaran *Passion* (✉ Belmont ☎ 784/458–3884), custom-built for day sailing, offers all-inclusive daylong snorkeling and/or sportfishing trips from Bequia to Mustique, the Tobago Cays, and St. Vincent's Falls of Baleine. It's also available for private charter. The Frangipani Hotel owns the **S. Y. Pelangi** (✉ Port Elizabeth ☎ 784/458–3255 ⊕ www.frangipanibequia.com), a 44-foot CSY cutter, for day sails or longer charters; four people can be accommodated comfortably, and the cost is $200 per day.

Diving & Snorkeling: About 35 dive sites around Bequia and nearby islands are accessible within 15 minutes by boat. The leeward side of the 7-mi (11-km) reef that fringes Bequia has been designated a marine park. **The Bullet,** off Bequia's north point, is a good spot for spotting rays, barracuda, and the occasional nurse shark. **Devil's Table** is a shallow dive that's rich in fish and coral and has a sailboat wreck nearby at 90 feet. **Moonhole** is shallow enough in places for snorkelers to enjoy. **The Wall** is a 90-foot drop off West Cay. Expect to pay dive operators $50 for a one-tank and $95 for a two-tank dive. Dive boats welcome snorkelers, but for the best snorkeling in Bequia, take a water taxi to the bay at Moonhole and arrange a pickup time.

Bequia Dive Adventures (✉ Belmont Walkway, Admiralty Bay, Port Elizabeth ☎ 784/458–3826 ⊕ www.bequiadiveadventures.com) offers PADI instruction courses and takes small groups on three dives daily;

harbor pickup and return is included for customers staying on yachts. **Dive Bequia** (⊠ Belmont Walkway, Admiralty Bay, Port Elizabeth ☎ 784/ 458–3504 ⊕ www.dive-bequia.com), at the Gingerbread Hotel, offers dive and snorkel tours, night dives, and full equipment rental. Resort and certification courses are available.

Beaches

ST. VINCENT St. Vincent's origin is volcanic, so its beaches range in color from golden-brown to black. Swimming is recommended only in the lagoons and bays along the leeward coast. By contrast, beaches on the Bequia and the rest of the Grenadines have pure white sand, palm trees, and crystal-clear aquamarine water; some are even within walking distance of the jetty. **Buccament Bay** is good for swimming. This tiny black-sand beach is 20 minutes north of Kingstown. South of Kingstown, **Indian Bay** has golden sand but is slightly rocky; it's a good place for snorkeling. **Questelle's Bay** (pronounced keet-*ells*), north of Kingstown and next to Campden Park, has a black-sand beach.

BEQUIA Bequia's **Friendship Bay** can be reached by land taxi. You can rent wind-surfing and snorkeling equipment at Friendship Bay Resort and also grab a bite to eat or a cool drink. Getting to **Hope Beach,** on the Atlantic side, involves a long taxi ride (about $7.50) and a mile-long (1½-km-long) walk downhill on a semi-paved path. Your reward is a magnificent crescent of white sand, total seclusion, and—if you prefer—nude bathing. Be sure to ask your taxi driver to return at a prearranged time. Bring your own lunch and drinks; there are no facilities. Even though the surf is fairly shallow, swimming can be dangerous because of the undertow. **Industry Bay,** a nearly secluded beach fringed with towering palms, is on the northeast side of the island and requires transportation from Port Elizabeth. This is a good beach for snorkelers, but there could be a strong undertow. Bring a picnic; the nearest facilities are at Spring on Bequia resort, a 10- to 15-minute walk from the beach. Wide, palm-fringed **Lower Bay** is reachable by taxi or by hiking beyond Princess Margaret Beach and is an excellent location for swimming and snorkeling. There are facilities to rent water-sports equipment here, as well as De Reef restaurant. Quiet and wide, with a natural stone arch at one end, **Princess Margaret Beach** is a half-hour hike over rocky bluffs from Belmont Walkway—or you can take a water or land taxi. Though it has no facilities, it's a popular spot for swimming, snorkeling, or snoozing under the palm and sea grape trees.

Where to Eat

A 7% government tax is applicable to your bill, and most restaurants add a 10% service charge in lieu of tip. If they do not, leave an appropriate tip; otherwise, anything additional is expected only for special service.

ST. VINCENT ✕ **Basil's Bar & Restaurant.** It's not just the air-conditioning that makes $–$$ this restaurant cool. Downstairs at the Cobblestone Inn is owned by Basil Charles, whose Basil's Beach Bar on Mustique is a hangout for the vacationing rich and famous. This is the Kingstown power-lunch venue. Local businesspeople gather for the daily buffet or a full menu of salads, sandwiches, barbecued chicken, or fresh seafood platters. Dinner entrées of pasta, local seafood, and chicken (try it poached in fresh ginger and coconut milk) are served at candlelit tables. There's a Chinese buffet on Friday, and takeout is available that night only. ⊠ *Cobblestone Inn, Upper Bay St., Kingstown* ☎ *784/457–2713* ⊟ *AE, MC, V.*

¢–$$ ✕ **Vee Jay's Rooftop Diner & Pub.** This eatery above Roger's Photo Studios (have your pix developed while you eat) and opposite the Cobblestone Inn offers downtown Kingstown's best harbor view from beneath a green corrugated-plastic roof. Among the "authentic Vincy cuisine" specials chalked on the blackboard are mutton or fish stew, chicken or vegetable rotis, curried goat, souse, and *buljol* (sautéed codfish, breadfruit, and vegetables). Not-so-Vincy sandwiches, fish-and-chips, and burgers can be authentically washed down with *mauby*, a bittersweet drink made from tree bark; linseed, peanut, passion-fruit, or sorrel punch; local Hairoun beer; or cocktails. Lunch is buffet style. ⊠ *Upper Bay St., Kingstown* ☎ *784/457–2845* ⌂ *Reservations essential* ⊟ *AE, D, MC, V* ☉ *Closed Sun.*

BEQUIA ✕ **Mac's Pizzeria.** Overheard at the dock in Mustique: "We're sailing over
☾ $–$$ to Bequia for pizza." The two-hour sunset sail to Admiralty Bay is worth the trip to Mac's, which has been serving pizza in Bequia since 1980. Choose from 17 mouthwatering toppings (including lobster), or select homemade quiche, conch fritters, pita sandwiches, lasagna, or soups and salads. Mac's home-baked cookies and muffins are great for dessert or a snack. To complement your meal, the outdoor terrace offers fuchsia bougainvillea and water views. ⊠ *Belmont Walkway, Admiralty Bay, Port Elizabeth* ☎ *784/458–3474* ⌂ *Reservations essential* ⊟ *D.*

San Juan, Puerto Rico

Although Puerto Rico is a commonwealth of the United States, few cities in the Caribbean are as steeped in Spanish tradition as San Juan. Within a seven-block neighborhood in Old San Juan are restored 16th-century buildings, museums, art galleries, bookstores, and 200-year-old houses with balustraded balconies overlooking narrow, cobblestone streets. In contrast, San Juan's sophisticated Condado and Isla Verde areas have glittering hotels, Latin music shows, casinos, and discos. Out in the countryside is the 28,000-acre El Yunque rain forest, with more than 240 species of trees growing at least 100 feet high. You can stretch your sea legs on dramatic mountain ranges, numerous trails, vast caves, coffee plantations, old sugar mills, and hundreds of beaches. No wonder San Juan is one of the busiest ports of call in the Caribbean.

Like any other big city, San Juan has its share of crime. Guard your wallet or purse, and avoid walking in the area between Old San Juan and the Condado.

CURRENCY The U.S. dollar is the official currency of Puerto Rico.

TELEPHONES Calling the United States from Puerto Rico is the same as calling within the U.S. You can use the long-distance telephone service office in the cruise-ship terminal, or you can use your calling card by dialing the toll-free access number of your long-distance provider from any pay phone. You'll find a phone center by the Paseo de la Princesa.

SHORE EXCURSIONS The following are good choices in San Juan. They may not be offered by all cruise lines. Times and prices are approximate. You can do your sightseeing in Old San Juan on your own, but if you want to see more of the island, you may be better off with a shore excursion from your ship.

El Yunque Rain Forest. A 45-minute drive delivers you to the Caribbean National Forest where you will independently explore along the trails, view the waterfalls, and can climb the observation tower. Usually includes a stop at Coca waterfalls. ☉ 5 hrs ⌑ $30–$39.

Kayaking. Paddle an ocean kayak along the coastline, passing white-sand beaches. ☉ 4–4½ hrs ⌑ $69–$79.

Old San Juan Walking Tour. After touring Fort San Felipe del Morro, your guide takes you for a walk along the narrow streets of historic Old San Juan, ending up at Christo's Chapel. ☉ 2½ hrs ⌑ $33–$39.

Rain Forest Nature Hike. After the 45-minute drive to the rain forest, you are joined by a guide who narrates your walk along selected nature trails-very similar to the El Yunque Rain Forest tours. ☉ 5 hrs ⌑ $39–$44.

San Juan & the Bacardi Rum Distillery. Take a narrated bus tour of San Juan and stop for a guided tour of the Bacardi Rum Distillery. After seeing how it's made, you can sample tropical rum drinks and shop for rum to take home. ☉ 3½ hrs ⌑ $30–$39.

Coming Ashore

Cruise ships dock within a couple of blocks of Old San Juan. The Paseo de la Princesa, a tree-lined promenade beneath the city wall, is a nice place for a stroll—you can admire the local crafts and stop at the refreshment kiosks. A tourist information booth is in the cruise-terminal area. Major sights in the Old San Juan area are mere blocks from the piers, but be aware that the streets are narrow and steeply inclined in places.

To get to Cataño and the Bacardi Rum Plant on your own, take the ferry (50¢) that leaves from the cruise piers every half-hour. Your best bet to reach Puerta de Tierra, Santurce, and Caparra (still within the San Juan metro area), other than an organized ship excursion, is to take a taxi. Taxis line up to meet ships. White taxis labeled TAXI TURISTICO charge set fares of $6 to $16. Metered cabs authorized by the Public Service Commission charge an initial $1; after that, it's about 10¢ for each additional ⅓₃ mi. If you take a metered taxi, insist that the meter be turned on, and pay only what is shown, plus a tip of 10% to 15%. You can negotiate with taxi drivers for specific trips, and you can hire a taxi for as little as $25 per hour for sightseeing tours.

Exploring San Juan

Numbers in the margin correspond to points of interest on the Old San Juan map.

OLD SAN JUAN Old San Juan, the original city founded in 1521, contains authentic and carefully preserved examples of 16th- and 17th-century Spanish-colonial architecture. Graceful wrought-iron balconies decorated with lush hanging plants extend over narrow, cobblestone streets. Seventeenth-cen-

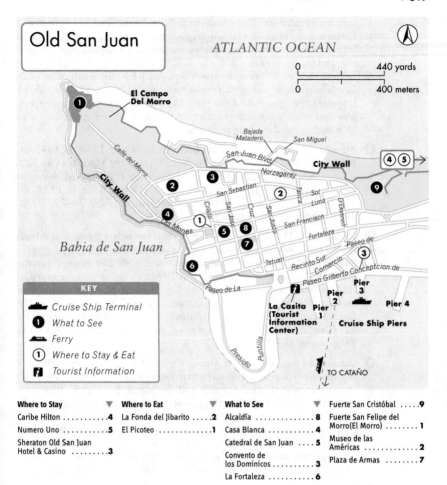

Old San Juan

ATLANTIC OCEAN

0 — 440 yards
0 — 400 meters

El Campo Del Morro

Bajada Matadero — San Miguel

San Juan Blvd

Norzagaray

City Wall

San Sebastian

San Justo

San Francisco

Fortaleza

Paseo de

Recinto Sur

Comercio

Paseo Gilberto Concepcion de

Bahia de San Juan

Tetuan

Paseo de La

Presidio

Puntilla

KEY
- Cruise Ship Terminal
- What to See
- Ferry
- Where to Stay & Eat
- Tourist Information

La Casita (Tourist Information Center)

Pier 1
Pier 2
Pier 3
Pier 4

Cruise Ship Piers

TO CATAÑO

tury walls still partially enclose the old city. Designated a U.S. National Historic Zone in 1950, Old San Juan is packed with shops, open-air cafés, private homes, tree-shaded squares, monuments, plaques, pigeons, people, and traffic jams. It's faster to walk than to take a cab. Nightlife can be quiet, but even during the low season you'll find some action on Calle San Sebastián, which has a row of restaurants, bars, and dance clubs. If your feet fail you in Old San Juan, climb aboard the free open-air trolleys that rumble through the narrow streets. Take one from the docks or board anywhere along the route.

❽ Alcaldía. The city hall was built between 1604 and 1789. In 1841 extensive renovations were done to make it resemble Madrid's city hall, with arcades, towers, balconies, and a lovely inner courtyard. A tourist information center and an art gallery are on the first floor. ⊠ *153 Calle San Francisco, Plaza de Armas, Old San Juan* ☎ *787/724–7171 Ext. 2391* ☜ *Free* ☉ *Weekdays 8–4.*

❹ Casa Blanca. The original structure on this site was a frame house built in 1521 as a home for Ponce de León who died in Cuba without ever having lived in it. His descendants occupied it for 250 years. From the end of the Spanish-American War in 1898 to 1966 it was the home of the U.S. Army commander in Puerto Rico. Several rooms decorated with colonial-era furnishings and an archaeology exhibit are on display. The lush garden is a quiet place to unwind. ⊠ *1 Calle San Sebastián, Old San Juan* ☎ *787/724–4102* ⊕ *www.icp.gobierno.pr* ☜ *$2* ☉ *Tues.–Sat. 9–noon and 1–4:30.*

❺ Catedral de San Juan. The Catholic shrine of Puerto Rico had humble beginnings in the early 1520s as a thatch-topped wooden structure. Hurricane winds tore off the thatch and destroyed the church. It was reconstructed in 1540, when the graceful circular staircase and vaulted Gothic ceilings were added, but most of the work was done in the 19th century. The remains of Ponce de León are in a marble tomb near the transept. ⊠ *153 Calle Cristo, Old San Juan* ☎ *787/722–0861* ⊕ *www. catedralsanjuan.com* ☜ *$1 donation suggested* ☉ *Weekdays 8:30–4; masses Sat. at 7 PM, Sun. at 9 and 11 AM, weekdays at 12:15 PM.*

❸ Convento de los Dominicos. Built by Dominican friars in 1523, this convent often served as a shelter during Carib Indian attacks and, more recently, as headquarters for the Antilles command of the U.S. Army. Now home to some offices of the Institute of Puerto Rican Culture, the beautifully restored building contains religious manuscripts, artifacts, and art. The institute also maintains a craft store and bookstore here. Classical concerts are occasionally held here. ⊠ *98 Calle Norzagaray, Old San Juan* ☎ *787/721–6866* ☜ *Free* ☉ *Mon.–Sat. 9–5.*

❻ La Fortaleza. On a hill overlooking the harbor, La Fortaleza, the western hemisphere's oldest executive mansion in continuous use and official residence of Puerto Rico's governor, was built as a fortress. The original structure constructed in 1540 has seen numerous changes over the past four centuries, resulting in the present collection of marble and mahogany, medieval towers, and stained-glass galleries. Guided tours are conducted every hour on the hour in English, on the half hour in Spanish.

✉ *Calle Recinto Oeste, Old San Juan* ☎ *787/721–7000 Ext. 2211 or 2358* ⊕ *www.fortaleza.gobierno.pr* 💲 *Free* ⊘ *Weekdays 9–4.*

🐾 ❾ **Fuerte San Cristóbal.** This 18th-century fortress guarded the city from land attacks. Even larger than El Morro, San Cristóbal was known in its heyday as the Gibraltar of the West Indies. ✉ *Calle Norzagaray, Old San Juan* ☎ *787/729–6960* ⊕ *www.nps.gov/saju* 💲 *$3, combination ticket including El Morro $5* ⊘ *Daily 9–5.*

🐾 ❶ **Fuerte San Felipe del Morro.** On a rocky promontory at the Old City's northwestern tip is El Morro, which was built by the Spaniards between 1540 and 1783. Rising 140 feet above the sea, the fort boasts six massive levels. It's a labyrinth of dungeons, barracks, towers, and tunnels. Its museum traces the history of the fortress. Tours and a video show are available in English. ✉ *Calle Norzagaray, Old San Juan* ☎ *787/729–6960* ⊕ *www.nps.gov/saju* 💲 *$3, combination ticket including Fuerte San Cristóbal $5.*

❷ **Museo de las Américas.** On the second floor of the imposing former military barracks, Cuartel de Ballajá, the Museum's permanent exhibit, "Las Artes Populares en las Américas," focusing on the popular and folk art of Latin America, contains religious figures, musical instruments, basketwork, costumes, and farming and other implements. ✉ *Calle Norzagaray and Calle del Morro, Old San Juan* ☎ *787/724–5052* ⊕ *www.museolasamericas.org* 💲 *Free* ⊘ *Tues.–Fri. 10–4, weekends 11–5.*

❼ **Plaza de Armas.** This is the original main square of Old San Juan. The plaza, bordered by Calles San Francisco, Fortaleza, San José, and Cruz, has a lovely fountain with 19th-century statues representing the four seasons.

NEW SAN JUAN In **Puerta de Tierra,** ½ mi (¾ km) east of the pier, is **El Capitolio,** Puerto Rico's white-marble capitol, dating from the 1920s. Another ½ mi (¾ km) east, at the tip of Puerta de Tierra, tiny **Fort San Jerónimo** perches over the Atlantic like an afterthought. Added to San Juan's fortifications in the late 18th century, the structure barely survived the British attack of 1797.

Santurce, the district between Miramar on the west and the Laguna San José on the east, is a busy mixture of shops, markets, and offices. The classically designed Universidad del Sagrado Corazón (Sacred Heart University) is home of the **Museo Contemporáneo del Arte de Puerto Rico** (Museum of Contemporary Puerto Rican Art; ✉ Av. Ponce de León at Av. R. H. Todd, Santurce ☎ 787/977–4030 ⊕ www.museocontemporaneopr.org). Closed Monday; free. The former San Juan Municipal Hospital is now the **Museo de Arte de Puerto Rico** (Museum of Puerto Rican Art; ✉ 300 Av. José de Diego, Santurce ☎ 787/977–6277 ⊕ www.mapr.org), which displays a permanent collection of Puerto Rican art and changing exhibits. Closed Monday; $5 admission.

SAN JUAN **Caparra Ruins.** In 1508 Ponce de León established the island's first set-
ENVIRONS tlement here. The ruins—a few crumbling walls—are what remains of an ancient fort, and the small Museo de la Conquista y Colonización de Puerto Rico (Museum of the Conquest and Colonization of Puerto Rico) contains historical documents, exhibits, and excavated artifacts,

though you can see the museum's contents in less time than it takes to say the name. ⊠ *Rte. 2, Km 6.6, Guaynabo* ☎ *787/781–4795* ⊕ *www. icp.gobierno.pr* ☒ *Free* ☉ *Tues.–Sat. 8:30–4:30.*

Casa Bacardí Visitor Center. Exiled from their homeland of Cuba, the Bacardí family emigrated to Puerto Rico and built this plant in the 1950s. It's one of the world's largest, with the capacity to produce 100,000 gallons of spirits a day and 221 million cases a year. Bacardí declared Puerto Rico the Rum Capital of the World when it created a modern multimedia center that includes everything rum, from the drink's history to slick video advertising. You can take a 45-minute tour of the bottling plant, the media center and museum, and the distillery. If you don't want to drive, you can reach the factory by taking the ferry from Pier 2 for 50¢ each way and then a public car from the ferry pier to the factory for about $2 or $3 per person. ⊠ *Bay View Industrial Park, Rte. 888, Km 2.6, Cataño* ☎ *787/788–1500 or 787/788–8400* ⊕ *www.casabacardi. org* ☒ *Free* ☉ *Mon.–Sat. 8:30–5:30, Sun. 10–5. Tours every 45 min.*

Shopping

San Juan is not a free port, so you won't find bargains on electronics and perfumes. However, shopping for native crafts can be fun. Popular souvenirs and gifts include santos (small, hand-carved figures of saints or religious scenes), hand-rolled cigars, handmade lace, carnival masks, Puerto Rican rum, and fancy men's shirts called guayaberas.

Look for vendors selling crafts from kiosks at the **Artesanía Puertorriqueña** (⊠Plaza Dársenas, Old San Juan, San Juan ☎787/722–1709) in the tourism company's La Casita near Pier 1. Several vendors also set up shop to sell articles such as belts, handbags, and toys along Calle San Justo in front of Plaza Dársenas. At the **Convento de los Dominicos** (⊠ 98 Calle Norzagaray, Old San Juan, San Juan ☎ 787/721–6866)—the Dominican Convent on the north side of the old city that houses the offices of the Instituto de Cultura Puertorriqueña—you can find baskets, masks, the famous *cuatro* guitars, santos, and reproductions of Taíno artifacts. **Nono Maldonado** (⊠ 1051 Av. Ashford, Condado, San Juan ☎ 787/721–0456) is well-known for his high-end, elegant linen designs for men and women.

Sports & Activities

CYCLING   Selected areas lend themselves to bike travel. In general, however, the roads are congested and distances are vast. Avoid main thoroughfares in San Juan: the traffic is heavy and the fumes are thick. The Paseo Piñones is an 11-mi (18-km) bike path that skirts the ocean east of San Juan. **Hot Dog Cycling** (⊠ 5916 Av. Isla Verde, Isla Verde, San Juan ☎ 787/ 982–5344 ⊕ www.hotdogcycling.com) rents Fuji mountain bikes for $30 a day and organizes group excursions to El Yunque and other places out on the island.

GOLF   Though there are no courses in San Juan proper, it's possible to do a golf outing to one of Puerto Rico's stellar courses as a day trip. Four world-class Robert Trent Jones–designed 18-hole courses are renowned classics at the **Hyatt Dorado Beach & Country Club** (⊠ Rte. 693, Km 11.8, Dorado ☎ 787/796–1234 Ext. 3238). With El Yunque as a backdrop, the two 18-hole courses at the **Westin Río Mar Beach Resort** (⊠ 6000 Río

Mar Blvd., Río Grande ☎ 787/888–6000) are inspirational. The River Course was designed by Greg Norman, the Ocean course by George and Tom Fazio. The 18-hole Arthur Hills–designed course at **Wyndham El Conquistador Resort and Country Club** (✉ 1000 Av. El Conquistador, Fajardo ☎ 787/863–6784) is famous for its 200-foot changes in elevation. The trade winds make every shot challenging.

Beaches

By law, all of Puerto Rico's beaches are open to the public (except for the Caribe Hilton's artificial beach in San Juan). Like Condado to its west, **Playa de Isla Verde** is bordered by resorts and has plenty of places to rent chairs and sports equipment or grab a bite to eat. There aren't any lifeguards, but the sands are white, and the snorkeling is good. East of Old San Juan and west of Ocean Park and Isla Verde, the long, wide **Playa del Condado** is often full of guests from the hotels that tower over it. Beach bars, sports outfitters, and chair-rental places abound, but there are no lifeguards. A residential neighborhood just east of Condado and west of Isla Verde is home to **Playa de Ocean Park,** a wide, 1-mi-long (2-km-long) stretch of golden sand. The waters are often choppy but still swimmable—take care, however, as there are no lifeguards.

Where to Eat

Tips of 15% to 20% are expected, and appreciated, by restaurant wait-staff if a service charge is not included in the bill.

$–$$$ ✕ **El Picoteo.** Mostly appetizers dominate the menu at this chic tapas bar. Entrées such as paella are also noteworthy. There's a long, lively bar inside; one dining area overlooks the hotel El Convento's courtyard, and the other takes in the action along Calle Cristo. Even if you have dinner plans elsewhere, consider stopping here for a cocktail or a nightcap. ✉ *El Convento Hotel, 100 Calle Cristo, Old San Juan* ☎ *787/723–9621* ▭ *AE, D, DC, MC, V* ☉ *Closed Mon.*

$–$$ ✕ **La Fonda del Jibarito.** Sanjuaneros have favored this casual, family-run restaurant for years. The back porch is filled with plants, the dining room is filled with fanciful depictions of Calle Sol, and the ever-present owner, Pedro J. Ruiz, is filled with the desire to ensure that everyone is happy. The conch ceviche and chicken fricassee are among the specialties. ✉ *280 Calle Sol, Old San Juan* ☎ *787/725–8375* ⌖ *Reservations not accepted* ▭ *AE, D, MC, V.*

Nightlife

Almost every ship stays in San Juan late or even overnight to give passengers an opportunity to revel in the nightlife—the most sophisticated in the Caribbean.

CASINOS By law, all casinos are in hotels. The atmosphere is refined, and many patrons dress to the nines, but informal attire is usually fine. Casinos set their own hours, which change seasonally, but generally operate from noon to 4 AM, although the casino in the Condado Plaza is open 24 hours. Other hotels with casinos include the Wyndham Old San Juan, Wyndham El San Juan, the San Juan Marriott, the Inter-Continental San Juan Resort & Casino, and the Ritz-Carlton San Juan.

A long line of well-heeled patrons usually runs out the door of **Babylon** (✉ Wyndham El San Juan Hotel, 6063 Av. Isla Verde, Isla Verde, San Juan ☎ 787/791–1000). Those with the staying power to make it inside step out of the Caribbean and into the ancient Middle East. Those who tire of waiting often head to El Chico Lounge, a small room with live entertainment right off the hotel lobby. **Café Bohemio** (✉ El Convento Hotel, 100 Calle Cristo, Old San Juan, San Juan ☎ 787/723–9200), a Latin restaurant, turns into a live jazz and Bohemian music club from 11 PM to 2 AM Tuesday through Friday (after the kitchen closes); Thursday night is best. **Candela** (✉ 110 San Sebastián, Old San Juan ☎ 787/977–4305), a lounge–art gallery housed in an historic building, hosts some of the most innovative local DJs on the island and often invites star spinners from New York or London. This is the island's best showcase for experimental dance music. The festive, late-night haunt is open Tuesday through Saturday from 8 PM onward, and the conversation can be as stimulating as the dance floor. At **Liquid** (✉ Water Club, 2 Calle Tartak, Isla Verde ☎ 787/725–4664 or 787/725–4675), the lobby lounge of San Juan's chicest boutique hotel, glass walls are filled with undulating water, and the fashionable patrons drink wild cocktails to pounding music. With a large dance and stage area and smokin' Afro-Cuban bands, **Rumba** (✉ 152 Calle San Sebastián, Old San Juan, San Juan ☎ 787/725–4407) is one of the best parties in town.

INDEX

FODOR'S KEY TO THE GUIDES

Caribbean

AMERICA'S **GUIDEBOOK LEADER** PUBLISHES GUIDES FOR **EVERY KIND OF TRAVELER**. CHECK OUT OUR MANY SERIES AND FIND YOUR **PERFECT MATCH**.

FODOR'S GOLD GUIDES
America's favorite travel-guide series offers the most detailed insider reviews of hotels, restaurants, and attractions in all price ranges, plus great background information, smart tips, and useful maps.

COMPASS AMERICAN GUIDES
Stunning guides from top local writers and photographers, with gorgeous photos, literary excerpts, and colorful anecdotes. A must-have for culture mavens, history buffs, and new residents.

FODOR'S 25 BEST / CITYPACKS
Concise city coverage in a guide plus a foldout map. The right choice for urban travelers who want everything under one cover.

FODOR'S AROUND THE CITY WITH KIDS
Up to 68 great ideas for family days, recommended by resident parents. Perfect for exploring in your own backyard or on the road.

SEE IT GUIDES
Illustrated guidebooks that include the practical information travelers need, in gorgeous full color. Perfect for travelers who want the best value packed in a fresh, easy-to-use, colorful layout.

FODOR'S FLASHMAPS
Every resident's map guide, with 60 easy-to-follow maps of public transit, parks, museums, zip codes, and more.

FODOR'S LANGUAGES FOR TRAVELERS
Practice the local language before you hit the road. Available in phrase books, cassette sets, and CD sets.

THE COLLECTED TRAVELER
These collections of the best published essays and articles on various European destinations will give you a feel for the culture, cuisine, and way of life.

At bookstores everywhere.   www.fodors.com/books